UNITED NATIONS CONFERENCE ON TRADE AND DEVELOPMENT

A POSITIVE AGENDA FOR DEVELOPING COUNTRIES:

ISSUES FOR FUTURE TRADE NEGOTIATIONS

GW00707526

UNITED NATIONS

New York and Geneva, 2000

Note

- Symbols of United Nations documents are composed of capital letters combined with figures. Mention of such a symbol indicates a reference to a United ations document.

- The views expressed in this volume are those of the authors and do not necessarily reflect the views of the United Nations Secretariat. The designations employed and the presentation of the material do not imply the expression of any opinion whatsoever on the part of the United Nations Secretariat concerning the legal status of any country, territory, city or area, or of its authorities, or concerning the delimitation of its frontiers or boundaries.

- Material in this publication may be freely quoted or reprinted, but acknowledgement is requested, together with a reference to the document number. A copy of the publication containing the quotation or reprint should be sent to the UNCTAD secretariat at: Palais des Nations, 1211 Geneva 10, Switzerland.

UNCTAD/ITCD/TSB/10

UNITED NATIONS PUBLICATION
Sales No. E.00.II.D.8
ISBN 92-1-112475-1

CONTENTS

III. OTHER ISSUES

ANNEXES

ACKNOWLEDGEMENTS

This compilation of technical papers reflects the third publication prepared by the UNCTAD Secretariat in relation with the support given to developing countries for their participation in the WTO and the formulation of a "positive agenda" in the multilateral trade negotiations. The papers compiled were prepared by DITC staff members and consultants during 1999, following specific requests of Member States or as background papers in the framework of regional and ad hoc meetings held in parallel with the preparatory process of the Third WTO Ministerial Conference.

This handbook is the result of a collaborative effort which has emerged from the experience of several years of work, in assisting developing countries to prepare for future trade negotiations. I wish to thank all those who have contributed to this volume with their research work or editorial support, and in particular, colleagues from the International Trade in Goods and Services, and Commodities Division, as well as a number of consultants and staff. Murray Gibbs, Head of the Trade Analysis and Systemic Issues Branch, co-ordinated and oriented the work related with the "positive agenda", to which the following staff members contributed: Ivan Anastassov, Philippe Brusick, Jolita Butkeviciene, Michiko Hayashi, Teresa Hinze, Ulrich Hoffmann, Stefano Inama, Veena Jha, Eila Jounela, Mina Mashayekhi, Josie Maximo, Sophie Munda, Marcel Namfua, Victor Ognivtsev, Bonapas Onguglo, Diego Oyarzun Reyes, Miho Shirotori, Erich Supper, Xiaobing Tang, Manuela Tortora, René Vossenaar, Tokio Yamaoka, Simonetta Zarrilli. While not all of these persons have been identified as authors of papers contained in the book, they have all made their contribution to the "positive agenda" process. A number of internationally recognized consultants also prepared some papers which were included in this book as written by them. These consultants are Carlos M. Correa, Rodney de C. Grey, Veena Jha, Tim Josling, Arvind Panagariya, Ashok Sajjanhar, Stephan Tangermann, Craig VanGrasstek, and Edwin Vermulst.

The views expressed in the papers included in this volume, are those of the authors and should not be construed as the official UNCTAD position on the issues concerned.

John D.A. Cuddy
Director
Division on International Trade in Goods
and Services, and Commodities
UNCTAD

FOREWORD BY THE SECRETARY-GENERAL OF UNCTAD
MR. RUBENS RICUPERO

When I attended the first WTO Ministerial Conference in Singapore, in December 1996, it was the first time I had participated in a meeting of the GATT/WTO since leaving my post as Ambassador and Permanent Representative of Brazil to the GATT shortly before the completion of the Uruguay Round. I was struck by the extent to which the WTO had evolved beyond the GATT, and in particular by the new and intensified challenges and opportunities facing developing countries in the multilateral trading system. Basing myself on the fresh and ambitious mandate UNCTAD had then recently received at its Ninth Conference, in South Africa, I decided to launch the "positive agenda" programme in UNCTAD, with a view to assisting developing countries to build their capacity to identify their interests, formulate trade objectives and pursue those objectives in international trade negotiations.

The scope of multilateral obligations, the technical complexity and sheer volume of the issues covered, the extraordinary work load on Geneva-based delegations and the administrative burden on capitals have placed most developing countries in a situation where participation in the system, let alone attempting to shape its future course, is almost beyond their means. However, at the second WTO Ministerial Conference in Geneva in 1998, the decision was taken to initiate a preparatory process that many countries understood to be leading to the possible launch of a new round of multilateral trade negotiations at the third Ministerial Conference. In response to the request of developing countries and the encouragement of our member States and of the General Assembly, UNCTAD began its work on the positive agenda over the period leading up to the Seattle Ministerial Conference of the WTO, which opened on 30 November 1999. This book represents a compendium of papers which were prepared by UNCTAD staff members and consultants in 1999, as part of that process.

The Seattle Conference did not launch a new round of multilateral trade negotiations, and did not achieve a clear consensus as to the appropriate follow-up. This poses a serious challenge not only to the WTO but to the international trading community as a whole, in which UNCTAD plays a particular role, that of ensuring the continuing strength and integrity of the multilateral trading system and its relevance for all countries. The factors which led to the inability to forge a consensus at Seattle must be analyzed so that corrective steps can be taken. UNCTAD X has a contribution to make in this respect. One issue is that of coherence in global economic policy-making, which must be seen in a broad perspective, involving the various agencies of the United Nations that deal with social, environmental and cultural matters. UNCTAD's particular role is to contribute to coherence between trade and development.

During the preparatory process leading up to the Seattle Conference, developing countries submitted well over 100 proposals for action, more than half the total. These proposals will require further supporting analysis and discussion. The papers in this book are meant to contribute to this objective, and it is hoped that the decisions taken at UNCTAD X will confirm and strengthen the role of UNCTAD in assisting developing countries in their efforts to shape a multilateral trading system that serves the interests of all.

CHAPTER I

A POSITIVE
AGENDA OVERVIEW

THE POSITIVE AGENDA AND THE SEATTLE CONFERENCE

Murray Gibbs, UNCTAD

The results of the Uruguay Round. contained certain major achievements by developing country negotiators. The MFA was terminated, an agreement on services was established that included movement of persons in the definition of trade in services and a structure that provided them with considerable flexibility to use liberalisation as a development tool. An agreement was reached on Agriculture which provided a framework for meaningful liberalisation in future. Provisions for differential treatment in their favour were achieved in many Agreements which, although phrased in best endeavour language, could be made more binding and operational in future. Even the TRIPS agreement, which is viewed with considerable trepidation in some developing countries, nevertheless incorporates certain provisions for flexibility which are available to developing countries to meet some of their particular needs. A number of developing countries were pleased that attempts to establish multilateral rules for investment had been deflected into the TRIMs Agreement. These accomplishments were in part due to the persistence of alliances of like minded developing countries, which formed around the various issues.[1]

On the other hand, the version of the "single undertaking" which underlay the establishment of the WTO, caused problems for many developing countries, who naturally did not want to be left behind in the old "1947" version of GATT. The large majority of developing countries, particularly the least developed countries (LDCs), did not possess the administrative, financial or human resources necessary to fulfill their new obligations, to exercise their new rights, or even to take advantage of the trade opportunities presented.

At Marrakesh in 1994, some countries pushed for the introduction of a future work programme for the new Organization, containing new issues which had not been dealt with in the Uruguay Round, as a component of the final package. A compromise was reached in the form of a statement by the Chairman of the Trade Negotiations Committee listing possible issues for inclusion in the work programme, which included the items proposed by developed countries, such as labour standards, investment, competition policy, but also some of interest to developing countries, including compensa-

1

tion for the erosion of preferences, commodities, financial issues, immigration etc.[2]

In the period between the entry into force of the WTO and its first Ministerial Conference, developed countries pursued the issues they had proposed for the work programme. The idea of negotiating multilateral rules for investment within the WTO attained a particularly high profile, due to the negotiations of the Multilateral Agreement on Investment (MAI) in the OECD. Developing countries had differing views as to whether it was advisable to bring the negotiations to the WTO where they would have some influence over the outcome, or to leave it in the OECD where it would not bind them. Many developing countries firmly opposed the inclusion of investment in any WTO work programme, and even more opposed any mention of labour rights; there was also significant resistance to further work on environment and even competition policy. During the period of negotiation of what was to become the Singapore Declaration, developing countries focussed attention on keeping these issues off the agenda.

Thus, many developing countries were somewhat taken by surprise when, from the opening statements of the Singapore Ministerial Conference, it became apparent that a major goal of the developed countries was the adoption of the Information Technology Product Agreement (ITA), and the rapid completion of the negotiations on financial services and basic telecommunications. Together these were seen as providing a legal foundation of the globalization process, which was presented as bringing benefits to all. The developing countries, by contrast, had not seen a need to formulate initiatives to obtain action in their favour, nor had they fully recognized the extent to which the WTO had become a forum for a continuous negotiating process.

Secretary-General Mr. Ricupero, an experienced trade negotiator himself, and who participated in the Singapore Conference, drew the conclusion that the developing countries needed a "positive agenda", in which they would systematically identify their interests and set realistic objectives with respect to all issues, not only those where they were "demandeurs", and pursue these objectives by formulating concrete, technically sound proposals in alliances with like minded countries. When a wide range of countries supported Mr. Ricupero's vision, the "positive agenda" thus became central to UNCTAD's work on trade for the next three years.

The exercise of supporting the developing countries in formulating their "positive agenda" was facilitated by the mandate which had been given to UNCTAD at the UNCTAD IX Conference which had been held in Midrand, South Africa in May 1996.[3] The Conference had assigned the Organisation a wide range of trade issues, including services, environment and competition policy, and instructed UNCTAD to study the implications of a possible multilateral framework for investment. UNCTAD had been given the specific task of examining the future trade agenda , and the mandate had been set in terms of "assisting developing countries to..." thus blurring the traditional differentiation between technical assistance and "regular work". The conference also created a new set of "expert meetings", which provided an opportunity to identify the interests of developing countries in a non-negotiating context, and became progressively an element of the positive agenda exercise.

Part of UNCTAD's mandate was directed towards an assessment of the impact of the Uruguay Round on individual developing countries. UNCTAD collaborated with the WTO and the ITC in the Joint Integrated Technical Assistance Programme (JITAP) and with a number of regional institutions such as the Latin American Trade Network which conducted highly original studies from the point of view of the private sector. At the request of developing countries, meetings were organized to assist them in the now rapidly proceeding negotiations on financial services, inviting lecturers from the Bank for International Settlements and other experts. And a series of dinner sessions were held at the invitation of several developing country delegations, at which papers were presented to facilitate the discussion on possible issues for future negotiation.

Preparations for Seattle

In the light of the results of the second (fiftieth anniversary) WTO Ministerial Conference, it was considered likely that the third Conference would launch a major trade initiative that was named by some the "Millenium Round". The Second Conference set up a preparatory process which would be "proposal driven", thus placing every WTO member under pressure to submit proposals to ensure that the trade issues of its specific interest would not be omitted in future negotiations. This impetus quickened the pace and sense of urgency of work on the "positive agenda".

During the summer and early autumn of 1998, a number of intergovernmental meetings were held in UNCTAD. The very enlightening expert meeting on trade in health services[4] was followed by similar meetings on tourism and related services, which among other things confirmed the significance of anti-competitive practices as an impediment to developing country suppliers gaining a fair share of the profits in this sector and suggested elements for a possible sectoral approach to future negotiations in this sector;[5] it also proposed that a expert meeting be held on air transport. Another expert meeting was held on environmental services, which suggested that further negotiated commitments in this sector could contribute to environmental protection if adequate funds were made available to developing countries.[6] In addition, much work was carried out on investment and competition policy, some in collaboration with WTO under the Singapore mandate where UNCTAD's role had been specifically recognized.

The third session of the Commission on Trade in Goods and Services, and Commodities focussed on GSP and on various trade in services issues, and instructed UNCTAD to organize expert meetings on trade in agriculture and on air transport, two sectors whose obvious sensitivity would have precluded them for consideration by UNCTAD a few years previously. In addition, UNCTAD was instructed to work with the WTO in preparing the assessment of trade in services (as required by Article XIX:2 of GATS), to study the problem of economic needs tests as a barrier to the movement of service suppliers as well as to identify barriers to trade in services so as to assist developing countries in preparing their requests in the next round of negotiations under GATS. Thus the intergovernmental work programme in UNCTAD came to coincide to an ever greater extent with the positive agenda process.

In mid September 1998, an Ad Hoc Expert Group was organized (under the specific authority given to the Secretary General for this purpose) as a follow up to a similar meeting which had been held in April 1997. The stated purpose of this meeting was to examine the analytical needs of developing countries in preparing for the possible future round of multilateral negotiations and initiate studies that could be of use to them in this process, the effectiveness of which would, it was hoped, be enhanced by networking among the organizations involved. The discussion at the Ad Hoc Expert Group was chaired by the Secretary-General and led by panellists from various UNCTAD divisions and other international organizations such as the World Bank, IMF, WIPO, UN Regional Commissions and research networks in Latin America and Africa. The free discussion which took place was found very useful by participants, and a publication was later issued, based on the debate at the Ad Hoc Expert Group, enhanced by further analysis by experts within UNCTAD.[7]

Developing countries began to take initiatives to coordinate their positions in preparation for the preparatory process for the third Ministerial Conference. The Group of 15 held a meeting in New Delhi in December 1998,[8] at which a number of participants put forward suggestions for improvements in the MTAs, based on experiences they had encountered in the implementation of the agreements. This effectively launched the work on "implementation" that became central to the preparatory process in the WTO General Council.

The positive agenda exercise intensified in early 1999, when a group of developing countries requested UNCTAD to arrange informal meetings in the Palais des Nations to support the preparation by developing countries for their participation in the preparatory process in the WTO General Council. These meetings, which were convened by different delegations in turn, examined the substance of all the possible issues on the table. They approached the problematique by identifying the "issue", the "problem" and the "solution", often using tabular presentations or proposed texts with detailed explanatory footnotes as working tools.

The intergovernmental process in UNCTAD continued to focus more directly on negotiating issues. The expert meetings on agriculture[9] and air transport[10] addressed specific negotiating issues in those sectors, the discussion being greatly enhanced by the availability of resources to finance the participation of developing country participants. Further impetus was provided by the decision of the UN General Assembly to attribute a significant amount of the savings achieved through greater efficiency to the organisation of three workshops, the preparation of technical studies and the conduct of advisory missions.

The first of these workshops was held in Seoul, Republic of Korea (an OECD member, it is worth noting) in June 1999, the second in Pretoria, South Africa in early July, and the third in Boca Chica, Dominican Republic during the first week of August. Government officials, trade practitioners and academics from developing and developed countries participated in these workshops.

Whereas the Seoul and Boca Chica workshops followed a strictly inter-regional format, the Pretoria workshop concentrated on identifying the African specificity of the proposals which had been submitted to that date, and provided many technical inputs into the process of formulating negotiating objectives in African capitals. It also examined the relationship between the proposals submitted to the WTO and the objectives of ACP countries in the negotiations of a successor to the Lome Convention. The Pretoria workshop had been immediately preceded by another meeting organised by UNCTAD in Sun City, South Africa which had involved senior trade officials from least developed countries. These senior officials had drawn up a clear statement of the objectives of the least developed countries in the future negotiations, which was submitted to the General Council, and which addressed a wide spectrum of issues, including that of bound, duty free treatment in favour of LDCs, a proposal which had been "on the table" since UNCTAD VIII.

The work in Africa was deepened by the organisation of sub-regional workshops for COMESA, ECOWAS, SADC and ECAAS, in collaboration with ECA and OAU/AEC. Three were held during the month of August 1999 and financed by the UNDP. A series of seminars at the national level and on specific subjects, (such as agriculture, textiles and sanitary regulations), were also carried out under the JITAP Programme (with the WTO and ITC) and responded to direct requests from individual African governments for advisory missions.

Developing countries continued their co-ordination process in various fora, seminars were organised by UN Regional Commissions, and the G15 held a Ministerial Meeting in Bangalore, India in mid-August.[11] At their pre-UNCTAD Ministerial Conference in Marrakesh, in September, the G77 Ministers drew up a "message" stating their objectives and concerns for the Seattle Conference that was submitted to the WTO. And African trade ministers met in Algiers to draw up a common African position stressing decisions that should be taken in Seattle ("deliverables").[12]

Almost 250 proposals were submitted in the preparatory process for the Seattle Conference, over one half by developing countries, often presented by alliances of like-minded countries. Developing country proposals focussed on essentially two aspects, (a) how to ensure that the built-in agenda negotiations on services and agriculture would focus on their particular interests, and (b) specific actions related to the MTAs including the mandated reviews, grouped together under the broad title of "implementation".

Within the category of implementation issues, proposals addressed the issue of differential and more favourable treatment in favour of developing countries (S&D) with the objective of elaborating more contractual language for "best endeavours" type undertakings. Implementation proposals also aimed at agreed interpretations of the MTAs to deal with specific problems which had arisen in practice, particularly those which did not take account of the special characteristics of developing country economies, administrations and enterprises, (e.g high interest rates, difficulties in identifying inputs).[13] Difficulties they faced in meeting the administrative and procedural obligations were also the subject of proposals, notably to extend the transitional periods for TRIPS, TRIMs, and Customs Valuation Agreements. An important element in their proposals was to give precision to the concept of "imbalance" in the rights and obligations, so that they could no longer be accused of adopting "polemical" positions. The TRIPS Agreement was the subject of particular attention, in reaction to pressures to forego the flexibility and S&D provisions which had been built into the Agreement, even those involving life-and-death health matters. Some developing countries wished to ensure that the TRIPS Agreement actually promoted the transfer of technology, as stated in its provisions.

Once stock had been taken of the proposals on the table, there was little time for the process of preparing a draft Ministerial Declaration for Seattle, a process made more difficult by the vacancy in the post of Director-General of the WTO until 1 September 1999. A comprehensive draft was circulated on 19 October, which incorporated all the proposals into a structured comprehensive text, but without any further drafting. Only on 17 November was the Chairman of the WTO Governing Council in a position to circulate, on his own responsibility, a partial text which reflected a certain degree of agreement, (albeit with square brackets and alternative wordings), but which omitted the key issues of agriculture and implementation. Thus, after well over a year of preparation, the WTO ministers went to Seattle without a broadly-agreed text and were unable at Seattle to reach agreement on a declaration launching the new set of negotiations.

Many factors contributed to the failure of the Seattle conference, but some lessons have been clearly learned. Firstly, substance cannot take a back seat to process. If the major trading countries cannot agree among themselves on major issues such as agriculture, services or anti-dumping, no amount of procedural manoeuvring will create such agreement. A second lesson is that it is no longer possible to assume that agreements can be negotiated among a small group of countries, in a non-transparent manner, and imposed on the majority of WTO members. Mr. Moore, the new Director-General of the WTO, was aware of this change in mentality, and attempted to open up the negotiating process by creating a set of open-ended negotiating groups. But with the initial negotiating text so unsatisfactory, it proved impossible for these groups to move rapidly towards agreed text, and under the pressure of time constraints, ministers rapidly fell back into the habits of the old GATT. This was clearly articulated in the strong statements circulated in Seattle by the Latin American and Caribbean, and African groups, to the effect that they would not be able to join a consensus on agreements in whose negotiation they were not fully involved. Under the WTO all countries have accepted roughly the same level of obligation and will be bound by the outcome of any negotiation. Developing countries have become "full stakeholders" in the system,[14] and thus cannot be marginalized from the decision making process. As the United States Trade Representative, chairing the Seattle Conference, pointed out, more imaginative techniques of negotiation and decision-making have to be devised.

Issues which remain unresolved

Special and Differential Treatment

The history of the GATT since 1947, up to and, in particular, including, the Uruguay Round, has been one of a continuous process of interpreting the rules, so as to deal with practical problems which have be encountered, and to tighten up best endeavour obligations to give them a more binding status. The problems identified by developing countries have real impact on their trade, and need addressing immediately. In many cases the proposals made by developing countries are intended to deal with problems deriving from the characteristics of an underdeveloped economy and imply no formal differential treatment in their favour. Others, however, are aimed at giving S&D provisions a more binding character, and would require a political decision as to whether S&D should constitute a permanent element in the system. While there is merit in hypothesis that ultimately all countries should be subject to the same obligations, it is also logical that they benefit from such differential treatment in their favour so long as it is required, not simply for a arbitrary transitional period.

Particularly disconcerting to the developing countries is the apparent reluctance of certain developed countries to provide bound duty free treatment to the exports of the LDCs. As LDCs largely receive duty free treatment under existing preferential schemes, it is the concept of "bound" that is crucial. If duty free treatment does not have the necessary contractual status that would permit LDCs to have resort to the dispute settlement mechanism if such bindings were breached, it would be of little additional value. Binding would not require amendment of the WTO Agreement: a protocol could easily be devised to provide de facto binding status to such commitments.

Accession

UNCTAD has been assisting countries of various sizes and levels of development, ranging from China and Russia, to several LDCs, in their accession processes. Most of the governments involved hope to become members of the WTO before the new round of negotiations, and many have been prepared to make significant concessions to accelerate their accession process so as to achieve this objective. This attitude is in sharp contrast to historical experience when countries timed their accession to GATT to coincide with multilateral rounds, so as to mitigate the unilateral nature of the accession negotiations, and to have their accession "entry fee" credited as their contribution to the overall package emerging from the round. The proposed fast track process of accession for the LDCs would help them to hasten their entry into the multilateral trading system.

Built-in agenda

The negotiations and mandated reviews under the built-in agenda will need to be initiated without delay within the structure of the responsible WTO Committees if the WTO is to recoup the momentum lost at Seattle. This would require no more than a decision by the Councils concerned. In fact, many of the proposals by developing countries were aimed at setting fixed deadlines for outstanding work, both negotiations and mandated reviews, (e.g rules of origin, export credits on agriculture).

Transfer of technology

The issue of transfer of technology permeated the discussions on various issues in the preparatory process and at Seattle. The Uruguay Round, particularly through the GATS and TRIPS Agreements, set up a legal framework that made it easier for enterprises possessing advanced technologies to take advantage of such technologies to expand their operations to a global scale. This was obviously necessary for the multilateral trading system to keep up with realities, and maintain its relevance. On the other hand, the majority of WTO members do not possess, nor have access to such technologies, and they consider that the system should equally serve their interests as well. This imbalance in the rights and obligations between the technologically weak and the technologically strong had provoked initiatives to introduce corrective measures, notably in the context of the built-in agendas of TRIPs and GATS.

NGO Protest

Most of the street protestors in Seattle had only a vague idea of what the WTO was, but viewed the Seattle Conference as an opportunity to express their concerns and frustrations over the impact of globalization in general, and their sense of anxiety over the growing impotence of individuals even those living under fully democratic regimes, to influence their destinies.[15] On the other hand, a large number of NGOs arrived in Seattle with well documented briefs on the impact of WTO rules and decisions on various aspects of the environment, health, small farmers, child workers etc. These issues are unlikely to go away in the foreseeable future.

It is evident that these issues are all part of the broader issue of coherence in global economic policy. The relevant Decision on coherence at Marrakesh is narrow and places coherence exclusively in the context of cooperation between the WTO and "the international organizations responsible for monetary and financial matters".[16] Subsequent experience has shown that other organizations in the UN system, such as the ILO, WHO, UNEP, UNESCO are equally relevant to "global coherence".

What has the Positive Agenda exercise achieved so far?

The impact of UNCTAD's positive agenda exercise should not be overemphasized. Many developing countries had little need of UNCTAD's assistance in preparing their proposals. However, many others drew upon the technical work of the secretariat and the consultants' studies, and most have derived benefit from the interregional, regional and sub-regional meetings, including those held in Geneva, which permitted them to exchange ideas, confirm the validity of their proposals, and form alliances.

More importantly, the positive agenda has acted as a catalyst for a new dynamism in the role of developing countries in multilateral trade negotiations. This new dynamism is based on four pillars, (*a*) that developing countries clearly identify their interests and formulate realistic, technically sound proposals to pursue these interests, (*b*) that they understand the positions and objectives of their major trading partners, as well as the underlying political and legal background, (*c*) that they seek to understand each others' positions so as to form alliances with like-minded developing countries, and compromises with "different minded" developing countries before entering into the multilateral negotiations with the major trading powers, and (*d*) that they do not adhere to any consensus on the results of negotiations in which they have not be permitted to effectively participate.

ELEMENTS OF A POSITIVE AGENDA[17]

What is a "Positive Trade Agenda" for Developing Countries?

UNCTAD began to stress the need for a "positive agenda" for developing countries in multilateral trade negotiations immediately after the experience of the first WTO Ministerial Conference in Singapore (December 1996). It was based on the perception that in the preparatory process leading up to the Conference, developing countries had been concentrating almost entirely on opposing the inclusion of certain issues in the WTO work programme, e.g. labour rights and investment, without formulating proposals or counterproposals for action on issues of interest to them. As a result, they found themselves, having to accept results in areas of interest primarily to developed countries, i.e. the ITA, financial services and basic telecommunications services without obtaining reciprocal commitments in their favour in areas of primary interest to them such as agriculture, textiles and clothing, and movement of natural persons. The Uruguay Round had also demonstrated that where a group of developing countries could put forward and maintain consistent proposals for trade liberalization, they could succeed in blocking less ambitious results, (such as the action of the Latin American members of the Cairns Group at Montreal and Brussels, as well as the group of developing countries that placed clear proposals on the table for the structure of the GATS agreement and the inclusion of the movement of natural persons on the definition of trade in services). The thrust of the positive agenda initiative was thus that developing countries should make an unprecedented effort to ensure that their interests would be taken up in any future multilateral trade negotiations so as to make them fully responsive to the concerns of developing countries. As a first step, it meant that they would submit detailed, technically sound proposals in the preparatory process for the Third WTO Ministerial Conference, and that UNCTAD should assist them in this endeavour.

The initial step in this process was the organization of two Ad Hoc Expert Group meetings under the responsibility of the Secretary General of UNCTAD to exchange views among international organizations and academic institutions both in developing and developed countries in order to identify the work that should be carried out to further the positive agenda objective. These meetings resulted in a wealth of ideas, which have been circulated in publications by UNCTAD.[18]

This work began in earnest, however, when developing countries requested UNCTAD officials to assist them in drawing up and refining proposals for the future trade agenda. This work was further enhanced by the decision of the UN General Assembly to use financing from the "savings resulting from the improved overall cost-effectiveness" for this purpose.[19] Following the instructions of the UNGA, three UNCTAD interregional workshops on the Positive Agenda were organized, in Seoul, Korea (8-10 June 1999), Pretoria, South Africa (29 June-2 July 1999) and Boca Chica, Dominican Republic (2-4 August 1999). Participants in these workshops included government officials (in their personal capacities), academics, trade consultants and practitioners from developed and developing countries, and members of UNCTAD secretariat and other international and regional organizations, including the WTO secretariat. UNCTAD also organized a high-level workshop for Least Developed Countries in Sun City, South Africa (21-25 June 1999). This workshop resulted in proposals agreed by LDCs covering all substantive areas in the WTO preparatory process.[20]

Subsequently, under the UNDP project on "Capacity Building for Trade and Africa", UNCTAD organized another three sub-regional seminars in Africa, in Harare for COMESA, in Abuja for ECOWAS, in Cape Town for SADC (and in Libreville for ECCAS), aimed at assisting these groups to prepare for the Third WTO Ministerial Conference.

Furthermore, work conducted by the intergovernmental machinery of the UN and UNCTAD have also contributed to the positive agenda process. This includes UNCTAD expert meetings held on health services (1997), tourism services (1998), environmental services (1998), agriculture (April 1999) and air transport (June 1999); the report, prepared by UNCTAD secretariat, to the 54th Session of UNGA on developments in the multilateral trading system (under Resolution 53/170), regional meetings organized in cooperation with UN Regional Commissions (ECA and ESCAP), etc. In addition, the preparatory process for the Tenth Session of UNCTAD—UNCTAD X (Bangkok, February 2000) also provided substantive inputs to the development of the positive agenda. Thus, preparatory Ministerial Meetings of African, Asian and Latin American countries, as well as the Ministerial Meeting of the "Group of 77" in Marrakech (September 1999)[21] formulated basic approaches of developing countries to the new multilateral trade negotiations and UNCTAD's role therein. A substantive part of the Report of the Secretary-General of UNCTAD to UNCTAD X was also devoted to the positive agenda.[22]

The following paragraphs summarize some of the main ideas which have emerged to date in the positive agenda process.

Third WTO Ministerial Conference and a New "Trade Round"

The preparatory process pursued in the WTO General Council since September 1998, as required in the Geneva Ministerial Declaration (May 1998),[23] was centered on several areas: (a) issues and proposals relating to the implementation of the WTO Agreements; (b) issues and proposals relating to already mandated negotiations on agriculture and services and "built-in agenda" in other areas; (c) issues and proposals relating to the follow-up to the High-Level Meeting on Least-Developed Countries (1997); (d) issues and proposals relating to other possible work on the basis of programme initiated at Singapore Ministerial Conference such as "new issues"[24] and (e) any other matters concerning multilateral trade relations of WTO members. Additional inputs to the preparatory process was expected from the separate work programme on electronic commerce and on issues where there was expectation that decisions or agreements could be reached at a time of Seattle Ministerial Conference (the so-called "deliverables"). The latter category included ministerial decisions regarding: (a) duty-free access for products exported by the least developed countries; (b) coherence of global economic policy-making, i.e. coordination of activities between the WTO, Bretton Woods institutions, UNCTAD, UNDP and other international organizations; (c) transparency in government procurement; and (d) decisions with respect to matters where outstanding deadlines have not been met (see paragraphs on Implementation below) , or where decisions were awaited, e.g. extension of moratorium on non-violation cases under the TRIPS Agreement. African countries also set out a list of issues on which they considered that decisions should be taken at Seattle.

Out of 135 WTO members, 97 are developing countries (or 71,8%), including 29 least developed countries. Furthermore, out of 30 countries which are now in the process of accession to the WTO, 16 are developing countries, including 7 least developed countries. As of end 1999 249 proposals had been submitted in the WTO preparatory process in more than 20 subject areas, of which more than 50% were coming from developing countries (including those proposals which developing countries submitted jointly with several developed WTO members). The greatest number of proposals were in the following subject areas: Agriculture - 46 proposals (18 - from developing countries); Services - 25 proposals (14 - from developing countries); Industrial products - 14 proposals (2 - from developing countries); TRIPS - 15 proposals (8 - from developing countries); and "New issues"[25] - 37 proposals (11 - from developing countries).

Many WTO members had expressed their support for launching a new round of multilateral trade negotiations at the Seattle Ministerial Conference and the failure of Seattle has not fundamentally altered those countries' perceptions of the need for such a Round. In particular, a round with a broad-based and balanced agenda to conclude within a three-year time-frame continues to be an objective of a number of developed and developing countries.[26] The main argument of the proponents for launching the new round has been to keep up the momentum of trade liberalization against protectionist pressures which risked becoming stronger around the world, as well as to provide the possibility for trade-offs that would facilitate concessions for different participants, including developing countries. Among the major trading countries, the European Union was the main proponent of a major "Millennium" Round.[27] The United States, on the other hand, was hindered from taking major initiatives by the failure of the President to obtain "fast track" legislation (or even legislation setting out negotiating objectives) from Congress, and has, thus, tailored its proposals to conform to its residual negotiating authority.

In contrast, some developing countries have considered that WTO work should concentrate on the full implementation of the Uruguay Round results and the "built-in agenda" which foresaw new negotiations on agriculture and trade in services, and reviews of several Multilateral Trade Agreements (MTAs) which could give rise to negotiations. These countries indicated that there was no consensus on structuring the future WTO work programme as another "round".[28] Other matters of priority for many developing countries were, among others: (a) the implementation of special and differential treatment in their favour as envisaged in various WTO agreements; and (b) correction of imbalances in several WTO Agreements, including on Subsidies and Countervailing Measures, Anti-Dumping, TRIPS and TRIMs which have major implications for development policies and/or export interests of developing countries.

Objectives of the Negotiations

Developing countries are of the view that any Ministerial declaration eventually launching the new negotiation should contain a statement of the "problematique" facing developing countries that would have to be addressed in those negotiations, a "diagnosis" of the overall problem which the negotiations should seek to correct. Otherwise, in their view, the negotiations would be conducted on the assumption that liberalization of world trade, and the tightening and extension of multilateral trade disciplines into new areas, was an end to itself, rather than a means to achieving the more rapid development of developing countries. In this context, the work leading up to UNCTAD X becomes directly relevant to the WTO preparatory process.

BOX 1

"G-77" Diagnosis:

Financial vulnerability, including persistent balance-of-payment problems and extremely high external indebtedness, as well as narrow export potential and high dependence on commodities for trade, production and employment and lack of access to technology and information networks and distribution channels remain major obstacles for many developing countries to integrate successfully in the multilateral trading system and benefit from trade liberalization. Developing country firms often confront a world market dominated by TNCs, and by developed country media. As a result, many developing countries have not been able to benefit from the new trading opportunities offered by the MTAs. Furthermore, major imbalances in the balance of rights and obligations exist in certain multilateral trade agreements, as well as in market access and rule-making areas which may erode their confidence in the multilateral trading system.

Global economic growth in the 1990s has remained below the post-war average, the income gap between the developed and the developing countries has grown wider, and the prospect of marginalization is becoming increasingly real. This has been accompanied by increasing income inequality within countries, along with increased job and income insecurity and financial instability. These tendencies have been compounded by a series of unexpected financial crises which have affected the global economy with increasing frequency and intensity in the 1990s.

Recent experience suggests that no simple economic policy will make developing countries converge automatically towards the income levels of developed countries. This is a result of the operation of market forces in a world of asymmetries and imbalances. The most striking asymmetry in the globalization process lies in the uneven distribution of economic power in the world economy. A second set of imbalances exists among the international economic forces themselves. The fast pace of financial liberalization has delinked finance from international trade and investment. A premium has been placed on liquidity and the speedy entry into and exit from financial markets in search of quick gains. The growing volatility of capital flows follows from these developments.

Given these asymmetries in the world economy, the extent and the ordering of liberalization have also tended to have unbalanced outcomes. In trade, despite the liberalization process, many areas of export interest to developing countries remain heavily protected. Equally, labour markets have also remained protected in the developed countries, while capital markets have opened up in the developing countries. This makes it more difficult for developing countries to compete in those sectors where real and sustainable growth opportunities are most likely.

(Continued on next page.)

(Continued from preceding page.)

Objectives common to many developing countries:

(1) the implementation of the rules and commitments agreed to during the Uruguay Round, as enshrined the Marrakesh Final Act, especially those in favour of developing countries,

(2) the launching of the negotiations on trade in services under Article XIX of the GATS and the continuation of the process of reform of trade in agriculture as provided under Article 20 of the Agreement on Agriculture, and the completion of the various reviews of provisions of the Multilateral Trade Agreements (MTAs) as mandated by the Agreements themselves,

(3) action in favour of the least developed countries (LDCs),

(4) action to advance accessions to the WTO,

(5) measures to improve coherence in economic policy-making between the WTO and other international organizations,

(6) reaching consensus on the future direction of the work programme established at the first and second Ministerial Conferences,

(7) new initiatives aimed at liberalizing world trade and adapting the multilateral trading system so enhance its support of the development process.

General principles governing negotiations

In particular, in the view of developing countries, efforts to correct this situation in multilateral trade negotiations should seek substantial liberalization of trade in a balanced manner covering all products, services sectors and modes of supply of export interest to developing countries. In this view, there should be "umbrella" negotiating groups which would conduct overviews of the progress in specific areas of the negotiations with respect to progress toward these general goals. For example, such a negotiating group on the Transfer of Technology has been suggested, to propose approaches in negotiations in various areas that would correct the current trend toward reduced access to technology for developing country firms arising primarily from the privatization of R&D in the developed countries.[29]

The state of implementation of many provisions intended to provide for special and differential treatment for the developing countries ("S&D" provisions) is a source of deep concern to many developing countries. In many cases, this is due to the fact that such provisions are phrased in vague, "best endeavour" language. Developing countries would like to see all special and differential provisions translated into concrete benefits for them. They would like the concept of special and differential treatment to be reconfirmed and closely adapted to the development policies of developing countries, so as to ensure enhanced coherence between trade and development policies, as well as to the realities of globalization. In this view, such treatment should take into account the changing methods by which international trade is actually conducted and attempt to correct the handicaps faced by developing country firms in competing in such trade, by modifying the MTAs where necessary. In doing so, all relevant provisions of the MTAs could be reviewed, with the objective being to reach agreements on all these issues at an early stage of negotiations.

Many developing countries are having considerable difficulty in fully complying with their obligations before the expiry of the transitional periods, and therefore consider that the transitional periods should be extended for a length of time that would reflect the availability to developing countries of the necessary financial resources and human capacities to implement these various agreements. In this view, if new negotiations are launched, they should therefore include a "peace clause" so that developing countries could not be challenged under the dispute settlement mechanisms while the negotiations were in progress. This would preempt a situation in which developing countries would find themselves negotiating under the duress of frequent resort to the dispute settlement mechanism against them. Developing countries believe that, as in previous negotiations, a "standstill" clause should apply, and that such standstill should refer to all market access conditions, including GSP and other preferential agreements. They are also of the view that developed countries should make a clear indication at Seattle that they are committed to meaningful trade liberalization in areas of interest to developing countries, including tariffs, agricultural subsidies, anti-dumping measures, etc.

Developing countries consider that credit to them for autonomous trade liberalization measures should be a general principle governing negotiations, in that the binding of liberalization undertaken since 1 January 1995 should be recognized as a concession on the part of developing countries. In their view, this principle, articulated in GATS Article XIX:3, should apply across-the-board.

It is widely agreed that the experience with the Uruguay Round implementation has clearly demonstrated that it is imperative to address administrative and other costs of implementing any Multilateral Trade Agreements at national level[30] as an integral part of negotiations,[31] to ensure that developing countries are able to implement them and to identify the amount of assistance that should be provided by the international community to support them.

Developing countries consider that there should be a reconfirmation of the commitment to devote special attention to the problems faced by the least-developed countries, and measures to prevent their marginalization in world trade. In their view, the eventual launching of the negotiations should result in a decision to establish schedules under GATT Article II to extend bound, duty free treatment in favour of the LDCs by developed countries, and developing countries in their position to do so; and this should be accompanied by appropriate flexibility in the rules of origin to enable LDCs to effectively benefit. The specific problems of the small vulnerable developing economies were recognized in the 1998 Geneva Ministerial Declaration. Developing countries consider that these should be addressed by identifying the specific concerns of these countries under the various MTAs and formulating proposals for action.

There seems to be growing support for the idea of a "single undertaking" as sectoral or partial approaches are seen as likely to result in developing country issues being postponed or ignored. Some developing countries have stated that they will not participate in sectoral negotiations. However, it is also recognized that the "single undertaking" does not automatically ensure a balance favourable to developing countries. The possibility of "early harvests" which, to a certain extent, qualifies the "single undertaking" approach, is gathering support in developing countries, who consider that results should be achieved on the implementation and built-in agenda issues before initiating, or at least before completing, negotiations in other areas. Some of the nervousness of developing countries with respect to the "single undertaking" results from their experience of the final stages of the Uruguay Round, where they were faced with a take-it-or-leave-it situation. It should be recalled that the developed countries had decided to withdraw from the GATT to set up the WTO (originally MTO—Multilateral Trade Organization) to avoid the necessity of amending the GATT. Developing countries were thus obliged to accept all the Uruguay Round MTAs or remain outside the WTO. Since the WTO now exists, this situation cannot arise in the future, and a single undertaking will have to be accepted by consensus or vote, as provided in Articles IX and X of the WTO Agreement.

BOX 2

The Single Undertaking

The implications of the single undertaking concept differ depending on the particular context and the result desired by the parties concerned.

In the Uruguay Round, the main protagonists of the single undertaking approach (the Cairns group) sought to preempt the situation where agriculture could be dropped from the liberalization process during the course of the negotiations, as had happened in previous rounds. Furthermore, in earlier rounds, the United States Executive had been able to obtain negotiating authority only on the condition that the MFA would not be touched. Some developed countries, the USA in particular, also wished to ensure that developing countries, which they claimed had been "free riders" in earlier rounds, were obliged to accept a higher level of multilateral trade commitments. The Punta del Este Declaration thus specified in Part I B (ii) that "the launching, the conduct and implementation of the outcome of the negotiations shall be treated as parts of a single undertaking".

The Tokyo Round had resulted in a series of Codes, some of which interpreted existing GATT rules to provide for more stringent disciplines on several key NTMs, as well as on specific product categories, (some of which were aimed at restricting trade and fixing prices). The Codes were accepted on an optional basis, and in practice developed countries (with few exceptions) had subscribed to the NTM Codes. Not all developing countries had accepted the Codes; for example, although many had accepted the TBT code, only one had accepted the Government Procurement Code.

It should be recalled , however, that the Tokyo Round was legally not a GATT negotiation, but open to all countries. Some non-GATT contracting parties at the time took an active role (e.g. Mexico), of which several negotiated their accession to GATT during the round (e.g. Thailand, Colombia).

Despite the Punta del Este single undertaking clause, there was an early harvest at Montreal where decisions with respect to LDCs and dispute settlement were taken and applied on a provisional basis until confirmed at Marrakesh.

The unique nature of the Uruguay Round single undertaking was that it was imposed by fiat. Faced with the impossibility of amending the GATT to incorporate all the MTAs, the developed countries had decided to withdraw from the GATT (termed GATT 1947) and establish a new legal framework, supported by a new organization, i.e. the WTO. Developing countries thus had little choice but to accept the "single undertaking", even though it included some agreements, e.g. TRIPS, that they would never have accepted had they had the choice.

In the Uruguay Round, the concern of developing countries was to ensure that certain key issues were not excluded. In the future round, their main concern may be to ensure that certain issues are not included. Thus the approach to the question of the single undertaking would seem to depend upon what is finally included within the scope of the negotiations. For example, some developing countries may wish to ensure that anti-dumping is included, but investment excluded.

Sectoral negotiations do not conflict with the single undertaking, if they are only used as a negotiating technique and not as a measure of excluding more "sensitive" sectors, as was the case with the "zero-for-zero" negotiations in the Uruguay Round, and do not define the scope of the negotiations (i.e. some sectors would be excluded) as seems to be the case in APEC. The APEC sectors targeted for advanced (or accelerated) liberalization reflect the United States Executive's residual tariff negotiating authority. Developing countries' concern with this approach is that experience has shown that the sectors of export interest to the major trading countries receive priority in such negotiations. Sectoral negotiations can be used to go beyond tariffs to address a variety of issues per-

—(Continued on next page.)—

(Continued from preceding page.)

taining to a particular sector, such as subsidies, technical barriers, etc. The proposals on the fishery and forestry sectors seem to be aimed at an agreement which would deal with a variety of issues, including subsidies and environmental issues. The examples from the Tokyo Round are rather mixed: the Civil Aircraft Agreement was trade liberalizing, while the now defunct Agreement on Dairy Products fixed prices of exports; the MFA was, in the perspective of many developing countries, a very bad sectoral agreement.

BOX 3

Summary of "General principles governing negotiations" as stated by many developing countries

(i) Conduct of the negotiations in a fully transparent and manageable manner to ensure the effective participation of all WTO members;

(ii) Single undertaking: The launch, conduct and conclusion of the negotiations should be aimed at a single undertaking. The results of the negotiations shall be adopted in their entirety and applied to all WTO Members;

(iii) Principle of differential and more favourable treatment for developing countries should be fully reconfirmed, converted into concrete benefits and closely adapted to development policies of developing countries. Considering the costs of implementing the MTAs at the national level should be made an integral part of negotiations;

(iv) Particular situation of the least developed countries should be taken into account;

(v) Special consideration should be given to the case of small and vulnerable economies;

(vi) Recognition of autonomous trade liberalization measures and provision of modalities for crediting developing countries for such measures. Binding of liberalization undertaken since 1 January 1995 should be recognized as a concession on the part of developing countries;

(vii) Standstill: Commencing immediately and continuing until the formal completion of the negotiations, participants should agree not to take any trade restrictive or distorting measures inconsistent with the provisions of the WTO Agreements and not to take any trade measures in such a manner as to improve their negotiating positions. Developed countries should additionally agree that they will exercise due restraint in taking any trade restrictive or distorting measure in the legitimate exercise of their rights under the MTAs. Such standstill should apply to all market access conditions, including the GSP and other preferential arrangements. This should be subject to multilateral surveillance;

(viii) Peace clause" should be agreed that would ensure that developing countries would not be challenged under the dispute settlement mechanisms while the negotiations are in progress.

Implementation and "Deliverables"

There are a number of areas where the deadline for action set in the Uruguay Round Agreements have not been met. These include, for example, the negotiation of an arrangement to limit export credits in agriculture, a GATS emergency safeguard clause, the completion of negotiations on rules of origin and anti-circumvention measures, etc. These will have to be addressed by the negotiations' launching process.

BOX 4

The Uruguay Round Unfinished Business and the Reviews of the Operation and Implementation of Certain Specific Provisions of the WTO MTAs

(a) Unfinished business and reviews under GATS

A working party on GATS rules was established in 1995 to negotiate rules and disciplines in the areas emergency safeguards, government procurement and subsidies for services.

It was agreed at the Singapore Ministerial Conference that the results of the multilateral negotiations on emergency safeguards (GATS Article X) should enter into effect not later than 1 January 1998 (paragraph 17 of the SMD). This deadline was not met then and later.

Article XIII:2 of GATS provided that "There shall be multilateral negotiations on government procurement in services under this Agreement within two years from the date of entry into force of the WTO Agreement." The negotiations on government procurement "should commence" within two years from the date of entry into force of the WTO agreement, that is not later than 1 January 1997. The SMD noted that "more analytical work will be needed" on this issue (paragraph 17 of the SMD). To date, these negotiations had not yet reached any results.

No precise timetable was set for the negotiations on Article XV of the GATS (subsidies to trade in services). The SMD noted that "more analytical work will be needed" on this issue (paragraph 17 of the SMD).

Development of disciplines in the area of professional services: a Working Party on Professional Services (WPPS) was established in 1995. Priority attention of the WPPS has been given to the accountancy sector. The SMD committed to complete "the work on accountancy sector by the end of 1997." The SMD encouraged "the successful completion of international standards in the accountancy sector by IFAC, IASC, and IOSCO." (paragraph 17 of the SMD). In December 1998, the Council for Trade in Services adopted the Disciplines on Domestic Regulation in the Accountancy Sector which had been developed by the Working Party on Professional Services.

(Continued on next page.)

(Continued from preceding page.)

GATS Article II provides that MFN treatment is unconditional and is to be treated as a general obligation. However, Article II.2 does provide for certain exceptions from this obligation, governed by the criteria of the Annex on Article II Exemptions. As regards MFN exemptions, members are allowed to benefit from an exemption for a period of not more than 10 years, with a review requirement after 5 years (i.e., 1 January 2000), although the possibilities of exception are rather broad. Given that the Annex on Article II Exemptions does not specify conditions and criteria on the basis of which the review could take place, thought will need to be given to the establishment of guidelines for determining whether an exemption is reasonable, legitimate and does not nullify the benefits of the GATS.

The Annex on Air Transport Services applies to measures affecting trade in air transport services and ancillary services. It excludes from GATS coverage traffic rights and directly related activities that might affect the negotiation of traffic rights. The GATS applies, however, to aircraft repair and maintenance services, the marketing of air transport services and computer reservation system services for which commitments have been made by many countries. Paragraph 5 of the Annex requires the Council for Trade in Services to undertake periodical review, and at least every five years, of the developments in the air transport sector and operation of this Annex with a view to considering the possible further application of the GATS in this sector.

(*b*) Anti-circumvention measures in relation to anti-dumping duty measures (Marrakesh Ministerial Decision)

This matter was raised by the major developed countries for negotiations and addressed unsuccessfully in the Uruguay Round. At the Marrakesh meeting, Ministers decided that the issue of circumvention of anti-dumping duties would be remitted to the WTO Committee on Anti-Dumping Practices. The informal consultations on this subject matter so far have been conducted within the context of the Committee on Anti-Dumping Practices with a view to reaching an agreement on a framework of understanding within which further informal consultations should be held. No results have been achieved to date.

(*c*) Harmonization of non-preferential rules of origin (Article 9 of the Agreement on Rules of Origin)

The WTO Agreement on Rules of Origin provided that the harmonized set of rules shall apply to all non-preferential commercial policy instruments, from MFN treatment to government procurement and trade statistics and such work programme should be completed within three years. The work programme of harmonization was initiated in July 1995 and the WTO Committee on Rules of Origin has received three reports from the WCO Technical Committee for consideration. In May 1996, the WTO Committee decided to establish an integrated negotiating text—a common working document with a view to enhancing efficiency and discipline in the negotiating process, and assisting delegations in assessing progress in the negotiations and problems that exist. Despite prolongation of the deadline for completion of these negotiations, no agreed outcome has yet been reached.

(*d*) **Development of internationally agreed disciplines to govern the provision of export credits, export credit guarantees or insurance programmes (Article 10 of the Agreement on Agriculture).**

Export subsidies are among the most trade-distorting measures as they allow subsidizing countries to displace efficient producers in world markets for agricultural products. Part V of the Agreement on Agriculture imposes multilateral disciplines on agricultural export subsidies for the first time (though it is very vague), beginning the process of reducing the use of export subsidies in agricultural trade. As part of its continuous work programme, Article 10.2 of the Agreement commits WTO members to work towards internationally agreed disciplines and to abide by those disciplines once they are established. This commitment provides an opportunity to establish additional limits on measures that can serve as indirect export subsidies with a view to preventing WTO members from circumventing the export subsidy commitments. However, despite some work conducted on this subject in OECD, no agreed outcome has yet been reached in the WTO.

(*e*) **Special review on non-actionable research and development subsidies (Article 8.2(a), footnote 25 of the ASCVM)**

Although such review should have been conducted within 18 months after the entry into force of the WTO Agreement (i.e., by the end of June 1996), in view of the lack of experience and the fact that no notifications of non-actionable research subsidies had been submitted, it was agreed that such review will be conducted at a future time if members wish to do so.

(*f*) **Export competitiveness provision for developing countries (Article 27.6 of the ASCVM)**

The operation of this provision should be reviewed five years from the date of the entry into force of the WTO Agreement (1 January 2000); this has not yet been done.

(*g*) **Article 6.1 on actionable subsidies and Articles 8 and 9 on non-actionable subsidies (Article 31 of the ASCVM)**

The operation of these provisions should be reviewed five years after the entry into force of the WTO Agreement with a view to deciding whether to extend their application. Such review is supposed to be conducted not later than 180 days before the end of this period (i.e. 1 January 2000); this has not yet been done.

(Continued on next page.)

(Continued from preceding page.)

(*h*) Geographical indications (Article 24.2 of the TRIPS Agreement)

The TRIPS Agreement establishes protection of the indications which identify a good as originating in a country, or a region or locality where a given quality, reputation or other characteristic of the good is essentially attributed to its geographical origin. Article 24.2 of the Agreement commits WTO members to keep under review of the application of the relevant provisions in the Council for TRIPS and the first such review was to have taken place within two years of the entry into force of the WTO Agreement. The review has been delayed and has not yet taken place.

(*i*) Patent or *sui generis* protection of plant varieties (Article 27.3 (b) of the TRIPS Agreement)

Patentable subject-matter was one of the most difficult issues in the Uruguay Round TRIPS Agreement negotiations. One of the main reasons is that intellectual property protection in this area of living matter is still in its early years of development. For that reason, the TRIPS Agreement called for a review four years after the date of entry into force of the WTO Agreement (i.e., not later than 1 January 1999); this review has not yet occurred.

(*j*) The non-application to TRIPS of GATT Article XXIII:1 (*b*) and (*c*) (i.e., non-violation provisions) with a view to examining the scope and modalities for complaints of the type provided for under GATT Article XXIII:1 (*b*) and (*c*) (Article 64 of the TRIPS Agreement)

While Article 64.1 of the TRIPS Agreement affirms the applicability of the DSU to the TRIPS Agreement, paragraphs 2 and 3 of Article 64 try to accommodate the inconclusive negotiations in the Uruguay Round regarding GATT Article XXIII:1 (b) and (c), which refer to non-violation and "any other situation", respectively. Thus, GATT Article XXIII:1 (b) and (c) will not apply to the settlement of disputes under the TRIPS Agreement for a period of five years from the entry into force of the WTO Agreement. During this five-year period, the TRIPS Council has examined the scope and modalities for these complaints made pursuant to the TRIPS Agreement, and was to submit its recommendations to the third Ministerial Conference for approval. No decision was taken on this issue at the Ministerial Conference. Therefore, unless a consensus develops on whatever is to be agreed for the future, paragraphs 1 (b) and (c) of GATT Article XXIII would cease to apply to the TRIPS Agreement.

(*k*) Standard of review for anti-dumping disputes, and consideration of the general application and the application to countervailing cases (Marrakesh Ministerial Decision)

The provision on standards of review in the Anti-Dumping Agreement obliges dispute settlement panels to defer to the decisions of the administering authorities if an alternative interpretation of the agreement is "permissible". In the Marrakesh Ministerial Decision, it was provided that the standards of review

(Art.17.6 of the Agreement on Anti-Dumping) should be reviewed after a period of three years with a view to considering the question of whether it was capable of general application. No further work on this subject has been conducted to date.

(*l*) Operation of TRIMs Agreement and consideration of whether to complement it with provisions on investment policy and competition policy (Article 9 of the TRIMs Agreement)

Although the scope and coverage of the TRIMs Agreement is circumscribed by Article 1 which stipulates that it relates to trade in goods only and its application is limited only to those measures that are prohibited by GATT Articles III and XI, as provided for in Article 2, Article 9 of the TRIMs Agreement on review of the operation of the Agreement provides for consideration as to whether the Agreement should be amended or complemented with provisions on investment policy and competition policy. This would mean that the TRIMs Agreement could be expanded to develop an investment regime and to add provisions to address the problems of anti-competitive practices of the transnational corporations, such as restrictive business practices.No such decision has yet been taken.

(*m*) Interpretation of the rules on modification and withdrawal of concessions—negotiating rights (Understanding on interpretation of GATT Article XXVIII)

Under the provisions of Article XXVIII of GATT 1947, there was no precise definition of "substantial interest" which is related to the "initial negotiating rights". The Understanding on the Interpretation of Article XXVIII (GATT 1994) created a new negotiating right for the country for which the product in question accounts for the highest proportion of its exports—(or the so-called "additional negotiating rights"). Such a country is deemed to have a principal supplying interest if it does not already have an initial negotiating right or a principal supplying interest (as provided for in Article XXVIII:1). Para. 1 of the Understanding provides for a review by the Council for Trade in Goods, 5 years after the entry into force of the WTO (i.e., by the end of 1999) to decide whether the criteria for determination of additional negotiating rights has worked satisfactorily in securing a redistribution of negotiating rights in favour of small and medium sized exporters. This has not yet been done.

(*n*) Grandfather rights (i.e. the US Jones Act) (Paragraph 3 of GATT 1994)

Under the GATT 1947 and its Provisional Protocol of Application , a number of "grandfather" rights were enjoyed by some GATT contracting parties. As provided in Para. 3 of the GATT 1994, the Ministerial Conference is to undertake a review of the only remaining such right, i.e. the US Jones Act (not later than 5 years after the entry into force of the WTO, i.e., by the end of 1999) for the purpose of examining whether the conditions which had created the need for the exemption still existed. Such review is now under way.

(Continued on next page.)

(Continued from preceding page.)

(o) Operation of TPRM (Section F of TPRM)

Section F of TPRM requires the WTO to undertake an appraisal of the operation of the TPRM not more than 5 years after the entry into force of the WTO Agreement and to report the results of the appraisal to the Ministerial Conference. It may subsequently undertake appraisals of the TPRM at intervals to be determined by it or as requested by the Ministerial Conference. The appraisal has not yet occurred.

(p) Dispute settlement rules and procedures (Marrakesh Ministerial Decision)

The Marrakesh Ministerial Decision on the Application and Review of the Understanding on Rules and Procedures Governing the Settlement of Disputes requires the Ministerial Conference to complete a full review of dispute settlement rules and procedures under the WTO within four years after the entry into force of WTO Agreement and to take a decision on the occasion of its first meeting after the completion of the review, whether to continue, modify or terminate such dispute settlement rules and procedures. Such review has not yet been completed, while its deadline expired on 31 July 1999.

(q) Implementation of TRIPS Agreement (Article 71.1 of the TRIPS Agreement)

Under Article 71.1 of the Agreement, the TRIPS Council is required to review the implementation of the TRIPS Agreement after the expiration of the transitional period (for developing countries, i.e., 1 January 2000). This has not yet been done. The TRIPS Council is also required, having regard to the experience gained in its implementation, to review it two years after that date, and at identical intervals thereafter. The Council may also undertake reviews in the light of any relevant new developments which might warrant modification or amendment of the TRIPS Agreement.

Developing countries see the most urgent objective in new negotiations as being to address implementation issues (see Box 5 below). As part of these, they consider that where S&D treatment has been expressed in terms of best endeavour clauses, there will be a need, before the negotiations are launched, to assess the extent to which the expected benefits have actually materialized in practice. These clauses include provisions of Article IV of GATS, the transfer of technology provisions of the TRIPS and SPS Agreements, Decisions on Measures in Favour of Least—Developed Countries and Net Food-Importing Developing Countries, and practically all provisions in the WTO Agreements related to technical assistance. The launching process might take separate Decisions aimed at ensuring the effective operation of these provisions (see Box 6 below).

BOX 5

Implementation Issues Raised By Developing Countries[32]

(1) **Agriculture**

—Developing countries with predominately rural agrarian economies shall have sufficient flexibility in the green box to adequately address their non-trade concerns, such as food security and rural employment.

If in the calculation of the AMS, domestic support prices are lower than the external reference price (so as to ensure access of poor households to basic foodstuffs), thereby resulting in negative product specific support, then Members shall be allowed to increase their non-product specific support by an equivalent amount.

—TRQ administration shall be made transparent, equitable and non-discriminatory, in order to allow new/small-scale developing-country exporters to obtain market access.

—To this end, notifications submitted to the Committee on Agriculture shall include also details on guidelines and procedures of allotment of TRQ.

—The Marrakesh Ministerial Decision on Measures Concerning the Possible Negative Effects of the Reform Programme on Least-Developed and Net Food-Importing Developing Countries (NFIDCs) shall be revised, before 1 January 2001, in order to ensure its effective implementation.

(2) **Services**

—Developed countries shall fully implement commitments undertaken by them in Mode 4. In regard to mode 4 commitments: (a) there shall be no application of the economic needs test; (b) there shall be automatic issuance of visas and exemption from work permit/residency requirements for short periods of presence, for the sectors where commitments have been undertaken by developed country Members.

—A monitoring and notification mechanism shall be established to ensure effective implementation of Article IV.

(3) **Anti-Dumping**

—No investigation shall be initiated for a period of 365 days from the date of finalization of a previous investigation for the same product.

—Under Article 9.1 the lesser duty rule shall be made mandatory.

—Article 2.2 shall be clarified in order to make appropriate comparison with respect to the margin of dumping.

(Continued on next page.)

(Continued from preceding page.)

—Article 15 of the Agreement on Implementation of Article VI is only a best-endeavour clause. Consequently, Members have rarely, if at all, explored the possibility of constructive remedies before applying anti-dumping duties against exports from developing countries. Hence, the provisions of Article 15 need to be operationalized and made mandatory.

—The existing de minimis dumping margin of 2 per cent of export price below which no anti-dumping duty can be imposed (Article 5.8), needs to be raised to 5 per cent for developing countries, so as to reflect the inherent advantages that the industries in these countries enjoy *vis-à-vis* comparable production in developed countries.

—The major users have so far applied this prescribed de minimis only in newly initiated cases, not in review and refund cases. It is imperative that the proposed de minimis dumping margin of 5 per cent is applied not only in ew cases but also in refund and review cases.

—The threshold volume of dumped imports which shall normally be regarded as negligible (Article 5.8) should be increased from the existing 3 per cent to 5 per cent for imports from developing countries. Moreover, the stipulation that anti-dumping action can still be taken even if the volume of imports is below this threshold level, provided countries which individually account for less than the threshold volume, collectively account for more than 7 per cent of the imports, should be deleted. Article 5.8 should also be clarified with regard to the time-frame to be used in determining the volume of the dumped imports.

—The definition of "substantial quantities" as provided for in Article 2.2.1 (footnote 5) is still very restrictive and permits unreasonable findings of dumping. The substantial quantities test should be increased from the present threshold of 20 per cent to at least 40 per cent.

—Article 2.4.1 shall include details of dealing with foreign exchange rate fluctuations during the process of dumping.

—Article 3 shall contain a detailed provision dealing with the determination of the material retardation of the establishment of a domestic industry as stipulated in footnote 9.

—As developing countries liberalize, the incidence of dumping in to these countries is likely to increase. It is important to address this concern, since otherwise the momentum of import liberalization in developing countries may suffer. There should therefore be a provision in the Agreement, which provides a presumption of dumping of imports from developed countries into developing countries, provided certain conditions are met. Presently there is a different and more restrictive standard of review pertaining to adjudication in anti-dumping cases. There is no reason why there should be such discrimination for anti-dumping investigations. Hence, Article 17 should be suitably modified so that the general standard of review laid down in the WTO dispute settlement mechanism applies equally and totally to disputes in the anti-dumping area.

—The annual review provided under Article 18.6 has remained a proforma exercise and has not provided adequate opportunity for Members to address the issue of increasing anti-dumping measures and instances of abuse of the Agreement to accommodate protectionist pressures. This Article must be appropriately amended to ensure that the annual reviews are meaningful and play a role in reducing the possible abuse of the Anti-Dumping Agreement.

(4) Subsidies Agreement

—Article 8:1 of the Subsidies Agreement dealing with non-actionable subsidies shall be expanded to include subsidies referred to in Article 3:1 of the Agreement when such subsidies are provided by developing country Members.

—Export credits given by developing countries shall not be considered as subsidies so long as the rates at which they are extended are above LIBOR.

—Any countervailing duties shall be restricted only to that amount by which the subsidy exceeds the de minimis level.

—Annex VII of the Agreement shall be modified to read as follows:

The developing-country Members not subject to the provisions of paragraph 1(a) of Article 3 under the terms of paragraph 2(a) of Article 27 are:

(i) The developing countries, including the least-developed countries, Members of the WTO that are included in the Low and Middle Income Category of the World Bank;

(ii) Countries indicated in paragraph (i) above will be excluded from this Annex if their GNP per capita has exceeded the top level of the Middle Income Category of the World Bank.

—The prohibition on using export subsidies under Article 27:6 shall be applicable to a developing country only after its export levels in a product have remained over 3.25 per cent of world trade continuously for a period of five years.

—Aggregate and generalized rates of duty rate remission should be allowed in case of developing countries even though the individual units may not be able to establish the source of their inputs.

—Developing countries should be allowed to neutralize the cost-escalating effect of taxes collected by government authorities at different levels i.e. the taxes such as sales tax, octroi, cess, etc. which are not refunded, without these being termed as subsidies.

—Article 11:9 should be modified to provide an additional dispensation for developing countries, in as much as that any subsidy investigation shall be immediately terminated in cases where the subsidy being pro-

(Continued on next page.)

(Continued from preceding page.)

vided by a developing country is less than 2.5 per cent ad valorem, instead of the existing de minimis of 1 per cent presently applicable to all Members.

—The present de minimis level of 3 per cent, below which countervailing duties may not be imposed for developing countries, needs to be increased (Article 27:11). Countervailing duty investigations should not be initiated or, if initiated, should be terminated, when imports from developing counties are less than 7 per cent of the total imports irrespective of the cumulative volume of imports of the like products from all developing countries.

—Article 27:3 of the Agreement allows a developing country to grant a subsidy for the use of domestic products in preference to imported products (defined in Article 3.1(b of the Agreement). There should be a clarification in Article 27:3 that it is applicable notwithstanding the provisions of any other agreement.

—The definition of "inputs consumed in the production process" (footnote 61) needs to be expanded to include all inputs, not just physical inputs, which may have contributed to the determination of the final cost price of the exported product.

—Annex I of the Agreement shall be amended to provide developing countries the flexibility to finance their exporters, consistent with their developmental objectives. Annex I shall clarify that developing countries shall not be compelled to conform to any undertaking or arrangement designed for developed countries which proves to be unrealistic given the difficulties and constraints confronted by developing countries.

(5) Sanitary and Phytosanitary Measures

—The provisions in Article 10 shall be made mandatory, including that if an SPS measure creates a problem for more than one developing country, then the country which has adopted it shall withdraw it.

—Article 10:2 provision shall be made mandatory for developed countries to provide a time period of at least 12 months from the date of notification for compliance of new SPS measures for products from developing countries.

—International standard-setting organizations shall ensure the presence of countries at different levels of development and from all geographical regions, throughout all phases of standard-setting.

—The provisions of paragraph 2 of Annex B shall made mandatory, and a "reasonable interval" shall mean not less than 12 months.

—Article 4 shall be clarified so that developing countries can enter into equivalency agreements.

—Though the SPS Agreement encourages Members to enter into MRAs, so far developing countries have not been included into such agreements. It is suggested that: (i) MRAs are developed in a transparent way; (ii) they should be open to parties that may wish to join them at a later stage; and (iii) they should contain rules of origin which allow all products which pass the conformity assessment procedures to benefit from the MRA.

—The definition of an international standard, guideline and recommendation (paragraph 3 of Annex A) needs to be revised so that a differentiation is introduced between mandatory international standards and voluntary international guidelines/recommendations.

—Article 12:7 provides for a review of the operation and implementation of the Agreement three years after the date of entry into force of the Agreement and thereafter as the need arises. This review shall be carried out once every two years.

(6) Technical Barriers to Trade

—International standard-setting organizations shall ensure the presence of countries at different levels of development and from all geographical regions, throughout all phases of standard-setting.

—A specific mandate shall be given to the TBT Committee as part of its triennial work programme to address the problems faced by developing countries in both international standards and conformity assessment.

—The triennial work programme of the TBT Committee shall as a matter of priority address the following issues and find solutions:

—Means have to be found to ensure effective participation of developing countries in setting of standards by international standard-setting organizations. It shall be obligatory for international standardizing bodies to ensure the presence of developing countries in the different phases of standard setting. Moreover, a clear provision that the international standardizing bodies must comply with the Code of Good Practice.

—Article 11 shall be made obligatory so that technical assistance and cooperation is provided to developing countries for upgrading conformity assessment procedures.

—Acceptance by developed-country importers of self-declaration regarding adherence to standards by developing-country exporters and acceptance of certification procedure adopted by developing country certification bodies based on international standards. Such a provision to be introduced in Article 12.

—A specific provision to be introduced in Article 12 that developing countries shall be given a longer time-frame to comply with measures regarding products to export of interest to them. Furthermore, a specific provision in Article 12 that if a measure brought forward by a developed

(Continued on next page.)

(Continued from preceding page.)

country creates difficulties for developing countries, then the measure should be reconsidered.

(7) Textiles

—Importing countries shall, on the first day of the 85th month that the WTO Agreement is in effect, integrate products which accounted for not less than 50 per cent of the total volume of the Member's 1990 imports.

—The importing countries to apply growth-on-growth for stage 3 with effect from 1 January 2000 instead of 1 January 2002.

—A moratorium shall be applied by importing countries on anti-dumping actions until two years after the entire textiles and clothing sector is integrated into the GATT.

—Any change in rules of origin shall be examined in the CTG for its possible impact on market access of exporting countries, before it is applied.

(8) Trade-Related Investment Measures

—The transition period mentioned in Article 5 paragraph 2 shall be extended until such time that their development needs demand.

—Developing countries shall have another opportunity to notify existing TRIMs measures which they would be then allowed to maintain till the end of the new transition period.

—Article 5.3, which recognises the importance of taking account of the development, financial and trade needs of developing-countries while dealing with trade-related investment measures, has remained inoperative and ineffectual. The provisions of this Article must therefore be suitably amended and made mandatory.

—Developing countries shall be exempted from the disciplines on the application of domestic content requirement by providing for an enabling provision in Articles 2 and 4 to this effect.

(9) Trade-Related Aspects of Intellectual Property Rights

—In the light of provisions contained in Articles 23 and 24 of the TRIPS Agreement, additional protection for geographical indications shall be extended for products other than wines and spirits.

—A clear understanding in the interim that patents inconsistent with Article 15 of the CBD shall not be granted.

—Article 64, paragraph 2 shall be modified so as to make it clear that subparagraphs (*b*) and (*c*) of Article XXIII of GATT 1994 shall not apply to the TRIPS Agreement.

—The provisions of Article 66.2 shall be made obligatory and shall be subject to periodical notification.

—The period given for implementation of the provisions of Article 27.3(*b*) shall be five years from the date the review is completed.

—The list of exceptions to patentability in Article 27.3(b) of the TRIPS Agreement shall include the list of essential drugs of the World Health Organization. Article 7 and 8 of the TRIPS Agreement to be operationalized by providing for transfer of technology on fair and mutually advantageous terms. Article 27.3(*b*) be amended in light of the provisions of the Convention on Biological Diversity and the International Undertaking, in which the conservation and sustainable use of biological diversity, the protection of the rights and knowledge of indigenous and local communities, and the promotion of farmers' rights, are fully taken into account.

Further, the review of the substantive provisions of Article 27.3(b) should:

—clarify artificial distinctions between biological and microbiological organisms and processes;

—ensure the continuation of the traditional farming practices including the right to save, exchange and save seeds, and sell their harvest; and

—prevent anti-competitive practices which will threaten food sovereignty of people in developing countries, as permitted by Article 31 of the TRIPS Agreement.

(10) Agreement on Implementation of Article VII of GATT 1994

—A multilateral solution that enables customs administrations of importing countries to seek and obtain information on export values in a time-bound manner, in doubtful cases, shall be included in the Agreement.

—The addition of cost of services such as engineering, development, and design work, which are supplied directly or indirectly by the buyer free of charge or at reduced cost for the production of goods under import, shall be included in Article 8:1(*b*)(iv).

—The residual method of determining customs value under Article 7 shall be inclusive of all residual eventualities, thus allowing valuation based on domestic market price or export price in a third country with appropriate adjustments.

—In order to avoid manipulation of import prices and enable a better approximation of 'transaction value', the Agreement should be amended to provide for the highest value when more than one transaction value of identical or similar goods is found.

—In order to address the problem of manipulation through artificially reduced re-invoice prices, mainly under-invoicing and the artificial splitting of value, especially when purchases are first made by buying agents and are re-invoiced to the importer, for the purposes of Article 8 of the Agreement, buying commissions should be taken into account in the determination of customs value of imported goods as it forms a legitimate component of the landed cost of imported goods.

(Continued on next page.)

(Continued from preceding page.)

—For the purposes of valuation of imports by sole agents, sole distributors, and sole concessionaires of large corporations, including transnational corporations, under Article 15.5 of the Agreement, and in order to shift the burden of proving that the prices quoted are not influenced by the relationship to the agents, distributors or concessionaires, as the case may be, persons associated with each other as sole agents, sole distributors, and sole concessionaires, howsoever described, should automatically be deemed 'related'.

(11) Agreement on Rules of Origin

—The CRO shall complete its remaining work on harmonizing non-preferential rules of origin by 31 July 2000.

—No new interim arrangements shall be introduced. Further, any interim arrangements introduced by any Member with effect from I January 1995 or any subsequent date shall be suspended with effect from 4 December 1999.

(12) Article XVIII and Balance-of-Payments Provisions of GATT 1994

—Only the Committee on Balance of Payments shall have the authority to examine the overall justification of BOP measures.

—The Committee shall keep in view that Article XVIII is a special provision for developing countries and shall ensure that Article XVIII does not become more onerous than Article XII.

—A complete review of Article XVIII shall be undertaken with a view to ensure that it subserves the original objective of facilitating the progressive development of economies in developing countries and to allow them to implement programmes and policies of economic development designed to raise the general standard of living of their people.

(13) Special and Differential Treatment

—In many areas of the WTO provisions, special and differential provisions are phrased only as best endeavour clauses, the implementation of which has remained ineffectual and has therefore been difficult to assess. All S&D provisions shall be converted into concrete commitments, specially to address the constraints on the supply side of developing countries.

BOX 6

"Best endeavour clauses"

Agreement on Agriculture (preamble): (*a*) in implementing commitments on market access, developed countries will take fully into account the particular needs and conditions of developing countries by providing for a greater improvement of opportunities and terms of access for agricultural products of particular interest to these countries, including the fullest liberalization of trade in tropical agricultural products and products of particular importance to the diversification of production from the growing of illicit narcotic crops. Account may also be taken of concessions and other liberalization measures implemented by developing countries.

Decision on Measures Concerning the Possible Negative Effects of the Reform Programme on Least-Developed and Net Food-Importing Developing Countries (paragraph 3): appropriate mechanisms will be established to ensure that the implementation of the results of the Uruguay Round on trade in agriculture does not adversely affect the availability of food aid at a level which is sufficient to continue to provide assistance in meeting the food needs of developing countries, especially least developed and net food-importing developing countries. It is envisaged that the provisions of the Decision will be subject to regular review by the Ministerial Conference.

Agreement on Textiles and Clothing (article 2.18; article 6.6 (*a*) (*b*) and (*c*)): meaningful improvement in access will be provided to those countries whose exports were subject to restrictions on the day before the entry into force of the WTO Agreement and whose restrictions represent 1.2 per cent or less of the total volume of the restrictions applied by an importing country. Least developed countries will be accorded treatment significantly more favourable than that provided to other groups. Small suppliers will be accorded differential and more favourable treatment in the fixing of restraint levels. In the case of wool-producing developing countries, special account will be taken of their export needs when quota levels, growth rates and flexibility are being considered.

Agreement on Anti-Dumping (Article 15): special regard should be given by developed countries to the special situation of developing countries when considering the application of anti-dumping measures. Possibilities of constructive remedies provided by the Code will be explored before applying anti-dumping duties where they might affect the essential interests of developing countries.

Agreement on Import Licensing Procedures (article 3, paragraph 5(*j*)): in considering the import performance of the applicant when allocating non-automatic import licenses, special consideration should be given to those importers that import products originating in developing countries, in particular the least developed countries.

Agreement on Subsidies and Countervailing Measures (article 27.15): upon request by an interested developing country, the Committee on Subsidies and Countervailing Measures will undertake a review of a specific countervailing measure applicable to this developing country.

Agreement on TRIPS (article 66, paragraph 2): developed countries will provide incentives to enterprises and institutions in their territories for the purpose of promoting and encouraging technology transfer to least developed countries.

Another issue relates to the so-called "deliverables", i.e. those agreements which could be undertaken at the launching process itself. A number of developed countries have made specific proposals in this respect. The United States in particular appears to attach very high priority to "deliverables". It has been the United States position that the biennial Ministerial Conferences should produce concrete results, (e.g. ITA at Singapore in 1996, moratorium on duties on electronic commerce in Geneva in 1998). The United States attaches particular importance to an extension of the moratorium on duties on electronic commerce, agreement on transparency in government procurement, a commitment to pursue the objective of zero duties in the APEC accelerated liberalization list (ATL), the expansion of the country coverage of the ITA (ITA II), increased technical assistance for developing countries for their implementation of the WTO Agreements, and provision for increased transparency of WTO operations. The EU has supported certain of the above with qualifications, while a key deliverable for the EU is a decision to provide duty free treatment to LDCs' exports, as well as endorsement by the heads of international organizations of capacity building for developing countries. From a developing country perspective, most "deliverables" are closely linked with implementation issues, while least developed countries expect that long promised duty free treatment of their exports would be among the "deliverables".

BOX 7

A. *"Deliverables" proposed by Developing Countries*

Extensions of the Transition Periods in the TRIPS and TRIMs Agreements, both of which expire at the end of 1999 (for developing countries, while LDCs have longer periods). Developing countries have proposed a five year extension of each. The proposed extension of the TRIPS Agreement has been linked to the fact that very few developing countries will be in a position to comply with all the enforcement provisions of that Agreement, and that an extension would be preferable to a situation in which the large majority of WTO members find themselves in a situation of being in conflict with their multilateral obligations, particularly when they are entering into new multilateral negotiations. The extension of the TRIMs Agreement has been proposed on the grounds that in any case, the agreement foresees the possibility of such extensions being granted on a case by case basis, but does not set out the criteria for granting such extensions. Developing countries have proposed that they be permitted to resubmit their notifications of TRIMs which would be covered by such extension. Mexico has indicated that it definitely will request such extension, motivated by the fact that the transitional period provided under NAFTA to TRIMs in the automotive industry is longer than that in the WTO TRIMs Agreement. Some developing countries (e.g. Philippines) have requested an extension on an individual basis, but others consider it preferable to provide a general extension at least until the relevant criteria have been agreed.

Accelerated Implementation of the Agreement on Textiles and Clothing. Developing countries have drawn attention to the fact that the implementation process to date has resulted in the major importing countries liberalizing only six percent of their trade under restriction under the MFA bilateral agreements. This contrasts sharply with the short transitional periods accepted by developing countries in other areas, and calls into question the political will to effectively implement the ATC at the end of the transitional period. The concerned developing coutries feel that a political gesture, which would provide real economic benefits to developing countries, is needed to manifest the commitment of the developed importing countries towards liberalizing trade in the sector of textiles and clothing, by agreeing to advance integration of restrained products as provided for in Articles 2. 10 and 2.15 of the ATC; such as: inclusion of at least 50% of the products under restraint, spread equally over all four groups, in the third phase of integration, i.e. by 1 January 2002; a decision to advance the third stage of the growth-on-growth provision to 1 January 2000, (instead of 2002), with any growth rates lower than 6 percent being increased to that percentage; and reaffirmation that the restraining countries would refrain from frequent and repeated recourse to safeguard actions/anti-dumping measures and other market restricting instruments.

Rebalancing the Agreement on Subsidies and Countervailing Measures. Several of the provisions of the Agreement are the subject of the mandated reviews, notably those on non-actionable subsidies which favour subsidy programmes which are generally applied in industrialized countries. Developing countries have noted one particularly striking imbalance with respect to export subsidies, where developing countries find themselves penalized by their lack of access to credit at the terms available to developed country firms. For this reason, they consider that an immediate Decision should be taken to interpret Annex I paragraph (k) of the Agreement on Subsidies and Countervailing measures to the effect that export credits offered by developing countries shall not be considered as subsidies so long as the rates at which they are extended are above LIBOR.

S&D for Anti-Dumping. Developing countries observe that not only are they the frequent target of anti-dumping actions, but also that the flexibilities provided to administrations in importing countries are being applied in such a manner as to further penalize their exporters, both in the determination of dumping and in the calculation of dumping margins. They point out that this is in contradiction with the provisions in Article 15 of the Anti-dumping Agreement under which "special regard" is to be given to the "special situation of developing countries", and "constructive remedies" explored before applying anti-dumping duties against "their exports. In order to prepare the ground for converting these best endeavour undertakings into concrete obligations, developing countries therefore consider that Ministers should decide to establish a special Working Group with the mandate of examining the special difficulties faced by developing country exporters in facing anti-dumping actions, and to submit its findings by 31 July 2000.

(Continued on next page.)

(Continued from preceding page.)

Export Subsidies on Agricultural Products. The reduction of export subsidies on agriculture is an inherent element of the continuation of the reform process set out in Article 20 of the Agreement on Agriculture. The fact that most developing countries have accepted to abandon export subsidies, while developed countries retain the right to massively subsidize agricultural exports and account for 90% of export subsidy commitments, causes great concern to developing countries. The elimination of export subsidies should therefore, in their view, be a priority objective in the continuation of the reform process. However, for them, the first step is to prevent the circumvention of existing commitments through the export credit mechanism; they note that the commitment in Article 10:2 of the Agriculture Agreement to negotiate internationally agreed disciplines to govern the provision of export credits, export credit guarantees or insurance programmes has not been respected. Thus, in their view, the Ministers should decide to establish a Negotiating Group on the Implementation of Article 10:3, in the WTO, to negotiate internationally agreed disciplines in these areas by 31 July 2000.

Implementation of Decision in Favour of NFIDCs and LDCs. The Net Food Importing Developing Countries are preoccupied by the failure to translate the Marrakech Decision into concrete measures, particularly in light of the continuous shrinking of food aid. This renders it difficult for them to take clear positions in support of agricultural reform. They therefore consider that Ministers should subscribe to a Decision to establish a fund that would be made available to NFIDCs and LDCs for the provision of food aid and for technical and financial assistance to improve their agricultural productivity.

TRIPS and Essential Drugs. Developing countries note that they have been facing difficulties in obtaining essential drugs at affordable prices and that, in certain cases, pressures have been exerted on their governments to refrain from resorting to their rights under Article 31 of the TRIPS Agreement even when health emergencies, such as the AIDS epidemic, arise. They are thus of the view that Ministers should make a clear Declaration recognizing the right of developing countries to access to essential drugs at reasonable prices, and reconfirm Article 31 of TRIPS. This would have the added advantage of providing a visible response to NGO criticism of the WTO.

Standstill and Due Restraint ("peace clause"). Previous negotiations, such as in the Punta del Este Declaration, provided for a "standstill" clause under which members would not take actions, whether or not in conformity with their multilateral obligations, that would serve to improve their negotiating position during the negotiations. In the view of developing countries, it is essential that Ministers take a Decision to this effect. In addition, given the dependence of many developing countries on tariff preferences such as GSP, Lomé etc, and the state of uncertainty which prevails regarding the future of these preferences, the standstill provision, they argue, should also cover preferential access, perhaps via a general waiver to preference granting countries.

Many developing countries also find themselves in a vulnerable position to the extent that they are having difficulty in implementing the obligations of the

MTAs, and in many cases it may be possible to identify aspects where they have not fully met these obligations. It would create extreme difficulties for developing countries, if they were to be obliged to defend themselves in dispute settlement cases at the same time that the negotiations were underway. Thus, developing countries consider that Ministers should decide to exercise "**due restraint**" in invoking the DSU against developing countries during the multilateral negotiations.

Coherence. Developing countries are calling for a clear endorsement by the heads of the international organizations of joint efforts in support of capacity building, so that developing countries can derive full benefits from a new round of trade liberalization.

There is also a view that there should be a paragraph in the Seattle Ministerial Declaration calling for the development of a work programme on coherence in parallel to the negotiations of the new round.

DSU review. The review of the Dispute Settlement Understanding (DSU) was scheduled to be completed by the end of July 1999, but was not completed on time. Developing countries consider that, at the launch of new negotiations, Ministers could agree on a continuation of the review, including the issue of implementation.

B. "Deliverables" proposed by Developed Countries

Tariff free treatment for products of least-developed countries. It was proposed by some developed countries (e.g. the European Union) that Ministers, make a commitment to ensure duty free market access no later than the end of the next round of negotiations for essentially all products originating in the least-developed countries. Such a commitment should, in their view, be made by industrialized countries, while the more advanced developing countries should also be invited to make a contribution.

Transparency in government procurement. Transparency was considered by developed countries as the basic building block of a stable and predictable procurement regime. They consider that all participants in the procurement process would benefit from the existence of transparency, whether it is the government as a purchaser, the government as a regulator, potential suppliers, those who must enforce the rules, or investors. The decision was taken at the WTO's First Ministerial Conference in Singapore to establish a Working Group to discuss this issue. Consensus may emerge on what the basic principles of transparency should be, to serve as one of the bases for future negotiations but not necessarily to be formally adopted at the launch of the new negotiations (EU position). From the perspective of some developing countries, the main objective is to prepare the ground for a substantive agreement and not seek a "quick fix". On the other hand, other developed countries (e.g. the United States) believe that an agreement for Ministerial approval should be negotiated, recognizing that such a free-standing multilateral agreement would neither prejudge

———— (Continued on next page.) ————

(Continued from preceding page.)

in any way participation in the plurilateral Government Procurement Agreement (GPA).

Transparency issues.   With regard to the derestriction of documents and consultations with civil society, many countries are of the view that the General Council should reach a decision before Seattle on a broader policy for the derestriction of WTO documents. This would include earlier derestriction of submissions by WTO Members, Secretariat background notes and minutes of WTO meetings, as well as the findings and conclusions of panel reports. At the launch of the new negotiations, in these countries' view, it should be possible to: (i) record the progress achieved in improving WTO transparency through a broader policy of document derestriction and informal means for dialogue with civil society, which should continue and intensify after the launching of the round; and (ii) agree to explore the possibility of further measures to enhance transparency of WTO operations. This would include consideration of means of enhancing dialogue with organizations of civil society.

DSU review.   Within the context of the DSU review, a number of changes in transparency procedures were inconclusively discussed. These include: (a) public release of Members' submissions; (b) opening panel and appellate body hearings to the public for attendance; (c) a procedure for the presentation of written submissions by interested Members of the public. Agreement before the launch of negotiations on a broad package of DSU reforms was considered necessary to encourage widespread support for improved transparency. Transparency in the context of the DSU review would, in some countries' view, need to be considered as a separate issue from the more general transparency question.

Electronic commerce.   In the view of the EU, agreement may be possible on a balanced package of trade principles covering inter alia issues such as domestic regulation, anti-competitive practices and clarifying the application of GATS rules. However, the EU would not agree to the prolongation of the standstill (moratorium) on duties on e-commerce, as would have wished the United States, unless there is agreement, by the launch of the new negotiations, on a satisfactory outcome of the work programme including a balanced package of trade principles. A possible outcome, in the view of some countries, could be the adoption of the trade principles including a continued moratorium on tariffs, to become definitive upon the completion of the work programme at some future stage.

APEC's "Accelerated Tariff Liberalization" (ATL) Initiative.   The United States, Australia, New Zealand and some other APEC members have insisted that WTO members should finalize, by the time of the launching negotiations, the APEC liberalization initiatives in the areas of: chemicals, environmental goods, energy-related goods, fish, forest products, gems and jewelry, medical and scientific equipment, and toys.

Built-in Agenda

Agriculture

The continuation of the reform process aims at the long-term objective to establish a fair and market-oriented agricultural trading system, through substantial and progressive reductions in support and protection in the agricultural sector. The targeted outcome of this round of negotiations on agriculture, while agreeing on the continuation of the reform process beyond this round, will be to integrate the agricultural sector with the rules and principles of GATT 1994, taking into account the need of the Net Food Importing Developing Countries and the need for S & D treatment by developing countries with large population in the agricultural sector as well as small and vulnerable economies, including small island countries.

In realizing the long-term objective, the negotiations of further reduction commitments will encompass the three major reform areas which resulted from the Uruguay Round Agreement on Agriculture, i.e. market access, domestic support and export competition, and will be made from the binding commitments made under the Agreement, supplemented by additional disciplines.

Negotiating initiatives in agriculture will logically follow the major reform areas within the structure of the WTO Agreement on Agriculture. Among the options which may be considered during the negotiations are:

Market access

- deep cuts to all tariffs, with an application of an appropriate tariff reduction approach which curtails tariff peaks and eliminates tariff escalation, as well as credits autonomous agricultural liberalization undertaken by developing countries; to provide for a greater improvement of opportunities and terms of access for agricultural products of particular interest to the members, including the grant of duty-free and quota-free access to all primary and processed agricultural exports of LDCs and NFIDCs;

- reductions in complexity of the agricultural tariff structure, including a conversion of *non-ad-valorem* rates to *ad-valorem* rates;

- progressive increases in the import quantities under tariff rate quotas and concomitant reductions in tariff rates within quotas;

- establishment of a guideline with regard to the administration of tariff rate quota system which will ensure trading opportunities to all members in a equitable manner;

- total elimination of the Special Safeguard (SSG) provisions by developed countries with the possibility of their use by developing countries to protect the livelihood of subsistence farmers.

Export subsidies

- complete elimination and prohibition of all forms of export subsidies within the time frame of the next reform process, thus bringing export subsidies in agriculture under the general rules of the Agreement on Subsidies and Countervailing Measures;

- strengthening the rules to prevent all forms of circumvention of export subsidy commitments, particularly through the establishment of effective international disciplines concerning export credits, export credit guarantees and export insurance programmes;

- establishment of disciplines concerning export restrictions and binding of export taxes.

Domestic support

- substantial progressive reductions of all forms of trade-distorting domestic support;

- flexibility to developing countries in the use of domestic support measures that are linked to their developmental objectives (e.g. improvement in agricultural production for the purpose of food security, securing employment to rural population, support to small-scale resource-poor farmers, etc.), through, *inter alia*, an increase in the *de minimis* limit applicable to developing countries; it should be noted that these concerns do not correspond to those of the developed countries as embodied in the "multifunctionality" concept, which aims at using trade measures to protect the income of a very small rural population in some wealthy countries;

- review of the criteria of exempt measures given in Annex 2 (Green Box) for it to reflect specific needs and conditions of developing countries, including full incorporation in it of those exempt measures specified in Article 6.2 of the Agreement;

- operational modification of the methods of calculation of the Aggregate Measurement of Support.

LDCs and Net-Food Importing Countries

The Marrakesh Ministerial Decision on Measures Concerning Possible Negative Effects of the Reform Programme on Least-Developed and Net Food-Importing Developing Countries should, in the view of developing countries, be revised during the negotiations, with a view to incorporating concrete, operational and contractual measures in the Decision that are both effective and responsive to the special needs of LDCs and NFIDCs that may be arising from the continuation of the reform process. It has been noted that the export subsidy regimes of developed countries do not do much to alleviate the problems of the NFIDCs as their mechanisms are such that export subsidies are not generally provided when world prices are high. If such concrete measures, including financial provisions were established, NFIDCs could support the abolition of export subsidies.

Other issues

Multilateral approaches should, in the view of developing countries, be adopted to address both new issues and those overlapping with other Agreements and provisions of GATT 1994 (for example, the Agreements of SPS, TBT and TRIPS), especially regarding new areas such as the use of genetically modified organisms.

Services

Developing countries consider that the services negotiations should encompass the progressive liberalization of market access and the development of the GATS framework disciplines. Major elements for GATS negotiating objectives could, in this view, include the following.

Existing Architecture of GATS/Respect for Articles XIX and IV

- As provided in Article XIX, the negotiations should be conducted within the existing architecture of the GATS, and ensure appropriate flexibility for individual developing country members for opening fewer sectors, liberalizing fewer types of transactions, progressively extending market access in line with their development situation and, when making access to their markets available, attaching to such access, conditions aimed at achieving the objectives referred to in Article IV. The negotiations could aim at the effective achievement of the objectives of GATS Article IV, reducing the current imbalance in commitments through a focus on the liberalization of market access in sectors and modes of supply of export interest to developing countries.

Priority to Movement of Natural Persons

- There should be a revision of the Annex on Movement of Natural Persons to ensure a substantially higher level of liberalization and effective market access through mode 4. Particular effort should be made to remove economic needs tests for specific categories of persons and to develop criteria for application of any economic needs test to other categories of persons.

Assistance to Develop Services Capacity, especially Electronic Commerce

- Specific additional commitments should be included in the Schedules of Commitments of developed countries and incentives should be provided by them to firms and institutions for the purpose of improving developing countries' access to technology and to distribution channels and information networks, particularly via electronic commerce. Relevant measures should be notified to the Council for Trade in Services on a regular basis. Concrete capacity building measures to assist in developing the services sectors of developing countries and benchmarks for imports should also be included as additional commitments.

Article VI Issues

- Disciplines should be developed under Article VI.4, taking into account the particular need of developing countries to exercise the right of members to regulate, and to introduce new regulations, on the supply of services within their territories in order to meet national policy objectives. These disciplines should not restrain developing countries in exercising policy flexibility for developing supply and export capacity and ensuring respect for the social aspects of services. The disciplines developed should apply to sectors where specific commitments have been undertaken.

Article VII MRAs

- Negotiations should proceed on recognition under Article VII and ensure the effective access of developing countries to mutual recognition agreements (MRAs) and the active pursuit of equivalence. Existing MRAs should be examined to ensure that such agreements do not have a trade distorting impact.

Emergency Safeguard Mechanism, Subsidies, Government Procurement

- Negotiations under Article X on emergency safeguard measures should be completed prior to the adoption of the results of the next round of services negotiations. Negotiations under Articles XIII and XV should continue on subsidies and government procurement, taking particular account of the trade distorting impact of subsidies granted by developed countries on developing countries' services exports.

Anti-Competitive Practices

- Article IX should be strengthened to ensure adequate control of the abuse of dominant position, inter alia through addressing specific private sector restrictive practices and establishing a notification requirement for restrictive business practices.

Electronic Commerce

- A review of the impact of electronic commerce on the GATS commitments should be conducted.

Negotiating Guidelines

- The negotiations should be pursued in accordance with Article XIX.2 under the principle of progressive liberalization. Negotiating Guidelines and a Work Plan for negotiations should be adopted expeditiously. These would provide for mechanisms to rebalance the commitments to ensure the implementation of the objectives of Article IV and the special treatment of least developed country Members in accordance with Article IV.3. The negotiations on commitments would be based on a request/ offer mechanism. Formula approaches could be used for the implementation of Article IV. The basis for negotiations should be the commitments contained in the schedules of commitments of members at the end of the Uruguay Round. The negotiations should provide for recognition and credit of liberalization undertaken autonomously by members since the Uruguay Round negotiations and the Guidelines should establish the necessary modalities for the grant of such credit. The results of the negotiations in all areas should be completed in the same time frame to ensure balanced results, except as otherwise provided for the negotiations on emergency safeguard mechanism.

TRIMs

Developing countries have difficulties in identifying their TRIMs and meeting their obligation of eliminating all TRIMs notified under Article 5.1, particularly the local content requirements. Moreover, such TRIMs, especially domestic or local content requirements are considered by many developing countries as a useful and necessary tool for development. Thus, they consider that there is a need to extend the transitional period for all developing country members, including the least developed countries, until the end of the negotiations. They also argue that developing countries which did not notify TRIMs that are not in conformity with the Agreement should be enabled to notify such TRIMs during the negotiations.

Some developed countries have proposed that the list of prohibited TRIMs should be extended to cover measures which do not conflict with GATT obligations. The review under Article 9 of the TRIMs Agreement should, in the view of developing countries, recognize the role of performance requirements in building supply and export capacity in developing countries and accept that use of such TRIMs by developing countries should not be further restricted. The mandated review in the same Article provides that investment policy and competition policy should be considered in parallel. This review would take into account the findings of the Working Groups on Trade and Investment and Trade and Competition policy established in Singapore and should, developing countries believe, focus on developmental needs and the necessary policy space for adoption of policies for developing countries.

The proponents of the negotiation of a multilateral framework for investment in the WTO have come forward with proposals which seem tailored to obtain greater acceptance by developing countries. There is a dramatic departure from the approaches taken in the OECD MAI. For example, the proposals generally recognize the need to maintain coherence with the GATS and to follow a positive list approach. It has been suggested that developing countries might wish to react to these proposals with coherent counterproposals at the appropriate time for alternative approaches to dealing with investment issues, such as taking them up in the context of existing MTAs.

Thus, a constructive approach to the review of the TRIMs Agreement and to possible new negotiations should, in the view of developing countries, be based on an assessment of the impact of current rules, the characterization of the possible negotiating scenarios and the identification of national (and regional) interests in relation to investment policies.

Empirical evidence about the impact of the TRIMS Agreement is scant. Very little data collection and research seems to have been done on the impact of the TRIMS Agreement since its adoption, so as to provide a solid basis for future action on the matter. Only twenty five countries had notified TRIMs in order to benefit from the transitional period provided for under article 5, and some of them face problems to phase out the notified TRIMs. The elimination, in particular, of local content requirements may have a negative impact on industrialization policies.

The debate on TRIMs has taken place in a spectrum between the position of the United States, which seeks to expand the list of prohibited TRIMS to include export performance requirements, technology transfer requirements and product mandating requirements, and that of certain developing countries, which seek greater flexibility in the use of already prohibited measures, notably local content requirements, and at least a five year extension of the transitional period with an opportunity to resubmit notifications. Mexico has indicated its intention to request an extension, motivated by the fact that the transition period in NAFTA is longer than that in the TRIMs Agreement.

A revision of the Agreement may also give the opportunity—though strong opposition by developed countries may exist—for dealing with investment incentives, which currently are not subject to specific multilateral disciplines. Developed countries offer in some cases incentives in a magnitude that developing countries are unlikely to match. In their view, developing countries may, therefore, benefit from international rules that introduce disciplines on incentives both on efficiency grounds and because of the competitive disadvantage that poorer countries face when subsidies determine location decisions. These measures could also be dealt with under the SCM Agreement.

Article 9 of the TRIMs Agreement provides that in the course of the review, the Council for Trade in Goods shall consider whether the Agreement should be complemented with provisions on investment policy and competition policy. The relationships between trade and investment policy and competition policy have been examined in the Working Groups on these two issues established at the first WTO Ministerial Conference (i.e. the "Singapore issues").

Multilateral Rules on Investment

Proposals have been made to begin negotiations on a multilateral framework of rules on investment. The EU and Japan have been the main proponents, supported by some other developed and developing countries. The EU has distanced itself from the defunct OECD MAI , stating that the MAI is "dead", and has submitted a proposal designed to take account of many of the preoccupations expressed by developing countries in particular. The EU envisaged an agreement which would deal only with FDI and not short term capital movements, recognize that host countries should retain the right to regulate the activity of investors, and address concerns regarding investors' responsibilities . The EU also suggests a "positive list" approach to commitments, following the GATS model. The Japanese proposal is similar, making specific reference to the need to discipline performance requirements while recognizing that they may be relevant to the development perspectives of developing countries. The Japanese proposal accepts the positive list approach for access but considers that national treatment should be a right once investors are established.

Many developing countries remain unconvinced that they have anything to gain from a multilateral agreement on investment in the WTO. Further, the United States has indicated that it has no interest in entering into early negotiations on investment. A compromise position could be the adoption of an intensified work programme, which might examine the implications of the proposals which have been submitted and perhaps include a procedure for notifying investment restriction measures, but postponing any decision to negotiate until the Fourth WTO Ministerial Conference.

BOX 8

Proposals on trade and investment[33]

The European Union, Japan, Korea and Poland pronounced for negotiation in the WTO on a multilateral framework of rules governing international investment, with the objective of securing a stable and predictable climate for foreign direct investment world-wide. Such a framework should focus only on FDI, to the exclusion of short-term capital movements. It should also preserve the ability of host countries to regulate the activity of investors (whether foreign or domestic) on their respective territories, taking also into account the concerns expressed by civil society in many WTO Members, including those regarding investors' responsibilities. The commitments should be negotiated on the basis of a "positive list" approach, although, national treatment would constitute a right once access was granted.

Switzerland proposed that negotiations should be more comprehensive with the aim to establish a multilateral framework of principles, rules and disciplines for international investment with the overall objective to increase legal security and predictability for governments and investors, as well as to favour international flows of investment, taking into account the work already undertaken in the WTO Working Party on the Relationship between Trade and Investment. Due consideration should be given to the WTO Agreement on Trade-Related Investment Measures with a view to supplement the list of measures which are inconsistent with WTO rules. In Swiss view, the negotiations should also ensure the coherence between the multilateral framework on investment and the relevant WTO agreements like the General Agreement on Trade in Services (GATS).

Hong Kong, China emphasized that the next round of negotiations should include negotiations on core rules and disciplines that should apply to foreign direct investments. The aim is to maximize allocative efficiency and to promote more trade and investment in a globalized environment while providing a level playing field with greater predictability and stability for investors. The negotiations should take into account the existing architecture of the WTO Agreements and the needs of all Members, and in particular the developing and least-developed Members.

Costa Rica proposed that a multilateral framework for regulating investment should be developed in the next trade negotiations in the WTO. A multilateral agreement of this kind should be based on the fundamental principle of non-discrimination so as to guarantee a more predictable and stable climate for worldwide investment, which would be of benefit both to international investors and to the host States. A greater degree of stability and predictability for investors and their investments would not only encourage investment but would certainly also contribute to the growth and development of the world economy.

Competition Policy

The symmetry between new rules on investment and on competition policy was inserted into the TRIMs Agreement by developing countries. It was felt that, as many TRIMs were used to preempt anti-competitive practices, stricter disciplines on investment measures should be accompanied by multilateral rules to prevent RBPs. Despite this, some developing countries seem to have lost their enthusiasm for such a multilateral framework, considering that it could serve more to further the penetration of TNCs into their markets than to discipline their practices. The European Union has proposed the launching of negotiations on a multilateral framework on competition policy that would contain a list of core rules, including a prohibition of price-fixing "hard-core" cartels and collusive tendering, and keep open discussions on more difficult issues, such as the control of vertical restraints, prohibition of abuses of dominant market power by enterprises and control of mergers. The proposal would include an undertaking, for countries which are ready to do so, to adopt and effectively implement national competition law, and provision of technical cooperation for those countries which wish to adopt legislation or improve existing systems. The United States has indicated that it was opposed, at the present time, to embark on negotiations which would lead to "watered-down" rules, much less effective than those they apply under the U.S. Antitrust rules.

Japan, supported by a number of developing countries, proposed to include in the discussions trade measures that also distort competition such as anti-dumping and countervailing duties. They consider that in particular, anti-dumping actions tend to preserve anti-competitive situations, while anti-dumping rules and legislation are inconsistent with competition principles, i.e. that actions which would be consistent with competition laws when practiced on the domestic market, are subject to anti-dumping actions when import competition is involved. It is this direct challenge to anti-dumping regimes that appears to have further hardened USA opposition to the proposals for a multilateral framework.

Recognizing that the negotiation of multilateral rules on competition policy will be a long term process, and recognizing the particular problems they face from anti-competitive practices in various service sectors, certain developing countries aim at strengthening GATS Article IX and drawing up sectoral "reference papers" to deal with anti-competitive practices in certain service sectors, notably for tourism.

Given the differences of views which have persisted, a continuation of the "learning process" undertaken under the WTO Working Group on the Interaction between Trade and Competition Policy seems likely for a given period of time, after which a decision might be taken to resume negotiations, if all parties agree. In any event, it should be recalled that in creating the WTO Working Group, it was decided in the Singapore Declaration, that "these Groups shall draw upon each other's work if necessary and also draw upon and be without prejudice to the work in UNCTAD and other appropriate intergovernmental fora. Work is under way, as provided for in the Midrand Declaration, and can make a contribution to the understanding of issues. In the conduct of the work of the working groups, cooperation with the relevant organizations to make the best use of available resources and to ensure that the development dimension is taken fully into account" (para. 20 of the Singapore Declaration of 13 December 1996)[34] would seem useful.

TRIPS

In view of major difficulties faced by developing countries in implementing the TRIPS Agreement, the following matters, they consider, merit attention: (i) extension of the transitional period to provide additional time in view of broadness and complexity of the reforms of IPR laws required for domestic industries to adjust; (ii) lack of technical and financial support to develop IPR rules adapted to domestic circumstances and stage of development and necessary institutional infrastructure; (iii) adoption of specific measures facilitating the use of compulsory licensing as a means to ensure the transfer of technology (including environmentally sound technologies), and to meet public health concerns (e.g. compulsory licensing regime for WHO listed essential drugs); (iv) shortening the term on patent, to bring the TRIPS Agreement into line with the Convention on Biodiversity; (v) inclusion of new provisions in the TRIPS Agreement relating to the protection of traditional and indigenous knowledge and works of folklore. In addition, developing countries consider provisions should be made to prevent any restriction on parallel imports and the TRIPS Agreement should be clarified to explicitly prohibit any rules and practices that amount to unilateral retaliation based on IPRs issues.

Further negotiations on TRIPS should, in the view of developing countries, be based on the recognition of the major difficulties faced by them with modernizing the administrative infrastructure, modernizing and drafting new laws on the granting and protection of intellectual property rights, strengthening institutions and creating a culture for the protection of intellectual property, and creating an appropriate framework for promoting research and development to ensure that they would not continue to be only consumers of foreign technology. They also argue that the transition period should be extended at least until the end of the negotiations.

There is lack of clarity on the criteria used to decide what can and cannot be excluded from patentability in Art. 27.3(b). By stipulating compulsory patenting of microorganisms (which are natural living things) and microbiological processes (which are natural processes), the provisions of Art. 27.3 contravene the basic tenets on which patent laws are based: that substances and processes that exist in nature are a discovery and not an invention and thus are not patentable. Moreover, by giving Members the option whether or not to exclude the patentability of plants and animals, Art. 27.3(b) allows for life forms to be patented. The exclusion of patentability of plants and animals should, in the view of developing countries, be extended to microorganisms as there is no scientific basis for the distinction.

Developing countries consider that TRIPS Article 27.3(b) should recognize the principles, objectives and measures planned and proposed under the CBD and the International Undertaking that Member countries exercise sovereign rights over their biological resources. They are of the view that the review process should seek to harmonize Article 27.3(b) with the provisions of the CBD and the International Undertaking, in which the conservation and sustainable use of biological diversity, the protection of the rights and knowledge of indigenous and local communities, and the promotion of farmers' rights, are fully taken into account. The right of holders of traditional knowledge to share benefits arising out of any related innovation through material transfer agreements/transfer of information agreements should, in the view of developing countries, be included in the provisions in Article 29, requiring a clear mention of the biological source material and the country of origin. They believe that domestic laws on biodiversity should ensure that prior consent of the country of origin and the knowledge holder of the biological raw material meant for usage in a patentable invention would enable the signing of material transfer agreements or transfer of information agreements.

The same degree of protection of geographical indications as granted to wines and spirits should, in the view of developing countries, be extended to cover other products, particularly typical products traditionally produced in developing countries.

The current procedure in Article 31 for the use of patents without authorization is highly restrictive. It limits the authorization to the supply to domestic markets and it provides for termination of the authorization if the circumstances which led to it cease to exist. Certain drugs are essential and, developing countries argue, any restriction on their production should be removed so as to make them available at reasonable prices. They also believe that there is a need for relaxation in exclusive rights of the patent holders in respect of the drugs listed as essential by WHO, and that there should be a provision authorizing countries to use automatic compulsory licensing for these drugs in the interest of their supply at reasonable prices.

The moratorium on the application of the non-violation remedy under the TRIPS Agreement should, according to developing countries, be maintained indefinitely until members agree by consensus that sufficient experience has been gained with the application of the Agreement and that the remedy if adopted will not increase Member's level of obligations.

Recognizing that the provisions of Article 66.2 are obligatory and that the provisions have not been effectively implemented, developing countries argue that guidelines on categories of incentives should also be established, and that the application of this Article should be extended to all developing countries. It has been noted that the technology gap between developed and developing countries is widening. Articles 7, 8, 40, 66 and 67 are important obligations that qualify other provisions of the Agreement. Effective transfer and dissemination of technology at fair and reasonable costs to developing countries constitutes one of the key elements in accelerating the pace of their economic and social development, and therefore developing countries are of the view that developed countries' should effectively implement their obligation in relation to transfer of technology.

Subsidies and countervailing measures

The reviews conducted under Articles 8.2(*a*), 27.6 and 31 of the Agreement on Subsidies and Countervailing Measures (ASCVM) should, in the view of developing countries, address the difficulties faced by many developing countries owing to the industrial subsidies (both export and domestic) generally used by developing countries for development of their industrial production and export fall in the "actionable" category. The review provides developing countries with leverage to include some of such measures within the non-actionable category. Developing countries have yet to identify clearly those subsidies which they consider essential to their development programmes.

Developing countries consider that the review should also examine the link between the ASCVM and the TRIPS Agreement with a view to facilitating the transfer of technology, and explore ways and means of making financial resources available to meet the special needs of developing countries, particularly with respect to the subsidies covered by Article 8.2(c) (adaptation to environment requirements). In particular, developing countries are of the view that several additions to Article 8.2 of the ASCVM could be considered, including:

- assistance for the acquisition of technical knowledge, consultancy and equivalent services or licenses of IPRs for the production of new or improved goods or services by a firm located in a developing country Member which is not an affiliate[35] of a foreign firm, if the assistance covers not more than 75% of the costs of acquisition, including equipment directly related to the transfer of technology.

- assistance for the provision of technical knowledge, licenses of IPRs, supply of consultancy and equivalent services to an enterprise which is not an affiliate of a foreign firm and which is located in a developing country, for the production of new or improved goods or services,[36] if

  (*a*) the assistance covers not more than 50% of the

  (i) costs of personnel engaged exclusively in the transfer of technology or supply of services;

  (ii) costs of equipment directly related to the transfer of technology or supply of services;

(*b*) the terms and conditions applied to the transaction are not less favourable than those applied by the same supplier to similar transactions.

• Such assistance may cover up to 75% of items (a)(i) and (ii) when the technology is transferred to LDCs in pursuance to Article 66.2 of the TRIPs Agreement.

Developing countries also believe that Annex I of the ASCVM should be amended to include provisions to allow developing countries to provide financing to their exporters in terms that are consistent with their development objectives, taking account of the fact that interest rates which prevail in developing countries are generally higher than those in developed countries. If the credits provided are not above LIBOR they should not, in this view, be considered to contain a subsidy element.

Developing countries consider that the provisions with respect to S&D treatment should be made more realistic. For example, the $1000 per capita income criterion could be replaced with a more relative concept, such as one based on the ratio to the per capita income in OECD countries. Also, in their view, if developing countries fall below the per capita limit, they should regain their exemption for the export subsidy prohibition.

Other market access and/or rule-making issues

Anti-Dumping measures

Among the proposals put forward by developing countries in the preparatory process under the General Council, the following main ideas were expressed.

Implementation and operationalization of Article 15 of the Agreement

Article 15 in the Agreement on Anti-Dumping (AAD) is devoted to developing countries, but it merely provides that special regard must be given by developed country Members to the special situation of developing country Members when considering application of anti-dumping measures and that constructive remedies provided for by the Agreement must be explored before application of anti-dumping duties where they would affect the essential interests of developing country Members. This is a "best endeavour clause" with, in developing countries' view, little practical meaning.

Article 15 commitment therefore, developing countries argue, should be made concrete, for example by providing higher de minimis dumping margins and imports' share thresholds in anti-dumping proceedings involving developing countries.

Application of lesser duty rule (Article 9.1 of the Agreement)

The Agreement provides for the possibility to apply a lower dumping margin when the lesser duty is adequate to remove the injury. This provision appears to codify the EC practice and was strongly opposed by the US during the Uruguay Round negotiations. Some commentators pointed out that it would be actually difficult to verify and control how this rule, if made compulsory, could be effectively implemented. In fact, injury calculations made by EC authorities are not disclosed to the defendants, making virtually impossible to ascertain the actual application of rule.

Therefore, in the view of developing countries, the application of the "lesser duty rule" should be made mandatory, but with a clear obligation of the investigating authorities to disclose the non-confidential part of the injury calculations.

Standing of the complainants

There is possible imbalance in the AAD when related to the provision contained in the Footnote 1 to Article 1 of the Agreement on Rules of Origin on the definition and coverage of the rules of origin which provided that the definition of "domestic industry" or "like products of domestic industry" fall outside the scope of the above mentioned article. Anti-dumping proceedings are normally initiated at the request of a complainant domestic industry against products originating in a certain country. Thus, a normal antidumping procedure requires that, besides other findings relating to dumping and injury, the investigating authorities have to determine the origin of the product exported from the third country. However, this is not always consistently carried out by the investigating authorities.

Thus, developing countries argue, Article 4 of the AAD and footnote one of Article 1 of the Agreement on Rules of Origin should be revised to include domestic industries subject to origin determination requirements.

Standard review as in Article 17.6 of the AAD

This article sets up an ad hoc and unique standard of review for disputes on AD limiting and/or guiding the area of interpretation of the panel, distinguishing it from other WTO Agreements. The special standard of review under Article 17.6 should, developing countries argue, be abolished.

Issues related to dumping margin calculations

During the forthcoming negotiations it has to be recognized that the character and patterns of trade and industry are changing rapidly. Internationally operating companies are seeking better opportunities to produce at low cost and to penetrate new markets. Classical production patterns of producing goods at one place are changing into a pattern of outsourcing and production at a global scale. Price differentiation as a pricing policy (as often used within domestic economies) is a widely used instrument to introduce products to new markets. Similarly, temporary sales below fixed costs (but above variable costs) are common in many industries during downturns in the business/product cycle. Yet, given the current structure of the Agreement, in such a period developing countries exports are likely to be affected by a surge of projectionist pressures.

Therefore, in the view of developing countries, key substantive concepts of the AD need to be revised to better reflect business realities in a globalized economy.

Comparison between export price and normal value

Article 2.4 of the AAD should, developing countries argue, be targeted for reform with a view to increasing transparency and reducing the scope of discretion in the application of this provision. Article 2.4 articulates the rather vague general guiding rule that the comparison between export price and normal value should be "fair". While further elaboration on the application of this concept is provided, developing countries consider that additional detailed rules should be included to reduce the discretion available to investigating authorities, in particular, findings of **negative dumping**, when these exceptions are not computed in the calculations of the dumping margins, resulting in higher dumping margins. Moreover the term "comparable" in article 2.4.2 of the antidumping agreement is interpreted as not allowing the offsetting of the different models of the finished products. This particularly affects the electronic industry where the business life of a product is limited to a life span of two or three years. The fact that "like" products are considered alike when computing prices does not take into account the evolving nature of the electronic industries.

The question of **credit terms** is also of extreme relevance. Normally export credits are netted back to the ex factory prices. However, current practices indicate that unless the credit terms are laid down in a contract or letter of credit they have to be disregarded.

In addition, further detailed rules may be necessary with regard to taking into account differences that affect price comparability. In this regard, it is noted that certain traditional users of anti-dumping measures in practice place the burden of proof squarely on the respondent with respect to demonstrating that differences in terms of levels of trade or other trade and business conditions affecting price comparability. In the view of developing countries, the provisions of Article 2.4 leave too much leeway to authorities to reject claims regarding such differences.

With respect to sales below cost, Article 2.2.1 provides that such sales may be disregarded for the purpose of determining normal value on condition that these sales are made over an extended period of time and in substantial quantities. The test for determining whether such sales are made in "substantial quantities" is that the weighted average selling price of the transactions under consideration for determining normal value is below the weighted average per unit costs, or that the volume of sales below per unit costs represents more than 20% of the volume sold in transactions under consideration for determining normal value. The threshold of 20% is, developing countries consider, too low and easily leads to arbitrary dumping findings and should be increased, e.g. to 40%.

Anti-circumvention

It has been argued that the question of anti-circumvention was not appropriately addressed since the existing multilateral rules contained sufficient elements to discipline adequately eventual cases of anti-circumvention, such as rule 2(a) of the Harmonized System and the harmonized non-preferential rules of origin. However, three broader elements have to be taken into account during the forthcoming negotiating process:

- The WCO negotiations on harmonized non-preferential origin rules are progressing very slowly, arguably in part because of the absence of a multilateral anti-circumvention provision;

- a substantial number of countries, including not only the United States and the EC, but also (Latin American) developing countries, have unilaterally adopted anti-circumvention provisions;

- (Non-harmonized) non-preferential rules of origin continue to be used to enforce anti-dumping duties and, consequently, to combat third country circumvention.

The main problem is related to the slow progress in the negotiations on rules of origin. Unless these rules are clearly defined and tailored to solve the question of anti-circumvention, the second element of the argument for the utilization of rule 2(a) and the rules of origin is lacking. The thorniest issue of residual rule of origin, which has now been debated for months both in Geneva and Brussels, is at the core of the problem. In particular, the US suggestion to move out of the scope of the Agreement on Rules of Origin the origin determination in AD proceedings, in spite of the clear provision of Art. 1.2 and 9.1 (*a*) that rules of origin should be applied equally for all purposes has to be read in this context and developing countries consider that it should be resisted.

Industrial tariffs

Some countries consider that the inclusion of industrial tariffs in the negotiations is essential to obtaining a balanced package that would address all the interests of developing countries. While noting that such negotiations are not part of the built-in agenda, the developing country proponents of such negotiations stress the need to achieve substantial tariff reductions on those products which face tariff peaks and tariff escalation. Tariff negotiations could adopt a simple and transparent approach (see the example of the Swiss reduction formula below), including appropriate methods to eliminate tariff peaks, tariff escalation and nuisance tariffs, as well as to credit autonomous liberalization measures adopted since 1 January 1995.

An Example of a Tariff Reduction Approach: Swiss Formula

$$T1 = CT0 / (C + T0)$$

Where:

$T0$ = initial tariff rate

$T1$ = tariff rate after reduction

C = reduction coefficient ($c > 0$)

Swiss Formula (SF) is one of a "harmonized" tariff reduction approach. Its characteristic is that the reduction of a tariff rate is larger (in absolute terms), the higher is the initial rate (T_0). The major objective of the application of SF is thus to reduce the degree of tariff dispersion. SF was used for industrial tariff reductions during the Tokyo Round.[37]

Developing countries consider that the negotiations should be accompanied by a comprehensive initiative to reduce/eliminate non-tariff barriers, so as to make sure that non-tariff concerns do not counter the benefits of further tariff reductions. The non-tariff initiative could be based on a rules approach, looking at horizontal issues such as licensing, rules of origin, product safety standards and certification procedures. The negotiations should, in their view, take into account special needs and conditions faced by developing countries.

In this context, developing countries argue that bound tariff-free and quota-free access to all products from LDCs should be implemented by all developed countries by the end of the new round of negotiations and that developed countries should also, where feasible, improve their autonomous provisions of significant margins of preferences in favour of developing countries in products of export interest for these countries, and simplify and harmonize the rules associated to such preferences.

TBT

It is recognized that the benefits of trade liberalization achieved by the Uruguay Round negotiations could be undermined by the protectionist use of technical regulations, standards and conformity assessment procedures. Therefore, certain provisions of the Agreement on Technical Barriers to Trade should, in the view of developing countries, be amended to ensure that the risk of using technical regulations, standards and conformity assessment procedures as border protection instruments is minimized, while all country members equally benefit from the Agreement.

Developing countries consider that technical regulations and standards should be harmonized through a fair international standard-setting process where all countries have equal opportunities to effectively participate and that international standardization activities should be carried out according to the principles of transparency and accountability, taking into account the special development, financial and trade needs of developing countries. Full implementation should, in this view, be given to the principles of transparency, least trade restrictiveness, non discrimination and special and differential treatment for developing country members. Developing countries argue that technical assistance should be provided by international organizations and developed country members to developing country members and that special efforts should be devoted to the least-developed country members but note that in no event should technical cooperation replace the removal of unnecessary trade barriers. The provisions referring to equivalency of technical regulations and mutual recognition of conformity assessment procedures should, in this view, be fully implemented to ensure the achievement of the goals of the Agreement, as well as flexibility for country members to select measures which are appropriate to their specific technological, developmental, environmental and socio-economic conditions. An increasing number of technical regulations and standards, including eco-labeling programmes, reflect environmental concerns, and developing countries consider it essential that environmental considerations should not be used as disguised barriers to trade.

SPS

The benefits of trade liberalization in the agriculture sector achieved by the Uruguay Round negotiations could be undermined by the protectionist use of sanitary and phytosanitary measures. Therefore, developing countries argue, certain provisions of the Agreement on the Application of Sanitary and Phytosanitary Measures should be amended to ensure that the risk of using SPS measures as border protection instruments is minimized, while all members equally benefit from the Agreement.

In the view of developing countries, this would mean that the following should be done: (i) SPS measures should be based on scientific evidence and harmonized through a fair international standard-setting process where all countries have equal opportunities to effectively participate. (ii) International standardization activities should be carried out according to the principles of transparency and accountability and should take into account the special development, financial and trade needs of developing countries. (iii) Full implementation should be given to the principles of transparency, least trade restrictiveness, special and differential treatment for developing country members, and adaptation to regional conditions. (iv) Technical assistance should be provided by international organizations and developed country members to developing country members and special efforts should be devoted to the least-developed country members which are approaching the end of the transitional period. (v) Technical cooperation should not replace the removal of unnecessary trade barriers. (vi) The provision referring to equivalency of sanitary and phytosanitary measures should be fully implemented to ensure a high level of health and sanitary protection and flexibility for country members to select appropriate domestic measures. (vii) Mutual recognition of conformity assessment procedures should be pursued to avoid unnecessary testing and certification costs.

Trade and Environment

There are widely divergent views between developed and developing countries' negotiators on whether trade and environment should be included in the mandate of the forthcoming trade negotiations. There are equally large differences of views between Northern and Southern NGOs on a range of issues. By and large, proposals by developed countries aim at (*a*) making environment an important cross-cutting issue throughout the negotiations; and (*b*) clarifying specific trade and environment issues, which may imply a further accommodation of environmental considerations into the multilateral trading system. Proposals focus on:

- "Mainstreaming" environmental considerations in WTO Committees and future negotiations.

- Clarifying the relationship between trade measures pursuant to Multilateral Environmental Agreements (MEAs) and the Multilateral Trading System (MTS).

- Examining the compatibility of eco-labelling schemes with WTO rules.

- Enhancing the role of environmental principles, such as the Precautionary Principle in WTO Agreements.

- Conducting sustainability assessments of the future trade negotiations.

- Increasing "transparency" and making further arrangements for the relation with Non-Governmental Organizations (NGOs).

While developing countries oppose linking market access with environment as well as any further accommodation of environment-related trade restrictions in the MTS, they have themselves made proposals on specific issues that have been discussed in the Committee on Trade and Environment (CTE). These proposals generally relate to environmental considerations in the implementation of different WTO agreements. Proposals largely focus on the following issues:

- The effects of environmental measures on market access.

- The issue of the export of domestically prohibited goods (DPGs).

- General issues stemming from the Agreement on Trade Related Intellectual Property Rights (TRIPS).

- Strengthening complementarities between the Convention on Biological Diversity (CBD) and the TRIPS Agreement, by reflecting the CBD principles in the TRIPS Agreement.

While there are strongly divergent views on the most of these proposals, there is a convergence of views between many developed and developing countries on:

- Pursuing the trade liberalization agenda in accordance with the objective of sustainable development.

- Identifying "win-win" situations, in particular with respect to agriculture, fisheries and environmental services, as well as in other sectors.

- Continuing the work of the CTE.

With regard to almost all of the above-mentioned proposals, proposals have been made, aimed at identifying points of convergence and divergence. Some consensus appears likely to arise on issues such as:

- a reconfirmation of the objectives set out in the Preamble to the Marrakesh Agreement Establishing the World Trade Organization, which includes inter alia promoting sustainable development and protection of the environment;

- some reference to the need to ensure that environmental and trade policies are mutually supportive and to enhance policy co-ordination at national and international levels;

- continuing the role of the CTE with its existing mandate and balanced agenda.

Possible advisory roles for the CTE and the Committee on Trade and Development (CTD) have been considered. One suggestion is that the CTE and CTD could each provide a forum to identify and debate the developmental and environmental aspects of the negotiations, including synergies between trade liberalization, economic development and environmental protection. The work of the two bodies would be complementary and would help to ensure that the negotiations reflect the preamble of the Agreement establishing the WTO and the objectives of sustainable development, while responding to the needs of developing countries, in particular the LDCs. The deliberations in the CTE and the CTD would provide useful inputs for national authorities. Developing countries are of the view that the role of the CTE, in building consensus before any negotiation on possible modification of trade provisions can be negotiated, should not be weakened.

It has been proposed that certain environmental issues be addressed on a sectoral basis. On fisheries, to deal with liberalization in the overall context of resource management (Japan), many countries (including USA, Australia, New Zealand, Norway, Peru Iceland and Philippines) have targeted fishery subsidies which have adverse effects on trade, environment and sustainable development and propose to elaborate WTO disciplines and commitments regarding their reduction or elimination. On forest products, Japan has proposed a similar resource management approach to liberalization, involving disciplines for exporting and importing countries. A Working Group on Biotechnology was proposed by Canada. Japan is also in favour of creating a "forum" to address new issues, including GMOs. This could be a sub-group of an independent negotiating group on agriculture to identify topics on food-related matters of GMOs, which should inter alia consider whether the relevant WTO agreements, such as SPS, TBT and TRIPS, are capable of responding to GMOs matters.

Free trade in environmental goods and services, which are on the ATL list, has been proposed by the USA (it will be recalled that UNCTAD organized an expert meeting on environmental services in 1998).

A hotly debated issue is whether and how sustainable development and trade should be reflected under the "principles governing the negotiations". However, developing countries currently are broadly of the view that there should be an inclusion of any specific issues (such as multilateral environmental agreements, eco-labelling or the precautionary principle) under "issues for negotiation". Their position seems to be strengthened by the fact that the United States also are not keen on negotiating specific issues, in part because of its fear that this could affect trade in GMOs.

The United States appears to believe that in any case it can pursue its environmental agenda through the development of case law. In fact, recent appellate body decisions have, in practice, ruled in favour of greater accommodation of environment-related trade measures in the MTS. Proposals to allow formally the submission of amicus curae briefs may be seen in that light; developing countries are, however, concerned that Northern NGOs would find it easier to take advantage of such options than NGOs in the South. The EU appears to want a very broad agenda in general, to negotiate concessions in the area of agricultural trade liberalization.

The challenge will be to ensure that progress made in understanding trade and environment is consolidated, perhaps by use of general language confirming the objectives of sustainable development and environmental protection, so that the agenda emerging from the convergence of views mentioned above is presented as a positive outcome. Furthermore, it is broadly agreed that capacity building to help promote policy co-ordination at national and international levels, including by UNCTAD, UNEP, UNDP and civil society, is essential. These institutions are currently stepping up their joint efforts; this is particularly important in the context of further trade liberalization that is likely to follow after the launch of the negotiations.

The fact that developing countries are opposing the inclusion of trade and environment in the negotiating agenda should not be seen as lack of priority for environment and sustainable development. Developing countries attach importance to environment and sustainable development, but oppose trade restrictive measures for environmental purposes. In fact, in the context of preparations UNCTAD X, the G-77 Plan of Action shows the developing countries' interest in integrating trade, environment and development.

Labour standards

It may be recalled that at the 1996 WTO Ministerial in Singapore, the following provision was included in the Ministerial Declaration:

"We (i.e. Ministers) renew our commitment to the observance of internationally recognized core labour standards. The International Labour Organization (ILO) is the competent body to set and deal with these standards, and we affirm our support for its work in promoting them. We believe that economic growth and development fostered by increased trade and further trade liberalization contribute to the promotion of these standards. We reject the use of labour standards for protectionist purposes, and agree that the comparative advantage of countries, particularly low-wage developing countries, must in no way be put into question. In this regard, we note that the WTO and ILO Secretariats will continue their existing collaboration."

Therefore, ILO's unique competence in this area was explicitly confirmed. The WTO Ministerial Conference did not give any mandate to the WTO in this area. On the other hand, the re-emergence of labour standards as a trade-related issue appears to be in response to a social reaction in some developed countries to the globalization and trade liberalization. However, labour norms are not a trade-related issue per se, and the concern of developing countries is that it is a very convenient cover for "new protectionist measures" against their competitive low-cost exports. This issue is a "coherence" problem and, in the view of developing countries, should be dealt with accordingly in cooperation with all relevant international organizations under the leadership of ILO.

The United States has been the most active in working to link observance of "internationally recognized workers' rights" to trade agreements.

First, the United States has conditioned eligibility for trade preferences within the Caribbean Basin Initiative (CBI), the Andean Trade Preference Trade Act (ATPA), and the Generalized System of Preferences (GSP) for each country on an examination of "whether or not such country has taken or is taking steps to afford to workers . . . internationally recognized worker rights." The GSP statute allows all interested parties to petition USTR to initiate a public review of whether a GSP country complies with the statute's worker rights requirements and mandates an annual report on the status of such rights in each beneficiary country. Such information is provided in the State Department country reports on human rights.

No country has been denied benefits on the basis of worker rights in the CBI or ATPA, though the threat of sanctions evidently induced improvements in labor standards in Haiti, the Dominican Republic, and elsewhere. Ten countries have been suspended from GSP beneficiary status as a result of worker rights violations, though most have been reinstated upon indication of progress.

A similar position has been adopted by the European Union which has included in its new GSP scheme an "incentive" aimed at observance of core labour standards. Beginning in 1998, the EU has tied additional tariff preferences to "acceptable behaviour" on worker rights.

Thus, these major WTO members are likely to continue their efforts to include, in some form, the issue of trade/labour linkage in the WTO work programme and eventually in the agenda of the next multilateral trade negotiations. President Clinton has stated (13 October 1999) that the WTO should create a working group on trade and labour. The EU mandate instructs their negotiators to seek a joint WTO/ILO working forum on trade, globalization and labor issues.

The US-EU summit meeting on 27 October 1999 emphasized "the goal of better addressing the social dimensions of trade by promoting a substantive dialogue with our partners, involving the WTO and the ILO, although we still differ on the modalities". "The dialogue would include an examination of the relationship between trade policy, trade liberalization, development and fundamental labor rights, so as to maximize the benefits of open trade for workers. The two leaders also agreed that the new Round should enhance the potential for positive synergies between trade liberalization, environmental protection and economic development".

Finally, on 30 October the United States submitted a proposal in the preparatory process on the establishment of a WTO Working Group on Trade and Labour at Seattle Ministerial.[38] The work of this Group is viewed as being limited to the following issues:

- *trade and employment*—examination of the effects of increased international trade and investment on levels and composition of countries' employment;

- *trade and social protections*—examination of the relationship between increased openness in trade and investment and the scope and the structure of basic social protections and safety nets in developed and developing countries;

- *trade and core labour standards*—examination of the relationship between economic development, international trade and investment, and the implementation of core labour standards;

- *positive trade policy incentives and core labour standards*—examination of the scope for positive trade policy incentives to promote implementation of core labour standards;

- *trade and forced or exploitive child labour*—examination of the extent of forced or exploitive child labour in industries engaged in international trade; and,

- *trade and derogation from national labour standards*—examination of the effects of derogation from national labour standards (including in export processing zones) on international trade, investment and economic development.

The objective of the Working Group in the first two years would be to produce a report on its discussions for consideration by WTO Members at the Fourth Ministerial Conference. In accomplishing its work, the Group would benefit from consultation and collaboration with the ILO, International Financial Institutions and UNCTAD. It is also proposed that the WTO would welcome a request by the ILO for observer status.

The European Union, on its part, submitted a communication from the EC Commissioner for Trade, Mr. Pascal Lamy,[39] proposing to establish a Joint ILO/WTO Standing Working Forum on Trade, Globalization and Labour Issues.

The EU emphasizes that the relationship between trade liberalization and, in more widespread respects, core labour standards is one that has attracted much public interest. The EU has sought to promote these standards through an incentive-based approach, under its system of generalized preferences. During the forthcoming review of the "enabling clause" and its re-negotiation, the EU would wish to achieve support within the WTO for this type of incentive-based approach for the promotion of core labour standards.

The EU also would like to make ILO/WTO co-operation more operational. To that effect, it is proposed that ILO and WTO organize a joint ILO/WTO Standing Working Forum on trade, globalization and labour issues, to promote a better understanding of the issues involved through a substantive dialogue between all interested parties, including governments, employers, trade unions and other international organizations. This dialogue should include an examination of the relationship between trade policy, trade liberalization, development and core labour standards and it should explicitly exclude any issue related to trade sanctions. The EU also proposed to host, no later than the year 2001, a ministerial-level meeting which would examine the work done in the joint standing working forum.

Broader systemic priorities

Special and Differential Treatment

Developing countries consider that the basic priority should be aimed at providing them with Special & Differential Treatment (S&D) in their favour, adapted to the realities of globalization and development strategies. The underlying need for S&D treatment in favour of developing countries has not changed in the post-Uruguay Round period. The disparity in per capita income between developed and most developing countries has actually increased since 1980, and many developing countries have fallen into the least developed category. Even those developing countries which have achieved growth success have nevertheless had their vulnerability demonstrated by the financial crisis. Developing countries also face major handicaps in implementing their multilateral trade obligations and in deriving benefits from world trade and from the trading system.

As the pressure to extend the "frontiers" of the trading system continues, developing countries argue that their right to take certain measures as essential components of their development policies should be preserved. Rather than relying on artificial and arbitrary time frames unrelated to need or performance, the expression of S&D treatment should, in this view, be tailored to the specific trade needs and development objectives of developing countries and there should be an understanding at the beginning of the new trade negotiations that such provisions would be included where a clear case for their need could be demonstrated. Pursuit of this approach would require a clear understanding as to what measures constituted such "essential policies" and factual demonstration of disadvantages faced by developing countries or their exporters.

For example, this could include examination of the following broad policy lines relating to S&D treatment: (i) basic rights of developing countries under Article XVIII, Part IV and the Enabling Clause which remain integral parts of GATT 1994; (ii) extension of Enabling Clause to cover also South-South provision of non-reciprocal preferences to LDCs; (iii) adequacy of transitional periods in some WTO Agreements that would be phased out by 2005 or earlier; (iv) revision and improvement of S&D provisions in WTO agreements on the basis of experience accumulated in their implementation (for example, establishment of new thresholds in application of anti-dumping measures to safeguard developing countries' export interests); (v) elaboration of additional S&D provisions providing emphasis on supply side measures in order to foster the development of internationally competitive export supply capabilities and to encourage product diversification; (vi) linkage of further trade liberalization to transfer of technology requirements; and (vii) definition of S&D aspects for LDCs, small and vulnerable States to redress their marginalization.

Accessions to the WTO

Another systemic issue relates to the problems faced by developing countries, especially the least developed among them, currently acceding to the WTO. Achieving the universality of the multilateral trading system will undoubtedly be a major objective of the new negotiations. However, the acceding countries are facing substantial difficulties in their attempt to benefit from some of the S&D provisions in the WTO Agreements. The negotiation of transitional periods, for example, is being strongly resisted by major developed countries. The acceding countries are also being required to accept obligations going beyond those of the original WTO members or the WTO Agreements themselves, for example in such areas as agriculture, privatization, export tariffs and the acceptance of optional plurilateral trade agreements. Moreover, they are facing extensive requests to liberalize market access in goods, and especially in services, which may not be consistent with their present development needs. The approach to acceding countries appears often to be motivated by geopolitical strategies and concerns to establish precedents. These imbalances should, in the view of developing countries, be corrected to avoid fragmentation of the trading system in terms of different rights and obligations for original members and newly acceded countries. This would also ensure that the new negotiations do not delay, but on the contrary advance, the accessions to the WTO, so that by their completion the WTO should become a truly universal organization.

Participation of acceding countries in new negotiations

It is likely that new negotiations would be open to: (i) all members of the WTO; (ii) States and separate customs territories that have already informed members, at a regular meeting of the General Council, of their intention to negotiate the terms of their membership and for whom an accession working party has been established. Decisions on the outcomes of the negotiations would, however, be taken only by WTO Members.[40]

This formula, which repeats the relevant provision of the Punta del Este Declaration, would mean that in the market access negotiations, countries in the process of accession would be granted participant status in the negotiations, replicating arrangements made during the Uruguay Round. Thus acceding countries would schedule commitments along with WTO Members, but with no right of veto over the eventual outcome. This opens a possibility that their market access obligations and concessions could be integrated in the final package of results of new multilateral trade negotiations alongside the similar obligations of current members. This would also mean that acceding countries would be able to table requests on goods and services to their trading partners (both WTO members and other acceding countries) which should better balance an entirely unilateral accession process. On the other hand, in negotiations on new rules, acceding countries would have only observer status, with the right to participate in all working groups, and to table proposals, but with no right of veto over the outcome.[41]

Coherence

The financial crisis once again brought into the picture relationships between trade, finance and development. The trading system was severely strained by the recent financial turmoil. To achieve greater coherence in global economic policy-making, which is one of the WTO functions, and make it more operational, WTO rules and disciplines should be taken fully into account by the international financial institutions when designing macroeconomic programmes and "rescue packages" for individual countries. In particular, it is clearly "incoherent" that developing countries should be obliged to abolish measures which are consistent with their WTO obligations, for example, with respect to non-specific subsidies and commitments on services.

Institutional capacities

Developing countries are traditionally confronted with weak institutional capabilities and lack of resources for sustaining effective trade policy formulation and coordination mechanisms. Financial assistance could be an important element in future to enable developing countries to implement their obligations and exercise their rights. Developed countries have traditionally resisted any notion that the multilateral trade agreements could include "financial windows". However, practice has demonstrated that without such assistance the possibilities of many developing countries to meet fully their obligations and effectively exercise their rights is very limited. In order to strengthen the credibility of a rules-based multilateral trading system, during new negotiations, developing countries are of the view that an attempt should be made to assess the administrative and financial burden of fulfilling multilateral obligations. For example, where new multilateral disciplines are accepted, there should be an "implementation audit" to estimate the financial and administrative cost of implementation for developing countries.

Chapter II

THE MULTILATERAL TRADE DISCIPLINES

SPECIAL AND DIFFERENTIAL TREATMENT IN THE CONTEXT OF GLOBALIZATION

Note presented to the G15 Symposium on Special and Differential Treatment in the WTO Agreements, New Delhi, 10 December 1998

Murray Gibbs, UNCTAD

This paper is a revision of an earlier paper prepared for the G77; it takes account of the recent debate on the issue and the papers circulated for this conference. It examines (a) the relevance of a continuation of S & D in its present form, (b) possible new forms of S & D called for by increasing liberalization and globalization.

Differential and More Favourable Treatment up to the Uruguay Round

" Special and differential" treatment[42] is the product of the coordinated political efforts of developing countries to correct the perceived inequalities of the post-war international trading system by introducing preferential treatment in their favour across the spectrum of international economic relations.

As early as the 1947-48 Havana Conference, developing countries (mainly Latin America at the time) challenged the assumptions that trade liberalization on an mfn basis would automatically lead to their growth and development. Their position gained greater political force with the independence of the developing countries of Asia and Africa. They argued that the peculiar structural features of the economies of developing countries and distortions arising from historical trading relationships constrained their trade prospects. This development paradigm was based on the need to improve the terms of trade, reduce dependance on exports of primary commodities, correct balance of payments volatility and disequilibria, industrialize through infant industry protection, export subsidies etc.

To a certain extent GATT rules reflected elements of this paradigm. Article XVIII of GATT, "Governmental Assistance to Economic Development",

under which developing countries enjoyed additional facilities to enable them
(*a*) to maintain sufficient flexibility in their tariff structure to be able to grant
the tariff protection required for the establishment of a particular industry and
(*b*) to apply quantitative restrictions for balance of payments purposes in a
manner which takes full account of the continued high level of demand for
imports likely to be generated by their programmes of economic development.

Developing countries enjoyed thus enjoyed considerable flexibility in
their trade regimes, primarily due to Article XVIII:B, but also to low levels of
tariff bindings,(although the latter could have been attributed to the lack of
benefits received in the earlier rounds of GATT negotiations). Many developing countries acceded to GATT under Article XXVI which enabled them to
largely escape the negotiations of bound tariff rates as part of their terms of
accession. This flexibility was facilitated by the incorporation in 1964 of the
"non-reciprocity" clause (Article XXXVI:8) of Part IV into GATT.

The UNCTAD II Conference (New Delhi 1968) led to the introduction
of GSP schemes by developed countries. These were covered by a GATT
waiver (not Part IV). During the Tokyo Round, developing countries' efforts
to legitimize preferential treatment in their favour across the whole spectrum
of trade relations resulted in the "Decision on Differential and More Favourable Treatment, Reciprocity and Fuller Participation of Developing Countries" (usually described as the "Enabling Clause"). This instrument pertains
specifically to (a) GSP, (b) NTMs in the context of GATT instruments, (c)
regional or global arrangements among developing countries, (d) special treatment for LDCs. The Tokyo Round resulted in enhanced disciplines in the form
of detailed Codes (e.g. subsidies, technical barriers to trade, customs valuation), but these were not accepted by the majority of developing countries.

Thus, S & D treatment rested on two operational pillars:

a) Enhanced access to markets (*a*) through preferential access under the
GSP, (*b*) the right to benefit from multilateral trade agreements, particularly
on tariffs in accordance with the MFN principle, without being obliged to offer
reciprocal concessions; (*c*) the freedom to create preferential regional and
global trading arrangements without conforming to the GATT requirements
on free trade areas and custom unions (Article XXIV).

b) Policy discretion in their own markets concerning (*a*) access to their
market (i.e. a right to maintain trade barriers to deal with BOP problems and
to protect their "infant" domestic industries), and (*b*) the right to offer governmental support to their domestic industries using various industrial and trade
policy measures that otherwise would be inconsistent with their multilateral
obligations.

Change of Direction

At the beginning of the 1980s, however, developing countries began to perceive that the positive discrimination received under S &D treatment had become outweighed by increasing negative discrimination against their trade. This was evidenced in such measures as: (*a*) voluntary export restraints and other "grey area" measures directed against their most competitive exports, (*b*) bilateral pressures by major importing countries aimed at obtaining trade concessions through the threat of trade sanctions, rather than the offer of reciprocal benefits, (*c*) the extension of free-trade agreements and customs unions among developed countries, (*d*) higher MFN tariffs on products of export interest to developing countries compared to those of interest to developed countries, (*e*) the proliferation of restraints on textiles and clothing exports under the Multi-Fibre Agreement; (*f*) the diminishing effectiveness of any GATT disciplines governing trade in agricultural products, and (*g*) increased harassment from anti-dumping and countervailing duties.[43] In addition, the GSP was beginning to be applied in a conditional and discriminatory fashion, being used more frequently by some preference-giving countries as a means of leverage to obtain other benefits, including measures outside the area of trade. The Tokyo Round codes, with their limited developing country membership, appeared to represent a major step towards the "GATT plus" approach, advocated in developed country circles in the early 1970s, according to which those countries would create an inner system of rights and obligations encompassing areas of mutual interest among themselves, and were leading to active consideration of the resurrection of the so-called "conditional" MFN clause (which would place the developing countries at a serious disadvantage).

In the early 1980s, as a consequence of this perception, the thrust of the developing countries' initiatives shifted; while seeking to preserve the differential treatment in their favour, they also began to defend the integrity of the unconditional MFN clause, obtaining MFN tariff reductions, and strengthening the disciplines of GATT (particularly in the product sectors mentioned above) so as to prevent the restriction and harassment of their trade. Particular emphasis was laid on an improved dispute settlement mechanism, as a means of defense against bilateral pressures from their major trading partners. At UNCTAD VI (Belgrade, 1983), all countries recognized the need to strengthen the international trading system based on the MFN principle.[44]

Meanwhile, the acceptance by many developing countries of IMF structural adjustment programmes, their adoption of an export-oriented development model and unilateral liberalization of quantitative import restrictions and reduction of tariffs, stimulated an enhanced interest on their part in export markets. The Uruguay Round was consequently viewed as a means of obtaining improved and more secure access for their exports, consolidating the liberalization undertaken unilaterally and obtaining "negotiating credit" from the countries that were benefitting from this unilateral liberalization.

The Uruguay Round (unlike the Tokyo Round) was open only to GATT contracting parties or to countries which committed themselves to negotiate accession to GATT during the Round; a large number of developing countries followed this course of action. Many of the developing countries which acceded to GATT either immediately before or during the Round accepted to bind up to 100 per cent of items in their tariff schedules.

As a result of "single undertaking approach", the Uruguay Round Agreements have been accepted by all developing countries. The MTAs provide for S & D treatment mainly in the form of time-limited derogations, as more favourable thresholds in the application of countervailing measures and for undertaking certain commitments, greater flexibility with regard to certain obligations and "best endeavour clauses". The time-limits for such derogations run from the point in time when the WTO Agreement came into force, and will be phased out in the context of WTO Agreements by 2005.[45] Only in the Agreement on Subsidies and Countervailing Measures is such S & D treatment linked to economic criteria. In the Agreement on Agriculture, the S & D provisions will be reviewed as part of the overall reform process. The experience in the implementation of S&D measures in the WTO has been extensively documented and reviewed in the excellent paper submitted by the delegation of Egypt.

As this Egyptian paper clearly documents, a large number of S&D provisions were incorporated into the Multilateral Trade Agreements (MTAs). However, this was accomplished in a somewhat ad hoc manner, not as a result of an underlying consensus as to how the trade needs of developing countries emanating from the development paradigm should be reflected in trade principles and rules. On the contrary this earlier paradigm did not enjoy a consensus even among developing countries, it was viewed as ideological baggage from the past by some, or described as a crutch which developing countries no longer needed and which was actually hindering their competitiveness. S & D was thus considerably eroded during the UR, because it was addressed separately in each negotiating group without an underlying conceptual framework. There was no overall consensus as to the trade measures required by developing countries as essential elements of their development programmes.

The challenge facing developing countries in future negotiations would seem twofold, (a) to maintain existing S&D measures where these are crucial to the success of development programmes, and (b) adapt the concept of S&D to the realities of globalization and liberalization.

Is S&D outmoded?

The arguments against S&D tend to emphasize the differences among developing countries with respect to their resource endowments, their production capabilities, their economic and social institutions and their capacities for growth and development. It is claimed that while some are economically weak, lacking the human and the material resources on which to base a sustained strategy of economic and social development; others have reached the "take-off stage" where the economy begins to generate its own investment and technological improvement at sufficiently high rates so as to make growth virtually self-sustaining; others are seen to advance further to a stage of increasing sophistication of the economy and are "driving to maturity". These categories are used to justify graduation and to abandon S&D.

However, what appears to have changed is more the political attitudes to S&D than the underlying reality. Some developing countries are joining the group of those economies which are "driving to maturity"; and in the case of a few of these, the economic disparity between them and developed countries is shrinking. However, in general, the disparity in per capita income between developed and developing countries has actually increased since 1980, and many developing countries have fallen into the "least developed" category. In addition, many newly independent "countries in transition" would fall into the GATT definition of a "less developed" country, in that they "can only support low standards of living". In fact, many of the developing countries "driving for maturity" have had their vulnerability and developing country status rudely demonstrated by recent events.

Article XVIII

Pressures have successfully been applied on a number of more advanced developing countries to disinvoke Article XVIII:B of GATT which permits under certain circumstances a developing country to apply quantitative restrictions or tariff surcharges for balance of payments purposes. The Republic of Korea gave up the benefits afforded to developing countries by Article XVIII during the Uruguay Round. It was followed by other countries, including Peru, Argentina and Brazil. India's resistance to this pressure led to it being brought before the dispute settlement mechanism of the WTO.

Accession of Developing Countries

Developing countries acceding to the WTO are facing difficulties in their attempt to benefit from some of the S & D provisions of the MTAs. In the present climate of "roll-back" of S&D treatment, even the negotiation of transitional periods is proving difficult in the accession negotiations. For example, the position of the Office of the United States Trade Representative (USTR) is that all transition periods in WTO Agreements should expire no later than 2005.[46] Not only are they being asked to forego the S&D provisions of the MTAs, but are even being required to accept obligations going beyond those of the original WTO members.

Regional Trade Agreements

A strong emphasis on reciprocity has emerged in North-South trade relations. Unilateral preferential schemes are being replaced by reciprocal free trade agreements. In NAFTA, for example, Mexico, previously a GSP beneficiary in Canada and the United States, has accepted roughly the same obligations as those countries (qualified by a series of reservations in the Annexes). The FTAA would establish a reciprocal free trade area for the whole hemisphere. The preferential schemes of the EU in favour of individual developing countries in the Mediterranean are being replaced by bilateral free trade agreements, which, building upon a system of cumulative rules of origin, aim at establishing a free trade area for the whole Mediterranean basin. While these agreements are reciprocal in the sense that the developing countries are committed to eliminate tariffs and other trade barriers, they benefit from measures on the part of the EU to encourage investment and upgrade their supply capacity. The Lomé Convention itself is presently covered by a waiver in the WTO and an intensive debate is underway as to how to eventually convert the Lomé Convention into a free trade area (or a series of FTAs) in the sense of GATT Article XXIV. At the same time, groups of ACP countries are intensifying their efforts to form effective sub-regional groupings, with the support of the EU.

Sub-regional free trade areas and customs unions among developing countries are expanding and deepening in Asia, Latin America and Africa. As stressed in the paper submitted by Zimbabwe, sub-regional groupings greatly enhance the negotiating leverage of their members in trade negotiations. They also provide an economic space, sort of a training ground for their manufacturing and services industries to build up their capacities. In certain cases, this integration process is encouraged by GSP donors, notably through the application of cumulative rules of origin. However, in other cases, the most successful sub-regional grouping among developing countries, notably MERCOSUR, have come under attack from the developed countries.

S&D in Future Trade Negotiations

In these circumstances, application of the principle of S & D in future trade relations and, in particular, in multilateral trade negotiations, seems to have been called into question. The following paragraphs address this question by examining (a) the relevance of a continuation of S & D in its present form, (b) possible new forms of S & D called for by increasing liberalization and globalization.

Access to markets

Tariffs

Although the progress in multilateral tariff liberalization and the extension of the regional agreements among developed, and between developed and developing countries has and will continue to erode preferential tariff margins, GSP and other unilateral schemes are needed to maintain access to markets and to reduce marginalization. All developing countries cannot participate in North-South free trade areas, and thus GSP treatment should be maintained or extended to ensure that the most vulnerable of them are not adversely affected, and that their access conditions are maintained (e.g. "NAFTA parity"). This process of conversion of unilateral schemes into FTAs could have the effect of eroding the efforts of developing countries to consolidate sub-regional integration agreements, and have the effect of exacerbating distortions of trade flows along North-South lines. Therefore S&D in the sense that North-South regional FTAs do not necessarily have to involve reciprocity by the developing countries should be established as a principle. Developing countries should have the opportunity to share in the dynamism demonstrated in the import growth of certain developing countries, thus the GSTP should be expanded within the framework of the "enabling clause".

The GSP can also play an important role in sectors where it has so far been applied on a very limited scale. The tariffication of QRs, VERs, etc. in the agriculture sector, and the high mfn tariffs in the textiles and clothing sector provide an opportunity for meaningful preferential tariff margins, and/or special tariff quotas which could provide a major impetus to the trade of developing countries.

Increasing tariff rates on imports from developing countries (whether termed "graduation" or otherwise) defies the basic logic of the value of free trade. It has never been successfully demonstrated that withdrawing GSP treatment from one developing country can stimulate the exports of another; nor is there any evidence that GSP benefits have dissuaded countries from participating in further trade liberalization at the multilateral or regional levels. From this perspective, it would seem that GSP treatment should only be withdrawn on the basis of safeguard-clause type of economic criteria based on injury caused to the donor country industry. Multilaterally agreed economic criteria could be developed for such competitive need or safeguard measures, as has been done in the Agreement on Subsidies and Countervailing Measures. In this sense, it would seem logical that the GSP should be "grandfathered".

Market Access under the MTAs

In terms of market access, certain MTAs (e.g. Agreement on Subsidies and Countervailing Duties) provide thresholds under which imports from developing countries cannot be subjected to countervailing duties. New thresholds might be negotiated in the MTAs, notably in the Agreement on Anti-Dumping where thresholds in favour of developing countries comparable to those in the Agreement on subsidies and countervailing duties could reduce the scope for trade harassment by protectionist interests. The paper submitted by India contains specific proposals for raising these thresholds.

While the transitional periods will result in most S & D treatment in the form of exemptions from the obligations being phased out by 2005 (with the exception of rules on export subsidies), Article XVIII, Part IV and the Enabling Clause remain as integral parts of GATT 1994. S & D treatment can be pursued through seeking extension and revision of the relevant provisions of the MTAs in the context of the "built-in" agenda. As noted above, the Agreements themselves foresee the possibility that the transition periods could be extended, e.g. subsidies, TRIMs, etc. In other Agreements, the experience with the S & D provisions may be such as to indicate that there could be considerable room for improvement. The papers submitted by India and Egypt make specific suggestions in this regard.

The documentation of developing countries' experience with the operation of the S & D provisions in the MTAs will provide elements for specific proposals for improvements and/or extension of S & D treatment which could support the proposals in the Egyptian and Indian proposals. There is a need to monitor the concrete measures taken by developed countries to implement each one of the S&D provisions and link their implementation with the obligations contained in the agreements as well as real trading opportunities.

Key areas can be identified in the area of TRIMs, agriculture and subsidies. In TRIMs, future initiatives under Article 9 of the Agreement seem likely to include (*a*) proposals on extending the prohibitions on local content and trade balancing requirements to cover measures not presently contrary to

GATT rules, (b) proposals to introduce provisions for market access (establishment) and national treatment. In agriculture, the issue arose during the Uruguay Round of the different impact of agricultural trade liberalization as between developing countries with the large majority of their populations employed directly or indirectly in the agricultural sector, and those (mainly developed) where such employment is well under 10 per cent.

In the case of subsidies, the Indian and Egyptian papers have pointed out that there would appear to be a bias against developing countries. The non-actionable categories are those most available to developed countries, while subsidies of key importance to developing countries fall in the actionable category. Furthermore, the non-actionable nature of the R&D subsidies permits firms in developed countries to have access to subsidies for the development of new products, for which they are subsequently given a monopoly under the TRIPs Agreement. In addition, the fiscal investment incentives offered by developed country governments to attract investment, often at sub-national levels are not effectively disciplined . As the continuation of the non actionable category requires consensus, developing countries have the opportunity of correcting this imbalance.

Trade in Services

The GATS establishes a different approach to S&D than other MTAs. The GATS structure provides for the integration of development objectives throughout the text of the Agreement. Market access and national treatment are negotiated concessions relating to a particular service sector/subsector on the basis of a positive list approach to allow for a more gradual liberalization, and the possibility for tradeoffs and obtention of reciprocal benefits. Moreover, Article XIX.2 provides for flexibility for developing countries for opening fewer sectors, liberalizing fewer types of transactions, progressively extending market access in line with their development situation and when making access to their markets available to foreign services suppliers, attaching to such access conditions (e.g. transfer of technology, training, etc.) aimed at achieving the objectives referred to in Article IV on Increasing Participation of Developing Countries. Article IV.1 provides that the increasing participation of developing country Members in world trade shall be facilitated through negotiated specific commitments, by different Members . . . relating to: (*a*) strengthening of their domestic services capacity and its efficiency and competitiveness, inter alia, through access to technology on a commercial basis; (*b*) the improvement of their access to distribution channels and informational networks; and the liberalization of market access in sectors and modes of supply of export interest to them.[47]

Experience so far suggests that the structure of the GATS has proven to be of greater utility to developing countries than declarations in their favour, such as GATS Article IV, which have not to date been effectively implemented.

The Annex on Telecommunications which provides for access to and use of public telecommunications transport networks and services for the supply of a service included in member's schedule of commitments, also recognizes the essential role of telecommunications for expansion of trade in services of developing countries and provides in section 6 (c) and (d) that members shall make available, where practicable, to developing countries information with respect to telecommunications services and developments in telecommunications and information technology to assist in strengthening their domestic telecommunications services sector. Members shall give special consideration to opportunities for the least-developed countries to encourage foreign suppliers of telecommunications services to assist in the transfer of technology, training and other activities that support the development of their telecommunications infrastructure and expansion of their telecommunications services trade.

The GATS thus contains concepts which foresaw the type of S&D treatment required in the context of globalization. The GATS also legitimizes investment performance requirements, measures which have been attacked in the TRIMs Agreement and particularly in the MAI.

The Enabling Clause

Preserving and adapting S&D in future negotiations would involve recognition that the basic elements of the "Enabling Clause" are still relevant and could be consolidated by their restatement and adaptation to the current context. This would entail:

a) recognition that GSP treatment should not be "rolled back", i.e. that access provided under GSP should be maintained (although "competitive need" criteria could be applied); in a world where target dates for free trade have been set for APEC and in the Western Hemisphere, and the possibility of "global free trade" is being seriously discussed, it would seem incongruous to impose higher tariffs on poorer countries on the basis of "graduation".[48]

b) extension of the time limits for S & D treatment in the context of the WTO MTAs where the need for such extension can be demonstrated.

c) encouragement of regional and interregional preferential agreements among developing countries under the Enabling Clause and provision to developing countries of differential and more favourable treatment in regional agreements with developed countries.

d) extension of duty and quota free access to all imports from LDCs.

Financial assistance could be an important element of S&D in future to enable countries to implement the obligations (e.g. trips) and exercise their rights (dispute settlement). There has been traditional resistance to any notion that the MTAs could include a financial window, however, practice has demonstrated that without such assistance the possibilities of many developing countries to fully meet their obligations and fully exercise their rights is very limited indeed.

"Supply Side" Measures

S & D treatment in the context of globalization should give heavy emphasis on "supply side measures" aimed at developing a competitive capacity at the national level. As the East Asian experience has shown, one of the most important aspects of special and differential treatment for assuring sustainable export growth, has been the policy discretion developing countries have been allowed to employ a variety of policy measures and incentives, targeted at specific sectors and industries, in order to foster the development of internationally competitive export supply capabilities. The success of those countries in increasing their participation in the globalizing world economy have been due largely to their successful use of policy instruments to build competitive export supply capacities and to encourage product diversification.

The tighter disciplines in the MTAs on the level and type of support (direct and indirect subsidies) that governments can provide domestic producers and exporters of agricultural and industrial products; and the reinforced disciplines on the use of certain trade-related investment measures (TRIMs) may have constrained the use of policy instruments that could be effectively applied by developing countries to develop sectors and industries with an export potential. In other cases, these policy measures may not be effective.

Future Negotiations

In future negotiations, S & D treatment could be pursued through (*a*) amendment of the MTAs, (*b*) special improvements in market access or (*c*) special provisions in the context of possible new rules in areas not presently disciplined by the WTO.

As the pressure to extend the "frontiers" of the trading system continues, developing countries will undoubtedly wish to preserve their right to take certain measures as essential components of their development policies. Rather than relying on artificial and arbitrary time frames unrelated to need or performance, the expression of S&D treatment in the rule making area would, in such a case, be based on economic performance based criteria. This could involve a "carve out" for certain measures, e.g investment performance requirements which would remain "untouched" in future extensions of rules on investment, subsidies, etc. Pursuance of this approach would require a clear understanding as to what measures constituted such "essential policy measures".

The concentration of technology alliances among companies with their home base in major developed countries has become an important feature of global corporate strategies, creating the danger of exacerbating inequality of access to technology. The ability to join these networks and to ensure that membership in a network enhances knowledge accumulation and flexibility in a participating firm is thus of strategic importance for firms in developing countries. In a globalizing world economy, presence of foreign firms in the market will be crucial to the trade, industrial and other economic development objectives of the host economy, but developing countries will continue to wish to be permitted to link liberalization to transfer of technology requirements.

The existence of IPR regimes in the host countries creates a sense of security for those transferring technologies. However, the role of IPRs in technology transfer varies across industries and activities. Patents are more important for transfer in industries whose technology can be easily copied; for other industries, trade secrecy protection may be more important. For example, IPRs are regarded as an important determinant of foreign investment in industries such as chemicals, pharmaceuticals and scientific instruments. As noted below, there are a number of aspects relating to special needs and interests of developing countries, including the protection of indigenous and traditional knowledge.

S&D relating to transfer of technology appears in several provisions in e.g. GATS (Article IV, Annex on basic telecommunications) and TRIPs. In particular, the TRIPs Agreement provides in Article 66.2 that developed country Members shall provide incentives to enterprises and institutions in their territories for the purpose of promoting and encouraging technology transfer to least developed country Members in order to enable them to create a sound and viable technological base.

The approach to S & D in the future will have to take account of the realities of globalized production and be directed to assist developing country enterprises to derive benefits from and successfully confront the challenges of globalization. This would require, in addition to ensuring improved and more stable access to markets, that of obtaining access to technology, an objective which is closely related to that of access to information networks and distribution systems. S & D treatment would need to recognize the real problems that face developing countries in dealing effectively with the fact that the global strategies of TNCs may not coincide with the development objectives of developing countries, and also may contain anti-competitive elements, as well as in maximizing the development impact of FDI.

Thus, in the context of globalization, emphasis would need to be given to building up strong developing country enterprises able to compete in the world market for both goods and services. This would seem to require less emphasis on "infant industry" tariff protection and more on subsidies and various performance requirements to encourage developing country firms to enter the world market, to underwrite some of the costs and risks of their doing so and to give them the means to compete in terms of technology and access to networks. Thus, future efforts at S & D on the "supply side", might include such elements as:

a) an extension of the 8 year transitional period for developing countries in Article 27.4[49] of the Agreement on Subsidies and Countervailing Measures.

b) extension of the transitional periods for the phase out of prohibited TRIMs (Article 5.3 of the TRIMs Agreement would seem to open the door to such an initiative).

c) recognition of the importance of investment performance requirements for the development programmes of developing countries and their right to impose such requirements to ensure transfer of technology, export-orientation, etc.

d) recognizing the importance of joint ventures in the development of supply capacities in developing countries and that in the context of future negotiations on trade in services (under GATS Article XI.X) or under TRIMs or other investment-related negotiations, no developing country should be constrained from limiting participation of foreign capital to 49%.

e) in TRIPS, extension of the transitional periods and measures facilitating the use of compulsory licensing as a means to ensure the transfer of technology (including environmentally sound" technologies), shortening the term on patents, to bring the TRIPS Agreement into line with the Convention on Biodiversity and new provisions relating to the protection of traditional and indigenous knowledge.[50]

In summary, S & D treatment can be pursued through (i) a restatement of the four main elements of the enabling clause, adapted to current realities, (ii) a "carve out" of essential policy measures aimed at strengthening the competitiveness of developing country enterprises from the disciplines of future MTAs.

However, the success of the targeted approaches suggested above, will be uncertain without the existence of an underlying consensus, at least among developing countries as to what is the problematic of development in the face of globalization, and which are the acceptable and effective measures that developing countries should use to ensure their economic and social growth and development in the next century.

The papers submitted by India and Egypt are action oriented, focussed on specific provisions of the MTAs, but from the various problems cited in these papers, an interesting problematic emerges. The problems cited include:

(a) the low level of industrialization in developing countries,

(b) inability to access advanced technologies,

(c) lack of domestic savings to invest,

(d) excessive dependance on primary product exports, declining terms of trade, volatility of export earnings,

(e) vulnerable BOPs situations, requiring sufficient reserves , not only to cover current imports, but for long term stability,

(f) high cost of capital, which is not taken into account for example in dumping cases against developing countries, nor in the rules on export subsidies,

(g) inefficient infrastructures, with the same implications,

(h) inefficient taxation systems in which it is difficult to calculate the rebate of indirect taxes, thus penalizing exporters, which is not taken into account in the Agreement on Subsidies (reminiscent of the "taxes occultes" debate of the late 1960's),

(i) inability to meet standards of developed countries and difficulties in preparing and enforcing the required technical regulations,

(j) import bias of foreign investors in developing countries leading to reduced positive impact of FDI , as well as BOPs problems,

(k) lack of access to distribution channels,

(l) high percentage of the population employed in the agricultural sector, mostly at subsistence levels,

(m) need to ensure food security for low income groups,

(*n*) lack of resources for subsidization,

(*o*) difficulties in protecting against theft of traditional and indigenous technologies.

What would seem required is to weave these 15 problems into a comprehensive statement of the TRADE problematique facing the DEVELOPMENT of developing countries, testing them against new developments such as electronic commerce, strategic alliances etc.

THE POST-URUGUAY ROUND TARIFF ENVIRONMENT FOR DEVELOPING COUNTRY EXPORTS: TARIFF PEAKS AND TARIFF ESCALATION

Erich Supper, UNCTAD

Executive summary:

This study analyses the post-Uruguay Round tariff situation that will prevail for products imported from developing countries, once all Uruguay Round concessions have been implemented, in the four developed country markets of Canada, the European Union, Japan and the United States, as well as in the four developing country markets of Brazil, China, the Republic of Korea and Malaysia. This paper was revised essentially to reflect updated data for applied tariffs and import charges for Japan after the new tariffications (2000) and for China (1998); new Generalised System of Preferences rates; as well as new estimates for ad valorem equivalents of specific post-Uruguay Round tariff rates based on average import unit values for 1996/1997.

Problems of high tariffs and tariff escalation remain widespread for developing countries even after the Uruguay Round. About 10 per cent of the tariff universe of the Quad countries will continue to exceed the level of 12 per cent ad valorem after full implementation of the Round and taking into account GSP rates. Quad countries maintain tariff peaks reaching as high as 350 per cent to 900 per cent for important export products of developing countries, essentially basic food and footwear. One fifth of the tariff peaks of the United States, about 30 per cent of those of Japan and the European Union and about one seventh of those of Canada exceed 30 per cent. The developing countries covered apply rates above 12 per cent more frequently than the Quad countries, but have fewer extremely high rates. Peak tariffs affect both agricultural and industrial products significantly. The main problems occur for major staple foods, such as sugar, rice, milk products, and meat; fruit, vegetables, fish, etc; food industry products; textiles and clothing; footwear, leather and travel goods; automotive products; and consumer electronics and watches. Peak tariffs are, for the time being, cumulated with the continued application of stringent textiles and clothing quotas by three of their most important developed country markets, as well as severe import restrictions maintained for reasons of plant and animal health. In addition to extremely high tariffs and other protection, tariff escalation remains a further important obstacle which makes it difficult for developing countries to enter into industrial exports. This is particularly pronounced in precisely those branches that offer a realistic chance for a successful start to a wider range among them: the food industry, textiles, clothing and shoe industries, as well as wood industry products.

Introduction

This study has been prepared by the secretariats of UNCTAD and the World Trade Organization (WTO) in the framework of their mutual cooperation programme. Its objective is to review the tariff situation in major developed and developing countries once all the tariff changes and quota phase outs agreed in the Uruguay Round (UR) have been fully implemented. The study analyses the tariff situation for developing country exports and focuses on two major aspects: (a) tariff peaks; and (b) tariff escalation. For this purpose it takes account of the concessions granted by preference-giving countries under their respective generalized system of preferences (GSP) schemes.

The study aims at improving the understanding of the dimension of the post-Uruguay Round tariff problems and at identifying the main sectors where exports of developing countries face high tariffs in their major markets. The study further illustrates, by the example of some major export products of developing countries, the patterns of tariff escalation that are encountered in the post-Uruguay Round situation. The results of this study are intended to contribute to preparations by developing and other countries for trade negotiations.

To this effect, substantial work has been initiated to improve and update UNCTAD and WTO databases on tariffs and trade to the post-Uruguay Round situation. This study uses the results of this work to date to project as realistically as possible the post-Uruguay Round tariff situation for exports to eight selected major markets: in the developed countries, Canada, the European Union (EU), Japan and the United States, and in the developing countries, Brazil, China, the Republic of Korea and Malaysia. These countries are major export destinations for developing countries and comprise some of the most dynamic developing country markets. Peak tariffs were defined as rates above 12 per cent ad valorem, which may still provide substantial effective rates of protection to domestic producers of up to 50 per cent. The tariff data reflect the final most-favoured-nation MFN rates resulting from the Uruguay Round negotiations, or the most recent (or final) GSP rates, or suspended MFN rates, whichever are the lower. In the case of MERCOSUR they reflect the ratified commitments for alignment to the MERCOSUR Common External Tariff by the year 2000.

A problem in carrying out a study of peak tariffs is that a substantial proportion of peak tariffs are specific rates or combined rates. This is the case for almost all products where post-Uruguay Round MFN rates (outside tariff quotas) exceed 30 per cent ad valorem. Due to the lack of the tariffs' transparency, ad valorem equivalents were estimated. They are generally based on import unit values by tariff line when detailed values were available from the country or from UNCTAD's Trade Analysis and Information System (TRAINS). In the other cases, average unit values were calculated for 1996 and 1997 by 6-digit harmonized system positions (1996 version) using the COMTRADE database for the country concerned. If imports of a product were insignificant or import values heavily biased, world market prices or average import values of the developed countries as a group were used instead. From the point of view of exporters, ad valorem equivalents vary considerably, however, from one transaction to the other and may significantly deviate from these annual averages for all trade throughout a full year. The incidence of specific tariffs on their prices and earnings fluctuates with world market prices and exchange rates: it will be the higher the lower the export price and fall with rising trade prices. Post-Uruguay Round tariff data in HS 96 nomenclature are available for the European Union; cooperation by the United States authorities with respect to preliminary estimates of 1997 MFN tariff rates and for import unit values facilitated substantially the estimation process.

Improvement of tariff transparency, particularly in the sectors of peak tariffs, and their comparability with trade data depends crucially on cooperation by the countries concerned. A methodology based on original country data for estimating ad valorem equivalents for specific tariff rates for negotiating and analytical purposes is superior to any other methodology. Nonetheless, comparisons with world market prices or other international prices are useful, where peak tariffs have reduced a country's imports to minimal levels or have allowed only imports of highest quality and highest priced products which can support such tariff rates and the resulting consumer prices for luxury products.

In conclusion, it seems necessary substantially to improve transparency of tariffs with regard to specific rates. In the first instance, ongoing work by WTO member countries regarding translation of post-Uruguay Round concessions into the most recent HS nomenclature should be concluded as rapidly as possible. It is also desirable for countries to provide information on *ad valorem* equivalents of specific rates currently applied and resulting from the Uruguay Round in order to increase transparency. For future trade negotiations, the option of converting all specific and combined rates into *ad valorem* rates should be further explored. The clear expression of specific duties in *ad valo-*

rem terms would substantially facilitate the evaluation of their incidence on prices and trade in the countries concerned and by their trading partners.

Tariff peaks

As a result of the Uruguay Round and national tariff reforms, average tariffs of many countries have now been reduced to relatively low levels. This has led to a widespread belief that tariffs are no longer a major problem for international trade, nor for the trade of developing countries.

However, this study shows that problems of high tariffs are still widespread. Even after the full implementation of all Uruguay Round concessions a substantial number of high tariffs will remain which provide for high levels of protection and affect international trade, including exports from developing countries.

Frequency

Both frequency and tariff levels are a matter of concern. About 10 per cent of the tariff universe of the Quad countries will continue to exceed the level of 12 per cent ad valorem after full implementation of the Round. This rate refers to the effectively applied tariffs for imports from developing countries. All presently applied tariff suspensions, as well as general GSP concessions as applied in favour of developing countries in 1998/1999, were subtracted. The Quad countries maintain an extremely large variation of tariff rates. In extreme cases, though for important products, their tariff peaks reach 350 to 900 per cent. The majority of their peak tariff ranges from 12 to 30 per cent. But one fifth of the peak tariffs of the United States, about 30 per cent of those of the European Union and Japan and about one seventh of those of Canada exceed 30 per cent (see tables 1 to 4).

Developing countries apply rates above 12 per cent ad valorem more frequently than the Quad countries but have fewer extremely high rates. In the four examples selected for this study, the proportion of peak tariffs ranges from 8 per cent in the Republic of Korea to 30 per cent in Malaysia and 60 per cent in Brazil and China. However, at the end of the implementation period no MFN tariffs will exceed 100 per cent in the Republic of Korea, and only very few rates will be above 20 per cent in Brazil, once the MERCOSUR Common External Tariff has been fully implemented. Malaysia's tariff will be 30 per cent or more for about one third of all peaks. This is still the case for one quarter of the peak tariffs in China, which is, however, engaged in negotiations for WTO membership and a progressive liberalization programme for its tariff and non-tariff measures (see tables 5-8).

Peak tariffs affect both agricultural and industrial products significantly. Agricultural peaks are important in all developed countries, the Republic of Korea and China. Their proportion is relatively low in Brazil and Malaysia. Industrial peaks are most frequent in the United States and Canada, and more generally in the developing countries. About one fifth of Japan's peaks are in the industrial field. They play a small role in the European Union, where GSP avoids rates exceeding 12 per cent for most industrial exports from developing countries, as well as in the Republic of Korea.

Main sectors

The problem of peak tariffs occurs in six sectors: (*a*) major agricultural staple foods products; (*b*) fruit, vegetables, fish, etc.; (*c*) the food industry; (*d*) textiles and clothing; (e) footwear, leather and travel goods; (*f*) the automotive sector and a few other transport and high-technology goods, such as consumer electronics and watches.

(a) *Major agricultural food and commodities*

The most important areas with the highest frequencies and the highest rates are the major agricultural staple foods, in particular meat, sugar, milk, butter and cheese, and cereal, as well as tobacco products. Tariffication of former quantitative restrictions, levies and similar non-tariff protection measures resulted in extremely high rates exceeding in most cases 30 per cent and reaching up to 900 per cent for MFN trade above tariff quotas (see table 9).

The tariff quotas for such products are intended to safeguard traditional trade flows and create new minimum access opportunities for the trade of all WTO members. While several of these tariff quotas do create new trading opportunities, a number lack dynamism or are limited in their use. Frequently, the volume of the tariff quotas does not increase during the implementation period. Quotas are often allocated mainly to traditional partners or are accessible under preferential arrangements. This risks pre-empting trading opportunities and leaves little room for imports from newcomers. Products benefiting from tariff quotas are often narrowly defined, exclude standard trade qualities, or are provided for industrial use. There are important cases where tariff quotas carry peak rates or even rates exceeding 30 per cent.

High MFN rates for these staple food products are often combined with country-specific special measures. In application of the special agricultural safeguard clause, the United States has throughout the period since the conclusion of the Uruguay Round stipulated additional duties in its customs schedule for above-quota imports of beef, sugar, milk and dairy products, cotton, groundnut products and others. These safeguard duties are levied if the price of a specific transaction is below the reference level and rise progressively the lower the import price. The European Union has throughout applied a system of additional duties for poultry meat, eggs and sugar (which amounted in the latter case to 65-120 per cent *ad valorem* in early 1999). Japan maintains a system with similar effects, as tariffs for certain meat products, for example, are defined as the difference between the import price and a certain standard price or a multiple thereof. Furthermore, state trading and the designation of sole import agencies are still important, in particular for cereals or dairy products, in such countries as Japan, Canada and the United States. Under such a system, Japan applies substantial import mark-ups, which raise the overall import charges for such products frequently to 200-900 per cent for major foods and their processed products, such as rice (after tariffication of the previous import quota). Levies have not fully disappeared either: the Japanese sugar levy raises the import charges up to 250 per cent; the European Union maintains levies on the sugar contents of processed sugar products, etc. The Republic of Korea continues to maintain import quotas for rice. All the price-based safeguards have had a long life: they may remain in place for the duration of the reform process, for which no termination date has been set as yet. Such a date may be determined in the course of the forthcoming negotiations scheduled under the WTO Agreement on Agriculture.

(b) *Fruit, vegetables, fish, etc.*

In these areas, MFN peaks are generally lower than in the above-mentioned major food sectors, but nonetheless very common; with some exceptions, there is a single rate without tariff quotas that would reduce their impact. In most cases, peak duties for major fruits, vegetables and some fish and crustaceans range from 12 to 30 per cent. This is frequently the case for oranges and other citrus fruit, pineapples, apples, some stone fruit, grapes and tomatoes in the high season, as well as for tuna and sardines (for consumption). In individual markets, high rates are also applied to a variety of other fresh or dried vegetables, such as asparagus, olives, mushrooms, garlic, etc. However, in some markets import duties for many fruits, vegetables and fish are substantially lower.

Special national features include the prohibitive tariffs for above-quota imports of bananas into the European Union (220 per cent): of dried beans and peas into Japan (370-530 per cent); and of groundnuts into the United States and Japan (132 and 470 per cent, respectively). The European Union replaced its former reference price system for fruit and vegetables by a system of tariffs which rise in parallel to lower import prices, so as to compensate any price differences below a threshold level: this is the case, for example, for oranges and other citrus fruit, grapes, apples, tomatoes, olives and cucumbers. The European Union's tariff quotas for fish for industrial processing remain subject to reference prices. Furthermore, seasonal tariffs are common in most countries: substantially higher rates apply in the high season, which hampers continuity of supplies and profitability of exports.

(c) Food industry

The food industry is a major area where tariff protection remains frequent and high in the major developed country markets, even after implementation of the Uruguay Round concessions. Tariff peaks and a range of additional measures extend far beyond the immediate first processing stages to the industry as a whole and its large variety of products. Peaks are also relatively frequent in the food industry of China and the Republic of Korea.

The European Union's food industry (beyond the stages of immediate processing industries) accounts for about 30 per cent of all tariff peaks, ranging with some exceptions from 12 to 100 per cent. There are several cases of additional duties to compensate processing industries for higher prices of agricultural inputs. Examples of products subject to particularly high rates include cereal and sugar-based products, fruit preparations and canned fruit juices. The food industry accounts for one sixth of all tariff peaks in the United States and these also fall mainly into the 12 to 100 per cent range. The United States applies a widespread system of combined MFN and tariff quota rates in this area, together with additional safeguard duties. Examples of products subject to United States tariff peaks include orange juice (31 per cent), peanut butter (132 per cent), and certain tobacco products (350 per cent). In Japan, the food industry accounts for 40 per cent of all tariff peaks throughout the various branches. Major product examples include margarine, canned meat and meat preparations, chewing gum and other sugar confectionery, cocoa powder and chocolate, pasta and other cereal products, preserved fruit and vegetables, fruit juices, coffee and tea syrups and extracts, cigarettes, smoking tobacco, and so forth.

In the four developing countries, the food industry accounts for 4 to 8 per cent of all tariff peaks in Brazil, Malaysia and China, and 30 per cent in the Republic of Korea. Major sectors affected are canned fruit and vegetables, beverages and tobacco.

(d) Textiles and clothing

In the United States, the European Union and Canada, large proportions of clothing and textile imports are subject to high tariffs. Most tariff peaks are in the 12-30 per cent range, with some exceptions such as certain woollen and synthetic clothing that are subject to rates of 32 per cent in the United States (see table 10). These high tariffs are, for now, combined with quantitative import restrictions. On the other hand, there are a number of textile products of major importance for developing country exports whose MFN or GSP rates are being substantially reduced or set to zero (such as tariffs on printed cotton fabrics in the United States). In the United States and Canada, MFN rates apply for most products, even for developing countries, as most textiles and clothing are not covered by the GSP. The European Union's GSP benefits for clothing and textile products are generally limited to a 15 per cent margin of the MFN rates and subject to several country-sector limitations. On the other hand, Japan has very few and relatively low peak tariffs in these two sectors and does not apply quantitative restrictions to developing countries' exports (except for a few voluntary export restraint (VER) agreements with such countries as China and the Republic of Korea).

In some of the developing countries, clothing and textiles are still largely protected by relatively high tariffs and in China by import licencing. The Republic of Korea is a notable exception, and in Brazil protection is limited to tariffs that will be reduced to 20 per cent by the year 2000.

(e) *Footwear, leather and travel goods*

Footwear of various types is still protected by high tariffs in most developed countries. Post-Uruguay Round MFN rates will reach about 160 per cent in Japan (for a pair of leather shoes valued at US$ 25), 37.5-58 per cent for certain rubber, plastic and textile shoes in the United States, and 18 per cent for shoes in Canada. MFN duties remain relevant, as GSP benefits are limited in this sector. In the United States and Canada, most footwear and leather products are excluded from the coverage of the scheme, so that MFN tariffs apply fully to developing countries. Japan generally grants a reduction of half of the MFN duty within the limits of binding tariff quotas and ceilings for travel and leather goods and footwear, which are usually rapidly exhausted soon after the opening of the quotas. With the exception of the Republic of Korea, the developing countries maintain relatively high duties on footwear and leather products.

Furthermore, Japan applies a rate of 30 per cent on tanned and prepared leather. The GSP rate is half of the MFN rates and subject to tariff quotas.

(f) *Automotive sector, transport equipment and electronics*

With the exception of Japan and the Republic of Korea, the countries reviewed maintain a high level of protection for one or the other branch of the transport industry. Most of the developing countries maintain high tariff protection, with rates rising above 100 per cent in their automobile industry. In the developed countries, MFN tariff protection is more selectively applied: 25 per cent for trucks in the United States; 22 per cent for trucks and 16 per cent for buses in the European Union; and 25 per cent for ships and boats, including fishing vessels, in Canada.

In addition, various developed and developing countries apply high tariffs on TV receivers, video recorders, TV picture tubes and some other high technology products, such as watches. The major developing country suppliers of electronic and automotive products are often excluded from GSP benefits. In addition, anti-dumping duties are frequently applied in these industries (as well as in steel, metal and textile industries).

Least developed countries

Due to the application of a more favourable GSP treatment, the post-Uruguay Round position of the least developed countries (LDCs) will be more favourable than that of developing countries in general. However, a substantial number of peak tariffs will continue to apply to their important export products in all major markets.

Most industrial exports from LDCs to the European Union are duty-free, as most of these countries are members of the Lomé Convention. The European Union Council of Ministers has decided to extend the preferential tariff treatment under the Lomé Convention to the other least developed countries by the year 2000. As a result, no industrial peak tariffs will remain in effect for LDC products. Japan's GSP exempts most LDC exports from virtually all industrial peak tariffs as well as tariff quota limitations. Therefore, LDCs can, *inter alia*, export leather products and footwear duty-free to Japan. In 1997, the United States extended the product coverage of its GSP in favour of LDCs. As a result, many more industrial and agricultural products can benefit now from duty-free entrance and significant tariff advantages vis à vis other suppliers. However, such major sectors as textiles, clothing, footwear and leather products, for which LDCs would otherwise have good chances for entering industrial exports, remain outside the scope of the United States GSP, even for LDCs. Furthermore, a number of LDCs are not beneficiaries of the special GSP provisions for LDCs, the GSP or even MFN treatment. Consequently, LDCs continue to face many MFN peak duties for their major industrial exports in that country. In Canada, certain peak duties will also remain in effect for imports of LDCs with regard to products not covered by its GSP, which are essentially in the same sectors as in the United States. In developing country markets, LDCs members of the Global System of Trade Preferences among Developing Countries (GSTP) will benefit from the results of the second round of GSTP negotiations, which have been concluded. Furthermore, LDCs are progressively benefiting from the special tariff concessions and other trade support measures that certain developing countries have introduced or plan to introduce in favour of LDCs; such schemes have already been put into place by Turkey and Egypt. They also benefit from the continuing tariff reforms ongoing in major developing countries on a national basis, as well as from progress in subregional trade liberalization and intensified trade cooperation within the subregional integration and cooperation groupings of which they are members.

The situation is different in the agricultural sector, as quite a number of peak tariffs remain applicable to LDCs in all major markets. Since 1997, the GSP scheme of the United States provides duty-free access for most agricultural exports from LDCs, including imports within tariff quotas. Consequently, LDCs can now obtain important tariff preferences for a number of products. On the other hand, the peak tariffs on exports above the tariff quotas remain applicable to LDCs. Japan grants duty-free treatment to LDCs for a substantial range of agricultural and food industry products. However, LDCs continue to face peak MFN rates for beef and other meat products, sugar and sugar products, various fruits and fruit juices, etc. The European Union applies extensive preferences to agricultural imports from African, Caribbean and Pacific (ACP) countries. But high tariffs, including MFN peak rates, remain in effect for a number of major food products, in particular for imports beyond limited preferential tariff quotas or past trade levels. For example, this is the case for bovine meat, sheep and goat and other meat and meat products; major cereals, such as rice, wheat and rye; and for several fruit, vegetable and food industry products. Many other agricultural products and processed agricultural products obtain only a partial reduction of the MFN duties. This rebate amounts for example to 16 per cent of the MFN rate applicable to sugar and its products, various canned meat products, certain milk products and butter, etc. Consequently, even many preferential ACP rates remain at peak levels.

Tariff Escalation

Not only the level of a tariff, but also the tariff structure may imply a distortion of international production and trading conditions and constitute additional barriers to market access. Tariff escalation occurs if tariffs rise with stages of further processing. Escalating tariffs provide additional protection to domestic processing industries, allowing them to produce at higher than international costs, and hence to increase artificially their value added as compared to that of efficient international competitors. This implies in turn for exporters that access to exports for processed industrial products becomes more difficult, and that vertical diversification of production for exports of higher value-added products is slowed down. In an attempt to capture these considerations, tariff escalation is frequently measured in terms of Effective Rates of Protection (ERPs). This measure relates the protection granted to the processed product, i.e. to the value added of the particular process involved, and deducts the protection for the input procured externally. De facto, many data, methodological and conceptual problems involved in the measurement of ERPs lead to the frequent use of nominal rates of tariff escalation as a proxy.

A note prepared by the WTO secretariat on tariff escalation in the context of the Committee on Trade and Environment (WT/CTE/W/25) arrives at the conclusion that in most countries studied (i.e, the Quad, Brazil, India, Indonesia, Malaysia, Poland and Hungary), bound post-UR tariffs imply a nominal tariff escalation in such sectors as metals, textiles and clothing, leather products, rubber products, and to some extent also wood products and furniture. The study further maintains that in view of the relatively large share of inputs in the value of the final product produced using natural resource-based products and textiles and clothing, the tariff escalation for these categories implies a substantially higher effective rate of protection. In view of the large market base of these countries, a decline in tariffs would imply a significant increase in market access for other countries supplying them with exports.

The Food and Agriculture Organization (FAO) study (1997) on the impact of the Uruguay Round on tariff escalation in agricultural products (ESCP No. 3) points out that as a result of the UR tariff concessions more than 80 per cent of nominal tariff wedges between raw materials and their processed products have decreased in nominal terms, creating some opportunities for developing countries to diversify their exports into higher-value processed products. However, for more than half of the commodities selected, a positive tariff escalation will remain in application and retain an important dimension. After full implementation of the UR concessions, these tariff wedges will reach, on average, 17 per cent nominally (as compared to 23 per cent in the base years 1986-1988) for the commodity pairs and the three markets selected: 16 per cent in the European Union (down from 23 per cent), 27 per cent in Japan (down from 35 per cent) and 9 per cent in the United States market (down from 12 per cent). The study also contains estimates for effective rates of protection of selected products. Post-UR ERPs, in the European Union for example, reach 44 per cent for wheat flour and 25 per cent for orange juice; in Japan, 30 per cent for refined sugar and 12 per cent for roasted coffee; and in the United States, 13 per cent for soya bean oil and 42 per cent for condensed milk. This study further finds that in certain cases ERPs will be negative, as the tariff for the agricultural raw material exceeds that for the processed product. This result is however due mainly to the fact that only bound tariffs were taken into account. In many cases, processing industries nevertheless have access to zero or low-duty imports of their raw materials under tariff quotas or autonomous tariff suspensions. Others are compensated for high domestic raw material prices by additional tariffs for their products. In actual fact, the effective protection for the industry will not be negative but may even reach substantial dimensions.

The FAO study concludes that tariffs and tariff escalation may present an important problem for diversifying exports of developing countries. Although food processing is a major export industry of developing countries, their exports are largely concentrated in the first stage of processing. More advanced food industry products make up only 5 per cent of the agricultural exports of LDCs and 16.6 per cent of those of developing countries as a whole, against 32.5 per cent for developed countries. There are a number of reasons preventing developing countries from establishing value-added industries and increasing their share of processed agricultural exports. FAO concludes that for some commodities, tariff escalation probably constitutes one of the major constraints to vertical diversification of their agricultural exports.

The analysis in this study complements the WTO and FAO studies by an estimation of ERPs for two major export products of developing countries which are followed through various stages of the production chain from raw materials through intermediate products to final industrial consumer goods: leather shoes and cotton shirts. These estimates meet the same problems as other studies in this area, such as the difficulty in translating estimated magnitudes into trade and resource allocation effects, as well as data problems for input-output coefficients, the selection of representative products in representative price ranges, or the need to apply restrictive assumptions (for example, that world market prices and production methods would not be affected by tariff changes). The results need therefore to be interpreted with all due caution.

Post-Uruguay Round ERPs for the production of leather shoes vary substantially between major markets. In terms of applied rates (as distinct from much higher bound rates or lower GSP and LDC rates), ERPs are relatively low for the final stage of shoe production in the European Union and the United States, with 9 and 12 per cent, respectively. Protection for men's leather shoe producers, however, reaches high levels in Canada, with 32 per cent; in Japan this rate is 28 per cent for shoes within the tariff quota and 260 per cent at the specific MFN rate for shoes priced at US$ 25 per pair (corresponding to the average import price of such shoes in the United States). At the lower rates, costs for domestic consumers in Canada and Japan reach by and large already one third of the value added. At the Japanese MFN rate, the protection implied can be compared with two and a half times the overhead cost and salaries of management and staff of a shoe factory. ERPs for leather shoes amount to 15 per cent in the Republic of Korea and 44 per cent in Malaysia. In the United States, the ERP is much higher for footwear of plastic, rubber or textiles than for leather shoes.

There appears to be no homogeneous pattern of increase of effective protection by stages in the shoe industry. Effective protection doubles in the United States and Canada from the stage of the leather industry to that of footwear production (from 7 to 12 per cent and from 15 to 32 per cent, respectively), and rises even more steeply in Malaysia (from 16 to 44 per cent). On the other hand, about the same level of protection is accorded to both industries in the Republic of Korea (15 per cent). In the European Union, protection is more pronounced for the leather industry than for shoe production (at rates of 14 per cent and 9 per cent). At a rate of 14 per cent, EPR may however still slow down entry of new potential exporters aiming for forward integration from efficient cattle production. It may also be recalled that most successful footwear exporters did not build up vertical integration through these stages, but started directly with shoe production under subcontracting and special tariff provisions for outward processing.

The non-linearity of effective protection along the processing chain is even more pronounced for cotton shirts. Effective protection of cotton shirts varies between 7 per cent in Japan and 35 per cent in the United States among the developed countries and amounts to 20 per cent in the Republic of Korea and 58 per cent in Malaysia. Effective protection remains relatively high at the first entry level to industry. Spinning is protected at rates of 25 and 28 per cent in the United States and Canada, 40 per cent in the Republic of Korea and almost 70 per cent in Malaysia. This compares with 14 per cent in the European Union and only 6 per cent in Japan. ERPs for the weaving stage are relatively lower and fairly similar in the European Union, Japan and the Republic of Korea (13-15 per cent), about half that level in the United States (8 per cent) and substantially higher in Malaysia.

As stated above, these estimates need to be interpreted with caution because of data problems. Another reason is that quantitative restrictions continue to provide additional protection for the textiles and clothing industry. GSP offers opportunities for lower tariff imports of intermediate inputs in some major markets. Both factors increase the ERP in further processing stages. On the other hand, special outward processing tariff provisions for the finished products, or certain intermediate processes such as cotton printing, diminish effective protection in the clothing and footwear industries. These results point nonetheless to the persistence of high levels of effective protection in these major consumer good industries which are of primary export importance to developing countries.

Overview

In spite of the substantial progress in trade liberalization resulting from the Uruguay Round, there remain an important number of products and sectors where peak tariffs, relatively high effective protection and significant tariff escalation will persist even once all agreed concessions are implemented, and even if one takes full account of GSP concessions.

While numerous peak tariffs were substantially reduced during the Round, this was not a general pattern. In effect, there are a number of products for which certain countries did not offer concessions at all, or only small reductions. The effects of the per se positive structural change in protection through tariffication have further created new peak tariffs throughout the agricultural sector and in large parts of the food industries. The reform process of agricultural protection, which comprises also the reduction of subsidies and domestic protection, should therefore be pursued intensively and rapidly concluded. The persistence of many high duties and the below-average reduction of many such rates is also a consequence of the fact that the Uruguay Round tariff negotiations did not establish specific targets for tariff harmonization, contrary to what had happened during the previous Rounds. Appropriate harmonization formulas which meet this new situation merit further consideration.

In the industrial sector, the high-tariff, high-escalation areas include many products where developing countries have a relatively high share in the imports of the major markets concerned. Footwear, clothing, textiles, etc. represent a significant proportion of exports of many developing countries. In the agricultural sector and in particular the food industry, the importance of peaks for exporters is often reflected by low levels of imports to major markets: where tariffs are very high, overall imports are frequently small. Imports from developing countries are absent over wide ranges of food industry products and sometimes even for their major agricultural export products in individual major markets. According to preliminary indications there seems to be little trade exceeding the tariff quota levels in agricultural and food industry products.

The effects of the Uruguay Round concessions should become transparent in the trade statistics. A preliminary review of trade data for broader product groups, including high-tariff products, tends to show that there have been substantial trade increases in some areas in major markets, and in particular the developing country markets selected. But this is by no means a general trend. There are several products and sectors where tariffs are particularly high and where trade has stagnated or even regressed between 1990 and 1996, sometimes contrary to the general trend of rapid growth of overall import demand. This has been for example the case of imports of beef and groundnut products into the United States and shoe imports into Japan. In the European Union, a significant reduction in imports of beef with bones, other meat, and a number of cereals has complemented the absence of significant imports of several other products from developing countries. It is not possible to attribute at this stage movements in trade to tariff changes resulting from the Round. Many other factors enter into account, in particular with respect to export capacities of developing countries and competitive strength and divergent economic growth in major markets. Other market access conditions also play an important role. For example, the sanitary and phytosanitary problems of many developing countries, and the way in which corresponding import restrictions are still applied by many importing countries, may provide some explanation for highly skewed trading patterns by destination.

The nature of the peak tariffs and their selective application would warrant complementing the existing tariff and trade database with detailed national trade data specifying for each tariff line the trade flows under the various tariff regimes and rates applied. This should include individual trade flows by partner countries under the MFN, GSP and LDC rates, preferential trade within free trade agreements, customs unions or other preferential arrangements, trade under outward processing regimes, and autonomous tariff rates. This work could be useful for backstopping future negotiations on agricultural and industrial products, including harmonization of peak tariffs. It requires the full cooperation of the WTO member States for supplying this information to the secretariats. The TRAINS system of UNCTAD is being adjusted for disseminating such information in a computerized format to member countries and private business.

References:

The Impact of the Uruguay Round on Tariff Escalation in Industrial Products, Jostein Lindland FAO, ESCP No. 3, Rome, April 1997.

Tariff Escalation Note by the WTO secretariat, WT/CTE/W/25, Geneva, 22 March 1996.

Tariff Escalation and Environment OECD Working Papers, vol. V, No. 10, Paris, 1997.

Tariffication in the Uruguay Round: How much Liberalisation Merlinda D. Ingco, Blackwell Publishers, Ltd., Oxford, 1996.

Strengthening the Participation of Developing Countries in World Trade and the Multilateral Trading System TD/375/Rev. 1, UNCTAD, Geneva, 1996.

The World's Leather and Leather Products Industry: A Study of Production, Trade Patterns and Future Trends Robert H. Ballance, Ghislain Robyn, Helmut Forstner, UNIDO, Vienna, 1993.

International Yearbook of Industrial Statistics 1996 UNIDO.

The Uruguay Round, Statistics on Tariff Concessions Given and Received.

J. Michael Finger, Merlinda D. Ingco, Ulrich Reincke, The World Bank, Washington, D.C., 1996.

THE INTERESTS OF DEVELOPING COUNTRIES IN THE NEXT ROUND OF WTO AGRICULTURAL NEGOTIATIONS

Tim Josling
Stefan Tangermann

Introduction

Developing countries make up the large majority of WTO members, and are increasingly active in the deliberations of that body. Recent economic policy changes in developing countries, emphasizing openness and market orientation, have given them a much greater stake in the outcome of trade talks. This, together with the emergence of global markets in sector after sector, has held out the prospect of productive participation in world trade as a viable path to development. But it has also increased the risks of exposing domestic markets and institutions to competition from abroad, and made countries with inadequate infrastructure and inappropriate policies vulnerable to marginalization in the global economy.

This paper attempts to define the interests of developing countries in the agricultural part of the upcoming WTO negotiations (the Millennium Round).[51] From the perspective of developing countries, five types of problems arise to cloud the enthusiasm for the continued reform of the agricultural trade system. Resolving these issues should go far toward defining the interest of developing countries in the agricultural talks. The first is that many developing countries have preferential access into the highly protected markets of the industrial countries. This degree of preference not only assures them access but also contributes to price stability. This implies that reform and liberalization, even if in the long run interest of all countries, can have negative impacts on the developing countries that currently enjoy the preference. Should developing countries therefore resist further liberalization, such as a reduction in the EU's high MFN tariff for sugar, on the grounds that preferential access to the EU sugar market is currently beneficial? To pose this problem suggests that ways may well have to be found to ensure that countries with a heavy dependence on such preferential treatment are compensated or otherwise encouraged to relinquish their special market access.

The second problem is that developing countries are particularly vulnerable to fluctuations in world markets. As importers of temperate zone agricultural goods developing countries often appear to benefit from cheaper sources of supplies when these are "surplus" to market requirements. Food aid represents a formal distribution of these surpluses, but the flood of subsidized exports from Europe and the US over the years has also resulted in cheaper commercial imports of grain, oilseeds, dairy products and meats. These low prices have kept import bills down but have also had some negative effects in developing countries, such as encouraging importer governments to neglect their own agricultural sectors. They have also been responsible in many cases for destabilizing the price structure in domestic markets. Often the subsidized imports seem to be available only when supplies on the world market are adequate, and dry up when prices firm. But support for further reform of agricultural trade, such as the removal of export subsidies in agricultural goods, may require firmer assurances that food importing developing countries will not be adversely affected by such a move. The Ministerial Declaration on this subject may need to be strengthened and some elements incorporated into the WTO rules. Some action may need to be taken to restrict the use of export taxes and embargoes, which reduce the reliability of world markets as a source of food supply.

A third problem is that developing countries themselves have high tariffs on agricultural goods. Sometimes the high tariffs are a result of protectionist policies in the past: at other times they represent an attempt to collect tariff revenue. Moreover, many developing countries use parastatal importing agencies to control imported foodstuffs and agricultural raw materials. Most developing countries, however, are in the midst of a radical transformation of their own trade and domestic agricultural policies. This means that actual tariffs are often lower than those bound in the WTO schedules. Regional trade agreements already allow imports from neighboring countries at rates well below the MFN level. For these countries the prospect of negotiations to lower the bound tariffs poses little or no threat to domestic producers. But for those countries that have not undertaken a trade liberalization program that extends to agriculture, the WTO negotiations on market access will directly impact the level of protection afforded to domestic agriculture. These countries may be tempted to withhold their agreement to improved market access. For these countries there are special problems of coordinating the external and dimensions of agricultural policy reform.

Fourth, as a somewhat more technical problem, there are some issues which are particularly relevant for the economic situation of many developing countries, and where rules of the URAA and the way they are interpreted and implemented can potentially cause more problems for them than for industrialized countries. For example, high rates of inflation in developing countries have in some cases eroded base period external reference prices to be used in calculating current domestic support. Coupled with low domestic support levels in the base period, which led many developing countries to declare zero accountable domestic support in the Uruguay Round, this can create a situation where countries appear to violate their domestic support commitments, without actually having granted much support to their farming sectors.

A fifth problem is more complex. The deeper integration of the world economy has facilitated and required a fundamental change in the nature of international trade negotiations. Whereas in the early post-war period the trade system was essentially concerned with trade policies operated at the border in the area of manufactured goods, the WTO and the regional pacts cover virtually all goods and services and relate to what might be considered "domestic" policies. The complexity of international rules and their implications for policies administered internally strain the resources and the governmental structures of many countries, but it puts increasing strain on small countries and on those that have under-developed domestic administrative infrastructure. Moreover the trade system for years was mainly concerned with the industrial countries, with developing countries as spectators. The much expanded WTO membership gives the opportunity for much wider involvement,. But the exponential growth of meetings and international negotiations strains the diplomatic budgets and human resources of all but the largest nations. This issue has considerable relevance to agriculture, as more aspects of rural and food policies become covered by international rules and as meetings on agricultural trade issues proliferate. The topics to be considered in relation to agriculture in the Millenium Round therefore, also, should include approaches to helping developing countries to cope with the growing demand for human resources and institutional arrangements required to conduct the negotiations and to implement their results.

The agricultural agenda can be conveniently broken down into four categories, inter-related but raising separate issues for developing countries. The first category is that of the "core" agenda, mandated by the URAA and representing a continuation of the process started in the Uruguay Round. This category contains the familiar topics of market access, export competition and domestic support. The second category of issues for negotiation includes those topics sometimes referred to as "new" issues, though they have strong connections with the core agenda items. Among the topics that could be grouped under this head are state trading; the administration of tariff rate quotas (TRQs) (which has been elevated from a technical issue to a political controversy by the WTO banana dispute); and the question of export restrictions, which was made more urgent by the policies of some countries during the high price period of 1995-96.

A third category of topics can be called "parallel" issues, having major implications for agricultural trade and policy but lying somewhat outside the URAA itself. This category includes such issues as the need for renegotiation of the SPS Agreement, the question of regional trade agreements and their relation to the multilateral system, and the issue of the future of commodity preferences. For many developing countries these topics will have more impact on their agricultural trade prospects than the core issues. A fourth category of topics one could call "related" issues, even further from the main agricultural talks but still of potential significance for the development of agricultural policies. These related items include the issue of intellectual property, made more relevant to agriculture as a result of the move toward the patenting of genetic material; competition policy, which could impinge on many areas of agricultural trade where competition is less than "perfect" and markets are not fully contestable; and investment policy, which touches the agricultural and food sectors increasingly as foreign direct investment becomes an important avenue for development in this area. Though these topics will typically be negotiated, if at all, by diplomats unfamiliar with agricultural conditions, it is important that those responsible for agricultural trade policy be aware of the linkages with these issues.

Taking all these elements together means that a complex set of issues has to be considered when looking at developing countries' interests in the agricultural part of the Millenium Round. In most of the four categories of negotiating topics, the five sets of issues mentioned above that are particularly relevant for developing countries have to be analyzed. To gain an overview of this complex structure, it may help to think of a four-by-five matrix where the concrete issues to be considered in preparing for the negotiations can be conveniently allocated to individual categories (see Table 1). In this paper, only some observations and preliminary comments on major elements of this matrix of issues can be offered.

TABLE 1

Matrix of Agricultural Issues and Perspectives of Developing Countries

Developing country perspective	Agricultural agenda			
	Core Issues	New Issues	Parallel Issues	Related Issues
Preferential Access into Developed and Regional Markets	Market Access	TRQ administration	Preferential systems, regional trade agreeements and GSP	
Reliability of Supplies and Market Distribution	Export subsidies	Export restrictions	Measures for least-developed and food-importing countries	

TABLE 1 (*continued*)

Developing country perspective	Agricultural agenda			
	Cores Issues	*New Issues*	*Parallel Issues*	*Related Issues*
High Import Tariffs and State Import Agencies	Market access	State trading	Reciprocal access	
Rules in WTO with differential effect on Developing Countries	Domestic support calculations		SPS Agreement	
Domestic Infrastructure and Administrative Weakness	Domestic support	State Trading	SPS Agreement	Intellectual property, competition policy, investment rules

The "Core" Issues

Overall Approach to the Negotiations

The core agenda for the next round of agricultural negotiations will in all probability follow closely in the steps of the Uruguay Round Agreement on Agriculture (URAA). The triad of "market access", "export competition" and "domestic support" will no doubt be used again, and the nature of approaches to be applied will be very similar to that used in the URAA. Hence, as far as the core elements of the URAA are concerned, major questions in the next round of negotiations will be the rates of reduction to be applied, and the timing of the new implementation period. Major countries are likely to have an interest in concluding the agricultural negotiations before the end of the year 2003.

Market Access

Developing countries have complex interests in the area of market access. Exporters of agricultural products have an incentive to see trade barriers lowered. On the other hand, many tropical products already enter duty free into the main industrial markets. In these cases expanded market access into industrial markets may have to come from actions other than tariff reduction, such as reducing domestic taxation. At the same time, access into the developed country markets for temperate zone products is often significantly restricted by high and sometimes prohibitive tariffs. It is in these areas where preferences have been particularly important. Reduction of MFN tariffs may have no positive impact on the exports from the preferred country, and could actually reduce sales and prices. Only when MFN tariffs are reduced so much that developing country exporters can also gain from better access at MFN rates, may the resulting market expansion offset the preference-reduction effect. Thus developing countries will want to establish their own preferred list of commodities where they are in favor of developed countries expanding market access through MFN tariff reductions, and the magnitudes of such tariff cuts that would be beneficial to them.

Developing countries have a clear interest in seeing the Special Safeguard provisions in agriculture eliminated, or at least greatly constrained so that additional duties can be less frequently imposed, and at lower rates. As importers, developing countries do not have access to the Special Safeguard provisions, but as exporters they can be hard hit when developed countries impose additional duties under these provisions.

As far as the lowering of tariffs in developing countries is concerned, a number of conflicting issues emerge. On the one hand high tariffs are a regressive tax on imported agricultural goods which place a particularly high burden on low-income consumers and at the same time distort domestic incentives and lead to wasteful resource use. On the other hand governments need to raise revenue and often feel that they have to protect the income streams of local producers for more or less defensible reasons. Trade policy reform, such as has been adopted by many countries, including many developing countries, involves the development of alternative revenue sources and the removal of the most distortive special interest protection. Those that have undergone this process may still have bound tariffs at a high level, but not be using all the protection in their WTO schedules. For them there is an opportunity to get "credit" for trade barrier reduction without having a major impact on domestic markets. For those that have not reduced tariffs unilaterally, the negotiations will provide an opportunity to build such tariff reductions into the process of domestic reform.

An issue of particular interest to developing countries is the use of variable tariffs in the context of fluctuating world market prices for agricultural products. Developing countries have a strong interest in stable world market conditions, and therefore want as many countries as possible to contribute to buffering world market instability. This speaks for limiting the use of variable tariffs, because they insulate the importer markets concerned and thereby aggravate instability on world markets. Developing countries will, therefore, have an interest in seeing the variability of tariffs that the EU uses in the cereals and the fruits and vegetable sectors eliminated. On the other hand a number of developing countries, in particular from Latin America, themselves use variable tariffs, in so-called price band schemes, to protect their domestic markets against price fluctuations in international trade. One possibility in the next round might be to treat this issue as an item under special and differential treatment, and allow the use of such variable tariff schemes only in developing countries.

Export Subsidies

Agricultural exporters among the developing countries have a strong interest in seeing developed countries' export subsidies further reduced in the next round of negotiations. Export subsidies in agriculture are largely a policy of developed countries. Thus by far the majority of exporting developing countries can only gain by seeing export subsidies further reduced in the next round, because this improves their competitive situation in international trade, without imposing any further constraints on them.

Those few exporting developing countries that have non-zero commitments on export subsidies would see the scope for their export assistance programmes further constrained if the next round should result in another step towards reducing, if not eliminating export subsidies. However, on balance even they are most likely to be better of with further reductions of export subsidies. This is not only because their own export subsidies are a drain on scarce government funds and distort the use of domestic resources. It is also true because their export subsidies are small as compared to those of some developed countries. As a result their exports are more likely to suffer from distorted competition with exports from subsidizing developed countries than they benefit from their own export subsidies.

Interests are different for importing developing countries that benefit from lower world market prices resulting from the export subsidies provided by other countries. However, these benefits are highly unreliable and therefore not a good guide in formulating the WTO positions for the negotiations. Indeed, when world market prices for agricultural products are high, and hence when importing developing countries might most want to benefit from subsidized shipments, export subsidies provided by the developed countries tend to be particularly low and therefore of little use to the importing developing countries. On the other hand, when world market prices are depressed, developed countries have tended to engage in particularly large export subsidization, depressing world prices even more and thereby potentially doing harm to domestic producers in importing developing countries.

Rather than opposing further reductions of export subsidies, developing country importers of agricultural products, and in particular those heavily dependent on food imports, are probably better off by supporting alternative approaches to improving their food security. These approaches should be considered in the context of the Ministerial Decision relating to the situation in the least-developed and net-food importing countries (see below).

Domestic Support

No more than 12 developing countries have non-zero commitments on domestic support. All other developing countries cannot grant any domestic support at all, with some important exceptions. One exception is the *de minimis* provision under which developing countries can provide product-specific support up to 10 percent of the production value and non-product-specific support up to 10 percent of the value of total agricultural production. Another exception relates to certain investment and input subsidies that developing countries can grant outside any WTO constraint. These exceptions are likely to remain untouched by any agreement on continued reduction commitments. Therefore, domestic support policies in a large majority of developing countries would not be affected by any further general reduction commitments on domestic support that may be agreed in the next round of agricultural negotiations. Hence the interest of the majority of developing countries regarding domestic support is rather clear - they should argue for large reductions and tight rules, as this will primarily limit the distortions that developed countries can cause.

However, some developing countries have difficulties with particular "technical" elements of the way domestic support is measured. One such difficulty exists in countries with high rates of inflation. The URAA contains a provision stipulating that "due consideration" should be given to the influence of "excessive rates of inflation" on the ability of the countries concerned to honor their domestic support commitments. In the next round of negotiations, there may be a point in finding a solution that goes beyond these vague terms. One possibility would be to allow all countries with rates of inflation above an agreed threshold to convert their external reference prices (and current administered prices) into a less inflationary currency, or into Special Drawing Rights, or to specify their commitments in real terms.

Another "technical" difficulty is that the presence of zero commitments in many developing countries requires them to keep support below the 10 per cent *de minimis* threshold for each individual product. As a result, these countries have less flexibility regarding policies for individual products than countries with non-zero commitments. If the next round of negotiations should make the domestic support commitments product-specific, then this asymmetry would disappear. However, if the domestic support commitments continue to be defined at the aggregate level, then developing countries may want to argue for some more flexibility regarding application of the *de minimis* provision. For example, a 5% aggregate *de minimis* could replace the current 10% product-specific *de minimis*.

Special and Differential Treatment

The general S&D provisions for developing countries' policies in the URAA may well survive the next round of negotiations unchanged. There is also not much reason for developing countries to try and change them (except possibly the *de minimis* rules, see above). Whether both lower rates of reduction and a longer period for making them in developing countries should also be agreed in the next round is a different issue. These two provisions taken together mean that the process of policy reform in developing countries, which eventually is in their own interest, gets increasingly out of line with that in the rest of the world. In particular, the longer implementation period for reductions in developing countries means that they will still be engaged in reductions while the next round of negotiations is already being conducted. If this approach is continued for a few more rounds of WTO negotiations, then the rhythm of policy reform in developing countries will become more and more asynchronous with the rhythm of WTO rounds. Lower rates of reduction in developing countries, on the other hand, do not create that type of problem.

The "New" Issues

State Trading

Many developing countries use state trading agencies to control domestic markets and to regulate trade. Any change in the WTO rules on state trading will thus have a direct impact on these countries. However, it is questionable whether it is in the longer run interest of developing countries to obtain exemptions from, or more flexibility in, applying the stricter rules on STE activities that may be negotiated in the next round. There is now widespread agreement that STEs have in many cases hampered economic development in developing countries, and added to distortions of incentives that reduce the efficiency of resource use. Many developing countries have therefore found it beneficial to leave trading activities increasingly to private enterprises, while influencing market conditions through conventional measures of trade and market policies such as tariffs and subsidies. If developing countries were to receive special treatment regarding the operations of their STEs, this could send the wrong signals regarding the longer run desirability of relying on state controlled monopolies in agricultural trade.

On the other hand, as was indicated earlier, this "intrusion" into the internal structure of markets in developing economies could pose problems for those for whom the infrastructure is still unable to support a competitive private sector fulfilling the many roles of importing and distributing agricultural and food products. In these cases it would be undesirable to compel privatization and other changes in the market system before it was able to support such a move. For some time to come, parastatals may therefore still have a place in developing country food trade and marketing in order to provide stability, administer nutritional programs and prevent the abuse of market power by private firms. This is another case where "special and differential treatment" may play an important role.

Administration of Tariff Rate Quotas

Developing countries have a direct interest in the administration of tariff rate quotas (TRQs). To allocate the TRQs to the exporting country government, as is done for instance in the case of US sugar imports, implies a deliberate attempt to influence the pattern of trade in favor of the recipient countries. This has in the past been done to target development aid or reward political friendship. Such non-market allocation schemes may have had their purpose. They do not, however, promote the competitive trade system that is the fundamental goal of the WTO. Efficient producers can make no headway against the assured market shares of the quota holders. Even allocating TRQs by country based on historical market shares does not ensure that the sourcing of supplies for the importer bears any necessary relation to the competitiveness of the supplier. Hence, even if developing countries on aggregate may have an interest in receiving specific allocations under TRQs, competition among them and hence benefits to those developing countries that have particular comparative advantages will continue to be denied if country-specific allocations of TRQs remain a widespread practice.

The best solution may in the end be to steadily increase the TRQs, until the issue of how to allocate them is rendered moot. But this will have major implications for the developing countries that consider their current market access "guaranteed" by TRQs. The TRQs that embody preferential access agreements for certain commodities are in place to ensure that the access quantity will not be reduced. This is not the same as guaranteeing preferential access relative to other suppliers. The TRQs emerging from the Uruguay Round are designed to open previously closed markets. They will tend over time to dilute the advantages of preferential access. Thus there could be a conflict of interest between the desire to use TRQs to expand market access and the fact that such an expansion will eventually remove the benefits of preferential access.

Export Restrictions

The practice of export taxes and export restraints through quantitative controls urgently needs to be addressed in the Millenium round. There is a clear conflict between the ability of exporters to withhold supplies to relieve domestic shortages and the reliability of the world market as a source of supplies for importers. In the next round of WTO negotiations, developing country importers have the opportunity to lead a movement to constrain the ability of exporters to restrict supplies. After all, restraints on exports are no less inconsistent with an open trade system than restraints on imports. Export taxes could be included under the same qualifications as quantitative restrictions. It seems inconsistent to leave in place the possibility of export taxes and quantitative restrictions that have an immediate and harmful impact on developing country food importers. Hence developing countries have a strong interest in banning export taxes on agricultural products in the next round of negotiations.

The "Parallel" Issues

Preferential Systems and the Lomé Convention

Contrary to the situation in industrial products, in agriculture many tariffs are still extremely high in the developed countries, not the least on products of particular export interest to developing countries. Hence there are still potential economic benefits that can be derived from preferential access to developed countries' agricultural markets. Under these conditions, a strategic question for developing countries is whether the "negotiating capital" they have is better used in WTO negotiations on further reductions of MFN tariffs in agriculture or in attempts at deepening and expanding tariff preferences under GSP schemes. Though the appropriate response to this question may differ from case to case, overall the MFN route is probably the more promising approach. Tariff reductions are more likely to be achieved in multilateral WTO negotiations, rather than in country-to-country negotiations on GSP schemes.

Moreover, the international trading regime for agricultural products is gradually moving towards a situation of lower tariffs. Hence, efforts to improve agricultural preferences should be seen as investing limited negotiating capital in a business that will not be very profitable in the long run. This is not to say that existing agricultural preferences under GSP schemes should be eliminated. As a matter of fact, it may be worthwhile to explore in the Millennium round the possibility of binding these so far unilateral preferences in the WTO.

The same fundamental considerations, of course, also apply to preferential schemes for selected groups of developing countries, such as trade preferences granted under the Lomé Convention, as to general preference schemes. However, there is an extra reason for skepticism regarding the longer run usefulness of trade preferences granted by developed countries under such closed-shop schemes, because they are likely to change markedly in the next decade. The Lomé Convention itself has been declared to be in contravention of international trade rules. It has been granted a waiver until the year 2000 from the obligation to conform with the WTO rules. If such a waiver is still required after that year it will have to be renewed annually. This will increase the pressure to bring the relationship between the EU and the ACP into conformity with global trade rules.

The approach considered as the longer run alternative to non-reciprocal preferences under the Lomé Convention is a free trade arrangement between the EU and the ACP countries, or a set of such arrangements between the EU on the one hand and individual groups of ACP countries on the other. Agriculture can no longer be excluded from such regional arrangements, and hence it is likely that one day in the not too distant future the agricultural preferences that in the past were granted under the Lomé Convention will be replaced by reciprocal regional preferences negotiated under free trade arrangements. This does not guarantee, though, that access to EU agricultural markets for the ACP countries will be wide open. However, it is difficult to imagine that any successor arrangement(s) to the Lomé Convention could include conditions for access to EU markets less beneficial than those provided under the Lomé Convention. In that sense, anything agreed on agriculture in the ongoing Lomé negotiations is likely to be a stepping stone for future negotiations between the ACP countries and the EU.

In the longer run any such preferences will lose value as preference margins will inevitably be eroded by MFN tariff reductions to be agreed in the next rounds of WTO negotiations. Which particular agricultural products are the most interesting candidates for further preferential treatment by the EU vis-à-vis the ACP countries is a matter of quantitative analysis, which will be provided in a future report following-up on this paper.

Where preferences for ACP agricultural exports to the EU are constrained by quotas, and where these quotas are fully utilized, the administration of licenses by the EU means that quota rents, and hence much of the benefit resulting from the trade preference, generally accrue to EU citizens. This is the case even though the beneficiaries of the preferential trade arrangement concerned are supposed to be the exporting country. ACP countries have good reason to argue that this is not appropriate, and hence that the regime should be changed such that these economic benefits flow to them. One way to achieve this is to agree with the EU that licenses for trade under preferential quotas are in future issued by the exporting ACP countries concerned, to ACP traders, rather than by the EU.

Sugar and beef are the two products under the core CAP regimes for which given ACP countries have received the most financially valuable preferences. However, any reduction of EU domestic price support in these two markets will directly reduce the economic benefits that currently accrue to the ACP exporters concerned. In the EU the position has been adopted that farmers' income losses resulting from price cuts under the CAP should be compensated, more or less fully, through direct payments. There is no reason why this option should not also be explored for ACP countries in negotiations with the EU. However, the sugar case appears more promising in this regard than that of beef. This is because the Sugar Protocol under the Lomé Convention provides for guaranteed prices on ACP shipments to the EU, while in the case of beef there is only an indirect and informal relationship between EU price support and export revenue of ACP exporters, working through the market price mechanism.

Measures for Least-Developed and Food-Importing Countries

Discussions about implementation of the Ministerial Decision on Measures Concerning the Possible Negative Effects of the Reform Programme on Least-Developed and Net Food-Importing Developing Countries, adopted at Marrakesh, have kept the WTO Committee on Agriculture busy at many of its meetings. However, it is still not clear whether the Ministerial Decision has had any noticeable effect on actual assistance provided to the developing countries concerned, through food aid or in other forms. The minimum annual contributions of food aid under the Food Aid Convention, which stood at 7.517 million tonnes of grains (wheat equivalent) under the 1986 Convention, were reduced to 5.35 million tons under the 1995 Convention. Actual shipments of food aid, which amounted to 9.66 million tonnes per year on average in the period 1990/91 to 1994/95, declined to 6.13 million tonnes per year on average in the period 1995/96 to 1997/98. The most recent Food Aid Convention, entering into force on 1 July, 1999, has further reduced the minimum annual contributions of cereals, to 4.9 million tonnes, though other foods have now also been included, with a value of shipments equivalent to $130 million. Under the new Convention, contributions can also be expressed in value, rather than in quantity terms. This could add to the tendency for shipments to be the smaller the higher are world market prices.

There may be a close relationship between willingness of food-deficit developing countries to support further liberalization of international agricultural trade on the one hand, and guaranteed access to food aid at time of

particularly high world market prices on the other hand. Thus firmer commitments of the developed countries not to reduce food aid shipments in periods of
high world market prices could be an item on the agenda for the next round of
WTO negotiations on agriculture.

The "Related" Issues

The globalization of the food and agricultural sectors that has taken place
over the past two decades has changed the policy environment in crucial ways.
Globalization brings new challenges and requires new policy approaches, both
domestically and internationally. Moreover the old policies often get in the way
of those that are needed for the new food system. Nowhere is that more clearly
seen than in the area of trade policies.

The main focus of international trade policy has traditionally been the
conditions of access into markets. As globalization has progressed so the scope
of trade rules has expanded. The new trade policy environment has a number of
different elements. These include the health, safety and environmental rules
that ensure quality and acceptability in discriminating markets; codes for the
treatment of foreign direct investment; and the codification of the rights granted
to the owners of intellectual property. To flag the relevance of these issues for
the next round of agricultural negotiations, some "new" facets of agricultural
trade policy arising from globalization are very briefly discussed below.

Intellectual Property

Among the newer aspects of international trade policy is the setting up of
rules regarding intellectual property. The emergence of international rules pre-
dates the GATT Uruguay Round, with the establishment of the World Intellectual Property Organization (WIPO), but there was insufficient incentive for
countries without intellectual property protection to join. But the breakthrough
came in the Uruguay Round when the negotiating countries signed the Trade
Related Intellectual Property (TRIPS) agreement. TRIPS brought a degree of
harmonization to the disparate treatment of patents, copyrights and trade-marks
in various trading countries.

One important area of the food and agricultural sector where the rules on
intellectual property are significant is in the input industries. The seed sector, in
particular, has already made use of such international facilities to try to reclaim
some revenue from farmers. The ability to patent plant varieties has been a controversial topic for some years. Now one has the possibility to patent particular
manipulations of genetic material that are the fruits of biotechnology. This
would give a much greater chance for companies to license new varieties to

others to plant. Though plant breeders rights have been recognized since the 1930s in the US, it has proved impossible to patent improvements that come through selection in the field (landrace crosses) and not easy to see the justification for doing so. But when the improvement comes in the laboratory, as a result of using particular genetic material in a biotech process, the pressure for and the feasibility of restricting unlicensed use increases.

This is of concern to those who fear that the highly concentrated seed industry could extract considerable profits from farmers world wide, as they would have to pay from season to season for planting even their own retained seed. Many developing countries have already expressed their worries on this score, and farmers have not been slow to voice their own fears. For continued progress in this important area of agricultural technology it is imperative that some agreement is reached which would allow research to continue and at the same time avoid the possibility of excessive rents from the ownership of intellectual property vested in natural materials.

Competition

It seems plausible that a global trade system needs global competition laws. This conclusion has had little effect so far on trade policy discussions. Whilst some countries are calling for full scale negotiations on international competition policy, others maintain that the most you can do is to make sure that each trading country has its own anti-trust policy in place. The minimalist approach is unlikely to be satisfactory in the long run. Trade itself is a stimulus to competition: the best policy for curbing misuse of market power in any one country is an open trade system. But the very openness of the trade system allows large firms to develop market power in the world market. Global competition policy will eventually be more about market power in world markets than about enforcing competition policy in each national market.

The issue of competition also is at the heart of another potential problem facing the agri-food system. State trading can lead to the lack of contestable markets, denying consumers of the benefits from competitive prices and levels of service. Importing parastatals have no need to keep margins down, and may not purchase the qualities that consumers would demand. Without the threat of failure the incentive to innovate is missing. Export agencies have often lagged in selling techniques, failing to develop new markets and new uses for products. In some cases they pay farmers less than competitive prices for their products and impose higher than necessary distribution costs on the sector. The question that such agencies pose is whether private or cooperative enterprises could perform the functions of the parastatal in a more efficient manner? If so, the problem remains how to devise international competition rules that would encourage such private activities without losing sight of social responsibilities?

Concentration of economic power is not confined to public agencies given monopoly rights in importing or exporting. Private firms can also have significant market power to influence prices. Privatization itself can lead to market dominance by a few private firms. Should there be any rules relating to the use of market power in international markets? What are the dangers that the rules are trying to prevent? Is the problem the withholding of supplies to raise the price of commodities? This seems relatively unlikely in the case of basic foods, but could happen with vital agricultural inputs. . Or is the problem one of dumping and market disruption? The incorporation of anti-dumping rules in a set of more comprehensive competition regulations has been suggested by many trade economists.

Whatever is agreed in the area of competition policies in the next round of WTO negotiations will have significant implications for global agriculture. Developing countries may have to play the role of watchdog in the area of competition policy. The majority of large firms, in agriculture and food as in other areas, are still based in the developed world. Concentrations of market power will therefore always have a tendency to be of benefit more to industrial countries. But domestic markets are often less than competitive in developed countries. A framework for competition policy thus could help developing countries in two respects: improving market structure at home and avoiding abuse of market position by others in world markets. Without such a framework, many of the benefits of an open trade system may be elusive.

Investment

The global system, whether in agri-food products or in automobiles or computers, depends on investment. Capital accumulated in one country is invested in others, to the mutual advantage of both economies. But global investment also requires rules, and these are not yet fully developed. Several issues are at stake in the area of investment. Among these are the assurance by the investor that the assets owned by foreigners will not be expropriated; that earnings from investments can be taken out of the country; and that there will not be undue restrictions (such as requirements to use domestic inputs or to export a share of output) on the foreign operation. To some extent markets already send signals about the requirements for a favorable investment climate. Firms have alternatives, and countries that maintain policies that are not investment-friendly may lose the opportunity to participate in the global division of labor regardless of international rules.

The development of a global food and agricultural sector has been largely stimulated by foreign direct investment (FDI). This has enabled developing as well as developed countries to establish modern food processing and retailing sectors. Supply chains, reaching from the raw material producer to the ultimate consumer, have been set up which cross borders and continents. If developing countries are to participate fully in this international food market the conditions have to be attractive for investment. The global reach of food retailing and processing requires the assurance that facilities abroad will not be expropriated and that undue restrictions are not placed on the repatriation of earnings. Supply chains also need the environment of predictability that comes from an open investment policy.

Some start to the forging of an investment policy was made in the Uruguay Round, with a limited agreement on Trade Related Investment Measures (TRIMS). More recently, the OECD countries have been trying to work out a Multilateral Agreement on Investment (MAI). At present the MAI is moribund, a victim of both bad publicity and unfavorable reactions from the non-OECD countries. It was widely characterized as a charter for the multinational corporations. But the EU has promised to raise the issue again for inclusion in the next Round of trade talks. Developing countries have an interest in seeing an investment regime that balances the interests of the investor in guarding against undue interference in commercial decisions with the concerns of the host country that the investment is beneficial in economic and social terms. The continued growth of the global food industry depends to an extent on the satisfactory resolution of this issue.

Conclusions

In assessing the interests of developing countries in the specific agenda for the new agricultural trade negotiations there are two kinds of questions to ask. The first is whether the measure contemplated, if implemented by others, has acceptable or beneficial consequences for developing countries or whether it tends to harm their interests? The second question, the other side of the coin, is whether developing countries themselves can accept the same measure applied in their own economies? Obviously the answer to these two questions may differ. This points up the key strategic issue for the developing countries as they approach the next round of agricultural negotiations. How can one support the continuation of desirable reforms in agricultural trade without at the same time paying a high price in terms of domestic policy autonomy and the structure of preferential access currently enjoyed.

One traditional way out of this dilemma is through "special and differential treatment" (S&D). If changes that are implied by a particular measure would be appropriate for developed countries but less applicable, or difficult to implement, for developing countries then S&D could be invoked. But there has always been an implicit cost to S&D, which inevitably shows up in terms of less influence over the agenda for those countries that choose to opt out of, or delay, certain disciplines. It may well be the time to redefine S&D to identify a small set of trade policy areas where developing countries have particular difficulties, and to forego the broader use of the concept as a way of delaying adjustment. Developing countries are the emerging markets that developed countries require for continued trade expansion, in food as in many other goods. Developing countries generally stand to gain from this process of trade expansion. It may be more advantageous to participate fully in the trade liberalization, ensuring that the products and markets of interest to developing countries are included, rather that take advantage of "opt out" provisions which essentially allow others to set the agenda.

It is apparent that the interests of all developing countries are not alike. The premise of this paper is that there are enough similarities of interest to define a "developing country" position on the major issues, even though the importance of individual issues may differ among countries and regions. The success of any strategy that is developed will depend on whether such a coincidence of interest exists. Developing countries will generally benefit from a continued liberalization in agricultural markets, involving further reduction of tariffs, an elimination of export subsidies and the tightening of constraints on domestic support in the industrial countries. Many of the problems of world trade in agricultural products stem from the policies pursued in industrial countries to support commodity prices. Developing countries have borne the brunt of the instability and unreliability of agricultural markets. Support for further efforts at reform would be in the general interest of developing countries.

Developing countries that have not yet completed the reform of their domestic and trade policies to take advantage of global markets and the decline of preferences will face a challenge from the continuation of reform. In these cases countries should seek time to coordinate this reform with WTO commitments. The benefits to the individual country from the continued improvement of market access and the curbing of disruptive subsidies are proportional to the extent of involvement in world markets. Domestic reforms thus play an essential role in the trade negotiation strategy of developing countries.

Current preferential systems should be reviewed both with a view to deriving lasting benefit from the access opportunities and with the prospect of inevitably declining levels of preference. Some erosion of preferences is inevitable, but this will be offset by the fact that such preferences are most valuable on products where protection is high (for example, sugar). In such cases the pace of liberalization is likely to be slow. As the value of such preferences will decline over time it is not worth expending a large amount of negotiating "capital" in preserving them at current levels. Settling the issue of the role of preferences in the trade system is essential to regain the stability needed for investment and growth.

Regional trade agreements offer a parallel trade policy path that should eventually lead to more open world markets. Developing countries should encourage the inclusion of agriculture in these agreements and should ensure that external protection is low enough that significant trade diversion does not occur. The conversion of current preferential agreements to reciprocal FTAs could be both a way to resolve the issue of preferences within the multilateral system and of strengthening regional cooperation and market integration.

Developing countries in the same region (and in particular when members of the same trade bloc) should consider pooling resources and negotiating positions in matters relating to agriculture, so as to avoid duplication of effort and under-representation at meetings. Developing countries should consider how to make use of established groups of countries, such as the Cairns Group, to maximize their effectiveness in the negotiations. If a parallel group of "food importing" countries were to be formed, it could be useful to agree on a strategy with the Cairns Group. Two or more competing groups of developing countries would effectively limit the impact on the agricultural negotiations.

NOTES ON THE IMPLEMENTATION
OF THE AGREEMENT ON AGRICULTURE

Miho Shirotori, UNCTAD

Introduction

The Agreement on Agriculture was first adopted at the Uruguay Round, with the objectives to: (i) bring the agricultural sector under the GATT disciplines; (ii) prohibit the use of non-tariff and reduce tariff barriers in the agricultural sector; and (iii) establish rules to restrain the use of domestic policy measures (i.e. domestic support and export subsidies) that have trade-distorting effects. The framework for trade liberalization and the commitments under the Agreement are not considered as the final and complete, and indeed Article 20 of the Agreement stipulates that new negotiations on agriculture would take place one year before the year 2000, with a view to continuing substantial progressive reductions in support and protection in the agricultural sector. Following the failure to reach agreement at the Seattle Ministerial Conference, the WTO General Council is expected early in 2000 to set out a programme for these negotiations.

Having completed the first five years of the implementation of the commitments, various aspects of the implementation experience that could form the basis of new negotiations had been identified and discussed officially among WTO member countries at the review process of the implementation of the Agreement (i.e. the four-time-a-year meetings of the WTO Committee on Agriculture; informal meetings of the Analysis and Information Exchange (AIE) Process since its establishment at the WTO 1996 Singapore Ministerial Conference), as well as independently at national, regional or international level.

The implementation experience confirmed qualitative gains to WTO Member countries from the rule-based agricultural trading environment—in particular, increased transparency and predictability in the pursuit of agricultural trade policy. The experience also showed, however, that quantitative gains to developing countries, in terms of substantial improvement in market access conditions, failed to materialize. Moreover, in some cases the implementation of the Agreement led to an increased imbalance in a country's legitimate use of "trade-distorting" measures. The following sections of this paper examine issues that have arisen from the implementation of the Agreement, and problems that have been faced by developing countries.

"Implementation Issues " of the Agreement on Agriculture

At the outset, a clarification should be made regarding the definition of so-called "implementation issues". They do not refer only to the difficulties in implementing the commitments under Agreements. When an issue concerning the implementation of the Uruguay Round Agreements is referred to, it should be understood in light of the paragraph 9 of the Ministerial Declaration at the second session of the WTO Ministerial Conference (Geneva, 1998) which stipulates that issues relating to implementation of existing agreements and decisions would be a part of possible future working programme, formulated under the WTO General Council and to be submitted to the Third Ministerial Conference, concerning the launching of further multilateral trade negotiations.[52]

Discussions on implementation issues are particularly relevant to the Agreement on Agriculture because, as stipulated in Article 20 of the Agreement, there will be a new set of multilateral negotiations so as to continue the reform process (i.e. substantial progressive reductions in support and protection). The Agreement was a "trial" - i.e. it was the first serious attempt to introduce a set of multilateral rules and disciplines to the agricultural sector; accordingly, it had been expected that five years of implementation experience would reveal the agenda and the direction of new negotiations. Subsequently, various implementation issues have been identified and discussed during the review process and in the preparation for the Third Ministerial Conference. Participation by developing countries in those discussions was active, as evidenced by the number of proposals submitted to the General Council in the preparation for the Third Ministerial—almost half of over 50 proposals on agriculture was submitted by developing countries.

Based on those discussions, the major implementation issues concerning the Agreement on Agriculture, particularly from the perspective of developing countries, could be summarized as the following:

(i) Market access commitments—developing countries are of the view that the implementation of the Agreement failed to reduce substantially the trade barriers in the agricultural sector;

(ii) Domestic support and export competition commitments—the implementation of the Agreement "legalized" the use of trade-distorting support measures mainly by developed countries while definitively limiting such use by many developing countries; and

(iii) Non-trade concerns—the implementation of the Agreement could not resolve the ambiguity with regard to what are legitimate non-trade concerns which should be taken into account in the implementation of certain commitments.

The following section examine those implementation issues for each area of commitments, i.e. market access, domestic support, export competition policy and non-trade concerns.

Market Access Commitment

The legal text referring to the market access commitments is very short. Article 4 of the Agreement of Agriculture only states that (i) Members' commitments (tariff bindings, tariff reductions and market access opportunities) had been contained in "Schedules", and (ii) Members could no longer revert to any non-tariff measures (NTMs). The details of the market access commitments are found in an informal document (so-called "Modalities of Concessions") which describes: the methods to convert NTMs to tariffs (i.e. tariffication); tariff reduction approach, i.e. average 36% (24% for developing countries) reduction; binding of tariffs; and the method to provide market access opportunities under the system of tariff rate quotas.

While those commitments undoubtedly improved the agricultural trading environment qualitatively, in terms of transparency and predictability of trade policies of the WTO members, various empirical studies of the post-Uruguay Round tariff environment indicate that the impacts upon actual improvement in the market access condition has been limited. First, the post-Uruguay Round agricultural tariffs at the bound level remain distinctively higher than industrial tariffs. The trade-weighted average of post-Uruguay Round bound tariffs on agricultural products is estimated at 32.4%, compared to 5.7% on industrial products or 6.5% on all merchandised products.[53] Moreover, the agricultural sector remains one of the sectors that are most affected by tariff peaks and tariff escalation problems. Second, the tariff structure in the agricultural sector remains complex, including the frequent use of non-ad valorem rates (such as specific rates and compound rates), which by nature discriminate against lower-price imports. Third, the market access opportunities, whose objective was to ensure a flow of imports previously discriminated against in favour of domestic products by means of non-tariff barriers, seem to have had limited impacts upon exports from developing countries.

High tariff barriers, tariff peaks and tariff escalation

Two aspects of the market access commitments in the "Modalities", that are the tariffication methods and the tariff reduction approach, are the main cause for persisting high agricultural tariff barriers as well as problems of tariff peaks and tariff escalation .

Tariffication—According to the "Modalities", NTMs should be converted to ad-valorem equivalents based on the price gap between the administered price (i.e. domestic price under NTMs) and the c.i.f. import price of the product concerned. During this process, many of 38 (mostly developed) countries which implemented the tariffication commitment had managed to calculate tariff equivalents resulted in a higher level of protection than the level under NTMs (so-called "dirty tariffication"). Those self-claimed tariff equivalents had been rarely challenged by other member countries during their exchange of concessions. Such exercises often resulted in prohibitively high rates (e.g. above 300%).

Tariff reduction formula—The Uruguay Round tariff reduction approach employed for the agricultural sector suggested that the overall result should achieve on average 36% tariff reduction, with an additional commitment to reduce each tariff line at least by 15%. That is to say, Member countries had flexibility to chose which tariff rates to reduce by how much, and many of them reduced the tariff rates of sensitive products by the minimum level of around 15%, and compensated for it by making larger cuts on low tariffs. This led to an uneven tariff cuts across different products, which consequently resulted in a larger degree of tariff dispersion.

Tariff peaks and tariff escalation are major problems in the post-Uruguay Round tariff environment in the agricultural sector. A joint UNCTAD/WTO study[54] shows that more than half of the peak tariffs of developed countries are found in the agricultural (including food industry) and fishery sectors. Major export products of developing countries such as sugar, tobacco and cotton, and those of potential export interest such as processed food, are frequently levied at some of the highest peak rates (e.g. exceeding 100%), as shown in Table 1. The study also finds that the tariff peak problem is more pronounced in developed countries: in the developing countries studied, agricultural tariffs above 100% are rare. Tariff escalation occurs when tariffs are increased as the level of processing in a production stages is increased. It is a major impediment to developing countries' efforts to diversify agricultural exports from primary commodities to processed products. Tariff escalation persists in the post-Uruguay Round tariff environment especially in a number of product chains that are of importance to developing countries including;

coffee, cocoa, oilseeds, vegetables and fruits and nuts. Escalation appears to be less significant in meat and dairy products.[55]

Agricultural tariff structure

In the agricultural sector, specific rates or other non-*ad-valorem* (NAV) rates are frequently used, which make the agricultural tariffs very complex.[56] To exporters, NAV rates can conceal the actual degree of tariff protection. An informal UNCTAD study made calculations of *ad-valorem* equivalents for various NAV rates in the agricultural sector, and found that a large portion of those NAV rates revealed the *ad-valorem* equivalents of above 100% as shown in the Table 2.[57] NAV rates may discriminate against cheaper imports, i.e. the degree of restrictiveness varies inversely with the unit import price. For instance, a NAV tariff of $2.00/kg has an *ad valorem* equivalent of 10% when the unit import price is $20.00/kg. If the unit import price falls to $15.00, the *ad-valorem* equivalent increases to 13%, and to 20% then the import price falls to $10.00.

TABLE 1

Selected Post-Uruguay Round Tariff Peaks (%)

	EU	Japan	USA	Canada	Brazil	Korea
Bovine meat, chilled	86	46	26	26	10	40
Bovine meat, frozen (boneless)	215	46	26	26	12	30
Pork, frozen	38	66	0	0	10	25
Chicken meat, whole, frozen	32	12	2	238	10	20
Milk (>3% fat)	113	280	66	241	14	36
Milk in powder, without sugar	66	80	55	213	16	40
Milk in powder, with sugar	54	85	179	243	16	40
Yogurt	69	370	63	238	16	36
Butter	68	105	70	300	16	40
Cheese	120	30	133	246	16	36
peas, dried	0	640	1	0	10	27
Manioc, dried	75	15	0	0	10	20
Bananas, fresh	180	23	0	0	10	30
Wheat	65	39	2	77	10	5
Maize	84	60	2	1	8	5
Rice, milled	71	550	0	1	10	5
Wheat flour	44	40	2	33	12	4
Maize flour	29	21	2	6	10	5
Wheat, groats and meal	74	25	1	50	10	5
Maize, groats and meal	24	21	0	3	10	5
Malt of wheat	52	42	1	25	14	30
Ground-nuts, shelled	0	550	132	0	10	40
Olive oil, refined	60	0	0	0	10	8
Margarine	31	21	10	56	12	8

Table 1 (*continued*)

	EU	Japan	USA	Canada	Brazil	Korea
Sausages	25	10	0	1	16	18
Pork hams, prepared	30	110	0	10	16	30
Beef meat, prepared	26	21	0	11	16	30
Cane sugar, raw	73	100	43	70	16	5
White sugar	71	59	41	70	16	8
Sugar confectionery	21	25	33	8	20	8
Cocoa powder with sugar	22	30	52	5	18	8
Chocolates, not filled	21	30	39	5	20	8
Pasta, uncooked, without eggs	39	22	0	7	16	8
Tapioca	34	10	0	0	16	8
Sweet biscuits, waffles, etc.	26	15	0	4	18	8
Fruits & nuts, preserved by sugar	33	13	16	10	14	30
Fruit jams, marmalades, puree	39	34	10	9	14	30
Peanut butter	13	12	132	0	14	50
Ground-nuts, roasted	11	21	132	0	14	50
Pineapples, preserved	25	110	1	0	14	45
Citrus fruits, preserved	21	30	14	0	14	45
Fruit mixtures, preserved	19	6	15	6	14	45
Orange juice	52	30	31	2	14	50
Grapefruit juice	44	30	19	0	14	30
Pineapple juice	46	30	12	0	14	50
Grape juice	215	30	14	10	14	45
Apple juice	63	34	0	9	14	45
Coffee preparations & extracts	9	130	27	0	16	8
Tea prep., essences & extracts	6	180	91	0	16	40
Tobacco, stemmed, stripped	5	0	350	0	14	20
Cigarette	58	0	10	13	20	40
Smoking tobacco	75	30	310	5	20	40

Source: UNCTAD, *The Post-Uruguay Round Tariff Environment for Developing Country Export: Tariff Peaks and Tariff Escalation*, UNCTAD/WTO Joint Study, (TD/B/COM.1/14/Rev.1), 1999.

TABLE 2

Incidence of *Non-Ad-Valorem* Rates in the Agricultural Sector

	Number of NAV tariff lines as per cent of the total agricultural tariff lines (HS 01-24)	Number of agricultural NAV tariffs as per cent of the total NAV tariff lines (HS 01-97)	Ad-valorem equivalent exceeding 50 per cent (100%), as per cent of total agricultual NAV tariff lines
Australia	4.3	63.3	42.0 (25.8)
Canada	22	89.3	3.8 (0.0)
Japan	22.6	50.3	62.1 (51.1)
New Zealand	1.3	4.7	50.0 (41.7)
Norway	63.2	55.2	35.6 (19.5)
Switzerland	96.4	26.6	25.4 (15.9)
United States	35.6	42	0.2 (0.03)
European Union	34.8	96.4	43.4 (18.1)

Source: UNCTAD *study (Computation of* ad-valorem *equivalents of specific tariffs), 1998; UNCTAD TRAINS database.*

Market access opportunities (Tariff rate quotas)

The aim of market access opportunities within the market access commitments was to ensure that: tariffication of NTMs would not reduce the "current" level of imports (the level of imports at the base period); or, for those products whose imports at the base period was insignificant, the "minimum" level of imports (3% of the domestic consumption in the base period) would be guaranteed. Member countries set quotas for those current and minimum level of imports, and imports within quotas are levied at substantially lower rates than their corresponding MFN rates (the tariff rate quotas (TRQs) system). The experiences in the implementation of TRQs, however, revealed that those quotas under TRQs have not been always fully utilized.

Tariff rate quota (TRQ) under-fill—WTO Member countries' notifications to the WTO Committee on Agriculture reveal that not all the quantities under the TRQ have been imported (i.e. some quotas have not been filled). The simple average fill-rates (imports made under a TRQ as a percentage of the base quantity as notified in a Member's Schedule of commitments) of notified quota imports were: 65% in 1995; 63% in 1996; and 46% in 1997.[58] Most-sited reasons for TRQ under-fill by importing countries was a lack of domestic demand for imports of product under TRQs. Exporting countries, on the other hand, suggested that the TRQ under-fill could have been directly or indirectly caused by the methods applied for the TRQ administration. For instance, when TRQs are administered under the system of import licensing, importing countries normally consider that TRQs are "filled" once all the licence for a respective year are allocated to importers, regardless to whether those licence holders actually make the use of it or not. The "Modalities" did not provide guidelines with regard to the TRQ administration methods. The Agreement on Agriculture does not penalize TRQ "under-fill", and no action has been taken against such incidence.

Preferential quota allocation—TRQs under the "current" access commitment are pre-allocated to specific suppliers on the basis of their market shares in the base-period, or as a result of bilateral negotiations held during the UR negotiations. 70 (out of the total 1370) TRQs had been specified as partially or totally pre-allocated to specific supplier countries in Members' initial commitments. TRQ under the "minimum" access commitment should in principle be treated as global quotas, and should be allocated to supplier countries on a MFN basis. However, some portion of the "minimum" access TRQs appear to have been earmarked for specific supplier countries under bilateral, regional or inter-regional preferential trade agreements. Members' Uruguay Round Schedules of Commitments do not always make a clear distinction between current access TRQs and minimum access TRQs.

TRQ administration methods—Since the start of the implementation of the TRQ commitments in 1995, exporting countries reported to the Committee on Agriculture of cases where certain TRQ administration methods allegedly presented difficulties in obtaining access to markets under TRQs. Problems of TRQ administration methods as identified by exporters include: (i) the existence of disparate types of the TRQ administration methods among TRQ-providing countries, or even among products within a country; and (ii) conditions attached to certain TRQ imports, that are seemingly restrictive against imports. First, there exist a variety of TRQ administering methods. An informal study made by the WTO for the AIE Process[59] groups those administration methods into 8 categories: applied tariffs (i.e. imports are allowed at the in-quota tariff rate or lower, with no quota quantity limitation); first-come-first-served; licences on demand; quota auctioning; quota allocation to historical importers; quota allocation to state trading enterprises (STEs); quota allocation to producer groups or associations; mixed allocation methods (and "other" category for those which do no clearly fall within any of the above categories). The study finds, based on the notifications of TRQs submitted by WTO Members during 1995-1997, that around the half of total 1370 TRQs committed in members' Schedules entered into the market under the applied rate (i.e. quota-free) condition, followed by the system of import licensing (25% of the total TRQs) and the first-come-first-served (7%). The study also provides average TRQ fill-rates for each classified administration method. Although the values vary slightly from one year to another, the fill-rates of three categories (licences on demand, auctioning and "other") were consistently below the overall average fill-rate for each of three years since 1995. Provisions of TRQs to STEs or to producer associations of the products concerned are sometimes viewed as an indirect restriction over TRQ imports, as those organizations may control the quantities or the market prices of imports under the quotas. The average TRQ fill-rate of the quota allocation to STEs in 1995 and 1996 were higher than the overall average (no allocation to STEs were reported in 1997). The average TRQ fill-rate of the quota allocation to producer associations was higher than the overall average in 1995 (74% to the overall average of 65%), but lower than the average in 1996 (53% to 63%). Second, exporters also suggested that additional conditions attached to imports of TRQs could have had a restrictive effect upon quota imports. Neither the Agreement on Agriculture, the GATT 94 nor other WTO rules stipulate any specific rules governing the use of TRQs stipulated. The above sited informal study by WTO identified five principal additional conditions to the TRQ administration, that are: domestic purchase requirement (e.g. concurrent purchase of domestic products); limits on TRQ share among importers; export certificates by the exporting country (for bilateral allocation of TRQs); past trading performance of importers. Throughout 1995 to 1997, approximately one in five TRQs were associated with an additional condition, including those TRQs imports under the applied rate method. The incidence of those additional conditions is highest in the case of the licence-on-demand method.

High in-quota tariff rates—The Draft Final Act of the Uruguay Round indicated that "minimum access opportunities shall be implemented on the basis of a tariff quota at a low or minimal rate". However, there is no guideline as to at which level rates are considered to be "low or minimal". The lack of ceiling to in-quota tariffs allowed a country to set prohibitively high in-quota rates such as 250%, considering that they are low or minimal compared to the above-quota (MFN) rate of, say, 300%. High within-quota rates, which are sometimes higher than a country's (simple) average agricultural tariff rate may have prevented the tariff rate quota-fill.

Market access—Use of the special safeguard (SSG) provisions

The limited use of SSGs raised a question as to whether this special provision of market protection should necessarily be continued beyond the current implementation years. 38 countries reserved the right to apply SSGs in their Schedules. In total, only 6 countries between 1995 and 1998 took either price-based SSG actions (affecting a total of 72 tariff items) or volume-based SSG actions (affecting a total of 128 tariff items) or both (as notified by October 1998). SSGs can only be levied on "tariffied" products, which are already protected by high above-quota tariff rates in most cases. SSGs thus grant a "double" protection to them, first with a high tariff rate and second with an additional duty.

The followings are the "problems" associated to the SSG provision, as identified by exporters in the implementation period since 1995:

- Volume-based trigger quantity could be below the level allowed under a TRQ for the product concerned, such that a minuscule level of imports could trigger an immediate SSG action.

- A product coverage for volume-based SSGs is sometimes set so broad that it may contain a number of tariff lines that are considered as "similar" products.

- Price-based SSGs resemble closely to variable levies, as the size of an additional duty depends (but is not equal to) on the difference between the import price and the trigger (reference) price.

- Trigger prices used for price-based SSGs are in many cases higher than those used for the tariffication process. Trigger prices that had been calculated discretionary by each country did not need verifying.

The SSG provision had been included in the Agreement on Agriculture to protect domestic producers from the impacts of tariffication, i.e. a possible influx of imports or a possible plunge of import prices. Some countries consider that, given the infrequent use of SSGs, the provision could be eliminated after the current implementation period. Some, however, consider that the continuation of the SSG provision would facilitate the acceptance of further negotiations on tariffs, as it would provide possible remedy against possible disruption of domestic market.

Domestic support reduction commitments

The AMS reductions commitments

The implementation problem associated with the domestic support commitment include: (i) unequal distribution of "rights" to use trade-distorting domestic support measures, in terms of the Aggregate Measurement of Support (AMS); (ii) ambiguous product specificity associated with the AMS commitment; and (iii) the AMS calculation concerning excessive inflation and "negative" AMS.

Concentration in the use of trade-distorting domestic support by certain developed countries

During the Uruguay Round negotiations, countries were suggested to submit the value of **Amber Box** (i.e. trade-distorting) domestic support measures used during the base period (1986/1988), which was taken as the initial AMS value from which the reductions of 20% (13% for developing countries) had to be made by the end of the implementation period. Only 28 countries (of the current 134 Members) specified positive base-period value. Majority of developing countries had claimed zero value in the base period, which limited their right to use Amber Box measures only within the de minimis limit. The reduction commitments hence resulted in imbalance between developed and developing countries in terms of their leverage to legally use trade-distorting domestic support.

The gap in the AMS values between developed countries and developing countries is considerably large - the base-period AMS of majority of developing countries was below 15% of their respective agricultural GDP, while that of thirteen out of seventeen developed countries exceeded 20% (of which eight exceeded 50%). In 1996, the aggregate current total AMS value of 10 developed countries accounted for 95% (of which the European Community accounted for 56% and Japan 28%) of the total value of US$103.7 billion notified by 24 countries.

Lack of product specificity

The commitment to reduce product-specific domestic support measures are made on the aggregated value (i.e. in terms of AMS), not on the level of support to each specific product. This provided countries with a flexibility to shift the values of available product-specific AMS among different products, i.e. as long as the Total Current AMS is within the bound level, it is left to each country's discretion to determine 'domestic support on which product should be reduced by how much' within the reduction commitment. The implication of this flexibility is that countries can have a right even to increase the support to sensitive products, by reducing the level of support to less sensitive products.

The method for the AMS calculation concerning excessive inflation and "negative" AMS

Several developing countries faced problems with the treatment of "excessive" inflation and the "negative" AMS in calculating the current total AMS. The calculation of the annual product-specific AMS value (which all the WTO member countries have to notify to the WTO Committee on Agriculture each year) is based on the difference between the administered price of each product concerned (i.e. the price set by the importing government for the domestic market) and the nominally fixed reference price, which is normally the c.i.f. import price in 1986-88. Thus, in a country which experienced a substantial rate of inflation since the base-period, the gap between the administered price in the current price level and the nominally fixed world be so large. This would result in a reduction in real terms of the annual AMS value given in a country's Schedule of Commitment if it specified a positive value for the base-period AMS. An average annual inflation rate in developing countries was around 30 per cent between 1990 and 1996, compared to 3 per cent in developed countries (20 per cent for East European countries).

A product-specific AMS for market support measures could be negative, when the administered price of the product concerned in any particular year was lower than the nominally-fixed reference price. Some developing countries suggested that such negative AMS be deducted from the total current AMS, as a negative AMS could be considered as an implicit tax on farmers, and the total AMS should by definition by the sum of all subsidies and taxes. The Agreement does not specify if and how the initial commitment may be revised due to excessive inflation.

Exempted domestic support measures

Another major questions raised over the effectiveness of the domestic support commitments concern the definition and the treatment of domestic support measures that are exempted from the reduction commitment, which are: domestic support measures within the de minimis limit; the **Blue Box** measures (i.e. direct payments under production-limiting programmes); and the **Green Box** measures.

Questions over the sufficiency and effectiveness of the de minimis limit

Countries are allowed to exclude domestic support measures that are within the *de minimis* limit, i.e. less than 5% (10% for developing countries) of the value of annual production of the product concerned. As the majority of developing countries claimed zero value for the base-period AMS, the value within the *de minimis* limit is the only amount of **Amber Box** type of domestic support to which they are legally entitled each year. An application of measure outside the *de minimis* limit could be subject to subsidies and countervailing actions under the GATT 94. The values under the *de minimis* limit for product-specific domestic measures could not be aggregated, thus countries cannot shift the value of the *de minimis* support among different products, unlike the flexibility given to the AMS reduction commitments. As regards non-product-specific *de minimis* support, 10% of the agricultural GDP of developing countries on average is roughly estimated to be US$800 million. The *de minimis* limit of 5%, on the other hand, provides the United States with the value of up to US$6,000 million, and Japan with the value of up to US$4,800 million.

Blue Box exemptions (Article 6.5)

Only four countries specified the **Blue Box** exemptions in their commitments (the EU, Iceland, Norway, and the United States). Major exporting countries, namely those in the Cairns Group and the United States (which abolished the use of Blue Box measures in the 1996 FAIR Act) suggest that the **Blue Box** exemption to be terminated at the end of the implementation period for the Uruguay Round commitments, as they consider the Blue Box measures to be a transitional mechanism, that had been included in the Agreement on Agriculture merely as a political compromise between the EU and the United States.

Criteria for the Green Box exemption

The major implementation problem with regard to the **Green Box** exemption is that each country may have its own interpretation of the criteria for **Green Box** measures. Developed country members of the Cairns group consider that the current criteria is too broadly defined that it allows countries to disguise domestic support measures which do not meet the basic principle of the **Green Box** criteria— i.e. having no or minimal trade distorting effect, and not providing price support to producers. The Agreement on Agriculture has no provision of a mechanism to assess conformity of those measures notified as **Green Box** measures.

Export subsidy reduction commitments

Reduction commitments

The export subsidy provisions is a special treatment within the WTO framework that is applicable only to agricultural products. The use of export subsidies in the industrial sector is prohibited. The legitimate value (i.e. within the reduction commitment) of export subsides at the end of the implementation period would remain at around US$13.8 billion, which accounts for 2.4% of the world total agricultural exports (US$579.9 billion) in 1997, or 63.6% of the total agricultural exports of Africa in the same year, though notifications submitted to the WTO Committee on Agriculture by member countries on the use of export subsidies reveal that countries did not always use export subsidies up to the annually allowed ceiling level.

The implementation problems identified in the export subsidy reduction commitment include: (i) concentration of the use of export subsidies among few countries; (ii) "roll-over" provision (Article 9.2(b)) for the use of export subsidies; and (iii) Circumvention of the reduction commitment.

Concentration of the use of export subsidies among few countries

Only 25 out of 135 WTO member countries, which are mostly developed countries, made reduction commitments in export subsidies. According to annual notifications submitted to the Committee on Agriculture on the use of export subsidies, subsidies provided by six industrial countries in 1995 accounted for more than 75% of the total value of the reduction commitments. The share of all developing countries combined, on the other hand, accounted for just over 20%. For the years 1995 and 1996, approximately 93% of export subsidies on wheat and wheat flour under the quantity reduction commitment were of the entitlement of three countries; 94% of the butter subsidies by three countries; and 92% of cheese by three countries. Countries that claimed zero value of the base-period export subsidies are prohibited to introduce new export subsidies.

"Roll-over" provision (Article 9.2(b)) for the use of export subsidies

This provision allows countries to "deposit" an unused amount of the export subsidies in a year, if the actual payment for export subsidies was below the annually committed level, for the use in the following year(s). For instance, if the world price of the product concerned is high in a given year, the government may set aside a part of the annually committed level of export subsidies which could be "rolled over" in the following year(s) if the world price level falls. Countries with no export subsidy commitments claimed in the Committee on Agriculture that the roll-over provision exacerbated the imbalance in the "benefits" accrued from the Agreement on Agriculture between those who those countries which continue to provide trade-distorting export subsidies and those who denounced the use of such subsidies, in favour of the former group of countries.

Circumvention of the reduction commitment

There were incidence of the use of "gray area" measures, which some countries considered as non-export subsidies (hence outside the scope of the reduction commitments), while the others considered as circumventing the reduction commitments. Measures in question include; multi-pricing system, price pooling and inward-processing methods.

Other export controlling measures (export credits, export prohibition, etc.)

WTO members failed to implement in the implementation period from 1995 to the end of 1999 the commitments to set the framework on the treatment of export credits and other export enhancing measures and measures controlling export quantities such as export prohibition.

Non-implementation of Article 10.2

Article 10.2 of the Agreement on Agriculture stipulates that WTO members should ". . . work towards the development of internationally agreed disciplines to govern the provision of export credits, export credit guarantees or insurance programmes . . " before the end of the Uruguay Round implementation. No agreement has yet been reached as of the end 1999. Export credits may impact the world market in a similar manner as export subsidies, as they may affect the quantity of exports and export prices. As export subsidies are subject to the reduction commitments, countries may increase the use of export credit programmes, to which no discipline applies under the framework of the Agreement on Agriculture, as a replacement of export subsidy programmes. Recent increase in the provisions of export credits to Asian countries during the 1997/98 financial crisis confirmed the concerns. Export credits, however, may be an essential measure for net food-importing developing countries, especially those low income countries, for securing the flow of food imports. In this connection, it was agreed in the Marrakesh Ministerial Decision on Measures Concerning the Possible Negative Effects of the Reform Programme on Least- Developed Countries (LDCs) and Net Food-Importing Developing Countries (NFIDCs) that any agreement relating to agricultural export credits should make appropriate provision for differential treatment in favour of LDCs and NFIDCs.

Disciplines on export prohibitions and restriction (Article 12)

Export prohibition is "illegal" under the GATT 94 Article XI:1, though Article XI:2 allows export prohibition to be "temporarily applied to prevent . . . critical shortages of foodstuffs or other products essential to the exporting contacting party". However, in the agricultural sector, there is no clear agreement within the framework of the WTO Committee on Agriculture nor at the OECD negotiations on this issue has yet been made. Export prohibition, restriction or export taxes could lead to an increase in the world price, if implemented by major suppliers. Net food-importing countries consider that export prohibition, restrictions and taxes could pose a serious threat to the food security of those countries, and clear disciplines should be set against those measures. Some net food-importing countries view this problem as an imbalance in rights and obligations stipulated in the Agreement on Agriculture between importing and exporting countries - while importing countries should be committed to lower tariffs and other boarder barriers, exporting countries face no disciplines on their use of such export control measures.

Non-trade concerns and other aspects included in article 20

The initial scope of the next negotiations on agriculture is stipulated in Article 20 of the AoA that "... the long-term objective of substantial progressive reductions in support and protection resulting in fundamental reform is an ongoing process". Article 20 also specifies the elements that should be taken into account in the next negotiations, which are: (i) the experience to that date from implementing the reduction commitments; (ii) the effects of the reduction commitments on word trade in agriculture; (iii) non-trade concerns, special and differential treatment to developing country Members, and the objective to establish a fair and market-oriented agricultural trading system, and the other objectives and concerns mentioned in the preamble to this agreement; and (iv) what further commitments are necessary to achieve the above mentioned long-term objectives.

Non-trade concerns

The treatment of "non-trade concern" has attracted a great attention both from developed and developing countries during the discussions at the AIE Process.

The concept of non-trade concerns (NTCs)

A principal notion of NTCs is that the agricultural activity not only produces marketable goods (i.e. harvests) but also provides the society with public goods and services that are "externalities", "by-products" or "joint outcome" of the agricultural activity, all of which are non-marketable. Such public goods and services include environmental benefits accrued from agriculture (e.g. landscape preservation, protection from natural hazards and disasters, maintenance of bio-diversity, etc.) and rural development (e.g. securing rural employment, balancing regional income distribution, etc.). The concept that agriculture has several different functions to play in the society is termed as the "multifunctionality" of agriculture.

Treatment of "multifunctionality" of agriculture in the next agricultural negotiations

There are divergent views regarding how the concept of multifunctionality should be incorporated in the next agricultural reform process. Countries such as the EU, Japan, Korea and Norway consider that NTCs, or the multifunctionality of agriculture, should form the basis in designing the structure of the next agricultural reform process. The main argument of countries such as the EU and Norway is that the multifunctional character of agriculture, in particular its capacity to provide public goods (e.g. environmental protection, preservation of rural landscapes, viable rural development including the generation of employment opportunities) cannot be ensured by market forces alone, thus public intervention (e.g. in a form of monetary or technical domestic support to producers) is required. They argue that the multifunctional nature is to an extent specific to the agricultural sector, given that: the agricultural production is more dependant on exogenous factors such as natural, geographical, demographical, economical and social factors than the industrial production; the agricultural production factors such as land and generally aged labour force (in developed countries) are less mobile than those in the industrial sector; and the production is closely linked to the concern of food security. An argument in this line claims that the positive externalities arisen from the agricultural activity could not written off by the envisaged allocative efficiency achieved from agricultural trade liberalization.

Major exporting countries, including members of the Cairns Group (e.g. Australia, Argentina, New Zealand) and the United States, agree that NTCs are important issues in the agricultural trade, but the Green Box provisions already contain sufficient and appropriate scope to accommodate the need to address NTCs in each country's domestic policies. Those countries suggest that some of the NTCs associated to agriculture, such as environmental protection, would be best taken care of by instruments that are specifically targeted at those issues, rather than resorting to production- and trade-distorting measures.

Issues regarding food security[60]

Food security is considered by most countries as one of the largest NTCs. The Agreement on Agriculture in its preamble recognize the need to take into account food security as a part of NTCs, and countries are allowed to exempt public stockholding for food security as a Green Box measure. Net food-importing countries express that the current Agreement on Agriculture however does not pay sufficient attention to increasing the "certainty" of the food supply to the world market (as demonstrated, e.g. by the lack of disciplines over export restrictions). They therefore consider that, in order to ensure food security, countries that are non major agricultural producers, or that are with high population growth, may have to resort to domestic support measures to ensure sustainable production, regardless to their trade-distorting impacts.

Special and differential (S&D) treatment to developing country Members

Implementation of the S&D provisions

The S&D provisions in the reduction commitments of the Agreement on Agriculture are technically non-ambiguous—i.e. they provide the numerical reference to the provisions, or nominate specifically which types of measures may be exempted from the reduction commitments. Few problem associated with the incorporation of the provisions in the reduction commitments of developing countries have been so far identified during the review process.

Adequacy of the current S&D provisions

During the Uruguay Round negotiations, the extent of the S&D treatment for developing countries concerning the reduction commitments (such as time limit derogation, more favourable thresholds and higher "*de minimis*" limit) were agreed at 30% less than the commitment level of developed countries. The agreement was not based on any analysis of the appropriateness of such values to special needs and concerns of developing countries. Such values are fixed at the same level for all developing countries regardless their differences in economic needs and conditions. The review process of the implementation of the Agreement on Agriculture lacks a framework for systematically examine whether the S&D provisions have been effective in enhancing the implementation of the commitments by developing countries.

Article 15 (*Special and Differential Treatment*)

The Objective of the Special and Differential (S&D) treatment for developing countries is to facilitate the implementation of the commitments by developing countries by providing them with differential and more favourable treatment that meet their specific needs and conditions.

The S&D provisions in the AoA include:

- time limit derogation (developing countries have flexibility to implement their commitments over a period of 10 years, instead of 6 years for developed countries, and LDCs are exempted of making reduction commitments in all areas of the AoA;

- more favourable thresholds for reduction commitments (the degree of reduction commitments for developing countries could be up to one third less than that specified for developed countries);

- higher "*de minimis*" limit in the domestic support reduction commitments; and

- flexibility in obligation and procedures.

Flexibility clause refers to: a developing country's choice to offer the ceiling bindings which could be higher than the base-year applied rates to previously unbound customs duties; exemption of certain domestic support measures (e.g. input subsidies generally available to low-income or resource poor producers and investment subsidies generally available to agriculture) and export subsidy measures (e.g. subsidies to reduce the costs of, *inter alia*, marketing agricultural exports, and international transport and freight) from their reduction commitments (Article 9.4).

Other objectives and concerns mentioned in the preamble to this agreement

The preamble to the AoA compels Members to take into account several factors in the implementation of the commitments. Those factors include: (i) the long-term objective to establish a fair and market-oriented agricultural trading system; (ii) a greater improvement of opportunities and terms of access for agricultural products of particular interest to these Members provided by developed country Members in implementing their commitments on market access; and (iii) an equitable reform programme among all Members, having regard to non-trade concerns (food security and the need to protect the environment), S&D treatment for developing countries, and the possible negative effects of the implementation of the reform programme on LDCs and NFIDCs.

A greater improvement of opportunities and terms of access by developed countries for agricultural products of particular interest to developing countries

The Agreement on Agriculture does not incorporate this factor into the market access commitments. Ambiguity thus exists as to how developed countries should meet this provision. Many developing country exporters claimed that developed countries have failed to implement this provisions. Such a S&D treatment targeted at a specific developing country (or a group of developing countries) could be considered as a barrier to trading opportunities to other developing countries.[61]

Ensuring an equitable reform programme among all Members

The term "equitable way" used in the preamble is not defined in the Agreement on Agriculture, and not associated with clear reference as to how such an equity should be established among countries.

Possible Negative Effects of the Reform Programme on Least-Developed Countries (LDCs) and Net Food-Importing Developing Countries (NFIDCs)

At the conclusion of the Uruguay Round Agreement in Marrakesh, Ministers of the WTO member countries acknowledged that the implementation of the Agreement on Agriculture, especially the commitment to reduce export subsidies, could have negative impacts through increases in the world food price level upon LDCs and NFIDCs, which may have a high dependence on imported food. Ministers thus adopted the Marrakesh Ministerial Decision on Measures Concerning the Possible Negative Effects of the Reform Programme on Least- Developed Countries and Net Food-Importing Developing Countries (NFIDCs) with a view to minimizing possible negative effects of the implementation of the Agreement on Agriculture.

Marrakesh Ministerial Decision on Measures Concerning the Possible Negative Effects of the Reform Programme on Least- Developed Countries and Net Food-Importing Developing Countries (NFIDCs)

The Decision commits food aid donor WTO Members to:

➢ establish a level of food aid sufficient to meet the needs of developing countries during the agricultural reform programme;

➢ adopt guideline to ensure that food aid provided to LDCs and NFIDCs will be in fully grant form and/or on appropriate concessional terms in line with Article IV of the Food Aid Convention 1986;

➢ give full consideration in their aid programmes to the need of LDCs and NFIDCs for technical assistance to improve their agricultural productivity;

➢ ensure that any agreement relating to agricultural export credits make appropriate provision for differential treatment in favour of LDCs and NFIDCs; and

➢ call for special consideration to be given by international financial institutions (e.g. IMF and World Bank) to the possible short-term financial difficulties that LDCs and NFIDCs may face in financing normal levels of commercial imports as a result of the Uruguay Round and hence their eligibility to draw on those institutions' resources under existing facilities.

LDCs countries are those 48 countries which are recognized by the Economic and Social Council of the United Nations. *NFIDCs* include *any* developing country Member of the WTO, which was a net importer of basic foodstuffs in any three years of the most recent five-year period, for which data are available and which notifies the Committee of its decision to be listed as a Net Food-Importing Developing Country (NFIDC). As of November 1998, those 18 NFIDCs include: Barbados, Botswana, Côte d'Ivoire, Dominican Republic, Egypt, Honduras, Jamaica, Kenya, Mauritius, Morocco, Pakistan, Peru, Saint Lucia, Senegal, Sri Lanka, Trinidad and Tobago, Tunisia and Venezuela.

The implementation of the Decision has been annually monitored at November meetings of the Committee on Agriculture. The following are the summary of implementation issues raised during the monitoring process. UNCTAD submitted its study to the annual monitoring exercise in 1998 on the evaluation the overall economic capacity of LDCs and NFIDCs to pay for the food imports, by looking at their changes in export earnings and the flow of external finances. The study, "Some Considerations Concerning the Availability of Adequate Supplies of Basic Foodstuffs from External Sources to LDCs and NFIDCs", is annexed to this document.

Provisions of sufficient food aid

The volume of food aid in cereals, in particular of wheat and wheat flour and coarse grains, had been reduced almost by half in the period between 1992 and 1997, and an annual decline in the volume continued throughout 1995 to 1997.[62] While many LDCs and net-food importing developing countries (NFIDCs) had depended large portion of their food imports on subsidized exports (as much as 26 per cent of their cereal export import bills for the LDCs and 46 per cent of NFIDCs in 1994/95), the implementation of the export subsidy commitment made it dropped to virtually nil since 1995/96.[63] Together with decline in the relative contribution of food aid to cereal imports, the burden of food import bills to those countries has been increasing since the start of the implementation of the AoA commitments. The ability of LDCs and NFIDCs to finance normal commercial imports of such basic foodstuffs, which depends crucially on their overall export earnings growth and changes in the terms of trade, has been declining in the last two decades.[64]

Provisions of technical assistance and financial assistance from the international financial institutions

It is not possible to evaluate to what extent the Decision has been taken into account in the development aid programmes of bilateral or multilateral donor countries. The Decision is a "recommendation" to food aid donors, and not an agreement with an enforcing power.

Appropriate provision for differential treatment in favour of LDCs and NFIDCs in any agreement relating to agricultural export credits

No agreement on export credits has been reached.

Further commitments necessary to achieve the long-term objectives

The following Issues have been identified in the Committee on Agriculture and the AIE Process as possible new areas for possible disciplines in the next reform process:

- activities of STEs and possible rules to discipline their activities in relations to TRQ administration, domestic support and export subsidies;

- activities of large private-sector trading companies (TNCs) on the agricultural trade;

- use of biotechnology, in particular the treatment of genetically modified organisms (GMOs); and

- extension of the Peace Clause beyond the year 2003, to protect the commitments under the Agreement on Agriculture from possible countervailing or other challenges under the GATT 94 and other relevant WTO Agreements.

- establishing increased linkages between the Agreement on Agriculture and other Agreements relevant to the trade in agriculture (e.g. Agreements o   n SPS and TBT, and TRIPs).

Issues for the next agricultural negotiations

Based on the implementation issues in the agricultural sector, the issues as listed in the following section, though by no means exhaustive, would be considered as possible elements to be taken into account in the next negotiations. Annex 1 provides excerpts of selected proposals concerning issues for the upcoming agriculture negotiations, submitted by developing countries to the General Council during the preparation for the Third Ministerial Conference.

Market access:

- the choice of the tariff reduction approach, including the ways to reduce problems of tariff peaks and tariff escalation;

- the choice of the "base-period", i.e. from which the next round of tariff reductions will be made;

- Whether the TRQs should be a transitory measure with a built-in phase-out period in a manner similar to the phase-out of the MFA (i.e. gradually increasing the quota quantity until the in-quota rate applies to all the imports);

- Whether to set a maximum ceiling on in-quota tariff rates;

- Possible guidelines on TRQ administration methods;

- Possible rules to the currently broad-defined product specification for products under TRQs.

Domestic support:

- The choice of approach for future reductions in domestic support;

- Possible modifications to the calculation of AMS;

- Addition of certain "flexibility" to the AMS reduction commitments to take into consideration the special needs and conditions of agriculture in developing countries (e.g. the right to introduce new the base-period AMS for those which had no AMS commitment in the Uruguay Round, or an increase in the level and the flexibility in use of the *de minimis* support);

- Continuation of the Blue-box provision;

- Need to modify the Green Box criteria

Export competition policies:

- Elimination or continuation of export subsidies in the agricultural sector;

- The choice of the reduction approach should export subsidies be further allowed;

- Types of anti-circumvention measures should be established;

- Time table for the treatment of export credits and export prohibition measures.

ANNEX 1

Excerpts of selected proposals submitted to the General Council

Market Access Commitments

Dominican Republic and **Honduras** (WT/GC/W/119), *Preparatory Process for the 3rd Ministerial Conference of the WTO*

"The Uruguay Round Agreement on Agriculture required the developing countries to comply with far-reaching commitments on market access and domestic political reform. However, the sudden liberalization of agricultural markets can also have a destabilizing effect on small and vulnerable rural economies, with serious social and political consequences for our countries. In order to avoid this situation, it is essential to ensure better market access for the agricultural products of countries which depend heavily on agricultural-based export industries for their future development and economic growth. Although the future opening up of world markets will have to take place in a balanced manner which provides all countries with an equitable opportunity to export agricultural products and takes due account of the needs of importing countries, special consideration will have to be given to agricultural products—including value-added products—from developing countries with small and vulnerable economies."

Indonesia, Malaysia, Philippines, and Thailand (WT/GC/W/331), *Special and Differential Treatment for Developing Countries in World Agricultural Trade and the Mandated Negotiations*

Market access

- As a general obligation, the negotiations must achieve more ambitious liberalization commitments in the area of market access than what was achieved in the Uruguay Round. This may include agreed minimum reduction rates that would result in the substantial reduction, if not elimination, of tariff peaks and escalation. This may also include a clarification of the continuation of the use of tariff quotas and, if so, ensuring the non-discriminatory allocation and administration of tariff quotas, involving inter alia disciplines in the operations of state trading enterprises.

- Developing countries, on the other hand, must be allowed adequate flexibilities in scheduling their commitments, including recourse to special safeguards for the duration of the reform process. This is in view of the fact that even in the event that agreement is reached to eliminate export subsidies and trade distorting support measures, any residual domestic support applied to exported products is not different from export subsidies. Thus, the playing field will remain uneven even after the negotiations because of the wide difference between developed and developing countries' capacity to provide domestic support measures. It is in this light that it may even be said that market access commitments by developing countries should be directly related to the outcome of reform commitments by developed countries on domestic support and export subsidies.

- The level of development of a developing country and its degree of competitiveness in the agricultural sector should be taken into full account in the negotiating process and in the outcome of the negotiations.

- Developed countries are encouraged to commit the unconditional binding of all GSP schemes for agricultural tariffs in the negotiations.

Domestic Support Commitments

Cuba, Dominican Republic, El Salvador, Honduras and **Nicaragua** (WT/GC/W/120)

Initial List of Items for Inclusion in the Forthcoming Negotiations on Agriculture

"Provide the developing countries with flexibility and facilities to assist them in using domestic support in the agricultural sector provided such support is aimed at improving marketing, transport and diversification of agricultural production or ensuring compliance with sanitary and phytosanitary regulations."

Pakistan (WT/GC/W/161)

Agreement on Agriculture

"The developing and least developed countries, in view of their special needs and different levels of development, require b*etter S&D disciplines and more flexibility* in the use of domestic support to the agricultural sector. The developing countries will look at mandated negotiations as an opportunity to minimize flexibility in domestic support by developed countries and providing more flexibility in this regard to developing and least developed countries. To this effect, an understanding should be reached that the restrictions available in Article 3 of the Agreement on Agriculture will not apply to the developing countries and that those developing countries which have already provided their schedules on reductions of domestic support and export subsidies shall be allowed flexibility to enhance the levels of these measures and to lessen the pace of reduction of such levels within their national policies to enable them to develop their agricultural sector and to ensure food security. Therefore, through a clarification or amendment of Article 3 or 4 of the Agreement, the developing countries should be excluded from the discipline of import control and domestic support in the food product sector."

India (WT/GC/W/152)

Issues under Paragraph 9a(ii) of the Geneva Ministerial Declaration—Mandated Negotiations

"It also needs to be said that agricultural self reliance forms a vital underpinning for the growth of the GDP of agrarian developing economies, since good agricultural production provides purchasing power to a large majority of the population, which in turn spurs industrial growth. Self-sufficiency in food production has therefore a specific developmental perspective as opposed to a purely commercial perspective. Hence, it is our view *that developing coun-*

tries need to be provided the requisite flexibility within the AOA to pursue their legitimate non-trade concerns. More specifically, developing countries need to be allowed to provide domestic support in the agricultural sector to meet the challenges of food security and to be able to preserve the viability of rural employment, as different from the trade-distortive support and subsidies presently permitted by the Agreement. It is therefore important that during the negotiations a differentiation is made between such domestic support measures which are presently being used to carve out a niche in international trade and those measures which would allow developing countries to alleviate rural poverty.

As already stated by us, the *only way that these concerns can be met is by providing a certain degree of flexibility to developing countries by appropriately modifying the provisions of the Agreement on Agriculture, particularly as far as domestic support and green box measures are concerned.* For instance, it would be important to recognize that in time to come the 10% de minimis level presently provided under the AMS may not be sufficient for developing countries to give the kind of support needed to alleviate poverty and sustain rural employment. Moreover, as has been discussed in the AIE process, specific guidelines would need to formulated on how to compensate for excessive rates of inflation and depreciation of currency - problems which developing countries face while calculating their AMS. Similarly, some aspects of the green box measures may also need to be reviewed in order to provide a certain degree of flexibility to developing countries. For instance, the restrictions on public holdings for food security purposes and domestic aid do not appear to be entirely realistic since at times it would be impractical to insist on hard and fast criterion for eligibility for distributing subsidized food grains, particularly in view of the geographical spread of the vulnerable sections of society. Moreover, certain other green box measures such as those related to de-coupled income support to producers for limiting production are geared more to meet the needs of developed rather than developing countries."

Bulgaria, Czech Republic, Hungary, Latvia, the Slovak Republic and Slovenia (WT/GC/W/217)

Negotiations on Agriculture: Domestic Support - Concerns of Transition and Post-Transition Economies

"Adequate ways and means should be identified and agreed upon that would enable transition or post-transition economies to introduce or continue to use support measures which are necessary for the economic transformation of their agriculture. Such mechanisms would serve the objective of assisting these countries in their efforts to establish and consolidate a market-oriented domestic agricultural sector by partly alleviating the extreme burdens associated with such a process and of allowing them to benefit from their comparative advantages."

Indonesia, Malaysia, Philippines, and Thailand (WT/GC/W/331), *Special and Differential Treatment for Developing Countries in World Agricultural Trade and the Mandated Negotiations*

Domestic support

- The "blue box" category of support measures, or those under production-limiting must be subject to substantial reduction commitments if not eliminated at the next phase of the reform process.

- The criteria for the "green box" category of support measures, or Annex 2 of the Agreement must be reviewed to ensure that they meet the basic requirement that they have no or at least minimal trade distorting effects on production and trade, and that they adequately address the trade, financial and development needs of developing countries.

- Developing countries, on the other hand, will require flexibility to rely on domestic support because of their long-term need to develop and benefit from their agricultural sector. While considered to be an essential feature of S&D, flexibility in terms of lower rates of reduction commitments and longer timeframe for implementation would not be adequate to address the development needs of developing countries.

- S&D in terms of domestic support must result in providing developing countries the flexibility to pursue WTO-consistent policies and strategies that would allow them to develop their potential in agriculture and address their non-trade concerns, including food security, rural development and poverty alleviation.

Export Subsidies Commitments

Dominican Republic and Honduras (WT/GC/W/119)

Preparatory Process for the 3rd Ministerial Conference of the WTO

"**Export subsidies**—Everyone recognizes that government export subsidies distort international trade, creating situations of unfair competition in which producers from developing countries have had to face serious difficulties in order to be able to compete on international markets. International organizations such as the OECD have reported with concern that there has been an increase in real terms of such income transfers with a highly damaging effect on market access possibilities for our countries. We must draw up clear objectives for the forthcoming negotiations, setting initial domestic assistance levels in view of their elimination by the developed countries at the next round of negotiations. We recognize, on the other hand, that the elimination of subsidies could, in the short and medium term, have a negative impact on the net food-importing countries, and that we should therefore provide for financial and technical assistance programmes to allow those countries to overcome such difficulties as they might encounter. There is a growing need for us to commit ourselves in that respect during the next negotiations.

"**Export credit**—We are equally concerned by the WTO Secretariat's note (document WT/L/271 of 7 May 1998) in which it reports that the work on the development of disciplines to govern the provision of export credit for agricultural products has not yet begun. The new agricultural round will have to tackle this issue, which has been pending since 1994."

India (WT/GC/W/152)

Issues under Paragraph 9a(ii) of the Geneva Ministerial Declaration - Mandated Negotiations

"Similarly, trade-distorting subsidies in some developed countries have had a disproportionately negative effect on trade in the many agricultural products on which developing country exporters are dependent. In fact, export subsidies is one area where we definitely feel that the playing field is not even, since developed countries who had notified their basic level of support can, and have, continued to provide large scale trade distorting export subsidies. On the other hand, some developing countries that were provided this facility as part of the special and differential treatment have been unable to do so because of the constraints on their resources. It is therefore imperative that the use of export subsidies be minimized and a suitable time frame determined for effective reductions in export subsidies so that the trade distorting effect of these subsidies is gradually eliminated. It would also be important to address these issues during the negotiations."

Least-Developed Countries (WT/GC/W/251)

Coordinating Workshop for Senior Advisers to Ministers of Trade in LDCs in Preparation for the Third WTO Ministerial Conference, Sun City, South Africa, 21-25 June 1999 (Communication from Bangladesh)

Proposals to be Submitted to the Preparatory Process of and to the Third WTO Ministerial Conference Section A

"Elimination of export subsidies by developed countries, within an agreed time period, particularly for agricultural products of strategic interest to LDCs."

Scope, Structure and Time frame of the Next Agricultural Negotiations

Argentina (WT/GC/W/118)

Agriculture: Continuation of the Reform Process

AGENDA FOR THE FORTHCOMING NEGOTIATIONS

(*a*) There are still some outstanding accounts which have to be settled before the new round of negotiations is begun. In agriculture, these include in particular the failure to fulfil the obligation under Article 10.2 of the Agreement relating to the adoption of disciplines on export credits, export credit guarantees and export insurance programmes. . . . Developing countries have access only to legitimate instruments of competition: quality and price. . . . We developing countries have already paid and are continuing to pay for this Clause every time we are displaced from a market, either through the use of subsidies or through the use of subsidized credits.

(*b*) A message was clearly delivered to all those present: the application of "special and differential treatment" for developing countries is far from allowing us to participate equally in the benefits of the Uruguay Round Agreements. During the forthcoming renegotiation of the Agreement on Agriculture this situation should be reversed. The first step is that the law must be the same for everyone. Export subsidies are an additional privilege, in favour of countries that do not need to add further privileges to their already privileged situation; they should be done away with immediately. ... The idea that "non-trade concerns" as mentioned in Article 20 of the Agreement should enable some developed countries to find new arguments to justify protectionism is unacceptable to us. Neither consumer concerns nor protection of the countryside, rural culture or the environment need to lead to mountains of surpluses that are subsequently tipped on the world market at prices with which we cannot compete and which ultimately generate yet more marginalization and poverty in our countries.

Dominican Republic and Honduras (WT/GC/W/119)

Preparatory Process for the 3rd Ministerial Conference of the WTO

Net food-importing countries:

We propose that the Decision on Net Food-Importing Countries be revised in order to bridge the gap between intentions and achievements. In doing so, we must take account of the points mentioned in paragraph 3 of this document and give due consideration to other specific conditions in the developing countries with small and vulnerable economies. ... Finally, in many developing countries the agricultural sector is not only the sector which occupies the largest portion of the population, but it is also crucial to their economic welfare, their export revenue, their social cohesion and their food security. We must acknowledge that the developing countries are at different stages of development, and therefore have different needs. We consider that the forthcoming negotiations should pay particular attention to the specific needs and conditions of the developing countries with small and vulnerable economies, ensuring totally free access to the products that are of the greatest interest to them.

Cuba, Dominican Republic, El Salvador, Honduras and **Nicaragua** (WT/GC/W/120)

Initial List of Items for Inclusion in the Forthcoming Negotiations on Agriculture

Special attention to the net food-importing countries:

Improved market access for products from the net food-importing countries so that they can increase their export earnings and hence be in a position to face the increases in the food-import bill. Financial and technical assistance commitments by the developed countries so that the developing countries can diversify and increase their productivity in the agricultural sector and hence be able to face the increases in the food-import bill.

Non-trade concerns of the developing countries, particularly those with small and vulnerable economies

Develop a package of measures aimed at improving the national food security situation, maintaining the standard of living of the rural population and preserving the environment, and exempt such measures from the reduction commitment. It goes without saying that these domestic support measures will bear no relation to export subsidies. . . . Allow countries that are victims of natural disasters flexibility in complying with agricultural provisions and permit the temporary application of domestic support measures with a view to reviving domestic production.

Pakistan (WT/GC/W/161)

Agreement on Agriculture

—Most of the net food-importing developing countries face balance of payments problems. In order to meet their rising import bills for food, the developed countries may take an initiative by contributing towards a revolving fund to help ease this problem. There should be a provision in the Agreement elaborating upon the criteria for contribution and the enforcement mechanism.

—The Agreement should envisage a technical assistance programme, whereby the developed countries may help the developing countries in increasing their productivity, storage, grading and packing facilities.

India (WT/GC/W/152)

Issues under Paragraph 9a(ii) of the Geneva Ministerial Declaration—Mandated Negotiations

Ensuring food security, that is the access of the population to sufficient food to meet its nutritional requirements, is a basic objective of governmental policies in agrarian developing countries. . . . This recognition of the importance of food security even for low potential areas clearly underlines a developmental perspective which goes beyond mere trade concerns, and is therefore germane to the outlook and interest of developing countries.

Countries which argue and support rapid liberalization of the agricultural sector contend that global food sufficiency would in a way ensure food security since countries could then produce what they are most competent and efficient in, while importing the rest of their food requirements. Such an argument presupposes that all countries would at all times have sufficient foreign exchange to procure their food requirements internationally. This assumption is obviously not true since not all developing countries would always be in a position to import food grains, even if these were available at competitive prices, due to their limited foreign exchange reserves. . . . we feel that low-income developing countries should be able to produce at least a certain minimum percentage of their annual food requirement. We feel this is an objective which needs to be pursued, particularly in light of the constraints that developing countries have faced in the past in procuring their food grains requirements from international markets. We feel that it would need to be recognized, in the WTO, that the small farmer would not be able to meet his principal responsibility without adequate support from government. Public intervention would therefore be necessary in order to achieve these goals. . . . Hence, it is our view that developing countries need to be provided the requisite flexibility within the AOA to pursue their legitimate non-trade concerns. More specifically, developing countries need to be allowed to provide domestic support in the agricultural sector to meet the challenges of food security and to be able to preserve the viability of rural employment, as different from the trade-distortive support and subsidies presently permitted by the Agreement. It is therefore important that during the negotiations a differentiation is made between such domestic support measures which are presently being used to carve out a niche in international trade and those measures which would allow developing countries to alleviate rural poverty.

Korea (WT/GC/W/170)

Agriculture

In order to achieve a balance of interests among Members, provisions on non-trade concerns and special and differential treatment to developing countries should be strengthened. The Agreement on Agriculture does not fully take into account the non-trade concerns and the special requirements of small-scale subsistence agriculture. As a result, it has failed to achieve a balance of interests between exporting and importing countries and between the developed and developing countries. The balance is tipped against developing countries and importing countries, which is highly undesirable. Sound reforms cannot continue at the expense of a particular group of countries. Korea makes the following suggestions to alleviate the difficulties of the developing countries and importing countries:

Non-trade concerns, especially the multifunctionality of agriculture and food security should be fully taken into account in continuing the reform process.

Ways to make the provisions on special and differential treatment of developing countries more operational should be devised. In particular, more attention should be given to the important role that governments can play in achieving this goal.

Disciplines against arbitrary export restrictions should be developed.

Kenya (WT/GC/W/223)

Contribution to the Preparatory Process

It is our view that while non-trade concerns such as food security has been mentioned in the preamble to the Agreement, very little has been done to address this issue. The agricultural liberalization advocated by the Agreement cannot by itself overcome the problems of food security for developing countries with sizeable rural population. It is therefore extremely important that a certain degree of flexibility be provided to developing countries for the adoption of domestic policies with the intention of providing continued food security and employment to a large segment of the population. This will improve the general levels of production and enhance the income levels of the rural poor.

The implementation of the Decision on Measures Concerning the Possible Negative Effects of the Reform Programme on Least Developed and Net

Food-Importing Developing countries (NFIDCs) has been a source of deep concern to them. The modalities of implementing the Decision require a close re-examination, particularly in the light of declining food aid.

ANNEX 2

ANNUAL MONITORING EXERCISE IN RESPECT OF THE FOLLOW UP TO THE MINISTERIAL DECISION ON MEASURES CONCERNING THE POSSIBLE NEGATIVE EFFECTS OF THE REFORM PROGRAMME ON LEAST DEVELOPED AND NET FOOD IMPORTING DEVELOPING COUNTRIES (NOVEMBER 98)

Statement by the representative of UNCTAD—Some Considerations Concerning the Availability of Adequate Supplies of Basic Foodstuffs from External Sources to LDCs and NFIDCs

The availability of adequate supplies of basic foodstuffs from external sources to LDCs and NFIDCs have depended both on commercial food imports and on food aid. Both of these sources have been indispensable elements in meeting the shortfall between domestic agricultural production and food requirements in many LDCs and NFIDCs.

Concerning food aid, as the data provided in WTO Secretariat document G/AG/W/36 show Food Aid Convention annual shipments of grains (in wheat equivalent) have been following a declining trend since 1990/91 falling by more than 50 per cent to around 5.5 million tons in 1997/98. As the data shows, the decline is due mainly to the substantial fall in shipments from the major donors—a 66 per cent decline in shipments from Canada, a 64 per cent decline in shipments from the United States and a 15 per cent decline in shipments from the European Communities. It should be noted that in the Food Aid convention of 1995, the total minimum annual contribution (MAC) was revised, downwards (by about 29 per cent) from a figure of approximately 7.5 million tons under the Food Aid Convention of 1986. Non-cereal food aid deliveries which are not covered by the Food Aid Convention also show an overall continuous decline between 1992 and 1997 of about 50 per cent. Table 1 highlights the decline, since the conclusion of the Uruguay Round, in cereal and non-cereal food aid deliveries to individual LDCs and NFIDCs.

With the decline in recent years in the volume of food aid, a greater volume of basic foodstuffs is now imported by LDCs and NFIDCs under commercial terms. The ability of these countries to finance normal commercial imports of such basic foodstuffs depends crucially on two factors: their overall export earnings growth, which is a principal determinant of their import capacity, and changes in their food import bills due, in particular, to price factors.

According to FAO data, from 1993/94 to the peak price year of 1995/96, both LDCs and NFIDCs experienced a substantial increase in their cereal import bills which rose by 85 per cent for the former group of countries and 68 per cent for the latter.[65] These higher import bills were due to a combination of factors: higher than trend prices due to a rundown of stocks and reductions in export subsidies and domestic support, lower food aid and a smaller volume of subsidized exports to LDCs and NFIDCs, and an increase in the underlying deficit in cereal production in these countries.[66]

This note seeks to draw attention in particular to the export earnings growth of, and the net flow of financial resources to, LDCs and NFIDCs which are important determinants of their import capacity and hence economic access to adequate food supplies from external sources. Before turning to this subject, the next section reviews briefly the dependence of LDCs and NFIDCs on food imports.

The food import dependency of LDCs and NFIDCs[67]

Globally, as shown in table 1, the overall share of food in merchandise imports stood at around 9 per cent in 1994.[68] While this share, reported in column (1) of table 1, had in general been decreasing through time, for both developed and developing countries in the aggregate, for the African region, which contains the largest number of LDCs and NFIDCs, the share rose from 15.8 in 1980 to 16.4 per cent in 1994. When food imports are taken as a ratio of total merchandise exports as reported in column (2) of table 1, while this share shows a decline over time at the world level as well as for developing countries in the aggregate, for both Africa and OPEC countries there is an increase. This suggests that a rising proportion of export earnings for these groups of countries has been devoted to the food import bill.

More detailed analysis at a country level confirms that food imports do weigh heavily on the trade balance of LDCs and NFIDCs. Table 2 shows the dependence of 45 LDCs[69] and 18 NFIDCs on net imports of basic foodstuffs as defined by FAO.[70]

With regard to LDCs, the share of net imports of basic foodstuffs in total merchandise imports exceeded 20 per cent for seven countries, ranging up to

50.4 per cent (in Sierra Leone). While six LDCs (Chad, Mali, Afghanistan, Laos, Myanmar and Nepal) are net exporters of basic foodstuffs in value terms, this is due in most cases to one or two export items. For NFIDCs the share of net imports of basic foodstuffs in total imports is highest for Senegal (21.8 per cent) followed by Egypt (15.3 per cent). While the exports of basic foodstuffs for four NFIDCs (Honduras, Kenya, Morocco and St. Lucia) exceed imports, these countries are all net importers of cereal, which account for a large portion of their net imports. The dependency of LDCs and NFIDCs on food imports is expected to persist, due to the fact that their average agricultural production growth has failed to keep pace with increasing food demand resulted from their high population growth. For example, while the per capita agricultural production in developing countries as a whole in the period between 1985 and 1995 increased by 13 per cent, that for LDCs in fact declined by 9.6 per cent.

Trends in the export performance and import capacity of LDCs and NFIDCs

As mentioned earlier, the ability of LDCs and NFIDCs to finance normal commercial imports of basic foodstuffs depends largely on their export earnings and the net flow of foreign exchange available to them. Table 4 provides a number of indicators of the import capacity of LDCs and NFIDCs.

The picture is mixed concerning the export earning growth of these two groups of countries in recent years. As will be noticed. a large number of LDCs have experienced negative annual average export earning growth between 1990 and 1996. Eleven African LDCs (for which data are available) and Haiti experienced a fall of export earnings in the period 1990 and 1996. The annual average export growth in NFIDCs were positive (except in Mauritius), ranging between 0.9 per cent (Côte d'Ivoire) and 12.9 per cent (Sri Lanka). However, even in those cases, because of deteriorating terms of trade, the purchasing power of exports has declined significantly since 1990.

Most LDCs. as well as NFIDCs. are financially heavily indebted. In 1996, the average debt/GDP ratio for LDCs was 90 per cent ranging from 23 per cent at the lowest (Kiribati) up to 538 per cent (Sao Tome and Principe). Twenty three LDCs (for which data were available) faced the debt/GDP ratio of above 90 per cent, seventeen of which faced the ratio above 100 per cent. Since all the debt has to be paid in foreign currency, the debt burden further constrains the availability of already limited foreign exchange from export earnings. As will be noticed from table 4, the debt service ratio has remained high for most LDCs as well as for NFIDCs, ranging above 25 per cent for a large number of countries. The debt service/export ratio is extremely high for a number of NFIDCs: six out of sixteen NFIDCs (for which data are available) face the debt service/export ratio of over 25 per cent; and five countries have a ratio of between 15 and 20 per cent.

Lastly, as Table 4 shows, since 1994, net financial flows to LDCs and NFIDCs have registered significant declines (in both real and nominal term) for the majority of countries in the former group and a number of countries in the latter group. Twenty African LDCs, Haiti and seven Asia/Pacific LDCs experienced a nominal decline in total financial flow between 1994 and 1996. Nominal declines in net financial flows were also experienced by seven NFIDCs (Côte d'Ivoire, Honduras, Mauritius, Morocco, Senegal, Sri Lanka and Trinidad and Tobago).

The recent and projected further slowdown of the world economy due to the Asian crisis is having a significant impact on the export earning prospects of LDCs and NFIDCs. This is particularly true for the commodity export dependent countries. First, many of the fast-growing economies in Asia had become major markets for a wide range of commodities (e.g. agricultural raw materials, metals and fuel), which are supplied by other developing countries including LDCs. For example, annual average export growth from Africa to South and South-East Asia during the period 1980-1994 was 7.9 per cent, while Africa's exports to the world fell on average during the same period. Growth of exports to Asia was especially high for agricultural raw materials, at 13.8 per cent, and for ores and metals, at 16.1 per cent. Second, the decline in commodity imports by the crisis-hit South-East Asian countries has had a substantial effect on demand/supply balance on many commodity markets. Table 5 provides an overview of changes in monthly prices for products of main export interest to developing countries since the beginning of the crisis. From mid-1997 to April 1998, the price of oil fell by 25 per cent, while commodity prices (excluding the price of oil) experienced an overall decline of over 10 per cent. with larger falls in agricultural raw materials and metals than in food and beverages. Price decreases, some of them very pronounced, were observed for many commodities, which altogether accounted for about one third of the non-oil primary exports of the developing countries. Of course, factors other than the crisis also contributed to these declines (e.g. the effects of the world business cycle largely reflecting the industrial slow-down and crisis in Asia, the appreciation of the dollar which tends to reduce commodity prices expressed in dollars, and supply considerations particularly new supply facilities for non-ferrous metals coming into production). However, there is no doubt that the prices of agricultural raw materials, timber, metals (particularly copper and nickel) and, to a somewhat lesser extent, energy products were adversely affected by the depressed demand resulting from the crisis. The fall in prices was quite widespread and affected both agricultural commodities and metals. However, while the prices of agricultural commodities appear to have more or less stabilized, albeit at lower levels than those prevailing in mid-1997, most metal prices and the price of petroleum continued to decline as of

TABLE 1

Food Aid Deliveries To LDCs And NFIDCs

	Cereals[a] (tonnes, in grain equivalent)		Non-Cereals[b] (tonnes in product weight)	
	1994	1997	1994	1997
I. LDCs	**4,871,094**	**3,089,340**	**525,590**	**301,280**
Africa:	**3,218,931**	**1,822,703**	**457,004**	**257,499**
Angola	278,985	152,793	50,229	27,789
Benin	13,567	29,642	4,614	2,080
Burkina Faso	29,592	32,673	7,629	6,863
Burundi	92,812	1,450	28,192	1,874
Cape Verde	68,632	61,549	3,516	3,815
Central African Rep	5,943	842	865	13,030
Chad	13,991	45,004	1,404	2,413
Comoros	6,209	3,100	519	-
Dem. Rep. of Congo	75,345	22,033	18,764	3,615
Djibouti	11,834	11,914	1,159	615
Equatorial Guinea	2,802	118	470	80
Eritrea	293,388	53,538	30,533	-
Ethiopia	905,277	368,585	44,585	20,116
Gambia	7,675	7,956	2,019	1,293
Guinea	38,570	4,611	1,600	1,327
Guinea-Bissau	3,964	5,622	895	325
Lesotho	30,897	7,092	3,585	1,861
Liberia		118,843		18,803
Madagascar	22,667	44,167	3,098	2,905
Malawi	131,951	42,627	9,080	2,187
Mali	25,772	25,209	1,320	655
Mauritania	22,407	36,339	3,036	2,625
Mozambique	347,499	165,295	21,840	11,690
Niger	42,900	58,952	4,593	4,443
Rwanda	178,531	227,099	93,380	71,071
Sao Tome and Principe	6,686	2,055	1,188	1,924
Sierra Leone	29,199	78,100	4,281	12,476
Somalia	52,413	4,054	12,712	1,416
Sudan	331,112	111,071	57,374	17,740
Togo	8,221	6,600	999	14
Uganda	46,106	64,447	19,545	11,177
United Rep. of Tanzania	78,023	19,000	18,852	7,994
Zambia	15,961	10,323	5,128	3,283
America:	**70,227**	**121,543**	**25,243**	**9,787**
Haiti	70,227	121,543	25,249	9,787
Asia & Pacific:	**1,581,936**	**1,145,094**	**43,343**	**33,994**
Afghanistan	65,120	166,728	7,133	15,014
Bangladesh	1,179,455	703,828	16,426	4,795
Bhutan	2,814	4,619	371	617
Cambodia	53,371	43,670	2,763	1,908
Kiribati	203,483	95,514	-	-
Laos	15,187	39,617	82	-

TABLE 1 (*Continued*)

| | Cereals*a*
(tonnes, in grain equivalent) | | Non-Cereals*b*
(tonnes in product weight) | |
	1994	1997	1994	1997
Maldives	1,370	2,740	-	-
Myanmar	1,500	8,195	455	-
Nepal	21,205	25,752	10,969	5,838
Samoa	-	-	-	-
Solomon Islands	-	-		
Tuvalu				
Yemen	38,431	54,431	5,144	5,8
II. NFIDCs	**1,627,819**	**574,795**	**170,470**	**109,107**
Barbados	-	-	-	-
Botswana	5,875	-	3,267	-
Côte d'Ivoire	55,139	15,507	715	-
Dominican Republic	7,196	1,348	6,940	1,242
Egypt	278,471	66,519	15,841	3,686
Honduras	111,259	27,573	4,807	939
Jamaica	69,800	15,495	300	1,561
Kenya	203,483	95,514	28,436	13,923
Mauritius	-	-	-	-
Morocco	87,594	14,267	16,221	1,599
Pakistan	97,837	177,317	42,811	4,733
Peru	352,436	55,350	39,312	76,282
Saint Lucia	3,000	-	-	-
Senegal	23,765	11,488	2,019	1,946
Sri Lanka	306,874	82,757	4,003	2,456
Trinidad and Tobago	-	-		
Tunisia	25,090	11,660	5,798	740
Venezuela				

a Include wheat, barley, maize, millet, oats, rye, sorghum, rice and pulses.

b Include dairy products, vegetable oils and fats, meat and fish.

Source: UNCTAD Compilation based on data provided in WTO document G/AG/W/36.

TABLE 2

Share of Food Imports to the Total Imports (1) and to the Total Exports (2)

| | 1980
(%) | | 1990
(5) | | 1994
(%) | |
	(1)	(2)	(1)	(2)	(1)	(2)
World	11.1	11.1	9.3	9.3	9.1	9.1
Developed countries	10.2	10.8	9.2	9.2	9.5	9.3
Developing countries	11.7	9.9	9.4	9.4	8.5	8.7
OPEC	13.6	5.7	13.7	8.8	12.8	8.9
Latin America	10.5	12.3	10.1	10.3	9.3	10.9
South and South-East Asia	10.3	7.0	6.5	6.3	6.3	6.3
Africa	15.8	14.0	15.6	17.0	16.4	18.0

Source: UNCTAD, *Handbook of International Trade and Development Statistics* (1995)

Table 3

Imports of basic foodstuffs (1990-92 average)[1]

	Net Imports of Basic Food[2] (million US$)	Net Imports of Cereals (million US$)	Share of Net Basic Food imports to Total Merchandise Imports (%)
I. LDCs[3]	**2509**	**1925**	**10.2**
Africa	**1619**	**1259**	**10.3**
Angola	237	63	14.5
Benin	65	40	17.4
Burkina Faso............	66	46	11.9
Burundi....................	17	6	7.3
Cape Verde	23	11	14.9
Cent. Afr. Rep.	8	7	6.1
Chad........................	-19	11	-7.3
Comoros	17	9	28.5
Dem. Rep. of Congo	163	73	40.1
Djibuti.....................	30	12	13.9
Ethiopia	166	148	22.2
Gambia	35	20	16.0
Guinea	70	63	9.7
Guinea-Bissau	11	17	15.1
Lesotho	87	19	10.6
Liberia	62	47	27.4
Madagascar..............	16	29	3.3
Malawi....................	67	55	10.0
Mali	-18	31	-3.2
Mauritania	42	51	8.5
Mozambique............	140	124	16.0
Niger.......................	18	34	5.1
Rwanda...................	24	7	8.2
Sao Tome and Principe	4	3	16.9
Sierra Leone	77	47	50.4
Somalia...................	17	61	2.3
Sudan	91	129	8.6
Togo.......................	37	15	7.8
Uganda....................	1	-1	0.4
United Republic of Tanzania	15	33	1.1
Zambia....................	50	49	4.9
America:			
Haiti	126	91	37.4
Asia & Pacific:	**764**	**575**	**8.8**
Afganistan	-1	61	-0.2
Bangladesh	346	202	9.6
Bhutan	4	7	3.5
Cambodia................	13	12	5.1
Kiribati....................	5	3	16.7
Lao People's Dem. ...	-5	8	-2.2

Table 3 (*Concluded*)

	Net Imports of Basic Food[2] (million US$)	Net Imports of Cereals (million US$)	Share of Net Basic Food imports to Total Merchandise Imports (%)
Maldives...................	15	5	9.2
Myanmar	-123	-47	-23.5
Nepal	-1	4	-0.1
Samoa.......................	8	3	8.5
Solomon Islands .. 13	8	12.6	
Vanuatu	5	4	5.7
Yemen	485	305	23.5
II. NFIDCs..............	**3035**	**2824**	**5.0**
Barbados..................	60	14	14.0
Botswana	65	36	3.4
Côte d'Ivoire	187	137	9.2
Dominican Republic...............	111	99	5.1
Egypt	1294	1019	15.3
Honduras	-323	30	-33.1
Jamaica	83	69	5.0
Kenya.......................	-29	65	-1.5
Mauritius	132	40	8.0
Morocco...................	-106	275	-1.5
Pakistan	13	-39	0.2
Peru.........................	387	341	9.3
Senegal	249	141	21.8
Sri Lanka	219	166	7.2
St. Lucia...................	-28	6	-9.6
Trinidad Tobago	137	45	9.7
Tunisia.....................	143	148	2.5
Venezuela	441	232	4.1

[1] Basic foodstuff (cereals. livestock, pulses, roots and tubers).

[2] FAO, "Definition of Net Food Importing Countries (ESC/M/95/4), Table 11, imports in c.i.f. value.

[3] LDCs for which data are available.

Source: UNCTAD compiled, based on FAO data.

TABLE 4

Indicators of ability to pay

	Export Value: Annual Average Growth Rate	Net Barter Terms of Trade	Purchasing Power of Exports	Debt Service/ Export ratio	Total Financial Flows	
	1990-1996 (%)	1995 1990=100)	1995 (1990=100)	1996 (%)	1994	1996
I. LDCs					**16,080**	**14,899**
Africa:					**12,115**	**11,448**
Angola	1.2	118	76	13.0	672	517
Benin	-13.9	114	182	8.0	258	298
Burkina Faso	-14.5	133	84	21.0	427	413
Burundi	-4.2	..	..	28.0	306	199
Cape verde	..	..	..	8.0	119	127
Central African Rep.	19.1	..	..	8.0	159	160
Chad	4.4	129	68	11.0	229	350
Comoros	..	..	..	..	42	40
Congo. Dem. Rep. ...	-4.8	95	21	..	213	228
Djibouti	..	..	..	7.0	123	116
Equatorial Guinea....	..	..	..	3.0	32	33
Eritrea	8.2	..	..	41.0	1,011	876
Ethiopia	-8.1	101	129	12.0	70	46
Gambia, The	..	..	..	13.0	370	231
Guinea	-2.8	..	..	38.0	107	204
Guinea-Bissau	..	..	..	28.0	-56	703
Liberia	21.7	..	..	4.0	228	171
Lesotho	1.2	108	86	11.0	265	318
Madagascar	-1.5	82	75	20.0	464	489
Malawi	6.2	95	104	21.0	460	558
Mali	..	89	87	21.0	247	279
Mauritania	1.1	104	108	33.0	1,295	1,055
Mozambique	1.6	62	84	39.0	376	219
Niger	-19.5	89	71	23.0	710	676
Rwanda	..	..	..	..	52	49
Sao Tome and Principe	-23.4	101	73	18.0	263	186
Sierra Leone	..	..	..	5.0	537	174
Somalia	-6.4	85	70	25.0	401	212
Sudan	9.6	91	52	11.0	116	156
Togo	29.1	88	116	18.0	895	701
Uganda	-4.1	90	112	19.0	940	928
Tanzania	8.7	74	96	19.0	626	579
Zambia						
America:					**596**	**380**
Haiti	-8.3	..	..	19.0	596	380
Asia & Pacific:					**3.369**	**3,071**
Afghanistan	..	..	..	..	172	198
Bangladesh	10.0	101	129	14.0	1,625	1,212
Bhutan	..	..	..	12.0	74	62
Cambodia	..	..	..	5.0	353	451

TABLE 4 (*Continued*)

	Export Value: Annual Average Growth Rate	Net Barter Terms of Trade	Purchasing Power of Exports	Debt Service/ Export ratio	Total Financial Flows	
	1990-1996 (%)	1995 1990=100)	1995 (1990=100)	1996 (%)	1994	1996
Kiribati.....................		..	..	5.0	-12	13
Lao PDR..................	30.3	..	..	4.0	219	334
Maldives.................	..	..	..	3.0	42	-62
Myanmar..................	14.9	69	176	10.0	171	142
Nepal	9.2	79	..	7.0	451	418
Samoa......................	..	..	..	7.0	48	34
Solomon islands	..	..	..	..	44	44
Tuvalu......................	..	..	..	..	8	8
Yemen, Rep.............	..	..	..	3.0	174	217
II. NFIDCs...........					**16,105**	**20,614**
Barbados..................	..	..	..	..	29	274
Botswana	7.9	154	..	4.9	9	60
Côte d'Ivoire...........	0.9	63	83	26.2	1,241	614
Dominican Republic	2.6	86	74	11.4	34	45
Egypt, Arab Rep.	8.5	67	86	11.6	2,598	2,642
Honduras	10.0	63	99	28.8	232	195
Jamaica	4.4	162	100	18.0	75	107
Kenya.......................	8.5	72	191	27.5	13	199
Mauritius	-2.1	126	116	7.2	125	116
Morocco...................	5.3	94	81	27,7	660	571
Pakistan	9.6	93	128	27.4	3,157	3,286
Peru.........................	11.1	63	107	35.4	4,909	6,070
Senegal	8.4	102	65	15.9	551	446
Sri Lanka	12.9	82	178	7.3	675	575
St. Lucia...................	..	..	..	..	54	82
Trinidad and Tobago	6.3	59	86	15.6	551	324
Tunisia.....................	8.9	69	110	16.5	660	941
Venezuela	6.7	49	86	16.8	533	4,067
Memo items:						
All LDCs				15.0	16,093	15,000
All developing countries				..	157,238	193,395
In constant 1980 dollars						
All LDCs					13,755	11,905
All developing countries					139,149	163,894

TABLE 5

**Changes in monthly price indices of selected primary commodities
June 1997-April 1998**

Commodity	Percentage Change
Tropical beverages	-19.3
Food	-6.7
Sugar	-17.7
Wheat	-10.1
Maize	-9.3
Tropical sawnwood	-32.7
Plywood	-27.7
Cotton	-14.6
Jute	-21.2
Hides and skins	-8.1
Minerals and ores	-17.3
Copper	-31.1
Nickel	-23.6
Zinc	-19.0
Lead	-7.0
Aluminium	-9.5
Crude petroleum	-24.6

Source: UNCTAD, *Monthly Commodity Price Bulletin*, May 1998.

GATS 2000: Progressive Liberalization

Mina Mashayekhi, UNCTAD

Introduction

New negotiations of specific commitments on services will be launched in the year 2000. The aim of the next round of services negotiations[72] in accordance with Article XIX.1 of GATS is to achieve a progressively higher level of liberalization of trade in services through the reduction or elimination of the adverse effects on trade in services of measures as a means of providing effective market access. The results of the negotiations should naturally promote the interests of all participants on a mutually advantageous basis, and secure an overall balance of rights and obligations, and with due respect for national policy objectives and the level of development of individual members both overall and in individual sectors. Article XIX.2 provides that there should be appropriate flexibility for individual developing country Members for opening fewer sectors, liberalizing fewer types of transactions, progressively extending market access in line with their development situation and, when making access to their markets available attaching to such access conditions aimed at achieving the objectives referred to in Article IV.

Developing countries are of the view that, to ensure that the above-mentioned objectives of the next round would be met, it would be important that the negotiations be conducted within the existing architecture of the GATS, giving priority attention to the imbalances (inter alia in terms of lack of concrete market access benefits accruing to developing countries), and ensuring that market opening by developing countries be determined solely by their national policy priorities given the role of services in development, whilst reaffirming the principle of gradualism and relative reciprocity/ flexibility for developing countries. In this view, negotiating guidelines and procedures for the next round would need to take into account the following:

♦ imbalance in terms of benefits achieved by developed and developing countries, as the commitments do not reflect the interests of developing countries in terms of commercially meaningful sectoral and modal coverage.

♦   full recognition of the need for flexibility as contained in Article XIX and other provision of the GATS.

♦   imbalance in negotiating leverage between developed and developing countries has made it difficult for developing countries to derive the expected benefits from the negotiations and provisions of Article IV and XIX.

♦   Major supply constraints preventing developing countries from benefitting from commitments.

This perspective would continue with the view that, to rectify these problems, there is need to (i) restore balance between the commitments in modes 3 and 4 and treat factors of production(capital and labour) in a symmetrical manner; (ii) ensure that services of export interest to developing countries (e.g. tourism, transport, construction, professional and business services (particulalrly computer services), health, education, audiovisual and energy-related services through in particular mode of supply of natural persons are included in the schedules of commitments of developed countries); (iii) consider commitments made by developing countries in the post Uruguay Round negotiations on financial and basic telecommunications services as well as their autonomous liberalization as a credit to the next round of negotiations; and (iv) provide a mechanism including financial resources to ensure implementation of the obligations contained in Article IV relating to building domestic services capacity and its competitiveness, access to technology and distribution channels and information networks.

Assessment of Trade In Services

As provided for in Article XIX.3 of the GATS for each round, negotiating guidelines and procedures need to be established. For the purposes of establishing such guidelines, the Council for Trade in Services is to conduct future negotiations to carry out an assessment of trade in services in overall terms and on a sectoral basis with reference to the objectives of the Agreements, including those set out in paragraph IV.1. At the Singapore Ministerial Conference, the Ministers endorsed an information exchange programme, as part of the requisite work to facilitate the negotiation of progressive liberalization of services. In June 1998, the Council on Trade in Services embarked upon a series of discussions on specific services sectors based on the list of sectors contained in MTN:GNS/W/120 and background sectoral notes prepared by WTO secretariat. The information exchange exercise dealt with questions such as: what are the regulatory authorities?, are there any special or common problems encountered as regards transparency or MFN application?, what are the most prevalent types of restriction on market access or national treatment?, are there other types of regulation e.g. in the area of licensing, technical standards or qualification requirements which commonly restrict trade in the sector? Some key issues of concern were identified during this exercise: (i) the need to improve classification of activities under particular sectors, (ii) Article VI type measures and disciplines needed to ensure that such measures would not raise unnecessary barrier to trade, (iii) presence of important obstacles to movement of natural persons, including restrictions on obtaining work permits and visas, recognition of qualifications, compulsory membership in professional associations, (iv) role of mutual recognition agreements (MRA), (v) non transparent and discriminatory taxation regimes, (vi) need for transfer of technology, (vii) issues relating to electronic commerce, (viii) important subsidies granted by developed countries and its impact on developing countries services sectors, and (ix) relationship between services sectors and services and goods sector and the need to remove barriers in the complementary sectors. Subsequently in the summer of 1999, the Council carried out discussions on the assessment of trade in services. This exercise has not led to clear cut conclusions in respect to contribution of GATS to increasing participation of developing countries.

An overview of information and statistics on services indicates the limitations of global data on trade in services, for the purposes of comparison, the contribution of services to the growth and transformation of developing countries, and the important role of services in employment creation. They also show that:

(a) Balance-of-payments statistics relate mainly to the cross-border mode of supply;

(b) Most developing countries have a deficit in trade in services, except in the areas of tourism and travel and worker remittances;

(c) For some developing countries, growth in imports of services is more important than growth in exports, as they depend to some extent on imports of professional and technical services;

(d) Since the adoption of GATS, developing countries' share of world service exports has increased by 6 per cent only , thanks to the export competitiveness of Asian developing countries;

(e) Developed countries account for three-quarters of world exports of services and most of the top 20 exporters are from developed countries;

(f) Infrastructural services particularly telecommunications, financial and transport services make an important contribution to the competitiveness of goods and services exports;

(g) The social dimension of services and the link between certain basic service sectors (infrastructural services as well as health and education) and sustainable development and public welfare needs to be recognized;

(h) Services also make a significant contribution to employment creation in developing countries;

(i) For many developing countries, the exports of services is their only means of diversification, and the only way they can move away from excessive dependence on export of primary commodities; and

(j) There is no empirical evidence of to link any significant increase in FDI flows to developing countries with the conclusion of GATS;

Given the paucity of disaggregated data any assessment of trade in services has to be based primarily on a qualitative analysis. The GATS commitments provide a substantial foundation for future efforts to liberalize international trade in services, providing unprecedented information on impediments.

Developing countries have made substantial commitments under GATS with respect to many service industries, often binding recently adopted legislation or pre-committing future policies without having had much experience in their implementation, and have undertaken a higher share of full bindings in market access under the cross-border and commercial-presence modes of supply. In contrast, they have not received concessions of any meaningful economic value under the movement-of-natural persons mode of supply.

Barriers to market access of developing countries

The lack of commercially meaningful commitments (except on intracorporate transferees) on the movement of natural persons, which is essential for the supply of a service by developing countries, has been highlighted in all the sectoral papers produced by UNCTAD as well as in the discussions at the sessions of the Commission and expert meetings. This lack of access creates a major imbalance in trade. Horizontal commitments have been made by ninety-two WTO member countries which do not refer to movement of natural persons in all categories and occupations. The main categories scheduled are limited to (i) intracorporate transferees (62 schedules) (ii) business visitors (32 Schedules) (iii) independent professionals including those providing services under a service contract (12 commitments). Therefore, developed countries who have a greater number of higher level personnel linked to mode 3 on commercial presence have largely benefitted from the GATS commitments on movement of natural persons. Barriers to this mode relate to the horizontal nature of the commitments (limiting access to intra-corporate transferees), strict and discretionary visa and licensing requirements, lack of recognition of qualifications and economic needs tests.[73] Transparency with respect to measures affecting the movement of natural persons is critical for increasing the participation of developing countries in international trade.

These barriers prevent technicians and businesspersons from developing countries' from participating in a variety of activitiesthat are essential to the penetration of world markets for services. Owing to their discretionary nature (especially where criteria are not clearly specified), economic needs tests represent a major barrier to trade in services, particularly with respect to the movement of natural persons, and are a source of considerable uncertainty as to the level of a country's commitment under market access. A commitment made subject to an economic needs test provides no guarantee of access. Reducing the scope of these rests and, scheduling specific criteria for their application and their eventual removal, particularly with respect to clearly identifiable categories of professions, will be central to future efforts to liberalize trade in services and to increase the participation of developing countries in it. The movement of service providers could also be facilitated by the use of "GATS visas" that would allow them to move in and out of markets for the purposes of business development and service delivery without time-consuming visa requirements or the need to have been invited.

Other critical market access barriers

A number of other barriers faced by service suppliers from developing countries have been identified in UNCTAD's sectoral analysis. They are:

(a) Prohibition of foreign access to service markets which reserved for domestic suppliers: nationality, residency or visa requirements can prohibit or limit the movement of natural persons;

(b) Price-based measures: entry and exit taxes and visa fees for the movement of natural persons; discriminatory airline landing fees and port taxes, licensing fees; tariffs on goods in which services are embodied or for goods that are necessary inputs in the production of services (e.g. films, television programmes computer software on disk, computers, telecommunications equipment and some advertising or promotional material);

(c) Subsidies granted in developed countries (e.g. for construction, communications, transport, health, or education), including for high-technology sectors, as well as horizontal subsidies and investment incentives that can have a trade-distortive impact on exports from developing countries. While financial constraints generally place service suppliers from developing countries at a disadvantage, enterprises from developed countries enterprises benefit from financial support from their Governments: for example, trade flows in construction services are affected by heavy government subsidies to export enterprises, tied aid, external financing packages and so on;

(d) Technical standards and licensing: in certain professional business services, the licensing of financial services and standard-setting have been used to restrict entry into the industry. Mutual recognition agreements are particularly important in facilitating trade. Non-participation in such agreements can result in effective exclusion from markets. Complex environmental and safety regulations, standardization and registration procedures all act as important deterrents to participation in the construction sector. The problem is compounded in some countries when these procedures vary from one state or region to another;

(e) Discriminatory access to information channels and distribution networks: for example, suppliers of the telecommunications network may discriminate by excluding certain users, charging higher fees or imposing restrictions on attaching equipment. In the air transport sector, discrimination in the availability and cost of ancillary services may reduce the competitiveness of an airline; slot allocations and the prohibitive cost of owning a slot in major airports, as well as access to computer reservation systems (CRS) and global distribution system (GDS) could also be used to exclude potential service suppliers, as could limitations on advertising and marketing;

(f) Lack of transparency in government measures (e.g. immigration legislation and procedures) and practices of mega firms are another major barrier to market access for developing countries;

(g) The growing importance of financing in winning projects in export markets and the difficulties developing countries face in trying to tap international financial markets; and

(h) Lack of access to government procurement orders e.g. in construction services).

Sectoral analysis

UNCTAD's sectoral analysis and the outcomes of the sessions of the Commission on Trade in Goods and Services, and commodities and of the expert meetings convened by the Commission demonstrate that there are niche opportunities for the expansion of trade in six sectors in which developing countries have an apparent or potential comparative advantage, particularly through the movement of natural persons. These sectors are professional and business services (such as computer and office services), health services, tourism, construction, audiovisual services and transport. However, niche opportunities change rapidly, driven in part by technological change and this requires a capacity to adapt promptly and rapidly to new market circumstances. The expert meetings revealed that several characteristics of these service sectors are probably shared with many other sectors.

Supply Constraints

Most developing countries face major supply constraints and do not satisfy the preconditions for building a competitive service sector. These preconditions are particularly important in ensuring that liberalization makes a positive contribution to the achievement of their social, developmental and environmental goals, as UNCTAD's national studies, particularly those undertaken within the CAPAS programme, have demonstrated. These preconditions include:

(a) Human resource development and technological capacity-building to ensure that professional and quality standards are met;

(b) Upgrading of the telecommunications infrastructure;

(c) A coherent pro-competitive regulatory framework for goods and services and trade and investment, which should include incentives to enhance the competitiveness of service firms;

(d) A national strategy for the export of services, to raise the profile of service industries and exports within the country so that everyone understands how vital they are to economic development;

(e) government support to help service firms, particularly SMEs, to improve the quality of the services they provide as well as to access new technologies and management techniques;

(f) The establishment of service industry associations as to introduce or reinforce codes of conduct for professionals, to put their members in touch with potential partners in target markets, and to voice the needs of the service industry they represent;

(g) An increase in the financial capacity of service firms;

(h) Promotion of their exports;

(i) A higher profile for telecommunication and information technologies to promote the export of labour-intensive services through the cross-border mode of supply;

(*j*) The use of new business techniques, such as the creation of alliances and consortia and networking;

(*k*) A presence in major markets;

(*l*) The capacity to exploit the opportunities offered by regional markets;

(*m*) The ability to offer a package of services; and

(*n*) The use of the knowledge and capacity built up in manufacturing and agricultural sectors to export service-related activities and to offer an integrated package of goods and services.

Given the above mentioned difficulties the implementation of Article IV and its strengthening based on specific benchmarks would require particular attention by developing countries in the next round of negotiations.

Preparations for the GATS 2000 Negotiations

Specific papers have been put forward by developed countries on assessment of trade in services, preparing for GATS 2000 negotiations and on the guidelines which refer inter alia to preserving the architecture of the GATS and increasing participation of developing countries as an objective of the round. These, however, (i) do not focus on principles of gradualism and relative reciprocity/flexibility for developing countries, (ii) see the benefits of GATS in terms of imports and attraction of FDI for developing countries, (iii) aim at initiating the round with binding of autonomous liberalization /status quo and achieving further liberalization through e.g. horizontal formulas, (iv) aim at comprehensiveness of commitments by reducing the current imbalance in commitments across countries and sectors, particularly in financial, telecommunications, express delivery services, distribution, construction, health, private education, energy and professional services, thus giving undue focus on reciprocity, (v) give primacy to regulatory disciplines to be developed under Article VI/procompetitive principles to ensure effective access, (vi) envisage understandings on interpretation and implementation of certain GATS provisions some of which could change the architecture of GATS by introducing notions of negative list approach e.g. distinction between modes 1 and 2, definitional and nomenclature issues, Disciplines on Domestic Regulations, distinction between market access and national treatment, GATS rules, Articles XXI and V, expanding the scope of negotiations from what is stipulated in Article XIX (vii) agreement on transparency in government procurement which would include services, (viii) emphasize commitments on commercial presence and cross border mode/electronic commerce in the context of the new round which includes proposals to extend the moratorium on duty on cyberspace, and (ix) do not refer to liberalization of mode 4 as a priority (ix) removal of MFN exemptions latest by 2005.

In this context, developing countries consider that the negotiations should pay attention to the following issues:

♦ maintaining the architecture of GATS intact

♦ clarifying the existing commitments through establishing a mechanism to undertake a comprehensive country by country review/ assessment of the schedule of commitments to identify patterns of bound commitments, the most important barriers/limitations/ restrictions, to clarify the extent of market access and national treatment and to see whether commitments meet the obligations contained in GATS e.g. Article IV and Mode 4,

♦ ensuring full transparency in respect to measures affecting supply of services including immigration legislation and labour market regime

♦ clarifing some of the provisions of GATS e.g. distinction between modes, nomenclature

♦ operationalizing Article IV and XIX through commercially meaningful commitments on movement of natural persons and capacity building measures, focusing on sectors of actual potential interest to developing countries

♦ achieving symmetry between capital and labour to ensure efficiency and economic welfare benefits through revision of the Annex on Movement of Natural Persons

♦ developing criteria in relation to MFN exemptions and removal of most MFN exemptions

♦ developing emergency safeguard mechanism to increase pace of liberalization and do away with ENT

♦ strengthening provisions on business practices/anticompetitive behaviour

♦ reviewing the Air Transport Annex with the objective of increasing the participation of developing countries along the lines of the Reference Paper on Basic Telecommunications

♦ providing initiative on Article VI which would give primacy to public policy objectives, equity, distributional issues.

♦ achieving liberalization in sectors where such liberalization can contribute to sustainable development

♦   recognizing the need for provisions on culture

Developing countries are also of the view that the results of the negotiations in all service related areas would need to be completed in the same time frame to ensure balanced results.

Mechanisms to achieve progressive liberalization

Global or Sectoral Negotiations

Another issue is whether negotiations would focus on selected sectors or all sectors in principle. To obtain reciprocal benefits it would be in the interest of developing countries to ensure that all services sectors and modes would be potentially subject to negotiations[74] otherwise the focus would be on sectors of interest to developed countries as post Uruguay Round negotiations have demonstrated. Although there seems to be a consensus that negotiations on services would cover all sectors, some proposals refer to "sectoral" negotiating modalities particularly for services which have intermediate function, which would imply priority attention being given to e.g. financial and telecommunications services. Moreover, it should be noted that the prerequisite to obtaining results in the next round would be identification of national interests by developing countries. Mechanisms to ensure cooperation between Government, private sector and academia would be crucial in this respect.

Commitment to status quo

During the preparation for Seattle various proposals by developed countries contained provisions on commitments to status quo at the initial phase of the round. By and large, such commitments would affect the basic principles of gradualism, relative reciprocity, and the need for developing countries to develop the appropriate policy, regulatory and institutional framework. Moreover, it has been pointed out by some developed countries that acceding countries, even at relatively low levels of development, have undertaken specific commitments guaranteeing open and non-discriminatory markets in a large number of sectors, in many cases beyond even what some developed countries provided in the Urugay Round and this indicates the direction of the next GATS round. Commitment to status quo particularly in respect to mode 4 would be a positive contribution by developed countries in building confidence in GATS and would improve the balance in the commitments. It is clear from the Preamble, Article IV and Article XIX that binding of status quo[75] can be seen as an objective to be achieved at the end of the negotiations if sufficient reciprocal concessions are obtained. Article XIX makes it clear that the starting point for the next round is the conclusion of the last round in that the binding of autonomous liberalization would be a concession in the next round. Given that services play a key role in economic and social development their liberalization could impact directly on national welfare so that liberalization under GATS will necessarily reflect national policy priorities and not go further than what the national regulatory/policy framework provide.

Modalities for negotiations

To ensure balanced results, consideration would need to be given to what kind of mechanism or combination of mechanisms should be used for achieving the aim of progressive liberalization e.g. request/offer, qualitative and quantitative formula approaches resulting in minimum access commitments[76] (sectoral/mode/multisectoral/horizontal) , model schedules (e.g. as in maritime transport, telecommunication), precommitment to future liberalization, zero for zero initiatives etc. In principle the request/offer approach would result in a more gradual liberalization. The question is whether adopting formulas (as was done in the Understanding on Financial Services, Reference Paper on basic telecommunications)could be in the interest of developing countries and how to undertake an evaluation of the impact of formula approaches proposed. The evaluation of the impact of a formula would require inter alia a comprehensive review of all schedules to identify prevailing pattern of bindings against the applied situation.

Formula approaches have been put forth to increase the pace of liberalization including through removal of certain measures from schedules e.g. performance requirements, limitation on equity etc.. Formula approaches as well as model/ uniformization of schedules of commitments could mean in effect switching to a negative list approach implicitly. Developing countries would need to consider seriously the impact of such approaches; for example in the case of the Understanding on Financial Services, the majority of developing countries decided to follow the GATS approach and not to apply the formula/negative list approach contained in the understanding.

On the other hand, the formula approach could have a liberalizing impact on Mode 4 in a selected number of categories of natural persons. In sectors where considerable commitments have been made, particularly in mode 3 such as tourism, financial services, professional and business services, telecommunications, liberalization of mode 4 could be taken as a priority. Pakistan's proposal could be taken as a basis for development of a formula approach to mode 4.

BOX ON MOVEMENT OF NATURAL PERSONS

A new approach to the negotiations on the movement of natural persons has been put forth by Pakistan which focuses on removal of economic needs test (ENT) along occupational lines, facilitate visa and work permit regimes and overcome barriers created by qualifications and licensing regulations.

Economic Needs Test

The ILO international Standard Classification of Occupation (ISCO) has established an internationally adopted classification of nine major groups: legislators, senior officials and managers, professionals, technicians and associate professionals, clerks, service workers and shop and market sales workers, skilled agricultural and fishery workers, craft and related trade workers, plant and machine operators and assemblers; elementary occupations. The classification could be used for establishing a list of occupations relevant for the international trade in services, as the UNCPC has been used to establish a list of service sectors. The list defines major and sub-major group titles which are further subdivided in the ISCO classification into the minor and unit group titles. Countries could agree on certain services sectors where the movement of the natural persons would be excluded from the general application of the ENT. The horizontal commitments on mode 4 would be supplemented by the list of service sectors where the ENT would not be applied to the movement of natural persons supplying services in that particular sector. The sector approach in establishing the ENT exemption list may seem too broad in some cases since commitments in mode 4 would apply to all natural persons in all profession supplying services in that sector. The ENT exemption list could include professions or trades implying that it would not be applicable tot he market access of the natural persons in these categories in any of the service sectors. The ENT exemption list could thus, be both occupation and sector specific, indicating that the ENT barrier does not apply for the selected profession in certain sectors. In addition authorization could be granted subject to a specific number of permits per annum.

To the extent that the remaining sectors and occupations would remain subject to application of ENT, efforts should be made to reduce the scope for arbitrary and discriminatory practices, provide greater transparency and introduce more neutral economic criteria. A reference paper could be drafted that would lay down the prinicples for application of ENTs. The prinicples should address: (i) definition of the economic needs test; (ii) criteria for the introduction of the ENT which could be quantitative and/or qualitative; (iii) procedures of the application of the ENT; (iv) duration or review of the ENT application; (v) guidelines for administration of the ENT; (vi) public availability of information; (vi) institutional provisions.

Visa Regimes

To render transparent and objective implementation of visa and work permit regimes, the following measures could be considered by members:

(Continued on next page.)

(Continued from preceding page.)

> publish the relevant legislation, implementating regulations, particularly the administrative rules that define the conditions of entry and national treatment. Without transparency on administrative rules, countries would retain a discretionary power to change rules and tighten up entry requirements, thus violating their bindings;

> establish a system allowing business persons to report to Trade authorities on examples of frustrations and abuses encountered as they seek temporary entry and stay under GATS

> bind their current immigration legislation related to all the relevant categories in their specific commitments.

Qualifications and licensing Regulations

Developed countries have set up regional and bilateral frameworks on licensing, qualifications and technical standards which exclude developing countries but promote labour mobility between them. The participation of developing countries in such agreements of mutual recognitions should be facilitated. International standards would facilitate the movement of labour and further liberalization in services. Harmonization, however, is slow, lengthy and difficult and therefore faster progress could be attained if harmonization were to be concentrated on industry-regulated services rather than state-regulated services. A system of partial mutual recognition of qualifications similar to the one installed by the European Union could be adopted as one of the steps towards international standards. This would allow the licensing authorities of individual countries to retain some control over the licensing requirements of foreign professions. Conditions regarding nationality and residency consitute a further barrier. In fact, professional services could often be performed more efficiently through cross-border trade with short visits rather then by the setting up of establishment. The distinction between consulting and practising could be further developed allowing movement of labour for consultancy while maintaining restrictions on establishing practice. The danger of international standards actually becoming another trade barrier must be avoided by ensuring that it does not imply a huge burden on developing countries to catch up with the standards of services in the developed countries.

Source: Pakistan Proposal submitted to General Council in the context of preparations for the Third Ministerial Conference.

Developed countries would be interested in putting forth a formula in relation to business visitors and intracorporate transferees. Removing certain restrictive measures across the board for all modes and sectors or particular modes and sectors e.g. economic needs test, equity limitations, could be another approach or agreeing to reduce a certain percentage of limitations/restrictions on market access and national treatment. Formula approach to sectors that are interrelated would also need to be considered, e.g. construction services and associated professional business and technical services or corporate law, auditing and taxation, management consulting and corporate financial advisory services. Formula approach could also apply to government procurement and standstill commitments, that is a critical mass of members could provide for access to governement procurement or agree to undertake standstill commitments.

Autonomous Liberalization measures

GATS Article XIX.3 provides that the negotiating guidelines should establish modalities for the treatment of liberalization undertaken autonomously by Members since previous negotiations. Recognition of autonomous liberalization in terms of receiving credit would provide countries with a strong incentive to unilaterally initiate liberalization and ensure that needed policy reforms are not postponed in anticipation of reciprocal trade concessions.

Classification and definitional issues

Nomenclature related issues would have to be given attention during the next round. The revised CPC list could be improved and supplemented by members' own definition. This could be more useful than the aggregated list contained in GNS/120. The approach proposed on "headnote", e.g. for environmental services, would broaden the definition of the sector to include all the related subsectors such as professional, technical and scientific services; this could lead potentially to treating certain subsectors differentially depending on their end-use. Issues have been raised in relation to definitions of financial services. Given the failure of negotiations on MAI at the OECD, developing countries are concerned that attempts might be made to introduce some of its elements into the GATS, for example by expanding the definition of commercial presence from an enterprised based definition to an asset based one.

Increasing Participation of Developing Countries

The negotiations are required to aim at the effective achievement of the objectives of GATS Article IV and to reduce the current imbalance in commitments by focussing on the liberalization of market access in sectors and modes of supply of export interest to developing countries. Developing countries have therefore to identify their national interests, which would require a review of existing policy/ regulatory framework and establishment of an effective domestic consultative mechanism to help define national objectives which may need to be reflected in a policy/regulatory reform exercise. The identified national interests would be the basis of their negotiating strategy and requests.

Mechanisms would need to be developed to ensure the effectiveness of Article IV as well as obtaining authoritative interpretation of the provisions relating to developing countries including the Annex on movement of natural persons. A monitoring and notification mechanism would need to be established to ensure implementation of Article IV obligation. Article IV provides that developed country Members shall undertake specific commitments to strengthen developing countries' domestic services capacity and its efficiency and competitiveness inter alia through greater access to technology and improved access to distribution channels and information networks,[77] which would be particularly important to enable developing countries to take advantage of the opportunities provided by electronic commerce. Positive measures could be taken by developed countries to implement Article IV, for example through encouraging investment in services sectors in developing countries, transfer of technology and access to distribution channels and information networks by providing incentives such as fiscal advantages for enterprises which undertake investment and facilitate access to technology and distribution channels and information network in developing countries.

Moreover, few developing countries have used the possibility of including access conditions (some use joint venture, employment, training requirements) aimed at achieving the objectives of Article IV e.g. training of local employees, transfer of technology and export performance requirements etc.

Modes of supply

Definition of modes of supply has given rise to difficulties relating to overlap between modes of supply, particularly as a result of the internet and definition of likeness. Several approaches to mode 1 and 2 distinction have been discussed in this respect, such as distinction on the basis of on whom the measure impinges, or on the basis of presence of supplier or consumer in the relevant market, whether there has been solicitation (mode 1, or solicitation has also been equated with commercial presence) or not (mode 2), or where the final consumption takes place. Distinction on the basis of where the final consumption takes place would mean that mode 1 would cover cases where there is no physical movement of the consumer and supplier and final consumption takes place in the territory of the member making commitments, and Mode 2 would take place where there is physical movement of the consumer and final consumption takes place in the territory of the member supplying/ exporting services. Issues of jurisdiction are also related to the modal distinctions.

Other approaches refer to collapsing modes, making commitments in modes 1 and 2 identical, or including a fifth mode. Some support the approach that one should follow the most liberalizing approach in relation of coverage of the modes of electronic commerce which would mean that Electronic Commerce would relate to consumption abroad (mode 2) as very few countries have scheduled limitations/ restrictions under mode 2. During the UR countries did not make commitments with Electronic Commerce intention. Collapsing modes could clearly lead to confusion. Instead, countries could review their schedules to clarify commitments they have undertaken under each mode. There would be a need to address issues relating to jurisdiction and origin of a service.

As to the issue of likeness of services and service suppliers, the problem relates to the possibility that a commitment on a particular service in one mode can be undermined by the absence of a commitment in another mode e.g. grant of subsidy or taxing , or by an interpretation of the relationship among modes that treats a given service as an unlike product by virtue of the fact that it is delivered via one mode rather than another mode. One view is that there is nothing in Article XVII which suggests that the mode of supply is the determining factor in defining the likeness. If this interpretation is pursued then the effects of an intervention under one mode on the value of a commitment under another would need to be tackled . Another approach, perhaps more in tune with the modal and positive list approach to services liberalization, would have likeness dealt with in a more specific manner and not across modes.

MFN Exemptions and grandfathering

The unconditional MFN principle which is the main pillar of the GATS ensures that the benefits of any agreement negotiated elsewhere on services would be granted to WTO Members. At the beginning of the Uruguay Round, developing countries opposed the idea of introducing "conditional MFN" into the Agreement. MFN exemptions have been sought by about 70 countries for some 380 measures. The coverage , content and time frame for such measures are not clearly defined. The next round of negotiations should aim at removal or narrowing of the scope of these exemptions and developing criteria for maintenance of the remaining exemptions for a defined period e.g. an additional 5 years.

It should be noted that during the negotiations, particularly on financial services, the possibility of retaining MFN exemptions appears to have been used as negotiating leverage to obtain additional concessions, rather than its original purpose of "grandfathering" existing preferential treatment or reciprocity requirements in domestic legislation. Moreover, it should be noted that

GATS Article XVI.1 clearly provides that the MFN exemptions cannot be applied to commitments included in the Schedules.

Developing countries wish to ensure that the MFN principle is not abused or weakened as it would weaken the benefits of a multilateralization of concessions and the multilateral trading system. They argue that negotiations should be on the basis of mutual benefit (Article XIX.1 of GATS and its Preamble paragraph 3) not threat of retaliation.The term "grandfather clause" has come to describe provisions which permit countries to maintain measures which otherwise would be prohibited, usually limited by time, in the GATT Protocol of Provisional Application or the MFN exemptions under Article II.2 of GATS. In the negotiations on financial services, the term "grandfathering" came to be used to apply to commitments not to roll back foreign ownership in specific firms, where these exceeded the bound limits. In the developing countries' view, such "grandfathering" discriminates against new entrants to the market which would only enjoy the right to the access provided in the schedules, in favour of established suppliers, increasing the economic rents of the latter.

During the financial services negotiations, which focused mainly on obtaining investment commitments, preserving the existing ownership rights of firms was an important objective for the United States. Malaysia refused to "grandfather" the existing ownership rights of AIG, given its national policy objective in relation to promoting economic balance between the major ethnic groups in Malaysia. The United States retaliated by including an MFN exemption in relation to forced divestiture of existing investment to the extent that acquired rights were not protected by bindings in insurance services.[78] The EC interpreted this MFN exemption in the sense that the circumstances addressed did not cover cases of nationalization of a sector or a subsector when the nationalization applied in the same manner to all companies independently of their nationality. The stance of Malaysia demonstrates that Governments are determined to defend the principle in GATS that their commitments do not extend beyond what they have included in their schedules and that certain national policy objectives override interests of existing ownership rights.

Domestic Regulation, Recognition and Transparency

The view has been put forward that work should be continued on Article VI.4 disciplines taking into particular account the right of Members to regulate, and to introduce new regulations, on the supply of services within their territories in order to meet national policy objectives and, given asymmetries existing with respect to the degree of development of services regulations in different countries, the particular need of developing countries to exercise this right. The focus of the work, in their view, should be on discriminatory measures with protectionist intention and should not a priori expand beyond this concern. Pursuit of public policy objectives, redistributional concerns, equity etc., need, on this view, to be given primacy and work to be limited to definition of some general principles, as in the case of accounting, since the best way to deal with protectionist domestic regulation is through dispute settlement and not development of detailed rules and disciplines on domestic regulation. In this context, it would seem that a horizontal approach to development of disciplines would be preferable to a sectoral approach, although some sector specific work may be required, and that the involvement of regulators would be key to obtaining results, as trade negotiators alone would not be able to negotiate multilateral liberalization and develop disciplines on domestic regulation.

One of the main negotiating objectives of major trading partners is to ensure major progress under Article VI. This would require adoption of least trade restrictive regulations based on a strict "necessity" test/proportionality. Criteria built only on narrowly-defined notions of economic efficiency could, of course, limit developing countries' flexibility to undertake policy/ regulatory reform, and meet public policy objectives, and could lead to harmonization of policies based on developed countries' policies. From the developing countries' perspective, the work on Article VI and VII would need to concentrate on achievement of fuller transparency of laws and regulations and generalizing the application of disciplines and guidelines on MRA developed for accounting to other professional services. In this view, it would be preferable that such disciplines apply only to sectors subject to specific commitments, as is clear from reading the subparagraphs of Article VI . Most of the paragraphs refer to specific commitments (in paragraphs 1, 3,, 5,and 6) only . Paragraph 5(a) provides "In sectors in which a member has undertaken specific commitments, pending the entry into force of disciplines developed in these sectors pursuant to paragraph 4. . . ."

The establishment of a monitoring and coordination mechanism for ensuring effective access to mutual recognition agreements is also important from the view point of developing countries since, as an exception to MFN obligation, the MRAs could have trade distorting impact. The accession clauses of these agreements would need to be examined to ensure that there is indeed possibility of joining under the same conditions as the members of the MRA, along the lines of "Members should ensure effective access of developing countries to mutual recognition agreements through inviting them to join such agreements and actively pursuing mutual acceptance of equivalence". Agreement on cross-border handling of conformity assessment and of professional liability issues that currently constrict the distance delivery of services would, in the view of developing countries, also require attention, since the implementation of any Article VI disciplines would be very difficult to apply in relation to cross border trade.

Market Access and national treatment

The issue of negative list /positive list approach applies also to market access and national treatment. The MAI negotiations have clearly demonstrated that the negative list approach does not necessarily create a pro-liberalization dynamic. The list of reservations and exclusions were quite important and far reaching.[79]

Some confusion has resulted from the scheduling convention in Article XX.2 which provides that where restrictive measures fall within the scope of both market access and national treatment, the measures should be inscribed in the market access column and it would be understood to provide a condition or qualification to Article XVII as well. Therefore as there is no indication whether the measures scheduled under Article XVI are discriminatroy or non discriminatory the scope of national treatment commitments remain ill defined. As a first step to solving this problem the schedules could be reviewed by members and if the scheduled market access measure relates to national treatment discriminatory measures this could be indicated by an asterisk.

Another problem identified by some countries is that when national treatment is undertaken in a sector/subsector and not full market access, it is not clear whether any unscheduled improvements to market access would have to respect national treatment. Various approaches have been set forth: (i) national treatment would apply to all present and future market access commitments with respect to entry and post entry operations e.g. as in MAI; (ii) national treatment would apply to market access commitments (present and future foreign entrants) entered into at the time the national treatment commitment itself was made but not to subsequent entry beyond scheduled commitments. This would need clarification particularly in respect to mode 3.

Competition-related Issues

Many markets for services are dominated by relatively few large firms from developed countries and a number of small players. This tends to lead in most service sectors to a position where the larger operators face little effective competition because the size of the next tier of competitors is so small. (For example, in tourism, 80 per cent of the market belongs to Thomson, Airtours, First Choice and Thomas Cook). Developing countries service providers, most of whom are SMEs, thus face competition from large service multinationals with massive financial strength, access to the latest technology, worldwide networks and a sophisticated information technology infrastructure.

This high degree of concentration is often a consequence of the enormous volume of capital and the complex networks of interdependent organizations needed to maintain technological advantage, to exploit several products simultaneously and to maintain economies of scale. For example, in advertising, auditing and management consulting, relations with customers are established on a worldwide basis, making it difficult for enterprises from developing countries to gain access to world markets.

The trend in mergers and acquisitions and strategic alliances has exacerbated this situation. UNCTAD's studies on health, tourism, air transport and construction have highlighted the possible anti-competitive impact of these new business techniques. For example, vertical integration between tour operators and travel agents creates considerable market power that puts competitors at a disadvantage.

A number of key competition issues are also raised by the manner in which distribution channels and information networks for several services are structured. For example, in tourism and air transport, the strategic global alliances and global distribution systems have restricted competition and have served as major barriers to market entry by developing countries. There have been significant problems with display bias on CRS and GDS screens, the global branding of flights to create consumer loyalty, and the tying-up of hub airports.[80]

Network affiliation can provide firms from developing countries with an international reputation, the benefits of research and development, and the possibility of moving more rapidly towards higher value-added products, training and soft technology transfer. It can also give their professional staff the opportunity to transfer to other markets. Firms can also join with like minded firms from other developing countries to form global networks that compete with the established service multinationals in niche markets. As the globalization of markets increases, it will become increasingly difficult for service firms to succeed without entering into some form of strategic alliance. However, as strategic alliances may develop into de facto industry standard-setters or price-setters—and thus will share the potential to erect new entry and access barriers—there is a need to pay particular attention to the design and development of national and international competition policies.

In view of difficulties resulting from abuse of dominant position of major service suppliers, Article IX needs to be strengthened to ensure control of abuse of dominant position through addressing specific private sector restrictive practices and establishing a notification requirement for restrictive business practices. Moreover, to tackle the abuse of dominant position of service suppliers from developed countries as well as the operators of distribution channel and information networks, procompetitive principles would need to be developed to control restrictive business practices and abuse of dominant position of services suppliers. An inventory of anticompetitive practices of service transnationals would also need to be drawn up. At the same time, specific provisions on anti-competitive behaviour could address the situation in certain sectors. The reference paper on basic telecommunication in an expanded more detailed form could be applied to other sectors such as tourism.

Electronic Commerce

The aim of developing countries is to integrate the negotiations on electronic commerce within the framework of GATS Article IV. The liberalization of electronic commerce would need to be linked with effective market access for developing countries' SMEs and the possibilities for them to develop local content. Moreover, unlike in voice telephony, the internet caller has to pay the full cost of the circuit. The issue of access to latest technology as well as costing of internet access services are particularly important. Ensuring technical and financial support through international financial institutions to fast-track improvements to the telecommunications and internet infrastructure in developing countries and strengthening of education/ training in disciplines related to Electronic Commerce need to be taken up jointly with issues related to market access. This liberalization would also require as a precondition competition policy related provisions. Implications of intiatives on distinction between modes 1 and 2, as well as technological neutrality and custom free cyberspace in relation to electronic commerce would require careful attention. The impact of these initiatives could be free trade in Electronic Commerce/ modes 1 and 2.

Technological neutrality

Technological neutrality has been used as an argument to expand the existing coverage of the commitments. The understanding reached in the context of basic telecommunications, which does not have a binding legal status, should not be confused with application of such a concept to GATS sectors and modes of supply in general. This understanding provided that any basic telecom service listed in the schedules of commitments may be provided through any means of technology e.g. cable wireless, satellites, unless otherwise noted in the sector column. This does not mean that the notion of technological neutrality and internet access is automatically applicable in all sectors/ modes without specific commitments in this respect. It should also be noted that the Annex on Telecommunications provides that each member shall ensure that any service supplier of any member is accorded access to and use of public telecommunications transport networks and services on reasonable and non-discriminatory terms for supply of services scheduled. The proponents of technological neutrality believe that if commitments have been made on fax, voice and data these services could be delivered through the internet even without express commitment in this respect. In view of the positive list approach to negotiations, a commitment to technological neutrality would need to be expressly included in schedules of commitments. Presently only 10 countries have made commitments on internet access services expressly. Restrictions on means of delivery of a service could, of course, be scheduled horizontally or as a national treatment restriction.

GATS Rules

Negotiations on the emergency safeguard mechanism (ESM) would need to be completed prior to the adoption of the results of the next round of services negotiations. Some developing countries have said that the provisions on ESM could be based on the Agreement on Safeguards. They argue that the existence of an ESM will help persuade domestic constituencies and trading partners to accept greater liberalization, in view of particular vulnerability of services sectors in developing countries which lack experience with open trade and size, and would provide time to domestic industry to undergo adjustment. ESM could be of particular importance in relation to impact of technological developments (e.g. ECom) on domestic industry. To ensure maximum impact, an ESM would need to be applicable across sectors (the disciplines would be horizontal and not sector specific) and modes of supply, be time bound, subject to progressive liberalization, and MFN based.

Negotiations will continue on subsidies and government procurement, and, in the view of developing countries, should take into particular account the trade distorting impact of subsidies granted by developed countries on developing countries' services exports, especially since technology related subsidies as well as investment incentives granted by developed countries could have major negative impact on developing countries' competitiveness. In this view also, subsidies granted by developing countries, should be excluded from application of national treatment, MFN sould apply to subsidies and national treatment apply to sectors which have been committed unless an entry has been made to specifically exclude application of national treatment.

On government procurement, one approach suggested is to have disciplines limited to purely transparency related provisions or to set out modalities for negotiating commitments in this area. Thus, government procurement could be dealt with in services through additional commitments (Article XVIII) with preference mechanisms for local suppliers in cases of developing countries and preference given by developed countries to suppliers from developing countries.

Air Transport

The Annex on Air Tranport provides in its paragraph 5 that the Council for Trade in services should review periodically, and at least every five years, developments in the air transport sector and the operation of this annex with a view to considering the possible further application of the Agreement in this sector. Recent developments relating to the structure of the market and the mode of operation of providers would need to be adequately reflected in the classification. The review would need to identify areas that lend themselves to multilateral liberalization for example in relation to commercial presence increasingly national airline companies are privatized through possibility of foreign equity participation. The structure of the market has changed as a result of open sky agreements and alliances. Moreover, efforts could be made to clarify the scope of services directly related to the exercise of traffic rights.

MOVEMENT OF NATURAL PERSONS UNDER GATS

Jolita Butkeviciene, UNCTAD

The growing importance of new technologies and new forms of business organization, are the factors behind the growing demand for specialized expertise, while the growing dynamism of the markets means shorter reaction time-span to problem-solving, which at times calls for the immediate availability of services professionals. Impact of new technologies could be seen, e.g. in the area of software development where the temporary movement of experts is taking place between the developed as well as between the developing countries—due to availability of different specialized software products and expertise in different countries. The movement of experts is also taking place in both directions between the developing and developed countries: on one hand it is investment-related movement into the developing country markets,[81] on the other—as a response to a growing demand for these types of services exacerbated by the need to adapt to the requirements of new technologies in developed countries.[82] Internet contributed to lowering costs and improvement in the dissemination of information in the process of work search by both, the prospective employees and employers, leading to ever decreasing tenure of the workers and expanding geography of employment.

The development of the cross-border trade via the telecommunication channels will have an increasing tendency to substitute for the cross-border movement of natural persons, but mainly with respect to the provision of standardized services. Example in this respect is the cross-border procurement of the construction projects via the telecommunication networks. These bids could be compared according to their standard features and reasonably assessed with respect to their quality/cost. Preparation of the project would involve limited need for the visits by specialists to the market of the consumer. This would be hardly possible in the case of architectural services, since the latter depend on the immediate contact, extended temporary presence and interaction between the customer and service provider and cannot be easily standardized and, thus, compared. As a result, the demand for the movement of natural persons will remain strong in the area of customized services, related after sale services and various other business services.

Furthermore, the development of the high-speed lower-cost transport services and communication networks may substitute for the need to hire staff locally with the supply of certain specialized or other services through the temporary movement of natural persons. The same factors would also make such temporary presence abroad of a shorter duration, making at the same time the temporary movement of natural persons even more important mode of trade.

Firms operating internationally, including in the implementation of services contracts, need to transfer expertise internationally through the temporary relocation of specialists and professionals. In addition, globalization calls for international management, which necessitates presence in decision-making process of the managers of different nationalities.

GATS view of the entry of foreign nationals for the supply of services

A major breakthrough in the Uruguay Round negotiations on trade in services occurred at the Mid-Term Ministerial Review Meeting held in Montréal in December 1988, when a formula was reached to include factor mobility in the definition of trade in services when such was essential to supply the service and providing for a symmetry between the movement of persons and the movement of capital (commercial presence).

Trade in services involving presence of foreign nationals abroad is defined in the GATS as so-called mode 4:[83] as the supply of service by a service supplier of one Member (say, country A)—through the presence of natural persons of a Member (country A or any other, but not B[84])—in the territory of any other Member (country B). To rephrase, the definition states that mode 4 is production, distribution, marketing, sale or delivery of a service abroad by a natural person or juridical person (to the extent the latter employs foreign nationals in the host country). This suggests that under the agreement covered are (*a*) natural persons who are independent service providers abroad, or (*b*) are employed abroad by service companies other than by host-country (where service is supplied) companies, i.e.: (i) are employees of the foreign (owned, controlled or affiliated) company established in the host country, or (ii) are employees of the foreign company which is supplying services under the contract. In effect, the case (b) is related to trade through commercial establishment (so-called mode 3), however, GATS allocates related presence of natural persons to trade in services involving mode 4. In both cases, services could be supplied as the final product for consumption or as an intermediary product. Thus, services could be supplied to the individual consumer or a company. As a result, where foreign natural person has a status of a juridical person, e.g. in the case of a number of occupations in professional services, he or she could sell services to the host country company under the agreement. The same would hold, if a foreign company as a service supplier wins a contract to supply services to the host company and brings a team to implement it.

Presence of foreign nationals abroad, though part of trade policy, involves issues of immigration law. To clarify this aspect, the developing countries, led by Mexico, and later by a group of like-minded countries (Argentina, Colombia, Cuba, Egypt, India, Mexico, Pakistan and Peru), submitted a text, which emerged as the Annex on the Movement of Natural Persons Supplying Services under the Agreement.[85] This Annex establishes a definition for the movement of natural persons as seeking non-permanent entry to supply services abroad. Non-permanent or temporary status may be interpreted by each member state and might be different for different categories of persons.[86] The scope of the Annex is somewhat different from the definition of mode four in the text of the agreement itself. The GATS refers to the 'presence', which is a stock of foreign service providers at any given period in time, while the Annex addresses their movement, i.e. the trade flow. Further, the Annex also extends to natural persons of all categories who could be employed by any—including the host country—service supplier in respect to supplying the service. However, according to the Annex such persons should not be seeking access to the employment market. This provision has to be clarified not to contradict to the definition of mode 4 in the GATS itself — where foreign nationals are covered by GATS as part of the employment (labor) market when employed by the foreign entity or as self-employed. The explanation rests in how the employment takes place. Those cases where the natural person engages in the active search and solicits employment abroad (i.e. 'seeking') are clearly outside the scope of the Annex. Thus, it is the service company that is looking for qualified persons: either through placing advertisements, reviewing information placed by the individuals on the Internet, etc. Those individuals who are hired for a temporary period of time as a result of this process are covered by the Annex.

Part III of the GATS establishes which measures affect market access for all modes, including presence of natural persons, and also conditions for their national treatment. Among them, mode 4 specific limitation is 'on the total number of natural persons that may be employed in a particular service sector or that a service supplier may employ and who are necessary for and directly related to, the supply of a specific service in the form of numerical quotas or the requirement of an economic needs test'. The only aspect of GATS, which relates to the movement of natural persons by service suppliers seeking market access are each member's specific commitments. The following discussion will refer to the contents of these commitments.

Since this is movement of people supplying services, their intended entry should fall under the provision of services in one of the industries classified as services sectors by the WTO. True, the GATS classification of services sectors is ill suited for detailed discussion of occupations, since many categories of persons could be providing services under each of the services sector. In fact, so far the coverage of the occupations for inclusion into GATS was limited to a few categories, which are discussed below, chosen at the discretion of each of the members.

Commitments under GATS: limitations on movement of foreign nationals

A number of studies[87] have indicated that commitments on trade in services have not achieved a balanced coverage with respect to all modes of supply. The sector specific commitments have covered measures (partially or in full) regulating commercial presence substantially more than the measures regulating movement of natural persons as service suppliers. Generally, countries in the sector specific commitments on mode 4 have not made any additional market openings.[88]

Horizontal commitments

Horizontal commitments concerning the presence of natural persons have usually stated the elements of the immigration and labor laws and regulations. It would be unlikely that Members would agree to fundamental changes in their immigration policies, and further liberalization would have to be achieved through negotiated commitments with respect to mode 4 in specific sectors or for selected categories of persons.

The present horizontal commitments do not refer to movement of natural persons in all categories and occupations. The main categories scheduled are limited to the following: (*a*) intra-corporate transferees; (*b*) business visitors; (*c*) independent professionals, including those providing services within a service contract. The movement of natural persons in these categories would be tied to commercial presence or establishment. Most of the commitments do not take into account sectoral specificities where the movement of natural persons in providing the service is crucial for delivery of the product.

Trade in services is not an issue of immigration policy, but it concerns some of its elements. For example, problems (e.g. delays, unreasonable criteria) associated with the issuance of visas present a barrier to the movement of persons, even for business persons. These can have serious repercussions for the competitiveness of firms seeking business contracts or investment opportunities.

Another measure included in the commitments is the requirement of residency for the supply of a service involving natural persons. However, it is questionable if the residency permit is to be required for the cross-border movement of foreign nationals in respect of the supply of service. As indicated, trade related movement of persons is of limited duration and implies only a temporary presence abroad, which may in principle be exempt from the residency permits. Furthermore, the Annex explicitly indicates that GATS will not apply to measures (in this case e.g., permit requirement) related to residency.

Another requirement referred to frequently by the members is that of a work permit. Countries usually have few categories of work permits, where some are directly GATS-relevant. Usually the system of work permits distinguish among those related to an offer of employment from a company established in a host country; an establishment or investment related employment; intra-company transfer or secondment; etc. If commitments would provide the information of the type and related numbers of available permits for GATS purposes, this would add to the predictability in the market access conditions, since these are the examples of measure that are limiting the number of people that could be employed in any of the service industries. Since GATS is silent as to what are the relevant occupations for each service sector, global quotas could be used as part of the horizontal or sectoral commitments. In addition the question remains if certain occupations could be exempt from the work permit requirement for the short periods of services trade-related presence in selected services industries. Clarification of these measures - already included into the commitments - would lead to improved clarity and consistency between the GATS commitments and domestic regulation and practice, making these commitments commercially significant.

Another measure adopted by a number of countries in their commitments concerning intracorporate transfers is the requirement that the enterprise in the foreign jurisdiction must have employed the applicant in the first place. From the policy perspective it might not matter for how long, however, a number of countries have indicated certain thresholds, e.g. of a year. What actually matters implicitly in this particular case is the applicant's ability to occupy the relevant position and to meet the qualification and experience requirements.

One of the distinct categories of the limitations on market access is the economic needs test (ENT). The majority of countries have maintained the right to use economic needs tests to regulate trade flows in their GATS schedules of specific commitments on services. Movement of natural persons supplying services is most frequently affected by the need to pass quantitative and/or qualitative tests. Only 22 WTO member countries[89] have clearly indicated those few categories of natural persons for which such tests do not apply. Those categories of persons are mainly limited to intra-corporate transferees, i.e. top managers and specialists with uncommon knowledge, and business visitors. Thus, these commitments indicate that only commercial-presence-related categories of persons are excluded from the application of the needs tests. In that respect, all trade in services based on mode 4 could potentially face economic needs tests which have not been explicitly spelled out in commitments but may be contained in the national legislation. Furthermore, unspecified general requirements of residency, authorization, approval, etc., could also contain elements of a needs test.

Of 134 WTO members, 67 have used economic needs tests to regulate trade flows in one or more modes and all or selected services sectors. Economic needs tests have qualified commitments on market access in all sectors in a few countries, but others may also apply them since no mechanism exists in GATS to limit the scope of their application. Some countries have identified categories of persons that are likely to be subject to needs tests in their horizontal commitments, but this does not mean that these and other countries would not apply needs tests to categories of persons not included in the schedules of commitments.

A few countries have also referred to the economic needs tests as qualifying their national treatment commitments. The GATS, however, includes economic needs tests among the market access barriers listed in Article XVI (Market Access). Also, the test seems less relevant in regulating market access at the horizontal (covering all sectors) level for commercial presence, where only three such cases could be found.[90]

Sector-specific commitments

The existence of economic needs tests can be found in the GATS schedules of specific commitments in various services sectors. However, their relevance differs from sector to sector. Financial services, including banking and insurance, is a sector where economic needs tests have been quite important, and a number of professional and business services in general have had a relatively high incidence of the application of economic needs tests. In particular, medical and educational services, due to their dual—social and economic—function, as well as retail services and transportation, have often been safeguarded by needs tests. Interestingly enough, the application of economic needs tests has also been frequent in the tourism sector with respect to hotels and restaurant services, even in countries, which have demonstrated strong export performance in the sector. Tourism creates significant spill-over effects for employment, and the role that economic needs tests play in these sectors is likely to be that of the safeguard measure. For cases like these, the availability of emergency safeguard mechanism in the GATS could eliminate the need for recourse to needs tests.

Developing countries have exhibited comparative advantage of trade in services through the movement of natural persons, but economic needs tests detract from the predictability of trading opportunities available to them. Further liberalization of trade in services cannot succeed without addressing the issue of economic needs test. Since many countries would hardly be ready to abandon the use of such tests at present, guidelines related to criteria, duration and procedures for application could be developed multilaterally. Furthermore, developing countries would benefit if - at least for selected categories of natural persons as service providers - non-application of economic needs tests were to be extended to selected services sectors. The use of economic or similar tests in other instruments regulating market access should be prevented. In addition, each WTO member country could establish thresholds below which such tests would not apply by way of minimum quotas for entry of natural persons supplying services.

Economic needs tests have been identified as a barrier to market access under Article XVI of the WTO General Agreement on Trade in Services (GATS). However, neither the definition of an economic needs test, nor the rules, criteria or procedures for its application were elaborated. As a result, economic needs tests may have a more or less distortive impact on trade depending on the manner in which they are implemented. At the same time, legal provisions are absent in the GATS to challenge any rejection on the basis of the economic needs test. This also limits the possibilities for comparison of the scope of needs tests among countries. Though economic needs tests are scheduled with respect to all GATS modes of supply of services, i.e. cross-border trade (mode 1), consumption abroad (mode 2), commercial presence (mode 3) and presence of natural persons (mode 4), the last of these is the one most frequently subjected to tests, whether the service concerned is supplied under mode 4 or in conjunction with mode 3. Thus, the presence of economic needs tests remains a major trade barrier to the movement of natural persons as service suppliers. Transparency is a prerequisite to being able to assess existing trading opportunities, but economic needs tests make this process less predictable and stable and more burdensome. The main issue is how to decrease the degree of subjectivity associated with economic needs tests.

The ENT or analogous requirements are features of several countries' regulations regarding selected service activities. These provision of their legal regimes are responses to diverse historical circumstances but reflect the view that on its own the interaction of competition and economic incentives cannot be relied on to prevent the imbalances in the social and demographic structure of the countries. The provisions to adopt more restrictive measures are justified by reasons of public policy and reflect the perceived need to protect jobs in certain sectors or to encourage selectively foreigners with high skills and experience not available locally.

It will be recalled that Article IV of GATS provides that "the increasing participation of developing country Members in world trade shall be facilitated through negotiated specific commitments...relating to the liberalization of members access in sectors and modes of supply of interest to them." The Schedules of Commitments show a bias against commitments in mode 4, which should be corrected in the future multilateral negotiations, through liberalization of the movement of persons in sectors or for categories of professions where such movement is critical for the export of services from developing countries.

Commitments in mode four

Definition of Service Suppliers on the basis of Occupations

The negotiations on the movement of natural persons could be based in a systematic manner on the occupational classification. The ILO International Standard Classification of Occupations (ISCO) has established an internationally adopted classification of nine major groups: (1) legislators, senior officials and managers; (2) professionals; (3) technicians and associate professionals; (4) clerks; (5) service workers and shop and market sales workers; (6) skilled agricultural and fishery workers; (7) craft and related trades workers; (8) plant and machine operators and assemblers; (9) elementary occupations. These groups are further sub-divided into sub-major, minor and unit group titles that have corresponding detailed definitions. Not all of these occupations are equally important to the movement of persons in the context of international trade in services. Agreement could be reached multilaterally as to which among them should be selected, and on that basis occupational list could be established. Occupational list would introduce greater comparability and balance in specific commitments for mode 4, since a single system of definitions would be adopted. It may be noted that a similar approach has been used in the GATS in establishing services sectoral classification list, which was based on the then Provisional UN Central Product Classification. The occupation list could also be used to identify those occupations for which economic needs tests could be waived in all sectors or in selected sectors, listed separately and subject to individual schedules of commitments. An example of those occupations that could be included initially for scheduling under the GATS includes: Computing professionals (ISCO 213); Architects, engineers and related professionals (ISCO 214); Health professionals (except nursing) (ISCO 222); Nursing and midwifery professionals (ISCO 223); Business professionals (ISCO 241); Writers and creative or performing artists (ISCO 245); Physical and engineering science associate professionals (ISCO 31); Artistic, entertainment and sports associate professionals (ISCO 347).

Improving transparency in regulating movement of persons

The issue of transparency in respect of the application of the GATS commitments is a key concept and a tool in promoting trade in services. In that respect, commitments in mode 4 are closely linked to the implementation of the relevant immigration regulations, policies and procedures in a clear and transparent manner. Publishing of the legislation and implementing regulations which significantly affect ability of the foreign nationals or permanent residents move across borders to supply services is a general obligation, since this is the way to limit the room for discretionary and procedural rules. The lack of transparency, clarity in the existence, implementation and application of policy guidelines affecting application for and consideration of temporary work permits, residency requirements of visas impede market access, effectively violating key GATS provision.

On the other hand, a number of countries have indicated or suggested criteria for the application of economic needs tests. Though factors with respect to which needs are evaluated are often sector-specific, common features may emerge. Based on these common elements, a general criterion for the application of economic needs test could be elaborated. Also, additional provisions could be developed which would prevent the introduction of economic or similar needs tests in any other instruments regulating market access. To the extent that the remaining sectors and occupations would remain subject to the application of economic needs tests, efforts should be made to reduce the scope for arbitrary and discriminatory practices, provide greater transparency and introduce more neutral economic criteria. A reference paper could be drafted that would lay down principles of application of economic needs tests. The principles would evidently need to address the definition and criteria for the introduction of economic needs tests, which could be quantitative and/or qualitative, applications, procedures, duration, etc. A number of elements are referred to in individual schedules in different services sectors, and where the establishment is subject to an economic needs test, the main criteria taken into account are:

➤ Population, the number of existing pharmacies and their geographical density;

> ➤ The number of and impact on existing stores, population density, geographic spread, impact on traffic conditions and creation of new employment:

> ➤ The number of service suppliers in the local geographic area;

> ➤ Existing public transport on the route concerned;

> ➤ The measured route capacity for number of vehicles;

> ➤ The need to provide protection for investment of operators in underserved areas/developmental routes.

> ➤ Size of fully paid-up capital; employment creation; extent of foreign investment; export promotion; transfer of technology; special needs of the management;

> ➤ Market needs and location of different categories of hotels;

> ➤ Geographical location, increase in the number and categories of tourists;

> ➤ Population, degree of built-up area, type of neighbourhood, tourism interests, number of existing restaurants.

It would seem extremely unlikely that WTO members would agree to dispense with the economic needs tests in their horizontal commitments. If the elimination of economic needs tests were adopted as a negotiating objective, it would have to be pursued on the basis of service sectors and/or categories of persons. One of the ways to reduce the scope for the application of economic needs tests could be for countries to agree on certain services sectors where the movement of the natural persons would be excluded from the general application of the economic needs test. The horizontal commitments on mode 4 would thus be supplemented by the list of service sectors where the economic needs test would not be applied to the movement of natural persons supplying services in that particular sector. For example, the liberalization negotiations in the environmental services sector could be extended to the removal of the economic needs test for mode 4, where the movement of those providing management consulting, setting up the establishment to provide the environmental services, performing related training of the personnel, etc., is an important component of the service. Concepts used elsewhere in multilateral trade agreements such as "minimum" market access or "current" market access could also be considered in this context in establishing a minimum quota for trade-related test-free market access of natural persons.

Still, the sector approach in establishing the ENT exemption list may seem too broad in some cases since commitment in mode four would apply to all natural persons of all professions supplying services in that sector. The ENT exemption list could be supplemented with the above occupation approach. The ENT exemption list could include professions (or 'trades' as they are defined in the ISCO) implying that the ENT would not be applicable to the market access of the natural persons in these categories in any of the service sectors. The ENT exemption list could be both, occupation and sector specific, indicating that the ENT barrier does not apply for the selected profession in certain sectors.

Facilitation of the movement of business visitors

However, even where persons meet the criteria set under mode 4, whether or not subject to an economic needs test, the administration of the visa regime can pose another barrier to trade through movement of persons. To streamline visa regimes when visa issuance is requested for the trade-related movement of persons, the categories of natural persons and occupations that are included into the schedules of commitments could be made to qualify for entry visas, i.e. GATS visas, either automatically or for multiple entries over a long period. Economic needs tests operate as a barrier to trade in cases where the persons involved are employed by an entity in the importing country (either a domestic firm or a foreign firm established there). However, visa regimes also affect business visitors whose travel is linked to making business contacts or setting up a new business. Initiatives in the regional context to improve the conditions under which business visitor visas are granted could be brought into the WTO. The question of issuing the work permit is also related to the administrative aspect, simplification of which could by itself add to the trade creation.

Measuring trade in services for movement of natural persons

Systems of most countries have failed to evolve so as to reflect the growing complexity of international population movements - and now the needs of GATS. No one international collection system gives the complete coverage necessary for measuring the GATS needs related movement of persons, however, some elements could be drawn from the balance of payments statistics (BPM5), System of National Accounts, UN Statistics of International Migration, International Labour Organisation's (ILO) employment statistics.

No internationally comparable measure of trade created through the movement of natural persons is available to date. The available statistical measures are at best incomplete or only indicative. The major source of information for international trade in services related statistics is the BMP5. However, at individual country level additional details could be made available. Since no one collection system in any country gives the complete coverage necessary for measuring the GATS needs related to the movement of persons to work abroad, and the migrant 'border' system (which is the most widespread generator of information on the international movement of workers) is not concerned with the trade value generated from such work, the information on the movement of migrant workers can only be used as an aid to assessments involving the use of further data collected within each country from unconnected systems such as enterprise, labour and household surveys.

The main preoccupation in GATS related statistics for movement of workers is the total numbers of persons working abroad, their countries of origin, occupation or status in employment in the receiving country, length of stay and total remuneration received. However, the BMP5 provides three types of information that may be relevant to the value of trade created by workers abroad. In some cases this information underestimates or overestimates the actual trade, however, if anything it confirms the importance of global labour mobility as the factor in trade. The principal variables to satisfy the GATS requirements are the numbers of persons working abroad, their gross earnings and the remittances they send back to their home country.

In the case of establishment of the foreign affiliate in a services industry, employment would normally be measured as the number of persons on the payrolls of foreign affiliates. However, this measure does not identify the number of foreign as opposed to local employees of affiliates, which is a measure of the GATS presence of natural persons mode of supply. Information in regard to employee compensation if available would also indicate the value of trade created by human factor.

When individuals work for less than one year in the economy where they are not residents, the balance of payments records their earnings under the 'compensation of employees'. The measure overestimates services value created since all employees, not only of services industries, are captured there, also seasonal workers,. GATS does not have a clear-cut definition for the period of stay, any individual who has not transferred his status to 'permanent' would be GATS-relevant for any—even extended—period of stay. Under the BMP5, these individuals whose stay abroad exceed one year are regarded as residents and their earnings are not recorded under 'compensation' and in that respect the measure underestimates.[91]

The balance of payments statistics provide two other measures—workers' remittances and migrants' transfers—which are indicative of the importance of trade related movement of persons. None of the two could be considered as a measure of trade in services since they capture any type of presence abroad, covering any industry, but exclude expenditures or retained (not transferred) income for GATS-relevant stay abroad. At the same time, this is the only measures that could be used for approximating the value created through the movement of persons and its relative significance in income flows of individual countries.

The data to be compiled for GATS will need to cover both the movement ("flow") in a given period and the presence ("stock") of service providers at a given time. Statistics collected on persons at the ports of entry are the most widespread sources of information on the movement of service suppliers. Measuring the "stock" of foreigners providing services poses real problems, because population registers, registers of foreigners or other surveys or administrative records do not provide a comprehensive way to trace and keep track of foreign service providers individually. In the GATS context the principal variables that relate to temporary worker movement are the numbers of persons working abroad, their gross earnings and the remittances they send back to their home country.

TABLE 1

Annual average growth rates of workers' remittances
(*Percentage*)

Region, coutry or area	1980-1990	1990-1998	1980-1998	1980-1985	1985-1990	1985-1995	1990-1995	1994-1995	1995-1996	1996-1997	1997-1998
Received											
World.....................	**3.8**	**5.1**	**4.6**	**-1.2**	**10.2**	**5.5**	**2.5**	**8.8**	**8.8**	**13.6**	**-5.9**
Developed Market Economy Countries..........	3.8	-0.5	3.5	-6.3	11.9	5.7	-0.2	2.2	1.8	-6.9	1.6
Developing countries and territories....	3.9	6.4	4.7	0.7	9.6	5.1	2.9	10.5	11.0	20.5	-8.1
Countries in Eastern Europe	..	..	..	..	..	..	..	35.5	13.7	-11.7	17.8
Paid											
World.....................	**4.9**	**3.8**	**6.0**	**1.5**	**10.2**	**8.8**	**6.5**	**-0.5**	**-1.3**	**1.7**	**0.9**
Developed Market Economy Countries..........	5.9	4.0	5.8	2.2	9.2	7.0	5.3	4.4	2.2	-0.8	4.2
Developing countries and territories....	3.6	3.6	6.3	0.6	11.7	11.3	7.8	-5.6	-5.5	5.0	-3.0
Countries in Eastern Europe	..	..	..	..	..	..	..	-4.7	-5.8	-32.0	1.3

Source: UNCTAD *secretariat calculations based on IMF Balance of Payments CD-ROM.*

NOTES: Growth rates based on standard regression results of data obtained from tables "WORKERS' REMITTANCES. . ."

TABLE 2

Top ten countries* in workers' remittances: *Paid*

Region, country or area	Millions of dollars										
	1980	1989	1990	1991	1992	1993	1994	1995	1996	1997	1998
Saudi Arabia	4094	8542	11236	13746	13397	15717	18102	16616	15513	15339	14983
United States	810	7925	8395	9051	9437	10205	10947	11846	12860	14132	15941
Germany	4437	3991	4379	3859	4384	4134	4633	5305	4919	4341	3946
France	3039	2228	2787	2754	3108	2761	2704	3146	3067	2875	3072
Japan	..	..	..	..	..	..	..	..	2785	2777	2601
Switzerland	603	1605	2116	2195	2276	2135	2311	2679	2480	1975	1940
Oman	397	830	856	910	1220	1423	1365	1537	1371	1501	..
Malaysia	..	..	..	..	..	..	..	1198	1192	1422	..
Kuwait	692	1283	770	426	829	1229	1331	1354	1376	1375	1352
Bahrain	96	199	332	369	336	396	431	500	559	635	725
Total Top Ten	**15167**	**29102**	**33572**	**36011**	**38184**	**41799**	**45622**	**46782**	**46123**	**46371**	**46802**
As a percentage of Total World	**72.4**	**87.5**	**86.4**	**87.8**	**87.9**	**88.1**	**88.2**	**90.9**	**90.8**	**89.8**	**89.8**

* Ranking according to data in 1997.

Source: UNCTAD *secretariat calculations based on IMF Balanced of Payments CD-ROM.*

TABLE 3

Top ten countries* in workers' remittances: *Received*

Region, country or area	Millions of dollars										
	1980	1989	1990	1991	1992	1993	1994	1995	1996	1997	1998
India	2756	2584	2352	3275	2891	3495	5782	6139	8453	10297	9453
Mexico	698	2213	2492	2414	3070	3392	3475	3673	4224	4865	5627
China	..	76	124	207	228	108	395	350	1672	4423	247
Turkey	2071	3040	3246	2819	3008	2919	2627	3327	3542	4197	5356
Egypt	2696	3293	4284	4054	6104	5664	3672	3226	3107	3697	3370
Portugal	2928	3562	4263	4517	4650	4179	3669	3793	3738	3231	3199
Greece	1066	1350	1775	2115	2366	2360	2576	2982	2894	2816	..
Spain	1649	1601	1886	1792	2173	1926	2167	2603	2747	2658	2944
Nigeria	13	10	10	66	56	793	550	804	947	1920	..
Morocco	1054	1336	2006	1990	2170	1959	1827	1970	2165	1893	2001
Total Top Ten**	**14929**	**19066**	**22437**	**23249**	**26718**	**26736**	**26740**	**28866**	**33489**	**39997**	**36933**
As a percentage of Total World**	**50.8**	**50.8**	**48.9**	**59.6**	**64.0**	**63.5**	**58.6**	**58.2**	**62.0**	**65.2**	**55.7**

* Ranking according to data in 1997.

** Includes estimates.

Source: UNCTAD *secretariat calculations based on IMF Balanced of Payments CD-ROM.*

THE AGREEMENT ON TEXTILES AND CLOTHING AND RELATED TRADE POLICY DEVELOPMENTS

Xiaobing Tang, UNCTAD

With the increasing globalization of production and the momentum of trade liberalization, world exports of textiles and clothing in 1997 stood at US$332 billion, an increase of 16 percent over 1992, of which 64 percent went to the developed country markets.

Since the beginning of the eighties, world production of textiles has increased on an average of 1.2 percent per year; however, the developing countries as a whole have registered an increase of 2.7 percent. Asian developing economies particularly have forged ahead with an average growth rate of 3.6 percent. Between 1986 and 1997, the world clothing trade increased 180 percent (from US$64 billion to US$177 billion). However, growth in the value of exports of developed countries was much less than that of the developing countries (around 65 and 200 percent, respectively).

The high growth in textiles exports by developing countries was mainly due to the success of the first-tire East Asian NIEs and their subsequent massive investment in other least-cost countries in East Asia and elsewhere. For example, between 1985 and 1990, the production of the Philippines, Indonesia and Malaysia increased by 139, 110 and 78 percent, respectively. Over the past decade, China has become the major world producer and supplier of clothing, now followed by India.

In 1997, US exports of textiles and clothing increased by 15.2 percent and US firms played a prominent role in supplying producers in other NAFTA countries and in Caribbean Basin Initiative (CBI) countries.

Within MERCOSUR, which groups Argentina, Brazil, Paraguay and Uruguay and became operational on 1 January 1995, Brazil, with its already wide network of clothing enterprises (more than 14 000 officially registered) is a major producer and exporter.

Central and eastern European countries, such as Bulgaria, Hungary, Poland, Romania and the Czech Republic have already become important suppliers to the EU market. This may be attributed to their long-standing textile tradition, their proximity, their economic reforms and their skilled and still relatively cheap labour force.

Turkey, since 1995, has moved up to first place among the top ten clothing suppliers to the EU market and accounted for a value share of 65 percent and a volume share of 67 percent of total imports into the EU. With the entry into enforce of the Customs Union Agreement between Turkey and the EU on 1 January 1996, the EU has abolished all quotas on textiles and clothing imports from Turkey which enhanced Turkey's competitiveness vis-à-vis other key suppliers in the EU market.

In Africa, Morocco, Mauritius, Tunisia and more recently Madagascar have become important clothing producers which export most of their products to the EU market.

For many developing countries, textiles and clothing are continuing to be the most important source of foreign exchange earnings. In 1996, developing countries' exports of textiles and clothing amounted around US$160 billion which represented nearly 20 percent of their total exports of manufactures and 13.2 percent of their total exports of goods. In 1996, 57.3 percent of developing countries exports went to developed country markets and 40 percent was among the developing countries themselves.

Although developing countries are traditionally considered as exporters of textiles and clothing, in recent years they have become increasingly significant importers, with a number of them emerging as important new markets for textiles trade. In 1996, developing countries as a whole imported US$101 billion worth of textile and clothing products, which accounted for 31 percent of world total imports. This was an increase of 18 percent over their imports in 1992 of US$87 billion. During the period 1992-1996, developing countries' imports of textile and clothing products from the developed countries increased around 15 percent from US$27 billion in 1992 to nearly US$38 billion in 1996.

The prospects for expansion of trade in textiles and clothing between the developing countries, particularly the emerging new markets in Asia and Latin America are also bright as most of these countries have simultaneously been taking steps for liberalization of their import regimes, and as rising standards of living would further increase demand for bought and non-traditional style clothing. Such expansion of trade in textiles and clothing have also created new opportunities for the international trading community, particularly for those developing countries that, until now, have been almost entirely dependent upon the markets of the developed countries.

For example, the annual growth rate of final fibre consumption of developed countries for the period of 1985-1995 was 3.2 percent while that of developing countries was 3.8 percent. Among the developing countries, by region, consumption in Latin America grew at 4.6 percent, in South Asia 5.1

percent, and East and South East Asia 6.7 percent. Thus, the fastest growth has been in developing countries, in particular East and South East Asia whose consumption per head increased by over 80 percent in ten years before the financial crisis (from 1985 3.6 kg per head to 1995 6.6 kg per head). According to an estimate by Textiles Intelligence, China's consumption per head will rise from 5.6 kg in 1995 to 6.4 kg in 2005. Because of the country's large population, a difference of only 0.1 kg per head in Chinese consumption means an increase or decrease of 120 000 tonnes in 1995 and 137 000 tonnes in 2005.

The implementation of the Agreement on Textiles and Clothing (ATC)

The WTO Agreement on Textiles and Clothing provides a legal framework for the phasing out of quotas, leading to the "integration" of this sector into GATT at the end of a 10-year transition period, when the same rules will apply to trade in textiles and clothing as to trade in other goods. This phasing-out process comprises two aspects: the integration of products into the GATT, through the elimination of restrictions on products covered by the bilateral agreements negotiated under the MFA, to be accomplished in four stages leading to their complete removal at the end of 10 years; and, within the 10-year period, increases in the quotas of the products remaining under restriction, at a fixed growth rate. Restrictions not covered by the MFA will have to be either brought into conformity with GATT 1994 within one year or phased out according to a programme to be presented to the Textiles Monitoring Body (which replaces the Textiles Surveillance Body of the MFA).

The ATC is a transitional arrangement with a finite life span set up to liberalize trade in this sector through the progressive phasing out of the discriminatory quota restrictions over a ten-year transition period. The ultimate success, delay or failure of the agreement will rely on how these commitments are implemented by the governments of the major industrialized countries. However, such implementation, so far, has been very slow. Since the implementation started almost five years ago, only few quotas have been removed by the major importing countries. This is mainly due to the "end-loading" feature of the integration process, which allows countries to delay the integration of most important products to the end of the transitional period. Thus, in the short run, the quotas still remain as a real obstacle. Furthermore, the so-called "transitional safeguard mechanism" is also a major problem of the implementation of the ATC. Under such mechanism new restrictions can continue to be imposed on a discriminatory basis on products not yet integrated into GATT 1994. Despite their successful challenges to such measures before the WTO Dispute Settlement Body (DSB) and the repeated calling for these measures be applied as sparingly as possible by the relevant WTO bodies, developing countries are faced with frequent resort to new restrictions under the "transitional safeguard" provisions of the ATC.

The process of integrating the textiles and clothing sector into GATT 1994

As to the first stage of the integration under the ATC, it was clear that the products integrated into the GATT 1994 were in the least sensitive areas, with no quotas being removed by the four WTO members maintaining restrictions carried over from the MFA (the European Union, the United States, Canada and Norway), with one exception in Canada (for work gloves).[92] For the second stage, although the products integrated included some of these that were subject to quotas, it is evident that for products that are of interest to developing countries only represent a very marginal share of trade. For example, the EU's integration programme in the second stage included more than 20 categories of products of which 14 were with quota restrictions accounting for less than 4 percent of the volume of EU's imports in 1990. The second stage integration programme of the United States also contained only a few products with quota restrictions, namely babies' garments excluding cotton diapers, down-filled coats and certain items of hosiery accounting for a mere 1.3 percent of the total volume of US imports in 1990.

Although as indicated Table 1 the major importing countries have met the integration target which was set in volume terms, there has been minimal integration of restricted products into the GATT 1994. Thus, they have respected the letter, but not the spirit of the ATC, as a result of which developing textile exporting countries have not obtained the expected benefits from the ATC.

"In order to facilitate the integration of the textiles and clothing sector into GATT 1994," Article 1:5 of the ATC states: "Members should allow for continuous autonomous industrial adjustment and increased competition in their markets." This was also reaffirmed by the Ministers at the Singapore Conference (paragraph 15 of the Singapore Ministerial Declaration).

During the first major review conducted by the Council for Trade in Goods (CTG) as required by Article 8.11 of the ATC, the CTG recalled that "Members should allow for continuous autonomous industrial adjustment and increased competition in their markets in order to facilitate the integration of the textiles and clothing sector into GATT 1994." The CTG noted that further information in this regard would facilitate the review of progress.

Developing countries are therefore of the view that the effective implementation of the integration programme should be accompanied by active steps taken by the developed importing countries with a view to facilitating full return of this sector to the GATT rules and to orienting their industries in the direction of structural adjustment, so that there will be no pressure on these governments in 2004 to continue with the restrictive regime.

Transitional safeguards

The application of the transitional safeguards has also presented problems for the implementation of the ATC. During the first four years, 34 transitional safeguard actions were invoked, including 28 by the United States affecting 14 exporters. Although most of these actions were taken during the initial period of the implementation their disruptive effects cannot be underestimated (Tables 2 and 3).

The successful challenges brought by developing exporting countries in two panel cases before the WTO DSB - Costa Rica's complaint regarding cotton and manmade fibre underwear, and India's complaint concerning woven wool shirts and blouses - have confirmed that the strict criteria for application of the transitional safeguard provisions must be fully complied with by the invoking country. The two panel reports as well as appellate body reports have further underscored the differences between the MFA which was a derogation from GATT obligations and the ATC as a transitional arrangement for a phased integration of trade in the textiles sector into the normal GATT disciplines.

In a recent case between US and Pakistan on combed cotton yarn, the TMB found that the restriction imposed by the United States could not be justified.

Anti-dumping actions against textile and clothing products

According to the available information, over the period of 1987 - 1998, there were about 160 anti-dumping investigations related to textiles and clothing, with more than 60 percent of these cases were initiated in recent years since 1993 and mainly targeted at the imports from developing countries (Tables 4, 5 and 6).

It is also interesting to note that the ratio between initiation of anti-dumping actions and final measures for textiles and clothing is around one third, the lowest among the key sectors involved.

Over the same period, among 355 anti-dumping actions initiated by the EU, 16 percent or more than 50 cases were targeted at textiles and clothing, mainly at developing exporting countries, and thus, made the EU the most frequent user of anti-dumping measures in the area of textiles and clothing.

Repeated recourse has been made to anti-dumping actions by the EU against the same products (e.g. grey cotton fabrics and bed linen) from a number of developing exporting countries whose exports of these products have already been under restraints. For example, in the case involving imports of grey cotton fabrics originating from six countries (i.e. China, Egypt, India, Indonesia, Turkey and Pakistan), the EU has repeatedly initiated several investigations over the past four years. These so-called "back to back" investigations, have caused even greater concern. As shown in Table 7 while the EU total imports of grey cotton fabrics declined by 6.52 percent its imports from the six countries targeted for investigations declined by over 33 percent.

As anti-dumping appears to be becoming a primary instrument of trade restriction, many small and medium size firms in developing countries have difficulty in defending their interests. This is because of the complexities of the system and the cost of compliance in investigation proceedings. For example, in Canada and the United States, it is not unusual for exporters to incur defence costs well in excess of US$500 000 to defend their interests. At such cost small exporting firms in developing countries are hardly able to take advantage of the procedural and substantive rights theoretically available to them.

The adverse impact of these investigations is much greater than the actual trade involved as the initiation can have an immediate impact on trade flows as it prompts importers to seek alternative sources of supply. In certain cases, petitioners initiate actions only to "harass" imports even through they are aware that their outcomes would be negative as they are not required to pay the legal fees of successful defendants.

Apart from the losses for businesses of these countries exporting to the EU market, these actions also have a significant bearing on the effective and smooth transition of the sector to GATT 1994. In this regard, some experts suggest that in the future reviews of the WTO Agreement on Anti-Dumping Measures and the forthcoming new round of multilateral trade negotiations, anti-dumping rules need to be improved with a view to reducing the discretion available to national anti-dumping authorities.

Rules of origin related to textiles and clothing

Another issue of concern is related to the United States *rules of origin* for textiles which entered into force on 1 July 1996. These rules, as codified in US Customs Regulation 102.21 (19 CFR 102 21), do not provide for cutting components or cutting and hemming to confer country of origin as under the previous rules. The basis of the 1996 rules is processing operations or assembly. For example, for fabrics, the country of origin is the country in which fabric woven, knitted or created by other fabric making process, rather than dying and printing. These changes are summarized in the table below.

Main category of textiles products	Prior to July 1996 Origin conferring operations	After July 1996 Origin conferring operations
Apparel	Cutting	Assembly
Fabrics	Diong of fabric and printing if accompanied by two or more finishing operations	Weaving from yarn

These changes have introduced great uncertainty for exports of a large number of countries to that market. The delay in concluding the negotiations on the harmonization of non-preferential rules of origin under the WTO Agreement on Rules of Origin could have serious impact on developing countries' trade in textiles and clothing.

Recent developments have indicated that the application of these rules have the potential to generate trade disputes. For example, a complaint[93] to the EC Commission was raised as early as October 1996 by the Italian Association of Textile Producers against the changes in the US textiles rules. Since the complaint contained sufficient evidence the matter was subsequently brought by the EU at WTO where consultations with the US authorities have been initiated.[94] The fact at stake is that the new rules refused to grant EU originating status to scarves which have been dyed, printed and finished in the EU on loom-state fabrics produced in third countries (mainly, China). A significant aspect of the complaint related to the requirement to label the products in question as originating in the country which produced the fabric with obvious consequences on the US consumer which may not concretely identify EU's products.

Although it may be difficult to quantify, it appears obvious that in the upper-textile market of haute couture brand name and mark of origin have a considerable impact on consumer choice which may justify the concern of producers of finished products. Although the globalization of production has outpaced the notion that a product is wholly produced and obtained in a country, consumers may still identify certain quality products with specific geographic region or countries. Moreover, the non-inclusion of design and style in expenses on advertising and research which may be incurred in fashion textile industry together with ownership of the manufacturing plant may not respect the "substantial transformation" concept.

In another related field, these changes introduced in the US legislation have caused changes of origin of products submitted to quotas such as textile and steel products. Decision on where the origin of the product is allocated among countries which are subject to quota may have a highly disruptive effect on production chains and relations established among different industries. In Asia, cutting of fabric into garments, a former origin conferring operation, used to take place in countries where quotas were under-utilized or in countries which had no quotas, while the assembly operations were performed in low-cost countries such as China. The new rules imply a change in origin allocation switching origin to countries such China, where most assembly operations are performed. This may ultimately result in new limitations if these countries' exports are subject to quotas where they are fully utilized. Notably China is not yet a member of WTO and thus its textiles and clothing exports do not benefit from the ATC. Thus, the changes in origin rules affect the pattern of production and investment in a whole region which may take considerable time and financing to adjust.[95]

Tariff reduction commitments by the major developed importing countries

Although MFA quotas are still the factor actually limiting the current exports of textiles and clothing by the developing countries to the major developed country markets, it is expected that, with the gradual integration of this sector into the GATT, tariffs eventually could become the main instrument of border protection. The post-Uruguay Round average tariff level of 12.1 percent in the textiles and clothing sector is still considerably higher than for all industrial products in the developed countries which is 3.8 percent.

Trade liberalization measures taken by developing countries

Another important feature of the Uruguay Round results is that developing countries have also made significant contributions by undertaking tariff reductions, tariff bindings, and the elimination of non-tariff measures.

In the past, many developing countries protected their domestic textile and clothing production from import competition or in pursuing an import-substitution policy on the basis of the infant-industry argument. Since the late seventies and early eighties, more and more developing countries have adopted trade liberalization as a general strategy to sustain economic growth. During the course of the Uruguay Round negotiations, almost all the Latin American countries had autonomously removed restrictions on the imports of the textile and clothing products. Several Asian countries had, at the same time, opened their markets to imports as a part of their programmes of economic liberalization.

Within the context of the Uruguay Round Agreements, developing countries have also made significant contributions by undertaking tariff reductions, tariff bindings and the elimination of non-tariff measures with respect to textiles and clothing. It is, however, not possible at this stage to calculate the average depth of cut in textiles and clothing tariffs for this group of countries because for many of them ad valorem equivalents of specific duties and trade-weighted averages of tariffs are not available. Nevertheless, it is noticeable that the reductions in the textiles and clothing sector in trade-weighted tariff averages range from 9 percent in Zimbabwe to 52 percent in India. Argentina, Brazil, Chile, Colombia, Costa Rica, El Salvador, Indonesia, Jamaica, Mexico, Peru, Uruguay and Venezuela have bound all their tariffs. The scope of tariff bindings of India, Turkey, Singapore, the Republic of Korea, Malaysia, Philippines, Thailand, and Tunisia range from 61 to 98 percent. Senegal and Zimbabwe have also bound 22 and 44 percent of their tariffs respectively.

In addition, India also agreed to liberalize its textiles import regime by removing all yarns, fibres, and some industrial fabrics from its restricted list of imports. For certain other fabrics and garments, the removal will start in 1998. Restrictions for most other garments will be phased out by 2002. As part of its Uruguay Round commitments, India agreed to reduce tariffs on various textiles items to 20 percent or less from the current 65 percent to 70 percent. As an intermediate step, tariffs on these products would be cut to 40 to 50 percent within three years.

The Government of Pakistan decided to phase out its concessional credit facility and dual cotton-pricing system, and to improve the access of textile and clothing industry to fibres, yarns and cotton substitutes by allowing imports at reduced tariffs. The tariffs on selected textile products would be reduced during the transition period of the ATC to 35 percent for clothing, 25 per cent fabrics and 15 percent for fibres and yarns.

It has been reported that the Egyptian Government cut import duties by five percent for most consumer goods as part of its programme to liberalize trade. These commitments by developing countries with respect to tariff reductions and tariff bindings together with the obligations of the phasing out of GATT-inconsistent non-MFA restrictions, and the strengthened GATT rules and disciplines, particularly in the areas such as safeguards, balance-of-payment provisions, notification procedures, etc., would no doubt bring increased security and predictability for access to their market of textiles and clothing.

Impact of regional agreements and arrangements

As of mid-1998, there were more than 100 regional trade agreements and arrangements in force. With the implementation of the ATC nearing its half-way mark and the elimination of MFA restrictions lacking commercially meaningful progress, these regional agreements and arrangements have had a significant effect on trade in textiles and clothing, and the related corporate activities. This is particularly true in the two major markets, the EU and the US.

This was mainly due to the enlargement of the European Union and its cooperation and association agreements and arrangement with "preferential" countries, e.g. Turkey, central and eastern European Countries, Morocco, Tunisia, Bangladesh, etc.; and the NAFTA and Caribbean Basin Initiative (CBI). Under these agreements and arrangements, the preference and rules of origin have played key roles, in particular those related OPT trade.

As a member of NAFTA, Mexico is now a privileged supplier of clothing to the United States and Canada. Foreign investors, who had foreseen the signing of the free trade agreement, have built up the clothing industry in Mexico which, with its 8 000 enterprises, is in a very strong position vis-à-vis other competitors.

In the late nineties, Mexico became the number one supplier of textiles and clothing; and Canada has become the number two supplier, to the US market. Their status as the top suppliers to the US market are testimony to the importance of duty rates as all shipments from Canada are duty-free, and beginning from 1 January 1999, most Mexican shipments are also duty-free.

The share of the CBI countries (mainly the Dominican Republic, Honduras, El Salvador, Costa Rica and Guatemala) in the total US imports of textiles and clothing at the end of April 1999 was almost 11 percent as compared to 14.13 percent for Mexico, 9.73 for Canada and 7.17 for China.

The return of grey area measures or comeback to VERS

During the course of the Uruguay Round, in addition to the commitments by the WTO members to dismantle the MFA, it was also agreed, under the Agreement on Safeguards to eliminate VERs over a four-year period and to prohibit new ones. However, the recent return to so-called grey area measures and VERs, or the comeback of "managed trade" in the area of steel products could have adverse implications for the effective phasing out of discriminatory quota restrictions under the ATC.

Other trade and trade-related policy developments

Social clause or labour standards

Although, the proposals and efforts to include the issue of core labour standards and their relationship to international trade were again rejected at the 1996 WTO Singapore Ministerial Conference, a provision concerning Labour Standards was introduced into the bilateral textile agreement between the United States and Cambodia (which is a non-WTO member in the process of acceding the WTO). In this provision, it was agreed that an increase of 14 percent quota levels for the following year should be implemented on the condition that Cambodia would respect and implement internationally recognized core labour standards. In the event of Cambodia becoming a WTO member, this provision would remain in force and be notified to the TMB.

Environmental measures

The application of eco-labelling and other environment quality requirements in textiles and clothing could also become a burden for many developing countries in their textiles trade. For example, following the ban on AZO dyes in Germany in 1996, textile manufacturers in Thailand switched to AZO-free substitutes with additional costs estimated at between 5 and 20 percent. Textile manufacturers in some other countries in the Asia-Pacific region, like India, encountered difficulties in obtaining substitutes. Small and medium enterprises were slower to adjust to eco-labelling demands and found the costs of adjustment difficult to absorb. Several of these enterprises preferred to divert sales to the domestic market or other overseas markets which have no eco-labelling requirements.

Summary

As a transitional arrangement with a definite life span, the ATC will liberalize trade in this sector through the progressive phasing out of the discriminatory quota restrictions over a ten-year transition period. However, this will not mean that the protectionism is going to retreat.

While the integration process under the ATC has not yet achieved any substantial liberalisation, developing countries are faced with the frequent resort to new restrictions under the "transitional safeguard" provisions, and the increased initiation of anti-dumping actions to "harass" their exports.

The changes made by the United States in its *origin rules* for textiles have introduced great uncertainty for exporters in a large number of countries to that market. The delay in concluding the negotiations on the harmonization of non-preferential rules of origin under the WTO Agreement on Rules of Origin could have serious impact on developing countries' trade in textiles and clothing.

With the gradual integration of this sector into the GATT, tariffs eventually could become the main instrument of border protection.

Currently, more than 100 regional trade agreements and arrangements are in force. These regional agreements and arrangements have had a significant effect on trade in textiles and clothing. This is particularly true in both the EU and the US markets, mainly due to the enlargement of the European Union and its cooperation and association agreements and arrangement with "preferential" countries, e.g. Turkey, Central and Eastern European Countries, Morocco, Tunisia, Bangladesh, etc.; and the NAFTA and Caribbean Basin Initiative (CBI). Under these agreements and arrangements, the preference and rules of origin have played key roles, in particular those related OPT trade.

Other trade and trade-related policy developments that may also affect trade in textiles are the so-called social clause and the application of eco-labelling and other environment quality requirements.

TABLE 1

The first and second stages integrated volume under ATC integration programme and their value equivalent by the US, EU, Canada and Norway

		Percentage of total imports in 1990					
		In volume[1]					In value[2]
	Integration stages	Yarns	Fabrics	Made-ups	Clothing	Total	Total
USA	1	8.46	1.65	4.19	1.92	16.21	6.62
	2	8.00	2.51	4.54	1.98	17.03	10.73
	Total	16.46	4.15	8.73	3.90	33.24	17.35
EU	1	4.39	8.14	3.48	0.38	16.38	8.70
	2	11.63	2.22	2.06	2.09	17.99	12.92
	Total	16.01	10.36	5.54	2.47	34.38	21.62
Canada	1	9.60	4.33	1.28	1.13	16.34	13.04
	2	0.64	2.09	14.30	0.24	17.29	16.70
	Tot4al	10.24	6.42	15.58	1.38	33.62	29.74
Norway	1	3.51	11.95	0.65	0.15	16.26	7.40
	2	6.58	2.38	11.14	4.16	24.26	16.55
	Total	10.09	14.33	11.80	4.31	40.52	23.95

NOTE: Totals may not tally due to rounding of figures.

Sources:

[1] ITCD Secretariat estimation based on information provided in G/TMB/N series.

[2] UNCTAD Secretariat estimation based on information provided in G/TMB/N series.

TABLE 2

Number of quotas eliminated

WTO Member	Total number of quotas*	Number of quotas eliminated			Notes
		By integration in Stages 1 and 2	By early elimination under Art. 2.15	Total	
USA	750	2	11**	13	Also integrated one category partially—babies' garments excl. diapers (cat. 239) for which 6 countries were restrained
EU	219	14	0	14	
Canada	295	29	0	29	Also eliminated quotas partially under Art. 2.15: on children's blouses &shirts of cat. 7.3& 8.1, WG knit blouses &shirts of cat. 8.1, WG blouses & shirts of silk & other vegetable fibres (17 QRs); babies' snowsuits, coats & jackets of cat. 14.1 (9 QRs); and rainwear of cat. 1.3 (11 QRs)
Norway	54	0	51	51	

* Total number of quotas includes specific limits and sub-limits therein only.

** These quotas have been eliminated only in respect of Romania.

Source: TMB notifications.

TABLE 3

Restrained trade freed of quotas (as percent of imports in each of the recent years)

	EU		USA	
Year	In volume	In value	In volume	In value
1995	4.74%	4.28%	6.23%	6.40%
1996	4.92%	4.34%	6.03%	6.14%
1997	4.77%	4.18%	6.00%	6.12%

Percentages derived from official US and EU data. For EU, Eurostat, Intra- and Extra-EU trade; for USA, US Department of Commerce, Office of Textiles and Apparel, TQ data for MFA product categories, 1997.

TABLE 4

Effects of anti-dumping actions (data in thousand tonnes)

	Total extra-EU imports			Imports from countries subject to anti-dumping actions		
Product	1996	1997	Change %	1996	1997	Change %
Grey fabric cotton	230	215	-6.52	132	88	-33.33
Bed linen	84	92	+9.52	48	48	-

Source: EUROSTAT data

TABLE 5

Tariffs in textiles vs. industrial tariffs (Trade Weighted Average Percentages)

	Overall industrial tariffs		Textile tariffs	
WTO Members	Pre-UR	Post-UR	Pre-UR	Post-UR
Canada..............................	9.0	4.8	21.3	14.5
EU....................................	5.7	3.6	11.0	9.1
USA..................................	5.6	3.5	16.7	14.6
Japan................................	3.9	1.7	11.3	7.6
Switzerland.......................	2.2	1.5	8.0	5.2
Norway.............................	3.6	2.0	18.1	10.6
All Developed....................	6.3	3.8	15.5	12.0

Source: WTO calculations, November 1994.

Table 6

Uruguay Round tariffs reductions (Trade Weighted Average Percentages)

	Overall industrial products	Textile and clothing products
USA....................................	35	13
EU	37	17

REVIEWING THE **TRIPS** AGREEMENT

Carlos Correa

The TRIPS Agreement brought about a "signal change" in the protection of intellectual property rights (UNCTAD, 1996, p. 18). This Agreement is, by its coverage, the most comprehensive international instrument on IPRs.

The Agreement establishes minimum standards on almost all areas of IPRs in terms of both the availability of rights and their enforcement. The inclusion of these latter type of provisions—one of the main innovations of the Agreement with respect to pre-existing conventions on IPRs—means that whenever the Agreement enters into force, the particular Member country must have in place the legal procedures and the administrative and legal infrastructure necessary to actually enforce the conferred rights.

Any deviation from the standards set forth by the Agreement may lead to a dispute settlement procedure within the WTO, in accordance with the Dispute Settlement Understanding (DSU). If the existence of a violation is determined, the affected country can apply trade retaliation against the non-complying country in any area covered by the WTO Agreement.

As a result of its broad coverage and the nature of its provisions, the implementation of the TRIPS Agreement requires dealing with a significant body of national legislation in terms of substantive as well as procedural rules. In many developing and least developed countries, such implementation called for massive changes in pre-existing laws.

The Agreement provides a framework for legislation and not operative provisions that may be directly imported into national laws. In some cases, there is considerable room for interpretation. For instance, the concept of "exclusive marketing rights" as contained in article 70.9 is undefined. Article 27.3.b) allows Members to develop an "effective *sui generis* regime" for plant varieties that may be designed without following any specific model. In other cases, the provisions explicitly determine options for legislation, such as article 34 on the reversal of the burden of proof.

Even in those cases where the standard of protection is clearly stated, Member countries must decide how to implement it according to their own

221

legal system (article 1). The implementation of the TRIPS standards, in sum, requires considerable deliberation and elaboration at the national level.

Identifying national interests

In order to comply with the Agreement, there is a need to assume a wide range of obligations in almost all areas of intellectual property rights. In many areas, the pre-TRIPS laws of developing countries require very substantial change, particularly in order to handle new issues, such as the protection under copyright law of computer programs and databases.

There are also areas in which no previous legislation existed at all, such as in the case of undisclosed information, integrated circuits and plant varieties.

As mentioned, the TRIPS Agreement includes enforcement rules and not just substantive provisions. Member countries do not only face the task of drafting and obtaining parliamentary approval of new legislation. Compliance with the Agreement also calls for the revision of national laws in respect of civil, criminal and administrative procedures, as well as redefining the role of the police and customs authorities. As illustrated by the UNCTAD study on TRIPS (1996), the costs of developing the institutional infrastructure to implement the TRIPS Agreement standards may be substantial.

Amending or developing new legislation on IPRs requires legal expertise in a number of fields, which is often lacking in developing countries and LDCs. The drafting of legislation needs the active involvement and cooperation of different State organizations, and also interaction with the private sector and society at large.

The adoption of new IPRs rules may affect different industrial and commercial activities in the country. Given the flexibility left by the TRIPS Agreement to deal with some issues (e.g., parallel imports, compulsory licenses) and the likely impact of different solutions, the appropriate involvement of the local private sector in the discussion of new legislation seems essential. Similarly, the strengthening of intellectual property rights may affect consumers and other groups (e.g., local communities).

Concerns have been voiced in many developing countries, for instance, with regard to the possible impact of the introduction of product patent protection in the pharmaceutical sector. Though the estimates vary significantly, several studies indicate that an increase in the prices of new medicines (as compared to a situation of open competition) will be the probable outcome of such an introduction, with a possible welfare loss for the particular country

(Scherer, 1999). Likewise, stronger protection of computer programs might reduce access to information technology systems by small and medium enterprises and educational institutions.

The TRIPS Agreement aims at balancing the interests of producers and users of technology (article 7). Developing the appropriate mechanisms to do so is quite a difficult task, for which adequate consultation processes, reliable data and deep knowledge of each particular area are required.

The process of drafting legislation to implement the TRIPS Agreement is, therefore, not only a complex technical problem. It also raises a number of public policy issues that need to be properly addressed.

Transitional periods

Developing countries and LDCs were accorded transitional periods (article 65) to implement the Agreement. Application of the Agreement will become obligatory for the former countries by 1 January, 2,000. Products that are not patentable at that date need to be protected from the year 2,005.

The provision of such periods was an important element in the delicate balance reached as the outcome of negotiations. They were included to allow developing countries time to elaborate and adopt the required legislation, and to design any other policies necessary to minimize the possible negative effects of new IPRs rules. This was particularly the case with regard to products which were not patentable (such as pharmaceuticals, agrochemicals and food).

Despite the automatic nature of the transitional periods, many developing countries have been under pressure by some developed countries to accelerate the pace of reforms, so as to give immediate application to the TRIPS Agreement standards. These pressures have complicated rather than facilitated the process of legislative change.

Though so far only one case relating to TRIPS has been decided under the WTO dispute settlement mechanism (USA-India on implementation of article 70.8), several complaints and requests for consultations have been filed during the last few months, including by the EU against Canada relating to the "early-working" exception for patents on pharmaceuticals (also known as the "Bolar" exception), Canada against the EU relating to the extension of the patent term for agrochemical and pharmaceutical patents, the USA against Argentina on the recognition of "exclusive marketing rights", and the USA against Canada relating to the extension of patents issued before 1989.

A significant number of developing countries have not been able to adapt their legislation to the Agreement's minimum standards yet, and are unlikely to do so before the end of the general transitional period on 31 December 1999. Even some developing countries that have made substantial steps to implement the Agreement have not been able to cover all areas (particularly those in which they had no legislation previously), or have not been able still to reform enforcement-related rules.

This situation will put such countries in a situation of violation on 1 January 2,000, which may lead to a large number of actions under the WTO dispute settlement mechanism against them. In fact, the US Trade Representative (USTR) has already announced that it will assess the situation at the end of 1999 in order to take action as of January 2,000.

In view of this situation, a possible approach may be to negotiate an extension of the transitional period as contained in article 65.2. Alternatively, proposals could be made in order to reach a consensus for non-action in cases of non-compliance with the TRIPS Agreement by developing countries, for a certain agreed period.

Built-in agenda

Geographical indications

Article 23.4 of the TRIPS Agreement obliged Members to undertake negotiations on the establishment of a multilateral system of notification and registration of geographical indications for wines.

Two proposals have been made on the subject. The European Communities proposed an international registration of geographical indications according to which registered indications would be automatically protected in the participating Members, subject to a procedure for dealing with oppositions from each Member who considers that a geographical indication is not eligible for protection in its territory. On the other hand, United States and Japan envisage the development of an international database of geographical indications to which Members would be expected to have reference in the operation of their national systems. Both approaches have support from some other Members (Otten, 1999, p.7).

The other area of work on geographical indications is the review of the application of the provisions in the Section on geographical Indications under Article 24.2. In this context and also in the context of the preparations for a new round, proposals have been made for the expansion of the product areas that must benefit from the higher level of protection presently only required under the TRIPS Agreement for wines and spirits to other agricultural and handicraft products, for example, rice, tea, beer, etc.(Vandoren, 1999, p. 30).

Several developing countries have indicated interest in a TRIPS-plus protection in the field of geographical indications. For instance, Egypt has proposed that the additional protection conferred for geographical indications for wines and spirits (Article 23.1) be extended to other products, particularly those of interest to developing countries (WT/GC/W/136).

Biotechnological innovations

Article 27.3.b) is the only provision in the TRIPS Agreement subject to an early review, in 1999. So far, there has been no agreement in the Council for TRIPS on the meaning of "review". Developed countries hold that it is a "review of implementation" which is called for, while for developing countries a "review" should open the possibility of revising the text.

Several proposals have been made, particularly by IPRs-concerned NGOs, for the revision of article 27.3.b), for instance, in order to ensure that naturally occurring materials are not patentable, and to recognize some form of protection for the "traditional knowledge" of local and indigenous communities. The aim of some developed countries, if a revision takes place, would seem to include the elimination of the exception for plants and animals, and establishing that plant varieties should be protected in accordance with the UPOV Convention as revised in 1991.

The outcome of a possible revision of this article is unclear. In the view of developing countries, it would be important to ensure that the exception for plants and animals is maintained, as is the flexibility to develop *sui generis* regimes on plant varieties which are suited to the seed supply systems of the countries concerned.

In the revision of this provision, the following elements may be considered:

a) to preserve the right of any Member country to exclude from patentability plants and animals and to develop a *sui generis* regime for the protection of plant varieties;[96]

b) to clarify that naturally occurring substances, including genes, shall remain outside the scope of any IPRs protection;

c) to determine the novelty requirement in a manner that excludes the patentability of any subject matter which was made available to the public by means of a written description, by use or in any other way in any country before the date of filing, including use by local and indigenous communities, or by deposit of a material in a germplasm bank or other deposit institutions where the said material is publicly available;

d) to establish commitments by governments not to grant, or to cancel ex officio or upon request, IPRs on biological materials obtained: i)from collections held in international germplasm banks and other deposit institutions where such materials are publicly available; ii)without the prior consent, where applicable, of the country of origin;

e) to ensure, as appropriate, compliance with the obligation to share benefits with the country of origin of a patented biological material.

A possible revision of article 27.3.b) may also include—though this would not be strictly necessary—a provision specifically allowing for an experimentation exception (including the breeding of new plant varieties).

Another important issue is the possible development of some form of protection for traditional knowledge. The adoption of the Convention on Biological Diversity has given impetus to this idea, by establishing the obligation to "respect, preserve and maintain knowledge, innovations and practices of indigenous and local communities embodying traditional lifestyles relevant for the conservation and sustainable use of biological diversity..." (article 8 j).

Many approaches and proposals have been developed to deal with communities' knowledge,[97] ranging from the creation of new types of intellectual property rights (IPRS) to the simple option of legally excluding all forms of appropriation, be it under patents, breeders' rights or other modalities of IPRs. Only a few countries have so far started to address the complex conceptual and operational problems involved in the recognition of communities' rights on their knowledge. For instance, "collective" intellectual property rights have been recognized by the Constitution of Ecuador (1998). The Biodiversity law of Costa Rica (1998) protects "sui generis community rights" (article 82), and a draft law in Brazil (Bill No, 306, 1995) recognizes the rights of local communities to collectively benefit from their tradtions and knowledge and to be compensated by means of intellectual property rights or other measures. The creation of a new, sui generis, form of protection has also been proposed in a draft bill in Thailand, which would recognize rights to traditional healers and on medicinal genetic resources.

At least some aspects of communities knowledge—the artistic components—may be protected as "works of folklore", in accordance with the UNESCO/WIPO "Model Provisions for National Laws for the Protection of Expressions of Folklore against Illicit Exploitation and other Prejudicial Actions" developed by a Committee of Governmental Experts in 1982. An interesting element of this proposal is that the unauthorized utilization of expressions of folklore with gainful intent and outside the traditional or customary context of folklore, can be prevented by the community concerned or a competent authority. Indigenous communities are not prevented from using their expressions or from developing them by continuous reproduction, recitation or performance.[98]

Any WTO Member may provide protection beyond the TRIPs Agreement standards (article 1), and it is fully empowered to create new titles of IPRs, or new forms of protection, to the extent that this does not diminish or neutralizes the protection to be granted in the areas covered by the Agreement. If such a new title or form of protection were established and a WTO Member did not apply the principle of national treatment, there would be no violation of the TRIPs Agreement or of any other international instrument. A good illustration of this possibility is the European Union Directive 96/9/EC on the Legal Protection of Data Bases, which created a new *sui generis* right for data bases, subject to the principle of reciprocity.

Developing countries may keep their right to deal with communities' rights at the national level, without submitting them to international rules. In order to get the recognition of such rights in other countries, however, some form of pluri - or multilateral agreement would be necessary.

A review of the TRIPS Agreement could explicitly recognize the Members' right to legislate on communities rights, for instance by indicating like in article 6 of said Agreement- that no Member could be submitted to a WTO panel based on the adoption of protection for traditional knowledge. A step further would be to develop in the Agreement itself certain elements of such a protection in order to get an international recognition of such rights. This would imply, however, the application thereon of the TRIPS Agreement's principles of national treatment and Most-Favored-Nation. Given the status of the debates on the matter, this latter approach seems unlikely to succeed, but discussions could be started by the setting up of a Working Group.

Non-violation clause

An issue to be dealt with by the Council for TRIPS is the treatment of "non-violation" complaints, which are not subject to the dispute settlement mechanism till the end of 1999 (article 64.2 and 3). A decision should be taken—by consensus—on whether to extend this period or to determine the disciplines to be applied. An extension of the transitional period seems advisable.

Moreover, a deeper examination of the implications of this clause in the IPRs field may be undertaken. IPRs are generally defined in a precise manner since they imply the stipulation of a right to prohibit third parties from using, producing or commercializing a product or service. Non-violation would open a window for challenging on discretionary grounds IPRs national regulations[99] and domestic policies in different areas beyond IPRs, such as price controls and regulations on royalty remittances. Hence, the application of the non-violation clause may create a gray area and provide a basis for challenging national policies beyond the scope of IPRs.

It should be noted that according to article 19.2 of the Dispute Settlement Understanding, the WTO adjudication process "cannot add to or diminish the rights and obligations provided in the covered agreements", and that in the USA-India panel on article 70.9[100] the Appellate Body rejected the "legitimate expectations" test derived from GATT jurisprudence on non-violation acts, thereby confirming that

> "the developing countries are free to adopt their own laws and policies with respect to all intellectual property issues that were not expressly harmonized in TRIPS standards themselves" (Reichman, 1998, p. 597).

Review of the Agreement

Article 71.1 provides for a review of the implementation of the TRIPS Agreement after the year 2,000, and for possible reviews "in the light of any relevant new developments which might warrant modification or amendment".

There are already several proposals, some formally submitted, to revise the TRIPS Agreement in a future round of multilateral negotiations. A preliminary question is, however, what should be the developing countries' strategy on this matter.

Negotiating strategies

A first strategy may aim at a comprehensive revision, in order to effectively implement through specific provisions articles 7 and 8 of the Agreement and strike a balance between the interests of producers and users of technology. The rationale behind this strategy would be that the Agreement, as it stands, primarily reflects patterns of IPRs protection suitable for developed countries, but which largely disregard the "development dimension".

A component of this strategy may be to **clarify** various elements of flexibility which are present in the text, but which are or may be contested, such as the right to allow parallel imports (article 6) including when originating from a compulsory licensee, the non-patentability of uses of known products (interpretation of articles 27.1 and 28), and the right to grant compulsory licences on different grounds to be determined by each national law (article 31). In addition, certain obligations may be clarified, such as developed countries' obligations under article 66.2 with respect to LDCs and article 67 relating to technical assistance.

This strategy may lead to an improvement of the present text from the perspective of developing countries. There is, of course, the risk that, depending on such countries' level of preparation and bargaining power, the revision of many provisions may lead instead to texts which are more restrictive than the existing ones. A careful political evaluation of possible scenarios is, therefore, needed.

A second strategy may, in contrast, be based on a de minimis approach, that is, opening for renegotiation as few provisions as possible. The rationale for this position would be that the TRIPS Agreement is not a uniform law, and that it leaves developing countries some room for manoeuvre that may be lost if the text is broadly revised. This position also assumes that the chances for developing countries to obtain favourable amendments are slim, given the sensitive nature of IPRs issues and the pressures exerted on developed countries' governments by powerful industrial lobbies.

Under this approach, only a few key provisions should be subject to re-examination, such as article 31 g) (termination of a compulsory licence) which seriously undermines the compulsory licensing system.

Finally, a third strategy may be based on a "policy" or "issues approach", that is, on a systematic review of the Agreement in the light of a particular objective. This strategy would be most effective if the review systematically covers **all** WTO agreements that may affect the attainment of a certain objective, and not only the TRIPS Agreement. For instance, when dealing with technology transfer, in addition to particular provisions in the said Agreement, relevant provisions may be considered in the Agreements on the Application of Sanitary and Phytosanitary Measures (article 9), Technical Barriers to Trade (e.g., articles 11 and 12), and Subsidies and Countervailing Measures (SCM) (e.g., article 8), and in the General Agreement on Trade in Services (GATS) (articles IV and XIX) be considered.

Policy-oriented approaches

It is possible to identify different approaches for a systematic review as proposed:

Transfer of technology

Several developing countries have stressed[101] the need to develop particular provisions in the TRIPS Agreement so as to ensure that the objective of fostering the transfer and dissemination of technology (article 7) is effectively realized. In fact, developing countries and LDCs face growing constraints in getting access to up-to-date technologies (Correa, 1994). Given that the issues at stake are complex, the development of a multifaceted and comprehensive approach is needed (Roffe, 1999).

The enhancement of technology flows to developing countries may require the revision of several articles of the TRIPS Agreement, such as article 27.1 (working obligations), article 31.b) (broader application of "refusal to deal" as an autonomous ground for compulsory licences), article 40 (specification of illegal restrictive business practices in voluntary licences) and article 66.2 (further specification of measures to be adopted to encourage the transfer of technology to LDCs).

This approach may be supplemented, as mentioned before, by an analysis of the amendments or new provisions that may be needed in other WTO agreements, such as GATS and the SCM Agreement. For instance, consideration could be given to the exemption under the SCM Agreement of subsidies related to the export of technology and associated equipment to developing countries.

Environment

Within the WTO Committee on Trade and Environment, India has already indicated the need to amend the TRIPS Agreement in order to facilitate the access to and use of environmentally sound technologies. The proposal requires the amendment of articles 31 (compulsory licences) and 33 (duration of patents), and suggests that patent holders should be subjected to an obligation to transfer environmentally sound technologies on fair terms and most favourable conditions. It also proposes a financial compensatory mechanism.[102]

Biodiversity

The reconciliation of the TRIPS Agreement with the CBD may be one of the main objectives of possible negotiations.[103] This may include the amendment of article 27.1 (requirement of universal novelty as a condition for patentability) and article 29 (obligation to prove that prior informed consent has been obtained with regard to claimed biological materials). A new provision on "traditional knowledge" may also be considered, though the complexity of this issue would justify the establishment of a working group to study and clarify possible options (see below).

Health

The implementation of public health policies may be restrained by the implementation of IPRs protection, if the latter is not designed in a manner that effectively takes into account the objectives of such policies. The TRIPS Agreement leaves some room therefor (Correa, 1997; Velasquez and Boulet, 1999).

Under an approach focused on public health, however, some articles may require revision, for instance, article 27.1 in order to exclude the patentability of "essential medicines" listed by WHO; article 30 so as to incorporate an explicit recognition of an "early-working" exception for the approval of generic products before the expiration of a patent; and article 31 in order to clarify the right to grant and the scope of compulsory licenses for public health reasons.[104]

Competition

The expansion and strengthening of IPRs in developed countries has taken place *pari passu* with an effective application of competition law. Illustrative of this linkage is the large number of compulsory licences granted in the United States in order to remedy anti-competitive practices.[105]

In developing countries, in contrast, IPRs protection is being enhanced in consistency with the TRIPS Agreement, but competition law is non-existent or weak in many countries.

Revision of the Agreement could be made with a view to strengthening the competition-related provisions thereof (such as article 40) and incorporating new disciplines, for instance those relating to measures to prevent and remedy abuses of IPRs. Specific work could be undertaken on vertical restraints, such as tying arrangements and restrictive practices in licensing agreements, as well as on horizontal restraints, such as pooling and cross-licensing and industry standardization.

Other issues

Some proposals have been made to revise the TRIPS Agreement in order to expand the special protection of geographical indications under article 23 (now limited to wines and spirits) so as to cover other products of export interest, such as *basmati* rice.[106] Such increased protection, if admitted and not subject to special and differential treatment, could benefit all Members; therefore, its net impact in developing countries would depend on the number and economic importance of such countries' indications vis-a-vis those of other Members.

Other possible amendments that developing countries may consider include:

- clarification of article 70.8 and 70.9 in the sense that the "exclusive marketing rights" should be conferred only in respect of new chemical entities and that only patents granted in another WTO Member with an examination system may be considered as a basis for granting those rights (Velasquez and Boulet, 1999, pp. 29-30);

- incorporation of the first-to-file principle[107] for patent applications;[108]

- development of rules for the protection of the works of folklore, as recommended by the UNESCO Model Law of 1989, and allowing any Member country to recognize and protect traditional knowledge.

Both the United States and the European Union have suggested[109] that a possible amendment to the TRIPS Agreement should incorporate the two conventions approved under the auspices of WIPO in 1996, that is, the WIPO Copyright Treaty and the WIPO Performance and Phonograms Treaty.[110] The WIPO Copyright Treaty reconfirms the pertinent provisions of the TRIPS Agreement on copyright. It also contains provisions particularly relevant to the use of works in a digital environment, like the "right of distribution" (article 6)[111] and the "right of communication to the public", including when "members of the public may access these works from a place and at a time individually chosen by them" (article 8).

References

Correa, Carlos, (1994), *Sovereign and Property Rights over Plant Genetic Resources*, FAO, Commission on Plant Genetic Resources, First Extraordinary Session, Rome.

Correa, Carlos (1994), "Trends in technology transfer: Implications for developing countries", *Science and Public Policy*, vol. 21, No. 6.

Correa, Carlos (1997), *The Uruguay Round and drugs*, WHO, Geneva.

South Centre (1998), *The WTO multilateral trade agenda and the South*, Geneva.

Posey, Darrell A. and Dutfield, Graham, (1996), *Beyond Intellectual Property. Toward Traditional Resource Rights for Indigenous Peoples and Local Communities*, International Development Research Centre, Ottawa.

Reichman, Jerome (1998), "Securing compliance with the TRIPS Agreement after US v. India", *Journal of International Economic Law*, pp. 585-601.

Roffe, Pedro (1999), "The implementation of the TRIPs Agreement and transfer of technology to developing countries" (mimeo), Geneva.

Scherer, F., (1999), "The patent system and innovation in pharmaceuticals", presented at the AIDE Conference on Pharmaceutical patents, Innovation and Public Health, 28-30 January, Toulouse, France.

UNCTAD, (1996), *The TRIPs Agreement and Developing Countries*, New York and Geneva.

Velasquez, G. and Boulet, P. (1999), *Globalization and access to drugs*, DAP Series No. 7 Revised, pp. 29-30.

Vinje, Thomas (1997), "The new WIPO Copyright Treaty: A happy result in Geneva", *EIPR*, No. 5.

TRADE-RELATED INVESTMENT MEASURES

Mina Mashayekhi, UNCTAD

Investment was a major issue during the Uruguay Round negotiations. The negotiations in the context of GATS, TRIMs, TRIPS, Government Procurement, and Subsidies, as well as the MAI and discussions at the WTO Working Group on Trade and Investment have demonstrated that many countries continue to have concerns with providing right of establishment to foreign investment, limiting use of performance requirements and incentives and consider it important to maintain flexibility in their economic and development policies. Different trade-related aspects of investment measures are presently covered by GATS, TRIMs, TRIPS and Subsidies Agreements.

All multilateral negotiations on this subject since the Havana Charter have been marked by the reluctance to subject investment policies to international rules and disciplines.[112] The negotiations in the OECD on a Multilateral Agreement on Investment (MAI) met with difficulties and in May 1998 ministers decided to suspend negotiations until October 1998. In October France withdrew from the negotiations and it was subsequently decided not to continue the negotiations. The draft MAI, which draws heavily on the investment provisions of NAFTA, is much less ambitious than envisaged by the main proponents of such an agreement, and thus was not acceptable to them, while opposition was mobilized, particularly at the provincial and state levels in federal countries. . The main reasons for the failure of the MAI relate to:

- The issue of extra-territoriality as reflected among others in the US' Helms-Burton and D'Amato legislation,

- The US' proposals to include labour and environmental standards,

- The proposal by France and Canada on cultural exception, and

- The European Union's insistence on exception for regional integration agreements.[113]

- Major exceptions / carve outs from national treatment

- The preference for the WTO as a forum for negotiations due to the fact that in the WTO the EC Commission negotiations on behalf of member states

The OECD members seem reluctant to accept further commitments to liberalize restrictions on foreign investment that go beyond what they have already accepted in the WTO or in free trade agreements.

The basic policy dilemma that developing countries face is that the attainment of economic and development objectives implies the need for sequencing the eventual full application of the principles of market access and national treatment, while with the phenomena of globalization, to promote international competitiveness more liberal FDI policies are required. Moreover, with the reduction of official aid, countries' need for private investment has increased. The TNCS favour establishment in countries with the least number of restrictions.[114] Liberalization of investment does not, however, guarantee establishment of foreign firms or development. This is demonstrated through the existence of regional imbalances in development, when examining national markets where perfect mobility of factors of production exists.[115]

Moreover, recent empirical research demonstrates that the impact of FDI on the development process is uncertain. In a sample of 183 foreign investment projects in some thirty countries over two decades, a majority did provide a positive benefit to host growth and economic welfare. But in a large minority of cases (twenty -five to forty five percent) foreign investment projects had a clear negative impact on host growth and economic welfare. Evidence shows that there is an important distinction between investors producing solely for domestic consumption in the host country and investors using the host country as a site (integrated into the global sourcing network of the parents) from which to strengthen their larger competitive position in world markets. Once the parent investors commit themselves to incorporate the output from a host country into a larger strategy to meet global or regional competition there is evidence of a dynamic "integration effect" which provides newer technology, more rapid technological upgrading, best management practices and high industry standards. (see foreign Direct Investment and Development, Theodore H. Moran, Institute for International Economics , December 1998).

The GATS provides for the abovementioned concerns through covering commercial presence as a mode of supply of services and separate provisions on market access and national treatment to be scheduled as negotiated commitments in the selected sectors and modes of supply. This allows for a process of progressive liberalization of market access adapted to individual country's state of development. In the sectors subject to specific commitment performance requirements could be scheduled as limitations to market access and therefore maintained.

The TRIMs Agreement prohibits those measures which are in contravention of GATT Articles III and XI which essentially disciplines local content and trade balancing requirements. The following paragraphs review the UR negotiations on TRIMs, difficulties with the implementation of the Agreement, importance of maintaining flexibility in relation to performance requirements and incentives, possible issues which could be taken up during the review of the TRIMs Agreement in the context of Article 9. Countries have to decide whether such review would be confined to discussion of performance requirements or would it deal with broader aspects of investment policy such as market access and national treatment.

Background to negotiations on TRIMS

Although investment has often been included among the "new issues" for the future WTO trade agenda, it must be recalled that multilateral principles for investment had been addressed as far back as the 1947-48 Havana Conference. With the failure of the Havana Charter to enter into force, multilateral investment issues were largely addressed in UN fora, notably the Commission on TNCs. However, the investment issue was brought back to the GATT in the early 1980s and was very much a subject for the Uruguay Round negotiations. The preparatory work leading up to the 1982 GATT Ministerial meeting[116] which, in turn, set out the work programme leading up to the Uruguay Round investment measures and trade in services were items for consideration. The initiative by the United States[117] to include investment per se did not enjoy much support and by the time of the Punta del Este meeting it was confined to "trade related investment measures"(TRIMs). Negotiations were supposed to elaborate, as appropriate, further provisions that may be necessary to avoid adverse effects on trade.

Two basic issues separated the participants in the TRIMS negotiations (i) whether the disciplines developed in this area should be limited by existing GATT Articles or expanded to develop an investment regime, (ii) whether some or all TRIMs should be prohibited or should be dealt with on a case-by-case basis demonstration of direct and significant restrictive and adverse effects on trade. In the TRIMs negotiations, certain developed countries, notably Japan and the United States, put forward proposals that implied the negotiation of new rules with respect to various aspects of investment policy, notably incentives and performance requirements.

The United States and Japan were in favour of an international investment regime that would establish rights for foreign investors and reduce constraints on transnational corporations. They believed that TRIMs had adverse trade effects and that this was a sufficient reason to make the case for applying general principles and disciplines to control them e.g. III and XI. The submissions by these countries enumerated a number of regulatory performance requirements adopted by governments of host countries, which were alleged to have trade-distorting and inhibiting effects, such as requirements for local content, export performance, trade balancing, domestic sales, manufacturing, product mandating, remittance restrictions, technology transfer, licensing and local equity. Their position was certain TRIMs should be categorically prohibited, and a test should be established to evaluate the adverse trade effects of other TRIMs, that a framework should be developed to phase out prohibited TRIMs.[118] The proposal by Japan also drew attention to the need for inclusion of both national and local government measures. Incentives granted by governments were included by the U.S because they allegedly led to distortions of trade flows.

The EC[119] focused on measures that had a direct and significant restrictive impact on trade and a direct link to existing GATT rules identifying eight TRIMs that met the criterion of being directed at the exports and imports of a company with the immediate objective of influencing its trading patterns (local content, manufacturing, export performance, product mandating, trade balancing, exchange restrictions, domestic sales, and manufacturing limitations concerning components of the final product). A distinction was made between the general issue of foreign direct investment, and the more specific issues of trade-related investment measures and therefore opposed the inclusion of right of establishment in the negotiations. They believed that direct and indirect trade effects of investment measures should be evaluated separately. Indirect trade effects in their opinion were caused by TRIMs related to licensing, local equity and technology transfer requirements, remittances and exchange restrictions, and investment incentives. TRIMs with indirect effects would be subject to consultation and dispute settlement procedure.

Developing countries called for strict adherence to the mandate and for limiting the negotiating exercise to the effects of investment measures or regulations that had a direct and significant negative effect on trade.[120] On the basis of an effects test, developing countries wanted to ensure that there could be no a priori presumption that investment measures were inherently trade restrictive or distorting. The effects test would require credible evidence based on a case-by- case examination of investment measures (as in the FIRA panel case) to establish whether a direct and significant adverse effect on trade existed. In such cases a clear causal link would need to be demonstrated between the measure and the alleged effect; and if such a link was established, the nature and impact on the interests of the affected party would need to be assessed and appropriate ways and means would have to be found to deal with the demonstrated adverse effects, including in relation to the treatment accorded when development aspects outweigh the adverse trade effects.[121] Developing countries also argued that they used TRIMs to offset the anti-competitive practices of the transnational corporations, and that these should be addressed(Annex I). Such measures were considered outside the scope of the negotiating mandate by the United States and the EC.

A group of like-minded developing countries were successful in preparing a joint counter proposal, which had the effect of blocking the negotiation of new rules on investment and confining the TRIMs agreement to a restatement of existing GATT rules drawing upon the results of GATT jurisprudence. In fact, the TRIMs Agreement actually permits developing countries, and particularly least developed countries to maintain prohibited TRIMs to year 2000 and 2002 respectively with the possibility of seeking extensions in individual cases. The real trade off in the TRIMs agreement was the decision to consider in 1999, the possibility that it could be "complemented with provisions on investment policy and competition policy". This symmetry was established at the insistence of developing countries which saw TRIMs as a means of pre-empting the use of certain anti-competitive practices by TNCs.

Implementation of the TRIMs Agreement

The TRIMs Agreement establishes the extent to which multilateral trade obligations cover investment measures. It is basically a codification of the findings in the FIRA case. It prohibits those measures which are prohibited by GATT Articles III and XI. The developing countries were thus successful in preventing the extension of trade obligations into the field of investment, and the incorporation of principles such as "right of establishment" and "national treatment" for investors into the trading system. Countries maintain their sovereign rights to regulate foreign direct investment so long as the TRIMs Agreement is not infringed. The Preamble of the TRIMs Agreement recognizes that certain investment measures can cause trade-restrictive and distorting effects.

The scope and coverage of the Agreement is circumscribed by Article 1 which stipulates that it relates to trade in goods only. It should be noted that the General Agreement on Trade in Services (GATS) covers investment liberalization as it includes commercial presence as one of the modes of supply of services, defined in Article XXVIII of GATS as "any type of business or professional establishment, including through the constitution, acquisition or maintenance of a juridical person, or the creation or maintenance of a branch or a representative office within the territory of a Member for the purpose of supplying a service".

Article 2 on National Treatment and Quantitative Restrictions in the TRIMs Agreement limits the prohibited TRIMs to those inconsistent with the provisions of GATT Article III on National Treatment on Internal Taxation and Regulation and Article XI on General Elimination of Quantitative Restrictions. The Agreement therefore recognizes that certain measures do violate GATT Articles but does not expand on the existing disciplines. The Annex to the Agreement contains an illustrative list of such TRIMs which are mandatory or enforceable under domestic law or under administrative rulings, or compliance with which is necessary to obtain an advantage.

An "advantage" is not defined in the Agreement and therefore its scope could be wide including, *inter alia*, subsidies. It has been argued that the TRIMS Agreement has interpreted the obligations of GATT Article III and XI to discipline measures which tie performance requirements to the provision of incentives. The Agreement on Subsidies and Countervailing Measures is also of interest in this respect as it disciplines trade-promoting investment measures or incentives. Moreover, it refers specifically to subsidies tied to export performance and domestic sourcing requirements in Article 3, paragraph 3.1: "Except as provided in the Agreement on Agriculture, the following subsidies, within the meaning of Article 1 above, shall be prohibited: (*a*) subsidies contingent, in law or in fact, whether solely or as one of several other conditions, upon export performance, including those illustrated in Annex 1; (*b*) subsidies contingent, whether solely or as one of several other conditions, upon the use of domestic over imported goods". Measures or programmes usually referred to as investment incentives could be legally defined as subsidies subject to the disciplines of the Subsidies Agreement (SCM). The SCM provides for non-actionable subsidies which have been mentioned during negotiations on investment: research and procompetitive development activities, regional aids, and adaptation of existing plants to new environmental measures.

The TRIMs Agreement does not give a definition of a TRIM or an objective test for identifying such measures. It is therefore for the notifying country to judge which of its TRIMs are illegal under the Agreement. Although the TRIMs Committee has entered into operation and many notifications and measures have been examined, there is still no clear guidance given on which measures are, strictly speaking, prohibited. There are naturally different interpretation and differences of opinion. It is clear that export performance requirements remain permissible under the WTO Agreements.[122] Most developing countries have export requirements and they are normally mandatory for most investments in free trade zones or exclusive economic zones. Several other measures which may appear controversial can be maintained by host countries because there are no explicit legal prohibitions against them.

Difficulties faced by developing countries in the implementation of TRIMs

The implementation of the TRIMs Agreement has posed the following problems for developing countries: (i) the identification of TRIMs disciplined by the Agreement and their timely notification to WTO, (ii) importance of local content requirements in development policies of several countries in particular in relation to the automotive sector, (iii) adequacy of the transitional period for phasing out of the TRIMs (iv) the need to rethink the approach taken in the TRIMs Agreement by concentrating on direct and significant adverse effects on trade, rather than outright prohibition of certain measures and to provide special and differential treatment in particular key sectors.

The timing of notifications in relation to the provisions of Article 5.1 which requires Members to notify any TRIM of general or specific application inconsistent with the Agreement within 90 days after the entry into force of the WTO has led to difficulties for some developing countries . Some developing countries have taken longer to identify and notify their TRIMS given their institutional constraints. Developed countries are not flexible with respect to the time limit set in Article 5.1. This is the kind of situation that can arise with the negative list approach to market access and national treatment, that is if countries do not include their reservations prior to entry into force they will not be able to do so subsequently. Delaying notification of a measure in the context of benefitting from special and differential treatment should not, therefore, in the view of developing countries, diminish the benefits that should accrue to them in terms of e.g. additional time granted to adjust and implement obligations contained therein. And in their view, the implementation of notification obligation should be linked to concrete technical assistance by developed countries.

The measures which have given rise to requests for clarifications mainly relate to automobile sector, agriculture and general provisions on local content in investment laws. The relationship between TRIMS, SCM, GATT, and Agriculture Agreement also requires clarification. It can be expected that the countries most opposed to TRIMs will initiate litigation in order to determine the frontiers of the Agreement, e.g. case brought against Indonesia in relation to the automotive sector. Developing countries lack the capacity to identify TRIMs used by developed countries particularly at subnational level.

The problems with identifying a measure as a TRIM and the relationship between GATT, TRIMs and SCM have come up in the context of the Indonesia-Certain Measures Affecting the Automobile Industry. Indonesia believed that its National Car Programme which included local content requirements did not constitute a TRIM and therefore withdrew a notification(submitted after the deadline indicated in the Agreement) it had made to the TRIMs Committee on particular aspects of the program and dealt with such measures in the context of the SCM Agreement. Therefore, Indonesia did not claim that disputed measures benefit from the transitional period under Article 5 of the TRIMs Agreement. The panel concluded inter alia that the sales tax and customs duty benefits contingent on meeting local content requirements under the car programmes constitute "advantages" in the meaning of the chapeau of paragraph 1 of the Illustrative List and the local content requirements are TRIMs covered by the List in point (a) and in violation of Article 2 of TRIMs Agreement.

The panel also concluded that the Indonesian tariff and luxury sales tax exemptions (incentives) provided through the National Car Programme are specific subsidies which has caused serious prejudice to the interests of the European Communities within the meaning of Article 5 (c) of the SCM Agreement. This demonstrates that trade-related issues relating to investment incentives can effectively be dealt with through the SCM Agreement.

Since neither GATT case history nor the WTO rules address the wide range of investment policy measures currently in effect in many countries, the status of several of these is unclear. A narrow interpretation of the rules would imply that any measure that is not covered in the TRIMs text, or the Agreement on Subsidies and Countervailing Measures and is not inconsistent with basic GATT principles, would be acceptable or legitimate. But the question is particularly complicated for voluntary programmes since the TRIMs Agreement specifies measures that are "mandatory or enforceable under domestic law or administrative rulings", but it also refers to obtaining an advantage. This "advantage" may not be formally linked to the investment measure concerned.[123] However, Article 6 provides strengthened obligations on transparency in the administration of TRIMs, and TRIMs that are not transparent are likely to face challenges from trading partners.

There is no reference to a case-by-case effects test or measures of subnational levels of government. Article 6, however, does provide for the notification to the WTO secretariat of the publications in which TRIMs may be found, including those applied by regional and local governments and authorities within their territories. Developing countries would also like to include a requirement for establishing adverse effects of a particular TRIM on a case by case basis, particularly given new empirical research which demonstrates concrete benefits accruing to developing countries by use of certain performance requirements. The removal of the particular measure would then be contingent upon such adverse effects being greater than the positive impact of such requirements on development of particular sectors in developing countries.

Developing countries are allowed five years and the least developed countries a seven-year transitional period for eliminating the prohibited TRIMs, which could be extended if they demonstrate particular difficulties in doing so, and taking into account the individual development, financial and trade needs of the members in question. TRIMs introduced less than 180 days before the entry into force of the WTO will not benefit from the transitional arrangements, and members should not modify the terms of any notified TRIM so as to increase the degree of inconsistency with Article 2. Such provisions amount to a standstill on the prohibited TRIMs. The TRIMs text, however, permits TRIMs to be levied on new investors in the transition period to protect existing investors. This addresses a major concern of current investors, particularly in the automotive sector, regarding possible serious disadvantages vis-à-vis new investors. Local content requirements and domestic sourcing are most prevalent in the automotive industry. Many countries experience difficulties in removing such measures in the transitional period. Some consideration needs to be given to the extension of this period for particular developing countries in relation to specific sectors. In the TRIMs Committee the United States requested countries having notified their TRIMs to also notify the measures they were envisaging to phase out such TRIMs. This was strongly opposed by developing countries as no such obligation is contained in the TRIMs Agreement.

Compared to the range of policy instruments at a government's disposal, the TRIMs Agreement does not significantly constrain the ability of any government to regulate foreign direct investment in its territory. However, the import-substituting measures of many developing countries are now more explicitly prohibited. In any event, the above investment measures were inconsistent with GATT principles and could have been challenged in a dispute. The WTO and the single undertaking clarify the application of these obligations to developing countries and transition economies, but further challenges will no doubt be made to establish the exact "frontier" of the prohibition beyond the scope of the "illustrative list".

Pre-Seattle Proposals

Many developing are now reconsidering the length of the transitional period for the TRIMs agreement as reflected in article 5.2 and looked for its extension as one of the 'deliverables' in Seattle. It should also be noted that in the context of Article 5.3 some developing countries have requested an extension of the trasition period. For example the Philippines has requested extension of the trims relating to local content and foreign exchange requirements under the Car, Commercial Vehicle and Motorcycle Development Programmes. Philippines provides explanations inrelation to developments, financial and trade needs particularly the impact of the 1997 Asian financial crisis, several contracted domestic market volume and displacement of workers. The extension would provide them with the indispensable period to institute further structural reforms and to implement enhancement capability programmes. There are also proposals to provide developing countries with another opportunity to notify existing TRIMs measures.It is worthwhile referring to the proposals put forward by India[124] and Brazil in the context of reviewing the TRIMs Agreement, India proposes that:

- The Agreement poses problems both with respect to the limited transition period available for removing TRIMs and the denial of freedom to countries to channel investments in such a manner that fulfils their developmental needs. There is therefore a need to review provisions in the Agreement relating to local content requirements as they affect the industrialisation process in developing countries. India feels that such instruments should remain at the disposition of developing countries as long as their developmental needs demand. Accordingly, the transition period mentioned in article 5.2 needs to be extended.

- Article 5.3, which recognises the importance of taking into account of the development, financial and trade needs of developing countries while dealing with trade related investment measures, has remained inoperative and ineffectual. The provisions of this article must therefore be suitably amended and made mandatory.

- The TRIMs Agreement should be modified to provide developing countries another opportunity to notify existing TRIMs measures, which they would be then allowed to maintain till the end of the revised transition period.

Brazil proposal provides that the disciplines of the TRIMs Agreement disregard obvious structural inequalities among countries which could not have been overcome within the transition period. Solutions would require long-lasting policies and adequate financing for their execution. Developing countries , in the opinion of Brazil must have some flexibility when making use of trade-related investment measures, to attenuate the negative effects of investment cycles, create a hospitable environment for foreign and domestic investors and promote social and economic development, also addressing the situation of impoverished regions. The proposal envisages review of the concepts that led to the acceptance of horizontal and uniform TRIMs disciplines without due consideration to needs and singularities of developing countries. Brazil believes that specific provision should be included to provide flexibility for developing countries.to implement development policies intended to address particularly social, regional, economic and technological concerns that may help reduce the disparities they face vis-à-vis developed countries.

Review of the TRIMs agreement

Article 9 provides for a review of the operation of the Agreement on TRIMs no later than five years after the date of entry into force of the WTO Agreement. During such a review, consideration will undoubtedly be given as to whether the Agreement should be complemented with provisions on investment policy and competition policy. It would appear that the extended list of TRIMS to be disciplined, as well as principles put forward by US namely non-discrimination, right of establishment etc. which were proposed during the TRIMS negotiations (note these were taken up during the MAI negotiations) could be considered as the objective of the negotiations foreseen in TRIMs Article 9 by developed countries.

Developing countries are considering different alternatives which could be pursued during the review process. One alternative is to confine the review to discussions relating to problems of phasing out the prohibited TRIMs and/or extension of the Agreement to include other performance requirements. Another alternative is to deal with broader aspects of investment policy which are appropriate to be taken up in the context of WTO. This could involve the negotiation of GATS style market access and national treatment commitments and/or negotiating disciplines on investment in the context of other Multilateral Trade Agreements. A further view is that any extension of the disciplines on investment should include as a quid pro quo inclusion of competition policy related issues as provided for in the TRIMs Agreement.

Review process confined to performance requirements and incentives[125]

Many developing countries use a combination of investment incentives and performance requirements to pursue a variety of development objectives: to orient resource allocations to sectors considered to have a particular growth potential, to build up a viable domestic private sector, to promote vertical integration, to attract foreign technologies or export-oriented investment, or to improve access to major markets and export marketing capacities. In many cases, moreover, since policy instruments to ensure free domestic competition are not sufficiently effective or enforceable vis-a- vis large foreign enterprises, investment measures are relied upon to correct market distortions created by these enterprises.

A combination of incentives and performance requirements[126] are used to ensure that the flow of investment would involve also transfer of a package of assets conducive to human capital development including managerial skill as well as transfer of hard technology e.g. information processing equipment.

Given the tendency of TNCs to internalize technological assets, developing countries use combinations of incentives and performance requirements to ensure externalization of such assets and domestic capacity building. Therefore, in their view, retaining the flexibility in using these policy tools is of particular importance to sustainable development.[127] The combination of a variety of incentives and performance requirements is aimed at securing a balanced regulation and enhancement of foreign direct investment in the host country.[128] Furthermore, the same mixture can ensure an adequate compromise between the interests of the host country and those of the investor.[129]

The availability of a diverse set of incentives and conditions provides flexibility in negotiations with potential investors, and may allow a bargain to be struck in which an incentive with high value to the investor and low marginal cost to the host country (such as access to the benefit of an existing free-trade zone) is traded for a performance requirement of low marginal cost to the investor but high real or perceived value to the host country (e.g. an agreed commitment for local expenditure on research and development).[130]

The TRIMS , the failed OECD MAI negotiations as well as regional and bilateral have demonstrated that whereas countries are open towards developing disciplines on certain types of performance requirements, they are more reluctant to discipline investment incentives. The draft MAI prohibits a list of performance requirements relating to goods and services which covers measures beyond not only those listed in the TRIMS Agreement, but even beyond those prohibited under Article 1106 of NAFTA. The NAFTA list is supplemented by certain concepts of limitations to market access taken form Article XVI of GATS (e.g. hire a given level of local personnel, to establish a joint venture, to achieve a minimum level of local equity participation) as well as others which are currently permitted under TRIMS and GATS (e.g. transfer of technology requirements, to locate its headquarters for a specific regions or the world market in the territory of that contracting party). The draft MAI provides that a party shall not in connection with the establishment, acquisition, expansion, management, operation or conduct of an investment in its territory of an investor of a party or of a non-party, impose, enforce or maintain any of the requirements listed, or enforce any commitment or undertaking. These provisions would of course limit the flexibility of countries in respect to their industrial policies and could mean that investment would not lead to learning effects and the important externalities in the rest of the economy (e.g. building of domestic capacities through transfer of technology, strengthening of management techniques, human resource development).

GATS legitimizes a list of performance requirements as subjects for liberalization negotiations enumerated in Article XVI. Moreover, it permits developing countries to attach conditions when granting access to their markets in Article XIX. The TRIMS agreement only confirms that local content requirements and some trade balancing requirements are prohibited by GATT, but does not prohibit other performance requirements.[131] In the negotiations on TRIMS, developing countries considered performance requirements necessary to channel FDI according to their national development policy objectives, to offset the preferential treatment/incentives and to offset or preempt the anti-competitive practices of TNCs (see Annex I on RBPs and TRIMs designed to deal with them) .

Recent studies indicate that location of FDI in particular in the automotive, petrochemical and computer/electronic industries has had less to do with comparative advantage than with host governments' forceful use of policies including export subsidies and export performance requirements. The successful use of export performance requirements to build supply capacity in these three sectors demonstrates that it has generated a new structure of internationally competitive production. This puts in question whether it would make sense categorically to prohibit any performance requirement without actually examining whether such a measure had significant and direct adverse effects on trade which outweighed its beneficial effect on development. Local content and trade balancing requirements of developing countries could then be examined on a case by case basis, instead of being prohibited.

Performance requirements which developing countries consider essential for development strategies and therefore need to be maintained, include export performance, a minimum level of local equity, joint venture, hiring of a given level of local/national personnel, transfer of technology, nationality requirement for senior management, achieving a given level or value of production, investment, sales, employment or research and development.

Many developing countries consider that they are hurt by the incentive programmes of developed countries[132] who have the resources to subsidize their industries and to attract investment but have not been able to use the Agreement to enforce their rights. This is clear from the implementation of SCM Agreement where none of the developing countries have been able to make any counter notification in relation to measures of another member having the effects of a subsidy in accordance with Article XVI.1 of GATT, 1994 and Article 25.1 of the SCM. Disciplines, therefore, in the view of developing countries, need to be developed to control these unfair practices.

Consideration of Broader Aspects of Investment Policy

The question arises as to whether a comprehensive set of principles dealing with all aspects of investment policy could appropriately be linked to trade obligations, or whether specific provisions could be elaborated in the Multilateral Trade Agreements to ensure that their objectives were not frustrated by restrictions or conditions on investment. Examples of such obligations could be provisions where denial of right of establishment and national treatment could frustrate trade objectives, for example in the allocation of agricultural tariff rate quotas,[133] or disciplines with respect to subsidy measures which distort the flow of investment, and not just investment measures which distort the flow of trade in goods, could be incorporated into the Agreement on Subsidies and Countervailing Measures. Another possibility which has been suggested is that provision for establishment and national treatment be linked to duty free tariff treatment to reduce the possibility of attracting investment behind a tariff wall. This approach would have the advantage of confining the new trade obligations to those necessary to deal with trade problems, without requiring countries to harmonize their policies across the board with the risks this might entail.

The above considerations suggest that the best approach to dealing with trade and investment issues in the WTO could be to examine the extent to which investment issues are already dealt with in the WTO agreements and the possibility of incorporating additional provisions on investment policy into these Agreements. One approach that could facilitate negotiations could be to disaggregate the MAI approach, in the sense that the various elements lumped together in the MAI could be addressed separately in the trade context. For example, establishment issues are covered by the definition of market access through commercial presence mode of supply in GATS, national treatment is also covered by the GATS- commitments in these areas could be exchanged for reciprocal commitments. Other aspects of the MAI also relate to WTO Agreements such as movement of persons (GATS) performance requirements (TRIMS), and fiscal incentives (Subsidies Agreements).

To maintain the coherence of the international trading system and the balanced results achieved during the Uruguay Round, it would seem preferable to build on the achievements of the Uruguay Round.

Negotiation of GATS style market access and national treatment commitments

The GATS structure ensured that the development objective would be integrated throughout the text of the agreement through provisions providing flexibility for developing countries and ensuring their increased participation in trade in services. The positive list approach to the negotiation of commitments increases the possibility for tradeoffs and allows obtention of reciprocal benefits, thus, facilitating the efforts of developing countries to liberalize their own services sectors. Experience to date suggests that the structure of the

GATS has proven to be of greater utility to developing countries, than declarations in their favour, such as in GATS Article IV. To ensure appropriate balance, any new disciplines in the area of investment would evidently need to provide a structure that would facilitate achievement of reciprocal benefits of liberalization in investment for liberalization in other service sectors or mode of supply or even in goods e.g. tariffs, agriculture.

In the negotiations on the GATS all the impracticabilities of the negative list approach were examined[134] and GATS adopted the positive list approach which facilitates the achievement of reciprocal benefits and reduces the risk of omissions.[135] One particular characteristic of a negative list approach is that new sectors which are rapidly arising as a product of information technologies, could be automatically covered by GATS disciplines, unless explicit action would be taken to exclude them. A negative list approach is thus most appropriate to a context where all parties have subscribed to a common objective, such as in the OECD Codes or in free trade agreements such as NAFTA.

Acceptance of a negative list approach for investment or services would only be coherent if free trade targets were also established for market access in goods. Application of a positive list approach to investment in the area of goods would involve agreeing on a market access article comparable to Article XVI of GATS (which allows for scheduling a list of limitations including performance requirements). Countries could make commitments on market access and national treatment (i.e. post establishment). A separate article comparable to Article IV of GATS and XIX.2 could provide for maintaining incentives and performance requirements for developing countries.

Under the GATS the most significant market access commitments have been obtained in relation to commercial presence, particularly in the post-Uruguay Round negotiations on financial services and basic telecommunications. Negotiations on liberalization through expanding the Schedules of Commitments will involve further commitments in the area of investment. Pursuing negotiations under this framework provides the possibility for trade offs as between services sectors, modes of delivery and trade in goods, which would seem to facilitate a more substantial liberalization. The positive list approach provides flexibility to make market access and national treatment commitments on commercial presence on those sectors where countries wish to attract investment, conditions for the firms benefitting from the access commitment could also be specified. In such a context, liberalization of commercial presence is viewed jointly with development.

It should be noted that the MAI approach (based on NAFTA and US BITs) of providing right of establishment by applying national treatment to the pre-establishment phase does not reflect general practice in most BITs. Moreover, the application of national treatment in respect of entry of foreign investments is far more difficult than its application to trade in goods in terms of establishment of similar situations. The BITs usually provide limitations to national treatment and apply the principle where domestic and foreign investor find themselves in "identical" or "similar situations", or "in like circumstances" or even to " similar activities". The draft MAI provides for application of national treatment and MFN in like circumstances. It deals with issues going beyond strictly market access issues e.g. protection of investment.

Moreover, although it provides obligations for host governments, it does not include disciplines for abusive behaviour of investors. Investors are provided with the possibility to take states to arbitration but governments are supposed to deal with problems they encounter with investors within the context of national legislations.

The question would also arise as to the relationship between any commitments on investment and the commercial presence commitments in the GATS. One could imagine a general investment agreement based on the positive list approach which would basically involve extending GATS to cover investment in goods production. As the distinction between trade in goods and trade in services is difficult to maintain for movement of persons, a certain symmetry could be maintained without drastic revisions to the GATS structure.

Competition policy related issues

The increasing importance of competition policy is related to the fact that although governmental trade measures are increasingly brought under multilateral disciplines, enterprise practices that distort or restrain international trade may be more important than before; the growing integration of the world economy with the consequence that anti-competitive practices have increasingly a transborder dimension and affect more than one country, development of obligations on countries concerning intellectual property and investment, and the thinking that competition policy provides the most appropriate remedy to anti-competitive business practices rather than antidumping rules (the Hong Kong initiative on globalization which proposes the replacement of antidumping rules with competition rules).

Any expansion of the TRIMS Agreement to include other trade-related investment measures should, in the view of developing countries, include in parallel and as a quid pro quo elements of competition policy.[136] These relate in particular to control of restrictive practices for which TRIMS are used by developing countries (See Annex). The provisions of the UNCTAD Set of Multilaterally Agreed Principles and Rules for the Control of Restictive Business Practices, and Draft code of conduct on transnational corporations and transfer of technology could provide elements for disciplines on anticompetitive behaviour.

Developing countries are also interested in issues relating to the effects on competition of important incentives offered by developed countries. International companies are making their locational decisions in the midst of a fierce subsidy war in which locational incentives of more than $50,000-$100,000 per job (as calculated by the OECD) are acting as tie-breakers (see Foreign Direct Investment and Development, Theodore. Moran, Institute for International Economics, December 1998).

A second area of concern is the use of protectionist and investment-diverting trade measures, most notably rules of origin and anti-dumping regulations in a discriminatory and demonstrably distortionary manner. Both EU and NAFTA rules of origin require that a substantial portion of inputs originate in the NAFTA and EU states to qualify for preferential treatment-to protect local industries and to shift foreign investment into member states. A review by the OECD of antidumping cases in Australia, Canada, the EU and the US found that 90 percent of the import sales judged to be unfair would have been legal under corresponding competition standards, that is they would be considered perfectly fair if undertaken by domestic firms making a domestic sale.

Antidumping actions divert investment by generating uncertainty for international firms interested in investing in potential export operations and causing the redeployment of production to the market protected by antidumping regulations. Locational incentives, rules of origin and anti-dumping regulations are used to recast the international economic landscape hindering economic activity from moving along the lines of comparative advantage. The need to offset these investment diverting policies on the part of developed countries explains the crucial role of export subsidies and particular performance requirements in inducing companies to include developing countries in their regional or global sourcing networks.

Although some disciplines on monopolies are included in the GATS, developed countries resisted the inclusion of disciplines on anticompetitive practices. Subsequent negotiations on basic telecommunications demonstrated that there was a need to include competitive safeguards and a reference paper was included in most commitments which included such safeguards.[137] However, some countries appear to be seeking commitment on competition policy issues on a sectoral basis rather than aiming at disciplines applying to all services sectors.

The existing asymmetry between the treatment of disciplines governing government practices and corporate practices would, in the view of developing countries, need to be tackled in future. In the draft MAI, investors are provided with the possibility to take states to arbitration but governments are supposed to deal with problems they encounter with investors within the context of national legislation relating to competition policy.[138]

Differences in the competitiveness of enterprises from different countries may lead to an uneven distribution among countries of the gains and losses from greater competition and this may be exacerbated by the uneven application of competition principles to different sectors or trade measures by multilateral instruments. Developing countries therefore consider that it would be preferable to have uniform and consistent application of competition principles within the context of the international trading system, while allowing for special and differential treatment to compensate for the handicaps which would preven developing country firms from taking full advantage of the new opportunities provided by more competition.

Developing country interests and concern in the area of competition policy which they would like to see reflected in any future disciplines include: (i) the non-discriminatory application of competition legislation might serve developing host countries to remedy their major FDI concerns in case they adopt a liberal FDI regime; (ii) allowing small economies to control possible abuses of dominant positions of TNCs; (iii) exempting SMEs when the impact of their RBPs is insignificant in the relevant market by the application of de minimis rules; (iv) granting time limited exceptions to certain specific dynamic and growth oriented sectors which are deemed to need temporary shielding from full-fledged competitive forces to allow infant industries to progress along the learning process; (v) the extent to which restraints linked to licensing arrangements should be deemed anticompetitive and prohibited, vi) possibility of prohibiting bans of parallel imports under certain conditions; (vi) adoption by governments of substantive provisions to control horizontal and vertical restraints, abuses of dominant positions, export cartels.

Several approaches have been taken to future initiatives in this area: enhanced bilateral arrangements and voluntary convergence of substantive standards where significant international effects exist, establishment of detailed international norms and the creation of a supranational authority for their administration, enhancement of international cooperation of a more binding nature on substantive standards and enforcement which could include improvement of the existing competition related provisions of WTO agreements.

The suggestion has been made that consideration be given to home countries of foreign firms assuming some responsibility for assisting developing countries in establishing their competition machinery, as well as taking action to deal with RBPs by their firms which adversely affect markets of developing countries. To this end, developed countries might take the initiative at the national level to apply their own competition laws to RBPs of their firms affecting international trade and development, along the lines of paragraph E:4 of the Multilaterally Agreed Set of Principles and Rules for the Control of Restrictive Business Practices (this states that "States should seek appropriate remedial or preventive measures to prevent and/or control the use of RBPs within their competence when it comes to the attention of States that such practices adversely affect international trade, and particularly the trade and development of developing countries"), and might also extend to developing countries the terms of bilateral cooperation which a few developed countries already extend to each other (thus accepting an MFN obligation).

This would involve the grant of "negative comity" (commitments to take into account another country's significant interests when investigating or applying remedies against RBPs), "positive comity" (commitments to take enforcement action if considered appropriate in response to requests from another competition authority to undertake enforcement against RBPs in the requestee's territory affecting the requestor's territory) and consultation and cooperation mechanisms to developing countries. Moreover, developed countries might also refrain from extraterritorial RBP control action (or trade-related competition action of the sections 301 type) affecting developing country markets where the conduct in question is lawful under the laws of the developing countries concerned, or where they are making efforts to effectively apply their competition laws in line with internationally agree commitments (para 6 of the SET).

New Proposals on Investment Negotiations

Proposals on negotiations on investment have been put forth by some countries e.g. EC, Japan, Switzerland, Korea ,and Poland in the context of preparations for the Third WTO Ministerial Conference. It is alleged that today the EC is more inclined and ready to curtail its ambitions as to the scope and coverage of the rules it would want to negotiate in the WTO compared to the MAI in OECD. As to protection of investment, EC believes that further reflection is needed on the question of investment protection rules, as rules of this kind, although enshrined in many bilateral or regional investment treaties, in some cases have been subject to unexpected and controversial interpretations. Thus , in their opinion, international rules on FDI should preserve the ability of all host countries to regulate the exercise of economic activity on their territory; but this should be done in a transparent fashion.

Moreover the EC proposes a positive list approach (bottom up), where only those sectors in which a country is ready to undertake commitments are listed in the schedules. EC proposal also provides that the rules must respond to the concerns expressed by civil society, concerning the impact on the environment and labour conditions.

Concluding remarks

Future approaches to dealing with the interface between international trade and investment will have to take account of (*a*) the structure, definitions and commitments including MFN obligations established by GATS, (*b*) the parallelism between competition policy and investment policy set out in the Agreement on TRIMs, (*c*) the initiatives to negotiate plurilateral or regional obligations on investment policy or to extend the scope existing regional arrangements incorporating such provisions, (*d*) treatment of sensitive sector, (*e*) subnational entities, (*f*) need to carve out a list of performance requirements necessary for meeting development objectives (*g*) national security exceptions, investment screening and incentives. They will also have to take account of growing but contradictory pressures for increased multilateral disciplines arising from concerns that (*a*) different treatment of investment as among countries can cause distortions to trade and reduce efficiency, and (*b*) the freedom of enterprises to invest and produce where the fiscal and regulatory systems are least constraining, are resulting in an erosion of the fiscal base of governments and the undermining of social welfare programmes.

In view of the above, any future framework for investment in the WTO needs to allow for trade offs and reciprocal benefits, as well as provide for movement of different factors of production, and permit the maintenance of key development oriented performance requirements by developing countries to maximize the welfare gains from liberalization. The positive list approach will permit flexibility to make market access and national treatment commitments on commercial presence in those sectors where countries wish to attract investment. Moreover, such access could be conditioned with certain performance requirements which could also improve welfare gains by encouraging for example transfer of technology and management techniques.

SUBSIDIES

Interregional Workshop on Development of a Positive Agenda for Future Trade Negotiations, Seoul, Korea, 8-10 June 1999

Ashok Sajjanhar

Introduction

The use of Government Subsidies presents one of the most difficult challenges in international trade rule-making. There is always a fine balance to be achieved domestically in deciding whether to use Subsidies to achieve a certain industrial or trade objective. The most appropriate instrument among the available means of intervention, both from the point of view of economic efficiency and as a means of achieving the most direct political impact, may be in contradiction of fiscal realities and it may need to be carefully circumscribed so as to avoid a rush of similar claims from other quarters in the domestic economy.

Having worked through this policy-making dilemma, the decision makers are thereafter confronted with the international dimension of the problem. Subsidy in various forms - from grants or loan guarantees to tax incentives, for the agricultural sector or for aircraft producers, to promote exports, to lower the costs of capital investment - have some of the most obvious damaging spill-over effects on trading partners. The damage is manifested in economic terms, through displacement of production as well as gives rise to political friction between the two countries. A second balancing act must therefore be performed. On the one hand, Governments have a collective interest in cooperating to limit the adverse effects of Subsidies on international trade as well as to keep their expenditure under tight control. On the other, they have a legitimate interest in seeking to influence economic activity within their jurisdictions. The realm of Subsidy hence provides perhaps the *clearest example of the basic tension in international trade rule making: Exercise of national sovereignty over politically charged decisions of domestic economic policy making coming into conflict with the maintenance of economically optimal conditions for the conduct of international trade.*

Historical perspective

Although subsidies have been utilised as a form of Government incentive since ages, it is only recently that they have come to the forefront of International Trade Policy making. On the other hand, tariffs and import duties which have co-existed with subsidies for an equal length of time, have received detailed and comprehensive treatment as a tool of trade policy as they originated primarily as a source of revenue. On account of this characteristic, foreign relations among several countries, particularly smaller countries, revolved around the levying of tariffs on each others' products and negotiating over tariff levels with other countries. In theory, it should have been possible to conduct such negotiations for subsidies also. From an economic theory point of view, it would have been desirable and more beneficial for international trade and production if this had been done. It is recognised that while tariffs tend to distort both consumption and production patterns, subsidies are less distortive as they only affect production patterns of particular products. As such, Government intervention through subsidies is less distortive for trade and production as compared to tariffs. Further, as noted earlier, tariffs have occupied the primary position of attention of countries because they serve as a source of revenue. Countries have welcomed tariffs not only to meet their expenditure for economic development and growth or protect their industries but also to acquire more territory and maintain law and order.

The basis of current international rules, both multilateral in the General Agreement on Tariffs and Trade/ WTO and, for the most part, bilateral and plurilateral subsidy regimes, is found in Articles VI and XVI of the General Agreement. Long before any multilateral attempts were made to discipline subsidies, at least one country had introduced provisions in its domestic laws to address the subsidy practices of its trading partners. Since the 1890s, the United States has maintained a countervailing duty law in its statutes. Originally applied to offset the benefit of any bounty or grant to exports that were dutiable in the United States, the law was extended to cover domestic subsidies in 1922. The use of this USA countervailing authority however, did not assume a large proportion until it was substantially revised in the Trade Act of 1974.

In the meantime, the negotiations of GATT 1947 attempted to come to grips with this volatile, tricky subject. Initially Article XVI which sets out the basic rules to discipline subsidies contained only one paragraph on notification and consultation provisions. By contrast, Article VI which authorises the imposition of countervailing (and anti-dumping) duties represented a more elaborate attempt at the time to delineate remedies based on the application of national law. Article VI.3 stipulates that countervailing duty shall not exceed the amount of a bounty or subsidy granted directly or indirectly on the manufacture, production or export of a product. Article VI.6 (*a*) goes on to require a determination of material injury to domestic industry prior to imposition of a countervailing duty. It is interesting to observe that in the absence of or inability to reach an Agreement on the issues relating centrally to the international discipline on subsidies, negotiations quickly resorted to the authorisation of counter-measures to be applied in the first instance unilaterally. Further efforts to address subsidies more directly led to extensive amendments of Article XVI in 1955, prohibiting export subsidies on non-primary products and setting out trade effects concepts in an attempt to limit the use of subsidies on the export of primary products. In 1960, further elaboration was provided through an illustrative list of export subsidies.

The provisions of Articles XVI and VI were drafted at a time when economic policy formulation was a more straightforward exercise than it has since become. It was much easier and far less dangerous in those times to employ a term like "subsidy" in an international agreement without even defining it. Government policies may have been as inconsistent and non-transparent then as they are now, but the kinds of subsidies that most concerned policy makers at the time were more along the lines of bounties or grants to stimulate the production of specific goods. The simple problem of subsidies was given the simple solution: countervailing duties up to the amount of subsidisation. In apparent recognition of the fact that not all subsidies affect international trade adversely - or perhaps as a sort of compensation for the lack of definition of what constitutes a trade-distorting subsidy- another simple, undefined term "material injury" was imposed as a pre-condition for levying countervailing duties.

The USA Trade Act of 1974 contained significant amendments to the American countervail regime, the effect of which was to lend an impetus to the negotiations on subsidies/countervail issues in the Tokyo Round. The most important change in the US law was to make automatic the private right of action in seeking countervail redress. This in turn, led to a dramatic increase in the number of countervail cases brought by the United States and hence escalated international concern appreciably.

The negotiations on subsidies and countervailing duties considered by many to be the key element in the Tokyo Round Negotiations as a whole sought to up date and codify the obligations and provisions which had been maintained by countries like the United States. The United States was required to conform to GATT Article VI by incorporating an injury test in its countervailing duty law in return for more stringent multilateral discipline on subsidies.

It was one of the stated objectives of the United States, Australia and Canada in the Tokyo Round that there should be more stringent rules to limit export subsidies on agricultural products.

The Tokyo Round Code of 1979 marked a broader attempt to codify subsidy disciplines internationally and at the same time to clarify the rules governing the countervail remedy. While described as an Agreement to interpret Articles VI, XVI and XXIII, it represented a far more comprehensive treatment of all of the elements relating to the field of subsidies, both procedural and substantive. In the area of export subsidies, it introduced the concept of price undercutting in Article 10.3. Beyond export subsidies, the negotiators tried to set out guidelines that would justify the use of subsidies to achieve certain objectives as stipulated in Article 11.1, but conditioned these by exhorting signatories to avoid adverse trade effects in the subsidies practices. On the remedies side, Article 6 elaborated significantly the standards to be met in the determination of material injury based on an examination of all relevant economic factors, and a demonstration that the subsidised imports were the cause of injury. Even more significant was the acceptance by the United States that they would apply the injury standards set out in the agreement to other signatories of the Code. Previously, the United States had claimed grandfathering rights to the injury obligations in GATT Article VI on the ground that their countervail law pre-dated the GATT.

The 1979 Subsides Code was essentially the result of compromise between two largely conflicting interests. On one side it reflected the concern, felt most strongly by the United States but shared in some measure by many countries, to limit what they saw as damage unfairly inflicted on their trade interests by the subsidies granted by other governments. On the other side, it was meant to respond to the belief that the threat or use of countervailing duties had too often been unfairly used, particularly by US industry, as an auxiliary means of harassing and limiting imports. Unfortunately, it failed to respond adequately to either set of concerns.

Hardly had the Agreement on Subsidies and Countervail measures come into effect before its rules were put to the severest of tests in some of the most contentious dispute settlement cases to be brought before the GATT. Most notably these related to the agriculture subsidy wars between the European Community and the United States. A brief over-view of some of the major cases reveals the inadequacy of these rules, particularly given the lack of precision in bringing the trade effects standards into play.

The first case related to the US demand to obtain redressal against the grain subsidies provided by the European Community. The complaint filed by the US in 1981 claimed that the EC subsidies on the export of wheat flour resulted in the EC having more than an equitable share of world trade in that product and in prices materially below those of other suppliers in the same market, in violation of Articles 10.1 and 10.3 of the Code. The United States further claimed that these subsidies were causing nullification and impairment of benefits to the United States under the GATT and serious prejudice to their interests in terms of Article 8 of the Code.

The panel established under the Dispute Settlement provisions of the Code considered the EC export refunds to be a form of subsidy subject to the terms of GATT Article XVI as interpreted by the Code. The panel found that the EC share of world exports of wheat flour had increased considerably over the period under reference. The panel however was unable to conclude that this resulted in the EC having more than an equitable share in terms of Article 10 because of the highly artificial conditions prevalent in the wheat-flour market. Moreover, the panel concluded that it could not find serious prejudice because of the lack of clarity in the provisions of Article 8.

While explaining its findings, the panel noted that the effectiveness of the legal provisions under consideration was highly unsatisfactory and suggested that relevant provisions of the Code be made more operational, stringent and effective in their application to find solution to the problems presented by these types of export subsidies.

This case was followed by another major dispute involving the same players over the effects on EC pasta export of the EC variable levy on wheat. In this case, the panel found for the United States and the EC blocked adoption of the report in the GATT Council.

In 1988, the United States requested the establishment of a panel to consider the effects of EC subsidies to its oilseed processors. The United States alleged that the granting of subsidies for the purchase of EC produced oilseeds that were not available for purchases of the like imported product, caused nullification and impairment of tariff concessions granted by the EC pursuant to Article II of the GATT, and the EC regime accorded imported products less favourable treatment than to products of EC origin in violation of Article III. The oilseeds panel found for the United States, but based its finding on a narrow application of the national treatment principle, rather than on the evidence presented regarding trade effects.

The United States, in particular, always felt that the code did not go far enough in limiting subsidies, and quite soon found, when it complained formally about practices which it though were covered by the code, that other participants disagreed and that it could not gain acceptance of its views through dispute settlement procedures. Other countries on their part, found that the new countervailing duty rules failed to end what they saw as harassment of their exports to the United States which continued to be by far the largest user of such duties. Both sides therefore brought to the Uruguay Round negotiations on subsidies, essentially the same conflicting concerns that had motivated them in the Tokyo Round. The most important difference in the new negotiations was that the United States convinced that the code had failed because its rules had concentrated on limiting the effects of subsidies, now sought to limit the use of subsidies themselves. But another difference also helped to push the negotiations toward a successful conclusion. Almost all governments were increasingly conscious of the burden which subsidies placed on their national budgets and taxpayers, and of the risk that any subsidy introduced to give a competitive advantage would only be matched by other countries, in, as United States put it, "a self-defeating spiral".

By the time of the launch of the Uruguay Round in 1986, the agenda for the subsidies element of negotiations was fairly obvious and clear. High on the list was the need to address the failings of the serious prejudice provisions of the Tokyo Round Code that had become apparent through the dispute settlement proceedings. These countries felt that the solution lay in strengthening and extending the scope of the prohibition on export subsidies. Others, notable among them the European Communities, advocated an approach based on a clear definition of the term subsidy and the elaboration of trade effects standards. Nearly, all the participants felt that improvements were required to the dispute settlement mechanism provided for in the GATT and in the Tokyo Round Code. Finally, the increasing recourse to domestic countervailing duties gave rise to concerns on the part of a broad range of countries, particularly developing countries, with constraining the scope of application of countervail and with the transparency and procedural fairness of countervailing duty proceedings. Developing countries also demanded that keeping in view their limited possibility of providing subsidies to the domestic producers and industry, as well as the beneficial effects of subsidies on their production and exports, appropriate flexibility and freedom be provided to them to grant, production and export subsidies. Developing countries also demanded that their products not be subjected to countervailing duties as their products constitute only a small proportion of total imports into large markets. They demanded that provisions be introduced in the Agreement on de-minimis margin of subsidisation, de-minimis market share etc. below which no countervail investigations should be initiated or, if initiated, should be immediately terminated. They also demanded to have clearer, fairer and more predictable laws and rules for calculation of the amount of subsidisation and determination of countervailing duties. Provisions of subsidies at the sub-federal level as well as dual pricing of raw materials used in production of goods also became important issues for the negotiations.

The European Community argued during the negotiations that the group should try to resolve the key questions left unanswered by the Tokyo Round. For instance: what measures are to be regarded as subsidies - only those that involve a financial charge on government (the EC and Japanese view) or also measures which in practice give a special benefit to the recipient? When are subsidies potentially trade-distorting, and hence potentially actionable ? How should they be measured?

The WTO Agreement on Subsidies and Countervailing Measures

The Agreement on Subsidies and Countervailing Measures reflects a carefully negotiated balance between more rigorous disciplines on subsidies and reforms of countervailing duty procedures and remedies. The Agreement addresses two separate but closely related topics: multilateral disciplines regulating the provision of subsidies, and the use of countervailing measures to offset injury caused by subsidised imports. Multilateral disciplines are the rules to determine whether or not a subsidy may be provided by a member. They are enforced through invocation of the WTO dispute settlement mechanism. Countervailing duties are a unilateral instrument, which may be applied by a Member after an investigation by that Member and a determination that criteria set forth in the Agreement have been satisfied.

Article 1: The definition of Subsidy

The most important achievement of the Uruguay Round negotiations is, the inclusion, for the fist time in any multilateral trade agreement, of a definition of subsidy.

Article 1 of the Subsidy Agreement defines the term subsidy (regardless of whether it is actionable or not) as applying to either of the two situations.

The first is a financial contribution by a Government or a public body within the territory of a Member if:

♦ The Government practice involves a direct transfer of funds (e.g. grants, loans and equity infusions) or potential direct transfers of liabilities (e.g. loan guarantees);

♦ Government revenue that is otherwise due is foregone or not collected (e.g. fiscal incentives such as tax credits);

♦ The Government provides goods or services other than general infrastructure, or purchases goods;

♦ The Government makes payments to a funding mechanism that carries out, or entrusts or directs a private body to carry out, one or more of the type of functions, illustrated in (*a*) to (*c*) above, which would normally be vested in the government and the practice, in no real sense, differs from practice normally followed by governments.

The second is any form of income or price support in the sense of Article XVI of the GATT.

For the practice to qualify as a subsidy in either situation, it must confer a benefit. Perhaps the most significant aspect of Article 1 is not included in the definition: **any government practice that does not meet one of the four criteria laid out therein cannot be considered a subsidy for the purposes of the Agreement.**

A key feature of the definition of subsidy is the further requirement that a benefit be conferred on the recipient. The concept of benefit is related to the provisions of Article 14 on the calculation of the amount of a subsidy. Article 14 is constructed in the negative, in that it sets out a number of tests that define circumstances in which a benefit shall not be considered to exist. It is important to note that Article 14 governs the calculation of the amount of a subsidy only for the purposes of countervailing duties. The quantification of subsidies for the purposes of serious prejudice is handled in a different fashion.

Article 2: Specificity:

For a subsidy to be countervailable, it must be found to be specific. Article 2 of the Subsidies Agreement provides that a subsidy is specific if it is explicitly limited to an enterprise or industry or group of enterprises or industries ("certain enterprises") within the jurisdiction of the granting authority.

Article 2 states that if the legislation or the granting authority explicitly limits the subsidy to certain enterprises, the subsidy is specific. The language tracks the de jure specificity analysis currently conducted by the US Department of Commerce (US DOC). However Article 2 provides that if the eligibility is limited based on explicit, verifiable and objective criteria (i.e. criteria or conditions which are neutral, do not favour certain enterprises over others, are economic in nature, and are horizontal in application), the programme is not specific so long as eligibility is automatic and the criteria are strictly adhered to.

Even if the programme appears to be non-specific, a member may determine whether the programme is de facto specific if there is reason to believe the programme may, in fact be specific. In such analysis, the investigating authority may consider the following factors:

- use by a limited number of certain enterprises;

- predominant use by certain enterprises;

- the grant of disproportionately large amounts of subsidy to certain enterprises; and

- the manner in which discretion is exercised by administering authorities.

The de facto analysis is similar to current USDOC practices. However the Subsidies Agreement puts restrictions on the application of this analysis not found in US law or practice. Specifically, the Agreement provides that in determining de facto specificity, the investigating authorities should take account of the diversification of economic activities in the subsidising country and the length of time the programme has been in operation.

Article 2.2 states that a programme available only to certain enterprises within a designated geographic region of the granting authority's jurisdiction is specific. This represents a significant lessening of discipline from the Dunkel Draft which made all subsidies by sub-national governments, even if available to all enterprises within a certain area of the jurisdiction, specific.

The regional subsidy issue was raised by the European Community and several developing countries who were particularly concerned that rules should bound not only central Governments but also, in federal states such as United States, Canada and Australia, governments of provinces, states and other sub-federal units which had resources and authority that in other countries were reserved only for central governments. It was argued that subsidies by regional or local governments were no different in their effect from central government subsidies and should, if they had an effect on international trade, be disciplined in the same way. Disciplines on regional subsidies, in the Dunkel Text were included under Article 2 on specificity by which they would fall under the prohibited or actionable categories. However, in the final text, discipline on regional subsidies is much weaker and ineffective as compared to the original provisions as it provides that a subsidy "limited to *certain enterprises* located within a designated geographical region" within the jurisdiction of the granting authority shall be specific.

Article 2.3 states that any prohibited subsidy as defined in Article 3 (including low-cost loans contingent upon export performance, transportation rates more favourable for export shipments than for domestic shipments, and the excessive remission of taxes upon export) is specific. This makes explicit an implicit assumption of the Tokyo Round Code that the export subsidies enumerated in the illustrative list annexed to the Code are specific.

Finally, Article 2 requires that any determination of specificity must be "clearly substantiated" on the basis of positive evidence. This final require-ment of positive evidence is a significant departure from current US practice. Currently, the US DOC presumes specificity unless positive evidence to the contrary is provided. The Subsidies Agreement changes this presumption to one of non-specificity.

Article 3: Prohibited Subsidies:

In the Tokyo Round Code, only export subsidies are prohibited. The Subsidies Agreement expands this prohibition to include both export subsidies and subsidies, the receipt of which is at least in part, contingent upon the use of domestic over imported goods.

This latter category significantly expands the definition of actionable subsidies. Under the Tokyo Round Agreement, no Code discipline is explicitly available against import substitution subsidies because such subsidies are not prohibited. Moreover, under US law, an import substitution subsidy would not be countervailable merely because it favoured domestic goods over imports. Under US statute, the practice would have to provide a specific, non-commer-cial benefit to a certain enterprise or enterprises to be countervailable. By con-trast, the language of Article 3 of the Subsidies Agreement might allow an import substitution subsidy to be countervailable regardless of whether it was either *de jure* or de facto specific or whether it provided a non-commercial benefit.

It would be observed that provisions of Article 3 are applicable both to developing and developed countries. This is a significant change from the Tokyo Round Code. In the Tokyo Round Code, the developing countries were permitted to maintain export subsidies. This flexibility has however been withdrawn from developing countries under the provisions of Article 3. More-over another potential wide ranging and compulsory provision has been added which would make it very difficult for developing countries to provide domes-tic production subsidies to promote the growth and development of their industry and economy. The argument on the basis of which this provision was introduced in the Agreement was that such subsidies are in any case violative of Article III of the General Agreement as had been determined by the findings of several panels particularly by the FIRA panel between USA and Canada. Moreover, prohibition of such action by the Governments had already been agreed to and accepted in the illustrative list in the Trims Agreement under clarification of Rules on Article III of the GATT. The developing countries were persuaded to accept this additionality in the list of prohibited subsidies on the specific understanding and commitment that greater flexibility and freedom would be made available to them towards utilisation of subsidies in specific provisions which would be introduced for developing countries in the context of the Agreement. As would be observed from the discussion below, this hope and confidence of the developing countries for a better and more development friendly regime in the area of Subsidies has to a large extent been belied.

Article 6: Serious Prejudice:

The efforts in the Uruguay Round Negotiations to develop a meaningful multilateral subsidy discipline partly flowed from a desire to create an alternative to the application of countervailing duties. This concern dictated a multilateral mechanism that was sufficiently attractive to Governments as a means of addressing trade friction, that they might use it in place of the countervail mechanism favoured by domestic industries. Such a direct approach holds the potential of avoiding some of the international political friction inherent in countervail proceedings. Here subsidy complaints are arbitrated unilaterally in the first instance with subsequent recourse to GATT dispute settlement in the event a subsidising government believes that domestic laws have been applied in a fashion that is inconsistent with multilateral rules.

The serious prejudice provisions of the Subsidies Agreement have made a start in this direction. Complaints that might otherwise be the subject of countervail proceedings may be brought to the WTO on the basis that subsidies have resulted in prices that undercut, depress or suppress those of unsubsidized like products, or result in lost sales (Article 6.3{c}). To support this complaint mechanism, the Agreement contemplates an information gathering process similar to that employed in countervail proceedings (set out in Annex V) and imports some of the procedural devices used in domestic countervail investigations, for example the drawing of adverse inferences from instances of non-co-operation by any party involved in the information gathering process (Annex V, paragraphs 7,8, and 9).

The main thrust of the Uruguay Round serious prejudice provisions, however, is to address effects of subsidies that are manifested in third country markets and in the home market of the subsidising country in situations in which countervailing duty remedies are not available. The Tokyo Round Code attempted to address these types of trade effects, but the inadequacies of the rules themselves and the lack of procedures to apply any remedy made the so-called Track-II provisions difficult for panels to work with in practice. Filling the resulting gaps in disciplines was a key objective for many countries going into the Uruguay Round negotiations and the Subsidies Agreement has gone some way toward achieving this.

The Agreement makes it clear that serious prejudice may be caused, and remedies sought, where subsidies to domestic producers displace imports or impede the progress of imports into the domestic market. The Agreement similarly provides for serious prejudice cases to be brought to the WTO where subsidies have displaced or impeded another country's export into third-country markets. This displacement or impeding effect of subsidies is further defined for cases of exports into third country markets (although not for cases involving home market effects) to include situations where the market share of the subsidised product has increased, or even where it has remained constant when it would have declined but for the effect of the subsidy, or even where it has declined but at a slower rate than would have been the case in the absence of the subsidy.

The serious prejudice provisions of the Agreement contain an important legal safeguard against abuse of the mechanism (one that is lacking in some domestic trade laws) in the form of a list of situations in which serious prejudice shall not be admitted to exist. This list includes, for example, situations where a decline in exports is voluntary, due to autonomous market decisions by firms diverting trade from that market, or where natural disasters or other force majeure are the cause of the trade disruption.

The Agreement offers an additional element in the bringing of a serious prejudice complaint through Article 6.1(a) which sets a threshold value of subsidisation at 5% ad valorem. Any subsidy that is shown to exceed this threshold is automatically deemed to be causing serious prejudice, unless the subsidising country can prove that none of the grounds for a serious prejudice complaint exist. The effect of this provision is to reverse the burden of proof regarding the existence of trade effects for any subsidy above 5% putting the subsidising country in the position of proving to the panel that neither displacement nor impedance has occurred in its home market or in export markets that prices have not been undercut, depressed or suppressed; and that sales have not been lost as a result of the subsidy. This provision offers countries, adversely affected by relatively large subsidies, the option of bringing an action based on the size of the subsidy alone, leaving the trade effects standards to be argued in the negative by the subsidising country in its defence.

The Agreement specifies that, for the limited purposes of determining whether the 5% threshold has been met, the size of the subsidy shall be calculated based on the cost to the granting government. This was intended to soften the blow that some participants in the negotiation felt the threshold would have, since this methodology could yield a smaller amount of subsidy than a comparison with the commercial cost of borrowing. The latter standard is provided for in Article 14 of the Agreement for purposes of calculating the amount of subsidy in countervailing duty cases and gives a more meaningful economic measure of a subsidy's potential for trade distortion.

It may be mentioned that there were a wide range of ideas on how the "dark amber" category of "non-prohibited but countervailable or otherwise actionable subsidies" (Article 6.1) be treated in the Agreement. One major difference of opinion, with the United States, Australia and New Zealand on the one side and most other countries opposed to them, concerned the long standing issue of how a subsidy would be measured. Most of the countries saw a subsidy as involving a "charge on the public account". The United States and its allies wanted the concept of subsidy to be extended to cover other measures that gave benefits to their recipients: for example, measures that restricted exports of particular inputs, with effect of making those inputs available cheaply to domestic producers in the country concerned than to producers elsewhere. The majority view remained that a subsidy had to involve a transfer of funds from public sources to the recipient either through direct subsidy or a concession on taxation otherwise due and that any wider definition could open the door to the subsidy rules being used as a general purpose mechanism for trying to solve all problems in international trade and to offset any government measures in support of its traders and producers. The United States also demanded that the number of specific domestic subsidies including grants to cover operative losses, direct forgiveness of debts and loan guarantees and equity capital provided at less than the Government cost should be covered in the list of prohibited subsidies. These measures are covered under Article VI in the "dark amber" category. The figure of 5% *ad valorem* subsidisation was arrived at through negotiations between the United States and the European Community in the final stages of negotiation in 1993. This figure is not based on any economic rationale, but as is usually the case, represents a figure to which both the parties could grudgingly agree to.

In order to ensure that determination of serious prejudice does not lend itself to subjective findings, detailed guidance is provided on arriving at such a determination. Remedies are provided in Article 7 for consultation among members, establishment of panels and other procedures in the event of injury to domestic industry, nullification or impairment of benefits or serious prejudice.

Article 8: Non-Actionable Subsidies:

The creation of a category of non-actionable subsidies in the Agreement marked a major departure from previous multilateral negotiations on subsidies. It is a counterpart to the "red light" prohibition of certain subsidies contained in Article 3. Any subsidy falling within one of the three non-actionable categories of Article 8 cannot be subjected to countervailing duties or to the Agreement disciplines.

Exemption from countervail and from serious prejudice for certain types of subsidies was a major priority for several participants in the negotiations, particularly, the European Community and Canada (especially with regard to regional development programmes). Driven largely by unhappy and politically charged experiences with US countervailing duty laws, these countries pressed for, and eventually obtained, non-actionable status for certain regional development and research and development subsidies. Environmental subsidies, which had been considered but subsequently dropped from the non-actionable category earlier in the negotiations, were written into the Agreement in a modified form in the last days of the negotiations, largely at the behest of Mexico.

It is important to recognise that the extent of subsidisation possible under the criteria set out in Article 8.2 of the Agreement is likely to be quite limited. The rules regarding regional development subsidies require that they not be specific to any one industry or group of industries within a designated underdeveloped region. Similarly, as regards environmental subsidies, it is unlikely that the technical and legal conditions for non-actionable status will be met by any large subsidy programme. Recognition of this may explain, in part, why many countries that initially strongly opposed non-actionable status for these types of subsidies, agreed to incorporate them in the Agreement in the end.

It however, needs to be noted that both the major proponents of inclusion and deletion of the "green category" viz. EC and USA were able to get what they wanted. The change in the position of the United States on subsidies for research and development, as is explained below, made it more amenable to accept the green categorisation for subsidies for economically disadvantaged regions and for protection of environment. It was also the realisation on the part of United States that without the inclusion of such subsidies in this category, it would not be possible for the Agreement to be accepted by a large number of other countries. Article 6 and 8 were offered as a package after a series of heated and intense negotiations and consultations between the US and the European Community. The United States was able to go back from the negotiating table with the distinct feeling that it had obtained what it had sought out to achieve in Article 6 and although it had agreed to relent on inclusion of the "green category" in the Agreement, the provisions were so stringent that it would be difficult for large programmes to be covered under this category. Moreover, it was also provided that countries would be able to use the green category only after prior notification. The Agreement also contains provisions whereby the Secretariat is enjoined to review a notification at the request of another Member. The Committee is thereafter required to review the findings of the Secretariat and give its determination promptly.

The three category classification of subsidies was not a new idea. The United States had put it forward in the Tokyo Round but had subsequently had misgivings and doubts about it, mainly because of uncertainty whether any subsidy practice could always be considered harmless. In the Uruguay Round negotiations however, this idea gained broad support and agreement right from the initial stages of the negotiations. It also became clear to the United States that it would be impossible for it to achieve agreement on a broad degree of prohibition of some categories of subsides and more stringent rules on the question of determination of serious prejudice unless it was willing to be flexible on the question of the green category.

Under Article 9, if such a programme is found by the Committee to result in serious adverse effects to the domestic industry, it would be necessary for the programme to be modified failing which countervail action would be authorised.

The provisions governing non-actionable status for research and development subsidies, which had been an important objective for the European Community from the outset of the negotiations, underwent a significant transformation in the final stages of the negotiations. This came about as a result of an unusual coincidence between an ideological shift in the leadership of one of the two most influential participants in the negotiations when most of the other participants had key, unmet objectives of their own and could afford to view the US demands on research and development as relatively low-cost. With the 1992 election of President Clinton, a new US policy advocating Government partnership with industry to develop "strategic technologies" and enhance the international competitiveness of US manufacturers emerged. As the Uruguay Round drew to a close in late 1993, the Clinton administration attempted to eliminate potential multilateral constraints on its domestic policy agenda by negotiating greater latitude under the GATT for R&D subsidies.

This shift evidently reflected the belated concern within the Clinton Administration over the effect that the 1994 Agreement could have on its R&D agenda. To appease critics who favoured the old US approach, the Agreement requires the WTO Committee on Subsidies and Countervailing Measures to review the R&D rules within eighteen months of the Agreement's entry into force. Members dissatisfied with this provision could therefore press for its revision by mid 1996. The criteria for research and development subsidies were thus enlarged significantly, both in terms of the types of activities eligible and the percentage of costs that could be subsidised. The result of non-actionable status for a potentially greater amount of subsidisation are arguably in a more contentious area of economic policy making, than is the case with the other two types of non-actionable subsidies.

It may be noted that both the numerical limits and the definitions in the WTO Agreement are considerably broader than the R&D green light category in the Dunkel Draft (which allowed assistance only up to 25 and 50% for cost of pre-competitive development research and cost of industrial research as compared to 50 and 75% in the final Agreement). Moreover, the Dunkel Draft stopped well short of allowing assistance for creation of a prototype.

The Subsidies Agreement is quite different from US practice regarding assistance for R&D. The United States currently will countervail assistance for R&D if it is specific and provides a non-commercial benefit, unless the results of the R&D are publicly available to all who choose to use those results.

The other category of non-actionable subsidies concerns aid to disadvantaged regions within the territory of a Member given pursuant to a general framework of regional development. For the subsidy to be non-actionable, each disadvantaged region must be a clearly designated, contiguous geographic area with a definable economic and administrative identity and must be determined to be disadvantaged based on explicit, verifiable, neutral and objective criteria.

The other non-actionable assistance covered in Article 8 is the subsidy to adapt to new environmental requirements so long as the assistance is limited to 20% of the cost of the necessary adaptation and is given on a one time only basis. This was the result of a last minute Mexican proposal, drawn from a 1989 EC proposal, that the United States was unable to block because its credibility in opposing green light status had been shredded by its changing stand on R&D subsidies.

To be considered non-actionable, green light subsidies must be notified in advance to the Committee on Subsidies. The Committee, upon request, will review the practice to determine if the requisite conditions have been met. Even if the conditions of Article 8 have been met, if a Member has reason to believe that its domestic industry has suffered serious adverse effects from another Member's green light programmes, that Member may request consultations and review by the Committee. If the Committee's recommendations are not followed, the Committee would then authorise the injured Member to take counter-measures.

It may be noted that no notification of subsidies under Article 8 has been received which would imply that no green subsidy has been introduced since the Agreement came into the force. There might be several explanations for such a situation. Firstly, Article 8.3 states that such notifications should be made in advance of implementation of the subsidy programmes which meet the relevant green light criteria. This would seem to deny the opportunity of notifying pre-existing subsidies, and there may be enough ambiguity about what would constitute a new programme to act as a disincentive against the simple re-enactment and notification of existing subsidy programmes which Members may believe are of a non-actionable character. Secondly, footnote 35 to Article 10 of the Agreement makes it clear that a Member need not notify a subsidy to the Committee under the green light provisions in order to mount a "green light defence" of that programme if it is investigated in a countervailing proceeding or challenged under the dispute settlement provisions. Therefore, some WTO Members may have concluded that it is preferable to take one's chances and argue a green light case only if a programme is challenged than to go through the intrusive and burdensome process of notifying the programme to the Subsidies Committee in order to earn the green light label. A third reason could be that the details required and expected for making a notification are so enormous that some Members may have concluded that Submitting a notification is more troublesome than it is worth.

In this context the provisions of Article 28 "Existing Programmes" should also be noted. Under this Article, provisions that are inconsistent with the new Agreement must be notified within 90 days of the entry into force of the WTO Agreement for that member country. Until such programmes have been brought into conformity with the Agreement (including notification and approval) they will continue to remain countervailable under United States law. There would hence be some incentive to bring regional aid, research and environmental subsidies into conformity with the criteria and conditions of Article 8 if the country is a significant exporter of the particular product to the US market.

Article 27: Differential and more favourable treatment of developing countries:

Part VIII, Article 27 of the Agreement deals with developing country members and outlines the provisions for special and differential treatment in favour of developing countries. The preambular provision in Article 27, paragraph 27.1 is similar to Article 14.1 of the Tokyo Round Code, in embodying the recognition by members that subsidies may play an important role in economic development programmes of developing countries.

Analysis of the two Articles through comparison of their provisions could lead to the conclusion that the Tokyo Round Code provided greater flexibility for developing countries as regards the maintenance of subsidies for economic development programmes. Article 14.5 of the Tokyo Round Code constituted a "best endeavour" formulation i.e. that a developing country signatory should "endeavour to enter into a commitment to reduce or eliminate export subsidies when the use of such export subsidies is inconsistent with its competitive and development needs". In practice, the flexibility provided by this provision was rendered ineffective in part, through the provisions of Article 19.9 of the Tokyo Round Code relating to non-application of the Agreement, which in practice, means non-application of the material injury test by the United States in applying countervailing duties. In the years immediately following the conclusion of the Tokyo Round negotiations, the United States sought and obtained bilateral commitments for phase-out and elimination of particular subsidy practices which the developing countries, the new signatories to the Code, claimed to have been instituted in pursuance of economic development programmes. In accordance with a commitment under Article 14.5 that was undertaken and applied multilaterally in the Tokyo Round Committee on Subsidies and countervailing Measures, developing countries benefited from the provisions of Article 14.6 and 14.8 to the effect that countermeasures in pursuance of Part II and Part VI of the Code would not be instituted against such countries.

It would hence be seen that the flexibility available to the developing country signatories of the Tokyo Round Code was in practice, rather limited in scope owing to the bilateral commitments extracted under threat of non-application by the United States. Under the Uruguay Round Agreement, the flexibility is delineated in more specific terms and all members are required to apply the provisions on countervailing duties, including the injury criteria. The special and differential treatment in favour of developing countries is predicated on specific and legally enforceable provisions for a special dispensation in their favour, including precise and objective "graduation criteria".

The implementation of the Agreement has however, thrown up several issues particularly with respect to the findings given by some of the panels with respect to provisions in this Article. It would appear to be necessary to give a further close look at the provisions to ensure that they provide the necessary flexibility to developing countries for taking measures for meeting their economic development and growth needs.

Some significant highlights of the Agreement as they apply to developing countries are given below:

♦ developing countries which fall into the following categories i.e.: (a) least developed countries and (b) other countries, so long as their GNP per capita remains less than US $ 1,000 per annum, are exempt from the blanket prohibition in Article 3, paragraph 3.1(a), which deals with subsidies contingent, in law or in fact upon export performance, including those in the illustrative list in Annex I to the Agreement. Other developing countries i.e. those countries which are not included in Annex VII will be exempt from this prohibition for a period of 8 years provided the subsidies are progressively phased out during this period. In addition, the other prohibition contained in Article 3, paragraph 3.1(b) regarding subsidies contingent upon the use of domestic over imported goods will not be applicable to developing countries for five years and for the least developed countries for a period of eight years from the entry into force of the WTO Agreement.

♦ Developing country members would be required to phase out export subsidies for products in which they have reached a state of export competitiveness, defined as a share of at least 3.25% in world trade of that product for two consecutive calendar years. Least developed countries and other developing countries listed in Annex VII are allowed flexibility to phase out such subsidies over a period of eight years while other developing countries have to do so in two years.

♦ During the period in which developing countries are permitted to apply otherwise prohibited subsidies, the remedies provided for prohibited subsidies in Article 4 will not apply; instead the remedies in respect of serious prejudice in Article 7 will be applicable.

♦ With respect to actionable subsidies in Article 6, there will be no presumption of serious prejudice in respect of subsidies granted by developing countries. Therefore the existence of serious prejudice would have to be determined and positively demonstrated. Similarly, these countries are entitled to additional flexibility to phase out the actionable subsidies.

There are a number of provisions in the Agreement which provide for thresholds under which no action would be permitted against imports from developing countries. These provisions have been incorporated in this Agreement by lifting them directly from the Agreement on Anti-Dumping. It is for the first time that such provisions on the level of subsidisation and market share have been incorporated in a multilateral Agreement. This was in spite of the stiff opposition from the United States and a few other countries who were determined that all such provisions should be kept out because "there was no economic rationale" for including such de-minimis provisions. In the ultimate analysis however, the United States was informed unambiguously that the developing countries would not be in a position to agree to a text containing provisions relating to Article 3 and 6 but where no relief was provided to them from the harassment and trade chilling impact of countervailing investigations. This resulted in a softening of the US stance through a recognition, acceptance and inclusion of the deminimis provisions in various areas of the Agreement. On the same basis, a higher threshold for level of subsidies (from

2% to 3%) for Annex VII countries was agreed to in the concluding phase of the negotiations by the United States, European Union and other countries. It would however be observed that the numerical figures for the deminimis provisions are rather inadequate and fail to provide any significant relief from the harassment of countervailing action.

It may also be mentioned that the figures advanced by the developing countries for the level of subsidies as well as volume of subsidised imports were much higher than those included in the Agreement. However, the figures in the Agreement were introduced as a compromise by the Chairman of the negotiating group and were retained by the Chairman of the rule making group in the final phase of the negotiations (except for the change from 2% to 3% in the level of subsidies as mentioned above).

The figure of US $ 1,000 which has been introduced to determine the cut off for developing countries for inclusion under Annex VII is an arbitrary figure which appeared reasonable at that stage and was agreed to between a few developing countries and USA and EC.

The concept of export competitiveness was put forward by the United States particularly to take care of imports in the area of textile and garments in which they argued, developing countries were already competitive and had a comparative advantage as was evident from the large and growing exports of developing countries in the sector. The United States was insistent on pegging this level at 1.5% of the world export of that product by the particular country. The initial position of developing countries was not to accept such a concept at all because it could be construed narrowly and hence be used to impede normal exports from developing countries. However, after considerable discussions, it was agreed to define a product as a Section Heading of the Harmonized System Nomenclature for the purposes of this provision. It was thus considered that such a definition of the term "product" would be broad enough to prevent its misuse as it would cover a significant proportion of the trade of a particular sector. The developing countries wanted this limit to be fixed at 5% and not 1.5% as demanded by the United States. As a result of intense consultations in the final stages of the negotiations, it was decided to agree to an arbitrary level of 3.25% for the export competitiveness threshold.

A few comments about the innovative provisions introduced with respect to countervailing investigations on a product originating in a developing country would not be out of place. The investigation will be terminated if it is determined that the overall rate of subsidisation granted to the product in question does not exceed 2% of its value calculated on a per unit basis, or the volume of the subsidised imports represents less than 4% of the total imports of the like products in the importing country, unless imports from developing country members whose individual share of total imports represents less than

4%, collectively account for more than 9% of total import of the like product in the importing country. For developing countries which have phased out their export subsidies within 8 years and developing countries covered by Annex VII, the figure of de-minimis subsidization will be 3% instead of the 2% mentioned above. It however, needs to be noted that these thresholds have failed to provide meaningful and real relief to developing countries in facing countervailing actions. Moreover, the Agreement codifies the practice of cumulative assessment of injury, which had been opposed by developing countries. To be "cumulated", imports should be less than the *de-minimis* values.

Another important aspect relating to developing countries is that countervailing duties in respect of actionable subsidies provided in Part III, will not apply to direct forgiveness of debt or to subsidies to cover social cost when these are granted within and directly to a privatisation programme of a developing country member, provided that both the programme and the subsidies involved are granted for a notified duration and that the programme results in eventual privatisation of the enterprise concerned. If privatisation is linked to foreign direct investment, it could lead to higher subsidisation.

Notifications:

Article 25.2 of the Agreement enjoins upon all members to provide information on all measures, practices and activities that meet the definition of subsidy as set forth in the Agreement and which are specific within the territory of that country. "New and Full" notifications are required to be submitted every 3rd year beginning in 1995, where as updating notifications (usually containing information solely on changes made to previously notified subsidies) are to be submitted in the intervening years.

In the review of notifications undertaken by the Committee on Subsidies and Countervailing Measures in 1988, some progress was reported in the compliance by smaller and developing countries with the Article 25 notification requirements. Greater transparency than ever before has been achieved with respect to the number of notifications received and quality of information provided. Most of the major trading countries have submitted their notifications at least up to 1997.

One of the important development in reporting in 1998 was the addition to the United States notifications of 210 separate measures provided or maintained by 43 US states. This is in pursuance of the requirement that subsidies provided by all levels of government within the territory of a country are covered and susceptible to notification. EU also provided information on subnational subsidies specially with respect to four members states that are federally organised i.e. Austria, Belgium, Spain and Germany. Subsequently other countries such as Canada and Australia have also started providing information about their provincial and state programmes in response to questions posed by the United States and other countries.

The Subsidies Committee will be taking a series of special meetings during 1999 to review the new and full notifications submitted by different countries in 1998.

Under Article 25.3 (v) members are required to notify the subsidy programmes with statistical data permitting an assessment of their trade effect. The experience in the Committee on Subsidies so far has demonstrated that this is indeed a arduous, complex and difficult task to accomplish, particularly for developing countries.

Under Article 25.10, members are allowed to make counter notifications in relation to measures of other countries having the effect of subsidies which have not been notified in accordance with article 16:1 of GATT 1994 and Article 25 of the Agreement. So far, such provisions have been mainly utilised by the large developed countries against other trading partners including several developing countries.

It would be observed that the notification requirements for developing countries are indeed very burdensome and difficult. Neither are developing countries adequately equipped to compile all the information, nor do they have the requisite manpower and expertise available to provide the highly time consuming and detailed requirements stipulated in the Agreement. It is essential to provide meaningful technical assistance to upgrade the national capacity of administrations of developing countries and remove the government's institutional constraints to enable them to meet their obligations under these provisions.

Developing countries are not able to make any counter notifications in relation to measures of other countries having the effect of subsidy which have not been notified in accordance with the provisions of GATT 1994 and the Agreement on Subsidies. Assistance in this area also needs to be provided under the technical assistance programme of the WTO.

Review:

There are several provisions in the Agreement which are required to be reviewed after a given period of time from the coming into force of the Agreement:

♦ *Article 8.2(a), footnote of the Agreement: review of non-actionable research and development subsidy.* Such a review was to have been conduced within 18 months after the entry into force of the Agreement i.e. by the end of June, 1996. In view of lack of experience and taking into account that no notification in this area had been submitted, it was agreed that such a review will be conducted at a future time if the members wished to do so. The review will now have to be conducted along with those of Articles 6.1 , 8 and 9 as provided for under Article 31.

♦ *Article 27.6 of the Agreement: export competitiveness provisions for developing countries.* It is stipulated that the operation of this provision should be reviewed five years from the date of entry into force the WTO Agreement. No experience regarding the applicability of this provision is available so far, as no notification has been submitted by any developing county nor has request for a computation been received. This provision may be allowed to continue with the added requirement that if the export of a developing country in a product were to go above the level of 3.25% in world trade and then subsequently fall below it after a period of time, the country would be permitted to use the export subsidies in this sector also.

♦ *Article 31 provisions of Article 6.1 on actionable subsidies and Articles 8 & 9 on non-actionable subsidies.* As stated above, Agreement on these 3 provisions was arrived at as a package principally between the United States and the European Community at a late stage of the negotiations. Since both these aspects viz., "dark amber" and "green category" have entered into a multilateral Agreement for the first time, no previous experience is available on the manner in which they will operate. It is hence not surprising that it has been provided that all these 3 provisions will be reviewed simultaneously after a period of 5 years. i.e., by the end of 1999.

As mentioned above, no notifications under Article 8 have been received so far. Article 6.1 has also not been put to test as yet. It might hence be appropriate to allow the continuation of these provisions with the clear understanding that Article 8 will be modified to include the subsidies of interest to developing countries. **There should be an added stipulation that subsidies of interest to developing countries for promoting their economic and industrial development included in article 8 should also be free from the threat of countervailing action.**

Recommendations for Developing Countries:

♦ There is an obvious imbalance in the Agreement as far provisions of Article 8 on non-actionable subsidies are concerned. It is indeed ironical that while the subsidies which are used by developed countries, like those for research and development, regional development and adaptation of environmental standards have been declared green and non-actionable, those which are normally employed by developing countries for development, diversification and upgradation are actionable in the sense that counter-action can be taken against them under certain conditions.

This imbalance should be removed and corrected at the first available opportunity through inclusion of such subsidies employed by developing countries for promotion and development of their industry and agriculture. In this category should be added measures such as provision of cheap finance for investment of working capital, financial support for absorption and adaptation of new and advanced technology, subsidy for diversification of market, help in market development etc. Such subsidy practices have always been recognised as valid instruments for development and growth of the economy of developing countries. The Uruguay Round Agreement on subsidies however, either prohibits them or makes them actionable. Industrial development programmes like setting up of Export Processing Zones (EPZs), Free Trade Zones (FTZs) etc. should be covered under Article 8 so that products exported from these facilities would not be covered under any of the provisions of Part II, III or V of the Agreement. These programmes have long been used and recognised as appropriate vehicles for industrial growth of developing economies.

No action should be permitted either through the trade effect rules or through the countervail actions provisions on such Subsidies.

Adequate parameters would need to be built into the Agreement as far as these Subsidies are concerned so that they can be freely utilised by the developing countries. For the green subsidies already included in the Agreement, viz. regional development, environment and research and development subsidies, greater flexibility should be provided so that they can be utilised by the developing countries for promoting their economic growth and development.

♦ Subsidies which are maintainable under the provisions of Article 27 are subject to countervailing measures in accordance with the provisions of Article 6 of GATT 94. The special dispensation and the resulting benefits from the provisions of Article 27 thus stand negated by virtue of the provisions relating to countervailing measures. It is, therefore necessary that countervailing measures are not allowed to be used by developed countries against subsidies maintained by developooing countries with the special dispensation provided under Article 27.

♦ Article 27.3 of the Agreement allows developing countries for a period of five years and least developed countries for 8 years to provide subsidies for the use of domestic products in preference to the like imported goods (covered in Article 3.1 (b) of the agreement). It should be reiterated that the import substitution subsidies are integral element of the developing process of developing countries and hence should be covered under the non-actionable category of subsidies for developing countries and be added to Article 8. Arguments that such subsidies and actions by the governments are contrary to the provisions of GATT 1994 or to the Trims agreement are neither valid nor convincing because such subsidies are essential aspects of the policy framework for industrial and economic growth and development of developing countries;

♦ Article 27.5 of the Agreement requires the developing countries to phase out export subsidies when they reach the stage of export competitiveness in a particular product as defined in Article 27.6. Thus an automatic exclusion from the benefit and flexibility to provide export subsides follows once the stage of export competitiveness is reached for two years in succession. Clarity needs to be provided by specifying that if in subsequent years the share of the concerned country in world trade for the particular product were to fall below the stipulated level, the country would once again become eligible for providing subsidies for export of that product;

♦ Annex VII countries are defined as those countries which enjoy special dispensation and flexibility in respect of providing subsidies if their per capita GNP is less than US $ 1,000 per annum. (These countries are in addition to least developed countries as defined by the United Nations, which are also included in Annex VII). If the GNP of the country were to rise above this level, it would be excluded from the definition under Annex VII and would hence lose the flexibility to provide support for promotion of its exports. Since the Agreement came into effect, GNP of a number of countries has increased above the US $ 1,000 level viz., Philippines, Indonesia etc. This has taken place not as a result of some radical or distinct improvement in the volume or value of industrial and economic production of the country but on account of some drastic exchange rate fluctuations which have affected several countries in the world. Clarification needs to be provided that such changes in the per capita GNP of the country should not result in exclusion from the category under Annex VII and denial of benefits which would otherwise be available to them. Close study and analysis needs to be made to determine whether living standards and per capita GNP has increased as a result of increase in productivity or has the increase in GNP taken place artificially on account of some large scale fluctuations without making any perceptible dent in the quality of life of the people. Before "graduating" a country out of Annex VII, it should be ensured that the increase of per-capita GNP represents a structural improvement in the economy of the country concerned and is not a temporary phenomenon. The increase should have an element of stability. Serious consideration also needs to be given to the fact that the limit of US $ 1000 for inclusion of countries in Annex VII should be increased to say, a figure of US $ 1,500. The increase can also be correlated to a certain proportion of the average figure for the GNP of OECD countries.

Moreover, if a country which is on the verge or border of the US 1,000 per capita GNP level and its GNP increases to marginally above US $ 1,000, provisions should be introduced whereby it would be allowed to graduate out of Annex VII only if its GNP were to stay above US$ 1,000 for atleast three years in succession. The same benefit would be made available to it subsequently if its GNP were to fall below the US $ 1,000 (or US $ 1,500, or some other figure if subsequently negotiated upwards) level.

♦ The dispute settlement process has become highly complicated and technical. Developing countries while initiating complaints about the subsidies of other countries are required to collect and analyse a large quantity of information on the subsidy practices of those countries. Likewise, when defending themselves against the complaint of other countries they are required to obtain detailed data on the existence of injury to the industry of these countries. The developing countries also need to examine the causal linkage between their exports and the injury which might have been suffered by the domestic industry. Collection of such information is a highly difficult and expensive proposition. This puts the developing countries in a position of disadvantage notwithstanding the improved features of the agreement which in any case have been constructed on the existing practices prevalent in the developed countries particularly the United States.

Provisions should be introduced whereby panels would exercise their power to collect by using their own mechanism and authority, the information which is required and considered relevant for the case of the developing countries. The WTO secretariat should also be granted the authority to collect such information at the request of the concerned developing country. It would need to be kept in mind that the initiation of a countervail case in itself results in an adverse impact on the exports of the developing countries due to the chilling effect of such investigations. Developing countries are put in a position of double jeopardy as a result of the fact that they are in addition required to engage expensive legal help in defending their positions. Better technical assistance provisions should be developed and evolved so that developing countries would be provided with necessary advice and concrete help in adequately defending their positions.

Consideration should be given to introducing provisions in the Agreement whereby if the developing country against whom a countervail action or a dispute has been initiated, were to win the case, adequate compensation would be provided to it by the other country. This would not only lessen the number of frivolous cases that might be initiated against developing countries but would also seek to compensate the developing country concerned for the adverse effect on its exports as a result of initiation of such investigations.

♦ Some provisions with respect to the countervailing duty provisions also need to be looked into.

- The de-minimis level below which countervailing duties may not be imposed has now been fixed as 4% for developing countries. There are several disadvantages faced by industries in developing countries as compared to their counterparts in developed countries. Many of the export products in developing countries are produced by labour intensive, small and medium enterprises. Imposition of countervailing duties or even the threat of imposition of such duties has a serious adverse impact on the functioning of such units. As a consequence, there is a fall in production, large un-employment, decline in incomes and increase in poverty levels. The high cost of capital low level of infrastructure development, inadequate integration and organisation of the economy, poorly developed information networks are characteristics of industry in developing and least developed countries. It is recognised by economic analysts that the state has to assume a more active and positive role in assisting its industry. In order to offset the many disadvantages that developing and least developed countries suffer from, it would be essential to raise the *de-minimis* level below which countervailing duty may not be imposed. In place of the present provisions, changes should be made to provide that countervailing duty investigations would not be initiated or if initiated, would be terminated when imports from developing countries are less than 7% of the total imports, irrespective of the cumulative volume of imports of the like products of developing countries;

• The countervailing duty should be restricted to the amount by which the subsidy to be calculated exceeds the *de-minimis* level when action has been contemplated in case of products from developing countries;

• Export credits given by developing countries should not be considered as subsidy so long as the rate at which they are extended are above LIBOR;

• Aggregate and generalised rate of duty rate remission should be allowed in case of developing countries even though the individual units may not be able to establish the source of their inputs;

• Developing countries should be allowed to neutralise the cost escalating effects of taxes collected by the government authorities at different levels i.e., taxes such as sale tax, octroi, cess etc. which are not refunded;

♦ The term "pre competitive development activity" should be defined in Article 8.2(a) under the provision on research and development subsidy, so as to permit subsidies which are used by developing countries for product development and export development, to be non-actionable.

♦ Relevant provisions should be incorporated in the TRIPs Agreement by which, through a cross reference with the Agreement on Subsidies and Countervailing Measures, it should be ensured that the results obtained through the non-actionable research and development subsidies would be made freely available to facilitate the transfer of technology developed with public funds.

♦ Special facilities should be provided to developing countries for incorporating technologies for preservation of environment. A special fund could be set up to assist the developing countries in this endeavour. This would stimulate trade in environmental services. Suitable cross referencing could be provided between the Agreement on Subsidies with GATS so that those countries which are willing to undertake greater commitments in the area, would be provided with additional concessional financing.

♦ Developing countries not included under Annex VII are required to phase out their export subsidies within a period of 8 years from the entry into effect of the Agreement. If a developing country deems it necessary to use subsidies beyond the 8 year period, it should enter into consultations with the Committee on Subsidies and Countervailing Measures not later than one year before the expiry of this period. With more than half this period of 8 years already over, developing countries need to give serious consideration to demanding an increase in this arbitrary 8 year limitation so that export subsidies are available to them for meeting their development and growth requirements for a considerably longer period. Increase in length of this period is justified as export subsidies are recognised to be valid instruments and an integral part of increasing competitiveness in world markets.

♦ Some moves have recently become visible whereby developed countries are seeking to include Privatisation Subsidies granted by developing countries under the purview of countervailing duties. This is unfair and unacceptable from the point of view of developing countries as the price paid for the enterprise by the owner for the privatisation of the enterprise is inclusive of the subsidy provided.

Conclusion:

The negotiations on the subject of subsidy were closely focused on the demands put forward as well as the practices followed by the United States.

In overall terms, the approach of the new Agreement is to give members three years to bring existing programmes into conformity with its provisions. During this period, members would not be subject to the provisions of Part II of the Agreement which deals with prohibited subsidies and the remedies for them. This period could be construed as a continuation of the status quo prevailing before the establishment of the WTO. Yet, considering the extremely difficult and volatile situation obtaining in the area of subsidies in international trade, and the natural reluctance of governments to take on vested interests which subsidies inevitably create, it is, in effect, a clear and positive step forward. Similarly the flexibility given to developing countries i.e., other than the countries listed in Annex VII, would exempt them from the blanket provisions on certain categories of subsidies for a period of eight years.

The main achievements of the Uruguay Round Negotiations on Subsidies may be listed as:

- the definition of a subsidy, which is the first for a multilateral trade agreement, and its related rules on measurement;
- the elaboration of a trade effects standard embodied in the serious prejudice provisions to be enforced by a multilateral mechanism as opposed to the domestic application of countervailing law;
- the creation of a non-actionable category of subsidies;
- the refinement of substantive and procedural rules governing countervailing duty investigations;
- refinement and greater precision for measurement of subsidies;
- inclusion of de-minimis market share and de-minimis level of subsidisation for initiating countervail investigations against goods originating from developing countries; and
- specifically in the case of countervail, more stringent disciplines and procedural requirements would ensure that fewer cases are initiated.
- Moreover a higher proportion of them are likely to fail because they would not be able to meet the somewhat tighter injury test requirement. The evidentiary standard in the agreement have been made clearer and more precise. This would imply fairer hearing for interested parties. Because of the sunset clause provisions, a significant proportion of the cases should be terminated after five years.

It would be observed that the Agreement strengthens the capacity of the Governments to resist demands for subsidisation in terms of practices which have been clearly prohibited. Moreover, the fact that actionable subsidies have been provided with comprehensive guidance on determination of adverse effects and serious prejudice has also introduced a degree of predictability into international trade in so far as governmental use of such subsidies is concerned. The Agreement provides for more detailed provisions than its predecessor in respect of initiation of countervailing duty investigations, calculation of amount of subsidy in terms of benefit to the recipient, and definition of injury to a domestic industry or undertaking.

It is recognised that developing countries do not have the capacity to indulge in competitive subsidsaiton because of the resultant fiscal strains and pressures on their national budgets. As such, enhanced discpilines on subsides would be helpful for them by ensuring that developed countries do not have full freedom to subsidise and displace thier products out of home or third markets. Developing countries have the capacity to provide limited quantities of subsides in certain given sectors for which some flexibility has been provided to them in the Agreement.

The provisions in the Agreement on Subsidies negotiated under the Uruguay Round would not be applicable to agriculture, production and trade in steel products and in civil aircrafts in which separate agreements were negotiated. In some areas like steel, parallel negotiations were conducted to conclude a Multilateral Steel Agreement. This agreement could however, not be signed. Agreement on Trade in Civil Aircraft is contained in Annex 4 of the WTO Agreement. As far as the contentious areas of agriculture is concerned, separate and very detailed rules have been negotiated to discipline subsidies which are covered under the Agreement on Agriculture. As in the case of steel, an agreement on ship building was negotiated in 1996 in the OECD with a view to dealing with the effects of subsidisation of low pricing in the ship building industry particularly from new comers such as Korea. This agreement has yet to come into effect, as the same has not been ratified by the US Congress. Other signatories are also not applying the agreement pending US approval. This also hence constitutes a major sector falling out of the purview of the Agreement on Subsidies and Countervailing Measures.

Rules on subsidies in the area of services have not been evolved as yet. Considerable work and negotiations would be required to develop rules in the different area of trade in services.

ANTI-DUMPING AND COUNTERVAILING DUTIES

UNCTAD Workshop on Development of Positive Agenda, Seoul 8-10 June 1999

Edwin Vermulst

Anti-dumping and anti-subsidy concerns for developing countries in the Millennium Round: key areas for reform

> *"An anti-dumping determination is the product of hundreds, if not thousands, of individual substantive and procedural decisions made during the course of an investigation, each of which may be subject to one or more provisions of the AD Agreement."*[139]

Introduction

There are now more than 50 WTO members, which have adopted anti-dumping legislation.[140] Of these, more than half have initiated anti-dumping proceedings.[141] While in the eighties more than 80% of the cases were initiated by the four traditional AD users,[142] recent years have seen developing countries become increasingly active. Thus, for example, in 1998, South Africa initiated 41 proceedings, India 30, Brazil 16 and Mexico 10.[143] Indeed, in 1998 the four traditional users were responsible for only 34% of all initiations.

Main *targets* of world-wide anti-dumping action in that same year were China (23 cases), Korea (22 cases) and the EC[144] Member States (42 cases). Of the 225 cases initiated during 1998, 143 targeted developing countries.[145]

A major recent study[146] examining the use of anti-dumping over the period 1987-1997 concludes, among others, that:

> *". . . developing countries now initiate about half of the total number of anti-dumping cases, and some of them employ anti-dumping more*

actively than most of the developed country users. This article also suggests that this proliferation of anti-dumping is not altogether negative, as it appears to have helped countries navigate from a controlled to a liberalized trading regime: the developing countries liberalizing most intensively, tend to be active users of anti-dumping."[147]

These observations, buttressed by the 1998 data, are important for two reasons. First, they show that developing countries are no longer just on the receiving end. Second, the apparent causal effect between trade liberalization and AD signifies that the exponential increase of AD action by developing country WTO members is not a temporary phenomenon, but, in fact, is likely to continue: trade liberalization and AD complaints paradoxically go hand in hand, as arguably the four traditional users have found out in the past decades.

I have previously[148] pointed out that the systemic fundamentals of anti-dumping action have an inherently limiting effect on the scope of remedial action, first, because anti-dumping investigations are by nature conducted as investigations into individual producers'[149] pricing and costs in two markets and, second, because the administering agencies must comply with a high level of regulation, both internationally and nationally.[150] In this regard, anti-dumping action from a pragmatic perspective is perhaps preferable to application of other trade laws, such as anti-subsidy[151] and safeguard actions.[152]

In the following, I will address shortcomings in the Anti-Dumping Agreement [hereinafter: ADA] and the Agreement on Subsidies and Countervailing Measures [hereinafter: ASCM] from the perspective of developing countries, it being understood, however, that such perspective is no longer solely that of developing countries as victims of anti-dumping actions, but also must encompass developing countries as active users of AD action themselves.[153]

In this regard, I continue to believe that the keys to current and future anti-dumping law and practice must be *(perceived) fairness* and *predictability*,[154] because this is in the interest of all WTO members. Post-Uruguay Round practice shows that the ADA continues to leave too much leeway to importing country administrative authorities and makes dumping findings too easy. Overall, therefore, my recommendations will aim to further rationalize and concretize the ADA. This paper will review key areas where change is needed; it is, therefore, not at all exhaustive.[155]

Article 2: the determination of dumping

Present anti-dumping legislation, based on the WTO ADA, conceptually distinguishes between two forms of dumping:

♦ Price dumping, i.e. the selling at a lower price abroad than in the home market;

♦ Cost dumping, i.e. selling below cost in an export market.

In addition, de facto a third form of dumping exists: Non-market economy dumping. Where a non-market economy is under investigation, dumping may be established in a special manner. In this paper, however, we will not address non-market economy dumping and the problems with establishing normal value in such cases.

In all three cases, the establishment of dumping supposedly[156] is a technical mathematical exercise, which focuses on facts, to wit the prices and costs of merchandise in two separate markets. If dumping and resulting injury are found, anti-dumping duties may be imposed to offset or prevent injurious dumping in the importing country market. Anti-dumping duties therefore are defensive (and not punitive) in nature.[157]

Systematic, as opposed to incidental, price/cost dumping presupposes separation of markets[158] and existence of a closed home market, through governmental or private sector action. These conditions make parallel imports impossible. It is perceived to be unfair not to allow competition in one's home market, yet to benefit from the openness of other markets to sell at low prices there. This notion of unfairness can be said to form the current[159] basis for anti-dumping legislation.

> However, economists have pointed out that the problem with such systematic dumping is not the low prices in the export market, which increases economic welfare in that market, but rather the closedness of the home market, which precludes foreign producers from competing in such market.[160] But then, the argument goes, imposition of anti-dumping duties as a defensive action is only a second-best solution and the preferable option would be to open the closed home market by offensive means. This is an important element of the contestability of markets theory. However, as is the case with predatory dumping, one runs into evidentiary problems because it would need to be proven that the home market is indeed closed through means, which violate the WTO rules. The recent Kodak-Fuji WTO dispute illustrates these difficulties.[161]

Although there is still a need for the anti-dumping instrument, today's trade relations have become more complex than ever. Character and patterns of trade and industry are changing rapidly. Internationally operating companies are seeking better opportunities to produce at low cost and to penetrate new markets. Classical production patterns of producing goods at one place are changing into a pattern of outsourcing and production at a global scale.

Price differentiation as a pricing policy (as often used within domestic economies) is a widely-used instrument to introduce products to new markets (however, the effect of such a policy is often balanced by parallel imports). Similarly, temporary sales below fixed costs (but above variable costs)[162] are common in many industries during downturns in the business/product cycle. Therefore, key substantive concepts of the ADA need to be revised to better reflect business realities in a globalized economy.

In the areas of *price* and *cost* dumping, WTO rules leave too much leeway for dumping to be found and anti-dumping measures to be applied in circumstances where domestic competition laws would not find objectionable conduct, *c.q.* where *systematic* dumping does not take place. I qualify such dumping as *incidental* dumping.

A finding of incidental dumping, as opposed to systematic dumping, may result from various factors, including, but not limited to:

♦ differences in economic or business cycles in two markets;

♦ price differentiation to initially enter a market;

♦ exchange rate fluctuations;

♦ technicalities of dumping margin calculation methods, such as asymmetrical comparisons between domestic and export prices, restrictive interpretations of allowances, systematic exclusion of sales below cost and use of remaining sales above cost as the basis for normal value, use of constructed normal values with unrealistically high profit margins, etc.

Definitions of price and cost dumping in the WTO need to be revised to target only systematic dumping and exclude situations of incidental dumping. In the long term, three important modifications seem in order:

♦ First, the focus for the determination of dumping could shift away from differences between foreign and domestic prices. Instead, below-cost export sales could become the standard for determining dumping;

♦ Introduction of a concrete requirement that the investigating authorities must establish, based on positive evidence, the closedness of the market of the exporting country, in addition to a pattern of below cost export sales.[163]

♦ Third, a further element of the dumping determination could be an assessment of whether there exists a monopolistic intent on the part of the exporting country producers driving any price differentials on foreign markets.[164]

However, major users of the instrument presumably would be unwilling to go this far in the Millennium Round. Below, therefore, we address more modest, albeit in practice extremely important, dumping margin calculation issues.

With regard to the comparison between export price and normal value, Article 2.4 of the ADA might be targeted for reform with a view to increasing transparency and reducing the scope of discretion in the application of this provision. Article 2.4 articulates the rather vague general guiding rule that the comparison between export price and normal value should be 'fair.' While further elaboration on the application of this concept is provided, arguably additional detailed rules should be included to reduce the discretion available to investigating authorities. Thus, for example, the general rule is that the dumping margins during the investigation phase should be established on the basis of weighted averages-to-weighted averages or on a transaction-to-transaction basis. However, there are exceptions to this principle which allow, under certain conditions, comparisons between individual export prices and weighted-average normal value. In certain jurisdictions, particularly the major developed users of anti-dumping laws, the application of this exception has arguably been excessive and authorities have been too willing to find that the criteria for the application of this method are fulfilled. In practice, the use of this method often results in higher dumping margins, as Annex 5 illustrates. Therefore, the exceptions should be abolished and it should further be clarified that weighted average-to-weighted average or transaction-to-transaction comparisons should be made both in original and in review investigations, and not only intra-model, but also inter-model, as far as the former method is concerned.

In addition, further detailed rules may be necessary with regard to taking into account differences that affect price comparability. In this regard it is noted that certain traditional users of anti-dumping measures in practice place the burden of proof squarely on the respondent with respect to demonstrating that differences in terms of levels of trade or other trade conditions in fact affect price comparability. The provisions of Article 2.4 leave too much leeway to authorities to reject claims regarding such differences. Annexes 2, 3 and 4 illustrate this with respect to duty drawback, credit terms and level of trade respectively.

With respect to sales below cost, Article 2.2.1 provides that such sales may be disregarded for the purpose of determining normal value on condition that these sales are made over an extended period of time and in substantial quantities. The test for determining whether such sales are made in 'substantial quantities' is that the weighted average selling price of the transactions under consideration for determining normal value is below the weighted average per unit costs, or that the volume of sales below per unit costs represents more than 20% of the volume sold in transactions under consideration for determining normal value. The threshold of 20% is too low and easily leads to arbitrary dumping findings, as Annex 6 illustrates, and should be raised, e.g. to 40%.

Article 3: the determination of injury

One possible issue for reform with respect to injury determinations would be to require in all cases that both the injury and dumping margin must be calculated, and that the anti-dumping duty must reflect the lower of these two margins. This provision might be coupled to more detailed provisions ensuring transparency with regard to the calculation of injury margins.

I note that GATT and WTO Panels have interpreted Article 3, in conjunction with Article 12, quite stringently. For this reason, I do not advocate further changes to Article 3. Any problems presently occurring do not appear the result of Article 3 itself, but rather of inadequate application of the Article 3 provisions in concrete cases.

Special and differential treatment for developing countries

The WTO recognizes the special position of developing countries by allowing them more time to bring down trade barriers, thereby effectively offering such countries the possibility to keep their market closed for a grace period. Thus, it could be said that the WTO legitimizes, at least transitionally, closed markets in the case of developing countries. Should such legitimization shield developing countries from the application of anti-dumping measures? The legal answer to this question under the Anti-Dumping Agreement is clearly negative. Article 15 in the ADA is devoted to developing countries, but it merely provides that special regard must be given by developed country Members to the special situation of developing country Members when considering application of anti-dumping measures and that constructive remedies provided for by the Agreement must be explored before application of anti-dumping duties where they would affect the essential interests of developing country Members.

However, in practice, major users of anti-dumping legislation do not distinguish between developed and developing countries in their application of the anti-dumping instrument.

The Article 15 obligation therefore should be concretized, for example by providing higher *de minimis* dumping margin and imports' share thresholds in anti-dumping proceedings involving developing countries. A higher *de minimis* dumping margin might be all the more appropriate as importing country authorities often resort to 'best information available' in cases involving indigenous producers (as opposed to subsidiaries of multinational corporations) in developing countries. Thus, for example, the *de minimis* dumping margin for developing countries could be raised to 5%.

Increased *imports' share* thresholds, conceptually an injury issue, to 4 and 9% for developing countries in the ADA could easily be justified by reference to the similar provision in the ASCM, see Annex 1.

Regardless of the outcome of an anti-dumping or an anti-subsidy proceeding, it is clear that the *initiation* of such a proceeding in itself may have a significant impact on the exporting industries targeted. The process of replying to questionnaires, possibly attending hearings in the country initiating the proceeding and related tasks often involves significant manpower and costs.

In addition, the initiation of proceedings itself may lead unrelated importers or purchasers in the initiating country to switch sources of supply in favor of suppliers which are not targeted. Needless to say, the implications of these financial and practical difficulties are often magnified in the case of developing countries' industries. While the particular circumstances surrounding individual cases may vary, it might be argued that, overall, the initiation of anti-dumping or anti-subsidy proceedings disproportionately burdens developing countries whether or not the final determination is affirmative or negative. From a legal point of view, it is clear that neither the ADA nor the ASCM provide for any special consideration for developing countries with regard to the decision to initiate anti-dumping or anti-subsidy proceedings.[165]

In this regard, one conceivable possibility would be to strengthen Article 15 of the ADA so as to provide for additional procedural requirements to be met prior to the initiation of anti-dumping proceedings against developing countries where the initiation would affect the essential interests of the exporting country. The additional requirements might take the form of an obligation on the part of the government of the importing country to initiate consultations with the developing exporting country and to request the latter to take action to correct the alleged dumping or subsidization. Following this request, the initiation of the investigation would be suspended for a fixed period of time, thereby affording the developing country in question an opportunity to take steps to improve any eventual dumping. Proceedings would then be initiated only if it is found, following the expiry of the grace period, that insufficient improvement has been made.[166]

Furthermore, the ADA provides no direct guidance with regard to establishing the appropriate investigation period (IP) for the purposes of dumping investigations. In this regard, where the IP established falls outside the normal accounting period in the exporting country, the added administrative burden is inevitably considerable. In the case of developing countries, these problems are often compounded by the relative lack of adequate computerization and sophisticated information management tools which might otherwise ease the task of organizing relevant data efficiently and cost-effectively. Account should be taken of the particular need to minimize administrative difficulties encountered by developing Members, where possible, and that the accounting practices of such Members should be considered when setting the IP.

With regard to the ASCM, Asia's sudden plunge into a deep and ongoing financial crisis has provided important lessons and has highlighted the need for additional safeguards and clarifications to be added to the special provisions governing developing country Members in this Agreement. In this respect, one of the most important provisions in the ASCM providing preferential treatment for developing country Members is the exemption from the prohibition in Article 3.1 (*a*) against subsidies contingent upon export performance.[167] Article 27.2 (*a*), which provides for this exemption, distinguishes between two categories of developing countries and applies different rules according to the applicable category. The first category[168] consists of the Members listed in Annex VII to the Agreement. For these countries, the operation of the exemption is in principle indefinite[169] (although, as noted below, certain countries will cease to fall under Annex VII upon attaining a certain level of GNP per capita). The second category[170] consists of 'other developing country Members' not referred to in Annex VII. For these countries, the exemption is qualified and ceases to apply after eight years have elapsed since the entry into force of the WTO Agreement.

In other words, the exemption is currently set to expire by the end of the year 2002. However, this provision was drafted at a time when many assumed that the significant and rapid growth experienced by many developing countries was virtually assured to continue progressing at a similar rate. The current turmoil in much of Asia has forced such assumptions to be reconsidered, at least partially, as the current crisis has proven to be both more severe and more tenacious than most economists would have predicted. For certain countries, the effect of this crisis will have lasting implications for several years, if not longer. In the light of these circumstances, the obvious solution would appear to be an extension of the eight-year deadline in Article 27.2(b), perhaps coupled with a new provision dealing with the progressive phasing out of export subsidies.

In addition, Annex VII to the ASCM further distinguishes between two sub-categories of developing countries. The first category is comprised of least-developed countries (which are designated as such under United Nations criteria). The second category consists of a specified list of named countries.[171] For those countries listed in the latter category, paragraph (*b*) of Annex VII provides that these countries will become subject to the provisions governing other developing country Members once GNP per capita in these countries has reached $1,000 per annum. Therefore, upon 'graduating' from this category, these countries are subject to the deadline noted above with respect to phasing out export subsidies. Moreover, once a country has graduated from this category by reaching the requisite GNP per capita, there is no provision which would automatically allow such a country to revert back to its former status in the event that a subsequent recession would again lower its GNP per capita below the baseline level. Thus, the provision operates as a 'one-way street.' In this regard, the provisions of Annex VII could be clarified to expressly provide that countries will automatically be included in this category again in the type of circumstances noted above. In addition, the provision could be expanded to provide that any country dropping below the GNP per capita level specified therein could benefit from the preferential treatment under Article 27.2(a) in order to avoid arbitrary exclusions. Finally, the baseline amount of $1,000 might itself be reconsidered.

The second provision under Article 27 providing significant preferential treatment to developing country Members is Article 27.3 which exempts such countries from the prohibition against subsidies contingent on the use of domestic over imported goods. Under this provision, developing countries are entitled to benefit from the exemption for a period of five years from the date of entry into force of the WTO Agreement. Least developed country Members are exempted for eight years. The same concerns with respect to the expiry of the special exemption from the prohibition on export subsidies are equally applicable to these benefits.

Procedural issues

A difficult challenge facing developing countries in formulating their positions in the run-up to the millennium round will be the task of striking an appropriate balance between the desirability of enhancing procedural safeguards and transparency in the application of anti-dumping and anti-subsidy laws on the one hand, and on the other hand ensuring that such procedural requirements are not so complex and sophisticated as to be unworkable from the perspective of developing countries as users of such tools.

Paradoxically, while some developing countries during the Uruguay Round argued for the establishment of more detailed rules in order to contain the use of anti-dumping measures, the changing dynamics in the adoption and application of anti-dumping laws now mean that these more detailed rules will be more difficult for these countries to abide by if they wish to take anti-dumping action of their own. Beyond the problems of limited financial resources and manpower, developing countries, which are mainly relatively new users of anti-dumping and anti-subsidy laws, have the additional disadvantage of lacking the years of application and refinement of such laws and resulting expertise which have benefited the traditional developed users. While this latter defect will likely be cured to a large extent through increased experience gained over the coming years, in the short-to medium-term, remaining difficulties can be expected. This in turn could lead to increased resort to dispute settlement procedures by both developed and developing countries against anti-dumping and countervailing duty determinations made by developing countries. The precise balance to be struck may furthermore depend to some extent on the relative level of development, experience of the application of such measures and other factors.

Nonetheless, the tightening or elaboration of certain procedural requirements contained in the ADA and the ASCM may well, on balance, be in the interests of developing countries.

In the context of the ADA, one issue that has been of concern to exporting industries subject to anti-dumping duties is the often unpredictable and lengthy duration of sunset or interim reviews. The principle promulgated by the ADA is that anti-dumping duties shall remain in force only so long as and to the extent necessary to counteract dumping which is causing injury.[172] Under Article 11.3 of the ADA, any definitive anti-dumping duty shall be terminated not later than five years from the date of its imposition or from the date of the most recent review under paragraphs 2 or 3 of Article 11. However, if the authorities determine in a review initiated on the authorities own initiative or following a substantiated request by or on behalf of the domestic industry within a reasonable period of time before this date, that the expiry of the duty would be likely to lead to a continuation or recurrence of dumping and injury, Article 11.3 provides that the duty may remain in force pending the outcome of the review. Reviews may therefore have the effect of extending the period of application of anti-dumping duties beyond the five year period, and, in addition, where the findings of the review lead to the continuation of the duty, the new five year period will start to run based on the timing of the review. Despite the importance of these factors, the ADA does not provide for strict mandatory time-limits for the conduct of reviews; Rather, Article 11.4 merely provides that any review shall be carried out "expeditiously" and shall "normally be concluded within 12 months of the date of the initiation of the review." Article 21 of the ASCM contains the same provisions with respect to reviews covering subsidization and injury. However, experience in the EU has shown that the duration of reviews can greatly exceed this recommended limit.[173]

A future item of review may therefore be the tightening of the time limits for the conduct and completion of sunset and interim reviews, possibly in the form of imposing a mandatory maximum duration of such reviews.

Anti-circumvention

In this respect, three broader elements must be considered:

♦ The WCO negotiations on harmonized non-preferential origin rules are stuck,[174] arguably in part because of the absence of a multilateral anti-circumvention provision;

♦ A substantial number of countries, including not only the United States and the EC, but also (Latin American) developing countries have unilaterally adopted anti-circumvention provisions;

♦ (Non-harmonized) non-preferential rules of origin continue to be used to enforce anti-dumping duties and, consequently, to combat third country circumvention.

Because of these broader concerns, a reasonable multilaterally agreed upon anti-circumvention provision seems preferable. The UR Dunkel draft provides a reasonable starting point for continued negotiations. However, on the one hand, the draft is on some points insufficiently precise while, on the other hand, further considerations could be taken into account. The following checklist of issues might be helpful:

♦ the product assembled or completed in the importing country or the product exported from a third country must be a *like product* to the product which is subject to the definitive anti-dumping duty;

♦ he assembly or completion in the importing country or in a third country is carried out by a *related party*;

♦ sourcing in the country subject to the anti-dumping duty from the exporters/producers subject to the definitive anti-dumping duty, its traditional suppliers in the exporting country, or a party in the exporting country subject to the anti-dumping duty supplying parts or components on behalf of such an exporter or producer;

♦ *Change in the pattern of trade* in the sense that the assembly or completion operations in the importing country or in the third country have started or expanded substantially and the imports of parts or components for use in such operations have increased substantially since the initiation of the investigation which resulted in the imposition of the definitive anti-dumping duty.

♦ *Causal link*: The authorities shall determine whether the change in the pattern of trade results from the imposition of anti-dumping duties or from other factors, including changes in the pattern of trade of other exports, changes in the pattern of consumption, developments in technology and the export performance and productivity of the domestic industry.

♦ the total cost of the parts or components is not less than 70% of the total cost of all parts or components used in the assembly or completion operation of the like product, provided that in no case shall the parts and components or the like product exported from the third country be included within the scope of definitive measures if the value added by the assembly or completion operation is greater than 25% of the ex-factory price of the like product assembled or completed in the territory of the importing or third country;

♦ Due adjustment for *start-up or expansion operations* so that cost calculations reflect the costs at the end of the start-up or expansion period or, if that period extends beyond the investigation period, the most recent costs which can reasonably be taken into account by the authorities during the investigation.

♦ *Evidence of dumping*, as determined by a comparison between the price of the product when assembled or completed in the importing country or the third country, and the prior normal value of the like product when subject to the original definitive anti-dumping duty;

♦ Evidence that the inclusion of these parts or components or the like product manufactured in a third country within the scope of application of the definitive anti-dumping duty is necessary to prevent or offset the continuation or recurrence of *injury*.

Furthermore, it would be essential to define precisely key terms such as 'related party', 'parts' costs', 'value-added', and 'ex-factory price'.[175]

Anti-Subsidies

As we noted before,[176] the subsidization calculations in anti-subsidy proceedings leave much to be desired and are in fact primitive when compared with dumping margin calculations. The need for improvement in the calculation of subsidization levels is therefore equally pressing as in the area of anti-dumping. The three points that we stressed before with respect to subsidies' calculations merit reproduction:

"—categorical classification of accelerated depreciation as a subsidy in the form of a grant rather than as a possible tax deferral measure depending on the concrete circumstances;

—extremely limited scope for deductions to the subsidy amount in Article 7 (1) of Regulation 2026/97; and

—apparent a priori refusal to consider the merits of an allowance for any tax effects of subsidies or for any other economic or time value effect other than what is provided in Article 7 (1)."[177]

In addition to these earlier observations, there are in fact two more aspects in the subsidies' calculation that equally merit serious attention in a new round of negotiations:

- There is no provision in the ASCM that the normal accounting records of the company ought to be accepted by the importing country authorities. Thus, for example, instead of using the depreciation period (useful life) of the company under consideration,[178] the EC will often apply the depreciation period of the industry;

- The EC will in almost all instances not restrict itself to the product concerned, but will calculate the subsidization at the company level, including all other products produced by the exporter.

- As far as the deviation from the company's own accounting records is concerned, the difference can hardly be more striking when compared with the relatively sophisticated Article 2.2.1.1 of the ADA. Since a subsidy is to be calculated for a certain company on the basis of the 'benefit to the recipient' theory, it makes no sense to deviate from the company's records and revert to industry practice.

ANNEX 1.1

Comparison of the provisions on *de minimis* dumping/subsidy margins in the WTO ADA, ASCM (and Safeguards Agreement)

| | De minimis *dumping/subsidy margins* | |
	Developed countries	*Developing countries*
WTO ADA	The margin of dumping shall be considered to be *de minimis* if this margin is less than 2%, expressed as a percentage of the export price (Article 5.8)	
WTO ASCM	*CVD investigations:* There shall be immediate termination in cases where the subsidy is less than 1% *ad valorem* (Article 11.9).	*CVD investigations:* Any countervailing duty investigation of a product originating in a developing country Member shall be terminated as soon as the authorities concerned determine that the overall level of subsidies granted upon the product in question does not exceed 2% of its value calculated on a per-unit basis (Article 27.10(a)). *However,* for those developing country Members other than those listed in Annex VII to this WTO Agreement which have eliminated export subsidies prior to the expiry of the period of eight years from the date of entry into force of the WTO Agreement, and for those developing country Members referred to in Annex VII, the number in paragraph 10(a) shall be 3% rather than 2% (Article 27.11).
WTO Safeguards	Not applicable	Not applicable

ANNEX 1.2

Comparison of the provisions on *de minimis* import shares in the WTO ADA, ASCM and Safeguards Agreement

| | De minimis *import share* | |
	Developed countries	*Developing countries*
WTO ADA	The volume of dumped imports shall be considered negligible if the volume of dumped imports is found to account for less than 3% of imports of the like product unless countries which individually account for less than 3% of the imports of the like product collectively account for more than 7% of imports of the like product in the importing Member (Article 5.8)	

ANNEX 1.2 (*continued*)

	De minimis *import share*	
	Developed countries	*Developing countries*
WTO ADA	The volume of dumped imports shall be considered negligible if the volume of dumped imports is found to account for less than 3% of imports of the like product unless countries which individually account for less than 3% of the imports of the like product collectively account for more than 7% of imports of the like product in the importing Member (Article 5.8)	
WTO ASCM	*CVD investigations:*	*CVD investigations:*
	There shall be immediate termination in cases where the volume of subsidized imports, actual or potential, or the injury, is *negligible* (Article 11.9)	Any countervailing duty investigation of a product originating in a developing country Member shall be terminated as soon as the authorities concerned determine that the volume of the subsidized imports represents *less than 4%* of the total imports of the like product in the importing Member, *unless* imports from developing country Members whose individual shares of total imports represent less than 4% collectively account for more than 9% of the total imports of the like product in the importing Member (Article 27.10(b))
WTO Safeguard	There is no *de minimis* provision	Safeguard measures shall not be applied against a products originating in developing countries as long as their share of imports of the product concerned in the importing Member *does not exceed 3%*, provided that developing country Members with less than 3% import share collectively account for not more than 9% of total imports of the product concerned (Article 9.1)

ANNEX 2

Article 2.4: Duty drawback example

Production of polyester staple fibers:

Output:	100 MT PSF:	60 MT exported
		40 MT sold domestically
Input ratios:	0.71 PTA	
	0.31 MEG	
Input:	71 MT PTA	- 42.6 MT imported
- 28.4 MT purchased domestically		
	31 MT MEG	- 18.6 MT imported
- 12.4 MT purchased domestically		

Non-separated warehouses and production lines

Problem: Linkage between imported PTA/MEG and exported PSF cannot be established

Domestic inputs for domestic production and sales

Problem: Import duties are not borne by like product when destined for consumption in domestic market.

ANNEX 3

Article 2.4: Credit Terms

(1) *Export sales*: 90 days

$$\frac{90 \times 6\%}{365} = 1.5\%$$

(2) *Domestic Sales*: 90 days, calculated as average balance accounts receivable.

If granted: $\frac{90 \times 16\%}{365} = 4\%$

Problem: Domestic adjustment may not be granted because no direct relationship.

ANNEX 4

Article 2.4: Level of trade

Related distribution in domestic and export markets

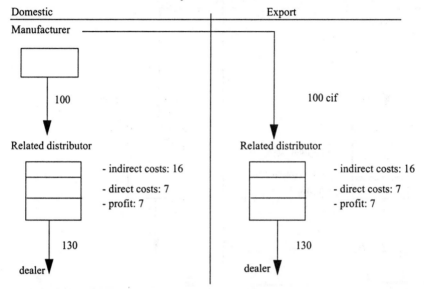

Domestic	Export
Manufacturer	

100   100 cif

Related distributor   Related distributor

- indirect costs: 16   - indirect costs: 16
- direct costs: 7   - direct costs: 7
- profit: 7   - profit: 7

130   130

dealer   dealer

Ex factory export price: 130 - 7 - 7 - 16 - 5 (cif costs) = 95
Ex factory domestic price: 130 - 7 = 123

$$\frac{123 - 95}{100} \times 100 = 28\%$$

Should be:

Ex factory domestic price: 130 - 7 - 7 - 16 = 100

$$\frac{100 - 95}{100} \times 100 = 5\%$$

ANNEX 4 (*Continued*)

Related distribution in domestic market

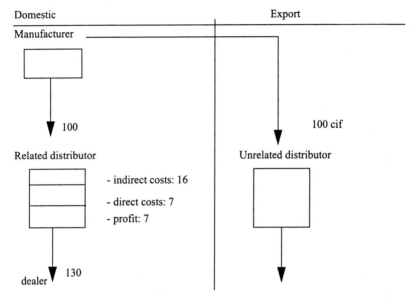

Domestic	Export
Manufacturer	

Ex factory export price: 100 -5 (cif costs) = 95
Ex factory domestic price: 130 - 7 = 123

$$\frac{123 - 95}{100} \times 100 = 28\%$$

Should be:

Ex factory domestic price: 130 - 7 - 7 - 16 = 100

$$\frac{100 - 95}{100} \times 100 = 5\%$$

ANNEX 4 (*Continued*)

Related distribution in export market

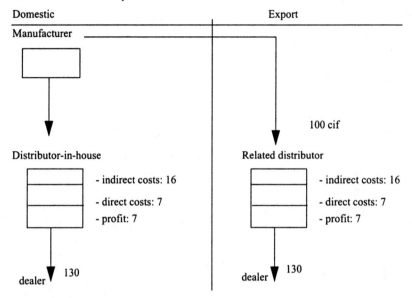

| Domestic | Export |

Manufacturer

100 cif

Distributor-in-house

- indirect costs: 16
- direct costs: 7
- profit: 7

dealer 130

Related distributor

- indirect costs: 16
- direct costs: 7
- profit: 7

dealer 130

Ex factory export price: 100 -7 - 7 - 16 - 5 (cif costs) = 95
Ex factory domestic price: 130 - 7 = 123

$$\frac{123 - 95}{100} \times 100 = 28\%$$

Should be:

Ex factory domestic price: 130 - 7 - 7 - 16 = 100

$$\frac{100 - 95}{100} \times 100 = 5\%$$

ANNEX 4 (*Concluded*)

Sales to domestic dealers and export distributors

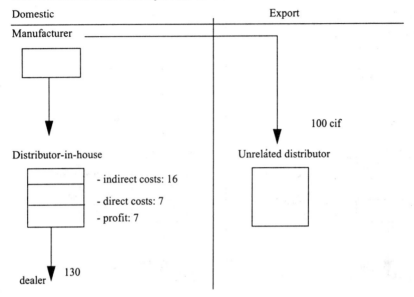

Domestic   Export

Manufacturer

Distributor-in-house   Unrelated distributor

- indirect costs: 16

- direct costs: 7

- profit: 7

100 cif

dealer 130

Ex factory export price: 100 - 5 (cif costs) = 95
Ex factory domestic price: 130 - 7 = 123

$\frac{123 - 95}{100} \times 100 = 28\%$

Should be:

Ex factory domestic price: 130 - 7 - 7 - 16 = 100

$\frac{100 - 95}{100} \times 100 = 5\%$

Note 1: The first situation is typical for Japanese cases, the second and fourth situations are typical for many developing countries, while the third situation is typical for Korea. The point is that the impact is basically the same in all four situations. This was arguably overlooked in the UR negotiations.

Note 2: The impact of the asymmetrical treatment of indirect expenses and profit on the domestic and the export side obviously depends on the level of such expenses and profit. Generally speaking, expenses will be higher for high tech products, such as consumer electronics and office automation equipment, and lower for more basic products such as steel and textiles.

ANNEX 5

Article 2.4.2: Negative dumping example

	Domestic	Export
(1) 1/6/99	50	50
(2) 10/6/99	100	100
(3) 15/6/99	150	150
(4) 20/6/99	200	200

(a) WA-to-WA comparison

(50 + 100 + 150 + 200 = 500 : 4 =) 125 - (50 + 100 + 150 + 200 : 4 =) 125 = 0

(b) T-by-T-to-T-by-T comparison:

50 - 50 =   0   150 - 150 = 0
100 - 100 = 0   200 - 200 = 0

(c) WA domestic price to T-by-T export price:

50 + 100 + 150 + 200 : 4 = 125
125 - 50 =   75 Dumping amount
125 - 100 =   25 Dumping amount
125 - 150 =   -25 = negative dumping = zeroed.
125 - 200 =   -75 = negative dumping = zeroed.
                        100 dumping amount

$\dfrac{100}{500}$ x 100 = 20% dumping margin

Apparent problems:

♦ Exceptions ADA are too broad;
♦ Inter-model offsetting not done;
♦ Sometimes only applied only in original proceedings (not reviews).

ANNEX 6

Article 2.2.1: Sales below cost example

	Domestic	Export
(1) 1/6/99	~~50~~	50
(2) 10/6/99	100	100
(3) 15/6/99	150	150
(4) 20/6/99	200	200

WAdomestic price: (100 + 150 + 200: 3 =) 150

150 - 50 =   100
150 - 100 =   50
150 - 200 =   0
150 - 200 = -50 = negative dumping = zeroed
                  $\overline{150}$ dumping amount

$\frac{150}{500}$ x 100 = 33% dumping margin

Even if averaging:
(150 - 125 =) 25 x 4 = 100 dumping amount

$\frac{100}{500}$ x 100 = 20% dumping margin

Problem: the 20% threshold is too low.

WTO SANITARY AND PHYTOSANITARY AGREEMENT: ISSUES FOR DEVELOPING COUNTRIES[179]

Simonetta Zarrilli, UNCTAD

Executive summary

Sanitary and phytosanitary (SPS) measures are typically applied to both domestically produced and imported goods to protect human or animal life or health from food-borne risks; humans from animal and plant-carried diseases; plants and animals from pests or diseases; and, the territory of a country from the spread of a pest or disease. To reach these goals, SPS measures may address the characteristics of final products, as well as how goods are produced, processed, stored and transported. They may take the form of conformity assessment certificates, inspections, quarantine requirements, import bans, and others. While some of these SPS measures may result in trade restrictions, governments generally recognize that some restrictions are necessary and appropriate to protect human, animal and plant life and health.

Sanitary and phytosanitary (SPS) measures are not a new issue in global agricultural trade. Because of the concern that SPS measures might be used for protectionist purposes, a specific Agreement on the Application of Sanitary and Phytosanitary Measures was negotiated during the Uruguay Round. The Agreement recognizes that countries have the right to maintain SPS measures for the protection of the population and the agricultural sector. However, it requires them to base their SPS measures on scientific principles and not to use them as disguised restrictions to trade.

Despite growing concern that certain sanitary and phytosanitary measures may be inconsistent with the SPS Agreement and unfairly impede the flow of agricultural trade, developing countries are not well positioned to address this issue. They lack complete information on the number of measures that affect their exports; they are not sure whether these measures are consistent or inconsistent with the SPS Agreement; they do not have reliable estimates on the impact such measures have on their exports; they experience serious problems on scientific research, testing, conformity assessment and equivalency. Developing countries are unable to effectively participate in the international standard-setting process and, therefore, face difficulties when requested to meet SPS measures in foreign markets based on international standards. Transparency-related requirements represent a burden for developing countries, while they are often unable to benefit from them, due to the lack of appropriate infrastructure. The provision of adaptation to regional conditions, which would be of great benefit to developing countries, has been little used because of the difficulties related with its scientific side. The provisions relating to special and differential treatment for developing countries remain rather theoretical and apparently have not materialized in any concrete step in their favour.

It is worth noting that, according to Article 12.7, the operation and implementation of the SPS Agreement was reviewed during 1998 and finalized by March 1999. However, the review was regarded as not exhaustive by Member countries, therefore it was agreed that at any time countries could raise any issue for consideration by the SPS Committee. Article 12.7 specifies that the Committee shall review the operation and implementation of the Agreement as the need arises. This opens the way to a proactive approach by developing country Members.

It is, however, important to keep in mind that, while all efforts should be made to limit the protectionist use of sanitary and phytosanitary measures and for this purpose some modifications of the text of the SPS Agreement may be worth considering, in many cases SPS measures reflect genuine concerns to protect health and safety. The present situation, where consumers are increasingly requesting governments to be vigilant and make efforts to minimize the risks of marketing and importing products which could jeopardize the health of people or animals or harm agriculture, is the result of several episodes—such as the so-called "mad cow" disease or the recent case of contamination by dioxin of a large number of agricultural products (and of the spreading of contamination through international trade)—where consumers have felt that health and safety were at risk. The spreading of the use of genetically-modified seeds and the perception that GM crops may negatively affect human and animal health and the environment contribute to a strong request for strict measures in the sanitary and phytosanitary field. For developing countries the best option is, therefore, to become able to respond to the exigencies which are emerging in their target markets as well as to the wishes and expectations of final consumers, by providing good quality and safe products. This implies building up knowledge, skills and capabilities. Strengthening domestic capacities in the SPS domain would also help developing countries to identify products that they may wish to keep out of their markets because of the potential negative impact on local people's health, animal health or the environment.

Developed countries and the relevant international organizations should be willing to support developing countries in this endeavour.

Introduction: the role of standards and regulations

Countries require that domestically produced and imported goods conform to regulations and possibly adhere to standards. The number of standards and regulations is constantly increasing in most countries because of the expansion in volume, variety and technical sophistication of products manufactured and traded. Nowadays, standards and regulations aim at complying with a variety of aims and tasks. Some of them are traditional—such as minimizing risks, providing information to consumers about the characteristics of products, providing information to producers about market needs and expectations, facilitating market transactions, raising efficiency and contributing to economies of scale. Other are less traditional—such as serving as benchmarks for technological capability and network compatibility and enhancing technology diffusion. Standards and regulations respond also to growing public demand, often voiced by consumer associations and environmental groups, to have in the market products which have minimum detrimental effect on the environment, display clear information regarding their possible impact on health and respond to high quality requirements. Because the tasks that standards and regulations aim to fulfil have expanded and deepened, the number of interested parties involved in setting-up standards and regulations is also increasing, with the participation of groups such as consumer and environmental organizations, which were not previously involved in these activities.

While standards and regulations, by satisfying the above-mentioned tasks, can promote economic development and trade, they may also be used as powerful tools to impede international trade and protect domestic producers, mainly through:

- unjustified different requirements in different markets;

- unnecessary costly or time consuming tests; or

- duplicative conformity assessment procedures.

The risk that countries resort to standards and regulations to maintain a degree of desired domestic protection is increasing, since more obvious trade barriers, such as tariffs, were reduced through several rounds of multilateral negotiations. This risk is particularly high in the agricultural sector where lowering the level of protection provided by tariffs and many non-tariff barriers would increase the importance of sanitary and phytosanitary measures as border protection instruments. Probably, the major difficulty in dealing with standards and regulations is to distinguish those measures which are justified by a legitimate goal from those which are applied for protectionist purposes.

Compliance with regulations is mandatory, therefore products which do not comply with regulations cannot be sold in a given market. On the other hand, standards are voluntary, therefore no product can be stopped at the border or refused access to the domestic market because of non compliance with standards. However, in practical terms, the distinction between standards and regulations is fading away, since adherence to standards is often a pre-condition for the acceptability of products by consumers and/or distributors. Moreover, insurance companies may request compliance with standards to reduce product liability exposure; importers may ask adherence to standards when there is a need for compatibility with a prevailing product in the importing market; and standards may be incorporated in regulations.

Conformity assessment measures are aimed at assessing the compliance of a product with a standard or a regulation. Conformity assessment can enhance the value of standards and regulations by ensuring that the required conditions are met by both domestic and imported products. Measures to evaluate and ensure conformity may be as significant as the standards and the regulations themselves, therefore they can also act as powerful non-tariff barriers if they impose costly, time-consuming and unnecessary tests or duplicative conformity assessment procedures. In the case of conformity assessment, as well as in the case of standards and regulations, the line between legitimate measures and measures aimed at discouraging imports and protecting domestic producers is very difficult to draw. However, statistics show that conformity assessment is a rapidly growing activity, especially in developed countries. According to a study carried out in the USA,[180] the activities of testing laboratories in the United States which carry out conformity assessment evaluation have been expanding by 13.5 per cent a year during the period 1985-1992. Adding the revenue from all firms involved in testing activities, the industry is estimated to involve around US$ 10.5 billion annually. The size of this activity mirrors its growing importance and gives an indication of the potential obstacle that multiple requests for testing and certification may represent for international trade.[181]

The agreement on the application of sanitary and phytosanitary measures

Negotiating history

When the Uruguay Round started, there was a consensus that the time had come for reform of international agricultural trade.[182] The Punta del Este

Declaration, which launched the Round in September 1986, called for increased disciplines in three areas in the agricultural sector: market access; direct and indirect subsidies; and sanitary and phytosanitary measures.[183] On the latter, the negotiators sought to develop a multilateral system that would allow simplification and harmonization of SPS measures, as well as elimination of all restrictions that lack any valid scientific basis.[184]

At the beginning of the Round the negotiating positions were the following. The United States and the European Communities (EC) were proposing broad harmonization efforts, based upon the expertise of international organizations. The EC was calling for all standards to be based on scientific evidence. The Cairns Group[185] endorsed the broad recommendations toward harmonization proposed by the EC and the United States. However, regarding the determination of what would be an acceptable level of sanitary and phytosanitary risk, it suggested that the burden of justification of SPS measures should be placed upon the importing country. Japan supported harmonization efforts based upon the work of international organizations; the improvement of notification and consultation procedures and of the dispute settlement mechanism; and special allowances for developing countries. However, Japan also supported the idea that international standardization bodies should develop guidelines rather than standards, thus providing countries with more flexibility in drafting SPS regulations. Developing countries strongly advocated the removal of sanitary and phytosanitary measures that acted as non-tariff barriers to trade. They supported the international harmonization of SPS measures to prevent developed countries from imposing arbitrarily strict standards.

In December 1988, at the Mid-Term Review of the Uruguay Round, it was agreed that the priorities in the area of SPS were: international harmonization on the basis of the standards developed by the international organizations; development of an effective notification process for national regulations; setting-up of a system for the bilateral resolution of disputes; improvement of the dispute settlement process; and provision of the necessary input of scientific expertise and judgement, relying on relevant international organizations.

The Working Group on Sanitary and Phytosanitary Regulations, which was formed in 1988,[186] produced a draft text in November 1990. First of all, the discipline related to SPS measures was included in a separate draft agreement. Secondly, a consensus was reached by the parties on the following points: SPS measures should not represent disguised trade barriers; should be harmonized on the basis of international standards, guidelines and recommendations and of generally-accepted scientific principles; special consideration should be taken of developing countries and their difficulties in meeting standards; transparency should be ensured in setting regulations and in solving disputes; and an international committee should be established to provide for consultations regarding standards. However, several areas remained unsettled: there was no agreement on whether and under what circumstances, countries could implement domestic measures stricter than international standards, or on whether economic considerations or consumer concerns, other than health-related concerns, should be taken into account in the risk assessment. The issues of inspection and approval still remained an area of dispute. It is worth noting that progress on SPS-related issues continued to outpace many other sectors within agriculture.

Due in large part to the agriculture deadlock, the Round, which was supposed to be concluded by December 1990, was adjourned. In December 1991 the so-called "Dunkel Draft" was issued by the Director General of the General Agreement on Tariffs and Trade (GATT) with the intention to move the talks toward completion. The draft incorporated proposals on sanitary and phytosanitary issues. The Dunkel text closely followed the draft text produced by the Working Group in November 1990, while providing for more stringent national regulations and excluding economic considerations. The final text of the Agreement on the Application of Sanitary and Phytosanitary Measures that was approved at the end of the Uruguay Round was largely based on the Dunkel text. It fulfils the general objectives of the Punta del Este Declaration in this area.

Salient features of the Agreement

The main goal of the SPS Agreement is to prevent domestic SPS measures having unnecessary negative effects on international trade and their being misused for protectionist purposes. However, the Agreement fully recognizes the legitimate interest of countries in setting up rules to protect food safety and animal and plant health.

More specifically, the SPS Agreement covers measures adopted by countries to protect human or animal life from food-borne risks; human health from animal or plant-carried diseases; and animal and plants from pests and diseases. Therefore, the specific aims of SPS measures are to ensure food safety and to prevent the spread of diseases among animals and plants. SPS measures can take the form of inspection of products, permission to use only certain additives in food, determination of maximum levels of pesticide residues, designation of disease-free areas, quarantine requirements, import bans, etc.

The Agreement provides national authorities with a framework to develop their domestic policies. It encourages countries to base their SPS measures on international standards, guidelines or recommendations; to play a full part in the activities of international organizations in order to promote the harmonization of SPS regulations on an international basis; to accept the SPS measures of exporting countries as equivalent if they achieve the same level of SPS protection; and, where possible, to conclude bilateral and multilateral agreements on recognition of the equivalence of specific SPS measures.

The Agreement requires countries to choose those measures which are no more trade restrictive than required to achieve domestic SPS objectives, provided these measures are technically and economically feasible (e.g. to apply a quarantine requirement instead of a ban). The SPS Agreement recognizes that, due to differences in geographical, climatic and epidemiological conditions prevailing in different countries or regions, it would often be inappropriate to apply the same rules to products coming from different regions/ countries. The SPS Agreement allows, therefore, countries to apply different SPS measures depending on the origin of the products. This flexibility should not lead to any unjustified discrimination among foreign suppliers or in favour of domestic producers. On the same lines, governments should recognize disease-free countries, or disease-free areas within countries, and adapt their requirements to products originating in such countries/areas.

The SPS Agreement allows countries to introduce sanitary and phytosanitary measures which result in a higher level of protection than that which would be achieved by measures based on international standards, if there is a scientific justification or where a country determines on the basis of an assessment of risks that a higher level of sanitary and phytosanitary protection would be appropriate. In carrying out risk assessment, countries are urged to use risk assessment techniques developed by the relevant international organizations. Since the drafting and entry into force of the SPS Agreement, a substantial amount of work has been undertaken in the area of risk analysis by the FAO/ WHO Joint Codex Alimentarius Commission, the Secretariat of the International Plant Protection Convention and the International Office of Epizootics.[187] On the other hand, the SPS Agreement permits governments to choose not to use international standards and adopt lower standards. The Agreement also permits the adoption of SPS measures on a provisional basis as a precautionary step, in cases where there is an immediate risk of the spread of diseases but where the scientific evidence is insufficient.

All countries must maintain an Enquiry Point, which is an office in charge of receiving and responding to requests for information regarding domestic SPS measures, including new or existing regulations and decisions based on risk assessment. Countries are required to notify the World Trade Organization (WTO) Secretariat of any new SPS requirement, or modification of existing requirements, which they are proposing to introduce domestically, if the requirements differ from international standards and may affect international trade. The WTO Secretariat circulates the notifications to all member countries. Notifications should be submitted in advance of the implementation of the measure, so as to provide other countries with the opportunity to comment on them. In cases of emergency, governments may implement a measure prior to notification. Countries are also requested to publish the sanitary and phytosanitary measures they have adopted.

The SPS Agreement provides for special and differential treatment in favour of developing countries and least-developed countries (LDCs). It includes, under certain circumstances, longer time-frames for compliance, time-limited exceptions from the obligations of the Agreement and facilitation of developing country participation in the work of the relevant international organizations.

The Agreement includes provisions for a two-year grace period for all developing countries (which expired at the end of 1997). However, this delay did not include the transparency provisions. For the LDCs, a five-year grace period, covering all obligations including the transparency ones, will expire at the end of 1999. One of the advantages of the transitional period is that countries are not required to provide a scientific justification for their SPS measures during this period, therefore, their measures can not be challenged on this basis.

Main differences between the SPS and TBT Agreements

While the SPS Agreement is a new agreement concluding during the Uruguay Round, a plurilateral Agreement on Technical Barriers to Trade (TBT), applying only to those countries which chose to accept it, had already been negotiated during the Tokyo Round (1974-1979). The TBT agreement, while not primarily negotiated having SPS concerns in mind, covered, nevertheless, requirements for food safety, animal and plant health measures, inspection and labelling. This Agreement was modified during the Uruguay Round and constitutes an integral part of the Final Act of the Uruguay Round, thus applying to all WTO Members. It covers all technical regulations and voluntary standards and the procedures to ensure that these are met, except when these are sanitary or phytosanitary measures as defined by the SPS Agreement. The TBT Agreement also covers measures aimed at protecting human health or safety, animal or plant life or health. To identify whether a specific measure is subject to the provisions of the SPS or the TBT Agreement, it is necessary to look at the purposes for which it has been adopted. As a general rule, if a measure is adopted to protect *human life* from the risks arising from additives, toxins, plant and animal-carried diseases; *animal life* from the risks arising from additives, toxins, pests diseases, disease-causing organisms;

plant life from the risks arising from pests, diseases, disease-causing organisms; and a *country* from the risks arising from damages caused by the entry, establishment or spread of pests, this measure is a SPS measure. Measures adopted for other purposes, to protect human, animal and plant life, are subject to the TBT Agreement. For instance a pharmaceutical restriction would be a measure covered by the TBT Agreement.[188] Labelling requirements related to food safety are usually SPS measures, while labels related to the nutrition characteristics or the quality of a product falls under the TBT discipline.

Disputes under the WTO involving violations of the SPS Agreement

Since the inception of the new Dispute Settlement Mechanism under the WTO in January 1995, three cases involving alleged violations of the SPS Agreement have reached the final stage of dispute resolution, that is, adoption of a panel/Appellate Body ruling by the Dispute Settlement Body (DSB). Moreover, in two additional disputes mutually acceptable solutions were found by the parties before the establishment of a panel.[189] In several other cases, consultations are still pending, as the parties have not found mutually acceptable solutions but have not asked for the establishment of a panel either.[190]

The first of the three cases that have reached the final stage of the adoption of panel/Appellate Body ruling by DSB were the complaints by the **United States** and **Canada** against a measure introduced by the EC prohibiting imports of bovine meat and meat products from cattle treated with six growth hormones. The EC forbade the use of such hormones in its territory and had prohibited "hormone-treated beef" imports since 1989, since, in its view, beef hormones might threaten human health. On the other hand, according to the United States and Canada, the use of hormones for growth promotion purposes in cattle was safe and posed no threat to human health. Therefore the EC measure, they contended, was scientifically unfounded and was designed to protect EC domestic producers from foreign competition. The panel reports, which were released in August 1997, found that the EC ban was inconsistent with the SPS Agreement, since it was neither based on international standards nor was it justified by a risk assessment (violation of Articles 3.1, 3.3 and 5 of the SPS Agreement). The EC appealed the panels' decisions. The Appellate Body (AB) upheld most of the findings and conclusions of the panels and concluded that the EC ban was inconsistent with the requirements of Arti- cles 3.3—as it was not based upon a risk assessment— and 5.1 of the SPS Agreement, which calls for the need for scientific justification for measures which imply a higher level of SPS protection than that included in international standards. In particular, the AB emphasized that nations have the right to set their SPS standards at higher levels than those set by accepted international organizations (in this case the Codex Alimentarius), provided a risk assessment has been carried out showing that a risk may indeed exist. However, the AB found that the EC import prohibition was not based on a risk assessment. The EC was given 15 months (expiring in May 1999) as a "reasonable period of time" for complying with the recommendations of the Appellate Body.

Since the AB report was issued, the EC has maintained that the AB ruling gives it the right to retain the ban while complementary risk assessments are performed to provide the necessary scientific evidence for permanently prohibiting "hormone beef" imports. According to the EC, the AB did not find that the import prohibition per se was inconsistent with the SPS Agreement, but only that the EC had violated its obligation under the Agreement by not conducting a proper risk assessment as the basis for the import prohibition. Therefore, by providing a more adequate risk assessment, the EC would put itself in compliance with the Agreement. According to the United States and Canada, the EC was free to conduct a risk assessment, but such a risk assessment would be irrelevant to the implementation of the recommendations of the AB and could not be used to delay compliance: the withdrawal of the ban would be the only action consistent with the WTO ruling.

While some preliminary results of the complementary risk assessment were made available in May 1999, the EC has recognized that the complementary risk assessment might not be finalized until the year 2000. The EC, therefore, has suggested three interim measures[191] to implement the WTO ruling. However, these proposed options have been rejected by the complaining parties. WTO arbiters are in the process of deciding the amount of the retaliatory measures which the United States and Canada will be authorized to apply starting in July 1999.

According to some, the attitude taken by the EC in this case may weaken the SPS Agreement, the WTO dispute settlement mechanism and the credibility of the whole WTO system. The lack of timely and full implementation of the Appellate Body's recommendations may prove that there are loopholes in the SPS Agreement and that member countries may circumvent the obligations they have undertaken under it. On the other hand, the WTO verdict has attracted wide-spread criticism from consumer associations and food safety groups who have accused the WTO of supporting "downward harmonization". As a consequence of this case, the debate about the possible inclusion in the SPS Agreement of economic considerations or consumer concerns or about the need to strengthen the precautionary principle may be reopened.

In 1997 a panel was established at the request of **Canada** regarding Australia's ban on the importation of fresh, chilled, and frozen salmon. Australia had maintained this prohibition since 1975 to protect Australian fish from up to 24 diseases that could enter the country through imported salmon from Canada. According to Australia, the establishment of these diseases could have damaging economic and biological consequences for Australia's fisheries. Canada claimed that the Australian measures were not scientifically justified and represented a disguised restriction on international trade. The panel's report, which was released in June 1998, found that Australia was in violation of the SPS Agreement as it did not base its measures upon a risk assessment (violation of Articles 5.1 and 2.2); was using its import restrictions on salmon in a way that resulted in a disguised restriction on international trade (violation of Articles 5.5 and 2.3); and was maintaining a SPS measure which was more trade restrictive than necessary to reach Australia's appropriate level of SPS protection (violation of Article 5.6). In July 1998 Australia announced that it would appeal the panel's decision. While the Appellate Body reversed the panel's reasoning with respect to certain SPS Articles, it nevertheless found that Australia had acted inconsistently with some Articles of the SPS Agreement, namely Articles 5.1 and 2.2—since the relevant measure was not based upon a risk assessment—and Articles 5.5 and 2.3—since the measure represented a disguised restriction on international trade.

In 1997 the **United States** introduced a panel against Japan regarding Japan's approval process for the importation of certain agricultural products. Japan prohibited the importation of eight fruits originating, *inter alia*, from the United States, on the ground that they were potential hosts of a pest of quarantine significance to Japan. The import prohibition on these products could, however, be lifted if an exporting country proposed an alternative quarantine treatment (i.e. fumigation) which achieved a level of protection equivalent to the import prohibition. The exporting country bore the burden of proving the efficacy of the alternative. In 1987, Japan's Ministry of Agriculture, Forestry and Fisheries developed two guidelines for the confirmation of the efficacy of the alternative quarantine treatment: a guideline which outlined testing requirement applicable to the initial lifting of the import prohibition on a product; and a guideline which set out the testing requirement for approval of additional varieties of that product (so-called varietal testing). The United states claimed that it took from two to four years to conduct the necessary varietal tests, that tests were expensive, and that Japan's policy adversely affected U.S. agricultural exports and violated Japan's obligations under the SPS Agreement. The panel determined that Japan's measures were violating several SPS articles, since they were not based upon scientific evidence (violation of Article 2.2) and were more trade restrictive than necessary (violation of Article 5.6). Moreover, since Japan had not published the measure, the panel held that Japan was also in violation of Article 7 and Annex B.1, both related to transparency. In 1998, Japan notified its intention to appeal the panel report. The Appellate Body upheld most of the findings of the panel and expanded them, confirming that Japan's varietal testing requirement could not be scientifically justified, was not based on a risk assessment and, therefore, was inconsistent with the SPS Agreement.

Main issues for developing countries in the SPS Agreement

The triennial review

According to Article 12.7 of the SPS Agreement, "the Committee shall review the operation and implementation of this Agreement three years after the date of entry into force of the WTO Agreement. . .". The SPS Committee agreed in July 1998 on a procedure to review the operation and implementation of the Agreement. The Committee finalized the Triennial Review in March 1999.[192] The SPS Committee did not recommend any modification of the text of the Agreement as a result of the review. However, since the review was not regarded as exhaustive, it was decided that Member countries could at any time raise issues for consideration by the Committee, as provided by Article 12.7.

Even though no modifications were introduced in the legal text, several issues have captured in particular the attention of country delegations and some suggestions to improve the functioning of the Agreement have been put forward.

International standards and international standardizing organizations

The divergence of standards and regulations creates costs for international trade. In some cases these costs are justified, since they arise from legitimate differences in societal preferences, technological development, environmental and health conditions. In these cases standards harmonization would not be a desirable solution, while mutual recognition of standards would provide a better option. On the other hand, where divergences are not justified, international harmonization of standards seems to be an appropriate solution. However, it is the efficiency and fairness of the international standard development process that is crucial for minimizing distortions to international trade. The benefits of harmonization may be impeded if the process is captured by special interests in order to exclude other market participants or if it is not adequately transparent.[193]

Article 3 of the SPS Agreement encourages countries to use international standards as a basis for their regulations. In Annex A it recognizes for food safety the standards, guidelines and recommendations established by the Codex Alimentarius Commission (Box 1), for animal health those developed by the International Office of Epizootics (OIE) (Box 2), and for plant protection those developed under the auspices of the Secretariat of the International Plant Protection Convention (IPPC) (Box 3). For matters not covered by these organizations, standards developed by "other relevant international organizations open for membership to all Members", as identified by the SPS Committee, are recognized. However, the Agreement does not specify the procedures that the relevant international organizations should adhere to in order to produce genuine international standards.

In the absence of more precise indications, standards developed by a limited number of countries or approved by a narrow majority of participants may get the status of international standards. Developing countries have repeatedly expressed their concern about the way in which international standards are developed and approved, pointing out how their own participation is very limited from the point of view of both numbers and effectiveness. As a consequence of the inadequacy of the process, international standards are often inappropriate for use as a basis for domestic regulations in developing countries and these countries face problems when they have to meet regulations in the importing markets developed on the basis of international standards.

Under the present rules, the Codex Alimentarius Commission and the OIE adopt standards, guidelines and recommendations by a simple majority of votes cast, when adoption by consensus proves to be impossible to achieve. Because of the simple majority rule, some Codex standards were adopted or rejected by a relatively small majority with a large number of member countries not voting in favour. Two recent examples illustrate this situation: the standard on maximum residue limits for growth hormones (beef) was approved by 33 votes in favour, 29 against and 7 abstentions. The revised standard for natural mineral waters was approved by 33 votes in favour, 31 against and 10 abstentions.[194] The way in which these standards were adopted has given rise to a number of criticisms and questions on the genuine international nature of Codex standards. As a result, the Codex Alimentarius Commission is in the process of analysing a number of options to improve the standard-setting process and to ensure that standards truly reflect the views of all member countries or, at least, of a large majority of them (see Box 4). On the other hand, in certain cases developing countries have been successful in urging the Codex Alimentarius Commission to develop standards on products of export interest to them, such as certain tropical fresh fruits and vegetables, and in ensuring that their concerns were taken into account while developing standards for products that they export, like in the case of sugars or edible oils.

BOX 1

The Joint FAO/WHO
Codex Alimentarius Commission

The Codex Alimentarius Commission's membership totalled 163 countries in 1998. The Commission has nine General Committees whose work is relevant to standards for all commodities, 16 Commodity Committees which have responsibility for developing standards for specific food or classes of food, and five Co-ordinating Committees, one per region, to ensure that the work of Codex is responsive to regional needs. A feature of the "Committee system" is that each committee is hosted by a Member country responsible largely for the cost of the committee's maintenance and administration and for providing the Committee's Chairperson. The Commission meets every two years. Depending on the need, meetings of Codex subsidiary bodies are held by host countries usually once a year. The Codex Alimentarius, which is a collection of international food standards adopted by the Codex Alimentarius Commission, includes standards for all the principal foods: processed, semi-processed or raw. To date, the Codex Alimentarius includes 4,821 standards. The main purpose of the standards is to protect the health of consumers and to ensure fair practices in the food trade. Standards are specified in the areas of Food Standards for Commodities, Codes of Hygienic or Technological Practice, Pesticides Evaluated, Limits for Pesticide Residues, Guidelines for Contaminants, Food Additives Evaluated, and Veterinary Drugs Evaluated.

BOX 2

The Office International des Epizooties (OIE)

The OIE has currently 151 Member countries. Its objectives and functions include the harmonization of health requirements for international trade in animals and animal products and the adoption of international standards in the field of animal health. The International Committee is the highest authority of the OIE. It comprises all the delegates of the Member countries and meets at least once a year. The Specialist Commissions, such as the International Animal Health Code Commission and the Standard Commission, are involved in the preparation of OIE recommendations. OIE has five Regional Commissions to study specific problems affecting veterinary services and organize co-operation within the regions.

In the case of the IPPC, a two-thirds majority for the establishment of a standard is required. However, passage by vote is allowed only when a draft has been presented twice to the Interim Commission on Phytosanitary Measures and no consensus has been reached. The Interim Commission, established in 1997 as a result of the revision of the IPPC, is pursuing the adoption of its own procedure for the elaboration of standards[195] and will discuss this topic at its next meeting (4-8 October 1999). Two concerns have strongly influenced discussions to date: increased transparency and increased participation by developing countries. Numerous changes to the present procedures are proposed to address these concerns.

BOX 3

The International Plant Protection Convention

The Secretariat of the IPPC was formed in 1993 and the standard-setting activity started the same year. The IPPC is responsible for phytosanitary standard-setting and the harmonization of phytosanitary measures affecting trade. To date, eight standards have been completed and 14 others are at different stages of development. The Interim Commission on Phytosanitary Measures has the responsibility for identifying the topics and priorities for the standard-setting activity. The IPPC is an international treaty for plant protection to which 107 countries currently adhere. The Convention came into force in 1952 and has been amended once in 1979 and again in 1997.

As pointed out in the previous paragraphs, standards formulation procedures vary among international standards setting organizations. Therefore, an initial step towards the establishment of a more coherent, transparent and effective system of international standardization would be the harmonization of the procedures. A second step would be to restate the principle that consensus should be pursued throughout the different phases of standard setting and that the participation of countries from different geographical regions and at different levels of development should be ensured. It would be useful to evaluate which initiatives have been taken up to now by international standardizing bodies to ensure the effective participation of developing countries in the adoption of standards and whether those organizations have taken into account the specific conditions of developing countries while setting standards. Acknowledging the concerns raised by developing countries in the review process, the SPS Committee has agreed to communicate these concerns to the Codex Alimentarius, the OIE and the IPPC, and has requested them to keep the Committee informed of any action taken in this regard.

The process of international standards setting is becoming increasingly politicized, with the inclusion of a large number of non-traditional stakeholders. This trend makes the adoption of standards more complex and time-consuming and implies that considerations of a non scientific nature may play a role. Some developed and developing countries have stressed the principle that domestic health and safety measures and international SPS standards must be based on science as a precondition for an effective implementation of the SPS Agreement. While strict adherence to this principle may help prevent the introduction of protectionist measures, developing countries have to be ready to demonstrate the scientific soundness of their own SPS measures, also through carrying out risk assessments, when these measures differ from international standards. They may also need to challenge the risk assessment carried out by their trade partners as the scientific basis for their SPS measures. Risk assessment may represent a major problem for developing countries, since they often lack the human and financial resources for it.

Box 4

Codex Alimentarius: some options to improve the standard-setting process

The Codex Committee on General Principles, at its Fourteenth Session, 19-23 April 1999, discussed the following options to improve its standard-setting process:

1. The Rules of Procedure could be amended to make it clear that every effort should be made to reach consensus on all matters, including the adoption of standards (at present any member has the right to call for a vote to be taken on any matter at any time);

2. The most desirable approach would be to try to avoid situations where voting on the adoption of standards is resorted to. In situations where consensus cannot be achieved and voting cannot be avoided, one possible approach would be to increase the majority required to a two-thirds majority. When the requirement of a two-thirds majority vote could constitute an undue block on the process of adopting standards, a two-thirds majority vote would be required on the first two sessions at which the standard is proposed for adoption. However, if the same standard is reconsidered for adoption at a subsequent session, only a simple majority would be required for its adoption;

3. Some measures could be taken to facilitate consensus building in the elaboration of standards: i. Reallocating work priorities to take into account the possibility of reaching consensus on particular subject areas; ii. Ensuring that the scientific basis is well established; iii. Ensuring that issues are thoroughly discussed at meetings of the Committees concerned; iv. Organizing informal meetings of the parties concerned where disagreements arise; v. Redefining the scope of the subject matter being considered for the elaboration of standards, in order to cut out issues on which consensus cannot be reached; vi. Ensuring that

matters do not progress from step to step until all relevant concerns are taken into account and adequate compromises worked out; vii. Emphasizing to the Committees and their Chairpersons that matters should not be passed on to the Commission until such time as consensus has been achieved at the technical level.

However, the Committee could not agree to change the simply majority rule to a two-thirds majority when consensus could not be found. Countries which opposed this change alleged that a two-thirds majority requirement would slow down Codex procedures and make it more difficult to propose new standards or to amend existing ones.

Source: Joint FAO/WHO Food Standard Programme, Codex Committee on General Principles, op. cit.

In the framework of the triennial review of the TBT Agreement, the issue of international standards and international standardization organizations was also addressed and some suggestions were put forward to eliminate or minimize problems related to it. It may be of interest to analyse these suggestions and assess whether they can usefully apply in the context of SPS. Ideally, a coordinated and common approach should be followed, given the similarity of the two Agreements.

In particular, in the framework of the TBT review, it was suggested that in the exchange of information evidence be included about the difficulties that countries face in relation with international standards, to encourage international standardizing bodies to follow the rules spelt out in the Code of Good Practice, and to invite them to a session of the TBT Committee[196] in order to give information on issues of particular concern to member countries. These concerns include, for example, transparency of procedures (e.g. publications or notifications of draft standards, availability of work programmes); openness in drawing up programmes (e.g. responsive to the needs of the market and regulators, and reflection of trade priorities); procedures for comments and decision making; percentage of standards developed by consensus and the definition of consensus; and whether and how account is taken of the special problems of developing countries. The EC has suggested that if international standards are to play the role assigned to them by the WTO Agreements, the international standardization bodies should remain accountable to the entire range of interested parties, and should achieve a high degree of effectiveness. The EC has spelled out some rules in this regard[197] and has suggested the establishment of some kind of formal code of procedures for observance by international bodies, along the line of the Code of Good Practice. The United States has stressed that international standardizing bodies should have established procedures to ensure that all interested parties have adequate notice, time and opportunity to make an input into the development of standards. It has also suggested that the TBT Committee articulate a set of principles and procedures to be followed by international standardizing bodies.

Equivalency

The SPS Agreement encourages countries to give positive consideration to accepting as equivalent the SPS measures of other members, even if these measures differ from their own or from those used by other countries, if the exporting country demonstrates that its measures achieve the importing member's appropriate level of sanitary and phytosanitary protection (Article 4.1). However, the implementation of this principle so far has been rather limited. Developing countries have reported that in several instances importing countries are looking for "sameness", instead of equivalency, of measures. The interpretation of equivalency as sameness is depriving Article 4.1 of its function, which is to recognize that different measures can achieve the same level of sanitary and phytosanitary protection and therefore countries can enjoy flexibility about the kind of measures to adopt to ensure adequate SPS protection.

Equivalency is the best option when harmonization of standards is not desirable or when international standards are lacking or are inappropriate. For developing countries, which face climatic, developmental, and technological conditions rather different from those prevailing in developed countries, the recognition of the equivalency of their SPS measures to those applied by the importing countries would represent a key instrument to enhance market access for their products.

Equivalency at regional level, in the framework of regional or sub-regional agreements, is easier to achieve. Developing countries may therefore have an interest in analysing the possibility of including reference to equivalency of SPS measures in the framework of regional and sub-regional groupings.

Equivalency of regulations is at present taking place in very special cases, as for example, among the Member countries of the European Community, among those of the North American Free Trade Agreement (NAFTA), and, more recently, between Australia and New Zealand. In the case of the EC, the concept of mutual recognition among Member countries was made explicit in the "Cassis de Dijon" decision by the European Court of Justice in 1979. The decision explicitly stated that nations were free to maintain and enforce their own regulations for products produced within their jurisdiction but that they could not legally prevent their citizens from consuming products that met the legal standards of another Member country of the EC, as long as they offered an equivalent level of protection of the public interests at issue. However, it seems that where technical regulations play a significant role in domestic markets, equivalency only works if there is either a formal arrangement, or harmonized standards have been developed. This is particularly the case when there are serious concerns about health and safety hazards.[198]

In February 1995, the EC Council agreed a mandate authorizing the Commission to conduct negotiations with a view to the conclusions of agreements with third countries on sanitary and phytosanitary measures. Following this mandate, the EC Commission has conducted negotiations with a number of countries. Agreements have been concluded with the United States, Canada, New Zealand and the Czech Republic, while negotiations are continuing with Australia, Uruguay, Chile and Argentina.

The Agreement between the EC and the United States on sanitary measures is aimed at facilitating trade in live animals and animal products between the two countries, by establishing a mechanism for the recognition of equivalence of sanitary measures. The procedure to reach recognition of equivalency is, however, rather complicated and consists of several steps. Basically, the importing country has to explain the objective of the sanitary measure for which recognition of equivalency is sought and identify its appropriate level of sanitary protection. The exporting country has to demonstrate that its sanitary measure achieves the importing country's appropriate level of sanitary protection. On the basis of the evidence provided by the exporting country, the importing country decides whether the foreign measure achieves its appropriate level of sanitary protection and, therefore, can be regarded as equivalent. The evidence that the exporting country may be requested to provide includes its domestic legislation regarding standards, procedures, policies, infrastructure, enforcement and control; the efficacy of its enforcement and control programme; and the powers of its regulatory authority. The agreement includes application of the principle of regionalization for the main animal diseases and lists those commodities for which equivalency is recognized. The other agreements negotiated by the EC are similar to the one described.[199]

The NAFTA Treaty provides for the mutual recognition of SPS measures if the exporting country's regulations achieve the importing country's appropriate level of protection. The burden of proof is on the exporter. If the importing country does not accept the exporting country SPS measure as equivalent, then it has to give reasons in writing upon request (Article 714). The final decision about equivalency stays with the authorities of the importing country who take decisions on a case by case basis.

Australia and New Zealand have agreed, under the 1996 Trans Tasman Mutual Recognition Agreement (TTMRA), to recognize each other's regulations in specific industrial sectors. This means that a product legally sold in one market can be also sold in the other without having to comply with additional requirements. In New Zealand, equivalency has also been provided in some cases by making reference to the applying national standards of other countries as means of compliance for regulations. In the food sector, the two countries have implemented mutual recognition of their respective regulations. However the next step will be the setting up of a joint food standards system which is expected to enter into force by the end of 1999.[200]

The recognition of the equivalence is not easy to achieve and usually implies the fulfiment of several requirements. However, for developing countries, this option is worth pursuing since it would greatly facilitate market access for their products.

Mutual Recognition Agreements

Mutual Recognition Agreements (MRAs) can take several forms. They can be limited to testing methods, they can cover conformity assessment certificates, or they can be full-fledged and include the standards themselves. MRAs of the first type entail only limited savings in international trade, but play an important role in building up confidence between laboratories in different countries and usually represent a necessary step towards the conclusion of broader MRAs. MRAs on conformity assessment improve market access by avoiding duplicative testing and the related costs, by reducing possible discrimination against foreign products and by eliminating delays. Moreover, they may represent crucial learning experiences, since they imply an intensive exchange of information and close contacts between relevant authorities. MRAs of the third type require that parties consider their domestic requirements as equivalent, with the consequence that a good which can be legally sold in one country may be legally sold in the other(s). Article 4.2 of the SPS Agreement makes reference to this last type of MRA.[201]

The limited capacity of several developing countries to carry out the functions of certification and accreditation of laboratory testing has serious implications for MRAs and for trade liberalization in general. This is reflected in the very small number of MRAs which involve developing countries. The lack of reciprocal recognition of standards and conformity assessment procedures on the national level has been mirrored on the regional level, where regional standardizing bodies in developing countries have accomplished relatively little during the history of their operation, due in part to the lack of dynamism and interest on the part of their members.[202]

On the other hand, in the framework of regional trade arrangements, there appears to be an increased acceptance of the advantages of mutual recognition as a means of advancing the objectives of integration and trade facilitation. Mutual recognition for conformity assessment is mandatory within the EC[203] and has been agreed as a basic principle within the Asia-Pacific Economic Co-operation (APEC), where the text of a model Mutual Recognition Agreement has already been adopted. The Free Trade Area of the Americas (FTAA), NAFTA, MERCOSUR, the Association of Southeast Asian Nations (ASEAN) and the Andean Group are also considering how to make progress in this area.[204]

The following measures could enhance the beneficial role that MRAs can play in international trade: MRAs should be developed in a transparent way (i.e., the SPS Committee should be informed of the intention of two or more countries to negotiate an MRA, the draft MRA should be notified to member countries for comments, the adopted text should be published); they should be open to other parties who wish to join them at a later stage; they should contain flexible rules of origin (i.e., the benefits of a MRA should be granted to all products which pass through the conformity assessment procedures of the contracting parties and not only to products originating in those countries). However, the costs in terms of the negotiation and implementation of such arrangements need to be taken into account.[205]

To alleviate the problem of non-recognition of developing country certificates, the pooling of human resources for research and laboratory development could be envisaged in regional and sub-regional agreements and the establishment of regional or sub-regional laboratories, certification bodies and accreditation institutions could be considered . These bodies could be granted international financing and be regularly supervised by the Codex Alimentarius Commission, the OIE and the Secretariat of the IPPC.

Transparency and notification provisions

Transparency is vital to make sure that SPS measures are scientifically sound and do not have an unnecessary detrimental impact on international trade. However, variations in the quality and content of the information provided by countries in their notifications, short comment periods, delays in responding to requests for documentation, absence, at times, of due consideration for the comments provided by other Members are recurrent problems limiting the effective implementation of the transparency provisions.

In order to improve transparency, some measures were agreed during the triennial review of the SPS Agreement. According to the Agreement, Members shall allow a reasonable interval between the publication of a SPS measure and its entry into force. This time frame is crucial for producers to adapt their products to the new requirements. An adequate time frame has also to be provided between the notification of a proposed regulation and its adoption, since this allows other Members to provide comments on the draft. Sixty days have been agreed as the appropriate time-frame in the latter case, while no decision has been taken for the first case. Language may be an obstacle to the effective capacity of countries to comment on draft regulations. Therefore, it was agreed that at least a summary of the proposed regulation in one of the official languages of the WTO should be made available by the notifying country.

At times, even when countries are able to provide comments on the draft, those comments are not taken account of by the notifying country and the whole exercise becomes worthless. A possible solution to this problem could be that when comments and suggestions are not reflected in the final text of the measure, the notifying country has to explain the reason.

As a means to improve the efficiency and the speed of the notification procedures, some countries, both developed and developing, have proposed the use of electronic transmission. While electronic means may in fact improve the system, it should be kept in mind that several developing countries still have limited access to INTERNET and that many enquiry points in developing countries do not have well-functioning e-mail systems. Therefore, not all countries would benefit from a switch from hard copy notification to electronic notification. A possible solution would be to make the two systems complementary. The SPS Committee has recommended Members to publish their SPS measures on the world wide web, in order to improve transparency.

The SPS Committee is a forum where countries can discuss the implementation of the Agreement, bring the difficulties they are experiencing in the field of sanitary and phytosanitary measures to the attention of other countries and challenge specific SPS measures proposed or already implemented by other Members. Developing countries are, unfortunately, making limited use of this forum, as well as of the other transparency provisions included in the Agreement. This may be due to the fact that the links between the public authorities and the private sector are only loose and, therefore public authorities are not fully aware of the difficulties that exporters face, while the private sector does not have appropriate channels to bring the difficulties it experiences to the attention of the competent authorities. Developing countries may, therefore, consider making the necessary efforts to strengthen these links.

Adaptation to regional conditions

Within a given country, the situation regarding plant or animal disease may not be uniform. The importing country should, therefore, consider whether there are zones within the exporting country which represent a lesser danger, either as a result of the prevailing natural conditions or because the exporting country has made efforts to eradicate the disease from such zones and has taken the necessary measures to prevent its reintroduction.

The adaptation to regional conditions, including the recognition of pest- or disease-free areas or areas of low pest or disease prevalence (Article 6), is of key relevance to developing countries, especially large countries where geographical, environmental and epidemiologic conditions may vary considerably from one region to the other. In some cases the provision of adaptation to regional conditions has facilitated trade in agriculture products (see Box 5). However, the efforts to eradicate a pest or disease from a specific area may imply large investment and the procedures to prove that an area is pest- or disease-free or is an area of low pest or disease prevalence are usually long and burdensome and often involve the need to provide complex scientific evidence (see Box 6). Developing countries have, therefore, not been able to fully benefit from this Article, despite the support provided by the relevant international organizations. Possible solutions include the simplification of the procedures, while maintaining them scientifically sound, and support for developing countries to prepare their submissions for the recognition of pest- or disease-free areas or of areas of low pest or disease prevalence (see Box 7). Developing countries have to determine when it is feasible and cost-effective to make efforts to eradicate a particular disease from a zone and whether they can get appropriate return on their investment. This is clearly an area where expert assistance would facilitate the actual implementation of the provision of the Agreement by developing countries. Once a country or an area within a country has been declared pest- or disease-free by the relevant international organizations, this status should not be questioned again by individual trade partners, which should refrain from requesting additional evidence of the status of a country or area free from pests or diseases.

BOX 5

Adaptation to regional conditions: problems and achievements

Brazil and the United States have held talks to liberalize imports of fresh bovine meat from certain southern states in Brazil which are aftosa-free. However, until now, the talks have been inconclusive. The same is happening in the case of Brazilian exports to Japan and Canada. Both countries are banning imports of fresh bovine meet from Brazil, including from the states of Rio Grande do Sul and Santa Catarina where no cases of aftosa fever have been reported since 1994. The EC has recognized that some Brazilian states are aftosa-free and is, therefore, authorizing imports from these states, but limited to bovine meat without bones only. In other cases the principle of adaptation to regional conditions has led to more concrete results: the United States nowadays allows imports of uncooked beef from regions in Argentina which have been recognized aftosa-free after a 80-year ban. The United States recently replaced a 83-year ban on imports of Mexican avocados with a process standard which allows avocados from a specified region in Mexico to be exported to the northeastern United States during winter months.

Special and differential treatment

Even though the SPS Agreement includes a specific Article (Article 10) on special and differential treatment (S&D) for developing countries and LDCs, the provisions of this article apparently have not been converted into specific obligations. Developing countries' agricultural exports are often concentrated in a few products and in a few markets. Each developing country could, therefore, prepare a short list of the main agricultural products it exports (perhaps a list of five to seven products), identify the main obstacles it faces in the principal countries of destination (again a list of five to seven markets) and request these countries and/or the relevant international organizations to provide assistance to facilitate the export of the listed products. Assistance would be multi-faceted and could include the following elements: help in eradicating a disease; help in proving that a country is free from a certain disease; support to improve packaging and transportation; support in the development of Good Manufacturing Practices for individual plants or for groups of products, such as meat and meat products, milk and dairy products, fish and fishery products; training of laboratory personnel who deal with the assessment of the exported products, etc.

BOX 6

Adaptation to regional conditions: the case of Egypt

Starting on September 1998, the EC has been banning potato imports from Egypt because of contamination from potato brown rot, in a derogation from recognized "pest-free areas". The decision taken by the European authorities has, therefore, changed the regime for Egyptian potato imports from all products considered disease-free unless proven otherwise, to all imports considered diseased unless proven to be disease-free. 133 dossiers for the recognition of pest-free areas were subsequently prepared by Egypt. However, only 23 were taken into consideration by the EC Standing Plant Protection Committee and ultimately only five pest-free areas were approved, while for other 14 areas additional documentation was requested. According to the EC authorities, the very low score of approval of disease-free areas was due to the fact that the documentation prepared by Egypt was inadequate (e.g. maps were not readable, documentation was in Arabic), which was due to the lack of technical capabilities in the country to deal with this issue. On the other hand, Egypt felt that the EC measure was unjustified. It claimed that brown rot was endemic in the EC and that it had actually been introduced in Egypt because of infected seeds imported from the EC. It also contended that the European authorities were much stricter with Egypt than with other suppliers. However, the EC ban is disrupting trade in a product which ranks third in Egypt for the generation of foreign exchange.

Source: findings from on-going research carried out by the Centre for Food Economic Research, Department of Agricultural and Food Economics, The University of Reading, United Kingdom.

BOX 7

Recognition of Foot and Mouth Disease (FMD)-free countries
by the International Office of Epizootics (OIE)

The International Office of Epizootics (OIE) had developed a procedure for the international recognition of Foot and Mouth Disease (FMD)-free countries. The procedure is voluntary and it is applied so that the OIE can recognize that the entire country or certain zones are free from FMD. Salient feautres of the procedure are as follows:

1.   The interested country sends a proposal to the Director General of the OIE, accompanied by a comprehensive report bsed on a model prepared by the OIE;

2.   The OIE Commission on FMD can support a country proposal to the Director General of the OIE, accompanied by a comprehensive report based on a motdel prepared by the OIE;

2.   The OIE Commission on FMD can support a country proposal at this stage, if it is convinced that the application is well-founded. Otherwise, it can decide not to support the proposal and request clarification or additional information. It can decide that the visit of a group of experts is necessary. The cost of a visit is borne by the applicant country;

3.   The Director General informs all OIE member countries of the Commission's support for a country's proposal. Countries have 60 days to inform the OIE of any objections they may have, based on scientific or technical grounds. The Commission then examines any objections received and decides whether or not to accept them.

4.   Each year, during its general session, the OIE adopts, by resolution, the list of recognized FMD-free countries and zones;

5.   Maintaining the FMD-free status is subject to continual observation of the OIE's rules and regulations and the declaration of any significant events likely to modify such status.

OIE' recognition of FMD-free status is not legally binding. However, if the WTO were called upon to resolve a dispute over the exporting country status regarding FMD, the country's recognition by the OIE could have a bearing on the panel's decision. The OIE has started performing similar tasks for other major diseases.

Source: T. Chillaud, R.E. Reichard, J. Blancou (1997), *The standardization activities of the Office International des Epizooties*, OIE, Paris.

Technical co-operation

The SPS Agreement was apparently negotiated and concluded with scant regard for the conditions necessary for its effective implementation, particularly in developing countries. Article 9.1, provides that the assistance that shall be provided to developing countries bilaterally or through the appropriate international organizations, may, inter alia, take the form of credits, donations and grants. The effective implementation of this provision would create a more substantial type of policy coherence since it would enable developing countries to establish the necessary infrastructural and other conditions necessary to the effective implementation of the Agreement. Technical co-operation and financial support, however, are not a panacea and should not be used to replace the removal of unnecessary obstacles to trade.

Technical co-operation could be extended to cover capacity building of the officials in developing countries in charge of the enquiry points, since transparency is proving to be a key issue for the correct functioning of the Agreement. Technical co-operation should in particular be extended to upgrade the technical skill of personnel working in laboratories, certification bodies and accreditation institutions in developing countries, since their having a certain level of qualifications and training is a precondition for the international acceptance of certificates issued by them and represents the basis for the negotiation of equivalence and mutual recognition agreements. Since developing countries experience difficulties in dealing with the scientific side of the Agreement, in particular risk assessment, technical co-operation should be extended on this matter.

According to Article 9.2, "where substantial investments are required in order for an exporting developing country Member to fulfil the sanitary or phytosanitary requirements of an importing Member, the latter shall consider providing such technical assistance as will permit the developing country Member to maintain and expand its market access opportunities for the product involved". This provision should be strengthened by, first of all, requesting the country which has implemented an SPS measure which creates particular difficulties for developing countries, to reconsider it. Secondly, if, after reviewing its implications, the importing country reconfirms the measure, then the provision of technical co-operation, including the transfer of the necessary technology, should be considered mandatory. Countries that experience the same trade problems in connection with a specific SPS measure may wish to join forces and table a common position. For developing countries it may be useful both to develop flexible alliances among themselves and with developed countries, considering that the latter are often more experienced in bringing specific cases to the attention of other countries or to the attention of the SPS Committee. The least-developed countries are approaching the end of the transitional period (31 December 1999), therefore, special efforts should be made to enable them to comply with the requirements of the Agreement. Since technical co-operation in the field of sanitary and phytosanitary measures is being provided by several international organizations and by a number of developed countries, better co-ordination among the different institutions would ensure that beneficiary countries fully benefit from these efforts.

Outstanding issues

The benefits of trade liberalization in the agriculture sector achieved by the Uruguay Round negotiations could be undermined by the protectionist use of sanitary and phytosanitary measures. The SPS Agreement was negotiated to limit this danger and represents a useful instrument for this purpose. However, this paper has identified some limitations of the Agreement. It could thus be worth considering the introduction of certain amendments to the legal text to ensure that the risk of using SPS measures as border protection instrument is minimized, while all countries benefit equally from the Agreement. In this context, the following articles would need attention.

Article 3.   Since developing countries feel that their participation in the international standard-setting process is not effective and, therefore, they face problems in complying with measures based on international standards, reference should be made in the Article to the need for international standards to be developed through a fair process, based on consensus, where countries at different levels of development and from different geographical regions are effectively represented. The SPS Committee could be encouraged to develop a set of rules that the relevant international organizations should adhere to in the process of standard-setting.

Article 4.   Equivalency is being interpreted as "sameness". This interpretation is depriving Article 4.1 of its function, which is to recognize that different measures may achieve the same level of SPS protection and, therefore, countries can enjoy a certain level of flexibility regarding the kind of measures to adopt. This could be spelled out more clearly in the Article. Moreover, due to the benefits which would arise from the participation of developing countries in bilateral or multilateral agreements on recognition of the equivalence of specific SPS measures, developed country Members should accept requests in this regard coming from developing country Members. Considering that one of the main difficulties developing countries face in this field is the lack of recognition of their conformity assessment certificates, the setting up of internationally financed regional or sub-regional laboratories, certification bodies and accreditation institutions should be included in this Article. These institutions would function under the supervision of the Codex Alimentarius

Commission, the OIE, and the Secretariat of the IPPC. Moreover, the scope of Article 4 could be expanded to include MRAs on conformity assessment.

Article 6.   The adaptation to regional conditions is of key relevance to developing countries, however the procedures to prove that some areas are pest- or disease-free or at low risk are usually long and burdensome and often include the need to provide complex scientific evidence. On the other hand, the eradication of a specific disease from an area may require a considerable investment and there is a need, especially for developing countries, to establish whether they can get appropriate return on their investment. Therefore, clear reference would need to be made in the Article to the effect that scientific and administrative support shall be provided by international organizations and developed countries to developing countries to facilitate the implementation of the provisions on adaptation to regional conditions. Moreover, if a country, or an area within a country, has been recognized free from a certain disease by the competent international organization, the disease-free status should also be recognized by all trade partners, without the need to provide additional evidence.

Article 9.   Technical assistance is essential to facilitate developing country fulfilment of the obligations of the Agreement. Since the Agreement puts emphasis on the scientific side, technical co-operation should be extended to this area. Article 9 should, therefore, make reference to the upgrading of personnel and equipment of laboratories, certification bodies and accreditation institutions and to strengthening developing countries' ability to deal with scientific issues, especially those related to risk assessment and to the recognition of pest- or disease- free areas and areas of low pest or disease prevalence. The provisions included in Article 9.2 could be strengthened by making technical co-operation mandatory in cases when a new SPS measure introduced by an importing country creates particular problems for developing countries and by linking the fulfilment of the sanitary and phytosanitary requirements of the importing countries with the transfer of the necessary technology. The connection between credits, donations and grants on one side, and developing country ability to establish the necessary infrastructural and other conditions necessary to the effective implementation of the Agreement, on the other, should also be stressed. Since the transitional period granted to LDCs expires at the end of 1999, special technical assistance efforts should be devoted to these countries to allow them to fulfil the obligations of the Agreement and benefit from it.

Article 10.   Developing countries should be entitled to receive special support from their trade partners and from the relevant international organizations in relation to agricultural products of particular export interest to them to ensure that SPS measures do not hamper their exports of these listed products.

This would be a way to convert the provisions for S&D into specific obligations.

Annex B. Variations in the quality and content of the information provided by countries in their notifications, short comment periods, delays in responding to requests for documentation, and absence of due consideration for the comments provided are recurrent problems limiting the effective implementation of the transparency provisions. The SPS Committee has agreed that 60 days represents a reasonable time-frame for providing comments on draft regulations. On the other hand, a particular time-frame has not been agreed for the interval between the publication of a measure and its entry into force. Developing country Members will have to evaluate whether the 60-day time frame for providing comments on notified measures is appropriate to their needs or whether it should be modified, and suggest which time frame they consider suitable as a reasonable interval between publication and entry into force of SPS measures. Article 10.2 specifies, however, that "where the appropriate level of sanitary and phytosanitary protection allows scope for the phased introduction of new sanitary and phytosanitary measures, longer time-frames for compliance should be accorded on products of interest to developing country Members so as to maintain opportunities for their exports". New language could be included in Annex B to stress the expectation that the comments provided on the drafts are reflected in the final texts and that, in the case they are not, explanations should be provided. The WTO Secretariat could be encouraged to set up a data base which includes SPS measures implemented by Members which could have a major impact on developing countries' exports.

List of abbreviations

FMD	Food and mouth disease
GATT	General Agreement on Tariffs and Trade
LDCs	Least-developed countries
MRAs	Mutual Recognition Agreements
S&D	Special and differential
SPS	Sanitary and phytosanitary
TBT	Technical barriers to trade
TTMRA	Trans Tasman Mutual Recognition Agreement

Organizations

APEC	Asia-Pacific Economic Co-operatioon
ASEAN	Association of South East Asian Nations
EC	European Communities
EU	European Union
FAO	Food and Agriculture Organization of the United Nations
FTAA	Free Trade Area of the Americas
IPPC	International Plant Protection Convention
MERCOSUR	Southern Common Market
NAFTA	North American Free Trade Agreement
OIE	International Office of Epizootics
UN	United Nations
UNCTAD	United Nations Conference on Trade and Development
UNDP	United Nations Development Programme
WTO	World Trade Organization

NON-PREFERENTIAL RULES OF ORIGIN

Stefano Inama, UNCTAD

Coverage and scope of the Agreement: harmonization work programme on non-preferential rules of origin and the Common Declaration on preferential rules of origin

Rules of origin have long been considered as a rather technical issue for the exclusive use by customs officials, having very little to do with the implementation of other trade policy measures. In the last decade, the realities of international trade have shown that origin determination may have far reaching implications on a number of cross-cutting issues throughout several WTO agreements, besides the more generally and easily perceived "mechanical" and administrative needs to determine the origin of the goods and the applicable tariff regime at the point of entry of the importing WTO member. Nowadays and following the WTO Agreement on non-preferential rules of origin, implications may go beyond border control mechanisms and extend to internal disciplines regulating the marketing of products to final consumers.

For instance, issues such as marks of origin, linkages with geographical denomination, definition of "domestic industries" may not be directly linked to the traditional view of origin limited to a border control device. In international trade, the difficulties in assessing the implications of non-preferential origin determination are mainly due to the fact that they may be considered as "secondary trade policy instrument". In fact, the relevance of non-preferential rules of origin may only be fully grasped when they are associated with primary trade policy instruments such as tariffs, contingency protection measures, etc. As shown in this paper, the implications of non-preferential rules of origin become immediately apparent when utilized in the context of anti-dumping and circumvention, remaining textile quotas and transitional safeguards under the ATC, safeguards, etc. where trade frictions have already shown in the past the extent of origin determination.

Rules of origin are very often being associated to preferential trade regimes, where their concrete effect is more evident. In the case of preferential rules of origin, the compliance with the rules awards a preferential tariff. One of the main differences between non-preferential and preferential rules of origin is that in the case of the former they should always provide for an exhaustive method to determine origin. In the case of preferential rules of origin, if the origin criterion is not met, the preferential tariff will just not be applied without any need to recur to alternative methods. In the case of non-preferential origin, in order to administer trade policy measures, if the first origin criterion is not met, there must still be a method to determine the origin of the good. Hence, other rules should be provided to determine origin when the primary rule has not been met. Customs administrations need to know always where the goods come from. These ancillary rules, that are used to determine origin whenever the primary rule is not met, are commonly referred to as "residual rules".

The Agreement covers the area of application of non-preferential rules and sets up a programme to negotiate, within the World Customs Organization and WTO, a harmonized set of non-preferential rules of origin. While covered by the Common Declaration on preferential rules of origin, the preferential rules of origin are neither subject to a harmonization programme nor to strict discipline. The Common Declaration mainly contains general guidelines.

According to Art. 1 of the Agreement, **non-preferential rules of origin** are to be utilized to determine the origin of goods for the following purposes:

1. MFN tariffs and national treatment

2. Quantitative restrictions

3. Anti-dumping and countervailing duties

4. Safeguards measures

5. Origin marking requirement

6. Any discriminatory quantitative restriction and tariff quotas

7. Government procurement

8. Trade statistics

Article 3, paragraph (a), states that, after the work programme on harmonization is achieved, this set will be **equally applied for all purposes**. Accordingly, the Harmonized Rules of Origin (HRO) will have to be used for all trade policy measures taken according to the WTO agreements. This excludes the past practices of some major trading partners where different origin criteria for non-preferential origin were utilized depending on the trade instruments. However this view may not be generally shared. For instance, a derogation to the general principle of "equally applied for all purposes" is contained in footnote 1 to Article 1 of the Agreement providing that the definition of "domestic industry" or "like products of domestic industry" fall outside the scope of the above-mentioned article. In the framework of contingency protection measures, such as safeguards and anti-dumping proceedings, such measures are normally initiated at the request of a complainant domestic industry against products originating in a certain country. On the other hand, a normal anti-dumping procedure requires that, beside other findings relating to dumping and injury, the investigating authorities have to determine the origin of the product exported from the country subject to investigation. Although this is not always consistently carried out by the investigating authorities, the footnote to Article 1 of the Agreement seems to exclude the application of the harmonized rules of origin to the "domestic industry" lodging the complaint against the imports from other countries, while the same rules will be applied in the context of origin determination to products exported from the country subject to investigation. This imbalance will have to be correctly addressed in the context of negotiations. On the other hand and as contained in the submission by India (attached) and the subsequent US[206] proposals to the Committee on Rules of Origin, the scope of application of the HRO on other WTO agreements, although spelt out quite clearly in the Agreement as mentioned above, is still to be discussed. Most likely, this will prove to be one of the most contentious issues during the forthcoming negotiations.

The definition and purpose of preferential rules of origin is contained in Article 2 of the Common Declaration with regard to **preferential rules of origin**. According to this article, preferential rules of origin serve to determine "whether goods qualify for preferential tariff treatment under contractual or autonomous trade regime leading to tariff preferences well beyond the application of article I", i.e. lower than MFN tariffs.

The following may be quoted as an example of preferential rules of origin:

1. Autonomous preferential tariff treatment:

    —GSP Rules of origin

2. Contractual non-reciprocal rules of origin:

    —Lomé rules of origin

    —CBI rules of origin

    —Caribbean rules of origin

3.   Contractual reciprocal rules of origin, i.e. free trade agreements:

—NAFTA rules of origin

—Protocol on rules of origin contained in Euro-Med or Europe agreements

—MERCOSUR/Andean Group/ASEAN rules of origin.

Progress and current status of the negotiations

One of the main objectives of the Agreement on Rules of Origin is to harmonize non-preferential rules of origin, as envisaged under Article 9 in Part IV of the Agreement. As such, the Agreement was established with a built-in agenda. The Harmonization Work Programme (HWP), which was launched on 20 July 1995, was scheduled for completion, pursuant to Article 9.2(*a*) of the Agreement, within three years of its initiation, i.e. by 20 July 1998. However, while the Committee on Rules of Origin (CRO) and the Technical Committee on Rules of Origin in Brussels (TCRO)—the body responsible for the technical aspects of the work—made substantial progress in the HWP during this three-year period, the work has not been completed as scheduled, mainly due to the complexity of issues. While recognizing that the CRO was mandated to complete the HWP within three years of its initiation and the importance of concluding its Work Programme, the Council for Trade in Goods (CTG) and the General Council, in July 1998, approved the recommendations of the CRO: (1) that it, in cooperation with the TCRO, should continue the work identified in Articles 9.2 (c) and 9.3 of the Agreement; (2) that Members committed themselves to make their best endeavour to complete the HWP by November 1999; (3) that the TCRO shall submit the final result of its work to the CRO by the end of May 1999 for final consideration by the CRO; (4) that the CRO shall report to the CTG on the progress of work in February, June and October 1999; and (5) that in June 1999 the CRO shall review the status of the HWP and make a recommendation on a deadline for completing that work.

At the CRO meeting in June 1998, it was thought that the work programme could have been completed by November 1999. At its November meeting, the CRO considered that very useful work and substantial progress had been made since July 1998. However, the remaining work could not be completed on a best-endeavour basis by November 1999.

During the preparations for Seattle, few specific proposals were made on the HWP as contained in the box below:

- Harmonization work programme to be concluded and results adopted by the time of the next Ministerial Conference (Bulgaria, Czech Republic, E.C., Hungary, Morocco, Poland, Slovakia, Slovenia)

- Developing countries to be assisted in strengthening their participation in the negotiations on the harmonization programme in both WTO and WCO (Egypt)

- Impact of harmonization work programme on Members" rights and obligations to be addressed adequately in the Committee on Rules of Origin, with particular focus on areas of interest to developing countries, such as textiles and clothing (Egypt)

- Results of the negotiations not to introduce additional burdens or impediments on market access of products of export interest to developing countries (Egypt)

- Lack of common understanding among Members as to implications of future discipline to "equally apply" harmonized rules of origin for "all purposes"; General Council to consider whether, pending further discussion in the Committee, divergent views on scope of application of results of harmonization work programme can be resolved by further consultations with other WTO committees or would require further negotiations (United States)

- Potentially significant lack of compliance with procedural disciplines designed to capture "best customs practices" and provide transparency to traders; urgent and immediate attention to this area needed to renew confidence

- Concern with respect to non-completion of work programme on harmonization of non-preferential rules of origin within stipulated time period (Brazil, Costa Rica, Guatemala, New Zealand, Norway, Switzerland, United States); this work to take precedence over other initiatives (Brazil); calendar of future WCO technical work to be requested to determine whether additional steps needed to enhance prospects for progress on technical work (United States)

- Scope of application of the Agreement to be extended to other areas such as services, information technology and intellectual property; high-level meeting on rules of origin to be organized to define new strategy on this theme as well as future work in this regard (Morocco).

At the last CRO meeting, the Indian Delegation proposed a new deadline for completion of HWP for July 2000. However, the draft Ministerial Declaration contained indications that negotiations may continue till 31 December 2000. The status of the negotiations is recorded in the "integrated negotiating text for the Harmonization Work Programme". The forthcoming meeting in January is expected to design a management plan to finalize negotiations.

Responsibilities and method of work of the TCRO and CRO

Part IV of the Agreement on Rules of Origin, entitled "Harmonization of rules of origin", deals specifically with, inter alia, the work programme for establishing a set of harmonized non-preferential rules of origin. While under Article 4 of the Agreement, the Committee on Rules of Origin was established, the actual elaboration of the harmonized rules was to be carried out by a technical committee "under the auspices of the Customs Cooperation Council" (now WCO) (see article 4, para. 2). According to Article 9, paragraph 2 (c), with reference to the work programme, the Technical Committee should first develop harmonized definitions of:

(i) Wholly obtained products and minimal operations or processes;

(ii) Substantial transformation - change in tariff classification, and

(iii) Other supplementary criteria, upon completion of the work under subparagraph (ii) and, on the basis of the criterion of the substantial transformation.

It is of paramount importance to note that the Agreement clearly stipulates that the Technical Committee will elaborate upon the issue of a change in tariff subheading or heading on the basis of the substantial transformation criterion. In addition, the work of the Technical Committee will be divided on a product basis taking into account the chapters or sections of the HS nomenclature.

Article 9, paragraph 2 (c) (iii), provides for the Technical Committee to consider and elaborate upon supplementary criteria to be used "when, upon completion of the work under subparagraph (ii) (i.e. the work based on the change of tariff heading criterion) for each product sector or individual product category . . . the exclusive use of the HS nomenclature does not allow for the expression of substantial transformation". Such supplementary criteria might be "ad valorem percentages and/or manufacturing or processing operations". From an outsider perspective, in this complicated wording, the Agreement and its work programme solve the unsettled question of the basis on which the harmonization of GSP rules of origin is to be carried out; the process criterion (change of tariff classification) is adopted as the main criterion, and the across-the-board percentage criterion is retained only as a supplementary criterion.

As regards the status of the work, substantial progress has been made, but it has been slow. Most of the technical work on the harmonization of rules of origin for specific products and sectors has been completed. The definitions of "wholly obtained" products and "minimal operations or processes" have been virtually completed, although further refinement is needed. What remains to be clearly defined is the overall structure of the harmonized rules of origin; in particular, work is still required on the content of and relationship between general rules, section (chapter rules /notes) and residual rules, although, remarkable progress has been achieved in the November meeting at the CRO on the issue of residual rules. The Agreement on Rules of Origin has largely guided the method of work adopted by the Technical Committee by putting at the core of its agenda the elaboration of the rules of origin on the basis of the change of tariff classification criterion. The structure of the harmonized non-preferential rules of origin, although still to be finally agreed, follows to some extent the pattern of the preferential rules of origin, which are based on conceptually similar principles of wholly obtained products and minimal operations and processes which are not considered by themselves as origin-conferring events.

It has to be noted that given the complexity of the issue, developed countries like the US, the EU and Japan, which had previously gained substantial experience in negotiating rules of origin in the context of FTA or, in the case of Japan, have been involved in several AD cases concerning origin issues, were better equipped from the outset to participate in the negotiations.

A preliminary analysis of the main implications and possible effects of the HWP of rules of origin on other WTO arrangements

Negotiations in the TCRO have been mainly driven by domestic industries and many debates focused on the technicalities of the Harmonized System and its suitability to determine origin. In the CRO, a more trade policy flavour was added to the technical debate. However, a somewhat striking aspect for the observer of the negotiations on rules of origin is the higher quality of the technical debate on what may be considered "substantial transformation" as compared to the absence, during the open debate, of the possible implications on trade policy of different proposed rules.

As previously mentioned, it was not before the Indian Delegation submitted to the consideration of CRO a series of illustrative self-explanatory examples of the possible implication of the HRO in the textile area that trade policy implications were openly addressed. In order to complement the issues raised in that submission, there might be other complementary systemic issues to be addressed as outlined below.

First, it has to be realized that a change in product-specific non-preferential rules of origin following the implementation of the HRO may affect the import rules currently applicable to certain products. For instance:

—Textile products not submitted to quotas under the ATC may be made subject to them. A change in the current rules of origin following the implementation of HRO may imply a switch of origin from country A not submitted to quotas to country B submitted to quotas under the ATC.

—Anti-dumping duties may be applied to imported products without conducting the necessary investigation on dumping margin and injury under anti-circumvention provisions. Obviously, this issue is strictly related to the unresolved status of anti-circumvention as discussed in the following pages.

—Since the Agreement strictly relates the question of customs origin to origin marking products may not continue to be marked as "made in . . . . ." when marketed in a certain country, unless they fulfil the rules as contained in HRO.

—The triggering thresholds and "graduation" provisions contained in the injury and de minimis thresholds as contained in several WTO agreements may be activated following the "revisiting" of trade statistics when the concept of customs origin of the HWP will replace the actual method of computing statistics according to the country of final exportation.

At general level, it may also be observed that in many instances, and especially in the agriculture and processed foodstuffs sectors, where developing countries are expected to have a comparative advantage, origin may be attributed to another country through relatively simple processing. This tendency has to be evaluated carefully against the background of the trade instrument which origin is designed to serve. For example, origin of foodstuffs and agricultural products may have implications with measures related to the Agreement on Agriculture, especially tariff quotas where origin may play an important role, or the Agreement on Sanitary and Phytosanitary Measures.

Although not directly an issue for negotiations in the context of the HWP, it has to be recalled that in the context of the agreements on mutual recognition of conformity assessment results, developing countries have advanced the view that these agreements, usually limited to cover only goods "originating" from signatories, should also be enlarged to cover goods originating in other countries that have undergone examination in one of the country signatories of the mutual recognition agreement. This issue may be eventually evaluated in the light of the fact that in some proposals concerning animal products, as submitted by developed countries, a relatively simple processing like the raising and fattening of animals and fish, slaughtering chicken, freezing, or salting fish, may confer origin.

Since the globalization of production is not only occurring in the machinery and electronic sector, this kind of operations may sound perfectly legitimate. However, a closer analysis should be able to identify what are the eventual implications on the SPS measures.

As the negotiations are mainly industry-driven, the final outcome of the Agreement may be similar to a worldwide origin map, whereby origin may be conferred on a certain manufacturing or processing operation, which could be concentrated in different countries or regions, depending on the rule adopted. Thus, careful attention needs to be paid to evaluation of the advantages and disadvantages of such concentration or diffusion of originating goods coming from certain countries in selected import-sensitive sectors. In so doing, it has to be considered that in certain sensitive sectors the stronger the concentration and the larger the volume of exports from one country in the trade statistics of the importing country, the higher the likelihood of triggering contingency protection measures in the importing country, when other requirements have been fulfilled as provided for in the respective WTO Agreements on Safeguards, Anti-Dumping and Subsidies and Countervailing Duties. For instance, depending on whether a particular rule of origin requires a high degree of manufacturing operations or a lower one, reflecting or not the industrial capacity of a country, the origin of a product may finally be concentrated in one country or scattered in several countries. If a rule of origin, such as one regarding manufacturing shoes from shoe parts, is adopted, the origin of shoes will depend on where the assembly operations are carried out. These operations may probably be carried out in many different countries, since producers may select the countries where assembly is more convenient. Such rules seem to be more suitable to the globalization of production and to a "diffusion" of originating shoes dispersed in many countries. Conversely, if origin rules are more stringent so as to exclude that kind of assembly, and require that origin depend on other manufacturing operations such as the making of shoe uppers, the production of shoes may result to be more concentrated in fewer countries, depending on the structure of this particular industry, eventually triggering contingency protection measures. Depending on the realities of production chains and industrial strategy, domestic industries may press for rules of origin that will reflect their capacity and sourcing of intermediate inputs. Ultimately, the trade effects of the final rules may affect the interaction with international trading system rules such as quotas, anti-dumping and mark of origin. If safeguards and anti-dumping may be triggered by a surge of imports originating in third countries, a set of rules of origin based on relatively simple operations may lessen the concentration of production and exports, making the injury test more difficult.

For example, if a country is a big producer and exporter of cotton fabrics, commonly an import sensitive product submitted to quotas under the ATC, that country may have an interest to support a negotiating position where printing and dying are origin conferring operations i.e. to lose origin as soon as its exported products are subject to processing or manufacturing operations in third countries before being imported as a finished product in certain import sensitive countries. Thus, if printing and dying are considered origin conferring operations, it may follow that all the cotton fabrics exported from this country to third countries for printing and dying will change origin in the third country where printing and dying are taking place and therefore its exports will result to be less concentrated and specialized when the finished product will be finally imported from a country maintaining quotas under the ATC. Ultimately, it may follow that exports of cotton fabrics from that country will be less likely to trigger trade contingency protection measures. On the contrary, if printing and dying are not considered as origin conferring, these operations even if carried out in third countries will be disregarded and origin will continue to be allocated and traced back to the country where the fabric originated. In this latter case, it is obvious that an importing country will be legitimately allowed to count exports from the third countries where printing and dying have taken place as exports coming from the country where the fabrics were originating. If one turns this example at the global level depending on the rules of origin utilized, we may have a concentration of exports of certain products in a restricted circle of countries from the importing country's point of view.

In some other cases, countries may be interested in "obtaining" origin even if the amount of working and processing carried out on the imported material maybe perceived as relatively simple. This is the case of many proposals launched in the case of agro-processing and foodstuff attracting particular qualities and/or fetching high prices when sold to the final consumers. For instance, during the TCRO negotiations, one delegation was of the opinion that drying and seasoning of imported meat was an origin conferring operation. Arguably, this negotiating position derived from the fact that this delegation defended the interests of domestic industries producing a regional and typical product consisting of dried and seasoned meat sold in the domestic market and not yet covered by geographical denomination. Thanks to its regional and typical identification in the domestic market the product usually fetched high prices since it was marketed to the final consumer as having a distinct character from other competitive dried meat preparations. Traditionally, the meat used for dried and seasoned was also originating in a particular region. However, in recent times, price/quantity/quality considerations have induced local manufacturers to utilize imported meat. If the proposal is accepted by other countries, the result may be that the dried and seasoned meat obtained from imported fresh meat could legitimately be sold as originating products from the region. This could imply a rent from the domestic producer of dried and seasoned meat since it could:

1) utilize cheaper imported meat outside the protected domestic market while retaining origin and labeling as producing high quality regional products

2) capture the highest peak of a value chain from raw meat to finished product while at the same time being protected by possible tariff escalation

Obviously this possible finding will have to be contrasted with national legislation on consumer views. In other cases a country may have an interest in "retaining" origin even if the exported product, in this case raw coffee from Colombia, is further processed in a third country before being sold to a final consumer. During the negotiations in the TCRO, the Colombian delegation strongly maintained that the process of decaffeination and roasting were not origin conferring operations while the US, EC and Japan had the opposite view. Leaving aside the technical consideration raised by delegations involved, one may consider that if roasting and decaffeinating is to be considered as origin conferring then the majority of Colombian coffee roasted or decaffeinated in the EC and US may be marketed as US and EC products without bearing indication that Colombian coffee was utilized. This fact may severely diminish the value of image and marketing potential of Colombian coffee as a quality product having a distinct character and taste from other coffees.

While it might be argued that some of the extreme implications indicated in the example may have a speculative character and have to be confronted with the structure of the particular industries and with other rules and regulations, such as national legislation protecting the consumer rights, it has been a fact that the technical issues involved provoked a wide debate during the negotiations.

Another example of the possible implications of the rules of origin may be drawn from the recent changes introduced to United States legislation, which implied changes to origin of products subjected to quotas, such as textile products. The decision on where the origin of a product is allocated among countries subject to a quota system may have a disruptive effect on production chains and relations among different industries. In Asia, the cutting of fabric into garments, a former origin-conferring operation, used to take place in countries where quotas were under-utilised or in countries which had no quotas, while the assembly operations were performed in low-cost countries such as China. According to some commentators, the new US rules conferring origin to assembly operations implied a change in origin allocation to China, a non-WTO member where the MFA quotas still apply. Thus by changing origin rules new restrictions were imposed.

To sum up, it may be said that one of the major issues is to decide when to "lose" or "retain" or "obtain" origin. The difficulty is that this has to be formulated in respect of single products or categories of products and is depending on industrial base of each individual country and in certain cases on industrial strategy considerations at global level. Subjecting trade statistics to the harmonized rules of origin, i.e. the fact that the same origin rules apply for both statistical and customs purposes, is almost unprecedented in world trade, since in the majority of the cases import statistics are classified according to the country of origin indicated in the invoice which is, in most of the cases, the country of direct importation and not the origin of the goods for customs purposes. This may lead to a revisiting of the current disputes about "trade surpluses" and trade negotiations in general, injury criteria, thresholds, etc. Some countries have already advanced the argument that their alleged "surpluses" are simply due to exports of goods which, although counted as originating in their country, are only subject to minor manufacturing operations conducted there where they do not gain any substantial economic benefit or technology transfer. These countries argue that they should not be charged the "trade bill", which should be imputed to other countries manufacturing the essential parts of the goods and deriving the substantial economic benefit of the sale of the finished product (see the Barbie doll case in "Globalization and the International Trading System", UNCTAD/ITCD/TSB/2, p.17).

Possible implications of the HRO on other WTO agreements

Besides the direct implications of the Agreement on Rules of Origin, it is worth noting at this stage the extension of the area of application of the concept of customs origin to marks of origin.

The linkage between customs origin and marks of origin derives mainly from the United States practice. The requirement to mark goods imported into the United States with their country of origin dates back to 1890, and has been reiterated since then. The purpose of this requirement was to inform consumers of a product's country of origin, but it could also have the indirect effect of favouring domestic products over competing foreign goods. Thus, as in many "buy national" campaigns periodically launched in certain countries, marks of origin may function as non-tariff barriers. However, in many WTO members, the issue of mark of origin, i.e. how a finished product was to be labelled before being marketed to the final consumer, was not directly linked and/or enforced to customs origin determination. The explicit link made by the Agreement between customs origin and marks of origin, as contained in Article IX of GATT 1994, may therefore be considered an innovation for many WTO members.

Thus, a change of the country of origin will also imply changing mark of origin with important and decisive consequences on consumer's choice especially where brand names or certain quality goods are commonly identified with certain countries. Moreover, environmental or humanitarian concerns may further influence the choice of the consumer to buy products from certain countries which are worldwide recognized as respecting human rights, labour laws and environmental treaties. Vice-versa, certain traditional products produced by developing countries which have been contending or are perceived to contest or apply deficient standards in these fields may suffer a set back.

Ample example in the literature and cases arising from this linkage may be drawn from the United States, where disputes on marks of origin, involving US customs and importers of foreign goods, have been the subject of several decisions in the United States courts. Usually, most disputes arose in sensitive sectors such as foodstuffs, textiles, steel products and footwear, where labelling, import sensitivity and consumer health considerations may have had a bearing on the final outcome.

Moreover, the recent trade dispute in WTO between the United States and the EC on rules and marks of origin on certain textile products may best summarize the implications of a change in rules of origin and consequently marks of origin, and on the international trading system open the way to further considerations regarding the impact on rules of origin.

Although it may be difficult to quantify, it is obvious that in the "upscale" textile market of haute-couture, brand names and marks of origin have a considerable influence on consumer choice, a fact which may justify the concern of producers of finished products. The globalization of production may have rendered outdated the notion that a product is wholly produced and obtained in a particular country. However, consumers may still identify certain quality products with specific geographical regions or countries. Moreover, the non-inclusion of design and style in expenditure on advertising and research which may be incurred in the fashion textile industry, together with ownership of the manufacturing plant, may not be in line with the "substantial transformation" concept.

The issue of origin may also be linked with the proposals made by developing countries on the issues relating to "traditional knowledge". Developing countries argue that some patents deriving from research in biotechnology and genetic engineering are based on plants and genetic resources, available mainly in tropical countries, and traditional knowledge. However, there is neither recognition nor reward for such traditional knowledge or materials used when they become the subjects of a patent. A specific proposal was advanced on Art. 27.3 of TRIPS and more specifically on the provision that plant varieties must be protected either by patents or by a "sui generis" system. Developing countries[207] have strongly advocated that where a country grants protection to plant-based inventions, it could impose obligations on holders of rights:

—to declare **the origin** of the materials and to demonstrate the prior consent of the country of origin and, where relevant, of the indigenous farming communities and;

—to pay compensation to the country or to the communities that had the material or the traditional knowledge used in the development of a new variety.

The relevant provisions of the Agreement on Rules of Origin do not explicitly extend the coverage of the HRO to IPRs. However, the explicit mention of origin in the text above may call for some consideration.

If the coverage of the Agreement is extended to TRIPS, then the mention of "origin" in this specific context may have a number of implications on this proposal. The present status of the rules suggests that unless specific provisions are formulated to take into account of this special case, the application of the current rules of origin may imply that origin could be lost when further processing is conducted in a third country. Since it is obvious that under these circumstances developing countries have an interest in retaining origin even if the plant and micro-organisms have been further processed in third countries some additional considerations and adjustments may be advanced in the context of the HWP process if the mention of "origin" is maintained in the context of Art.27.3 of TRIPS as proposed by developing countries.

Moreover, the question of marks of origin may extend its implications to geographical indications as contained in Art. 22 of TRIPS. This article clearly refers to "indications which identify a good as "originating" (emphasis added) in the territory of a member". This question has already been raised by the Swiss Delegation during the negotiations on origin determination for watches. According to this delegation, the mark of origin "Swiss made" was covered by Art. 22 of TRIPS and even if the watch movement was manufactured in another country, the assembly and testing of the watch carried out in Switzerland was sufficient to confer Swiss origin to the finished watch and the protection provided for in Article 22.

The overall question is obviously related to the marketing value and power of certain goods which customarily relate to a certain country for reasons of tradition, habits, quality, reliability, etc.

In a world of globalized production, the "image" of a product, distinguishing it from its competitor often fetches higher prices. Marks of origin usually play a significant role in the consumer's choice from buying vegetables at the supermarket to purchasing a car. Watches are commonly made in Switzerland, certain fruits come from exotic countries, hi-fi and electronics are made in Japan, fashion clothes in Italy or France, etc. Most recently certain mobile phones made in Nordic countries have acquired a certain status symbol even if the majority of their parts are made in a variety of other countries.

Then the real matter of this globalized production chain which ends with a finished product marked with "made in . . . ." is to determine where the substantial economic benefit of this process is going to.

As mentioned above, in the agricultural sector, where developing countries retain a certain comparative advantage, origin may change quite easily. According to certain proposals, roasting or decaffeination is a substantial transformation. Thus, coffee grown and harvested in Colombia when roasted in the US, becomes a US product which may be legally marketed and branded. Switzerland does not grow coffee; however, its biggest TNC is currently one of the major producers of instant coffee.

According to other proposals, fresh fruits, vegetables, spices bought in bulk in developing countries simply seasoned, dried, mixed, etc. may change origin and be marketed after packaging under a different mark of origin.

While it is legitimate that foreign companies retain their profits for overhead costs, profit, marketing skills, etc., one may wonder if this should also imply that origin or identity should also be lost by the seller.

In classical terms, this issue may remind of the perennial problem of the low value added of the exports from developing countries fetching lower prices than the finished products. In this case, the loss of mark of origin may be considered as tantamount to additional loss of potential value added.

In this picture it has also to be considered that in their continuous search for efficiency and competitiveness, some companies which have already moved ahead on the course of globalization have already shifted their strategy from a simple diversification of site of production and management of manufacturing assets to a more complex array of services going beyond the simple production of goods. The increased reliance on brand name and the management of servicing of finished products undertaken by these companies bypass some of the traditional trade concepts. For these companies, the importance of brand names and marks of origin carrying global reputation of quality and superior technology is progressively becoming the most important strategy. Global companies may thus start to produce goods and services tailored to global supranational taste sourcing their inputs and having the manufacturing facilities with the most comparative advantages. Traditional trade barriers may be either eliminated or obliterated by a combination of intellectual management of services, brand and corporate strategy.

In the middle of this picture it is difficult to assess precisely the direct implications for every product. However, developing countries should consider carefully how to secure a balanced share in the participation to the globalization process. In some cases and for certain products the loss of origin and marks of origin may have far-reaching implications in the next century.

The issue of residual rules

The rationale for "residual rules"

The issue of "residual rules" is strictly related to the objective of non-preferential rules of origin. As mentioned above, the main purpose of preferential rules of origin is to ensure that tariff preferences are confined to goods originating in the beneficiary countries to the exclusion of others. Thus, if the origin criteria are not met, the goods are simply not entitled to preferential treatment and no alternative option or origin determination is needed. Non-preferential rules of origin are aimed at assigning origin to all goods imported into a country. Thus, there must be an origin outcome, in all cases, as the customs authorities should be in a position to ascertain the origin of the goods to administer the trade policy instruments. If the main origin criterion is not met, other residual rules should be devised to determine origin. This issue is all the more relevant at present times when finished goods are the result of multi-stage, multi-country manufacturing operations. Thus, in the context of non-preferential rules of origin, failing to provide exhaustive residual rules would leave a loophole in the predictability of the harmonized set of non-preferential rules of origin.

Status of negotiations and relevance of "residual rules"

The basic question confronted by the negotiators is how to determine the sequence of application of these residual rules and their implementation, i.e. what happens when the goods do not meet the specific rule of origin and the residual rules come into play. Two basic approaches were being discussed. According to the original US and other delegations" positions, if the primary rule is not met, then the same primary rule should be applied in any preceding country to first ascertain if the rule has been met in any of them. Only when the primary rule has not been met in any preceding country, the use of residual rules is warranted. One may define this as "tracing-back" option. According to the second approach, mainly supported by the EC, the utilization of primary rule is limited to the country where the "last production process has taken place". Thus, if the primary rule has not been met in the country where the last production process has taken place, residual rules should be utilized.

Obviously, there are pros and cons in both proposed solutions. The important point is, however, to assess the potential implications which may derive at the time of implementation of the rules. Following the US tracing-back proposal, the customs administration at the time of importation will have, where applicable, to trace back on the basis of the available documentation the origin through the preceding countries. In some cases, this procedure may not be as easy as it appears since a variety of reasons may affect the capacity to produce origin certificates for the different manufacturing stages a finished product has undergone. Commercial reasons may also be an impediment to this tracing-back method. For developing countries exporters, producers and administration the application of this rule may also demand a certain degree of custom co-operation. Moreover, the provision of relevant information and documentation may require an extensive knowledge of the rules and awareness of the possible implications on the part of exporters, producers and customs administration.

Under the EC approach, origin determination seems to rely to a greater extent on the ability of customs administration to determine origin at the time of importation. If the primary rule is not satisfied, the customs official will have to immediately resort to general residual rules which according to the proposal are based on a percentage criterion. This approach may also have considerable implications since it seems to empower the customs authorities at the time of importation with a final origin determination.

One of the thorniest issues of contention was that depending on what approach was used, the origin outcome of a finished product will change accordingly and all the HWP process should have been revisited in a new perspective. At the latest November meeting in 1999, a partial agreement was reached after almost a year of negotiations on the adoption of the concept that if the primary rule is not met in the first country then residual rules come into play and there is no need to trace back if the primary rule has been met in any other country. However, the tracing-back method is still present in the residual rules which apply when the primary rule is not met in the last country of production. Moreover, there is still no agreement on the content and sequencing of application of these residual rules.

The direct implications of residual rules: anti-dumping and anti-circumvention measures

Anti-circumvention and rules of origin

Once the harmonized programme is achieved, some commentators are of the opinion that rules of origin may bring a definite answer to the unsolved issue of anti-circumvention. Since one of the main objectives of the rules is to provide for a predictable and transparent method to determine origin, discretionary utilization of "Ad Hoc" origin criteria will not be possible any more. Moreover, the utilization of "residual""rules of origin coupled with rule 2 (A) of the Harmonized System[208] could be adopted as the starting point of the negotiations on anti-circumvention. It would be hard to explain why after having negotiated on the residual rules for such a long time there would still be a need to establish specific circumvention provisions and not to take stock of the results achieved in the HRO.

In general, it has been argued that the question of anti-circumvention was not appropriately addressed during the Uruguay Round of negotiations since the existing multilateral rules contained sufficient elements to discipline adequately eventual cases of anti-circumvention, such as rule 2(a) of the Harmonized System and the harmonized non-preferential rules of origin. Other commentators have argued that three broader elements have to be taken into account during the negotiating process on anti-circumvention.

—The WCO negotiations on harmonized non-preferential rules of origin have progressed so far very slowly, arguably in part because of the absence of a multilateral anti-circumvention provision.

—A substantial number of countries, including not only the United States and the EC, but also (Latin American) developing countries, have unilaterally adopted anti-circumvention provisions.

—(Non-harmonized) non-preferential rules of origin continue to be used to enforce anti-dumping duties and, consequently, to combat third country circumvention. Moreover, penalties for false declarations of origin may also be relevant when following investigation of origin determination during an AD proceeding, a different origin outcome from the one declared by the importer has been determined.

According to these views, the main problem is related to the slow progress in the negotiations on rules of origin. Unless these rules are clearly defined and tailored to solve the question of anti-circumvention, the second element of the argument for the utilization of rule 2(a) and the rules of origin is lacking. The thorniest issue of residual rule of origin, which has now been debated for months both in Geneva and Brussels, is at the core of the problem and it is clearly related to the implications of the Agreement on Rules of Origin on other WTO agreements. In particular, it was rumoured that this issue could be raised by some delegations to move out of the scope of the Agreement the origin determination in AD proceedings in spite of the clear provision of Art. 1.2 and 9.1(a) that rules of origin should be applied equally for all purposes.

The first solution, i.e. utilization of harmonized non-preferential rules and rule 2(A) of the harmonized system should be preferred during the ongoing negotiations on rules of origin. In the case where such standing prove unworkable and to avoid a protracted legal vacuum which may have adverse effects a fall back position on the basis of the Dunkel draft may be considered.

This being said some lawyers consider that the UR Dunkel draft still provides a reasonable starting point for negotiations. However, on the one hand, the draft is on some points insufficiently precise while, on the other hand, further considerations could be taken into account. The following checklist of issues might be helpful:

—The product assembled or completed in the importing country or the product exported from a third country must be a **like product** to the product which is subject to the definitive anti-dumping duty.

—The assembly or completion in the importing country or in a third country is carried out by a **related party**.

—Sourcing in the country subject to the anti-dumping duty from the exporters/producers subject to the definitive anti-dumping duty, its traditional suppliers in the exporting country, or a party in the exporting country subject to the anti-dumping duty supplying parts of components on behalf of such an exporter or producer.

—**Change in the pattern of trade** in the sense that the assembly or completion operations in the importing country or in the third country have started or expanded substantially and the imports of parts or components for use in such operations have increased substantially since the initiation of the investigation which resulted in the imposition of the definitive anti-dumping duty;

—**Causal link**: The authorities shall determine whether the change in the pattern of trade results from the imposition of anti-dumping duties or from other factors, including changes in the pattern of trade of other exports, changes in the pattern of consumption, developments in technology and the export performance and productivity of the domestic industry.

—The total cost of the parts or components is not less than 70% of the total cost of all parts or components used in the assembly or completion operation of the like product, provided that in no case shall the parts and components or the like product exported from the third country be included within the scope of definitive measures if the value added by the assembly or completion operation is greater than 25% of the ex-factory price of the like product assembled or completed in the territory of the importing or third country.

—Due adjustment for **start-up or expansion operations** so that cost calculations reflect the costs at the end of the start-up or expansion period or, if that period extends beyond the investigation period, the most recent costs which can reasonably be taken into account by the authorities during the investigation.

—**Evidence of dumping**, as determined by a comparison between the price of the product when assembled or completed in the importing country or the third country, and the prior normal value of the like product when subject to the original definitive anti-dumping duty.

—Evidence that the inclusion of these parts or components or the like product manufactured in a third country within the scope of application of the definitive anti-dumping duty is necessary to prevent or offset the continuation or recurrence of **injury**.

Furthermore, it would be essential to define precisely key terms such as "related party", "parts" "costs", "value added", and "ex-factory price".

Implementation aspects of the Agreement

Business life evolves at a faster pace than multilateral trade negotiations. However, customs and trade officials at the borders in industrialized countries will always have to determine origin, apply the rules and enforce them. This may be one of the reasons why the elaboration of the harmonized rules has reached a level of technical details and sophistication almost unrivalled in other multilateral agreements.

The basic question is that the current rules of origin under negotiations are tailored to the industrial and technological processes existing in developed countries that do not necessarily mirror the needs, ability and resources of developing countries and administrations. The transparency and predictability of the rules, as advocated by major negotiators, are certainly a positive issue for the multilateral trading system. However, when translated into a WTO commitment, they may become an additional burden for those administrations which are not adequately equipped.

Conclusions

As emerged in this paper, it is impossible to determine the best rules of origin or the best proposal on the table without being product, country and industry specific. A country may have a specific interest on a product for a variety of reasons mostly of an industrial nature. Moreover, negotiations involve more than 8,000 or 10,000 specific sub-divisions each one involving a certain industrial process. This being said, some general guidelines may be drawn from the negotiating process.

The most important inputs in determining which rules are best for a given country are those provided by the domestic producers concerned or in their absence importers/exporters. The input of the domestic producers is decisive since they are the only ones who are in a position to know what the imported inputs used in the manufacturing process are, the production chains, the cost structure, industry performance and finally the implications of the possible origin outcome proposed by their competitors.

It is almost impossible to define implications abstractly unless they are focused at product specific level. It has also to be realized that the current negotiations cover all goods from agricultural to industrial products, thus the implications and trade policy interests need always to be analysed at product specific levels, except where so-called horizontal issues are involved. Such horizontal issues mainly concern general rules which govern the application of the product-specific rules, the sequence of their application and other ancillary criteria.

The question of the impact of "retaining", "obtaining" or "losing" origin of a product needs to be carefully evaluated at country and subregional level to better define the possible implications in respect of other WTO agreements and the implications on origin marking, statistics, etc. The networking and elaboration of contributions as led by the Colombian delegation in the case of coffee in the early stages of the negotiations should be extended to other categories of products and issues.

Early consideration should be given to the implementation aspects of the agreement. As mentioned above, the harmonizing set of rules is a sophisticated and highly technical instrument requiring a highly trained administration and private sector. The design of the rules is largely inherited from the institutional memory and domestic "acquis" of the major trading partners which scarcely exists in developing countries.

Finally, a step towards sounder multilateral rules could be the design, within subregional trade agreements, of a regional model of rules of origin which although inspired and drawing from the positive aspects of the EC, US and multilateral models, is tailored to the economic and industrial capacity of the region where the rules should apply.

Excerpt from document G/RO/W/42: Proposal from India on Implications of certain major proposals from harmonized rules of origin from access under the agreement on textile and clothing: an analysis of possible effects"

Textiles and clothing products are normally grouped under four different headings: yarns, fabrics, made-up articles, and clothing. With respect to each one of these products, proposals have been made by a number of countries. Within the short span of a few pages, it is not possible to analyze each and every proposal. It is, therefore, essential to group them under two broad headings. One set of proposals that recognizes most processing operations such as dyeing, printing, finishing, designing, cutting, sewing, embroidering, assembling and other making-up as origin conferring. The other set that recognizes only some of these processing operations as origin conferring but not the others.

The above distinction holds true of each of the four segments of the textile sector. Thus, for example, certain proposals do not recognize some operations that go into the making of some garment items (like assembling of knit-to-shape components into finished ready-to-wear garment products) as origin conferring. Similarly, some proposals do not recognize the conversion of fabrics to such varied set of articles as tents, embroidered products, table/bed linen, home furnishing items, etc., as origin conferring. Finally, a number of proposals seek to ignore processing of fabrics and yarns by dyeing, printing and finishing as origin conferring.

Each one of the above processing operations involves sufficient working to secure new and distinct articles. In an ever increasing system of global manufacturing, industrial and business operation are often designed and developed to optimize the advantages by manufacturing various articles in different locations. It is true of textiles and clothing as for any other sectors of trade.

If some processing operations are not recognized as origin conferring, they are bound to have adverse effects for the exporting countries concerned with respect to virtually all the articles of the ATC. Such adverse implications are highlighted hereunder.

Examples:

Assume that the rule of origin for a knitted garment is harmonized on the basis of where the fabric was knitted rather than where the garment is made. Likewise assume that the rule for dyed and printed fabric is where the grey fabric was made rather than where it is processed by dyeing and printing. Also, assume that a made-up article (for example, a tent or bed/table linen) is conferred origin on the basis of where the component fabric was made rather than where the made-up article is obtained.

Also assume that the above products are under quota restrictions for some WTO Members.

Implications under the ATC:

(a) *For Existing Quota Access*:

If a country exports any of the above basic products (knit fabrics, grey fabrics, etc.) to a second country which, in turn, processes it into another article and exports it to a third country which applies quotas against these products, the third country will deem the product to have originated in the first rather than in the second country and therefore charge it to the first country"s quota. This obviously is against the interests of the first country because its exports to the second country are adversely affected.

If in this example the second country is unable to export to the third country, the second country"s interests are also adversely affected.

(b) *For Administration of the Quotas*:

The ATC provides that the exporting Members shall administer the quotas. In the above example, if imports from the second country are debited by the importing country against the quota for the first country, the administration by the first country of its quota becomes unmanageable.

(Continued next page.)

(Continued from preceding page.)

(c) *New Restrictions under ATC Safeguard Mechanism*:

Assume that the first country is not currently under quota and is exporting only to the second country, which exports to the third country. If the third country invokes a safeguard action under Article 6 of the ATC, the imports from the first country could be placed under quota even though it may not have exported to the third country at all.

(d) *Circumvention of Quotas*:

Even when the second country is the actual exporter to the third country, the first country could be accused of circumventing the quotas without its knowledge or intent.

It can also happen that the second country may not be a WTO Member. In this case, curiously, the first country - a WTO Member - may be held responsible for exports from a non-WTO Member.

(e) *Integration Process under the ATC*:

Assume that in the above example, an imported product (say, a tent or quilt) the making of which is not considered to be origin conferring, has already been integrated into the GATT. In this case, the quota for the basic product (that is, the component fabric) could be debited thereby creating a situation where integrated products would effectively stand as not having been integrated.

Summing up:

The above analyses reveal that if the origin rules are harmonized in such a way that they ignore some important processing operations they are likely to have adverse implications for the implementation of a number of ATC provisions. Conversely, the more the process that are recognized as origin-conferring, the greater would be the certainty in the administration of restrictions applied to the products covered by the ATC as well as smooth implementation of the integration process under the agreement.

Implications under the Agreement on Safeguards:

The above analyses would be equally valid for cases of WTO Members under a system of quotas allocated according to the provisions of the Agreement on Safeguards.

Implications for Anti-dumping Cases:

Assume that, in the above example, an anti-dumping action is initiated by the third country against a company exporting from the second country. In this case also the first country"s interests may be adversely affected even when it may not have any direct involvement in dumping.

A footnote at the end of Article 1, paragraph 2 of the Agreement on Rules of Origin states that: "it is understood that this provision is without prejudice to those determinations made for purposes of defining "domestic industry" or "like products of domestic industry" or similar terms wherever they apply".

Could it mean that the Member applying a restriction might define domestic industry by a criterion that is different from the rule of origin applicable to the products in question" This could lead to a situation of domestic industry appearing to suffer greater damage than may be the case if the domestic production were defined according to the harmonized rules of origin.

If for purposes of anti-dumping the terms of "like product" may be defined differently than for the harmonized rule, then it would be contrary to the principle of applying the harmonized rule for all trade policy instruments.

Implications for Countervailing Duty Cases:

Article 11:8 of the Agreement on Subsidies and Countervailing Measures provides that "in cases where products are not imported directly from the country of origin but are exported to the importing Member from an intermediate country, the provisions of this Agreement shall be fully applicable and the transaction or transactions shall, for the purpose of this Agreement, be regarded as having taken place between the country of origin and importing Member".

In the example given above, the countervailing duty measure by the third country could be visited on the first country although the product may have been processed in the second country and exported to the third country.

Implications for Origin Marking Requirements:

In the above scenario, assume that the second country owns intellectual property rights with respect to particular designs incorporated in the processed product. However, since it is not treated the country of origin of the product exported to the third country, does it follow that the product exported by it would have to be marked as the product of the first country?

CHAPTER III

OTHER ISSUES

TRADE, ENVIRONMENT AND DEVELOPMENT

Veena Jha
Rene Vossenaar, UNCTAD

Part I

This Chapter consists of two parts. Part I by and large reproduces a paper written in July 1999.[209] Part II briefly examines developments during the preparatory process as well as the Seattle Ministerial Conference itself.

Introduction

Developing countries have had apprehensions about engaging in a discussion on trade and environment. While the issue has already been on the multilateral trade agenda for some time, work has so far focused on discussions aimed at clarifying trade and environment issues -a process that is still ongoing-, not on negotiations. However, there is now some pressure to "mainstream" Trade and Environment in several WTO agreements and to include the theme - in one way or another - in future trade negotiations.

The recent trade and environment debate creates both risks and opportunities for developing countries. There is no doubt that developing countries are fully committed to both trade liberalization and enhanced environmental protection. The UN General Assembly's Special Session (UNGASS), in its first five-year review of progress in the implementation of Agenda 21, recognized that "(t)he multilateral trading system should have the capacity to further integrate environmental considerations and enhance its contribution to sustainable development, without undermining its open, equitable and non-discriminatory character."[210] However, developing countries have to strive to ensure that any further accommodation of environment into the multilateral trading system is achieved in a balanced manner and that it takes account of their own environmental and developmental conditions. They may therefore have to resist certain proposals that may run counter to their interests. In particular, developing countries should firmly resist unilateralism and other measures that threaten to undermine the multilateral trading system.

A key to thinking about trade and environment is the concept of sustainable development, which includes both protection of the environment as well as the eradication of poverty. Basic parameters have been set by the UN Conference on Environment and Development, in particular through the Rio Declaration and Agenda 21. Thus, work on trade and environment should promote positive interactions between economic activities, particularly international trade, the multilateral trading system and the environment. Essentially, it should:

- contribute to the further integration of developing countries, particularly the LDCs, into the world economy as well as to their growth and development in the short-term and the long-term;

- help to achieve environmental and sustainable development objectives based on multilateral co-operation and the principle of common but differentiated responsibilities.

These objectives can be achieved only by considering trade and environment interactions within the broader context of development. Recent analysis and debate have indicated that strategies to achieve such objectives may be rendered more effective by:

- strengthening policy co-ordination at the national and multilateral levels;

- strengthening capacities in developing countries to deal with trade-related environmental and environment-related trade issues;

- promoting multi-stakeholder approaches to identify cost-effective and development-friendly options for trade and environment policy integration;

- implementing positive measures, in particular as outlined in Agenda 21

Although focusing on the trade and environment debate in the WTO, this paper also emphasizes the WTO's limitations in resolving trade and environment problems. Consequently, the paper also examines the role that UNCTAD, UNEP and the Commission on Sustainable Development can play in further integrating trade and environment in the pursuit of sustainable development.

Background

Following the first WTO Ministerial Conference in Singapore in 1996, interest in trade and environment first seemed to have diminished somewhat. Today, however, the intensity of the trade and environment debate, as measured for example by the number of meetings, seminars, research papers and technical co-operation projects, seems to be higher than ever before. Much of the renewed interest is focusing on the WTO and how trade and environment will evolve in the context of the multilateral trading system.

Developing countries, however, have expressed grave concerns about recent developments in the debate. Most of them are strongly resisting the inclusion of this issue in future trade negotiations. An important question thus becomes whether their present position obviates the need for attention to trade and environment in the WTO context. Developing countries may have sound reasons to oppose broad WTO negotiations based on environmental considerations. In addition, they may have had sound strategic reasons to oppose the inclusion of environment in the build-up to the Seattle Ministerial Conference. However, this Chapter argues that it may be very difficult for them to sustain their opposition to the entry of environment in future trade negotiations for a number of reasons.

First, the recent Appellate Body decision on Shrimp/Turtle has generated new uncertainty on how the multilateral trading system will further accommodate environmental concerns. While many observers in developed countries have welcomed the decision as a demonstration of the ability of the multilateral trading system to incorporate environmental considerations, others have expressed renewed concern over the effects of environmental policies, particularly the use of trade measures related to process and production methods (known as PPMs), on developing countries. Developing countries may be brought to a situation where they either have to resort to a litigious regime (involving clarification of trade and environment issues on the basis of case law rather than a broad-based consensus) or to a precautionary exploration of trade and environment issues to avert conflicts. In the latter case a Positive Agenda would be of some help.

Second, proposals have been made to "mainstream" trade and environment issues into existing WTO Agreements. This would imply that environment would be addressed in practically all relevant WTO committees, including in the context of work related to the built-in agenda and planned reviews of agreements.

Third, the Seattle process has triggered renewed concerns about the possible environmental effects of further trade liberalization and hence calls for environmental impact assessments of trade policies and agreements. Similarly, it has generated new expectations as well as interest in the NGO community to propose issues to be included in future trade negotiations. Both phenomena may add their own dynamics to future negotiating processes. Formulating a positive agenda or alternative positions may help to prevent that developing countries are taken by surprise in crucial negotiations.

With regard to specific trade and environment issues, pressures from developed countries and which are of particular concern to developing countries centre on three issues:

- A review or interpretation of GATT Article XX, to provide further accommodation of trade measures (including discriminatory trade measures against non Parties) pursuant to multilateral environmental agreements (MEAs). This may have implications for the use of unilateral measures;

- Accommodation of trade measures based on non-product related PPMs on environmental grounds, particularly in the context of eco-labelling.

- Greater scope for the use of the precautionary principle.

Developing countries have been concerned that any or all of these may go against their economic and trade interests. There may be two ways of dealing with this pressure. One is to resist the entry of issues by referring back to the Singapore report (and the Rio Declaration and Agenda 21), or to propose solutions outside the multilateral trading system Another option for developing countries would be to develop their own environmental agenda so that if this issue comes up for negotiations, they can pursue issues which can yield certain benefits to them. (On many issues, it may be possible to find alliances with certain developed countries).

There is also pressure for greater NGO inputs to the WTO processes, in particular its dispute settlement mechanism. Civil society, both NGOs and the business community can play an important role in promoting a balanced Trade and Environment agenda. However, there is a risk that certain proposals that may be labelled under the heading "transparency", such as the those facilitating the submission of amicus curiae briefs dispute settlement panels, could, in practice, accentuate certain imbalance in the agenda. This is because NGOs in the South have less financial resources to avail themselves of such opportunities.

Environmental considerations have also emerged in the debate on agricultural subsidies, one of the most important issues in the built-in agenda. The Cairns Group and other like-minded countries have used the CTE as yet another forum to strengthen the case for elimination of environmentally harmful subsidies. Future trade negotiations, combined with the strong public interest in environmental protection and sustainable development, could provide an opportunity to gain support for the elimination or reduction of some existing trade policy failures in particular in developed countries, such as trade restrictions and trade-distortive and environmentally harmful subsidies in agriculture and fisheries. These are areas where consensus has already been built between a range of developed and developing countries. Identifying "win-win" scenarios can constitute part of a positive agenda, provided that due attention is paid to possible adverse short-term economic effects on certain developing countries. Due attention should also be paid to food security objectives.

Except for issues that should be clearly resisted, proposing their own agenda may be a desirable option for developing countries. These countries now have an opportunity to bring greater balance in the treatment of different issues already on the agenda, as well as adding new issues. This should help to strengthen the development dimension in the trade and environment agenda.

It is important to understand some of the developing countries' legitimate apprehensions about the WTO debate and work out those aspects of the current debate that could yield potential benefits. Section II therefore analyses some of these concerns in the current and future discussions at the WTO and elsewhere for developing countries. It is in this framework that developing countries should assess the costs and benefits of engaging in discussions on trade and environment.

After such an assessment has been completed, they should then examine the current discussions and see whether there is scope within the current framework to accommodate their concerns. Section III deals specifically with the issue of mainstreaming. Section IV examines some key trade and environment issues with a view to highlighting some questions and issues that developing countries can legitimately ask. It also highlights their points of entry into a discussion which has so far been polarized.

The issues relating to trade and environment are, however, not limited to the arena of the multilateral trading system, but also span national and regional policies and include the private sector players. These different approaches have been discussed in section V. Section VI draws some broad conclusions.

Concerns of developing countries

Trade and environment is an important theme for developing countries. Indeed, starting from a position where several developing countries had argued that there was essentially no linkage between trade and environment issues, developing countries have not only acknowledged such linkages, they are proposing a constructive agenda on dealing with these linkages. For example, several of the "points of entry" described in the next session had already been flagged by developing countries in the CTE. And, as will be pointed out in Part II, developing countries submitted a number of proposals on these issues in the built-up to the Seattle Ministerial Conference. The great interest in technical assistance for capacity building also demonstrates developing countries' interest in further articulating a proactive agenda. However, it is necessary to redress first and foremost the imbalances in the agenda on trade and environment.

Need for balance in the trade and environment debate

Lack of balance in the discussions on trade and environment has led developing countries to adopt defensive postures in international debates.

For example, there is considerable dissatisfaction with the fact that for the most part, the trade and environment debate has explored only some aspects of the linkages. The CTE discussions, for example, have focused largely on issues such as the need to accommodate trade measures pursuant to multilateral environmental agreements (MEAs) as well as eco-labelling based on non-product related PPMs. While it is important to ensure a harmonious relationship between MEAs and the MTS, as well as between transparent and non-discriminatory eco-labelling programmes and the MTS, it should nevertheless be noted that "developing country issues", such as safeguarding and further improving market access, controlling export of domestically prohibited goods and promoting technology transfer, appear to have received far less attention.

Thus, although in the developed countries there is pressure to accommodate the use of trade measures for environmental purposes within the framework of WTO rules, it appears that there is no concomitant effort to actually control exports of environmentally harmful products and obsolete technologies to developing countries.[211] This is shown by the fact the issue of exports of domestically prohibited goods seems to have been set aside too early as a priority issue for the WTO. Developed countries have argued that this is a technical issue and other fora are better equipped to deal with it. It should be noted, however, that same arguments could be used to refer a great deal of the discussions on the use of trade measures pursuant to MEAs to the Conferences of Parties (CoPs) of the Conventions.

A challenge for developing countries is to develop a system that facilitates trade restrictions if necessary in such environmental "bads". It is interesting to observe that at the High Level Meeting on Trade and Environment several governments and NGOs called upon the trade community to re-orient the trading system to promote safe products and discourage or bar trade in harmful products.

Another feature of the trade and environment debate is that, although there is continuous pressure to legitimize the use of trade restrictions (including unilateral and extra-territorial restrictions), based on non-product related process and production methods (PPMs), much less attention is given to encouraging the dissemination of environmentally sound technologies (ESTs) that would help developing countries in moving towards more environmentally friendly PPMs. At the High Level Symposium a prominent NGO (Third World Network) pointed out that rather than being subject to trade sanctions, developing countries must benefit from access to sophisticated environmental technology, technical and political support from the international community and funding for environmental protection from multilateral lending institutions. The representative of the World Bank noted that allowing unilateral sanctions against pollution or environmental degradation in another country would fundamentally shift the trading system towards one based on power rather than on rules.

Similarly, although some would like an explicit recognition to extend the coverage of the TBT Agreement to include eco-labelling schemes (including non-product-related PPMs), there seems to be much less effort to examine how developing countries can benefit from trade in inherently environmentally friendly products which use traditional and indigenous knowledge. This may be a serious shortcoming to the extent that it can be argued that, whereas eco-labelling is a tool to provide information to the consumer as well as some market advantages to products which are relatively less environmentally-benign, the promotion of the sustainable trade in products based on indigenous knowledge actually foster conservation. Not only should products produced by using indigenous knowledge be excluded from patentability (which prevents developing countries from obtaining the full benefits from exporting these products), an effective branding and labelling scheme should help promote markets for such products.

Furthermore, while some want to accommodate eco-labelling using life cycle analysis in the TBT Agreement, it has not been possible to make progress on guidelines on eco-labelling of genetically modified organisms (GMOs) whose environmental and health effects may become known only after several years.

Need to strengthen financial and technological capacity to address environmental concerns

Whereas there has been a lot of attention for the environmental effectiveness of trade and other measures, the capacity-building needs to enable developing countries to meet stricter environmental norms and enhance environmental performance has been underestimated. It is not lack of interest that hinders faster progress on trade and environment integration in developing countries, but the inability of many of these countries to bear the related adjustment costs. Measures and timetables to address global environmental problems may not take sufficient account of the lack of implementation and monitoring capacities of developing countries. Thus whereas trade measures may be effective in inducing changes in developed countries, incapacity to monitor would imply that, whereas the economic effects of trade restrictions are felt by developing countries, the expected environmental improvements do not necessarily occur.

Expectations of some may have been geared too much towards blunt policy solutions, such as trade measures, whereas the complexity of the issues seems to impose a gradual approach and a priority for enabling measures which create conducive economic conditions for dissemination and effective use of ESTs. In particular, environmental problems created by the informal sector receive insufficient attention. This is the case although the informal sector often accounts for 50 per cent and more of the management of environmentally problematic natural resources, such as heavy metals or hazardous chemical, and is a key source of pollution.

Developing countries also lack capacity to build credible certification bodies with the result that their firms often encounter problems in certifying compliance with international standards. Enforcing environmental standards and norms and monitoring them is also an enormous problem for developing countries. Lack of finance, extension services, coordinating agencies etc are also severe bottlenecks in moving towards higher standards.

Although the "precautionary principle" plays an important role in environmental policy making, this should not prevent devising comprehensive and balanced packages of policy instruments to address all aspects of an environmental problem. There has often been insufficient time to study the underlying economics of environmentally motivated trade measures or other environmental measures that affect trade. In fact, there is a general lack of information on analysing the economic and social adjustment costs in developing countries.

Need for political will

These imbalances in the agenda become especially important because there has been little progress in implementing supportive mechanisms at the multilateral and national levels. The recent assessment of progress in the implementation of Agenda 21 by the United Nations General Assembly showed that little progress has been made on what Agenda 21 calls "implementation issues" such as finance, access to environmentally sound technologies and, perhaps to a lesser extent, capacity-building. Imbalances in the trade and environment agenda can only be addressed if sufficient attention is placed on the development and implementation of such measures.

If the ultimate objective of the trade measure is to fulfill environmental objectives, then such objectives cannot be met by the trade measure alone. In fact. trade measure without supportive measures (such as capacity building, finance and access to technology) may further hamper the capacity of developing countries to move towards sustainable development. The argument that supportive measures lie outside the purview of the WTO is no longer sustainable because the purview of WTO has been broadened considerably by the Uruguay Round Agreements such as trade-related intellectual property rights, special and differential treatment (S&D) and other provisions concerning technical assistance. The provisions on S&D have so far turned out to be largely empty boxes and compliance with these provisions by developed countries would allay some fears of developing countries about the use of environmental measures as protectionist devices.

Notwithstanding these concerns developing countries have to identify the points of entry into the current debate on trade and environment. While countries may resist on some issues, there are some others where both trade and environmental gains may accrue to developing countries.

Points of entry into the agenda of the Multilateral Trading System

This section provides a short overview of some of the key issues in the trade and environment debate and possible of entry for developing countries.

Trade provisions in MEAs and the provisions of the MTS

Summary of the discussions so far

The international community has fully recognized the important role that Multilateral Environmental Agreements (MEAs) play in addressing transboundary and global environmental problems, based on international cooperation and the principle of common but differentiated responsibility. There has been considerable debate, however, on the policy instruments used to achieve the objectives of MEAs. Discussions in the CTE have focused on the relationship between trade measures pursuant to MEAs and the provisions of the multilateral trading system.[212] Some developed countries may continue to press for an adaptation of GATT Article XX to further accommodate the use of trade measures specifically mandated by MEAs. Recent decisions by the Appellate Body may have reduced such pressure, although the Appellate Body decision on Shrimp/Turtle may have shifted attention away from the subparagraphs (*b*) and (*g*) (or the introduction of a new subparagraph) to the headnote of Article XX.

Points of entry for developing countries

- Improving of the implementation of supportive measures under MEAs as well as examining to what extent the multilateral trading system can help to remove possible obstacles to better implementation. This would be particularly relevant for the transfer of technology provisions in the MEA.

- Strengthening co-operation between MEAs and the WTO to avoid future conflicts. This would also obviate the need for Article XX amendments. Such co-ordination could also examine other WTO rules and aim at strengthening the compatibility of the transfer of technology provisions in MEAs with WTO rules.

- Examining the consistency of TRIPs provisions and the Convention on Biological Diversity.

- Avoiding unilateral and extra-jurisdictional trade measures to address issues of global environmental concern, including the use of the chapeau test of Article XX to allow trade measures that constitute arbitrary or unjustifiable discrimination or a disguised restriction to trade. This includes trade measures implemented by one or several countries, purportedly "pursuant to" an MEA, but that may be considered arbitrary or unjustifiable by other countries.

The Agreement on Trade Related Intellectual Property Rights (TRIPs)

Summary of the discussions so far

Of special concern to developing countries are provisions in the TRIPs Agreement that deal with transfer of technology and the protection of biodiversity. Developed countries have emphasized that this agreement is meant to foster innovation. Some have noted, however, that in several cases there may be a trade-off between positive effects of IPRs on the generation of ESTs and the negative effects of IPRs on dissemination of technologies. The TRIPs agreement, including through its review mechanism, must find ways and means of balancing these two effects. It is important to bring to the discussion the empirical evidence gathered on the dissemination of environmentally sound technologies (ESTs) in relation to the use of IPRs. Trademarks and trade secrets may also affect the dissemination of ESTs.

In the manufacturing sector the TRIPs Agreement may:

- adversely affect technology transfer, for example by restricting the use of compulsory licensing mechanisms by governments of developing countries;
- increase the price of goods and technologies because of increased concentration of industries;
- have negative effects on innovation, particularly in developing countries, including in the area of environmentally sound technologies.[213]

Several developing countries argue that the agreement, and more specifically its implementation, does not necessarily promote the dissemination of environmentally sound technologies or the protection of biodiversity.[214] The system of intellectual property protection should also find a way of recognizing indigenous technologies, knowledge and systems of species preservation as these may be of considerable value in protecting biodiversity. Ironically, the system of IPRs could have adverse effects on research and development on account of some factors. First, traditionally innovations in biotechnology for the agricultural sector have been dependent on land races. Without granting adequate protection to land races TRIPs may erode the very germplasm which forms the basis of biotechnological innovations. Second, granting protection to plant varieties would imply that plant breeders and researchers would be forced to buy patented material at exorbitant prices if they are allowed access to it at all. This would discourage research especially in developing countries where there is a cash crunch. Third granting broad-based protection to life forms instead of genes that produce those characteristics would discourage further research into effective ways of producing those characteristics. This would have a chilling effect on public research for which funding is in most cases difficult to obtain and justify.

Points of entry for developing countries

- Exclusion of all life forms and related knowledge from patentability, as is currently permitted under the WTO.[215]
- Further analyses of different options for the implementation of effective sui generis systems, as called for by Article 27.3(b). In particular, the implications of using the UPOV (Union for the Protection of New Varieties of Plants)[216] model for PVP (Plant Variety Protection) needs careful examination. Harmonizing *sui-generis* systems to UPOV 91, which *inter alia* imposes genetic uniformity as a legal requirement for IPRs, could be inappropriate for developing countries, which would work to have different options for the implementation of effective *sui*

generis systems. For example, they could consider systems such as FAO 1983, which protects land races and traditional medicinal plants as intellectual property. Other *sui-generis* systems that meet national conservation objectives could also be encouraged.

- Seeking additional time for examining the full implications of Article 27.3(b) as well as for a consideration of different options for implementing *sui generis* systems, and giving priority to further examination of the relationship between the provisions of the Convention on Biological Diversity (CBD) and the TRIPs Agreement.

- Making the WTO TRIPS Agreement consistent with relevant provisions of the Convention on Biological Diversity (CBD) especially in the areas of biological resources and traditional knowledge systems.[217]

- Studying the application of Article 27.2 which can exclude from patentability technologies which can harm the environment. This would particularly apply to genetically modified organisms (GMOs) which are known to be harmful. It may be necessary to build some scope for a precautionary measure in this Article too.

- Indicating, in all patent applications for biotechnological innovations, the country of origin of the germplasm and whether prior informed consent was obtained for the biological genetic resource or traditional knowledge so that mutual benefit-sharing arrangements can be made. Such documentation would need to be attached to the patent application.

- Fully implementing Articles 66.2 and 67 of the TRIPs Agreement. Article 67 obliges developed country members to provide, on request and on mutually agreed terms and conditions, technical and financial cooperation to developing countries. Article 66.2 obliges developed country members to provide incentives to enterprises and institutions in their territories for the purpose of promoting and encouraging technology transfer to least developed countries. Reviews of the implementation of these two Articles by developed countries could emphasize that these are binding obligations and not only best endeavour clauses. Examining what forms of recourse would be available to developing countries in case of non-implementation of these Articles would be another "entry point".

Market access

Summary of the discussions so far

Market access remains an issue of key concern to developing countries. Safeguarding market access for products exported by developing countries has been discussed extensively at the WTO. It has been pointed out that developing countries may be more vulnerable because of the composition of their exports to environmental measures. They may also find such standards difficult to meet on account of several constraints, many of which have to do with the nature of operation of small and medium enterprises (SMEs) that account for a large share of exports from developing countries.

Preferential market access and other trade preferences are of key importance for many developing countries, in particular the least developed amongst them. The erosion of such preferences, which may be accentuated as the result of future trade negotiations, may have adverse effects of the exports of certain developing countries and reduce their ability to achieve sustainable development through trade.

A lot of emphasis has been placed in this context on identifying win-win opportunities in trade and environment. 'Win-win" situations arise when the removal or reduction of trade restrictions (high tariffs, tariff escalation and remaining non-obstacles to trade) and distortions has the potential to yield both direct economic benefits for developing countries as well as positive environmental results.[218] Much of the discussion so far has concentrated on removing trade distortions in sectors such as fisheries, agriculture and energy. More research is needed to identify further examples of products where the removal of trade restrictions and distortions may result in "win-win" situations.

With regard to eco-labelling, discussions in the CTE have focused on multi-criteria eco-labelling schemes, especially those that are based on non-product related PPMs. The effects of "type-1" eco-labelling on the market place and international trade, particularly imports from developing countries, have so far been limited.[219] It would appear that the interest in eco-labelling in the context of international trade is at least in part attributable to the fact that, from a conceptual and trade-policy point of view, it involves many complex issues, such as PPMs, the definition of international standards and equivalency. So far, little progress has been made in dealing with the PPM issue in the context of eco-labelling (see below). In particular, the debates in the WTO and International Organization for Standardization (ISO)[220] have made very little progress on developing the concept of "equivalency".

Points of entry for developing countries

- Devising under the existing code of good practices, a mechanism for voluntary measures, aimed at avoiding the use of trade discriminatory measures based on PPM-related requirements.

- Introducing greater accountability and WTO discipline for NGO campaigns and policies of local governments—for example in the context of the Plurilateral Agreement on Public Procurement—that might may have a potentially significant adverse impact on developing country exports, such as bans on the use of tropical timber imposed by several municipalities.

- Building consensus on certain concepts to be taken into account in the development and implementation of newly emerging environmental measures with potential trade effects, particularly for developing countries, including the role of sound science and the concept of risks that non-fulfillment may create, particularly with a view to understanding the appropriate balance between reducing and environmental and health risks and adverse effects on trade. Measures that incorporate both these concepts are specially valid for agro-based products and marine products, areas that contribute a significant amount of export earnings to developing countries.

- Examining the concept of proportionality, which is implicit in national environmental policy making, in the context of international trade rules.

- Examining whether differential treatment for SMEs is available within the existing framework of WTO rules.

- Developing guidelines to ensure that eco-labelling processes are transparent and non-discriminatory, and capable of dealing adequately with the trade implications of the use of criteria based on non-product related PPMs, drawing on concepts such as equivalency.

- Defining what is "an international standard" which ensures effective and representative participation of WTO member States at all levels of development, as well as the effective participation of developing countries in international standard setting.

Domestically prohibited goods

Summary of the discussions so far

Many developing countries are concerned about the health and environmental effects of exports to their markets of goods, where the domestic sale of such products has been prohibited or severely restricted in the exporting country (DPGs). Developing country importers need adequate information about the risk that such products could pose to public health and the environment. Apart from information problems, developing countries may also lack the infrastructure (including testing facilities) and other capabilities to monitor and control imports of DPGs. Developed countries on the other hand argue that a number of multilateral agreements and instruments already address this issue. Although duplication is to be avoided, there is a need to examine whether existing instruments, such as the prior informed consent (PIC) procedure, are sufficient from the perspective of developing countries, in particular with regard to product coverage and procedures. In addition, membership of several multilateral agreements and instruments may be limited, and thus the only option for resolving disputes may be in the WTO. In this regard, the following points have been raised:

Points of entry for developing countries

- Clearly establishing and agreeing upon the definition of DPGs and which of the existing DPGs should be considered at the WTO.

- Identifying possible gaps, in terms of product coverage (for example certain cosmetics and other consumer goods) in existing agreements and corresponding international notification procedures.

- Designing and implementing concrete mechanisms for enhancing transparency and reviewing the DPG notification system established by a Ministerial decision that had been in existence between 1982 and 1990.

- Providing technical assistance to assist developing countries in strengthening their technical capacity to monitor and, where necessary, control the import of DPGs.

Environmental review of trade agreements

Summary of discussions so far

As mentioned above, the possibility of a new round of multilateral trade negotiations (a "Millennium Round") has triggered renewed concerns about the possible environmental effects of further trade liberalization, and hence calls for environmental impact assessments of trade policies and agreements. It is widely recognized, that trade liberalization should be accompanied by environmental and resource management policies in order to realize its full potential contribution to improved environmental protection and the promotion of sustainable development through more efficient allocation and use of resources.

Several suggestions have been made so far. One set of suggestions deal with examining the sustainability implications of new trade negotiatios (The European Commission and the United States have already announced that they will carry out "sustainability impact studies") and another deal with examining the environmental implications of existing agreements. It has also been suggested that an environmental impact assessment of the Uruguay Round and its agreements should be carried out, in order to draw lessons for future negotiations.

Several developed countries have suggested that an environmental impact assessment of trade policies be included in the Trade Policy Review Mechanism of the WTO. Many developing countries argue that while EIAs may be useful domestic policy instruments there may not be a need to multi-lateralize them.

So far, EIAs have been used mainly in the evaluation of projects. There is little practical experience, particularly in developing countries, with environmental impact assessments (EIAs) of trade policies. The challenge is to promote the integration of environment and economics and to anticipate potentially adverse scale effects of trade liberalization. However, there is a need to avoid undue pressures to carry out overly complicated environmental impact assessments that might adversely affect further trade liberalization and distract from emerging efforts in developing countries to integrate environmental considerations into economic policy-making.

Some points need to be stressed.[221] First, It is generally recognized that any assessment of environmental effects should be carried out under the responsibility of national Governments. Secondly, EIAs are not only a tool for the minimization of negative environmental impacts; their principal objective is to focus on and to be used in promoting sustainable development. In a broad sense, EIAs promote the integration of environment and economics. Thirdly, EIAs should not narrowly focus on scale effects, but also examine income and technology effects. It may also be necessary to examine "with" and "without" scenarios, i.e. what would be the environmental effects of economic growth patterns that would evolve in the absence of the proposed trade agreement?

Points of entry

- Strengthening capacities of developing countries to integrate environmental considerations into economic policies.
- Proposing an environmental review of the TRIPs Agreement.

- Carrying out an environmental review of the Agreement on Subsidies, especially those relating to agriculture.

- Proposing an environmental review of trade in "environmental bads" and DPGs.

Integrating trade and environment at national and regional levels in developing countries

Integrating trade and environment concerns in developing countries has emerged as one of the priority areas in moving towards sustainable development. Intensive debate and dialogue as well as pilot projects at the national and regional levels have led to the evolution of possible strategies, elements of which are slowly becoming visible. It is now becoming clear that integrating trade and environment in a development friendly manner needs concrete mechanisms which span several aspects of national and international economic activity. The national and international debate on these issues has also highlighted the fact that integration of trade and environment is often intrinsically linked to the culture of operation of economic activities at the national level. Hence mechanisms to integrate trade and environment should include initiatives which deal with national and international legislation, national and international policy-making, business partnerships, infrastructure building, civil society participatory activities and other related activities.

Better policy co-ordination at national level can help prevent or defuse conflicts at the multilateral level, as well as maximize benefits (or minimize the adjustment costs) of measures taken pursuant to multilateral environmental agreements as well as environment-related measures with potential trade effects adopted in developed countries.

Agenda 21 already proposed an international agenda on trade and environment.[222] However, the implementation of that agenda has been disappointing. It seems appropriate to renew commitments as well as to develop new proposals for pragmatic approaches to trade and environment integration. Such an agenda could *inter alia* include the following:

National legislation and policy making

- promoting policy co-ordination at the national level;
- identifying packages of measures for SMEs to meet environmental challenges;

- developing legislation and initiatives to mitigate adverse environmental effects of trade in DPGs;

- identifying packages of measures aimed at supporting developing countries' efforts to join MEAs and complying with national obligations.

- developing effective *sui generis* systems for the protection of traditional and indigenous knowledge as well as effective implementation of Article 27.2 which excludes environmentally harmful technologies from patentability

Building business partnerships and civil society participation

- identifying how to enhance the contribution that foreign direct investment (FDI) can make to the dissemination of environmentally sound technologies (ESTs) and better environmental management through the supply chain in the host country.

- building supply capacities for enhanced environmental management at the national and regional levels

- widening trading opportunities for "environment-friendly" products and services in the context of the greening of consumption patterns in developed countries.

- developing multi-stakeholder approaches in moving towards environmentally friendly production processes and sustainable resource management

Integrating trade and environment through regional co-operation agreements

- inter-regional co-operation in developing common positions and approaches in dealing with third countries;

- inter-regional co-operation in developing mechanisms to cope with national and regional trade and environment problems.

Conclusions

From the analysis presented in previous sections, the conclusion could be drawn that several steps should be taken to make progress in the Trade and Environment debate:

- There is a need for greater balance in the trade and environment debate, because it pays insufficient attention to issues of concern to the developing countries;

- The debate should provide more attention to the constraints facing many developing countries in responding to environmental challenges, such as the lack of technical, institutional and supply capacities, and that many environmental problems in developing countries are of a very different nature;

- There should be sufficient political will to take account of the previous points in building a broad-based agenda on trade and sustainable development in several fora;

- Developing countries need to identify a positive agenda such as that outlined above and to start a process of consensus-building along these lines.

Progress in constructing a more balanced agenda and strengthening the development dimension, can be made only to the extent that countries, in particular developed countries, show greater political will. This includes, for example, the full and timely implementation of the developed countries' Uruguay Round commitments in areas such as textiles. Governments have to adopt larger responsibilities, for example with regard to notification of exports of DPGs and in reviewing TRIPS for facilitating technology transfer to developing countries. But such political will also has to be shown outside the WTO context, for example through greater progress in providing finance, facilitating access to and diffusion of ESTs and capacity building, supported by multilateral and bilateral aid programmes.

Developed countries should be aware of the implications of their environmental policies on developing countries and avoid unnecessary adverse effects on developing countries' exports. It is necessary to develop a better understanding of the production conditions in developing countries, their legal systems and their monitoring capacities. Any calculation of incremental costs under MEAs should take account of these differences.

The role of national governments

The trade effects of environmental standards and requirements raise issues in the area of development and/or *trade promotion policy* as well as in the area of *trade policy*.

In the area of trade promotion policies, for example, governments and the business sector can adopt several policies and measures aimed at promoting standards and quality with a view to enhancing competitiveness. These include *inter alia* establishing and/or improving supporting infrastructure (e.g. appropriate testing, certification and accreditation facilities), the dissemination of information, promoting co-operation between the Government and the business community, promoting co-operation between retailers/importers and producers/exporters, as well as special measures in favour of SMEs. International organizations as well as bilateral and multilateral aid agencies can play important roles in establishing and upgrading national capacities in promoting quality, testing and certification

In the area of international trade policy, the emphasis is on reducing the likelihood that standards will restrict trade. Such trade policy measures include the harmonization of product standards whenever appropriate, the maximum possible recognition by importing countries of tests conducted by testing bodies in exporter countries, and the recognition that standards which may have significant effects on trade should be subject to trade rules and disciplines, including provisions for consultations.

The role of UNCTAD

As UNCTAD's special role in the area of trade and environment is to examine issues from a development perspective, it should play an important role in strengthening the development dimension in the trade and environment debate and in helping to identify issues of interest to developing countries.   .

UNCTAD's work on capacity building can be of key importance.[223] Strengthening capacities for policy analysis and better co-ordination between trade and environmental policies could help to reduce some of the obstacles to the achievement of sustainable development in developing countries. Multi-stakeholder approaches are important, in particular where interests of different groups have to be weighed. UNCTAD's work, including joint activities with the United Nations Environmental Programme (UNEP), shows that multi-stakeholder approaches may also help to find packages of measures to anticipate economic and social implications of globalization and trade liberalization and, where necessary, identify suitable packages of measures. The role of UNCTAD is crucial in this context. In particular, UNCTAD, in close cooperation with the WTO secretariat, can play a vital role in research and capacity building, including on issues listed in the next section.

UNCTAD and UNEP could establish a joint programme of capacity building on trade, environment and development. To help implement such a programme, the two institutions could set up a task force with the explicit aim of building capacity through the pooling of technical expertise of these two organisations. It could be envisaged that a trust fund might be set up to support technical co-operation activities. The pooling of expertise could assist the two organizations to promote:

- public awareness sessions for policy makers;

- national and regional training workshops for trade and environment officials and civil society;

- demonstration projects to address the environmental and economic effects of trade liberalization at the national level;

- the design of appropriate packages of economic instruments and other policy measures to promote sustainable development;

- developing countries' access to environmentally sound technologies (ESTs) as well as the strengthening of capacities for their indigenous development.

The aim of this task force would be to build capacity for promoting trade expansion in an environmentally friendly manner and to build capacity for trade and MEA negotiations.

Trade and Environment at the WTO

Finding a balance in the terms of reference of the CTE has been a difficult task. This balance could be lost if issues of concern to developing countries were to receive less attention than other issues. In addition, greater attention must be given to measures which take account of the difficulties of developing countries in integrating trade and environment, such as S&D provisions, measures which provide better access to information such as transparency and notification provisions and measures which may assist small and medium sized enterprises in responding to environmental challenges. Furthermore, it is important to ensure that all aspects of the issues on the agenda receive adequate attention. For example, attempts to clarify possible inconsistencies between MEAs and the rules of the multilateral trading system should also include full consideration to the concerns of many developing countries and NGOs in these countries with respect to differences in the IPR concepts and regimes in the Convention on Biological Diversity on the one hand and the WTO TRIPS Agreement on the other.

Several specific issues and approaches merit consideration and could be pursued in the WTO. For example:

- reconfirm the Rio Declaration and Agenda 21, in particular as they relate to WTO rules;

- strengthen the role of the CTE in clarifying trade and environment linkages, taking into account the need for a balanced and integrated approach as well as the importance of building consensus;

- promote market access for products from developing countries, through safeguarding existing market access (e.g. through an interpretative statement on the concept of proportionality) and additional market access including for environmentally friendly products.

- examine "win-win" areas, taking into account effects of individual countries, including the net food importing countries;

- enhance transparency of trade in DPGs, including the revival of notification provisions;

- promote compatibility between the TRIPS Agreement, the diffusion of environmentally sound technologies and mutual benefit-sharing agreements as prescribed by the Convention on Biological Diversity;

- seek accommodation in the WTO rules for the special environmental problems and lack of capacity of SMEs.

- promote capacity building to strengthen capacities for national and regional coordination on trade and environment policies.

- promote a coordinated approach to finding better forms of S&D and for implementing the existing provisions of S&D.

A co-ordinated agenda in several fora

Developing and implementing a trade and environment agenda based on the concept of sustainable development requires coordinated efforts in several fora. For example, the WTO debate on the relationship between trade provisions in MEAs and the provisions of the MTS would be more balanced if supportive measures were pursued in forums such as the UN Commission on Sustainable Development, UNEP, UNCTAD and the relevant Conventions. These forums could also co-operate in promoting policy co-ordination as a means to help prevent conflicts between trade measures in MEAs and the rules of the multilateral trading system, thereby obviating the need for a modification or interpretation of GATT Article XX. The WTO, UNCTAD, UNEP and other institutions could co-operate in the identification of incentives and supportive measures (rather than trade restrictions) to address issues such as PPMs.[224]

Part II

This part reflects on developments that took place in the preparatory process as well as during the Conference itself. It is hoped that this exercise will provide some indications of the future trade and environment debate and the possible implications for future work on the positive agenda in the area of trade and environment.

The preparatory process

Proposals submitted by WTO Members

In preparation of the Seattle Ministerial Conference, WTO Members tabled a large number of proposals on issues that had been discussed in the CTE, as well as other issues that have come up in the trade and environment debate. Developed countries, in particular Canada, the European Community, Japan, Norway, Switzerland and the United States submitted proposals under the heading trade and environment. Canada, Japan and United States made proposals concerning biotechnology. In addition, Australia, Iceland and New Zealand submitted proposals related to environmental benefits of removing trade restrictions and distortions ("win-win" or "double dividend" scenarios). Developing countries also submitted a large number of proposals, although they were not tabled under the heading trade and environment. Proposals were made by the African Group, Bolivia, Colombia, Cuba, the Dominican Republic, Ecuador, El Salvador, Honduras, the LDCs, Kenya, India, Nicaragua, Pakistan, Peru and Venezuela. In addition, the Philippines and Peru joined developed countries in proposals concerning fisheries subsidies.

By and large, proposals by developed countries aimed at (a) making environment an important cross-cutting issue throughout the negotiations; and (b) clarifying specific trade and environment issues, which might imply a further accommodation of environmental considerations into the multilateral trading system. Proposals focused on:

- "Mainstreaming" environmental considerations in WTO Committees and future negotiations.

- Clarifying the relationship between trade measures pursuant to Multilateral Environmental Agreements (MEAs) and the Multilateral Trading System (MTS).

- Examining the compatibility of eco-labelling schemes with WTO rules.

- Enhancing the role of environmental principles, such as the Precautionary Principle in WTO Agreements.

- Conducting sustainability assessments and national environmental reviews of the impact of trade policies and agreements.

- Increasing transparency and making further arrangements for the relation with Non-Governmental Organizations (NGOs).

Most developing countries' proposals focused on specific issues that had been discussed in the CTE and generally related to environmental considerations in the implementation of different WTO agreements. Proposals largely focused on the following issues:

- The effects of environmental measures on market access.

- The issue of the export of domestically prohibited goods (DPGs).

- General issues stemming from the Agreement on Trade Related Intellectual Property Rights (TRIPS).

- Strengthening complementarities between the Convention on Biological Diversity (CBD) and the TRIPs Agreement, by reflecting the CBD principles in the TRIPS Agreement.

While there were strongly divergent views on most of these proposals, there was a convergence of views between many developed and developing countries on:

- Pursuing the trade liberalization agenda in accordance with the objective of sustainable development.

- Identifying " win-win" situations, in particular with respect to agriculture, fisheries and environmental services, as well as in other sectors.

- Continuing the work of the CTE.

Draft ministerial texts

In the preparatory process, two draft Ministerial Declarations were released, on 7 and 19 October respectively. Both texts included reaffirmation of promoting sustainable development and the protection of the environment, in accordance with the Preamble to the Marrakesh Agreement Establishing the World Trade Organization, as well as the need to ensure that trade and environmental policies are mutually supportive under the "objectives and priorities for the negotiations". In addition, the 19 October text included different alternatives to sustainable development enhancing synergies between trade liberalization, environmental protection and economic development among the "principles governing the negotiations".

Both texts also referred to the CTE and the Committee on Trade and Development (CTD) in the negotiations . For example, according to the 19 October text, the CTE and the CTD could each provide a forum be identify and debate the developmental and environmental aspects of the negotiations, including synergies between trade liberalization, economic development and environmental protection. The work of the two bodies would be complementary and would help to ensure that the negotiations reflect the preamble of the Agreement establishing the WTO and the objectives sustainable development, while responding to the needs of developing countries, in particular the LDCs. One unresolved issue was to whom the CTE would report on his work as an advisory body. The 19 October text mentioned that the CTE and the CTD would provide useful inputs for national authorities. A draft circulated at Seattle clarified that the two committees would report regularly to the Trade Negotiations Committee. On the insistence of developing countries, both texts included the words "within their respective mandates" to delineate the scope of any role of the CTE.

While the 7 October draft text did not mention specific trade and environment issues, the 19 October included language on almost all issues referred to in the different proposals mentioned in the previous section, including in the areas of MEAs, eco-labelling and the precautionary principle. However, this text clearly stated that it was "aimed at identifying points of convergence and divergence", and there were clearly divergent views on most items.

The 19 October draft ministerial text also referred to the possible working groups, in particular:

- A Working Group on Fisheries, to identify subsidies which have adverse effects on trade, environment and sustainable development and to elaborate WTO disciplines and commitments regarding their reduction or elimination;

- A Working Party on Biotechnology.

In the context of "coherence", it was also proposed that "the relationships between appropriate trade, developmental, social and environmental policy choices in the context of the experiences of and challenges faced by all WTO Members in adjusting to globalization" be studied in a possible new Working Group.

Seattle

With regard to trade and environment, the text that circulated at the closing day of the Seattle Ministerial Conference (3/12 - 05.45), contains a number of paragraphs on trade and environment. While the status, if any, of this text is unclear, some comments can be made. Most references to specific issues that had been introduced - although all in square brackets - in the 19 October draft had been dropped. References to environment in the context of a proposed working group on globalization had also been dropped.

The preamble part contains one paragraph on trade and environment (paragraph 12), in square brackets. Other references to trade and environment include the following:

Principles Governing the Negotiations

- *Sustainable development: negotiations shall promote sustainable development and aim to make trade liberalization, economic development and environmental protection mutually supportive* (paragraph 21).

Structure, Organization and Participation

- *"Role of Committee on Trade and Environment and the Committee on Trade and Development: The Committee on Trade and Environment and the Committee on Trade and Development, within their respective mandate, will each provide a forum to identify and debate the developmental and environmental aspects of the negotiations in order to help achieve the objective that sustainable development is appropriately reflected throughout the negotiations. The two committees will report regularly to the Trade Negotiations Committee"* (paragraph 22).

Other references to trade and environment issues are included in the sections on:

- Non-trade concerns in the context of agricultural negotiations (paragraph 26);
- Subsidies and countervailing measures, as follows:
  —The text explicitly includes "certain subsidies that may contribute to over-capacity in fisheries and over-fishing" in the review, and, where necessary, amendments of the WTO rules on subsidies and countervailing measures (paragraph 34).

—The Annex on Possible Decisions at Seattle on Implementation Section , in its section (b) on subsidies instructs the Committee on Subsidies Countervailing Measures to extend the application of Article 8 of the Agreement, which includes environmental compliance subsidies, until the end of the Fourth Session of the Ministerial Conference.

- TRIPS. In accordance with paragraph 45, taking into account the work done under the built-in agenda in the Council for TRIPS, the Council shall:

—Examine, in cooperation with other relevant international organizations, the scope of protection covering intellectual property issues relating to traditional knowledge and folklore and other currently available legal means and practices, both national and international;

—In undertaking the review of the implementation of the Agreement provided for in its Article 71.1 and pursuing the review of Article 27.3 (*b*), examine, on the basis of proposals by Members, ways of enhancing the extent to which the Agreement responds fully to its objectives and principles contained in its Preamble and its Articles 7 and 8 as well as to new international legal and technological developments and practices.

Views expressed by developing countries

Developing played an active role throughout the negotiating process, including with regard to trade and environment. They strongly opposed the inclusion of the environment under issues for negotiation. Developing countries nevertheless made a relatively large number of proposals on issues that had been discussed in the CTE, in particular in the areas of TRIPS and biodiversity. This is illustrated in table 1, which summarizes proposals grouped by CTE agenda items. In fact, developing countries' proposals outnumbered proposals made by developed countries.

Developing countries very much stressed the need for balance in the trade and environment agenda. For example, developing countries argued that the balance, as represented in the CTE work programme, would be lost if only some specific issues were selected for negotiation, as had been proposed by some developed countries.

Similarly, developing countries argued that making reference to the only some of the Principles in the Rio Declaration was unbalanced. For example, they emphasized that the Precautionary Principle is only one of the set of Rio

Principles and that it would be more appropriate to refer to the Rio principles governing multilateral cooperation, in particular Principle 7 on Common but Differentiated Responsibilities.

Developing countries also stressed the importance of balance as one important benchmark to assess different proposals regarding mainstreaming and the role of the CTE.

TABLE 1

Proposals by CTE items

Item of the CTE agenda	WTO Members	Source
Items 1 and 5: The relationship between the provisions of the MTS and trade measures pursuant to MEAs	EC Norway Switzerland LDCs (positive measures) Rep. of Korea	WT/GC/W/194 WT/GC/W/176 WT/GC/W/265 WT/GC/W/251
Item 2: The relationship between environmental policies and MTS NOTE: this includes proposals concerning sustainability impact assessments and environmental principles	EC Japan Norway Switzerland United States	WT/GC/W/194 WT/GC/W/145 WT/GC/W/176 WT/GC/W/265 WT/GC/W/304
Item 3: Environmental requirements for products, including eco-labelling	EC Norway Rep. of Korea	WT/GC/W/194 WT/GC/W/176
Item 4: Transparency of env. measures	-	-
Item 6a: Environmental measures and market access. NOTE: This includes subsidies for environmental compliance and sustainable development	India LDCs (subsidies) Cuba, the Dominican Republic, El Salvador, Honduras and Nicaragua (subsidies)	WT/GC/W/223 WT/GC/W/251 T/GC/M/39
Item 6b: Environmental benefits of removing trade restrictions and distortions.	United States Australia, Iceland, New Zealand, Norway, Peru, Philippines and United States	WT/GC/W/304 WT/GC/W/303 WT/GC/W/229 (Iceland) WT/GC/W/292 (New Zealand)
	Canada	WT/GC/W/221
	Cuba, Dominican Republic, El Salvador, Honduras, Nicaragua and Pakistan (domestic support programmes)	WT/GC/W/163

Item of the CTE agenda	WTO Members	Source
	Rep. of Korea (negotiating group on fishery and forestry products)	W/GC/W/368
Item 7: Exports of DPGs	Kenya	WT/GC/W/233
	LDCs	WT/GC/W/251
Item 8: Trade-Related Aspects of Intellectual Property Rights (TRIPS) and the environment;	African Group	WT/GC/W/302
	India (TRIPS and MEAs)	WT/GC/W/225
	India (TRIPS and CBD)	WT/GC/W/147 WT/GC/W/225
	Kenya	WT/GC/W/233
	Venezuela	WT/GC/W/282
	Cuba, the Dominican Republic, Honduras and Nicaragua (compulsory licensing)	TD/GC/M/39
NOTE: Proposals on the TRIPs Agreement in general and proposals concerning the relationship between TRIPS Agreement and the Convention ion Biological Diversity are presented separately.	Cuba, the Dominican Republic, Honduras and Nicaragua (TRIPS and the CBD)	TD/GC/M/39
	Bolivia, Colombia, Ecuador, Nicaragua and Peru	WT/GC/W/362
	LDCs	WT/GC/W/251
Item 9: Services and environment	-	-
Item 10: Relationship with NGOs	United States	WT/GC/W/304

Developments in the trade and environment debate

The preparatory process for Seattle showed several developments in the trade and environment debate. First, developed countries' strategies changed gradually from a focus on specific issues to a larger emphasis on horizontal issues. This may be explained first by the opposition of developing countries to the inclusion of specific issues in the negotiating agenda and second by the lack of consensus among developed countries. For example, the United States showed little interest in pushing specific issues. This could be attributed both to the belief that trade and environment issues would, in any case, be clarified through the development of case law as well as the fear that certain proposals might go counter to the US export interests in the area of genetically modified organisms (GMOs).

Second, the mainstreaming debate gradually moved from an emphasis on factoring environmental considerations in different negotiating groups to a discussion on the role of the CTE. This might be contributed to the insistence by developing countries that the role of the CTE, as provided by the Marrakesh Ministerial Declaration should not be reduced. In fact, developing showed strong support for the work of the CTE, with its current mandate and balanced agenda.

Most of the points of convergence and divergence between developed and developing countries became clear well before the Seattle Ministerial Meeting. Although the environment was an important issue in the context of street protest in Seattle, trade and environment did not figure among the most hotly debated issues at the Conference itself.

Trade and environment in the built-in agenda

Although the Seattle Ministerial Conference failed to launch a new round of negotiations, environment may nevertheless require increased attention from WTO delegations. The built-in agenda already includes important trade and environment issues. For example, issues such as pursuing "win-win" results may come up in the context of the already mandated negotiations on agriculture and services. Similarly, biodiversity-related aspects of the TRIPs agreement play a key role in the planned review of that agreement. In the context of the Agreement on Subsidies and Countervailing Measures, WTO Members will have to take decisions on the future of non-actionable subsidies for environmental compliance purposes.[225] Finally, under the Agreement on Agriculture, decisions are due on the future of "green box" policies, which *inter alia* include domestic support measures under environmental programmes.[226]

Several trade and environment issues are relevant in the context of already mandated negotiations and planned reviews. However, other issues, in particular the relationship between trade measures pursuant to multilateral environmental agreements (MEAs) and the provisions of the multilateral trading system, are less likely to be discussed outside the CTE. With regard to specific trade and environment issues, the following comments could be made:

- *The relationship between and trade measures pursuant to MEAs and the provisions of the multilateral trading system.* None of the WTO committees responsible for existing UR Agreement would have a specific responsibility in this area. Thus, the issue is unlikely to be raised in the context of review processes of existing UR Agreements.

- *Eco-labelling.* The WTO compatibility of eco-labelling using criteria for non-product related processes and production methods (PPMs) has already been discussed in several WTO committees: the CTE and the TBT Committee, including in joint sessions. In principle, the WTO compatibility of voluntary labelling could be raised in the TBT Committee, which has the technical expertise to deal with this issue. However, as there is no consensus on the WTO compatibility of non-product-related PPMs, it may be difficult to initiate negotiations in the context of a review process, without a recommendation of the CTE (through the appropriate channels) to do so.

• *Environmental benefits of removing trade restrictions and distortions.* The issue of pursuing "win-win" results in sectors agriculture and services can already be pursued in the context of the built-in agenda. Win-win results in other sectors can be pursued in the context of negotiations on tariffs and non-tariff obstacles to trade.

• *Subsidies and Countervailing Duties.* The Committee on Subsidies and Countervailing Duties will have to consider the future of environmental compliance subsidies under Article 8.2.(c). It may be asked to examine subsidies issues related to fisheries.

• *The issue of exports of domestically prohibited goods (DPGs).* DPGs are already covered by a Ministerial Declaration, which has never been revoked. Thus, Members can pursue the effective implementation of the notification provisions contained in the Ministerial Declaration without the need for a new mandate.

• *Trade related intellectual property rights.* There is some debate about whether Article 27.3(b) provides for the review of the *implementation* of the provisions therein, or for the review of the *substantive provisions* of the Article itself. Some, mainly developed countries, see it only as a review of the extent to which the provisons have been implemented. Others, mainly developing countries see it as a review of the provisions themselves that could lead to revision of the text.[227]

• *Environmental reviews*: the European Community, the United States, Canada, Norway and some other developed countries have announced that they will carry out "sustainability impact studies" of forthcoming trade negotiations. This issue has been discussed in the CTE under item 2. Environmental reviews can be a useful tool at the national level and WTO Members are free to carry out national reviews.

Mainstreaming

The discussions and drafts of ministerial texts circulated so far would indicate that some degree of mainstreaming of environmental considerations in the WTO may be imminent. This issue requires further examination. In particular, developing countries should have full understanding of any changes in the scope and modalities of WTO work on trade and environment. In particular, an open-ended agenda may imply a risk to developing countries. Thus, if the WTO mandate on trade and environment were to be renegotiated, it should nevertheless remain specific and represent a balance of interests of both developed and developing countries.

Calls for mainstreaming environmental considerations in future trade negotiations seem to be inspired by two concerns.[228] One is the perceived lack of progress achieved in the CTE. Several proponents of mainstreaming argue that transferring specific issues to negotiating bodies may facilitate quicker progress. They also argue that in a process of negotiations, covering a wide range of issues, trade-offs can be identified. The other concern is to ensure that trade liberalization to be achieved in future trade negotiations should fully enhance its potential contribution to sustainable development.

With regard to the first concern, developing countries argue that the trade and environment agenda requires greater balance if progress has to be made. Developing countries strongly oppose transferring specific issues from the CTE to negotiating bodies. Concerns of developing countries include the following:

- This form of mainstreaming could affect the balance of interests of developed and developing countries, as established in the CTE work programme.

- It could affect the consensus-based process.

- Mainstreaming would diffuse the WTO work on trade and environment and make it more difficult for developing countries experts with environmental expertise to participate effectively.

With regard to the second concern, both developed and developing countries attach great importance to promoting the integration of trade and environment in the pursuit of sustainable development. This would require attention to proposals to:

- Strengthen the role of the CTE in clarifying trade and environment linkages, taking into account the need for a balanced and integrated approach as well as the importance of building consensus;

- "Mainstream" supportive measures, such as transfer of technology and technical assistance, through effective, binding provisions in several WTO Agreements;

- Promote the integration of trade and environment through better policy coordination at the national and international levels as well as supportive measures. This includes capacity building.

In any case, it would be important to establish clear hierarchy between the deliberations of the CTE and those of the negotiating groups in future trade negotiations.

Implications for the debate

Recent developments in the trade and environment debate point to continued need for capacity building as well as co-operation and co-ordination between WTO, UNCTAD, UNEP and other institutions.

Developing countries will evidently continue to emphasize the need for balance in assessing risks and opportunities of further developments in the trade and environment agenda. Attention will also be given to how specific language, for example in a future Ministerial Declaration, may impact on future development of case law.

The Positive Agenda, work in the area of trade and environment

The UNCTAD secretariat prepared several papers on trade and environment issues that were discussed with developing country delegations, both in Geneva as well as in capitals. Meetings in the context of the positive agenda on trade, environment and development were held, for example, in Cairo (Government of Egypt), Manila (Government of the Philippines and other stakeholders), New Delhi (government of India) and Suva (FORUM island countries). The UNCTAD secretariat provided substantive support to conferences and seminars held in preparation of the Seattle Ministerial Conference. These include meetings held in Beirut (with the secretariat of the Economic and Social Commission for Western Africa, for ESCWA countries), Caracas (with the International Centre for Trade and Sustainable Development, ICTSD, for Venezuela), Cairo (with the League of Arab States and UNEP, for Arab countries) and Manila (for 10 developing countries). UNCTAD staff also participated in meetings organized by civil society in developed countries, including Bonn, London, Paris and Washington. The above-mentioned meetings also benefited from the participation of representatives from the WTO, UNEP and civil society.

Activities envisaged to promote the effective participation of developing countries in multilateral deliberations on trade and environment include:

- Preparation of issues papers, in close coordination with policy makers in developing countries
- National and regional seminars
- Policy dialogues

The UNCTAD secretariat is cooperating with the WTO, UNEP, UNDP, other institutions and civil society in the implementation of such activities.

There may be an increased need for consensus building, through discussions in the CTE and elsewhere, to diminish pressure to resort to unilateral actions and to prevent overloading the WTO dispute settlement mechanism. Consensus building efforts may also be preferable to the clarification of trade and environment issues through the development of case law.

Developing countries will undoubtedly continue to carry out analysis and building consensus on the points of entry mentioned in Part I of this Chapter and the various proposals submitted by different (groups of) developing countries in the WTO Council in the pre-Seattle process. This remains particularly relevant for certain issues in the area of implementation, form example in the context of the review of Article 27.3(b).

It is also important to draw lessons from the civil society protests in Seattle. Although large part of the movement against the launching of a new round on negotiations appears to be based on incorrect information and analysis, concerns about the impacts of globalization on the human wellbeing and environmental quality have to be taken serious. However, in addressing these issues, the WTO's limitations in resolving trade and environment problems need to be emphasized.

The WTO has been perceived as one of the few multilateral institutions dealing with trade and environment that "has teeth". Therefore, many look at the WTO as the institution that will eventually resolve trade and environment issues. However, expectations are often too high. In its background note for regional seminars, the WTO secretariat itself emphasizes "that the WTO is not an environmental protection agency, and that its competence for policy coordination in this area is limited to trade policies, and those trade-related aspects of environmental policies which may result in a significant effect on trade". The WTO secretariat goes on stressing that in addressing the link between trade and environment, WTO Members do not operate on the assumption that the WTO itself has the answer to environmental problems. However, they believe that trade and environmental policies can complement each other. To address this complementary, the WTO's role is to continue to liberalize trade, as well as to ensure that environmental policies do not act as obstacles to trade, and that trade rules do not stand in the way of adequate domestic environmental protection.

The above implies that larger attention should be given to addressing trade-related environmental problems and environment-related trade problems outside the WTO framework. Strengthened policy coordination at the national level as well as international cooperation are particularly important in this context. UNCTAD X could promote capacity building efforts in these areas.

The 8th session of the Commission on Sustainable Development, in April/May 2000, could be another opportunity to promote future work, in particular in the areas of building confidence and promoting consensus between developed and developing countries, policy analysis, capacity building, institutional co-operation and cooperation with civil society.

MULTILATERAL DISCIPLINES ON COMPETITION

Philippe Brusick, UNCTAD

Efforts by the international community to adopt multilateral rules on trade and competition date back to the Havana Charter, which in 1947 gave birth to the General Agreement on Tariffs and Trade. Rules on competition, or restrictive business practices as the anti-competitive practices were called at the time, were already foreseen in Chapter V of the Charter. Chapter V could not be agreed upon by the founding fathers of the GATT, and it was never adopted. However, in a comprehensive multilateral trade agreement as that contemplated in the Havana Charter, a chapter on competition and enterprise practices or behavior made a lot of sense.

Trade barriers and distortions are primarily the result of State action at the border, such as quantitative restrictions, tariffs, and other non-tariff barriers. But, even in a market hypothetically free from State measures, it has now largely been proven and admitted by policy-makers, that enterprises themselves can considerably distort trade flows to their advantage, when not subject to competition rules. It is no mystery that from its inception, the European Community seeking to create a "common market", then a "single market", etc., has adopted and vigorously enforced Articles 85 and 86 of the Treaty of Rome in order to ensure that free trade among its members would not be hampered by enterprise distortions as soon as State measures were reduced or eliminated. It was felt also that for a Union among larger and smaller States, common rules were necessary, to protect the interests of smaller viz. larger partners. Competition rules are exactly doing that: irrespective of the economic power of the member States where the firms originate, they seek to challenge abuses of dominant power and monopolization attempts by enterprises, the main criteria being that of economic efficiency and consumer welfare. By maintaining open and efficient markets, the overall effect on the Union should be to accelerate optimal allocation of resources and achieving faster development for the Union as a whole. In any free market, even with competition rules, certain regions will likely develop faster then others, hence the risk of marginalization. To redress this, the European Union applies regional aids and subsidies. For a world of free trade under competition rules, attention should be given to measures aimed at alleviating marginalization and poverty, which should be complementary to any worldwide "free-trade-and-competition" system. Hence, the need for an effective, but also *equitable* competition regime.

It was the developing countries, concerned by the rising powers of multinational corporations viz. the powers of the State, who in the early seventies requested, *inter alia*,[229] international rules on restrictive business practices.

Work on restrictive business practices at UNCTAD, followed by negotiations of a code, led to the unanimous adoption, in 1980, of the UN Set (The Set of Multilaterally Agreed Equitable Principles and Rules for the Control of Restrictive Business Practices).[230]To a certain extent, the objectives of Chapter V in the Havana Charter were achieved. The Set contained basic rules on the core provisions of any Competition Law, namely on cartel agreements and abuse of dominant position, and in addition, it called for all countries, including developing countries, to adopt competition rules and to enforce them effectively; it called for international cooperation in the challenge of anti-competitive practices, including both positive and negative comity, even before these terms became part of the competition vocabulary, and set up the basis for consultation procedures on competition and monitoring of the application of the Set inter alia by the UNCTAD secretariat, where an annual Group of Experts was established. Also, most important for LDCs, the Set recognized the principle of preferential or differential treatment for development. The Set, however, had one very important limitation: it was in the form of a recommendation to States and hence, it had no binding force.

It is therefore no surprise that at the first UN Conference to Review All Aspects of the Set, in 1985, the developing countries, as well as the centrally planned economies of the time, requested that the provisions of the Set should be made binding. This request was rejected by the developed countries and the First Review Conference ended in a deadlock.

In 1986, at the Punta del Este Conference, which launched the Uruguay Round of multilateral trade negotiations, some developing countries, led by Brazil and India, requested that restrictive business practices be one of the new subjects to be discussed under the new Round. By the time the round started, the issue was not kept explicitly as one of the themes for negotiations. It is very important to note, however, that in the resulting Uruguay Round Agreements, the cross-cutting issue of competition is present in most sectoral agreements. It is strongly present in GATS, and in subsequent agreements such as Telecoms and financial services; it is also present in antidumping and countervail, as well as safeguards, TRIMs and TRIPs. It is not our purpose here to review the competition-related elements contained in each of these agreements, as it is easily available in other studies and reports.[231] Nevertheless, it is questionable whether a sectoral approach can lead to optimal results, in the absence of a comprehensive agreement on competition as part and parcel of the WTO trading system. First of all, references to competition in existing agreements are sketchy and not bound by a common understanding of definitions and references to competition. In various WTO agreements, they are subject to a wide array of interpretation. For many developing countries, where a competition culture does not exist, or is a new subject, notions such as dominant position of market power and attempts to monopolize are unfamiliar, hence difficult to interpret in a meaningful way when it comes to defend their interests under the *existing* WTO rules. Even the US and Japan, when Kodak tried to use the WTO Dispute Settlement Mechanism in its row against Fuji, were unable to settle the issue under WTO, as the Panel declared itself incompetent under existing WTO rules. Clearly, for the international trading system as represented by the WTO rules to be effective and consistent, competition disciplines will need to be adopted sooner or later. Developing countries should make all efforts to ensure that those disciplines take full account of the development dimension, as is the case in the UN set.

The need for a "multilateral framework" on competition

If the 1985 request of the developing countries to turn the UN RBP Set into a binding instrument is still valid today, then a multilateral agreement on Competition at the WTO, under its Dispute Settlement Mechanism, would have the advantage of being mandatory. The force of agreements of the WTO is that in the event of disputes, cases can be brought before the WTO Dispute settlement panels. Of course, as is the case for any of the other agreements at WTO, panels would obviously not always rule in favor of developing countries. But at least, developing countries, as well as all other member countries, could have recourse to a rules based mechanism to settle disputes, rather than simply submit to the weight of the most powerful. A first concern in this respect for developing countries, is that they would not want to find themselves trapped in an agreement which they were not fully prepared to negotiate and in which the DSM would be mainly used against them, to force them to open their markets to the powerful multinationals, to stop protecting domestic industry, and to refrain from authorizing mergers among domestic firms seeking to strengthen their position on international markets. Therefore it is very important at the outset, before deciding whether to seek negotiations on competition or not, for developing countries to have the best possible idea of what type of an agreement they should seek to obtain from such negotiations, and what are their chances of obtaining such an agreement.

Urgency in the preparation for the Seattle Ministerial, and calls for limited duration (3 years) for the future Round, in addition to the principle of "single undertaking" (a package of agreements to take or to leave as a block) added to the concerns of many delegations, which found themselves insufficiently prepared to enter negotiations on a subject as complex as competition policy at the world level and feared rightly that they could well be trapped into giving up important components of their economic sovereignty.

Need for adopting multilateral rules

The problem here is that unless negotiations are launched on a specific issue like competition, delegations of developing countries which are often small and receive limited support from their capitals, will not be ready for such discussions, because they will have to concentrate their limited resources on the issues which are placed on the agenda of negotiations, and not on potential issues which might be on the agenda of some future round in the future. What is important here is that further delaying the adoption of multilateral competition disciplines will clearly limit the possibility for developing countries (and the world in general) to benefit from this application, while at the same time enterprises, and especially the large multinationals, will be able to dominate every day more markets where they remain unchallenged.

It is clear that every day that passes, witnesses a list of mega-mergers and takeovers, increasing concentration of market power in global markets and what is more, an ever widening gap between developing-country enterprises and the might of global firms. It is true that national competition authorities in developed countries, and in developing countries when they have authority to control mergers, are consciously checking whether such mergers and acquisitions have anticompetitive effects on their domestic markets, and if so, they may prohibit them. But national competition authorities' powers, especially in developing countries, only apply in these countries' domestic markets. They are usually unable to act against international mergers having adverse effects on their domestic market, when the mergers in question take place abroad. It is only the EU and the US which so far have been able to take effective action against mergers or anticompetitive practices such as cartels, originating from outside their borders. (See, for example, the Boeing-McDonnell merger and the vitamins cartel case.) Moreover, effects of mergers differ from one market to another. It may well be that the effects of a given merger are not substantially anticompetitive in large, open markets, while they may be devastating in closed, small developing-country markets, where the only competitors are the subsidiaries of the now merging companies. The extent to which the national competition authority (if it exists) will be able to act effectively depends to a large extent on the will to cooperate of the governments (or competition authorities) of the countries where the headquarters of the merging firms are located. Of course, if the merging firms have subsidiaries in the country, they could be ordered to divest certain operations by selling them to other companies, in order to maintain effective competition. But in developing countries, it is not always obvious to find a buyer for such a subsidiary.

Therefore, the extent to which cooperation takes place internationally is essential. The same may be true of an international cartel affecting the domestic market of a developing country, but originating from abroad. First, cooperation might be needed with foreign competition authorities in order to gather evidence located overseas. For example, the international cartel might block exports of a developing country, or dominant firms abroad may hinder access to those markets of products exported by a developing country. In the absence of any bilateral or multilateral cooperation agreement, effective action for the competition authority of a developing (or other country as well, be it developed or an economy in transition, for that matter) might be impossible.

Moreover, even legitimate action by a national competition authority might be challenged by foreign countries, when it is taking action against a foreign firm. In the case of smaller trading partners, such as developing countries or economies in transition, unilateral pressures might be such on the government that the decision of the competition authority is overruled on the basis of "other" considerations, (e.g. threats of canceling a badly-needed loan or an employment-creating FDI project).

The benchmark effect

The mere existence of specific multilateral rules and disciplines might allow the weaker partners in this case to defend national competition in a more effective way. The multilateral rules would have a benchmark effect. Newly created, semi-independent competition authorities in developing countries and economies in transition may sometimes be placed under such pressure from both national interests as well as foreign, lack of understanding by Ministers, or the Presidency directly threatened or pressured by large foreign interests, that the competition authority may become "unzealed". The existence of multilaterally-respected rules and the possibility to appeal to an outside DSM may be instrumental in redressing the balance in favor of national competition authorities - first in proving to their own government that their action is fully compatible with international norms, and second, in taking necessary action to redress the imbalances in the global playing field.

Bilateralism or multilateralism?

Bilateral cooperation agreements are more likely to be passed between partners of relatively balanced strengths and interests. In fact, the main agreements in existence today are among developed nations, in particular US-EU, US-Australia, Japan, Germany, etc. To date, only countries interested in either joining the EU, or signing a free-trade agreement with it have competition cooperation agreements as part of a wider Treaty. The same with Mexico with respect to NAFTA. But bilateral cooperation agreements specifically on competition policy between developed and developing countries have not yet been passed. Perhaps one could contemplate in a not too distant future such agreements between EU, US and developing countries having very large markets, such as China, India or Brazil. But it is less likely that such treaties involving large developed trading partners on one side and smaller partners on the other, could be achieved for lack of some sort of balance. In fact, one concern of the smaller partner (developing country) in this case, would be that its small competition authority's human resources might be overwhelmed by requests for cooperation from foreign competition authorities requesting specific information related to opening of their domestic markets, while they would be unable to undertake their own research into practices affecting competition in their own markets, such as abuses of dominant positions, for example. Finally, a proliferation of different bilateral agreements, on top of creating enormous burden to competition authorities, would create a very complex network of agreements with often non-harmonized provisions resulting in considerable difficulty of implementation. Multilateral rules instead, would resolve the problem of harmonization, and would at the same time limit the burden of multiple reporting or notification for enterprises willing to merge or to launch a takeover bid. Finally, the question of imbalance of powers would be reduced, if an impartial Dispute Settlement Mechanism could be resorted to.

What type of multilateral agreement could be sought after?

What would be needed therefore, is an instrument that would complement the existing international trading system with competition principles and rules, in order to avoid - or at least to reduce - present inconsistencies of the existing system. The present system contains numerous competition-related provisions, as in GATS, in specific services agreements (telecoms), as well as in the agreements on antidumping, safeguards, etc. But such competition-related provisions are scattered within the various agreements and are not explicited in any part of the existing rules, leading to varying degrees of interpretation and understanding. Obviously, developed countries which are familiar with competition issues should be able to make use of competition-related clauses, while countries unaware of the finesses of competition law and policy would find themselves unable to use such provisions. Moreover, definitions of competition issues might vary from one WTO Agreement to another, necessitating some sort of harmonization between the various agreements. A comprehensive multilateral competition instrument therefore, would help define and harmonize the multiple references to competition issues which are presently scattered around in WTO agreements.

By doing so, it would also establish a benchmark for countries newly adopting competition law and policy, strengthening the hand of their domestic competition regimes. Further, it would reconcile the blatant inconsistencies between trade and competition rules, and bridge the gap between existing WTO rules and basic competition principles.

The UN RBP set

It is untrue to say that there is no multilateral agreement on competition principles and rules. The UN Set dates back to 1980, but irrespective of its sometimes old-fashioned language, it contains the basis for a modern competition framework, and this has been unanimously agreed by all States participating in the UN Conferences to Review All Aspects of the Set (1985, 1990, 1995) and in the work pursued by the UNCTAD Intergovernmental Group of Experts on Competition Law and Policy.

A further review of the Set will take place in September 2000, at the Fourth UN Review Conference. If the WTO agrees to continue the educational process which has been going on at the WTO Working Group on Trade and Competition, UNCTAD's role to ensure that the development dimension is taken fully into account, would be essential. It should be mentioned in this respect, that the UN RBP Set provides for special and differential treatment of developing countries, and in particular LDCs, in certain circumstances (Section B6, and 7 of the Set, in particular). This is in line with the WTO Trading System itself, which also has, as one of its principles, S&D treatment for developing countries. What, then should be embodied in a possible future WTO multilateral framework to ensure that the development dimension is taken into account?

A multilateral competition framework including a development dimension

First, the main WTO principles of MFN, non-discrimination, national treatment, transparency *and* special and differential treatment should be made to apply fully in the context of such a competition framework. The WTO Dispute-Settlement mechanism would have a procedural task to ensure the implementation of these basic trade principles in the treatment of competition. The DSM would, hence, be operational in procedural cases relating to the basic trade principles listed above.

In any case, the WTO or its DSM would not be entitled to second-guess substantive cases decided by national competition authorities, except in blatant cases of discrimination against a foreign competitor. The groundwork decisions of competition authorities would obviously not be subject to the DSM. The substantive part of the framework could contain a list of voluntary provisions and recommendations, such as those found in the OECD recommendation on hard-core cartels, the UN RBP Set on the core prohibited practices, abuse of dominance, an undertaking to effective enforcement of national rules by all nations, advanced cooperation, consultations among competition authorities—subject to the necessary confidentiality safeguards—including provisions for traditional, positive and/or negative comity principles. The "voluntary" part of the agreement would be subject to a continued (longer-term) "educational process" at WTO and in other fora, such as UNCTAD's Intergovernmental Group of Experts on Competition Law and Policy, with the understanding that once multilateral agreement is reached, for example, to prohibit hard-core cartels and collusive tendering (bid-rigging), the WTO Agreement may be revised and such a prohibition included.

Agreement on such a competition framework would strengthen the present WTO trading system and strengthen the positions of smaller and weaker trading partners viz. large trading partners and global firms. It would also probably result in a revision of the other Agreements of WTO, such as the Agreement on Subsidies and Countervailing Measures or the Anti-dumping Agreement, to make them compatible with the competition disciplines.

What special and differential treatment for developing countries?

The present WTO system, especially with the Uruguay Round, has relied mainly on transition periods, broadly 5 years for "developing countries" and 10 years for LDCs, after which all partners are considered "equal under the law". Even after 5, 10 or perhaps longer periods of time, there is no guarantee that a level playing field will result from applying *equal* rules to *unequal* players. What is contemplated in the possible competition framework, and what should be sought by developing countries, and especially by LDCs, is that the "special and differential treatment" in the case of competition, should include the right for these countries to exempt from full fledged competition, certain sectors of their national economy where market failures exist, and where protection might need to be warranted for some time, for e.g. in case of an important national resource deemed essential for development (e.g. oil, coffee, cocoa, copper, etc.). Also, a certain magnitude of flexibility should exist in favor of infant or "sunrise" industries. Obviously, it would be in the interest of the incumbent country to limit such exemptions in time, if it becomes evident that that sector is never going to become internationally competitive and it might come to the conclusion that it is not effective to distort resources any longer. Hence, the extent of flexibility should be left in the hands of the developing country in question which would be well advised to review its validity periodically. This should not pose immense problems for an Agreement, as developed countries themselves have exempted from their competition laws entire sectors—and while they have seriously reduced such exemptions in recent years as a result of the deregulating process, they have nevertheless had exempted sectors for as much as 40-50 years (roughly between late 1940s and fifties, when they gradually adopted competition laws, and the early nineties when they started to implement deregulatory measures). The same degree of flexibility should be afforded to developing countries: nothing more than what developed countries have been doing so far. Therefore, apart from specific sectors which would have to be notified and could be treated with some flexibility, developing countries would place their economies under general competition principles and rules for all sectors other than those where S&D is considered a necessity. The more developed a country, the less it would need to exempt entire sectors from application of free competition rules.

THE RELATIONSHIP BETWEEN ANTI-DUMPING POLICY AND COMPETITION

Rodney de C. Grey

Purpose

The purpose of this report is to examine the scope for devising provisions under the aegis of the World Trade Organization (WTO) which would bring anti-dumping policy into a greater degree of consistency with competition policy. Anti-dumping policy is directed at reducing the impact of an anti-competitive practice : namely, selling abroad for less than in the domestic market. Thus anti-dumping policy is, in a rather special sense, a part of competition policy. Competition policy is usually directed at actions taken in regard to the domestic market, and, commonly, by domestic firms. However, all countries with properly articulated competition policies address actions taken abroad, often by foreign-controlled and foreign-based entities, which have anti-competitive effects in the domestic market. Thus the question arises as to whether the anti-dumping system in any given country could be subsumed by that country's competition law and policy, along with other measures against other anti-competitive practices by foreign entities. A more modest question is: why are the standards and administrative rules of the anti-dumping system not more consistent with competition law?

These questions present themselves in the context of the forthcoming multilateral trade negotiations (MTN) to be launched by the WTO, in which it is assumed that a number of countries will seek changes in the GATT "Anti-dumping Agreement"[a], an agreement which is designed to provide uniform rules for the use of anti-dumping duties, the accepted method for sanctioning injurious dumping.

Put more specifically, the issue is why one particular type of anti-competitive practice—price discrimination—should be dealt with under different rules, tests and standards when it is practiced by exporters in other countries than when it is practiced by domestic firms. Can anything be done to reconcile the two approaches? In fact, the standards and texts of anti-dumping policy diverge from those of competition policy only for historical reasons: anti-

413

dumping measures evolved in a trade and tariff policy context, by different administrative agencies than those that addressed competition policy issues.

Before stating some specific proposals, offered in the context of the next MTN, certain working assumptions of this report should be made clear.

Assumptions:

One key assumption is that in so far as the anti-dumping system penalizes price discrimination in import trade more severely than similar price discrimination in domestic commerce (under competition law), the anti-dumping system is protectionist, to that extent and by design. This seems to this writer to be a self-evident proposition, acceptable both to those who seek to make the anti-dumping system less restrictive, and those who wish to maintain and strengthen the anti-dumping system. And to the extent that the anti-dumping system is more restrictive then the competition policy system, its application would appear to be in breach of the National Treatment obligations of the GATT (Article III). [One says "would appear" because one could conceivably argue that GATT Article VI, the article conferring authority to levy anti-dumping duties, can be read as an exception to Article III. Only a WTO panel looking at a test case could decide; however, it seems to this writer that Article III overrides Article VI, and that Article VI does not permit the levying of a tax on imports which is in excess of that levied, *in parallel circumstances*, on domestics products.]

Another assumption is that governments may quite properly to take some offsetting action or remedial action when there is a sharp increase in the volume of imports at prices which appear unusually low and which displace domestic production *to an intolerable degree.*

In such circumstances a government has to determine whether this intolerable surge in imports is due to an essentially anti-competitive action by a foreign firm or firms, or whether it reflects longer-term and relatively permanent changes in the structure of production. In the former case measures designed to offset the anti-competitive action may be appropriate; in the latter case governments should focus on adjustment measures - particularly those designed to protect the labour force from the effects of decisions to invest in productive facilities which they could not reasonably be expected to have foreseen when they accepted employment. Of course, price competition, perhaps to a very uncomfortable degree, may be the result of dislocations in the world economy, such as sharp changes in exchange rates and sharp changes in demand in particular markets, as have been manifested during the past year or so by dislocation in the world markets for steel products. Measures designed to deal with anti-competitive actions are not well-adapted to dealing with problems of adjustment to major changes in the structure of production of a particular product, nor to dealing with dislocations in markets due to rapid and substantive changes in exchange rates (a detailed review of the use of anti-dumping measures in the steel sector—in the US, since 1969—will make this all too clear.)[b] The purpose of any proposals here is not to preclude action by governments to deal with dislocations in domestic markets which impose unreasonable burdens on workers, or which are manifestations of anti-competitive actions. However, as to how governments should best intervene, this writer accepts the logic of what has been called the "injury only" view : that is, that the essential task of the trade policy administration is to consider to what extent an industry is "injured", to then assess what measures of adjustment are reasonable in the circumstances, and only then to decide what, if any, restriction (or tax) an imports is justified. This view was expressed many years ago by a distinguished US. trade policy lawyer, Noel Hemmendinger:

> "My thesis is that the Antidumping Act and the Countervailing Duty Law [●], are seriously defective in conception and need to be fundamentally reexamined. This is true in two respects. First, they attempt to deal with international economic conflicts through adversarial litigation, hobbling the essential elements of administrative discretion and negotiated solutions. Second, they assume an economic world free of governmental interventions, which has never existed, and more to the point [●] a world of fixed currency rates more or less rationally related to comparative advantage, which has been non-existent at least since 1971. I suggest that a variation on the Escape Clause would be the appropriate U.S. legal mechanism for addressing import trade problems." [c]

Put in GATT terms, this is the thesis that restrictions in imports which cause intolerable problems of adjustment to domestic producers should best be dealt + under the safeguard provisions of Article XIX, rather than under Article VI. Clearly, this is not a negotiable solution to the problem, but the "injury only" view, so expressed, is a valuable and reliable perspective on how problems of import competition should best be addressed.

Yet another assumption, or working premise, is that the option of simply subsuming measures against international price discrimination under competition law and polices is not, at this stage, a realistic goal in WTO negotiations. One reason for this, which many would advance, is that in many countries—notably the U.S., Canada, the E.U., Australia, and more recently, in a number of developing countries—business men have become strong—too strong—supporters of the anti-dumping system. They realize it gives them protection against imports and they like that. The rhetoric of " fair trade " has convinced them that they are entitled to such protection—and it is substantial—as is afforded them by invoking anti-dumping measures. This is a practical, political reason why the anti-dumping provisions simply can't be scrapped, and subsumed under the competition policy apparatus.

A second, and equally cogent reason, is that competition law is itself— as between jurisdictions—neither always fully developed—nor is there international agreement on policy. This reflects the fact that within many countries there are sharp, and often highly politicized differences of views about the economic and legal rationales of competition policy. The focus of this paper is on the reform of anti-dumping policy, under the aegis of the WTO, rather than on the reform of competition policy ; it is sufficient to note that competition policy varies widely from one WTO member to another. We shall, none the less, look briefly at some features of the competition law system addressed to price discrimination, to see whether they might be adapted to the anti-dumping system.

A fourth working premise of this report is that, at the very least, the anti-dumping system should not itself involve or encourage actions which are anti-competitive. This is particularly the case in regard of the use of "undertakings"[d] by exporters to raise prices, to cease dumping (or "injurious" dumping). Undertakings involve, in practice, the creation of combinations of exporters to fix export prices (and, no doubt, to allocate markets) in the importing countries. These are arrangements which were they not entered into under the aegis of the administrative authorities of the importing country, would be actionable offenses under the competition laws of most countries with developed competition law regimes. Further, such "undertakings" often involve the informal or tacit participation and agreement of the "injured" domestic industry, under the umbrella of the administrative authorities. They are thus no more than thinly-veiled conspiracies to raise prices. Thus the fourth premise or working proposition of the report is that the least that should be done to bring the anti-dumping provisions into some measure of conformity with competition law is to avoid the use of the anti-dumping system to encourage anti-competitive practices, i.e. market restriction or allocation by foreign cartels.

In the balance of this paper we examine some specific issues which will have to be considered, and perhaps negotiated, to bring the anti-dumping provisions of the WTO A/D Agreement somewhat closer to competition law concepts. We will need to look at the concepts of price discrimination under the two systems, at the concept of predatory pricing, particularly as shown by competition policy in practice (drawing mainly an U.S. and Canadian practice), at the concept of an "injury" to an industry and "injury" to competition —two quite different concepts, at the concept of "cause" under the various national anti-dumping regimes, and at the related concept of "material" injury. Finally, we should consider suggestions as to how developing countries might negotiate to narrow the very large gap between anti-dumping law and competition law. But before doing so perhaps two disclaimers are in order, and we will need some brief comments on the history of the anti-dumping provisions of the GATT/WTO.

Disclaimers:

The first disclaimer relates to the question of how and where to discuss the issues of detail which, of course, arise when negotiations are put in hand. A good deal of the literature—both the literature supporting the anti-dumping system as a necessary good, and those opposing it as an unnecessary evil—address the elements that are involved in the measurement of price discrimination (that is, of the "margin of dumping"). Such an approach will inevitably involve prolonged negotiations and minuscule improvements in detail. The Uruguay Round made that quite clear. Insofar as such detailed aspects of the techniques of price comparison may be involved, it may be sufficient to note that, since the Tokyo Round, if not before, there has been created a very extensive literature on all the separate components of price. These issues cannot be summarized usefully—they are extremely detailed—and the "devil is in the details". (There was a time, prior to the Kennedy Round, when it was possible for one person to be familiar with all the literature on anti-dumping, with all the statutes, and with most if not all the jurisprudence. Even before the Tokyo Round, this became no longer possible; major studies of anti-dumping are, increasingly, the work of groups of experts). Fortunately, a number of recent studies include detailed bibliographies, which enable specialists to look at specific issues, particularly issues affecting price comparison.[e] The second disclaimer is as much the same lines: it is not possible, in this short paper, to make any detailed examination of how price discrimination is addressed in the competition law systems of major trading countries. This is, like the calculation of the " margin of dumping", a matter of great detail (and, in any event there are detailed studies available of this aspect of competition law in various jurisdictions (e.g. U.S., EU, Canada). We will note some major questions which arise, but a cursory review of the literature of anti-dumping and the literature of price discrimination might well suggest that to embark on an attempt at reconciliation between the two systems, on this issue, would be an enormously detailed, time-consuming exercise (supposing the major negotiating countries were willing to undertake it) and probably prove in the end to be a blind alley.[f]

Price discrimination and predation:

The anti-dumping provisions (that is, the Agreement and national legislation) is not directed at predatory dumping, but at any dumping which causes injury, or threatens injury, to a domestic industry. In fact, there are few, if any, cases of anti-dumping action in the U.S., in Canada, or in the EU, where it is clear that predation—which involves intent—is evident. Predatory pricing is pricing designed to eliminate a business competitor, and thus is anti-competitive in nature. But how (unless there is documentary evidence) can we establish intent or design? (This was part of the problem with trying to enforce the U.S. anti-dumping legislation of 1916.) Thus there has been a search for some sat of objective test of predatory intent, in the context of competition law. As opinion has evolved, it has become accepted that sales below marginal costs suggest predatory intent, but not necessarily sales below total average cost but above marginal costs.[g] To put the issue more exactly the key academic text is that by Richard Posner :

> "[. . .] the most useful definition of predatory pricing is the following : pricing at a level calculated to exclude from the market an equally or more efficient competitor. Only two practices fit this definition. The first is selling below short-run marginal cost. There is no reason consistent with an interest in efficiency for selling a good at a price lower than the cost that the seller incurs by the sale [. . .]

> The second practice that is predatory under my definition is selling below long-run marginal cost with the intent to exclude a competitor. Long-run marginal costs are those that must be recovered to stay in business for the more or less indefinite future." [h]

It is readily apparent that this is a different standard than applied in the anti-dumping provisions. At issue is the calculation of the exporter's price in his domestic market; Article 2 of the Code deals with this issue. As summarised by a U.S. lawyer:

> "Article 2:1 continues the limitation of the Tokyo Round Code that the home market (or third-country) sales used for comparison to export prices be made "in the ordinary course of trade". Unlike the Tokyo Round Code, however, the Uruguay Round Code makes explicit that sales below total cost are not "in the ordinary course of trade". These sales may be disregarded in determining normal value if they are made "within an extended period of time in substantial quantities and are at prices which do not provide for the recovery of all costs within a reasonable period of time."[i]

This is manifestly far from the standard of predatory pricing as proposed by Posner, and generally accepted in U.S. competition law. It is also far from the standard of predation in Canadian law. There predatory pricing is defined in the Competition Act as:

"a policy of selling products at prices unreasonably low, having the effect or tendency of substantially lessening competition or eliminating a competitor, or designed to have such effect."

and the Canadian courts have held that:

"[i]f an article is sold for more than cost, it can never be held to be unreasonable."[j]

We need not pursue the comparison between predatory pricing, as addressed in competition law, and dumping prices, any further; sufficient to say that anti-dumping deals with price discrimination, not predatory pricing. If the predatory pricing standard were to be applied in anti-dumping cases, it would be sufficient defense against the charge of dumping to show that the prices at issue were above marginal cost. Clearly this is, for the present, not a negotiable approach.

"Injury" and adverse effects on competition :

The anti-dumping provisions speak of "injury" to the domestic industry, and this, as a practical matter, means some firms in the industry having to reduce prices and or lose sales.

In the U.S. system, if there is dumping, and if there is the condition called "injury"—that is, the domestic producer finds he must cut prices or lose sales, the test of "injury" is met, although the dumped imports may be only one of a number of factors influencing the market behaviour of the domestic producer. (This aspect of the anti-dumping system is examined below under causality. The EU and Australia are said to apply a more rigorous standard.) But whether one looks at the U.S. system, which appears to be the most trade restrictive, or at others, this is a very different approach from how the effect of price discrimination in domestic markets is considered in competition law. The relevant U.S. law (Section. 2 of the Robinson—Patman Act) makes it unlawful to engage in price discrimination

"[. . .] where the effect of such discrimination may be substantially to lessen competition or tend to create a monopoly in any line of commerce, or to injure, destroy, or prevent competition with any person who either grants of knowingly receives the benefit of such discrimination, or with customers of either of them:"[k]

On the face of it, this is an "injury to competition" or "injury to the structure of competition" test, not merely a question of whether the competing domestic industry has had to cut prices or lose sales. However, a close examination of case law shows that lost sales, or forced price cutting, as a result of price discrimination, may go some way to meeting the test of injury to "competition".

The essential view of competition law authorities in the U.S. is, however that of the Attorney General's 1955 National Committee to Study the Antitrust Laws :

> "[T]his Committee recommends that analysis of the statutory "injury" center on the vigor of competition in the market rather than hard-ship to individual businessmen. For the essence of competition is a contest for trade among business rivals in which some must gain while others lose, to the ultimate benefit of a consuming public. Incidental hardships to an individual businessmen in the normal course of commercial events can be checked by a price discrimination statute only at the serious of risk stifling the competitive process itself."

The anti-dumping concept of injury is simpler than the typical competition law test, but in practice the difference may not be as great as critics of the anti-dumping system have suggested.[1] The problem with the anti-dumping concept of injury to domestic producers is better discussed as the issue of "causality", but here we should note that "injury" to an industry is taken, in U.S. law and in other jurisdictions, to mean the existence of a member of negative developments lost sales, reduced market share, reduced profits that is, an assessment of the general health of the industry, rather than the notion of a specific adverse effect, such as is implied when we speak of an individual having been injured by a particular or specified external factor or event, such as being hit by an automobile.

Another way of stating this is the assertion that injury is "separable" concept—that is, an industry can be suffering from various injuries, from various causes. This is, indeed, the layman's view of what is an injury. In the Tokyo Round negotiation (of the Subsidies—Countervail Agreement—in which this issue arose) the U.S. representative agreed that "injury" is a "separable concept" and indeed that phrase was advanced by the U.S. representative. If injury is separable, then the issue is the general state of health of the industry is, strictly speaking, irrelevant—and the injury test would then seem radically different, and rather less easy for domestic producers to satisfy.

"Causality" or "Minimum cause":

The solution to the dilemma of "cause" could go some way to make the anti-dumping provisions less restrictive of legitimate trade and more nearly consistent with competition law standards. The issue is not simple. This writer's view of the meaning of the relevant phrases of GATT Article VI is that the dumped imports must be shown to be the cause of a material injury to the domestic industry. This view of the causal link is apparently accepted by the EU administrative officials, but only a detailed examination of EU anti-dumping cases could show whether this is so in practice. The Australian practice is described as follows:

> "It is not sufficient that the local industry be suffering detriment and that there be some dumping and/or subsidization of the imported goods. It is necessary that the dumped or subsidized goods themselves be the cause of the material injury."[m]

U.S. practice is quite different. The key phrase in the Code is in Article 3.5 : "It must be demonstrated that the dumped imports are through the effects of dumping [●] causing injury within the meaning of the Agreement. ".What is at issue. In the U.S. view—as shown in a long series of U.S. International Trade commission decisions in anti-dumping, subsidy and escape clause cases—in that injury is being in a state of ill-health, or having suffered some adverse effects; it is not, as we noted above, a reference to a particular harm or damage that can be attributed to a specific event, whether internal (e.g. mismanagement) or external (e.g. a change in demand).Given this rather elastic concept of "injury", the important question then is to decide on the causal connection. Article VI of the GATT, and Article 3.5 or the Agreement deal, inter alia, with the causal relationship. The provision reads as previous:

> 3.5: "It must be demonstrated that the dumped imports are, through the effects of dumping causing injury within the meaning of this Agreement. The demonstration of a causal relationship between the dumped imports and the injury to the domestic industry shall be based on an examination of all relevant evidence before the authorities. The authorities shall also examine any known factors other than the dumped imports which at the same time are injuring the domestic industry, and the injuries caused by these other factors must not be attributed to the dumped imports. Factors which may be relevant in this respect include, inter alia, the volume and prices of imports not sold at dumping prices, contraction in demand or changes in the patterns of consumption, trade-restrictive practices of and competition between the foreign domestic producers, developments in technology and the export performance and productivity of the domestic industry".

The more-recent, and authoritative discussion of this provision (which this writer has written about elsewhere) is the 1995 article by David Palmeter. As he points out, the U.S. ITC position is that "the Commission must determine whether imports are a cause of material injury", and the U.S. Court of International Trade has stated that "A cause which even minimally contributes to material injury is sufficient. "Palmeter sums up the issue:

"The key to the issue is how the seemingly innocent phrase, "a cause of material injury", is interpreted. One way of interpreting it would be to emphasize the adjective "material" as in "whether imports are cause of Material injury". Under this interpretation, the injury caused by the dumped imports alone must be Material. This would seem to be the interpretation closest to thement of the first sentence of Article 3:5 : "It must be demonstrated that the dumped imports are, through the effects of dumping• casing injury within the meaning of this Agreement."

under the minimal cause doctrine, the ITC reads this phrase differently to emphasize the indefinite article "a" as in:

"whether imports are a cause of material injury" under this interpretation, of imports are one of a thousand causes+ then they are a cause, and the requirement of Article 3:5 has been met [•]. This practice goes a long way toward reading the causation requirement of Article 3:5 completely out of the Code. None the less, it is a practice which, the United States argues, received the sanction of the panels formed to review the ITC's decision in Fresh and Chilled Atlantic Salmon from Norway".[n] (Emphasis added).

The wording referred to (Article 3.5) is not significantly different from the wording of the Tokyo Round version of the Agreement, which was in turn an attempt to clarify what had been agreed in the Kennedy Round. Speaking as one of the negotiators of the Kennedy Round Agreement and of the Tokyo Round Agreement, this writer wishes to confirm the view expressed by Palmeter above as to the requirement of Article 3.5. As for the proposition that the GATT Anti-dumping Committee Panel on Norwegian Salmon confirmed the U.S. view, it is now possible for outside observers to decide for themselves whether or not this is the case, because the Panel reports have now been published.[o] Palmeter argues that, in effect, the Panel did not deal properly with this issue, and a close reading of the Reports confirms this. (That is not to say that this case at issue—Norwegian salmon—was a good case with which to examine the issue, but in this writer's view the Panel did not address the legal argument adequately.)

"It is virtually self-evident that, if the Australian / EU interpretation of the causality obligation was adopted by all signatories, the provisions would be less restrictive of trade and would be more consistent with the approach in competition law to assessing the causal connection between an instance of price discrimination (in the domestic market) and the alleged impact on competition."[p]

The related issue of injury which is "material":

This issue is noted by Palmeter in the citation above. It seems preferable, for analytic purposes, to discuss this as a separate question. The issue above is: Has the dumping been the cause of an injury to an industry? Here the question is. Is that injury material? (And how does it differ from serious injury, under Article XIX?)

The various degrees of injury at issue under the two key GATT articles, (VI and XIX) and the Agreements could be more clearly set out. As this writer sees the matter,[q] at one extreme there is that degree of adverse impact on domestic producers which is "negligible", which does not warrant any intervention, which should not be actionable. We are considering, not the quantity of imports, nor the margins of dumping, but the degree of impact : how much injury? Further along in the progression there is that degree of adverse impact which is "material", that is the key word in Article VI, and in the Agreement. Nothing in the GATT wording or in the history of the drafting of these provisions (at least, in the experience of this writer) suggests that "material" begins where "negligible" ends, although such an approach, of course, commends itself to protectionists. In the absence of any GATT (or Article VI Agreement) provision defining "material", the U.S. Congress legislated a definition in the Trade Agreements Act of 1979: "in general, the term 'material injury' means harm which is not inconsequential, immaterial or unimportant."[r] Given that precedents and practices under the two GATT Article Vi Agreements tend to become internationalized (that is, given the likelihood of producers seeking definitions, precedents and standards in the practices of other countries), this U.S. definition is a definition which has created a "merely more than de minimis" injury test.

Further along in this progression of adverse impacts, there is that degree of impact which is "serious" and which under GATT Article XIX may justify the withdrawal of a tariff concession. It is implicit in the GATT that the withdrawal of concession can be justified only by a degree of impact considerably greater than that which has to be determined to exist to warrant action against "unfai" imports.

It should be dear from these few comments that it would be in the interests of developing countries, and perhaps of developed countries as well, that the word "material" be given a positive and meaningful sense—to signify a degree of adverse impact that is substantially more than merely trivial or negligible. As matters stand, in U.S. practice, at least, the word "material" is without meaning.

"Conditions of Competition"

The wording of the Uruguay Round Anti-dumping Agreement appears to make it mandatory that domestic authorities, when investigating the impact of dumping, consider "trade restrictive practices of and competition between the foreign and domestic producers●" This phrase is from Article 3.5. Not all countries (e.g. Canada) have taken all Agreement provisions into their domestic legislation ; accordingly, in domestic law in those countries there may be no requirement that the requirements of Article 3.5 be considered by the administrative authority. Clearly, here is one step that could be taken to bring competition policy considerations into anti-dumping policy without changing the international rules : all that appears to be required is that the existing Agreement provisions be properly implemented. (The same reasoning applies in relation to the application of countervailing duty).

It is not clear however, that the wording of the Agreement requires domestic administrative authorities to deny the protection of the anti-dumping provisions to a domestic producer which is a monopoly, or which is in a dominant position in the domestic market. On this point, it would have appeared that the EC Extramet decision, requiring the EC authorities to take into account EC competition policy rules when assessing injury by dumping, would have set an important precedent. In the case before the European Court of Justice, in June 1992, it was held that the institutions, of the Community must take into account EC competition rules when determining damage by dumped imports (the Extramet decision.⁵) Prior to this decision, the EC Commission appeared to give little weight to competition policy rules in making anti-dumping decisions. In one case, the Commission held that the Community producers had been injured, despite the fact that some aspects of their pricing policy had been criticized by the French anti-trust authorities. What was involved was a refusal to supply a product by the sole producer in the EU. The customer switched to imported supplies and the producer lodged a complaint of dumping. The customer charged the supplier with abuse of a dominant position, under the EU competition law provisions. The Commission imposed an anti-dumping duty on the customer who had turned to imports: this was appealed to the ECJ, which made the decision noted above. All well and good—competition law policy could not be ignored in anti-dumping cares. But the Commission anti-dumping authorities were not prepared to be disciplined by the Court. As Patrick Messerlin reported:

> "[●] without any formal re-initiation of the case, the Commission reopened the file and quickly ended it with dumping margins six times higher than those assessed in the initial case-despite the strong anecdotal evidence that the anti-competitive behaviour of Pechiney was still going on " (emphasis in original).ᶠ

If it were to be agreed that firms in a dominant position, or firms held to be abusing market power in the domestic market, should be denied the protection of the Agreement provisions, there would be some logic in considering just what of sanctions should be applied when the dumping at issue is being carried out by a firm in the exporting country which exercises market dominating power, or, for example, is able to dump exports because it serves a protected domestic market—protected by tariffs, quantitative restrictions, procurement preferences, and the like, which enable it to charge higher prices. Should the anti-dumping system, in taking competition policy into consideration, distinguish between price discrimination in an import market by an exporter in a relatively competitive domestic market, and price discrimination by an exporter which enjoys a highly protected domestic market or a position of domestic market dominance. One could envisage that remedies more effective (and less cartelizing) than anti-dumping duties, such as "cease and desist" or "exclusion" orders, might be invoked. One should recall that anti-dumping provisions, when first proposed by Canada in the early part of the century, were held to be necessary because of the export practices of protected "trusts or combinations".

Set out above are the issues which could be negotiated to achieve the stated objective : to make anti-dumping policy more consistent with competition policy. We will summarize them, in the form of a conclusion, and make some additional proposals. But before doing so, it would be useful to look briefly at the history of the GATT/WTO Anti-Dumping Agreement, in order to better understand how the issues set out above have arisen. That history may provide some guidance, some clues, for the next attempt at revising the Agreement.

The Evolution of the Anti-Dumping Agreement

The Anti-Dumping Agreement negotiated in the closing phases of the Kennedy Round—in the winter of 1966-67—was the first attempt under GATT auspices to create a binding code of conduct, a set of contractual rules, governing the use of what was labelled a 'non-tariff barrier'. Previous GATT negotiations, apart from the drafting of the GATT Articles (which derived from the commercial policy provisions of the Havana Charter) and the GATT revision in 1955, had focussed on tariff rates. Reductions in tariff rates could be negotiated in what appeared to be a quantifiable fashion, the agreed results could be set out in schedules of rates, and simple rules could be developed for the conduct of negotiations. However, it was obviously more difficult to assess benefits and cost (to adopt the mercantilist language of GATT negotiations), or of concessions obtained and concessions given, when formulating a set of common administrative rules. Each major participant had to consider just how the emerging set of rules could be presented as an achievement by its negotiators. And there were some sharp differences as to objectives as between the major negotiating parties. The GATT member country which initially pressed for the negotiation of a set of rules governing the administration of anti-dumping duties was the U.K. (not at that time a member of the European Community). The principal objective of the U.K. was to set some limits on the ability of the US authorities (the Treasury, and its Bureau of Customs) to hold a given category of goods being imported 'subject to appraisement' if it later appeared that they were dumped and that there was injury to domestic producers by reason of' that dumping. There were no rules requiring that this very disruptive administrative measure be limited to a fixed period of time. Most importers, if they wished to continue to import, either built up large contingent liabilities for duties, or came to terms with the authorities—even if they felt that the dumping of which they were being accused was not injurious. The U.K. wanted to set some limits on this US practice, and US representatives were prepared to concede, in the context of the GATT multilateral agreement, that some limits should be placed on the duration of 'provisional measures'. The U.K. was also interested in getting the Canadians to adopt an overt test of injury - and the Canadians were prepared to concede that - if they could secure some reform of the US system. The Canadians were believed to have a so-called 'automatic' system, without an overt and open public inquiry into whether or not domestic producers were being injured by dumping. The U.K. and the US both argued that the Canadian system, which relied on the application of a number of complicated legal tests, did not meet the injury requirements of the GATT Article VI. The Canadians were prepared to follow the US model (the Tariff Commission, later the International Trade Commission) of an independent inquiry, and reduce the discretion of the customs authorities in regard to dumping, if they were allowed to act against so-called 'sporadic' or hit-and-run dumping and if the US was prepared to limit harassment of legitimate or non-injurious dumped imports. The Commission of the EC, for its part, realized that the creation of a GATT agreement requiring application to the Community as a single market, would add to the powers of the Commission. Behind the Commission, only the French were really active users of anti-dumping measures. For the French, the main problem—as they saw matters— was the scope for French subsidiaries of foreign firms to compete in the French market by importing components at artificially low transfer prices from their parent firms (i.e. from their US parents). This was the problem of 'hidden dumping'. It is unlikely that at the time of the Kennedy Round EC officials could foresee that anti-dumping would become the protectionist 'weapon of choice' for EC producers and the principal device which the Commission could use to meet domestic producers' complaints about import competition.

The Kennedy Round agreement, and its subsequent application by major GATT signatories, revealed a number of not entirely foreseen results.[u] One was that as each major negotiating party insisted on incorporating in the Agreement the special features of its domestic law which it wished to preserve, all parties to the agreement acquired rights to use all the various different devices. Thus the US kept the right to apply 'provisional' measures, and so did every other country. The Canadians insisted on provisions in regard to 'sporadic' dumping (Article 10.6, .7, .8), and so other countries acquired the same right. The US insisted on a regional industry provision (Article 4.1 (ii)), and so did Canada.[v] The EC opposed the concept of an independent outside body inquiring into injury (as that would severely limit the discretion and authority of the Commission) and so no such institutional provision was put into Article 6.

A second feature of that negotiation was that the drafting was not always very precise, or alternately, where it was precise the words meant different things in different legal systems (e.g. the concept of cause, discussed above). The Agreement was, in effect a compromise between the detailed precise drafting of the US, which the Canadians also favoured, and the much looser legal drafting of the European Commission. Much of the later disputes about anti-dumping resulted from this rather loose drafting- and, of course - once administrative practices developed which relied on the imprecision in the Agreement, administering officials developed vested interests in those practices. For example, it took until 1994—27 years—to add precision to the concept of sales below cost and to the concept of 'the ordinary course of trade' (Article 2)—even if that precision authorized a basis for price comparison quite different from the standards of competition law (as noted above).

Experience with this first GATT non- tariff agreement might be compared with other agreements in the area of trade law and international commercial law. 'For example, most conventional trade agreements have relied on phrases and expressions which have been in use—and been tested—since the late 18th century. Other instruments, such as the UNCITRAL agreement on sales contracts, are the results of accumulated commercial practice and detailed drafting over a period of years. The Anti-Dumping Agreement, as a legal instrument, suffers in comparison.

Yet another result of the Agreement, which should have been foreseen, was that once the Agreement was in place, it would become the preserve of the administering officials, rather than of trade policy or economic policy officials. Only the administrators, and trade policy consultants and members of the trade law bar, now understand the various anti-dumping systems—so, as a practical matter, they have captured these systems. (Accordingly, it will be important to those countries which may wish to reform the system—that is, to liberalize the system, to make it less restrictive - that they endeavour to get the negotiation into the hands of policy officials and out of the grip of professional anti-dumpers.)

One development after the Round was that the US Congress was unwilling to make the changes in legislation (particularly on the issue of "cause") which the Agreement entailed. This was in part a quarrel between the Administration and the Congress over turf—resulting from what appeared to have been a failure on the part of officials to consult Congressional leaders fully before and during the negotiations ; it was also in part a difference over policy—the Administration was less protectionist that some Congressional leaders.[w] This was all unexpected by the negotiators of other countries, who had assumed, quite properly, that the US negotiators had cleared their lines with domestic business groups and with the Congress. The result of this confusion was that the US implemented only those administrative changes which could be achieved by regulation, not requiring Congressional approval. The further result was that Congress became much more aware of the possibilities of the anti-dumping system being used to meet pressures for protection, and much more determined to keep control of trade negotiations. (It was thus that the so-called 'fast track' system was invented.)

In the years between the Kennedy Round Agreement (and its non-implementation by the US) and the launching of the Tokyo Round, in 1975, the use of anti-dumping measures—by Canada, the US, by Australia, and by the EC—increased significantly. It was as though the Kennedy Round Agreement had become a sort of open, general hunting license—for a perfectly legal way to harass importers and impose a discriminatory duty on imports.

Negotiations in the Tokyo Round focussed on subsidies and countervailing measures; the group of anti-dumping measures was not very active, and it was only after the Tokyo Round Agreement on Subsidies and Countervailing Measures had been virtually completed that the negotiators turned their attention to bringing the wording of the Anti-Dumping Agreement (on 'cause' and on 'injury') into line with the language agreed in regard to countervail. The most important of the changes was the dropping of the Kennedy Round language about 'principal cause'. This followed a detailed (but informal) discussion in the countervail group. There it was argued that what was at issue was injury which resulted solely from the subsidization (or dumping) of imports, that injury was a 'separable concept'—to use a phrase of the US representative. Like most of the real negotiation of this and other non-tariff issues, this discussion took place, not in a plenary meeting, of which there would be a record, but in an informal group (but attended by the GATT Secretariat). Somehow this understanding among the main negotiators did not survive the voyage to Washington, and no trace of it appears in the Congressional documents, in the Statement of Administrative Action, nor in the account by two American officials which was later published.[x] Hence the continuing confusion, and differences of interpretation, on these issues, in regard both to anti-dumping and to countervail. The other major development was the introduction of the world 'material' into US legislation. As we have indicated above, the insistence of the EC that the US legislation be so amended was counter-productive.

After the Tokyo Round, and leading up the Uruguay Round, there was extensive use of anti-dumping (and of countervail, by the US) and extensive discussion in GATT groups of experts of various aspects of the anti-dumping system, or systems. These discussions were between professional anti-dump-ers—who were thus enabled to exchange much information about how to make their various systems more precise, more detailed—and thus more per-fectionist. It is this sort of discussion that must be curtailed if there is to be any serious negotiation leading to the anti-dumping regime becoming less protec-tions (i.e. more consistent with competition policy). The Uruguay Round negotiation led to minor improvements ; that they were only minor was to be expected from the tenor of discussions in the groups of experts referred to above, and given that no major negotiating country was committed to liberal-izing the system. The protectionism that has previously been contained by the tariff system had been diverted into a new channel—involving much more detailed administration, and much to the profit of the rapidly enlarging trade law bar in Brussels, Washington and elsewhere. Thus in addition to the obvi-ous interest of producers in finding some device affording protection against imports, two new and powerful interest groups were created in the period from the end of the Kennedy Round to the end of the Uruguay Round—the admin-istering officials and the trade law bar.

The Uruguay Round did produce, as we have said, some detailed, mar-ginal changes: the rules on 'standing'— that is, who has the right to launch a complaint of dumping, and certain precise reforms in the techniques of calcu-lating the margin of dumping, notably, the rules regarding the margin as between an import price and the average value of goods sold in the exporter's domestic market.[y] These changes did little more that add a further measure of legitimacy to a system which provided administered protection.[z]

As for the definition of the de minimis margin of dumping (2% of the export price) introduced into the Agreement (Article 5), US trade experts explained in testimony before a House of Representatives Committee that this would "have no impact on the vast majority of US cases."[aa]

Proposals for Negotiation:

The very brief comments set out above on what is in fact a long, compli-cated and essentially unrecorded history, retained only in fragmentary accounts of a few plenary meetings, evasive agreed texts, and the fading rec-ollections of negotiators, should serve as warning to negotiators who may for-mulate the more ambitious objective of moving the GATT/WTO Agreement on Anti-Dumping in the general direction of competition policy. Set out below are some suggestions.

- To concentrate on the minutiae of the calculation of the margin of dumping would not be profitable. Negotiators should not be diverted into such a detailed and time-consuming exercise. As long as markets are protected by transportation cost, by the existence of established brands and trade marks, by the existence of distribution systems which are even partly in the control of domestic producers, there will be dumping, and it will not be beyond the wit of administrators to find a positive measure of such dumping. The calculation of margins is not a major issue, it is subordinate, but it is what professional anti-dumpers will be prepared to talk about and around for the duration of the next MTN.

- Another issue which might be thought negotiable, but which might turn out to be a blind alley, is the question of 'injury' to what, and to whom. Academic critics of anti-dumping never titre of pointing out that the anti-dumping provisions (GATT Article VI and the Agreement) speak of injury to the 'industry' in the importing country, in contrast to competition law which addresses injury 'to competition'. As suggested above, this difference is perhaps less evident in practice: under competition law evidence of injury to competitors would be lost sales, lost market share, and being obliged to cut prices. If competitors are injured, then competition is injured. It might thus well be that trying to reconcile the two apparently different approaches to injury would merely serve to emphasize that injury under the anti-dumping provisions is not all that different conceptually from injury to competition under competition law.

- What might be more profitable would be to seek agreement that only a really intolerable impact on domestic producers warrants the application of a discriminatory duty—that is to say, the adjective 'material' should be given some real meaning. This will not be easy to negotiate, given that it was the US Congress (i.e. the Senate) which put in place the definition of material which governs in US law. But if it could be argued that 'material' injury is an adverse impact substantially more than merely 'immaterial', something much more that what in effect is merely the normal manifestation of competition. That would move the anti-dumping provisions a useful distance toward the more rigorous standards of competition law. A negotiation of this issue would necessarily involve consideration of the difference between material injury, under GATT Article VI (and in the two Article VI Agreements) and the concept of 'serious injury' under Article XIX —the so-called 'safeguard' provision. This will be difficult negotiating ground, but logic and reason would be on the side of those who would wish to make the 'material injury' test a standard of adverse impact that would be meaningful. As noted above, it is this writer's view that there is a progression in the GATT language about the adverse impact of imports on domestic producers. Because dumping is thought of as an uncompetitive practice, the degree of adverse impact justifying action against the imports in question is logically less than that degree of impact which justifies action against 'fairly traded' imports—i.e. imports which are coming in at prices and in quantities which have an intolerable impact on domestic producers (and on their employees) - and thus which justify the withdrawal of a concession (but on a non-discriminatory basis). Beyond that there is that degree of disruption of markets which has been held to justify restrictive action not provided for in the GATT, for example, the actions taken against textiles and garments under the MFA and prior agreements in this sector. But this does not amount to saying that the lesser degree of adverse impact from 'unfairly traded' imports is properly defined as merely more than 'immaterial'. The application of a discriminatory duty to imports can only be warranted if the impact on the domestic producers is something more than that following from normal competition for markets.[bb] Now that those signatories of the Agreement which have been majors users of the anti-dumping provisions are finding that they face action by other countries they may be more willingness to consider making the system more realistic and therefore, less protectionist. A working group could be established to draft an interpretative note putting some needed flesh on the word 'material'.

- Another profitable area for the next negotiation is to sort out the confusion between the notion of injury being done to the domestic producers or the domestic industry, and the notion of the general health of the industry. In US practice, injury means much the same as ill-health—or what has been called 'overall injury'. What Article VI (and the Agreements) speak of is 'injury' caused by dumping (and that injury must be material). This writer described the issue in the following terms, after the Kennedy Round:

"What is at issue is that a practical matter, an industry seeking relief from dumping is likely to be under the influence of various adverse factors—changes in demand, changes in costs, or changes in the character of import competition. Some of these are external factors impinging or having an impact on the fortunes or health of the industry. Others will be in a sense internal factors. But whether or not the industry is healthy or depressed, it is entitled to relief from dumping if injury—say a marked decline in profits, in employment, and in sales—can be shown to have been caused by dumped imports. Having satisfied themselves that there is an injury caused by the dumped imports and not by some other factor, the authorities must then decide whether or not such injury was maerial.*"cc

Put another way, this is the question of whether 'injury' is a separable concept. This is a major issue for negotiation ; sorting this out will, as a practical matter, move the anti-dumping provisions an important distance toward the concepts of competition law (even though the language may be rather different).

- Finally—and it will be perceived that these issues are closely related—there is the problem of 'cause'. As explained above, that word means, in US dumping law, that the dumping was a cause of injury, it was one of the causes. Thus injury is the sum of the effects of all the adverse factors impinging on producers, and dumping, if it is one of those factors, is a cause of injury. This is the most protectionist interpretation of the wording possible, but in this writer's view, it is not consistent with Article VI of the GATT. It has not been effectively challenged because the professional anti-dumpers who dominated the Uruguay Round discussions did not want to attack it, and, in any event, the attention being given to a major agreement on subsidies virtually precluded real reform of the injury and causality concepts being employed by the USITC. All students of law are aware that causality is an extraordinary difficult concept; there is an extensive literature. It would be a mistake to import this legal hair-splitting into a negotiation of these GATT phrases. The GATT Articles are attempts to find some relatively simple language which could mean the same things to administrators in many different jurisdictions - it should be interpreted with common sense. An understanding that when real damage, in an economic sense, is being inflicted on an industry or on producers by dumped imports because they are dumped—whether or not that industry is suffering from other outside or inside events, and if it is clear that it is the dumping which gives rise to the competitive harm, then it should be permissible to apply anti-dumping remedies. To achieve this result will require, not a simple change in the wording of the Agreement, but an extensive interpretive note.

Summary/conclusion:

It is the conclusion of this paper that reform of the GATT anti-dumping provisions to bring the somewhat nearer the concepts of competition law—

and incidentally make them less protectionist in effect—will turn on careful reworking of the concepts of cause, of injury, of material. They are the substantial concepts of Article VI, and only more defensible interpretations of those concepts will make the application of that Article more consistent with competition law, and thereby less protectionist.

Postface

Much criticism of the GATT/WTO Agreement, and of the various national anti-dumping systems derived from it, has focussed on the cost to a national economy of such a system. Attempts have been made to calculate the costs to consumers, and, more particularly, to down-stream users of the allegedly dumped imports. E.g. the controversial USITC study3[dd]. There has been much criticism of the more bizarre aspects of the calculation of the margin of dumping, which, it is alleged, leads to findings of dumping when there is no dumping. Economists concern themselves with these elements in the system perhaps because they can be expressed numerically, with the appearance of precision. It is clear that is very difficult to measure the various costs imposed by an anti-dumping duty, and thus defenders of anti-dumping policy are able to make fairly damaging criticism of such attempts at measurement. It is evident, of course, that anti-dumping, like other barriers to trade, may impose costs—but it is difficult to be really precise as to their magnitude in the longer term. As for the rules about calculating margins, some of the more obviously protectionist practices were negotiated away in the Uruguay Round. It is suggested in this paper that a further round of detailed negotiation of such matters between professional ant-dumpers is likely to yield meager results. This writer has taken part in two rounds of GATT anti-dumping negotiations and has drafted legislation on anti-dumping and has advised various governments on anti-dumping policy. Careful reading of the discussions in legislative bodies (e.g. the US Senate Finance Committee, the Trade Policy Sub-Committee of that Committee), intensive discussions with senior members of such bodies (e.g. US Senators Long and Ribicoff), with their staff and with senior members of the trade law bar in Washington and Brussels—and examination of USITC reports on such matters—have persuaded this writer that it is only by reworking the Agreement texts on cause, on material, on injury, that the system will be materially altered. Of course, these issues arise in regard to the application of countervailing duties as well.

References

a.   "Agreement on Implementation of Article VI of the General Agreement of Tariffs and Trade 1994" in The Results of the Uruguay Round of Multilateral Trade Negotiations (GATT Secretariat, Geneva, 1994) (Results) pp. 168-196 (The "Anti-dumping Agreement")

b. For a description of earlier U.S. measures in the sector, see Hufbauer, Berliner, Elliot : Trade Protection in the United States / 31 case studies, Washington, Institute for International Economics, 1986, pp. 154-184. (This account has extensive bibliographical references, including in regard to so-called "trigger-price" mechanism.)

c. Noel Hemmendinger : "Shifting Sands: An Examination of the Philosophical Basis of U.S. Trade Laws", in Jackson, Cunningham, Fontheim (eds): International Trade Policy: The Lawyer's Perspective, New York, Matthew Bender, 1985, pp. 2-1 - 2-10. The "injury only" view is argued, in the subsidies context, in John J. Barcelo III, "An Injury-Only Regime (For Imports) and Actionable Subsidies", in Wallace, Loftus, Krikmian (eds.): Legal Treatment of *Domestic Subsidies*, Washington International Law Institute, 1984. A more recent, and vigorous statement of this view is Robert B. Reich: "Trading Insecurities", in Financial Times, May 28, 1999.

d. "Undertakings", in the sense discussed in this report, are provided for in Article 8 of the Anti-dumping Agreement. No provision was made for such "undertakings" when Canada introduced revised anti-dumping legislation following the Kennedy Round negotiation. Not surprisingly, after the Tokyo Round, when some revisions to that legislation were required, there was pressure from domestic industry to incorporate a provision for accepting "undertakings". The possibilities of thus creating legalized expert cartels in countries exporting to Canada, with the consent or, at least, the tacit acceptance of the terms of such "undertakings" by Canadian competitors, was attractive to the business community.

e. We may note three recent studies: James Bovard: The Fair Trade Fraud, New York, St-Martin's Press, 1991 (A biography is to be found in the extensive chapter end-notes, and they includes useful references to newspaper articles); Richard Boltuck, Robert E. Litan (eds.); Down in the Dumps, Washington, Brookings, 1991 (a work by various authors, but without a bibliography); Greg Mastel: Antidumping laws and the U.S. Economy, Armonk (N.Y.) and London, M.E. Sharpe, 1998 (a vigorous defence of the U.S. anti-dumping system) with an extensive bibliography Richard M. Hockman and Petros Mavroids: " Dumping, Anti-dumping and Antitrust", in Journal of World Trade, ●, pp. 27-51 (contains a useful short list of references); J. Michael Finger (ed.): Antidumping / How It works and Who Gets Hurt , Ann Arbor, University of Michigan, 1993 some useful references). See also the annual volume of the Fordham Corporate Law Institute, published by Matthew Bender, New York, for the Institute.

f. For the U.S. system, see the classic work by Earl W. Kintner: A Robinson—Patman Primer / a Guide to the Law Against Price Discrimination, New York, Macmillan, 1979 (2nd Edition). This contains a detailed bibliography and texts of relevant U.S. legislation.

g. See the discussion in Kintner, op. cit., beginning at p. 127. For a general discussion, see OECD Secretariat: *Predatory Pricing*, Paris, 1989; the references constitute a useful bibliography.

h. Richard A. Posner: Antitrust Law / An Economic Perspective, Chicago, University of Chicago Press, 1976, pp. 188-189.

i. David Palmeter : "United States Implementation of the Uruguay Round Antidumping Code" 29 Journal of World Trade, N) 3, 1995, p. 46.

j. Canadian Competition Act Sector 50 (1) and Director of Investigation and Research: Predatory Pricing Enforcement Guidelines, Ottawa, 1992, pp. 2-3.

k. Cited Kintner, op. cit., p. 366, and see Chapter 5.

l. See Kintner's discussion of "injury to competition" under the Robinson-Patman Act, loc. cit.

m. Cited Palmeter, op. cit. ; this article by Palmeter is the clearest discussion of this issue.

n. Palmeter, op. Cit. P. 6.

o. Contracting Parties: Basic Instruments and Selected Documents (BISD), Supplement no 41, vol. 1, pp. 229-450.

p. See Kintner, op. cit., p. 140; p. 146, and Canada: Predatory Pricing, p. 13.

q. See Rodney de C. Grey: Injury, Damage, Disruption, UNCTAD / MTN 217, Oct. 1981 for a fuller discussion.

r. U.S.: Trade Agreements Act, 1979; See also Rodney de C. Grey : United States Trade Policy Legislation / A Canadian View, Montreal, Institute for Research on Public Policy, pp. 43-46 for a detailed discussion of "material" during and after the Tokyo Round.

s. "Extramet Industry SA v. Council of the European Communities" [No C-358-89] 11 June, 1992.

t.   Cited Hoekman & Mavroides, op. cit. p. 48

u.   For a short account of the Kennedy Round negotiations of an anti-dumping Agreement, the only one by a participant, see Rodney de C. Grey: The Development of the Canadian Anti-Dumping System, Montreal, Private Planning Association, 1973. See also the *Report of the U.S. Tariff Commission* to the Senate Finance Committee on this negotiation: "Committee Print", 90th Congress, 2nd Session, March 13, 1968.

v.   Grey, op.cit., note 21, p. 48, p. 73

w.   There is an extensive literature; see Grey, op. cit, note 18 for a discussion and references.

x.   Richard R. Rivers and John D. Greenweld : "The Negotiations of a Code on Subsidies and Countervailing Measures: Bridging Fundamental Policy Differences" in 11 Law and Policy in International Business, 1979, pp. 447-95.

y.   Palmeter: op. cit.

z.   loc. cit.

aa.   See "Testimony of Counsel to ECAT Before the Committee of Ways and Means / Sub Committee on Trade, U.S. House of Representatives" Jan. 23, 1992

bb.   See Grey, op. cit., note 17

cc.   See Grey, op. cit., note 21

dd.   USITC: The Economic Effects of Antidumping and Countervailing

---

ANTI-DUMPING POLICY IN THE COMPETITION POLICY CONTEXT

If anti-dumping policy is to be made more consistent with competition policy, the following related steps should be taken:

(1)   The concept of 'injury' to a domestic industry occasioned by price discrimination in import trade (i.e. dumping) should be made more consistent with the concept of 'injury to competition'. This means treating 'injury' as separable, not as the result in total of all the various negative factors affecting producers.

(2)   The *degree* of 'injury'—the extent of the adverse effect on domestic producers of dumping, should be defined in a more meaningful fashion. Com-

petition policy distinguishes between the effects of price competition and the effects of price discrimination. This distinction should be brought into anti-dumping policy: this means defining 'material' more substantively.

(3) The 'causal' connection between the alleged dumping and the injury alleged to exist should be more carefully defined—in order to make clear that what is at issue is the effect of the dumping only. As in competition policy, what should be at issue is the effect of the price discrimination, and only that.

(4) The competitive position of firms seeking anti-dumping relief should be taken into account. A monopoly, or a firm in a dominant position in a given market, might not be accorded the benefit of the anti-dumping provisions. Further, a firm convicted of a competition law offence might be denied recourse to anti-dumping relief for a stated period. This would bring anti-dumping policy into direct relationship with competition policy.

(5) By the same token; if the dumping at issue is by a firm which enjoys a dominant position in its domestic market, the importing country might issue a 'cease and desist' order, or impose a prohibition on imports from that firm. If the firm had been convicted of a competition policy offence in its domestic market, or in the importing country the sanction should be more severe. Such a firm should not be able to profit by giving an 'undertaking' not to dump.

(6) The concept of 'undertaking' in the anti-dumping system should be reworked to minimize the possibility of creating export cartels, and facilitating market allocation, under the cover of 'undertakings'. Anti-dumping policy should not explicitly encourage such anti-competitive practices.

TECHNOLOGY TRANSFER IN THE WTO AGREEMENTS

Carlos Correa

Introduction

Technology has been recognized as an essential element in any developmental strategy (Unctad, 1993). Though different technological packages are needed at different levels of development, the access to appropriate technical knowledge is key, not just to succeed in the market place, but also to survive in a context of trade and investment liberalization.

Developing countries have expressed their concerns with regard to one of the visible unbalances in the WTO system: while such countries have been required to expand and enhance their intellectual property regimes, very little is in the WTO agreements to effectively facilitate and promote the access to technology.

This paper briefly describes, first, the current global scenario with respect to the generation of technology, the technological demands of countries at different level of development, and the role of foreign direct investment (FDI) and licensing in the transfer of technology to developing countries. Second, possible elements for consideration in future negotiations within WTO are examined.

The global scenario for the transfer of technology[233]

Concentration of R&D capacity

Research and development (R&D) expenditures have significantly grew in developed countries since the 1970s,[234] with an increasing share of the private sector in total R&D.[235] On a world scale, R&D expenditures are very asymmetrically distributed: developing countries, on the most generous estimates, account for about 6 per cent[236] of global R&D expenditures (Freeman & Hagedoorn, 1992, p. 10).

R&D capacity is, in fact, largely concentrated in a small number of developed countries. Seven countries account for around 90% of total OECD expenditures, and United States alone for 47% of the total (OECD, 1992b, p. 113). Moreover, in the latter country 28 large corporations accounted for about half the total private R&D expenditures at the beginning of the 1990's (UN/TCMD, 1992, p.136). The upsurge of mergers and acquisitions that has taken place during this decade 1990s—which accounted for 58% of foreign direct investments in 1997[237]—has given further impetus to the concentration of R&D in a limited number of firms.

Decentralization of R&D activities

The apparent "globalization" of R&D activities has created some expectations as to the transfer of R&D capabilities to developing countries. Unfortunately, they are not justified. Large firms are decentralizing part of their R&D activities in foreign countries, but R&D is less internationalized than all other dimensions of corporate activity, such as production and sourcing. Overall, foreign ownership is either not significantly or is negatively correlated to R&D performance (Dunning, 1993, p. 304).

In addition, decentralization is done through foreign subsidiaries and branches mainly established in other developed countries. The transfer of R&D activities to subsidiaries in developing countries has been made on a very limited scale, basically in relation to adaptive tasks (UN/TCDM, 1992, p.147; OTA, 1994, p.87-89).In 1989 some 95% of the foreign R&D expenditures of US firms were concentrated in industrialized countries, whereas only 78% of the output of goods was (Dunning, 1993, p. 304).

As a result, R&D remains highly centralized across the industrialized countries; R&D activities by foreign firms in developing countries are very scarce. According to a study on US firms,

"R&D globalization is occurring at a moderate pace. Most industrial R&D is still performed in the company's home country . . Despite a few interesting countries—Korea and India most notably—developing countries are often left out of the R&D globalization process. Multinational corporations are primarily expanding their research and development activities to other first world countries" (Callan, Costigan and Keller, 1997, p. 2-3).

This situation is not likely to change in the near future (Pavitt and Patel, 1999, p. 94).

Technological alliances

In addition, large firms of developed countries have been able to develop a complex network of cooperation in technology through "strategic alliances", that further enhance their dominant role in technology generation and use.

Strategic alliances provide an increasingly important channel for the acquisition and exchange of technology in order to face technological and competitive challenges.[238] Such alliances have become common in the field of information technology[239] and biotechnology, but are also present in many other sectors (Unctad, 1996). They are based on the cooperation between equals, unlike conventional licensing agreements that occur between partners of unequal technological level. Some firms in developing countries have been able to participate in such strategic alliances (Unctad, 1998, p. 27-29), but they are beyond the reach of most firms in those countries.

In sum, the asymmetric distribution and high concentration of R&D capabilities, the limited decentralization of R&D activities by TNCs, and the establishment of technology-related strategic alliances, indicate that developing countries—with a few exceptions—continue to play a marginal role in the creation of technology. Those countries, however, need to ensure access to technology in order to advance their developmental objectives.

Technology demand

The demand for technology transfer varies as the firms and the industry evolve through different technological stages. At an initiation stage, mostly "mature" technologies are incorporated by firms in developing countries, such as for the production of food and textiles. At this stage, the main modes of transfer of technology include:

- informal transfers through the acquisition of machinery and equipment;

- imitation through reverse engineering;

- technical assistance provided by Original Equipment Suppliers (OEM) (Kim and Dahlman, 1992, p. 439).

"Informal" modes of transfer of technology predominate at this stage. However, technologies need to be acquired through more formal modes, including turn-key agreements and licenses, in cases relating to large scale industries (e.g. steel, petrochemicals) where complex processes and plant layouts are difficult to imitate.

Foreign direct investment (FDI) also is an usual mode of technology transfer at an early development stage, when local absorptive capabilities for unbundled technologies are limited. Latin American countries have heavily relied on this form of transfer during their import-substitution period. FDI has also been a dominant transfer mode in "second-tier" Asian countries (Malaysia, Thailand, Philippines).

As the industrialization process advances, and firms move along technology learning curves, the utilization of formal modes grows. Once firms have already "mastered the operation technology, the focus of technological efforts changes from the mastery of operation and low-level design technology in the initiation stage to the mastery of production-related technology such as manufacturing equipment, plant engineering, etc. and high level design technology" (Lee, Bae and Choi, 1988, p. 242). At this stage, foreign direct investments and licensing become more important modes of technology transfer.

The role of FDI

Foreign direct investment (FDI) has been generally recognized as an important channel for the international transfer of technology. However, the role of FDI in the transfer of technology to developing countries is subject to a number of limitations.

Developing countries' share in total FDI inflows drastically fell over the 1980's, from 25% to 17%. They accounted for around 20% of the world in 1997. A significant part of new FDI in the 1990's in such countries has be linked to the privatization process or consisted of the acquisition of local private firms. In addition, FDI is concentrated in a small number of developing countries. For instance, in Asia and the Pacific, FDI overwhelmingly concentrated in 1997 in China, followed by Singapore, Indonesia, Malaysia, Thailand, India, Honk Kong, Korea and Taiwan. In Latin America, Argentina, Brazil and Mexico accounted in the same year for 62% of total FDI inflows to the region, and those countries plus Venezuela, Peru, Colombia and Chile, for 88% of the total (Unctad, 1998, p. 16, 21, 198, 244).

There are also important changes in FDI patterns in the context of current globalization: "increasingly, companies began investing overseas as part of an integrated global production strategy which relies on significant cross-national transfers of intermediate and final products " (Wint, 1992, p. 1516). In some cases, such strategies go beyond setting up factories to take advantage of low-cost labor. Foreign companies are also looking to benefit from design and engineering by locals, such as in the case of Motorola in Singapore and Malaysia (and more recently, China), and IBM in India (in the software area).

FDI may be regarded as a modality of transfer of technology alternative to licenses and other non-equity forms. FDI inflows to developing countries grew during 1985-1990, faster than any other indicator of technology transfer, such as royalties and fees, capital goods imports and technical cooperation grants, (UN/TCMD, 1992,p.321).

A decline in the importance of contractual or non-equity modes of technology transfer has been observed in several studies (Kumar, 1997). Internalized forms of technology transfer (i.e. those taking place intrafirm) are more likely to be preferred by technology holders when the technology changes rapidly and when potential recipients may pose competitive threats in world markets as future competitors (Lall, 1992, p.4-6). Several other factors seem to reduce transnational corporations choice for externalized modes of transfer:

"For one, recent developments in information technologies tend to increase the internationalization advantages of Transnational Corporations (TNCs). Those developments facilitate and cheapen the cost of intra-firm communication, coordination and control. The high costs of development and rapid obsolescence are likely to reinforce efforts of TNCs to secure a quicker pay-back through internationalization. Futhermore, the internationalization of the R&D expenditure noted earlier and the trend towards strategic alliances among TNCs in respect of the development and transfer of technologies limit the plurality of sources in the technology market. The deceleration in the growth of external resource inflows through official development assistance and private flows other than FDI would limit the ability of developing countries to acquire unpackaged technology. Finally, recent policy changes in developing countries in favour of FDI tend to reduce the cost of internationalization. Those factors are likely to increase the importance of FDI as an instrument of technology transfer" (UN/TCMD, 1992, p. 154-155)

In addition, a significant part of technology in use is of "tacit" nature, such as many details and materials specifications and expertise at the floor level. The transfer of "tacit" knowledge may eventually be secured through well drafted contracts; but the direct involvement of the technology supplier through FDI or joint ventures may be crucial.

According to a generally accepted view, joint-ventures offer greater opportunities for the transfer of technology than other modalities, since domestic and foreign partners share in the ownership and management of the enterprise. Though a systematic assessment of the comparative advantages and disadvantages of this modality has not been conducted, it seems to lead to mixed results depending, among other factors, upon the terms of the particular agreements. The equity participation of the technology holder does not necessarily mean that he is actually committed to the success of the venture and to the transfer of technology.

In conclusion, FDI not only plays an important role as a means of technology transfer at earlier stages of development; it is also likely to growingly become a substitute for unbundled licenses as far as state-of the-art technologies are involved.

Licensing and contractual means

Licenses may provide an economical way of transfer—from the transferor viewpoint—of standardized, relatively simple and mature, technologies to recipients having absorptive capabilities. Licensing will also be the first option for small and medium enterprises lacking the financial resources to enter into equity ventures or FDI. Licensing is also likely to be used in transactions between large industrial groups with comparable technological levels (UNCTAD, 1990, p. 13).

However, innovative firms may prefer FDI when new technologies are ay stake, in order to ensure control over their application. The cost of R&D has increased, and fierce competition has shortened the life cycle of technologies.

Relying on licensing alone (from the point of view of the recipient) may limit access to state-of-the-art technologies. On the one hand, financial constraints make technology transfer without capital investment less feasible for developing countries. On the other, technology suppliers' concern with confidentiality issues and intellectual property has increased significantly, as discussed below. FDI ensures a tighter control over critical technology assets.

Several studies indicated that large industrial firms systematically exploited their licensing potential during the 1960s and 1970s via transferring mature technologies to developing countries. Negotiations with licensees usually occurred only after the R&D effort was completed and the product or process standardized (Contractor, 1981, p. 40). In this situation, the recipient firms need to find "compensating advantages" to meet the competitive disadvantages arising from time lags in the transfer of technology. In Cooper's view "the existence of these compensating advantages in import substituting economies is all too obvious: they take the form of effectively captive markets" (Cooper, 1991, p. 14).

Many developing countries have undertaken since last decade drastic reforms aimed at liberalizing and opening their economies to foreign products, technologies and investments. Local firms will find more difficult, if it is possible at all, to compensate the referred competitive disadvantages, not only because they would have to compete with foreign products on the domestic market but also because they will often need to export in order to make their operations profitable.

In this context, the possibility of a successful and rapid "catching up" process by developing countries, mainly based on the acquisition and imitation of foreign technologies, is strongly reduced. Access to scientific knowledge is also more problematic: "the growing economic relevance of research...increases pressures to limit the free dissemination of research results and to constrain the traditional openness of university laboratories where most basic research is performed in Western countries" (Skolnikoff, 1993, p. 118).

The integration of technology transfer with deliberate and endogenous technological efforts seems indispensable, particularly as a country advances in the industrialization process (Unctad, 1993, p. 24). The opportunities that are opened by various channels of technology transfer and diffusion will be more and more confined to those countries and firms that are able to develop their own technological capabilities (Lall, 1995, p. 21) .

It should be noted, lastly, that most of the countries that during the 1970's established regulations on technology transfer in order to improve the conditions for access to technology under contractual modes, have flexibilized or abolished the control of such transactions. There is very little statistical information on the number, subject matter, and other elements of arrangements for the transfer of technology to developing countries.

In sum, a globalized economy with an exacerbated competition is changing the patterns of technology transfer and, in particular, the relative importance of FDI and licensing. Open economies are likely to have a greater reliance on informal transfers of technology, i.e, those taking place through the import of equipment and capital goods, since neither the producers of said equipment nor those that may provide supportive services (engineering and consultancy firms) compete in the markets where the eventual recipients operate.

The advances in the industrialization process in some developing countries has led -in the light of the previous analysis- to changes in the content and modes of technology demand. As new industrializing countries reach higher levels of technological development, they have a more sophisticated demand for technologies which have not yet reached the "maturity" stage. Unlike mature technologies, which are relatively easy to acquire, technology which is still changing and profitable is more difficult to be obtained.

Changes in intellectual property protection

Attitudes and strategies on transfer of technology by innovative firms are growingly influenced by perceptions of and limitations on the appropriability of technological advances. The importance attributed to intellectual property rights has been fully recognized by the adoption of the TRIPS Agreement as a component of the Final Act of the Uruguay Round.

A few studies have attempted to assess the weight of IPRs on transfer of technology decisions. It is arguable that IPRs protection will constitute a precondition for innovators to license their technology. It is unclear, however, whether the introduction or strengthening of such protection would increase the net flows of technology flows (Nogues, 1991), since the patent holder may prefer the direct explotation of the invention through exports or subsidiaries (United Nations, 1993, p. 20).

Arguments on the relevance of adequate intellectual property protection in connection with transfer of technology are particularly strong where high, easily imitable, technology is at stake, such as in the case of biotechnology and computer software. It is also possible to argue that in cases where "tacit", non codified, knowledge is essential to put a technology into operation, the transfer is more likely to take place if it is bundled with the authorization to use patents and other IPRs. If protection of such rights and of trade secrets in the potential borrowing country are weak, the originating firms are unlikely to enter into transfer of technology contracts.

Changes in intellectual property legislation may also affect the bargaining position of potential contracting parties and can make access to technology more problematic (Skolnikoff, 1993); but, at the same time, the lack or insufficient protection may actually pose a barrier to obtain the required knowledge.

Stronger (or expanded) IPRs may imply higher costs in terms of royalties and other payments, which may in turn reduce the resources available for local R&D. If, as it is likely, a strengthened and expanded intellectual property regime leads to an increase in royalty levels, borrowing firms will find more difficult to compete, particularly in an open, globalized, international market. Higher levels of protection could also deepen negotiating imbalances and lead to the imposition of abusive practices that restrain competition.

In sum, the implementation of the TRIPS Agreement standards is likely to affect transfer of technology in an ambivalent way, by creating favorable conditions ,on the one hand, for such a transfer to take place, but by eventually impairing, on the other, the bargaining position of recipients in developing countries. While the recognition of intellectual property rights may be seen as a condition for the transfer of technology to take place, as stated by Maskus, "economists cannot be entirely optimistic about the implications of stronger IPRs for technology transfer" (Maskus, 1997, p.16).

New disciplines on transfer of technology in WTO?

Given the developing countries' concerns relating to the transfer of technology, how can such concerns be addressed in the framework of the WTO agreements and their possible review?

It is necessary to bear in mind that WTO agreements deals with **practices by governments**, while technology (except if in the public domain) is under the possession or the property rights of private or public entities.[240] Hence, the WTO framework may be too narrow to comprehensively deal with technology transfer issues.

In addition, as mentioned before, technology transfer should be strongly linked to the indigenous development of technology. Any policy relating to the former should be integrated in a broader technology policy aiming at the absorption of foreign technologies and the building up of local capabilities. Technology transfer alone would be insufficient to develop a viable technological infrastructure (Unctad, 1993).

TRIPS Agreement

One of the specific objectives of the TRIPS Agreement is the "transfer and dissemination of technology" (article 7). As examined elsewhere,[241] it leaves WTO Members certain room to adapt the national legislation to their particular needs and policy objectives. In implementing the Agreement, hence, it is important to take into consideration those aspects that may promote technology transfer and development.

Patents

In the patent field Member countries have flexibility to decide on aspects such as:

- the provision of an exception for experimental use, including for commercial purposes, of an invention;
- the establishment of compulsory licenses, for instance, due to non-working;
- the admissibility of improvement patents;

- the protection of "minor" innovations through utility models;
- the definition of the scope of claims and of non-literal infringement (Correa, 1998);

Legislation on these aspects may be adopted in the context of the existing rules of the TRIPS Agreement. However, the impact of some of these provisions on technology development and transfer may be enhanced with some changes in the current text. For instance, an explicit recognition of "refusal to deal"[242] as a ground for compulsory license may be included. Article 31. g) may also be revised, since the obligation to terminate a compulsory license when the reasons that justified its granting have ceased to exist, if literally applied, may constitute a strong disincentive to request a compulsory license and, in fact, undermine the whole compulsory licensing system.

Restrictive business practices

Article 40 of the TRIPS Agreement permits to apply competition rules to restrictive business practices in voluntary licensing agreements.[243] Some examples of restrictive business practices are given (exclusive grant-back conditions, conditions preventing challenging to validity and coercive package licensing). One of the purposes of Article 40 was to restrict the possible ways in which Member countries may control restrictive business practices and, in particular, to prevent developing countries from applying a "development test" to judge such practices, as proposed during the unsuccessful negotiations of an International Code of Conduct on Transfer of Technology.

Said article also provides for a "positive comity", that is, the obligation by a Member to consider requests for consultations by another Member relating to such practices. The Member to which a request has been addressed has the "full freedom of an ultimate decision" on the action to be taken.

Future negotiations in this area may aim at clarifying and expanding the rules relating to restrictive business practices in licensing agreements. It should be borne in mind that despite the failure of the initiative to establish an International Code on Transfer of Technology,[244] in December 1980 the UN General Assembly adopted by Resolution 35/63 a "Set of Multilaterally Equitable Agreed Principles and Rules for the Control of Restrictive Business Practices".

The Set is applicable to all transactions in goods and services and to all enterprises (but not to intergovernmental agreements). It deals with horizontal restraints (such as price-fixing agreements, collusive tendering, and market or customer allocation agreements), and with the abuse of dominant position or market power through practices such as discriminatory pricing, mergers, joint ventures and other acquisitions of control (Section D, paragraphs 3 and 4).

Developing countries have actively promoted -in the Review Conference convened in 1985- the upgrading of the Set to a *binding* instrument and of the Intergovernmental Group of Experts to a "committee". These initiatives failed, and the developed countries repeatedly (at the five-yearly review conferences) turned back the efforts by developing countries to make the code a binding international legal instrument.

Transfer of technology to LDCs

According to Article 66.2, developed Member countries are obliged to provide incentives under their legislation to enterprises and institutions in their territories for the purpose of promoting and encouraging the transfer of technology to LDCs "in order to enable them to create a sound and viable technological base".

At its meeting of September 1998, the Council for TRIPS agreed to put on the agenda the question of the review of the implementation of article 66.2 and to circulate a question on the matter in an informal document of the Council.

Future negotiations on this provision may aim at specify the obligations of developed countries under article 66.2 of the Agreement, for instance, in respect of the transfer of environmentally sound technologies and other "horizontal" technologies that may contribute to develop a solid and viable technological base, such as technology for quality control and good manufacturing practices. LDCs may also aim at reviewing other WTO agreements in a manner that facilitate compliance with article 66.2. Thus, the Agreement on Subsidies and Countervailing Measures (which currently permits subsidies for research and development under certain conditions), could be reviewed so as to explicitly allow for subsidies for the transfer of technology and associated equipment to LDCs.

Technical assistance

The supply of technical and financial cooperation for developing and least-developed countries is mentioned in article 67 of the Agreement, but no specific obligations or operative mechanisms are provided for. The provision of the assistance is on request and subject to "mutually agreed terms and conditions".

Such cooperation shall include assistance in the preparation of laws and regulations on the protection of IPRS as well as on the prevention of their abuse, the establishment or reinforcement of domestic offices, including the training of personnel. The Council for TRIPS has on many occasions reviewed information on assistance provided to developing and least developed countries, including by intergovernmental organizations.

Future negotiations in the framework of the TRIPS Agreement may aim at further specifying the obligations under this article.

Environmentally sound technology

A topic of particular importance is the impact of the WTO rules on the transfer of environmentally sound technology (EST). Chapter 34 of Agenda 21 recognized the need of a favorable access to and transfer of EST, in particular to developing countries, including on concessional and preferential terms. That Chapter also incorporates a detailed provision on action to be undertaken to support and promote the access to and use of EST.

Despite the clear justification and purposes of these provisions, little has been done to implement them. Moreover, the strengthening of IPRs in accordance to the TRIPS Agreement has reinforced the power of private parties to control the use and eventual transfer of ESTs.

Said Agreement has set forth high standards of protection for patents and "undisclosed information" whereunder title-holders may retain their technologies or charge high royalties for allowing access to them.

A good example is provided by the case of a substitute to chlorofluorcarbons (CFCs). India has found difficulties to get access to technology for HFC 134 A, which is considered the best available replacement for certain CFCs. That technology is covered by patents and trade secrets, and the companies that possess them are unwilling to transfer it without majority control over the ownership of the Indian company.

The access to technologies developed with public support is limited for foreigners in some countries, such as in the United States.[245] According to US law, exclusive licenses cannot be granted unless the licensee agrees that any product embodying the invention or produced through the use of the invention will be substantially manufactured in the United States. In addition, the guidelines on university technology transfer developed by the Council on Governmental Relations, provides that universities should be "extremely cautious in considering foreign licensees, especially if the research was funded by the United States Government".[246]

Under multilateral environment agreements (MEAs), obligations have been adopted in order to phase out the use of certain substances or technologies. Despite some measures to support developing countries in that process, technologies remain under the power of patent holders.

Similarly, there are standards adopted at the national level that ban imports if not complying with certain environmental requirements. Here, again, the lack of access to alternative EST pose an additional barrier to exports from developing countries.

The TRIPs Agreement contains some provisions that may be applied to deal with environmental concerns, notably:

- the possible exclusion from patentability of inventions which may cause serious prejudice to the environment;
- the possible exclusion from patentability of plants and animals;
- the right to confer compulsory licenses on grounds determined by national legislation.

As recommended by Agenda 21, compulsory licenses grounded on the protection of the environment may be specified in national legislation. These measures, however, may be insufficient to ensure the transfer of EST, as needed by developing countries. In line with proposals made by India during discussions of the WTO Committee on Trade and the Environment, the TRIPS Agreement may require changes in order to actually promote the transfer and use of ESTs.

TRIMs Agreement

The TRIMS Agreement only applies to trade-related investment measures. It does not prevent any Member from establishing performance requirements, for instance, in relation to transfer of technology and local R&D.

However, in the draft Multilateral Agreement on Investment (MAI), negotiated within OECD, it has been proposed to prohibit performance requirements relating to

- "transfer of technology, a production process or other proprietary knowledge to local persons or enterprises, unless this is enforced by a court or competition authority to remedy violation of competition laws, or this concerns the transfer of intellectual property and is undertaken in a manner consistent with the TRIPS Agreement"; and
- achieve a certain level or value of R & D in its territory.

Such requirements would be permitted, nevertheless, if linked to an "advantage", that is, some type of incentives.

In a possible review of the TRIMs Agreement, the unconditional right to apply these type of performance requirements should be retained.

Other Agreements

In the context of a systematic approach on development and transfer of technology issues, other WTO agreements need also to be considered.

Agreement on Subsidies and Countervailing Measures

The SCM Agreement considers as "non-actionable" "assistance for research activities" up to 75% of the costs of industrial research and up to 50% of "pre-competitive development activity"(article 8.2. a). Developed countries have, with this provision, created a "safe harbor" for a substantial part of the activities on which the competitive strength of their firms rely. While this provision may certainly benefit R&D in developing countries, it would not allow to exempt the assistance for the acquisition of technology, which is essential for developing countries. Such an exemption may be considered in the framework of a special and differential treatment for developing countries.

As mentioned above, the admissibility of subsidies conferred in developed countries in relation to technology transfer of technology (including equipment) to developing countries, may also be considered.

GATS

Article IV.1.a) provides that the increasing participation of developing countries in world trade shall be facilitated through negotiated specific commitments by members relating to the strengthening of their domestic services capacity and its efficiency and competitiveness, inter alia, "through access to technology on commercial basis". Article IV.2 obliges developed countries to establish "contact points" to facilitate access to information, including on the availability of services technology.

In establishing the negotiating guidelines and procedures for future rounds (article XIX.3) due attention should be paid to the referred provision, in order to make it operative.

It should be noted that the GATS Annex on Telecommunications also contains, under article 6 ("Technical Cooperation") obligations to assist developing countries in the access to information and LDCs in the transfer of technology.

TBT and SPS Agreements

Technical assistance, including to producers that wish to have access to systems for conformity assessment, is contemplated in article 11 of the Agreement on Technical Barriers to Trade. Besides, the Agreement on the Application of Sanitary and Phytosanitary Measures, stipulates the provision of technical assistance, especially to developing countries, such as in the area of processing technologies and research (article 9.1). The operationalization of these provisions may also be considered.

Conclusions

Technology plays a growing role in the creation of competitive advantages and in any development strategy. The generation of technology is overwhelmingly concentrated in developed countries and privately-held. Despite recent trends towards decentralization of R&D activities by large companies, little localization of R&D is taken place in developing countries.

The patterns of technology transfer have significantly changed with respect to those prevailing until the 1980's, when local technology recipients could enjoy "compensating advantages" and apply relatively mature technologies in markets with limited exposure to foreign competition. The access to relatively mature technologies may be obtained through equipment, technical assistance and engineering services. However, given the key importance of technology as a competitive asset, FDI is likely to growingly be a substitute for unbundled licensing whenever state-of-the-art technologies are involved.

The strengthening and expansion of intellectual property rights has reinforced the technology owners' capacity to control the use of their intangible assets, including whether to transfer it or not to third parties. The access to technologies developed with public funding may also be limited to foreign parties.

Any future action concerning technology transfer within WTO should recognize the strong linkages existing between the transfer and local technological capacity building, which remains a main responsibility of host countries. While certain provisions in existing agreements may be clarified or revised, the improvement of the conditions for access to and effective use of foreign technologies will require a broader approach.

The WTO agreements by their very nature address practices by governments and aim at preventing certain government measures that may distort or restrain trade in goods or services. Though some agreements may be improved or supplemented, they provide a too narrow framework to comprehensively deal with the issues at stake in the area of transfer of technology, particularly if the aim were to increase access to assets under private control.

Despite this, there is some room to reflect in such agreements -notably the TRIPS Agreement- the needs of developing countries in terms of technology transfer. This may be done by reviewing some existing provisions or incorporating new rules. If negotiations on new issues were undertaken (such as on investment)developing countries should be careful not to assume commitments that may limit their room to implement technological policies, including by means of technology-related performance requirements.

References

Callan, Bénédicte; Costigan, Sean and Keller, Kenneth, (1997), *Exporting U.S. High Tech. Facts and Fiction about the Globalization of Industrial R&D*, Council of Foreign Relations, New York.

Contractor, F. (1981), *International Technology Licensing, Lexington Books*, Lexington, Massschusetts.

Cooper, C. (1991), *Are innovation studies on industrialized economies relevant to technology policy in developing countries?*, UNU/INTECH, Maastricht.

Correa, Carlos, (1994), "Trends in technology transfer: Implications for developing countries", *Science and Public Policy*, vol. 21, No.6, Surrey.

Correa, Carlos, (1997), "New international standards for intellectual property: Impact on technology flows and innovation in developing countries", *Science and Public Policy*, vol.24, No.2, Surrey.

Correa, Carlos; (1998), "Implementing the TRIPs Agreement in the patents field—Options for developing countries", *The Journal of World Intellectual Property*, Vol.1, No.1, Geneva.

Dunning, John, (1993), *Multinational Enterprises and the Global Economy*, Addison Welswy, Suffolk.

Eisenberg, Rebecca (1997), *Ownership, commercial development, transfer and use of publicly-funded research results: The US legal regime* (study prepared for Unctad), Michigan.

Freeman, C. and Hageddorn, J. (1992), "Globalization of technology", A report for the FAST Programme, MERIT, University of Limburg.

Kim, L. and Dahlman, C., (1992), "Technology policy for industrialization: an integrative framework and Korea's experience", *Research Policy*, N 21.

Kumar, Nagesh, (1997), *Technology Generation and Technology Transfer in the World Economy: Recent Trends and Implications for Developing Countries*, The United Nations University, Institute of New Technologies, Maastricht.

Lall, S., (1992), *The interrelationship between investment flows and technology transfer: an overview of the main issues*, Unctad, ITD/TEC/1, Geneva.

Lall, Sanjaya, (1995), *Science and technology in the new global environment: Implications for developing countries*, Unctad, Science and Technology Issues, New York and Geneva.

Lee, Z., Bae, Z. and Choi, D., (1988), "Technology development processes: a model for a developing country with a global perspective", *R&D Management*, vol. 18, N 3.

Maskus, Keith, (1997), *The international regulation of intellectual property*, prepared for the IESG Conference "Regulation of International Trade and Investment", University of Nottingham, Nottingham.

Mytelka, L. (1992), *Technology transfer trends. An overview of strategic partnering, paper prepared for the Technology Development and Promotion Division*, UNIDO.

Nogués, J., (1991), "El rol de las patentes en la industria farmacéutica: el caso de la Argentina", in *El Comercio Exterior Argentino en la Década de 1990*, Ediciones Manantial, Buenos Aires.

OTA—Office of Technology Assessment (1994), *Multinationals and the U.S. Technology Base. Final Report of the Multinationals Project*, Washington, D.C.

OECD (1992a), *Technology and the economy*. The key relationship, Paris.

OECD (1992b), *Science and Technology Policy*, Paris.

OECD (1996), *Technology and industrial performance*, Paris.

Pavitt, Keith and Patel, Parimal, (1999), "Global corporations and national systems of innovation: who dominates whom?", Archibugi, Daniele; Howells, Jeremy and Michie, Jonathan (Eds.), *Innovation Policy in a Global Economy*, Cambridge University Press, Melbourne.

Reichman, J., (1996/1997), "From free riders to fair followers: global competition under the TRIPs Agreement", *New York University Journal of International Law and Politics*, vol. 29, No.1-2.

Roffe, Pedro (1998), "Control of anticompetitive practices in contractual licenses under the TRIPS Agreement", in Corre, C. and Yusuf, A. (Eds), *Intellectual property and international trade. The TRIPS Agreement*, Kluwer Law International, London.

Skolnikoff, Eugene (1993), "New international trends affecting science and technology", *Science and Public Policy*, vol. 20, N 2.

UN/TCMD (Transnational Corporations and Management Division), (1992), *World Investment Report 1992. Transnational corporations as engines of growth*, New York.

UNCTAD (1990), *The relevance of recent developments in the area of technology to the negotiations on the draft international code of conduct on the transfer of technology*, TD/CODE TOT/55, Geneva.

UNCTAD (1993), *Fostering technological dynamism: evolution of thought on technology capacity building and competitiveness. Summary of the review and analysis of the literature (draft)*, Report by the Unctad Secretariat, TD/B/WG.5/7, Geneva.

UNCTAD (1996), *Emerging forms of technological cooperation: the case for technological partnership*, New York and Geneva, 1996.

UNCTAD, (1998), *World Investment Report. 1998 Trends and Determinants*, New York and Geneva.

United Nations (1993), *Intellectual property rights and foreign direct investments*, New York.

Wint, A. (1992), "Liberalizing foreign direct investment regimes: the vestigial screen", *World Development*, vol. 20, N 10.

ELECTRONIC-COMMERCE, WTO AND DEVELOPING COUNTRIES

Arvind Panagariya

Introduction

There are currently six different mediums of electronic commerce (e-commerce): telephone, fax, television, electronic payment and money transfer systems, Electronic Data Interchange (EDI) and Internet.[247] It is fair to say that even though phone, fax and television remain the most widely used electronic mediums to promote or conduct commerce, much of the current excitement, confusion and debate on e-commerce is the result of the rapid ascendancy of Internet in the field. Internet has made possible international transmission of services in ways and on a scale that was not possible via traditional modes such as fax, phone and television. It is being used today to buy abroad many back-office services such as electronic publishing, website design and management, customer call centers, medical records management, hotel reservations, credit card authorizations, remote secretarial services, mailing list management, technical on-line support, indexing and abstracting services, research and technical writing, and technical transcription. Internet has also become a medium for electronic transmission of many products, traditionally traded in the form of goods. For instance, books, CDs, movies and computer programs can now be transmitted internationally in digital form.

From the viewpoint of multilateral rules of international trade as well as national economic policy, this medium gives rise to issues somewhat different from those faced with respect to other mediums. For instance, the WTO members must decide whether the GATT or GATS discipline should be applied to international trade via Internet. To the extent that some of the trade via this medium has a counterpart that is traded physically as is true of books, computer programs, music and movies, one may apply the GATT discipline. But to the extent that such counterparts do not exist, as is the case with the back office services mentioned above, it will make more sense to apply the GATS discipline. From the viewpoint of national economic policies, especially in developing countries, the potential for development, offered by this medium, increases the urgency of developing the telecommunications industry and creating financial infrastructure that facilitates electronic transactions(for example, credit cards).

In the present paper, I discuss these and other aspects of e-commerce from the viewpoint of developing countries.[248] In Sections 2-5, I offer an analytic discussion of multilateral rules likely to be applicable to Internet commerce. Special attention is paid to issues of taxation and access to e-commerce. In Section 6, I focus on the implications of e-commerce for developing countries and discuss possible policy measures the countries may wish to take in order to maximize the benefits from it. The paper is concluded in section 7.

Which multilateral discipline: GATT, GATS or both?[249]

To what degree countries can regulate international trade via Internet, what taxes they can impose on it, and in what way they can discriminate in favor of the domestic suppliers of similar items will depend on the WTO discipline the member countries decide to apply to it. The WTO report mentioned in footnote 2 [WTO (1998) henceforth] raises the possibility that, in principle, the "digits" traded on Internet could be viewed as goods, services or even something else. Which of these characterizations is chosen determines whether this trade is subject to the rules laid down in the General Agreement on Tariffs and Trade (GATT), General Agreement on Trade in Services (GATS), a combination of these two or an entirely new agreement.

It may be noted at the outset that there is no ambiguity at present regarding the status of the goods ordered and paid for on Internet but delivered physically in the conventional manner. Except for the order and payment themselves, these transactions are treated as goods trade and the GATT discipline applies to them. The ambiguity arises only when the goods are delivered on Internet.

On the face of it, any deliveries made by Internet would seem to resemble services. Nevertheless, as already noted in the introduction, there are products delivered by Internet that have counterparts in physical, merchandise trade. The obvious examples are books, videos, music CDs and computer software. When imported in physical form, these products are treated as goods with the GATT discipline applied to them. But can they be treated as services when delivered by Internet? Or, in conformity with their physical counterparts, should they be treated as goods?

One extreme possibility is to characterize all transmissions on Internet as goods with GATT discipline applied to them. Such a characterization accompanied by a ban on custom duties on the transmissions, currently in place, would amount to the WTO members committing themselves to complete free trade I transactions routed by Internet. This is because national treatment and MFN status are general obligations under GATT. By accepting the GATT discipline, under national treatment, the member countries would give up their right to discriminate against Internet imports as far as domestic taxes are concerned. In addition, the ban on custom duty would bind their tariffs on Internet imports at zero. At present, no one is considering such a proposal, however. The member countries made their commitments in the UR and post-UR negotiations in services based on the assumption that most of those transactions were services rather than goods.

At the opposite extreme, we could abandon both GATT and GATS and develop an entirely new discipline for Internet trade. Once again, virtually no one is advocating this position. For the search for a new discipline for e-commerce makes little sense. Internet services, which include Internet service providers and phone lines on which transmissions flow, are already subject to GATS and the Agreement on Basic Telecommunications. All electronic transmissions that flow on Internet, on the other hand, have counterparts in either goods trade or services trade. As such, the rules necessary to regulate that trade can be found in GATT or GATS.

Thus, the real choice is between applying GATS to all Internet trade or GATT to that trade for which physical counterparts also exist and GATS to all other e-trade. In my judgement, on balance, it makes more sense to define all electronic transmissions as services. At one level, it may be argued that at the time Internet transmissions cross the border between two countries, they do not have a physically traded counterpart. The eventual transformation of the transmission into a good such as a book or CD does not negate the fact that at the border the transmission did not have a physically traded counterpart. Indeed, in many cases, the transmission may not be turned into the physically traded counterpart at all. For example, the recipient may continue to store it in the digital form with books read on the screen and music played directly on the computer.

But this is not the primary reason why I lean in favor of treating all Internet trade as service trade. The key advantage of adopting the across-the-board definition is that it is clean and minimizes possible disputes that may arise from countries wishing to have certain transmissions classified as intangible goods and others as services. Under a mixed definition, in any trade dispute involving Internet trade, panels will have to first decide whether the object of dispute is a good or a service to determine whether the rules of GATT or GATS are to be applied in evaluating the dispute. The adoption of the across-the-board definition automatically resolves this issue.

The across-the-board definition, nevertheless, raises some efficiency issues that must be addressed. Thus, consider first the issue of tariffs, which are applicable to products imported in physical form but not when transmitted electronically. As long as the cost of electronic transmission is lower than that of physical delivery, the presence of tariffs on the latter poses no problem. Effectively, the electronic transmission offers the product to the country at a price lower than that available through physical delivery. This change is equivalent to an improvement in the country's terms of trade and, leaving aside some general-equilibrium considerations, improves welfare unambiguously.

But for many countries, especially developing ones, this is an unlikely scenario. In these countries, most consumers do not have computers or Internet access. A likely scenario, therefore, is one in which a handful of independent entrepreneurs will receive the product by Internet, convert it into physical form such as CDs and sell the latter to consumers. But this activity may itself be costly, using up real resources.

A possible outcome of the proposed regime in many developing countries can be represented stylistically, therefore, with the help of Figure 1. In the figure, DD gives the demand for a specific compact disc (CD) and GG its supply when imported in physical form, as a good. It is assumed that the country is small so that the supply is perfectly elastic. In the absence of Internet transmission, the quantity purchased is given by Q_0 and tariff revenue by $ABGG_t$.

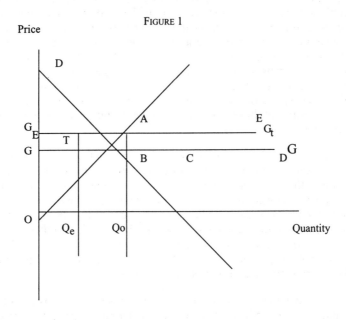

FIGURE 1

Suppose we next introduce Internet transmission. Assume, as is true currently, that if music is transmitted electronically, no tariff is paid. Competitive entrepreneurs import music electronically, convert it from digitized form into CDs and sell them to consumers. The marginal cost of conversion and distribution is positive and rising, leading to the supply curve EE. It is then immediate that quantity OQe will now be imported by the electronic medium with QeQ0 continuing to come in physical form. The tariff revenue collected previously on the quantity OQe disappears. Of the lost revenue, area marked 1 goes to cover the higher costs of supply by Internet and is a deadweight loss. The remainder of the lost revenue becomes a transfer to exporters.

This is the standard story from the smuggling literature that arises when there are two sources of supply and the more expensive source is not subject to a tariff but the less expensive source is. It should, of course, be clear that if the cost of Internet transmission were low such that the Internet supply curve crossed the demand curve below GG, this problem would not arise. Internet supplies will eliminate physical shipments and the price will be below GG, benefiting the consumers by more than the lost tariff revenue.

This analysis shows that subjecting like products, delivered by different means, to different disciplines can potentially result in harmful efficiency effects. This is not an inevitable outcome, however. There are at least two solutions to the problem. First, the country could choose to eliminate the tariff on physical deliveries, thus, eliminating the efficiency loss such as that represented by area 1 in Figure 1. Indeed, this will lead to a net efficiency gain of triangle ABC. Second, if the tariff on physical supplies cannot be eliminated because of fiscal considerations, the country could choose to impose a higher VAT or excise tax on music CDs supplied by Internet by an amount equal to the tariff on physical deliveries. As long as the country has not already committed itself to giving national treatment to imported music services, this option is available within GATS.[250]

It is useful at this point to return briefly to the temporary ban on custom duties on all electronic transmissions mentioned earlier. While this ban would be meaningful if all e-commerce is classified as goods trade, its continued existence and the current U.S. proposals to make it permanent are puzzling. At present, the only feasible method of charging a custom duty on electronically supplied foreign services is to subject them to a higher domestic tax relative to the identical, domestically supplied services.[251] As long as a country has not committed itself to giving national treatment to the foreign service in question in its national schedule, it is free to impose a higher domestic tax on electronically supplied services from abroad. The existing ban on custom duty and the U.S. proposal to make the ban permanent do not and cannot forbid countries from subjecting an imported service to a higher VAT or excise tax than equivalent domestically supplied service. The discriminatory treatment is forbidden only if the Member commits to giving the imported service national status in its national schedule. But in that case, the current ban on custom duty and the US proposal to make it permanent have no additional impact. In either case, the ban is meaningless and entirely vacuous.[252]

A second difference between GATT and GATS discipline from the viewpoint of efficiency is that the former does not allow quotas while the latter does. In the particular example I have discussed above, in principle, if WTO members decide to apply GATS discipline to services traded electronically, a country will have the option to limit the number of CDs that could be transmitted by Internet. It is not immediately clear how this restriction can be enforced. But assuming that it could be done, trade will be diverted to shipments in physical form, which may be an inferior mode of delivery. At present, such a quota is not enforceable. If it does become enforceable, the outcome can be inferior to that obtainable under the GATT discipline. This will be a cost of the clean definition I have advocated.

Mode 1 or mode 2?

The General Agreement on Trade in Services classifies services according to the mode of delivery. It distinguishes four modes: cross-border supply (mode1), consumption abroad (mode 2), commercial presence (mode 3), and the movement of natural persons (mode 4). Assuming the GATS discipline is applied to electronic trade, for transaction that do not take place either through commercial presence or the movement of natural persons, the member countries will still need to decide whether they are to be treated as cross-border trade (mode 1) or consumption abroad (mode 2).[253] There are no clear-cut objective criteria that can be brought to bear on this classification. Therefore, it is likely to be negotiated as a part of the next round of negotiations. The choice of classification has two principal implications.

First, the classification will determine the liberalizing impact of the commitments made in the UR and post-UR GATS negotiations on services. In these negotiations, countries have already made commitments based on the modes of supply of services. Therefore, it matters whether electronic trade is treated as being supply by mode 1 or mode 2. For example, if a country gave full market access under mode 2 for a particular financial service that is traded electronically, the commitment would have no liberalizing impact if electronic commerce is classified as supply under mode 1 rather than 2. Thus, the liberalizing impact of previous commitments will depend on the mode supply under which electronic commerce is classified. It is my impression that countries undertook more obligations for liberalization under mode 2 than under mode 1. Accordingly, the liberalizing impact of the commitments will be greater if electronic commerce is classified under mode 2. Developed countries, which are net exporters of electronic services, stand to gain greater market access if these services are classified as being supplied under mode 2.

Second, the classification determines the country of jurisdiction for purposes of regulation and dispute settlement. For supply under mode 1, the transaction is deemed to have taken place in the country where the buyer resides. Therefore, it is the regulatory regime of the importing country that applies to the transaction. In contrast, for supply under mode 2, the relevant regulatory regime is that of the country where the supplier resides. If countries feel that they want to protect their buyers' interests, they are likely to opt for mode 1. Thus, there is some tension in the choice of classification depending on the objective. The market access objective pulls towards mode 2 while consumer protection objective pulls towards mode 1.

To the extent that in making their liberalization commitments in the UR and post-UR negotiations, countries viewed the electronic transactions between providers and recipients in different countries as cross-border transactions, it makes sense to treat them as such. Otherwise, actual liberalization is likely to end up being at variance with what the countries intended.

Access to e-commerce

Access to e-commerce, which in the WTO parlance often means access to e-exports, has two components that must be distinguished sharply: access to Internet services and access to services that can be traded electronically. The former deals with access to Internet infrastructure while the latter relates to specific commitments in electronically tradable services (for example, commitments in financial services under modes 1 and 2). In goods trade, we can liken these components, respectively, to access to transportation networks (including ports, ships, roads, railways and air transport) and access to specific goods markets through a lowering of trade barriers such as tariffs and quotas. For lower trade barriers to result in more imports, access to transportation networks is necessary. Similarly, for specific commitments in various services sectors under modes 1 and 2 to result in increased flow of imports, access to Internet facilities is essential.

Access to Internet Services

The access to Internet infrastructure depends on two factors: (i) availability of communications networks, hardware and software and (ii) access to the existing communications networks. Let us consider briefly each of these factors.

Availability of Infrastructure, Hardware and Software

At the basic level, access to Internet by the residents of a country depends on the level of development of the telecommunications sector and the availability of hardware and software. In the remote villages of many developing countries, even the basic telecommunications service may not exist. To bring Internet and, hence, e-commerce to these villages, one will need to first bring telecommunications services there. But even when telecommunications services exist, additional hardware that links up the individual user to Internet must be put in place. Finally, one needs to ensure access to equipment such as computers, modems and software. Generally speaking, an open trade regime with respect to information technology equipment is likely to facilitate access to this equipment. This is perhaps the reason why some countries chose to sign the Information Technology Agreement (ITA), which requires the signatories to free up trade in a large number of information-technology products.

Access to Communications Networks

There are three principal WTO provisions that govern access to communications network: GATS Article VIII on monopolies and exclusive service suppliers, GATS Annex on Telecommunications, and the Reference Paper on regulatory principles in the Agreement on Basic Telecommunications. In addition, specific commitments on national treatment and market access made by countries in basic telecommunications sector have implications for access to Internet.[254] GATS Article VIII and the Annex apply to all WTO members uniformly. The Reference Paper applies to approximately 60 countries that incorporated it into their specific commitments in the agreement on basic telecommunications services. A total of 69 countries made specific commitments in basic telecommunications sector. Of these, ten countries made specific commitments with respect to Internet access providers.

Article VIII, which applies to all services, is designed to deal with monopoly suppliers who can potentially frustrate a Member's MFN and specific market access commitments. For instance, suppose telephone lines in a Member country are owned by a single entity and the Member has made market access commitments to other countries in the provision of Internet services. Article VIII requires this entity not to limit access to phone line to service suppliers from other Members or discriminates among them. It also requires this entity to ensure that the commitments made by the Member in other service sectors are not frustrated.

Article VIII is limited in its application to cases in which a monopolist supplies the service in question. GATS negotiators recognized, however, that basic telecommunications services are central to the smooth flow of trade in a large number of other services. Therefore they introduced further provisions in the Annex on Telecommunications to widen access rights in the use of public telecommunications transport networks and services (PTTNS).[255]

The Annex requires each Member government to ensure that suppliers of other Members are given reasonable and nondiscriminatory access to and use of PTTNS *for the supply of a service included in the Member's schedule.* The term "nondiscriminatory" is defined here to include *both national treatment and MFN.* The Annex, thus, goes beyond Article VIII in two respects. First, for a service listed in the Member's schedule, it gives foreign suppliers nondiscriminatory access to PTTNS even though the Member has not committed to national treatment in that service.[256] Second, the access provision applies to PTTNS irrespective of whether these services and networks are supplied by a monopolist or competitive firms.

The concern that telecommunications markets would be dominated by large operators, capable of frustrating market access commitments, remained central during basic telecommunications negotiations. This led the participants to lay down a set of regulatory principles, aimed at reigning in the behavior of the major suppliers of telecommunications services, in a Reference paper. Some 60 participants incorporated this Reference Paper into their commitment schedules.

The regulatory principles in the Reference Paper oblige major suppliers to provide interconnection on nondiscriminatory terms. They are to also provide services in sufficiently unbundled form that those seeking interconnections do not have to pay for unnecessary components and facilities. The Reference Paper also lists rules governing anti-competitive cross-subsidization, the misuse of information, licensing criteria and transparency.

Finally, Internet access also depends on the degree of liberalization undertaken by Members in basic telecommunications. 69 countries signed the Agreement on Basic Telecommunications in February 1997. Counting the European Communities as one, this produced 55 schedules. Many of the negotiated undertakings represent a pre-commitment to liberalize in the future.

A key area of liberalization from the viewpoint of Internet access is that of Internet Service Providers (ISP). In many countries, telecommunications services are supplied by a public monopoly, which often also becomes the monopoly provider of Internet access. In countries, which have liberalized their communications regimes, competing ISPs exist and offer different bundles of Internet services. In future negotiations, it will be worthwhile to incorporate ISP as an explicit sector into national schedules of commitment. This may induce further liberalization in many countries in this key area. There is no compelling argument against permitting multiple ISPs or foreign entry even in countries with monopoly provision of other telecommunication services.

Access to Electronically Traded Services

In addition to Internet access services just discussed, Internet offers the opportunity for trade in two additional areas. First, many services outside of telecommunications sector such as those in banking, insurance and computer programming sectors can be delivered electronically. Second, Internet can be the vehicle for the provision of distribution services with goods and services purchased through Internet but delivered by other means. For transactions in the first category, GATS discipline applies fully. In contrast, transactions in the second category are similar to those by telephone or mail order. When delivered physically, goods are subject to the usual GATT discipline including customs duties.

While national treatment and market access commitments in national schedules do matter in that they restrain the importing country's ability to discriminate in its tax policies in favor of domestic suppliers or among various foreign suppliers, in the case of Internet trade, they play a less crucial role. To the extent that governments do not have effective control over what gets traded on Internet, especially when transactions are from business to consumers, the value of these commitments is limited.

Instead, the bulk of the expansion of e-commerce will depend on countries granting recognition to the education or experience obtained, requirements met, or licenses or certificates granted in another country. Article VII of GATS allows for such recognition even on a discriminatory basis in the sense that it allows Members to extend such recognition on a selective basis. For instance, the United States may give recognition to accountancy degrees from Europe but not India. This could signal potential buyers that it is hazardous to buy accountancy services in India even though the latter may be capable of supplying them competitively. Article VII gives some flexibility to excluded countries in this regard which developing countries should exploit as much as they can. In particular, if a Member gives recognition to the standards prevailing in another Member in a specific area and a developing country's standards in the same area happen to be at par, under Article VII provisions, it should be granted similar recognition.

Intellectual property rights

The Trade Related Intellectual Property Rights (TRIPs) Agreement applies as much to transmissions on Internet as through other mediums. Copyright, trademark and geographical indications must be respected in Internet transmissions the same way as in other mediums. In December 1996, two new treaties came into existence under the auspices of the World Intellectual Property Organization (WIPO), which deal specifically with Internet transmissions. These are WIPO Copyright Treaty and WIPO Performances and Phonograms Treaty. These treaties are to enter into force three months after 30 countries have deposited the instruments of ratification or accession have been deposited with the Director General of WIPO.

The new WIPO treaties further strengthen the rights of authors, performers and phonogram producers. The treaties recognize the role that technological measures used by rights holders have in facilitating effective protection. A variety of technologies that help control access or limit copying of work transmitted via electronic means already exist and are being continuously developed. The signatories to the treaties must provide adequate legal protection and effective legal remedies against the circumvention of these effective technological measures used by authors, performers and producers of phonograms.

Technologies also exist for incorporating into digital copies of works and other material digital envelopes and watermarks that identify the work, its author and any other right holders, the terms and conditions of use of the work, and any other information. The treaties require signatories to provide adequate and effective remedies against any person, who alters or removes such information or distributes copies of protected material knowing that such information has been removed without authority.

At present, these treaties are in WIPO and have not come into force. But they can be eventually expected to be brought into WTO and incorporated into TRIPs. This may pose a problem for developing countries given their capacity to enforce disputes. In many developing countries, courts have already been stretched well beyond their capacity and it is unlikely that they will be able to deliver developed-country standards in the area of enforcement. As may turn out with the existing enforcement provisions in TRIPs, meeting the standards of developed countries in will give foreign rights holders a favored treatment relative to domestic rights holders who will likely be subject to domestic pace of dispute resolution. Developing countries will need to take into account these considerations and possible threats of the denial of Internet access by developed countries in making their decisions regarding these treaties as and when proposals are made to incorporate them into WTO.

E-commerce and developing countries

It is perhaps not an exaggeration to say that, from the viewpoint of commerce, Internet is the most important inventions of the last two decades. This medium of "transportation" has opened markets that were previously closed, speeded up transactions like no other medium has done in the past, and made the delivery of some products almost instantaneous.

In this section, I discuss the issues more directly relevant to developing countries. I begin with an analytic discussion of the ways in which Internet generates benefits for the countries and interacts with other modes of delivery of services, especially the movement of natural persons. I then consider policy actions that developing countries may consider taking to enhance the benefits from e-commerce.

The Gains from Internet to Developing Countries

While virtually all countries stand to gain from the opportunities offered by Internet, according to one view, developing countries stand to gain more from it than developed countries. The argument is that these countries are far behind developed countries in terms of information-technology infrastructure. Given the cost savings offered by Internet technology and relative ease with which it can be provided, they can now skip several stages of technological development through which developed countries had to go. Stated differently, developing countries are much farther inside the current technological frontier and, therefore, have larger potential benefits from moving to it.

In the long run, this is a defensible statement. But it must be acknowledged that the benefits of e-commerce are distributed unevenly not only across countries--both between and among developing and developed countries--but also over time. Given that three fourths of the current e-commerce is concentrated within the United States, perhaps this single country has benefited most from it. In contrast, for many poor countries in Africa, the telecommunications infrastructure is so poorly developed that it will take a long time before they are able to benefit significantly from e-commerce.

The benefits from e-commerce to a particular developing country, both domestically and internationally, depend on the volume of demand for and supply of goods and services that can be potentially traded on Internet. Despite all the excitement surrounding Internet, it is likely that for many developing countries the demand and supply factors do not promise large gains, at least in the foreseeable future. Due to a lack of electronic means of payment such as credit cards, payments will still have to be made by conventional means. This factor alone is likely to limit considerably the scope of domestic electronic transactions. Moreover, the domestic demand for services that are electronically delivered is likely to be limited. Due to low costs of internal movement of natural persons, even businesses, which have heavy needs for customized software, are likely to rely on the physical presence of the personnel. In these countries, even if Internet was widely available, e-commerce, as distinct from email and other communications, will not achieve big success immediately.

In assessing the potential benefits from international e-commerce to a country, analysts often focus only on the goods and services that it can export. This is an incorrect approach, however, since benefits can arise from a reduction in the cost of imports as much as from an increase in the price of exports received. Even if a country does not export any services, it can benefit from imports of services, paying for them in terms of goods. Cheaper availability of medical, engineering and architectural services, long-distance learning and reduced costs of transactions can confer benefits even if the country does not immediately export the services traded through Internet.

To the extent that Internet effectively opens markets that were previously closed, it is tempting to think of it as another form of trade liberalization. But, in fact, it is much more: it amounts to a technical improvement that lowers costs of transaction and, as such, generates far larger benefits than the triangular efficiency gains from trade liberalization. Indeed, the decline in costs increases potential benefits from trade liberalization in many services sectors.

Among developing countries, the countries best situated to benefits from e-commerce through export expansion are those with a substantial pool of skilled labor, capable of working on or near the frontier of computer technology. The case of India, which is already benefiting from e-exports in a big way, best illustrates this point.

I had long held the view that India had greatly over-invested in higher education. At one extreme, the most talented individuals left the country in search of better opportunities abroad and, at the other extreme, the country was stuck with a large pool of educated workers whom the economy could not absorb. Even today, the lowest-level clerical jobs attract large number of applications from graduates and post-graduates.

The advent of computer technology in general and Internet in particular threatens to prove my view to be incorrect, however. The migration of some of the country's most talented individuals to developed countries notwithstanding, the country has the world's second largest pool of English speaking scientific manpower. Each year, Indian universities graduate as many as 115,000 engineers. This pool, Internet and the opening to direct foreign investment by India have combined to yield annual exports of as much as $4 billion.[257]

Because the international movement of natural persons is subject to severe restraints, the value of marginal product of skilled labor in developed countries is far higher than in developing countries. Though numerical estimates are not available, the potential gains from increased mobility of the movement of natural persons are astronomical. Developing countries in general and India in particular have long sought a relaxation of restrictions in developed countries on the movement of natural persons. But they have not achieved a notable success in this effort.

By making the sales of skilled labor abroad possible without actually moving natural persons physically, Internet has at last brought developed-country demand for skilled labor to developing countries. This has resulted in a large capital gain on the investment India has made in higher education during the last four decades. Thus, what had seemed to be a poor allocation of resources for decades, *ex post*, promises to turn into an excellent investment.[258]

Figure 2 offers an analytic representation of the benefits from the opening of the market for skilled labor through Internet. For simplicity, divide the world into two countries and call them the United States and India. Use an asterisk to distinguish the variables of the United States from those of India. Let M^*M^* represent the potential excess demand for skilled labor in the United States and EE the excess supply of it in India. In view of the fact that the United States is very large in economic terms, M^*M^* is shown to be relatively elastic.

In the absence Internet and the movement of natural persons, skilled wages in the United States and India settle at W_A^* and W_A, respectively. The introduction of Internet allows "trade" in skilled labor between the United States and India provided the United States has opened up its imports of some services through modes 1 and 2. To the extent that Internet is an imperfect substitute for the movement of natural persons and trade in services under modes 1 and 2 is not entirely free, we will not expect the equilibrium to move to the fully integrated equilibrium, I. Instead, trade is likely to be limited up to, say, Q_1, generating gains from trade equal to the area between M^*M^* and EE over quantity OQ_1.

The important question is how these gains are going to be divided between the United States and India. The answer to this question depends on where the wage settles. When natural persons are allowed to move, the answer is clear. The wage is determined on the demand curve, M^*M^*. This is because the U.S. firms must compete for the limited number of workers who have been granted the entry visa. It is also the case because the U.S. laws do not permit local firms to hire foreign workers at a wage lower than what is paid to U.S. citizens to ensure that firms do not opt for the former because they can employ them cheaper.

FIGURE 2

Skilled Wage

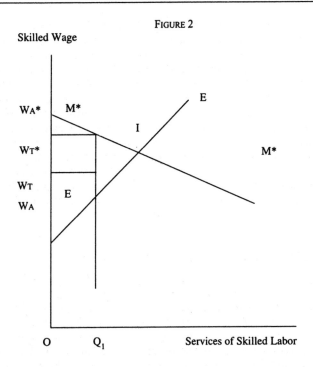

O　　Q₁　　　　　Services of Skilled Labor

The outcome is likely to be different when Internet is the medium of exports of skilled labor. Now the wage will be closer to the export-supply curve, EE. This is because the wage must be determined within the Indian market based on how much can be exported. The more liberalization in services the United States undertakes under modes 1 and 2, the greater the demand for the Indian skilled labor and the higher the wage. Thus, benefits to India depend directly on the extent of liberalization undertaken by the United States in services that can be potentially exported by India on Internet.

This analysis is, of course, highly stylized. Cross-border trade will not substitute for the movement of natural persons in all cases. Often confidentiality or security considerations require consultants to move to the site where service has to be provided. The most striking recent example relates to the Y2K contracts. In other circumstances, the movement of natural persons may even be complementary to exports via Internet. For instance, installation and maintenance of software may require physical presence of the supplier. Finally, natural persons may also be employed in sectors that remain largely non-traded. This is clearly true, for instance, of medical and health services.

We may also ask whether trade on Internet might substitute for direct foreign investment. Sometimes it is suggested that if the delivery by modes 1 and 2 becomes a substitute for delivery by mode 3, Internet will become a substitute for direct foreign investment. Although examples of modes 1 and 2 deliveries substituting for mode 3 deliveries are not pervasive, this does not rule out the possibility that Internet may have an adverse impact on direct foreign investment. Substitution between modes impacts only sectoral composition of direct foreign investment, not its aggregate level. Instead, the aggregate level will depend on whether Internet raises the return on capital more in the source countries or the host countries. If the former as is likely at least in the short run, more capital will choose to stay in the source countries. This is clearly an empirically testable hypothesis and is worth studying further. Internet has expanded sufficiently already in developed countries that its impact on investment abroad may be detectable in the data.

Policies for the Expansion of E-commerce

Development of e-commerce should not be treated as a goal in itself. Some countries are better positioned than others to achieve a rapid expansion of e-commerce for the same amount of resource invested. Since resources have alternative uses, one must compare the rate of return in e-commerce to those in other activities before committing resource in this sector. This consideration remains valid even if investment decisions are made by private agents but the policies chosen by the government have significant effects on those decisions. For instance, policies facilitating the development of e-exports are likely to yield higher returns in a country like India, which has a significant pool of skills to export, than in a country lacking such skills.

For developing countries that find the expansion of e-commerce a desirable instrument of achieving its social and developmental goals, action must be taken at three levels. First, the hardware and software necessary to develop electronically sellable services should be available at reasonable prices. Second, basic infrastructure necessary for smooth functioning of Internet must be in place. Here "infrastructure" is defined broadly and includes facilities to conduct financial transactions on Internet. Finally and most importantly, developing countries must negotiate access to developed country markets in sectors in which they can export service by the electronic medium. Let me take each of these areas in turn.

Countries can ensure the access to hardware and software by liberalizing the imports of the relevant products. This, in turn, can be accomplished by either signing the Information Technology Agreement or liberalizing the imports of the relevant products selectively, outside of that agreement. Note here that this recommendation is made taking as given the desirability of the expansion of e-commerce in the first place. We must bear in mind that when there are high trade barriers on other products as is likely in many developing countries, this liberalization itself may misallocate resource and the consumer expenditure. In such circumstances, the benefits from the expansion of e-commerce must outweigh the costs of the misallocation.

It is presumably in the area of infrastructure development that developing countries need to do most to assist in the development of e-commerce. Without adequate telecommunications system and the availability of inexpensive telephone service, Internet and e-commerce cannot flourish. At present, the telecommunications network in many developing countries is rather poorly developed. A large majority of individuals do not have access to even telephones.[259] And those who do must pay very high rates on telephone calls. Unlike in the United States, local telephone calls are metered and charged at fairly high rates so that even if the Internet access is cheap, the expenses on local telephone calls, necessary to connect to the internet access provider, can raise the overall cost of Internet use.

There is also the issue of power supply. In India, for instance, publicly supplied power has been sufficiently unreliable that many software firms in Banaglore had to resort to their own generators to ensure continuous flow of power. Frequent and long interruptions in power flows can have a devastating effect on the transmission of data.

At present, in the large majority of developing countries, Internet access is also expensive and unreliable. Often telecommunications services are supplied by a public monopoly, which also becomes the monopoly provider of Internet access. Unable to expand service sufficiently, under public pressure, it finds itself giving many more connections than the capacity of the system. The result is a failure of many customers to access the service for which they have paid.

The solution to this problem is to simply allow private Internet service providers into the market. As long as these access providers can be obliged to give inter-connections to one another through proper regulation, there are no benefits to having a monopoly supplier of the access service. This is clearly an area in which private market can function efficiently.

Prevalence of a legal framework, centered on paper-based contracts and handwritten signatures can also impede the growth of e-commerce. The United Nations Commission on International Trade Law (UNCITRAL) had drawn attention to this issue as early as 1985 and called upon Governments to consider the possibility of permitting, where appropriate, the use of electronic means of authentication. Subsequently, UNCITRAL has developed a Model law on Electronic Commerce, which was approved by the United Nations General Assembly in December 1996. The Model law lays out what constitutes the equivalent of a written document, signature and original in the electronic environment. It also sets forth rules governing the admissibility and evidential weight of electronic messages, the retention of data messages, the formation and validity of contracts, and attribution. Many countries have either adopted the Model law or introduced legislation related to electronic facilitation issues. The countries that have not yet introduced legislation along these lines are likely to need to do so.[260]

Finally, assuming the provision of reliable Internet service at reasonable rates domestically can be ensured, additional policy measures are required to facilitate e-commerce. In many developing countries, electronic means of payment, including credit cards, are virtually non-existent. This means that even when products can be ordered or services delivered by Internet, payment must be made by conventional means. This slows down the completion of transaction considerably, reducing potential benefits.

In the case of foreign purchases, this problem becomes even more acute. Many developing countries do not have current-account convertibility so that ordering goods on Internet from abroad is not a practical option except perhaps in the case of large firms, which may have ready access to foreign exchange. Even in countries such as India, which have current-account convertibility but not capital-account convertibility, individuals do not have ready access to foreign exchange. Thus, as far as imports of goods and services are concerned, the Internet option is likely to remain limited to larger firms. The solution here is not entirely clear since the issue of giving access to foreign exchange to individuals has serious implications for the ability to control capital outflows, especially in times of a crisis. Even if the access is provided for current-account transactions only, it becomes easy to disguise capital-account transactions as current-account transactions. This may be even easier when the purchase is that of a service rather than good.

Ready access to foreign exchange is not a problem, however, in so far as exports are concerned. Normally, exports require receipt of foreign exchange for which restrictions on electronic transmission are likely to be less of a problem. Moreover, exports are likely to be undertaken almost exclusively by commercial entities rather than individuals, which are generally equipped to deal in foreign exchange. Even if they need to import certain products, they are likely to be able to make payments electronically in countries with current-account convertibility.

The final step in ensuring access to international e-commerce is to have access to communication networks and markets for electronically tradable goods in foreign countries. The access to communication networks is essentially guaranteed under GATS and the Agreement on Basic Telecommunications as discussed in Section 5.1 of this paper. At present, there is sufficient excess capacity in the networks in developed countries. Therefore, the access is unlikely to be a problem. It is possible, however, that as the use of Internet grows worldwide, the expansion of capacity may fail to keep up with demand. Normally, one will expect that price mechanism will work to clear the access demand but there may be phases when networks begin to congest heavily. Under such circumstances, developing countries will need to ensure that their access rights are not violated. While, personally, I do not expect this to turn into a serious problem, some caution in this regard may prove valuable.

The more important access issue relates to liberalization commitments by developed countries in the services that developing countries can export electronically. To-date, liberalization commitments by both developed and developing countries have been concentrated in services traded by mode 3. In these services, developing countries are largely importers. Commitments in electronically traded services, which developing countries can potentially export have been limited.

For some developing countries, the potential for exports of services through electronic means is very substantial. For instance, the market for customized software alone is growing at more than 20 percent annually and is projected to reach $250 billion by the year 2000.[261] Back office services offer another area in which developing countries can and have been supplying services to developed countries. Starting with simple data entry services in the 1980s, the supply of back office services from developing countries has grown to include electronic publishing, website design and management, customer call centers, medical records management, hotel reservations, credit card authorizations, remote secretarial services, mailing list management, technical on-line support, indexing and abstracting services, research and technical writing, and technical transcription.

As reported in UNCTAD (1998), based on OECD (1997), the global market for back office services (including Y2K code conversion) that can be potentially supplied by developing countries amounted to as much as $438 billion in 1998.[262] This figure is at least 20% of total 1996 exports of developing countries. The United States corporations alone spend $50 billion a year on information processing, of which at least 20% can be provided in a back office environment.

Developing countries should also identify sectors in which they could export services electronically and have not been liberalized so far by developed countries. One such area would seem to be accountancy services. Negotiations in this are could potentially be extremely beneficial to some of the developing countries since this is a very large market.

Internet also offers developing countries the opportunity to become exporters of products purchased by foreign governments. In the past, it would have been difficult for potential developing country suppliers to find out information on these purchases. But many developed country governments are now beginning to post tenders for procurement of goods and services on Internet. This gives suppliers from developing countries a better access to yet another sector in developed countries. Though the establishment of credibility may take some time for the small and medium firms, large firms in developing countries can certainly bid and compete successfully for these contracts.

Conclusions

In this paper, I have discussed the main economic issues relating to e-commerce from the viewpoint of developing countries. The first set of issues discussed in the paper concerns the WTO discipline on this trade. Several points can be made in this context. First, all things considered, it will be most appropriate to classify e-commerce as trade in services with GATS discipline applied to it. Since this matter is still under negotiation, developing countries should be sure that e-commerce is not classified as goods trade with zero custom duty pact made permanent. Such an outcome would liberalize all e-commerce by default, undermining their bargaining power.

Second, at present there is some disagreement about whether the Internet transactions in which the provider and recipient of a service are located in different countries should be classified as cross-border trade or consumption abroad. In making their commitments in the UR and post-UR negotiations in services, countries presumably viewed these transactions as cross-border trade. For if they are defined as consumption abroad, the category described as cross-border trade in services will be virtually vacuous. In view of this fact, it can be argued that the transactions under consideration be classified as cross-border trade.

Third, in the area of intellectual property protection, developing countries must eventually confront the possibility of two WIPO treaties, concluded in December 1996 but yet to come into force, being brought into the WTO. These treaties have strong enforcement commitments that developing countries will need to study carefully. Many of the countries may lack the ability to enforce and deliver the settlement of disputes in this area.

Finally, developing countries such as India that have the capacity to export skilled services through Internet should aggressively negotiate market access with developed countries in the forthcoming round. This involves negotiations on two fronts. One, they should seek liberalization by developed countries in sectors in which they have comparative advantage. And two, they should seek recognition of their education, qualifications, requirements met, or licenses or certificates granted in the markets of other countries.

Policy issues confronting developing countries in e-commerce are not limited to the negotiating issues, however. Indeed, for most developing countries, the binding constraints on the development of e-commerce are internal. These countries lack adequate telecommunications facilities with the density of telephone lines being less than three per one hundred people. E-commerce can, of course, grow rapidly even when this density is low as the Indian experience testifies. But such growth is likely to be confined to an enclave and will fail to achieve its full potential. It can be argued that with superior telecommunications infrastructure and regular power supply, even the Indian software exports could have grown at a much faster pace than they did. Efficiency considerations dictate that, assuming e-commerce lowers costs of transactions, its expansion should not be confined to external trade but also extended to domestic trade. That, in turn, requires an expansion of telecommunications facilities. Also critical to the expansion of both internal and external e-commerce are financial sector reforms. In particular, unless electronic means of payment such as credit cards are developed, the expansion of e-commerce will be slow.

Electronic commerce offers unprecedented opportunities to both developing and developed countries. In the short run, the gains are likely to be concentrated in developed countries but, in the long run, developing countries have more to benefit. This is because, in the short run, developing countries lack the infrastructure necessary to take full advantage of Internet. But in the long run, they can leap frog, skipping some of the stages in the development of information technology through which developed countries have had to pass.

NOTES

[1] See the Assessment of the Uruguay Round conducted by the UNCTAD Secretariat TDR/14 and TDR/14/Supp.1

[2] See, GATT document MTN.TNC/MIN(94)/6—Concluding remarks by the Minister of Foreign Affairs of Uruguay. Chairman of TNC, Marrakesh, 15 April 1994.

[3] See MIDRAND DECLARATION AND A PARTNERSHIP FOR GROWTH AND DEVELOPMENT *Adopted by the United Nations Conference on Trade and Development at its ninth session*, Midrand, 27 April 1996, TD/377 of 24 May 1996.

[4] See joint UNCTAD/ WHO publication "International in Health Services—A development perspective", Geneva 1998, UNCTAD/ITCD/TS B/5 and WHO/TFHE/98.1.

[5] See UNCTAD secretariat's background note for the expert meeting on Tourism and Tour Operators TD/B/COM.1/EM.6/2 and agreed conclusions TD/B/COM.1/EM.6/3.

[6] See UNCTAD secretariat's background note for the expert meeting on Environmental Services TD/B/COM.1/EM.7/2 and agreed conclusions TD/B/COM.1/EM.7/3.

[7] See UNCTAD publication on "Preparing for Future Multilateral Trade Negotiations: Issues and Research Needs from a Development Perspective", UNCTAD/ITCD/TSB/6.

[8] See paper on Special and Differential Treatment in the Context of Globalization .... elsewhere in this publication.

[9] See UNCTAD secretariat's background note for the expert meeting on Agriculture TD/B/COM.1/EM.8/2 and agreed conclusions TD/B/COM.1/EM.8/L.1.

[10] See UNCTAD secretariat's background note for the expert meeting on air transport services TD/B/COM.1/em.9/2 and agreed conclusions TD/B/COM.1/EM.9/L.1.

[11] See, G15 website, "http://www.sibexlink.com.my/g15/pulications/wpno6.htm".

[12] See, Statement of the OAU/African Economic Community Conference of Ministers on Trade on the Third World Trade Organization (WTO) Ministerial Meeting Seattle, USA, November 30-December 3, 1999.

[13] See the preceding paper for more details on this issue.

[14] A term coined by Mr. Sergio Delagdo in "La Ronda Uruguay, el Desarrollo de America Latina" Patricio Leiva editor, Santiago de Chile,1995.

[15] In interviews of the farmer's protest on local television, one demonstrator indicated that he was protesting against barriers and subsidies to trade in agricultural products, another stated that he was protesting against the liberalization of agricultural trade which placed small family farms in jeopardy. I was approached by a young female protestor who asked me politely if I thought that the protests had had an impact, "will this stop the WTO from killing people?" she questioned.

[16] See Decision on the Contribution of the World Trade Organization to Achieving Greater Coherence in Global Economic Policy Making, paragraph 5.

[17] This paper is based on the various ideas which emerged during the positive agenda process in 1999, it was prepared by Victor Ognivtsev, incorporating also contributions from Murray Gibbs, Mina Mashayekhi, Xiaobing Tang, Simonetta Zarrilli, Miho Shirotori and Stefano Inama, reflecting the discussion in the many meetings held with developing countries.

[18] See, UNCTAD/ITCD/TED/2, 1997, UN sales no. E.97.II.D.14; and UNCTAD/ITCD/TSB/6, 1999, UN sales no.E.99.II.D.17

[19] See, GA Doc. A/52/898, 13 May 1998, p. 7.

[20] The proposals by LDCs were submitted to the WTO preparatory process, see doc. WT/GC/W/251, 13 July 1999.

[21] See, African Ministerial Declaration on UNCTAD X and Africa's Development Challenges, August 1999; Lebanon Declaration 1999 (AS/MM/77(IX)/3), August 1999; Santo Domingo Declaration (LA/MM/77(IX)/1), August 1999; draft Bangkok Consensus (TD(X)/PC/5), October 1999; Marrakech Declaration (TD/381), October 1999 and Plan of Action (TD(X)/PC/4), October 1999.

[22] See, doc. TD/380, 29 July 1999, pp. 44-45.

[23] WT/MIN(98)/DEC/1, 25 May 1998.

[24] These include: trade and investment; trade and competition policy; transparency in government procurement and trade facilitation.

[25] It is meant that "New issues" include: Trade and investment; Trade and competition policy; Transparency in government procurement; Trade facilitation; Electronic commerce; and Labour rights.

[26] See, "The 33rd Quadrilateral Trade Ministers Meeting", Tokyo, 11-12 May 1999, Communiqué of the OECD Council meeting at ministerial level, 27 May 1999; and G-8 Summit Communiqué, 20 June 1999. Also WTO Doc. WT/GC/W/230, 6 July 1999, in which Argentina, Australia, Chile, Costa Rica, Czech Republic, Hungary, Korea, Mexico, Morocco, New Zealand, Singapore, Switzerland, Thailand, Uruguay, Hong Kong and China have proposed to launch a new comprehensive round of multilateral trade negotiations; and Declaration of APEC Summit, Auckland, New Zealand, 13 September 1999.

[27] See "The EU Approach to the Millennium Round: Communication from the Commission to the Council and the European Parliament, Brussels 8 July 1999".

[28] See, WTO Doc. WT/GC/W/255, Communication from Dominican Republic, Honduras and Pakistan, 16 July 1999.

[29] See Carlos M. Correa, "Technology Transfer in the WTO Agreements", UNCTAD August 1999.

[30] In the view of developing countries, financial assistance should be an important element of S&D in future MTAs ("financial windows") to enable countries to implement the obligations and exercise their rights.

[31] Implementation of MTAs has demonstrated that without financial assistance the possibilities of many developing countries to fully meet their obligations and fully exercise their rights are very limited .

[32] "Implementation Issues" are described in proposals from a group of 12 developing countries (docs. WI/GC/W/354 and 355. Some of these "Implementation Issues" may also coincide with "Deliverables" (See, Box 7 below).

[33] The following proposals were tabled in the preparatory process: European Union – doc. WT/GC/W/245 (EC Approach to Trade and Investment); Japan—doc. WT/GC/W/239 (Agreement on Investment); Switzerland—doc. WT/GC/W/263 (Negotiations on Trade and Investment); Korea—doc. WT/GC/W/267 (Trade and Investment); Hong Kong, China—WT/GC/W/268 (Negotiations on Trade and Investment); Poland—doc. WT/GC/W/277 (Investment); Costa Rica – doc. WT/GC/W/280 (Negotiations Relating to a Multilateral Framework for Investment).

[34] It should be recalled that the UN Set of Multilaterally Agreed Equitable Principles and Rules for the Control of Restrictive Business Practices is to date, the only fully multilateral code on competition in existence, and that it is in the form of a recommendation unanimously agreed by the General Assembly, and that three UN Review Conferences have reconfirmed their unanimous acceptance of the Set, and of UNCTAD's mandate in the field of competition law and policy (in 1985,90 and 95, respectively), and that a Fourth Review Conference on the Set is convened by the General Assembly to take place in September 2000. The "preferential and differential treatment for developing countries" which is an agreed principle under the Set, could find a natural home under any possible framework in WTO, where the S&D Treatment for developing countries is also an agreed principle.

[35] "Affiliate" could be defined according to Article XXVIII of GATS.

[36] "New or improved goods or services" means goods or services that are new or improved for the recipient firm.

[37] The structure of the Swiss formula is as follows: $T_1 = c\,T_0\,/\,(c + T_0)$, where $c = $ reduction coefficient ($c > 0$); $T_1 = $ the tariff rate after reduction; and $T_0 = $ the initial tariff rate. The smaller the reduction coefficient, the larger the rate of reduction.

[38] Doc. WT/GC/W/382.

[39] Doc. WT/GC/W/383, 5 November 1999.

[40] Draft Ministerial Declaration, 19 October 1999.

[41] It is noted that during the Uruguay Round, acceding countries were excluded from participation in negotiations relating to the amendment or application of GATT provisions, or the negotiation of new provisions. (MIN.DEC, Part I, F, (b)). Participation in the negotiations on Trade in Services was subject to the same provisions as for GATT negotiations.

[42] The correct term is "Differential and More Favourable Treatment".

[43] These elements were clearly recognized in the resolution emerging from UNCTAD VI.

[44] For example, in resolution 159(VI), para. 14.

[45] There are only few exceptions under which developing countries, and particularly LDCs may obtain an extension of the transition periods. LDCs may, under the TRIPS Agreement, if their request is "duly motivated", obtain extension of the transitional arrangements. Developing countries may also request the Council for Trade in Goods to extend the transition period for the elimination of TRIMs. Under the Agreement on Subsidies and Countervailing Measures, LDCs and low-income developing countries (less than $1,000 per capita) are exempt from the prohibition of export subsidies contingent upon export performance, while others must phase out export subsidies over an eight year period,,i.e. by the end of 2003. However, a developing country may request an extension of this eight-year period from the Committee on Subsidies and Countervailing Measures.

[46] *USTR Strategic Plan, FY 1997-FY 2002*, Office of the United States Trade Representative, 30 September 1997.

[47] The negotiations on movement of natural persons have so far yielded limited results. Access to distribution channels and information networks e.g. CRS and technology has not yet been facilitated.

[48] The discussion in the GSP context appears to be out of date when viewed against the general acceptance of the benefits of trade liberalization. GSP is seen as a "burden" by donor countries, and as a loss of fiscal revenue.

[49] For developing countries which so request the Committee on Subsidies and Countervailing Measures before the end of 2002.

[50] Article 71.1 of the TRIPS Agreement provides for reviews, beginning in 2000 in the light of any relevant new developments which might warrant modification or amendment of the Agreement.

[51] For a survey of the treatment of agriculture in the GATT, with an extensive description and analysis of the Uruguay Round Agreement on Agriculture, see Josling, Tim, Stefan Tangermann and Thorald K. Warley (1996), Agriculture in the GATT. Houndmills, London, and New York: Macmillan Press.

[52] Ministerial declaration stipulates that the General Council work programme encompasses the following areas: (*a*) recommendations concerning: (i) the issues, including those brought forward by Members, relating to implementation of existing agreements and decisions; (ii) the negotiations already mandated at Marrakesh, to ensure that such negotiations begin on schedule; (iii) future work already provided for under other existing agreements and decisions taken at Marrakesh; (*b*) recommendations concerning other possible future work on the basis of the work programme initiated at Singapore; (*c*) recommendations on the follow-up to the High-Level Meeting on Least-Developed Countries; (*d*) recommendations arising from consideration

of other matters proposed and agreed to by Members concerning their multilateral trade relations.

[53] Finger, J.M., Ingco, M.D., Reincke, U., *The Uruguay Round - Statistics on tariff Concessions Given and Received*, World Bank, 1996.

[54] UNCTAD, *The Post-Uruguay Round Tariff Environment for Developing Country Exports: Tariff Peaks and Tariff Escalation*, UNCTAD/WTO Joint Study, (TD/B/COM.1/14/Rev.1), 1999.

[55] OECD, *The Uruguay Round Agreement on Agriculture and Processed Agricultural Products*, 1997.

[56] Specific rates are expressed as a fixed monetary amount per physical unit of the product imported (e.g. $20 per kilogram). Other type of non-*ad-valorem* rates include compound rates (a combination of *ad-valorem* and specific rates) and mixed rates (*ad-valorem* rate or specific rate, whichever is higher).

[57] "Computation of *ad-valorem* equivalents of specific tariffs", UNCTAD informal study, 1998.

[58] Not all the quota utilizations has been notified. As of May 1998, notifications had been received on 996 TRQs implemented in 1995 (out of total TRQs of 1261), 989 TRQs in 1996 (out of the total 1278), and 163 TRQs in 1997 (out of the total 1207). In 1995, 85% of countries (28 out of 33 countries) with notification obligation notified the TRQ utilization, The figures were lower for 1996 (74%, or 26 out of 34 countries) and for 1997 (33% or 12 out of 36 countries), reflecting delays in notification for the more recent years.

[59] WTO, *Tariff Quota Administration Methods and Tariff Quota Fill*, (AIE/S4/Rev.1), 1998.

[60] The definition officially endorsed at the 1996 World Food Summit is that food security is ensured when *all people, at all times, and physical and economic access to sufficient, safe and nutritious food to meet their dietary needs and food preferences for an active and healthy life.*

[61] On 7 December 1998, Brazil made a complaint to the Dispute Settlement Body that the EU's provision of the S&D treatment provided to the Andean Group of countries and the Central American Common Market countries under its GSP scheme (a duty free access to soluble coffee), in association with those grouping's programmes to combat drug production and trafficking, adversely affected Brazil's exports to the EU (WT/DS154/1).

[62] Detailed statistical information on the changes in the availability of food aid is given in: WTO, "Review of Food Aid Levels: Note by the Secretariat" (G/AG/W/36), November 1998.

[63] Konandreas, p., "Issues related to the continuation of the reform process in agriculture" (a paper submitted to UNCTAD Ad-hoc Expert Meeting on Preparing for future multilateral negotiations: Issues and research needs from development perspective, September 1998).

[64] UNCTAD, "Some considerations concerning the availability of adequate supplies of basic foodstuffs from external sources to LDCs and NFIDCs", contribution to the Seventeenth meeting of the WTO Committee on Agriculture (17-18 November 1998).

[65] See Panos Konandreas (FAO), "Issues related to the Continuation of the Reform Process in Agriculture". Paper presented to the Ad Hoc Expert Group of the Secretary-General of UNCTAD on Preparing for future multilateral trade negotiations: Issues and research needs from a development perspective, UNC TAD, Geneva, 21–21 September 1998.

[66] Ibid.

[67] As of November 1998 NFIDCs include: Barbados, Botswana, Côte d'Ivoire, Dominican Republic, Egypt, Honduras, Jamaica, Kenya, Mauritius, Morocco, Pakistan, Peru, Senegal, Sri Lanka, St. Lucia, Trinidad and Tobago, Tunisia and Venezuela.

[68] The "food" items included here covers products that are: SITC (Rev.3) 01 (food and live animals, including fish, sugar, coffee, tea and animal feeds); 1 (beverages and tobaccos), 22 (oil seeds and oil fruits); and 4 (animal and vegetable fats).

[69] Data were not available for the remaining three LDCs; Equatorial Guinea, Eritrea and Tuvalu.

[70] The FAO defines basic foodstuffs as cereals, livestock, pulses, roots and tubers including other vegetables and fruits. The table used the average import values of "food" in the years 1990-1992 as given in the table 11 of a FAO document, "Definition of net food importing countries" (ESC/M/95/4, November 1995).

[71] UNCTAD, Trade and Development Report 1998, p.42.

[72] The process of progressive liberalization is supposed to be advanced through bilateral, plurilateral or multilateral negotiations (Article XIX.4).

[73] See UNCTAD, AInformation on the temporary migration regime in force in selected developed countries@ and AHarmonization and recognition of professional qualifications@.

[74] This would mean that in principle all modes and sectors are subject to negotiations. It does not mean that schedules of commitments resulting from the negotiations would necessarily be comprehensive.

[75] Status quo commitments at the initial phase of the round can not reasonably be expected from developing countries, particularly because of the lack of competitive capacity to supply and export. In many countries the appropriate policy and regulatory framework for developing supply and export capacity is not in place. In many cases also no experience with recently adopted regulatory reform has been accumulated and social and economic costs of liberalization have not been properly analysed and determined

[76] Formula approaches multilateralise the request-offer process across members, sectors and modes of supply. The purpose is to identify a set of subsectors and commitments on market access and national treatment by mode and measure that would be assumed by all members or a critical mass of members. US has proposed a formula approach to electronic commerce to remove all restrictions relating to it. Removal of all nationality and residency requirements has been proposed by Australia,Chile and New Zealand. A cluster approach to environmental and tourism services has also been proposed as well as a formula approahc to increase foreign equity participation by a certain percentage.

[77] The aim is to translate the provisions in Article IV into more binding commitments. Specific provision could also be added along the lines that "To achieve such access specific additional commitments should be included in the Schedules of Specific Commitments of developed countries and incentives should be provided to firms and institutions for the purpose of encouraging transfer of technology and access to channels and networks". Concrete capacity building measures to build services sectors of developing countries and benchmarks for imports should be included as additional commitments. The effectiveness of the GATS contact points in providing relevant informati"n to developing countries would require a review.

[78] The text reads "Measures according differential treatment in regard to the expansion of existing operations, the establishment of a new commercial presence or the conduct of new activities, in a circumstance in which a member adopts or applies a measure that compels, or has the effect of compelling a person of the United States, on the basis of its nationality, to reduce its share of ownership in an insurance services provider operating in the Member's territory to a level below that prevailing on 12/12/97". For example in the insurance sector Philippines provides for grandfathering by including in its schedule "limitations in market access listed ...shall not apply to existing wholly or majority-owned authorized insurance/reinsurance companies as of the entry into force of this WTO Financial Services agreement." These limitations relate mainly to equity participation (limited to 5% in life and non-life and 40 percent in auxiliary services and reinsurance). Thailand in relation to Banking and other financial services (excluding insurance) commercial presence for foreign bank branches provides no limitation for existing foreign bank branches under present share holding structure. Moreover under local incorporated banks it is provided that the Bank of Thailand may relax limits on maximum foreign equity participation and combined shareholding of an individual and related persons, subject to the terms and conditions announced by the Minister of Finance. . . such equity participation will be autho-

rized for a period of up to 10 years with foreign shareholders who enter in this period being grandfathered thereafter with respect to the absolute amount of their equity holding."

[79] Another example is NAFTA where an agreement among 3 countries required hundreds of pages of reservations.

[80] The barriers to access have been identified in the paper entitled "Ways of enhancing access to and use of information networks and distribution channels", (TD/B/CN.4/42).

[81] In the context of a developing country, severely short of foreign direct investment and advanced labour skills, prospective foreign suppliers of service are not the types of individuals that compete with domestic unemployment.

[82] The problem of attracting and retaining employees in the IT industry firms is increasingly difficult. For example, Intel needs to recruit 7,500 technical and managerial staff members each year, according to the International Herald Tribune, Oct. 5 1999 while the average worker in information technology professions switch jobs every six months leading to the generally accepted turnover of 50%.

[83] Throughout the text reference is made to Articles and provisions of the General Agreement on Trade in Services, The Results of the Uruguay Round of Multilateral Trade Negotiations, The Legal Texts, WTO 1995, pp.: 325-351.

[84] This would imply nationals working for the foreign affiliate, which is not part of trade in GATS mode 4.

[85] Annex on the Movement of Natural Persons Supplying Services under the Agreement, The Results of the Uruguay Round of Multilateral Trade Negotiations, The Legal Texts, WTO 1995, p. 353.

[86] The Annex is very clear, the GATS does not apply to measures affecting natural persons seeking access to the employment market of a Member, nor shall it apply to measures regarding citizenship, residence or employment on a permanent basis, nor shall it prevent a member from applying measures to regulate the entry of natural persons into, or their temporary stay in, its territory, including those measures necessary to protect the integrity, of and to ensure the orderly movement of natural persons across its borders. In addition, the sole fact of requiring a visa for natural persons of certain Members and not for those others shall not be regarded as nullifying or impairing benefits under specific commitment.

[87] As has been shown in the recent sectoral studies by the secretariats of UNCTAD and the WTO.

[88] In the aftermath of the Uruguay Round extended Negotiations on the Movement of Natural Persons continued, resulting in modest commitments by 6 WTO members of which four have specified these commitments for selected services sectors or professions.

[89] Australia, Austria, Czech Republic, European Union (12), Finland, Iceland, Israel, Norway, Slovakia, Slovenia, South Africa.

[90] Grenada, Kuwait, Netherlands with respect to Netherlands Antilles.

[91] The one-year rule does not apply to students and medical patients, who remain residents of their economies of origin even if the length of stay in another economy is one year or more.

[92] See earlier UNCTAD analysis on the first stage of integration as contained in TD/B/WG.8/2 of 19 June 1995 and UNCTAD/ITD/17 of 6 October 1995.

[93] See O.J. C.351 of 22 November 1996.

[94] See commission decision of 18 February 1997 on the initiation of international consultation ad dispute settlement procedures concerning changes to Untied States rules of origin for textile products resulting in the non-conferral of Community origin on certain products processed in the European Community, O.J. L 62 [1997] and WTO document G/TBT/D/13 of 3 June 1997, "United States Measures Applying Textile And Apparel Products: Request For Consultation by the EC." It was reported that some interim arrangements were agreed between the United

States and the EU with regard to the dispute pending a final solution to be found in the context of the harmonization process under the WTO Agreement on Rules of Origin.

[95] For a more illustrative analysis of the interaction between origin and quotas on textile products, see document CR/XXV/SLV/6 of 20 May 1997 of the International and Textile Clothing Bureau presented at Council of Representative XXV session, San Salvador, 10-13 June 1997.

[96] See the position submitted by the government of Egypt in document WT/CG/W/136. In contrast, the United States has already indicated that the Council for TRIPS should inititate work "to consider whether it is desirable to modify the TRIPS Agreement by eliminating the exclusion from patentability of plants and animals and incorporating key provisions of the UPOV agreement regarding plant variety protection" (document WT/CG/W/115).

[97] For an analysis of different approaches, see Correa, 1884; Posey and Dutfield, 1996.

[98] Several countries (e.g. Tunisia, Bolivia, Chile, Iran, Morocco, Algeria, Senegal, Kenya, Indonesia, Niger, Panama) protect such works under national copyright law .

[99] See South Centre, 1998, p. 26.

[100] See Panel Report USA v. India, WT/DS50/R, 5 September 1997 (WTO 97-3496) and WT/DS550/AB/R, 19 December, 1997 (97-5539).

[101] See the submissions by the Dominican Republic and Honduras (WT/GC/W/119), Egypt (WT/CG/W/136) and, notably, India (WT/GC/W/147).

[102] See WTO/CTE/1, 12 November, 1996.

[103] For a justification and proposals on this issue, see the Indian submission as contained in WT/GC/W/147.

[104] It should be noted that the WHO Assembly approved in May 1999 a resolution giving WHO the mandate to work on issues relating to the implementation of the WTO agreements as it may affect public health.

[105] See Chapter III.

[106] See Indian submission WT/GC/W/147.

[107] According to this principle, applied by most countries in the world, the right to a patent corresponds to the first applicant. In the United States, a patent is granted to the "first inventor", a principle that allegedly leads to complex controversies and an unnecessary burden on inventors.

[108] This is also proposed by the European Union (WT/GC/W/193).

[109] See WT/GC/W/115 and WT/GC/W/193.

[110] For an analysis of these treaties, see Vinje, 1997.

[111] This right may be subject to the principle of exhaustion (article 6.1).

[112] In his speech to the National assembly announcing that France was no longer taking part in the negotiations, the Prime Minister of France explained that the process of consultations and evaluation of the negotiations led to the conclusion that there were some fundatmental problems with the draft MAI as it placed private interests above State sovereignty. France, he noted would propose the fresh start of the negotiations in a forum where all actors, notably the developing countris could be associated..

[113] "The Uruguay Round Negotiations on Investment: Lessons for the Future" by Murray Gibbs and Mina Mashayekhi (14 May, 1998).

[114] Removal of restrictions, however, is not sufficient condition for attracting investment. Important factors relating to locational decisions relate to size of the market, geographical location, political and social stability appropriate legal and physical infrastructure, quality of labour force.

[115] See Trade and FDI Policies: Pieces of a New Strategic Approach to Development, Manuel R. Agosin and Francisco J Prieto, March 1993.

[116] Trade-related investment measures first made an appearance as a specific issue for debate in GATT in 1981. This was in the context of discussions on structural adjustment and trade policy. In the Consultative Group of 18 the United States submitted a report on investment performance requirements and incentives. In the report the US expressed concern that the increasing world wide use of such measures might also effect third countries' trading interests, even to the point of impairing benefits negotiated under the GATT. Report of the Consultative Group of Eighteen, GATT Doc. No. L/ 5210 , reprinted in GATT BISD 28th Supp. at 75-76 (1982).

[117] In an attempt to ensure that the investment issue is addressed specifically in the GATT, the US requested on 31 March 1982 that the GATT Council establish a panel "to examine certain trade distorting practices in the implementation of Canada's Foreign Investment Review Act (FIRA)" It also made concrete proposals for negotiations to take place on investment see GATT Doc. No. Prep.com (86)/W/35 (June 11 1986).

[118] The United States attempted to categorize the effects of TRIMs as those which: (i) prevent, reduce or divert imports by limiting the sale, purchase and use of imported products; (ii) restrict the ability to export of home and third country producers; and (iii) artificially inflate exports from a host country, thereby distorting trade flows in world markets. It also requested that the applicability of some trade policy concepts to TRIMs should be considered, namely non-discrimination (MFN and national treatment), prohibition (as implicit in Articles I, II, XI, and XVI), transparency, and dispute settlement.

[119] See submissions by the EC, documents MTN.GNG/NG12/W/8, W/10 and W/22, and the submissions by the Nordic countries, documents MTN.GNG/NG12/W/6 and W/23.

[120] See meeting of 30 October - 2 November 1987, document MTN.GNG/NG12/4, pp. 11-12, where some developing countries' positions have been summarized.

[121] See submissions by Malaysia, Singapore, India, Mexico and Bangladesh (MTN.GNG/ NG12/W 13, 17, 18, 19, and 21). Mexico proposed that the effects of two TRIMS i.e. export performance requirements and local equity requirements be empirically tested. See also joint submission by developing countries (Argentina, Brazil, Cameroon, China, Colombia, Cuba, Egypt, India, Tanzania and Yugoslavia) and draft declaration on TRIMs submitted by Bangladesh, Brazil, Colombia, cuba, Egypt, India, Kenya, Nigeria, Pakistan, Peru, Tanzania and Zimbabwe (MTN:GNG/NG/W/25 and 26).

[122] Although subsidies linked to such requirements would be covered by the discipline of the Agr3ement on Subsidies and Countervailing Measures.

[123] The 1990 Panel on EEC-Regulation on Imports of Parts and Components suggested a broad scope for the application to Article III. The Panel ruled that the comprehensive coverage of all laws, regulations or requirements affecting the internal sale, etc., of imported products suggests that not only requirements which an enterprise is legally bound to carry out, such as those examined by the FIRA Panel, but also those which an enterprise voluntarily accepts in order to obtain an advantage from the government constitute requirements within the meaning of that provision. The Panel noted that the EEC made the grant of an advantage, namely the suspension of proceedings under the anti-circumvention provision, dependent on undertakings to limit the use of parts or materials of Japanese origin without imposing similar limitations on the use of like products of EEC or other origin, hence dependent on undertakings to accord treatment to imported products less favourable than that accorded to like products of national origin in respect of their internal use. GATT, *BISD*, Thirty-seventh Supplement, pp. 132, 197.

[124] Communication from India entitled: "Proposals regarding the Agreement on Trade Related Investment Measures in terms of paragraph 9 (a)(I) of the Geneva Ministerial Declaration" fothe Preparations of the 1999 Ministerial Conference.

[125] Developing countries tend to use TRIMs that impose requirements on investors e.g. to export or fiscal incentives, developed countries often use TRIMS in the form of subsidies to encourage investors to export or grants given their access to finance. During the TRIMs negotiations the US proposed a list of fourteen types of TRIMS including incentives to be limited. Jap-

anese government was supportive of this list except it did not wish to limit incentives. EU proposed a list of eight measures and did not include provision concerning incentives, technology transfer, or licensing because of the use of such measure in the context of national and EU level industrial policies and regional development policies.

[126] TRIMs are not unique in imposing conditions of performance. A "pure" investment incentive involving, for example, a tax rebate depending on the size of local operations, or including labour-training grants depending on the size of the labour force at the local plant, behaves like a performance requirement. These kinds of *quid pro quo* can be found in several countries, both developed and developing.

[127] Incentives (defined as the grant of a specific advantage arising from public expenditure [a financial contribution] in connection with the establishment, acquisition, expansion, management, operation or conduct of an investment) is one of the most difficult issues to be tackled in the negotiations on MAI. There are divergent views on whether a specific text is needed. Some have proposed a built--in agenda for future work in this area which is the same approach taken in the GATS and TRIMs. The draft text that has been included is that national treatment, MFN and transparency apply to incentives. Many believe that not all incentives are bad and inefficient and that the distorting effects of investment incentives on investment decisions should be balanced against their possible benefits in achieving legitimate social objectives regional development, environmental or R&D policies etc. The potential overlaps with the SCM and the GATS will also have to be considered. consideration has to be given also to the fact that most incentives are granted at sub-federal level and include tax measures on which the MAI contains a carve out.

[128] United States Department of Commerce, *The Use of Investment Incentives and Performance Requirements* (Washington, D.C.: 1977), pp. 1-2. The 1977 benchmark survey of the United States Department of Commerce, which provided elements for the formulation of a United States negotiating position on this issue, found that 27 per cent of United States affiliates in the developing countries received one or more incentives to invest, while the figure was 25 per cent for developed countries. However, developing countries imposed performance requirements on United States firms more often than other developed countries - 29 per cent as against 6 per cent.

[129] Hardeep Puri and Delfino Bondad, "TRIMs, development aspects and the General Agreemen", *Uruguay Round: Further Papers on Selected Issues* (UNCTAD/ITP/42), 1990, p. 55.

[130] Theodore H. Moran and Charles S. Pearson, "Tread carefully in the field of TRIP (Trade-Related Investment Performance) measures", *The World Economy,* Vol. 11, No. 1 (1988), p. 121.

[131] The MAI widens the list of performance requirements including many currently permitted under GATT and GATS, but some of them would be allowed if linked to the grant of an advantage. The MAI prohibits local content and export performance requirements.

[132] The Office of the United States Trade Representative, in its *1994 National Trade Estimate Report on Foreign Trade Barriers*, identified 24 developed and developing countries that use at least one TRIM (Washington, D.C.: 1994). A UNCTC/UNCTAD study reported that European Governments offer cash grants up to 60 per cent of the cost of the entire investment; state governments in the United States have given as much as $325 million per project (or $108,000 per job) to foreign firms. While no explicit domestic content or export-performance regulations are involved, it would be disingenuous to argue that such efforts were not trade-related investment measures. The Federal Reserve Bank of St. Louis found a positive statistical correlation between the expenditures of individual states in the United States on investment promotion, on the one hand, and exports from those states, on the other. No less real is the import-substitution dimension of such policies among the developed nations. The trend, moreover, is worrisome. Average state expenditures in the United States to induce inward investment and to promote exports have grown over the past decade by more than 600 per cent. *The Impact*

of Trade-Related Investment Measures on Trade and Development (United Nations publication, Sales No. E.91.II.A.19), 1991, p. 9.

[133] See Stefan Tangermann, Implementation of the Uruguay Round Agreement on Agriculture by Major Developed Countries, UNCTAD/ITD/16.

[134] For example under the negative list approach long list of reservations would be submitted , or new services would be automatically covered by GATS discipline unless explicit action would be taken to exclude them.

[135] NAFTA has adopted the negative list approach and it contains hundreds of pages of Annexes of reservations. This shows the difficulties encountered with the negative list approach for WTO. The MAI has also adopted the negative list approach which already has resulted in 600 pages of reservations for a few of the OECD countries only.

[136] Hardeep Puri and Philippe Brusick, "Trade-related investment measures: Issues for developing countries in the Uruguay Round", *Uruguay Round: Papers on Selected Issues* (UNCTAD/ITP/10), 1989, p. 219.

[137] The reference paper is designed to ensure that the advantages of the former monopoly operator are not used to the detriment of new entrants on the telecommunications market through competitive safeguards. On the prevention of anti-competitive practices, the reference paper provides that appropriate measures shall be maintained for the purpose of preventing suppliers who, alone or together, are a major supplier from engaging or continuing anti-competitive practices. These practices include engaging in anti-competitive cross-subsidization, using information obtained from competitors with anti-competitive results and not making available to other service suppliers on a timely basis technical information about essential facilities and commercially relevant information which are necessary for them to provide services.

[138] There was a proposal that this issue could be part of the built-in-agenda of MAI. The same issues have arisen during the MAI negotiations. The draft MAI contains provisions on monopolies etc. but there is no text on corporate practices.

[139] Guatemala-Anti-dumping investigation regarding portland cement from Mexico, WTO, WT/DS60/R, 19 June 1998, at para. 5.25 (description of the third party submission of the United States).

[140] These and the following data in this section come from the Rules Division of the WTO.

[141] In 1998, the following WTO members initiated anti-dumping proceedings: Argentina, Australia, Brazil, Canada, Chile, Colombia, Costa Rica, Czech Republic, Ecuador, EC, India, Indonesia, Israel, Korea, Malaysia, Mexico, New Zealand, Nicaragua, Panama, Peru, Philippines, South Africa, Trinidad & Tobago, Turkey, USA, Venezuela.

[142] Australia, Canada, EC, USA.

[143] This compares with the USA 34, EC 22, Australia 13 and Canada 8.

[144] The EC as such was a target in one additional proceeding.

[145] For this purpose, we considered Argentina, Brazil, Bulgaria, Chile, China, Colombia, Costa Rica, Croatia, Czech Republic, Ecuador, Egypt, Honduras, Hong Kong, Hungary, India, Indonesia, Kazakhstan, Korea, Macedonia, Malaysia, Mexico, Nicaragua, Panama, Peru, Philippines, Romania, Russia, Slovakia, Slovenia, South Africa, Thailand, Trinidad & Tobago, Turkey, Ukraine, Venezuela and Zimbabwe as developing countries.

[146] Miranda, Torres, Ruiz, The International Use of Anti-Dumping—1987-1997 32:5 Journal of World Trade, 5-72 (1998).

[147] *Id.*, at 64.

[148] Vermulst, Waer, EC Anti-Dumping Law and Practice, at 2 (1996).

[149] But note the practice in some jurisdictions of imposing residual or 'all others' anti-dumping duties on countries.

[150] See also Vermulst, Adopting and Implementing Anti-Dumping Laws—Some Suggestions for Developing Countries, 31:2 Journal of World Trade, 5-24 (1997).

[151] Once subsidies have been determined to exist in a certain country in a specific proceeding, copycat complaints often result.

[152] Safeguard actions must in principle be taken on a non-discriminatory basis.

[153] In this regard, it is significant that the first three AD/CVD disputes in the WTO all concerned developing countries' application of AD/CVD measures, respectively Brazil (desiccated coconut), Guatemala (portland cement) and Mexico (high fructose corn syrup).

[154] Vermulst, Waer, EC Anti-Dumping Law and Practice, at 3 (1996).

[155] I note that, although it may be in developing countries' interests to seek substantive amendments to the provisions of the ADA as well as the ASCM, it might prove counter-productive to advance specific proposals for reform *at this stage*. In particular, the United States has expressed reserve with regard to the need to negotiate reforms to these Agreements. By advocating concrete amendments too far in advance of any negotiations, this might have the unwanted effect of alienating the United States (among others) and lead it to further distance itself from any negotiations in these areas. Therefore, the appropriate approach at this point, from the perspective of developing countries, could be to ensure that issues which are of concern are placed firmly on the agenda of the Seattle meeting for future discussion, but to avoid taking specific positions on potential amendments until such time as these future negotiations have been assured. Thus, developing countries could, for the time being simply table two agenda items in the context of the Ministerial meeting: implementation issues and special treatment for developing countries.

[156] In reality, importing country authorities have much discretion in deciding on the calculation details. Furthermore, indiscriminate use of the *best information available* rule, especially against companies in developing countries, may lead to findings of dumping where none might exist.

[157] They are not punitive and in fact, there is no prohibition of dumping in the GATT/WTO:

> *"[t]he drafting history of Article VI was also relevant. The intention of the drafters of the Article had not been to condemn dumping itself but to limit the possibility of taking measures to counteract dumping and subsidization. The history also showed that there had never been agreement, including during the Tokyo Round negotiations which eventually led to the adoption of the Anti-Dumping Code in 1979, to encourage or justify actions by the exporting country to prevent dumping."*

See Japan - Trade in Semiconductors, Report of the Panel Adopted on 4 May 1988 (L/6309), GATT, B.I.S.D., 35th Supp., 116-163, at 128-129 (1989).

[158] Partly for this reason, some free trade agreements, e.g. ANZCERTA, the EEA (and Mercosur?), preclude use of anti-dumping actions among FTA members. Compare Hoekman, Competition Policy and Regional Integration Agreements (World Bank 17/2/1998).

[159] When anti-dumping laws were originally enacted in the beginning of this century, their rationale arguably was to counter predatory dumping.

[160] Compare Hoekman, Mavroidis, Dumping, Anti-Dumping and Antitrust, Journal of World Trade, 27-52 (1996); Messerlin, Should Anti-Dumping Rules Be Replaced by National or International Competition Rules?, World Competition, 37-54 (1995). But see Miranda, Should Anti-Dumping Laws Be Dumped?, 28:1 Law and Policy in International business, 255-288 (1996).

[161] See also Tharakan, Vermulst, Tharakan, Anti-Dumping and Competition: A Case Study, The World Economy (1998); Mavroidis, Van Siclen, The Application of the GATT/WTO Dispute Settlement Resolution System to Competition Issues, 31:5 Journal of World Trade, 5-48 (1997).

[162] In the area of EC competition law, see, *e.g.*, Case 62/86, AKZO Chemie v Commission, [1991] ECR, at 3359; Tetra Pak International SA v Commission, [1994] ECR, at paras. II-147-149.

[163] However, it is clear that in many circumstances it would be difficult to conclusively prove that the exporting countries market is closed, and to what degree, particularly where the market is *de facto* restricted. In addition, if such a positive requirement were introduced, the central challenge would be to establish a workable model for making such determinations. A model would need to be established which achieves an appropriate balance between being transparent and objective on the one hand, while not being reduced to a rigid procedural model that no longer conforms to economic reality or market conditions. An additional consideration would be that the imposition of such a requirement would add a significant burden on the investigating authorities of developing countries.

[164] In this regard, there has been much debate concerning the introduction of competition law concepts in the context of anti-dumping actions (or even the replacement of anti-dumping through the establishment of a multilateral competition regime). It has been suggested that many practices with respect to import sales which are currently caught under anti-dumping laws would not be considered objectionable under domestic competition law. However, many observers agree that the establishment of comprehensive multilateral rules on competition would, at the least, be a formidable task and it is therefore unlikely that such competition disciplines will replace anti-dumping measures in the short-to-medium term.

[165] Indeed, as noted above, Article 15 merely calls for special consideration with regard to the *application* of anti-dumping duties.

[166] However, such an approach would not be without potential pitfalls, notably that where proceedings are nonetheless initiated following a finding of insufficient or no improvement, the total duration and workload for the exporting industry may actually increase.

[167] Note that this applies only to the multilateral track and not to the unilateral track (imposition of countervailing duties).

[168] Article 27.2 (*a*).

[169] Under Article 27.5, however, a developing country Member referred to in Annex VII which has reached export competitiveness (as defined in Article 27.6) in one or more products, export subsidies on such products shall be gradually phased out over a period of eight years.

[170] Article 27.2 (*b*).

[171] The following countries are listed under paragraph (*b*): Bolivia, Cameroon, Congo, Côte d'Ivoire, Dominican Republic, Egypt, Ghana, Guatemala, Guyana, India, Indonesia, Kenya, Morocco, Nicaragua, Nigeria, Pakistan, Philippines, Senegal, Sri Lanka and Zimbabwe.

[172] Article 11 (1), ADA.

[173] For example, in *Potassium chloride originating in, inter alia, Belarus,* an interim review initiated in August 1995 was only completed in February 1998, i.e. a duration of 30 months.

[174] At the moment of writing, notably in the areas of machinery, textiles and agriculture.

[175] Past practice has shown that the absence of precise definitions of these terms can easily lead to abuse.

[176] Waer, Vermulst, EC Anti-Subsidy Law and Practice After the Uruguay Round: A Wolf in Sheep's Clothing?, 33:4 Journal of World Trade (forthcoming 1999).

[177] *Idem.*

[178] Assuming such useful lives have been established in accordance with the GAAP of the country concerned.

[179] The author wishes to express her thanks in particular to K. Bergholm, T. Chillaud, M. Gibbs, R. Griffin, J. Magalhães, M. Shirotori and the staff of the South Centre for the useful information and comments provided.

[180] National Research Council (1995), *Standards, Conformity Assessment, and Trade,* Washington D.C., National Academy Press.

[181] S. M. Stephenson (1997), *Standards, conformity assessment and developing countries*, Organization of American States, Trade Unit.

[182] Stewart, T. P. Editor (1993) *The GATT Uruguay Round: A Negotiating History*, Kluwer Law and Taxation Publishers, Deventer - Boston.

[183] The text of the Punta del Este Ministerial Declaration states, with respect to agriculture, that "Negotiations shall aim to achieve greater liberalization of trade in agriculture and bring all measures affecting import access and export competition under strengthened and more operationally effective GATT rules and disciplines, taking into account the general principles governing the negotiations, by: ...

> (iii) minimizing the adverse effects that sanitary and phytosanitary regulations and barriers can have on trade in agriculture, taking into account the relevant international agreements".

[184] The SPS negotiations were led by Argentina, Australia, Canada, the EC, Japan, New Zealand, the Nordic Countries and the United States.

[185] At the time of the UR negotiations the Cairns Group comprised Argentina, Australia, Brazil, Canada, Chile, Colombia, Hungary, Indonesia, Malaysia, New Zealand, the Philippines, Thailand and Uruguay. The composition of the Group has changed meanwhile, since South Africa has joined, while Hungary has left.

[186] The United States requested the Negotiating Group on Agriculture to establish a working group to address sanitary and phytosanitary measures, which, due to their technical aspects, were not well-suited to multilateral negotiations. According to the US, the results of the working group could then be incorporated into an overall draft text emerging from the agriculture group.

[187] According to Annex A of the Agreement, risk assessment is "the evaluation of the likelihood of entry, establishment or spread of a pest or disease within the territory of an importing Member according to the sanitary or phytosanitary measures which might be applied, and of the associated potential biological and economic consequences; or the evaluation of the potential for adverse effects on human or animal health arising from the presence of additives, contaminants, toxins or disease-causing organisms in food, beverages or feedstuffs".

[188] See: WTO (1999), *Understanding the WTO Agreement on Sanitary and Phytosanitary (SPS) Measures.*

[189] First complaint was introduced by the **United States** in 1995 with respect to requirements imposed by the Republic of Korea on imports from the United States of shelf-life of products. The US questioned the scientific basis for uniform shelf-life requirements and claimed that the measure had the effect of restricting imports. The United States alleged violations, inter alia, of Articles 2 (Basic Rights and Obligations) and 5 (Assessment of Risk and Determination of the Appropriate Level of Sanitary and Phytosanitary Protection) of the SPS Agreement. However, the parties reached a mutually acceptable solution: South Korea agreed to allow manufacturers of frozen food and vacuum-packed meat to set their own use-by dates. A similar case introduced by **Canada** about Korean regulations on the shelf-life and disinfection of bottled water was also solved by the parties.

[190] In 1996, the **United States** complained about Korean measures aimed at inspecting and testing agricultural products imported into Korea. According to the United States, those measures restricted exports and appeared to be inconsistent with Articles 2 (Basic Rights and Obligations) and 5 (Assessment of Risk and Determination of the Appropriate Level of Sanitary or Phytosanitary Protection) of the SPS Agreement. In 1997, the **European Communities** complained about a ban on imports of poultry and poultry products imposed by the United States. The EC contented that, although the ban was allegedly on grounds of product safety, it did not indicate why EC poultry products had suddenly become ineligible for entry into the US market. Therefore, it claimed that the ban was inconsistent, inter alia, with Articles 2 , 3 (Harmonization) , 4 (Equivalence), 5, 8 and Annex C (both Article 8 and Annex C deal with Control, Inspection and Approval Procedures) of the SPS Agreement. In 1998, **India** complained about the restric-

tions allegedly introduced by an EC Regulation establishing a so-called cumulative recovery system for determining certain import duties on rice. According to India, the discipline introduced through the new Regulation restricted the number of importers of rice from India and had a limiting effect on the export of rice from India to the EC. India claimed violation, inter alia, of Article 5 of the SPS Agreement. In the same year, **Switzerland** complained about measures concerning the importation of dairy products and the transit of cattle imposed by the Slovak Republic. Switzerland alleged that these measures had a negative impact on Swiss exports of cheese and cattle and were inconsistent, inter alia, with Article 5 of the SPS Agreement. In 1998, **Canada** questioned certain measures implemented by the European Communities regarding the importation into the EC market of wood conifers from Canada. Canada alleged violation of, inter alia, Articles 2, 3, 4, 5 and 6 (Adaptation to Regional Conditions) of the SPS Agreement. In the same year, **Canada** complained about measures imposed in one state of USA prohibiting entry or transit of Canadian trucks carrying cattle, swine and grain. Canada alleged, inter alia, violations of several Articles and of Annexes B (Transparency) and C of the SPS Agreement.

[191] These are, to pay compensation through trade concessions, most likely by increasing market access for other US agricultural products; transforming the present ban into a provisional one on the basis of available pertinent evidence; lifting the ban on imports and applying a mandatory labelling system which would specify that cattle have been treated with growth hormones.

[192] SPS Committee, *Review of the Operation and Implementation of the Agreement on the Application of Sanitary and Phytosanitary Measures*, G/SPS/12, March 1999

[193] OECD (1997), *Product standards, conformity assessment and regulatory reform*, TD/TC/WP(96)49/Rev2.

[194] Joint FAO/WHO Food Standard Programme, Codex Committee on General Principles, *Improvement of procedures for the adoption of Codex standards and measures to facilitate consensus*, CX/GP 99/5, March 1999.

[195] The Commission is presently working under the interim procedures established by FAO.

[196] An information session was held in November 1998.

[197] Openness should be provided in the drawing up of programmes and in the approval of standards so as to ensure reconciliation of conflicting opinions. The work programme of international standardizing bodies should reflect trade priorities; up-to-date international standards should be delivered in due time; and the activities of international standardizing bodies and the standards they produce need to be coherent both internally and with other bodies, and kept up to date. See: TBT Committee, Note from the European Community, G/TBT/W/87, 14 September 1998.

[198] According to the "New Approach", which the EC embraced in the mid-80s, legislative harmonization is limited to the adoption, by means of directives, of the essential requirements with which products put on the market have to conform. The task of drawing up the technical specifications is entrusted to the EC standardization organizations, such as CEN (Comité Européen de Normalisation) and CENELEC (Comité Européen de Normalisation Électrotechnique). The technical specifications are not mandatory and maintain the status of voluntary standards. See: W.S. Atkins (1996), The Single Market Review Series, Sub-series III—Dismantling of Barriers: Technical Barriers to Trade, Web site: europa.eu.int/comm/dg15/studies.

[199] *Sources*: Web sites: europa.eu.int/scadplus/leg/en/lvb/l21021.htm and, europa.eu.int/scadplus/leg/en/lvb/l21002.htm

[200] TBT Committee, *Equivalency of standards: an interim measure to facilitate trade in the absence of relevant international standards*, Note from New Zealand, G/TBT/W/88, 15 September 1998.

[201] "Members shall, upon request, enter into consultations with the aim of achieving bilateral and multilateral agreements on recognition of the equivalence of specified sanitary or phytosanitary measures".

[202] S.M. Stephenson (1997), op.cit.

[203] The "Global Approach" to testing and certification was developed by the EC to facilitate mutual recognition between the testing or certification bodies, and the European Organization for Testing and Certification was set up to provide the necessary infrastructure.

[204] For detailed information on the regional trade agreements see: S.M. Stephenson, op. cit.

[205] The TBT Committee has decided to address the problems associated with MRAs and may draft guidelines on MRAs. See: TBT Committee, *First Triennial Review of the Operation and Implementation of the Agreement on Technical Barriers to Trade,* G/TBT/5, 19 November 1997.

[206] See document G/RO/W/32 of 23 May 1998.

[207] Excerpt from Preparations for the 1999 Ministerial Conference: non paper on implementation issues. Communication from Zambia, Jamaica, Kenya, Pakistan, Sri Lanka, Tanzania, JOB(99)/3169 of 3 June 1999.

[208] The first part of Rule 2 (*a*) extends the scope of any heading which refers to a particular article to cover not only the complete article but also that article incomplete or unfinished, provided that, as presented, it has the essential character of the complete or finished article. The second part of Rule 2 (*a*) provides that complete or finished articles presented unassembled or disassembled are to be classified in the same heading as the assembled article. When goods are so presented, it is usually for reasons such as requirements or convenience of packing, handling or transport.

[209] This Chapter is largely based on Veena Jha and René Vossenaar, "Breaking the Deadlock, a Positive Agenda on Trade, Environment and Development?" in Gary P. Sampson and W. Bradnee Chambers, *Trade, Environment and the Millennium.* United Nations University, 1999.

[210] United Nations, Earth Summit+5, Programme for the Implementation of Agenda 21, June 1997. Paragraph 29.

[211] However, some progress has been made in designing multilateral agreements and instruments to regulate trade in DPGs. These include the Rotterdam Convention on Prior Informed Consent, the proposed Convention on Persistent Organic Pollutants (POPS), and the Basel Convention.

[212] Forums such as the CSD, UNCTAD and UNEP have emphasized the importance of supportive measures (such as capacity-building, improved access to finance and access to and transfer of technology) to assist developing countries in meeting multilaterally-agreed targets in MEAs, in keeping with the principle of common but differentiated responsibility. It has also been stressed that MEAs may use packages of instruments (which could contain both supportive measures as well as trade measures) to achieve their objectives. Finally, UNCTAD and other institutions have also stressed the need to examine the trade and economic effects of different policy instruments used or proposed in MEAs on developing countries

[213] See UNDP Human Development Report 1999, Chapter 2 on "New Technologies and the Global Race for Knowlwdge".

[214] In accordance with the TRIPS Agreement, in order to be patentable, an invention must be new. involve an inventive step and be capable of industrial application. It has been argued that the TRIPS Agreement seems to contemplate only the Northern industrialization model of innovation. It fails to address the more informal, communal system of innovation through which farmers in the South produce, select, improve and breed a diversity of crop and livestock varieties. Thus, Southern germplasm achieves an inferior status to that of contemporary biotechnologists' varieties. The intellectual property of Southern farmers is apparently denied recognition, and hence protection. WWF, The UN Biodiversity Convention and the WTO TRIPS Agreement, Discussion Paper

[215] Unless Article 27 of the TRIPS Agreement is interpreted broadly, the patenting of genetic materials could turn more and more life forms into patentable commodities, with long-term environmental, economic, cultural and ethical impacts. WWF, op. cit.

[216] UPOV governs an international system of PVP. Some 37 countries, mainly developed countries, are members. The 1978 treaty of UPOV allows certain exceptions for farmers and breeders to use protected materials. However, the treaty is being replaced by its 1991 successor, which eradicates the farmer's privilege and gives breeders control over further use of farmer's harvest of protected seeds. The 1991 treaty came into force on 24 April 1998. As a result, the 1978 version will be closed to further signature one year later, on 24 April 1999. See: <http://www.opov.org>.

[217] The international law of treaties uses various criteria to determine which treaty takes priority. Under the rule *that later treaties take priority over earlier treaties*, the TRIPS Agreement (which was agreed at the end of the Uruguay Round in December 1993 and signed in April 1994) would take priority over the CBD (which as agreed in May 1992). However, under the rule that *more specific treaties take priority over general treaties*, since the CBD's language on IPRs in the context of transfer of technology for biodiversity diversification is more specific than that of the TRIPS Agreement, the CBD would take priority. It is also to be noted that Article 16.5 of the CBD states that "The contracting parties, recognizing that patents and other intellectual property rights may have an influence on the implementation of the convention, shall cooperage in this regard subject to national legislation and international law in *order to ensure that such rights are supportive off, and do not run counter to, its objectives*". (emphasis added). WWF, op.cit.

[218] WTO/CTE/W/67

[219] "Type-1" eco-labels, in the terminology of the ISO, may be awarded by a third party to products that meet (multiple) preset environmental criteria, generally following a "life cycle" approach.

[220] In the ISO, progress has been made in developing guidelines on transparency, conformity assessment and mutual recognition.

[221] Rene Vossenaar, UNCTAD work on strategic environmental assessment, in Ole Christian Fauchald and Mads Greaker (editors) , *Environmental assessment of trade agreements and policy.* Nordic Council of Ministers. TemaNord 1998:551.

[222] For example, Agenda 21 called upon all countries to collaborate on global environmental problems on the basis of "common but differentiated responsibilities". It was recognized that developing countries should be provided improved market access, access to and transfer of technology, and finance.

[223] See "Building Capacity in Trade, Environment and Development, UNCTAD's Technical Co-operation Programme", UNCTAD/DITC/TED/Misc.7

[224] Rene Vossenaar, Process and Production Methods, Sizing up the Issues from the South. In Halina Ward and Duncan Brack (editors), *Trade, Investment and the Environment.* The Royal Institute of International Affairs. Earthscan Publications Ltd. London, 1998.

[225] Article 8.2 (*c*) of the Agreement on Subsidies and Countervailing Measures allows, under certain conditions, for "assistance to promote the adaptation of existing facilities to new environmental requirements imposed by law and/or regulations which result in greater constraints and financial burden on firms". Article 31, however, stipulates that the provisions of certain Articles, including 8.2 (*c*), shall apply for a period of five years from the entry into force of the WTO and that, not later than 180 days before the end of this period, the Subsidies Committee will review the operation of these provisions "with a view to determining whether to extend their application, either as presently drafted or in a modified form, for a further period."

[226] Article 13 of the Agreement on Agriculture specifies that during the implementation period (i.e. until 1 January 2001) domestic support measures that fully comply with the provisions contained in Annex 2 of the Agreement (support measures with minimal impact on trade, known as "green box" policies) are excluded from reduction commitments. These include expenditures under environmental programmes. These "green box" measures are due to expire by the end of the year 2000, unless they are renewed.

[227] The African Group, for example, has emphasized that the wording of the last sentence of Article 27.3(b) makes it clear that the mandate of the Council is to review the substantive provisions of this Article, and that the mandated review cannot be meant to be confined to the implementation of the subparagraph

[228] Veena Jha and Rene Vossenaar, "Mainstreaming environment in the WTO: Possible implications for developing countries. Paper prepared for the workshop on trade and environment held in Los Baños, Philippines, from 11 to 13 November 1999. UNCTAD/FIELD Project on Strengthening Research and Policy-Making Capacity on Trade and Environment in Developing Countries (Project INT/98/A61).

[229] Ref. to UNCTAD Code on Transfer of Technology, UN Code on TNCs etc.

[230] The Set was unanimously adopted by the General Assembly of the United Nations in Resolution 35/63 of 5 December 1980.

[231] See for example Annex 3 to UNCTAD, The outcome of the Uruguay Round: An initial assessment. Supporting papers to the Trade and Development Report, 1994, doc. UNCTAD/DR/14 (Supplement) ISBN 92-1-112362-2 UN Sales publication No. E.94.II.D.28.

[233] See OECD 1992a; OECD 1992b; OECD, 1996.

[234] In the United States, for instance, 61% of R&D expenditures were financed by the private sector and 73% performed by said sector in 1996 (Callan, Costigan and Keller, 1997, p. 8). The corresponding figures for Japan were above 70% (OECD, 1996. p. 31).

[235] If China is excluded this percentage is reduced to 4%.

[236] UNCTAD, 1998, p. 19.

[237] For a comprehensive analysis, see Mytelka, 1992

[238] For instance, IBM alone joined over 400 strategic alliances.

[239] Even the technologies developed with public funding or by public institutions are generally held as a proprietary asset by the respective institutions. A publicly held technology is not equivalent to a technology in the public domain, that is, free for use by any interested party.

[240] See, for instance, Correa, 1997; Reichman, 1997.

[241] As accepted under many national laws, a license may be granted for "refusal to deal" when the patent holder has refused to grant a voluntary license on reasonable commercial terms, particularly when this prejudices the development or establishment of a commercial or industrial activity or the supply of an export market (see. e.g. UK Patent law, article 48.3.d)..

[242] For an analysis of this article, see Roffe, 1998.

[243] Chapter IV of the draft Code contained detailes provisions on restrictive practices in technology transfer arrangements.

[244] The Federal government financed 34% all R&D expenditures in the United States in 1996 (Callan, Costigan and Séller, 1997, p. 8).

[245] See on this subject Eisenberg, 1997.

[246] Created by the trucking industry in the United States in the early 1970s, EDI entails the exchange of documents and information between the computers of two businesses without human intervention. Stores such as WalMart use the technology to link their suppliers directly into their stock databases. Through the link, suppliers are automatically notified and authorized to send shipments when the shelves are bare. According to the *Economist* (May 10, 1997), 95% of the *Fortune* 1,000 companies use EDI.

[247] The reader may find it useful to acquire some background information on various electronic mediums from the more comprehensive study, *Electronic commerce and the role of the WTO*, Special Studies 2 (Geneva: World Trade Organization), 1998. Additionally, the *Economist* has published two detailed surveys on e-commerce in issues dated May 19, 1997 and June 26, 1999.

[248] In writing this section, I have benefited greatly by email exchanges with Aaditya Mattoo and access to his ongoing research with Ludger Schuknecht for a forthcoming paper entitled "Trade Policies for Electronic Commerce."

[249] The absence of trade taxes on services is an important and entirely neglected problem. If tariffs are imposed to raise revenue, efficiency dictates that services are brought into the tariff net as well. Yet, this issue has received no attention in the academic or policy literature presumably because academics still like to think of services as non-traded and policy analysts do not want to scare away foreign investors by taxing the services supplied by foreign sources at higher rates.

[250] Even this option is available in the case of business-to-business transactions only. When a foreign business sells a product electronically directly to domestic consumers, it is not clear how the transaction can be subject to any domestic taxes.

[251] One possible explanation is that in the Seattle Round negotiations, the United States may still be intending to get Internet trade classified as goods trade. And if by then the countries have already committed to a permanent ban on custom duty, Internet trade will automatically be freed of all border restrictions.

[252] Though the discussions on e-commerce are often focused on cross-border method of delivery, it can and does take place through commercial presence (mode 3) as well as the movement of natural persons (mode 4). For example, when a foreign bank offers electronic banking services to the residents of a country, the transaction is classified under mode 3. Likewise, when computer programmers move to another country and offer their services electronically there, such e-commerce will be classified under mode 4.

[253] For completeness, mention may also be made of GATS Article IX on business practices, which provides for consultation and information exchange between affected Members when suppliers resort to anti-competitive practices.

[254] As defined in the Annex, a public telecommunications transport 'service' is any telecommunication transport service, offered to the public, involving the real-time transmission of customer-supplied information without any end-to-end change in its form or content. Public telecommunications transport 'network' refers to public telecommunications infrastructure permitting telecommunications between and among network termination points.

[255] This means that if a country lists internet service supplies in its national schedules even without committing to national treatment, foreign suppliers are to be given nondiscriminatory access to PTTNS. Discrimination against foreign suppliers is still possible in other areas (for example, taxation) as long as the country has not committed to national treatment in internet service supplies.

[256] This information was provided by Dewang Mehta in his presentation at the WTO conference "Potential for Electronic Commerce for Businesses in Developing Countries" on February 19, 1999 and summarized in the WTO document WT/COMTD/18.

[257] The simultaneous liberalization of direct foreign investment has also helped this process. The presence of foreign firms in India has played an important role in linking the demand for various services in their source countries with the supply in the host country (i.e., India).

[258] In China and India, there are 2.3 and 1.1 telephones per one hundred inhabitants. This compares with 59.5 telephones per hundred inhabitants in the United States. Among developing countries, only Hong Kong and Singapore have telephone availability that is comparable to that in developed countries. See Table 2, p. 7, WTO (1998), *op. cit.*

[259] For further details, see UNCTAD, *Legal Dimensions of Electronic Commerce*, may 4, 1999, TD/B/Com.3/EM.8/2.

[260] The information in this and the following paragraph is taken from UNCTAD, July 27, 1998, *Scope for Expanding Exports of Developing Countries in Specific Service Sectors*, TD/B/com.1/21.

[261] OECD, 1997, *The World in 2020: Towards a New Global Age.*

ANNEXES

ADDRESS BY THE SECRETARY-GENERAL OF THE UNITED NATIONS

Mr. Kofi Annan

Let me begin by thanking the city government and people of Seattle for hosting this very important, but evidently very controversial, conference. I wonder if they realised what they were letting themselves in for!

Personally, I am delighted to be here, and deeply honoured to be invited to address this gathering, which is indeed very important. I hope and believe it will be remembered as the Conference which launched the "development round", and laid the foundations of a world trade system which will be fair as well as free.

In the past, developing countries have been told time and again that they stand to benefit from trade liberalisation, and that they must open up their economies.

They have done so, often at great cost. For the poorest countries the cost of implementing trade commitments can be more than a whole year's budget.

But time and again, they have found the results disappointing—not because free trade is bad for them, but because they are still not getting enough of it.

In the last great round of liberalisation—the Uruguay Round—the developing countries cut their tariffs, as they were told to do. But in absolute terms many of them still maintain high tariff barriers, thereby not only restricting competition but denying crucial imports to their own producers, and thus slowing down economic growth.

Even so, they found that rich countries had cut their tariffs less than poor ones. Not surprisingly, many of them feel they were taken for a ride.

Industrialised countries, it seems, are happy enough to export manufactured goods to each other, but from developing countries they still want only raw materials, not finished products. As a result, their average tariffs on the manufactured products they import from developing countries are now *four times* higher than the ones they impose on products that come mainly from other industrialised countries.

Ever more elaborate ways have been found to exclude third world imports; and these protectionist measures bite deepest in areas where developing countries are most competitive, such as textiles, footwear and agriculture.

In some industrialised countries, it seems almost as though emerging economies are assumed to be incapable of competing honestly, so that whenever they do produce something at a competitive price they are accused of dumping - and subjected to anti-dumping duties.

In reality, it is the industrialised countries who are dumping their surplus food on world markets—a surplus generated by subsidies worth 250 billion dollars every year—and thereby threatening the livelihood of millions of poor farmers in the developing world, who cannot compete with subsidised imports.

So it is hardly surprising if developing countries suspect that arguments for using trade policy to advance various good causes are really yet another form of disguised protectionism.

I am sure that in most cases that is not the intention: those who advance such arguments are usually voicing genuine fears and anxieties about the effects of globalisation, which do need to be answered.

They are *right* to be concerned- about jobs, about human rights, about child labour, about the environment, about the commercialisation of scientific and medical research. They are right, above all, to be concerned about the desperate poverty in which so many people in developing countries are condemned to live.

But globalisation must not be used as a scapegoat for domestic policy failures. The industrialised world must not try to solve its own problems at the expense of the poor. It seldom makes sense to use trade restrictions to tackle problems whose origins lie not in trade but in other areas of national and international policy. By aggravating poverty and obstructing development, such restrictions often make the problems they are trying to solve even worse.

Practical experience has shown that trade and investment not only bring economic development, but often bring higher standards of human rights and environmental protection as well. All these things come together when countries adopt appropriate policies and institutions. Indeed, a developing civil society will generally insist on higher standards, as soon as it is given the chance to do so.

What is needed is not new shackles for world trade, but greater determination by governments to tackle social and political issues directly—and to give the institutions that exist for that purpose the funds and the authority they need. The United Nations and its specialised agencies are charged with advancing the causes of development, the environment, human rights, and labour. We can be part of the solution.

So too can the private sector. Transnational companies, which are the prime beneficiaries of economic liberalisation, must share some of the responsibility for dealing with its social and environmental consequences.

Economic rights and social responsibilities are two sides of the same coin. This is why, earlier this year, I proposed a Global Compact between business and the United Nations, under which we will help the private sector to act in accordance with internationally accepted principles in the areas of human rights, labour standards and the environment. The response so far has been encouraging, and I believe we can achieve a great deal by working together more closely.

But *this* meeting, and *this* Organisation, must not be distracted from their vital task—which is to make sure that this time a new round of trade negotiations really does extend the benefits of free trade to the developing world. Unless we convince developing countries that globalisation really does benefit them, the backlash against it will become irresistible. That would be a tragedy for the developing world, and indeed for the world as a whole.

Trade is better than aid. If industrialised countries do more to open their markets, developing countries can increase their exports by many billions of dollars per year—far more than they now receive in aid. For millions and millions of poor people this could make the difference between their present misery and a decent life. And yet the cost for the rich countries would be minuscule.

In fact, industrialised countries might even be doing themselves a favour. It has been calculated that some of them are currently spending as much as six or seven per cent of their gross domestic product on various kinds of trade protection measures. No doubt some of their citizens are benefiting from this, but surely there must be a cheaper and less harmful way for the rest of the population to help them!

This time, tariffs and other restrictions on developing countries' exports must be substantially reduced. For those of the least developed countries, I suggest, duties and quotas should be scrapped altogether.

And developing countries should receive technical assistance, both in the negotiations themselves and in implementing and benefiting from the agreements once reached. At present, some of them do not even have missions in Geneva. But UNCTAD—the United Nations Conference on Trade and Development—is there to help, if given the resources to do so.

In exactly one month we shall leave the twentieth century behind. The first half of it saw the world almost destroyed by war, partly as a result of its division into rival trade blocs.

The second half, by contrast, has seen an unprecedented expansion of global trade, which has also brought unprecedented economic growth and development, even if as yet very unequally distributed.

That expansion did not happen by accident. After the carnage and devastation of the Second World War, far-sighted statesmen deliberately constructed a postwar economic and political order governed by rules which would make free trade possible and thereby, they believed, make future wars less likely. Broadly speaking, they were right.

Several factors combined, at that time, to make such a liberal world order possible. One of them was a broad consensus on the role of the state in ensuring full employment, price stability and social safety nets. Another was that most big firms were still organized within a single country—so that international economic relations could be negotiated between states, each of which corresponded to a distinct national economy, and could be controlled by raising or lowering barriers at national frontiers.

And that in turn made it relatively easy to put in place a set of international organisations which were based on, and in their turn supported, the economic order: the World Bank, the International Monetary Fund, the General Agreement on Tariffs and Trade, and the United Nations.

Today's world is very different. Today, networks of production and finance have broken free from national borders, and become truly global. But they have left the rest of the system far behind.

Nation states, and the institutions in which they are represented, can set the rules within which international exchanges take place, but they can no longer dictate the terms of such exchanges exclusively among themselves. Economic life is no longer embedded in a broad framework of shared values and institutionalised practices.

The result is that, on top of the gross imbalance of power and wealth between industrialised countries and developing ones, there is now a second imbalance: the gap between the integration of the world economy and the continued parochialism of political and social institutions. While economics is global, politics remains obstinately local. It is for this reason, I believe, that so many people, even in the industrialised world, feel vulnerable and helpless.

And that, Excellencies, is why this is such a historic moment.

It will depend on what we decide here, and in a few other crucial meetings over the next few years, whether the twenty-first century will be like the first half of the twentieth, only worse—or like the second half, only better.

Let's not take the onward march of free trade and the rule of law for granted. Instead, let us resolve to underpin the free global market with genuinely global values, and secure it with effective institutions.

Let us show the same firm leadership in defence of human rights, labour standards and the environment as we already do in defence of intellectual property.

In short, let us emulate the wisdom, and the will-power, of those who laid the foundations of the liberal world order after the Second World War. They made change work for the people—and we must do the same.

STATEMENT BY THE SECRETARY-GENERAL OF UNCTAD

Mr. Rubens Ricupero

On the way to Seattle we have heard much talk about making these new trade negotiations into a Development Round. Our central objective must be to change that rhetoric into substance - in the agreements themselves. This is the way to give practical effect to the efforts by developing countries to become full-fledged—not shadow—members of the system.

UNCTAD is doing precisely this: encouraging developing countries to take a pro-active attitude in redressing the imbalances and shaping a better system through the "Positive Agenda Programme", whose impact can already be measured by the fact that half of the 250 proposals in the preparatory process came from those countries.

The developing countries in the past have been likened to the "free-riders" in the system. This was never true, and by their actions, the developing countries have shown just how wrong this view is. They have liberalized faster and further than any other countries. And in the preparatory process for Seattle, they have submitted more than 110 detailed and concrete proposals for dealing with the specific problems which they have identified as impeding their ability to participate fully and effectively in the multilateral trading system.

This is not only the best, but the only, way to deal with the problem of legitimacy, which stands now at the very heart of the trade debate —as anyone can see just by glancing through newspaper editorials or watching the street demonstrations.

At the root of the problem lies globalization and its disruptive effects: job security, increasing inequality among nations and inside them, the pervasive fear that people are losing control over their own lives. The backlash against globalization finds expression in shifting targets. First, it was the NAFTA, then the investment negotiations in OECD. Now WTO's turn has come. In this sense, it is suggestive and perhaps ironic that the home town of Microsoft, the symbol of the globalized economy, should become the setting for demonstrations against global trade, even if most participants in the protests come from elsewhere. It would be a serious mistake to brush aside the significance of these demonstrations. They have to be taken seriously.

For any international organization, legitimacy depends on three main components: universal membership, participatory and effective decision-making, and fair sharing in the benefits of the system. WTO's universality has just received a big boost from the breakthrough on China's accession, which will hopefully soon put an end to the long wait of one fifth of humanity.

We are still a long way, however, from ensuring that the accession process will become fairer and quicker. This requires agreeing to a "fast track" for those 19 least developed countries who remain in the waiting room. It also means not making demands on acceding countries, beyond those requirements already imposed on the current members. Now that the US and China have agreed upon terms for China's accession, there is no more reason for a geo-strategic game which has had serious knock-on effects for many acceding countries.

But as the organization grows more universal, it also gains in size, complexity and heterogeneity. The club-like decision-making process of the old GATT served well for an entity of a few like-minded countries, but it no longer fits one with 140 member nations, China among them, with different interests and development levels. As a former participant in the green-room system of the Uruguay Round, I have to admit that it was less than fair or transparent to the many excluded Contracting Parties. Since the end of that round, and because of the way it ended, complaints have been accumulating about the lack of participation and transparency in decisions. There has been a clear pattern of complaints leading to disappointment, and this in its turn is generating a sense of a "legitimacy deficit" for the whole system in the public eye. The net result has been a growing perception that the system could become more and more difficult to manage, as suggested by a series of painful episodes culminating in the inconclusive pre-Seattle preparatory process in Geneva.

A sure way of making things even worse would be to produce an artificial consensus on the basis of texts negotiated by a few key players. In due course, this will only turn disappointment into disaffection. In effect, it is not size that makes the process cumbersome, but the one-sided promotion of the interests of just one group of countries, and the persistent refusal to acknowledge the legitimate interests and well-founded concerns of developing nations. This is precisely what we have been seeing in relation to the genuine difficulties these countries have been facing with the implementation of some provisions in TRIPS and TRIMs, among others.

The implementation problem is but the last one in the long list of imbalances that have been distorting a system which was for many years aimed at the reduction of industrial tariffs among advanced economies. It was perhaps understandable, in that light, that agriculture would be kept largely outside the disciplines of a system that had to accommodate the construction of the European Common Market and its CAP, or Common Agricultural Policy. This was achieved, by the way, not through the official free trade philosophy of the multilateral system but very in spite of it. Massive subsidies and State intervention turned the market upside down, disproved all the predictions of the reputable economists of 80 years ago and made Europe into one of the largest agricultural exporters in the world. The first waiver in agriculture was granted to the US in the early 50s, while the first "short-term" arrangement for cotton textiles that would later develop into the Multifiber Arrangement occurred in the latter part of that decade: In one case, nearly half a century ago, and in the other, more than 40 years ago. And the nations which after all those years say they are not yet ready fully to liberalize agriculture or textiles trade are often the very same ones that feel it would be much too lenient to grant developing countries more than five years in which to adapt to the complex changes in intellectual protection.

In order to deserve to be called a "development round", future negotiations would have to redress those imbalances, as a bare minimum. More specifically, they would first have to eliminate the most glaring example of imbalance, the freedom of developed countries to subsidize massively their exports of agricultural products, and to place their industrial subsidies in the nonactionable category. Secondly, they should accelerate the dismantling of the Multifiber Arrangement, where only 6 per cent of the value of restricted items has been liberalized so far. Thirdly, it is time to get rid of tariff peaks and tariff escalation in a large array of products where developing countries are competitive, and to grant bounded free market access to LDCs exports.

There is no alternative to the multilateral trading system, but this does not mean we have to resign ourselves to its current imbalance. After the two decades of the Tokyo and Uruguay Rounds, the vast majority of developing countries have ended up with more trade deficits - 3 per cent more than in the 70s - and less economic growth - 2 per cent less than before. This is in part the result of inadequate domestic policies, although as I mentioned earlier, most of those nations carried out serious adjustment programmes and can no longer be called "free riders" after the rapid opening of these markets. There are other reasons: the sluggish growth of the economies and import demand of advanced countries, the fall in commodity prices and consequent deterioration in terms of trade. But a significant cause of this worrying state is certainly the asymmetries in the balance of mutual rights and obligations, including market access, that must finally be set right.

There are only two options before us. The first is to persist with the mercantilist approach of pressuring developing countries to further open markets that will soon become non-existent, as those nations will not be able to get through exports the resources they need to pay for their imports. The second is a "lift all boats strategy" that will allow developing economies to export their way out of poverty and underdevelopment, earning them the money to finance their imports of capital goods and technology from industrial countries, without increasing their debt. I hope that Seattle will choose the second road, the only one that can close the "legitimacy gap" and update the old UNCTAD slogan, "trade, not aid", with two new formulas: "market access, not speculative capital and debt; trade, not hot money".